CONTESTED SKIES

CONTESTED SKIES

Trans-Australian Airlines
Australian Airlines
1946–1992

John Gunn

University of Queensland Press

First published 1999 by University of Queensland Press
Box 42, St Lucia, Queensland, Australia
Reprinted 1999

Typeset by University of Queensland Press
Printed in Australia by McPherson's Printing Group

Distributed in the USA and Canada by
International Specialized Book Services, Inc.,
5804 N.E. Hassalo Street, Portland, Oregon 97213–3640

Cataloguing in Publication Data
National Library of Australia

Gunn, John, 1925– .
Contested skies

Bibliography.
Includes index.

1. Trans Australia Airlines — History. 2. Aeronautics, Commercial — Australia — History. I. Title.

354.790994

ISBN 0 7022 3073 1

To John Watkins
who did so much for
the early TAA

Contents

Preface

When Trans-Australia Airlines was founded in 1946 civil aviation was, despite a quarter of a century of development, still in its infancy as a global industry. Qantas had made its first overseas departure from Darwin to link Australia and England by air in February 1935. The aircraft it operated was a DH86 biplane, its forty-six-foot fuselage an unobstructed plywood box with spruce stiffening and fabric outer covering. The romantic Qantas flying boat service that followed operated for only a little over a year when, in 1939, World War II brought it to an end. Qantas then had ten captains and ten first officers. War brought Australian civil aviation to its knees. At the end of 1943 only twelve Australian-owned civil transport aircraft were in service, and in the words of the director-general of civil aviation at the time, civil aviation in Australia was expiring month by month.[1]

When the war ended one domestic airline, Australian National Airways, dominated the existing trunk routes and feeder lines. Australia's Labor government, with a firm commitment to socialist ideals and public ownership, regarded air transport, like the railways, as a public utility. It was not prepared to countenance the emergence of a private ANA monopoly in Australian air transport.

Out of this political commitment was born the government-owned Trans-Australia Airlines. Its history, as a result, has been remarkable for both its contribution to Australian civil aviation and its role as a focus for sustained and intense ideological political debate. As Sir Peter Abeles (chief executive of TAA's competitor, Ansett) later remarked: 'For the fifteen years from 1957 civil aviation was undoubtedly the most debated subject in the Federal Parliament ... it attracted Parliamentary attention far beyond its true significance because aviation had become a battle ground for politicians of all colours.'[2]

This history of Trans-Australia Airlines — later to be renamed Australian Airlines — records the growth of the airline from its modest postwar beginnings using DC3s, through its rapid expansion as a formidable competitor to Australian National Airways, to its emergence as an airline with a large fleet of jet aircraft, respected internationally for its operational achievements, technical expertise and safety record. It records also how changes in the Australia's economic and political environment led to its absorption, in 1992, into our international airline, Qantas, and its demise as a separate entity. Under a Labor government no longer driven by the ideology of public ownership the expanded Qantas, combining the domestic network created by TAA–Australian Airlines with its international services, passed into full private ownership in 1995.

In writing the history I have been helped by many people who were intimately involved in the creation and development of TAA. Their recollections have been valuable in giving perspective and balance to events. But though I knew all TAA's general managers from Lester Brain (the first) through John Ryland and Lyn McKenzie to Frank Ball, as well as many of the senior people who helped shape the airline, I have gone to the the documents of the day and the written word to uncover the complexities and detail of events as they unfolded. That research included an examination of all TAA–Australian's board papers and supporting documents throughout the life of the airline, all relevant Qantas board papers, the archives of both airlines, the voluminous and valuable Hudson Fysh Papers in the State Library of New South Wales, the resources of Australian Archives and the relevant files of the department of transport, the fine collection of material in the Airway Museum, Melbourne, of the then Civil Aviation Authority (including the valuable papers of the late Captain Edgar Johnston), and the extensive coverage and commentary on aviation by the specialist and general media over almost half a century.

I have many people to thank, some of them involved from the very beginning of TAA. Doug Laurie, who filled many senior roles, provided the anecdote with which this history starts; Lyn McKenzie and Frank Ball, who rose through the ranks to head the airline, gave me wise counsel; John Watkins, former director of engineering and a key figure in the selection of the aircraft that made it a dominant force for many years, lent me his papers as well as his time. Others who gave their time and help were Sir Kenneth Vial, TAA's longest serving chairman; Roger Meyer, custodian of the Airway Museum in Melbourne; John Tilton, TAA public relations manager for many years; Tony Dignam, TAA assistant general manager; Stanley Brogden, whose expert aviation journalism has covered half a century; John Schaap, former general manager and chief executive of Australian Airlines, and John Ward, former chief executive officer of Qantas. I would also like to thank James Strong, former chief executive officer of Australian Airlines and now chief executive officer of Qantas for his support. I am grateful to Captain Warwick Henry, who provided me with much information on the Northern Territory Aerial Medical Service, 1952–80. That service, however, deserves its own history, and space has precluded its inclusion in this work. I am also grateful to the then minister for transport, Laurie Brereton, for providing special access to files under thirty years old and to the department of transport for their generous cooperation in providing both access to their voluminous records and office space in which I could examine them, as well as to the then Civil Aviation Authority for similar assistance. Finally I would like to acknowledge the central and sustained contribution of my research assistant, Joanna Wills, throughout the project, and the contributions of Vikki Plant and Eleanor Bridger in its initial months.

Aviation started as romantic adventure, underwent rapid technological advancement in wartime and was soon vigorously exploited for its commercial possibilities. The rapid development of civil aircraft gave aviation for decades a glamour and excitement that never failed to engage the public imagination. When the jet engine brought civil aircraft speeds to their present high subsonic plateau that aura of glamour faded. Air travel, with ever larger jet aircraft, became an accepted means of mass transport, a routine and reliable convenience. TAA was born and grew in the era of excitement.

CONTESTED SKIES

John Gunn is the author of twenty books, his subjects ranging from widely translated children's books and adult fiction to the history of Qantas. Having served as a destroyer navigator in World War II and later a Fleet Air Arm pilot, he furthered his interest in aviation by working as a consultant to Rolls-Royce, British Aircraft Corporation, TAA and other companies. He has also written for the *Australian Financial Review*. His first volume on the history of Qantas, *The Defeat of Distance* (UQP 1985) was named the best Australian book of 1985 by the Townsville Foundation for Australian Literary Studies and also won the H. T. Priestly Memorial Medal. The third volume, *High Corridors: Qantas 1954–1970*, was published in 1988. His play *Hildegard*, a dramatic portrait of the twelfth-century saint and visionary, was premiered in St Stephen's Cathedral, Brisbane, in May 1999.

PROLOGUE

1920–46

The proper monopoly

On 2 September 1946 a small group of men charged with bringing into being a new, government-created airline met in Melbourne under the chairmanship of Arthur Coles, founding chairman of the Australian National Airlines Commission, founding director of the retail giant G. J. Coles & Co., former Lord Mayor of Melbourne, chairman of the Civilian Food and Clothing Rationing Commission during the war, chairman of the War Damage Commission, tireless contributor to Australian public affairs and trusted confidant of the Labor prime minister, J. B. Chifley.

'Gentlemen,' he said, 'the Government want us us to start services as soon as possible. There is a Federal election on 28 September. If we don't have an airline up and running by then and Labor loses the election there'll be no airline. We'll be out of a job.' He surveyed the group for a few moments. 'Any suggestions?"

The Commission members and newly appointed airline executives, all men of achievement in their fields, put their views. The recently formed Australian National Airlines Commission had a name for its airline, Trans-Australia Airlines, but no formal organisation, no sales staff, no ground facilities, no documentation; not even tickets. It did have some trained aircrews and aircraft. There was general consensus that with concentrated effort they could achieve the planned starting date for services of 7 October.

'I have news for you', said Coles quietly. 'We start next Monday.'[1]

Civil aviation in Australia, as it emerged from World War II, was pitifully weak. Before the war, at the end of 1938, Australia had ranked seventh in the world by the yardstick of airline route mileage and sixth in the total number of air miles flown by regular air transport companies. In the decade from 1929, air route mileage had risen worldwide by some 130 per cent, miles flown by 200 per cent. Australia had experienced double these rates of increase. It was hardly an exaggeration to say that in the pre-war years Australia, with the extraordinary record of its aviators in pioneering world air routes and the expansion of its civil aviation industry, was the most air-minded nation in the world.[2]

The great progress in military aviation in World War II did not produce aircraft suitable for civil use, but some were modified to become the only types available, both in Australia and other countries. Many years were to pass before aircraft designed specifically for commercial airline use were produced. The Commonwealth government took its first initiative for the development in Australia of civil aviation in 1921 with the formation of the Civil Aviation Branch, under the control of the Department of Defence. It was decided that government should control private flying, enforce safety regulations and establish aerodromes and landing grounds throughout the country, as well as provide financial assistance for the establishment of regular airline services in selected localities. It was at that time by no means a vision for the introduction of air links between large cities; railways (in which large sums of government money had been invested) were seen as the primary means of such public transport. The government's aim was to provide the benefits of air travel to centres in Australia's outback not served by other means of transport — and not competing with the railways. 'In no districts perhaps are these benefits more real', said an inter-departmental committee report as late as 1932, 'than in outback parts where other means of transport do not provide reasonable facilities'.[3]

The first of these regular air services in Australia began on 5 December 1921 between Derby and Geraldton, Western Australia, serving the main coastal centres between, on a route of 1,211 miles. The operator that won this service by public tender was Captain Norman Brealey's Western Australian Airways Limited. On 17 January 1924 this service was extended to Perth (1,467 miles from Derby) and was subsidised by five shillings and threepence per mile flown (or £25,000 per annum) in the first contract year. (The subsidy dropped to 2 shillings and sixpence per mile, or £19,213 per annum, in the final year, 1931–32). In addition to the subsidy, the Commonwealth guaranteed an overdraft of £8,000 at the Commonwealth Bank for purchase of initial equipment, which was repaid in eight monthly instalments. From the outset, civil aviation in Australia (as with the railways) meant expenditure of public money and close government involvement.

In Queensland two former officers of the Australian Flying Corps, Hudson Fysh and Paul McGinness, began joy-riding and aerial taxi activities that developed (with the support of grazier Fergus McMaster) into the Queensland and Northern Territory Aerial Services Limited (registered in November 1920). Qantas, as it became known, survived until a government contract with a subsidy of £12,000 per annum was provided to operate, from 2 November 1922, the 560-mile route Charleville–Longreach–Cloncurry (with intermediate stops). At the end of January 1925 this service was extended from Cloncurry through Mount Isa to Camooweal, a total route mileage of 825.

The first contract for an air service between capital cities was entered into on 21 December 1921, when Larkin Aircraft Supply Company won a public tender to fly between Adelaide and Sydney (790 miles) with a subsidy of £17,500 per annum, but that service did not start until 2 June 1924. Even then, in the words of a Civil Aviation Department report, 'it was found

... that the two days journey could be shortened by using the night train service between Cootamundra and Sydney and the latter section [Cootamundra–Sydney] was discontinued on 21 July, 1925'. A further contract with Larkin provided branch services from 4 July 1925 between Melbourne–Hay and Broken Hill–Mildura. These were the government-supported operations that introduced regular air services to Australia. They were the only ones until, on 30 August 1928, Western Australian Airways became the successful tenderer for a weekly service between Perth and Adelaide (1,435 miles). The service began on 2 June 1929 with a subsidy paid at the rate of twelve shillings and eightpence per pound of mail carried (with a guaranteed minimum payment of £380 per single trip).[4] Although community benefit was the core factor in the selection by government of airline routes to be flown, the contracts given to the airline operators always related to the carriage of mails.

Many other unsubsidised services began as the twenties ended — Brisbane–Townsville (728 miles) by Queensland Air Navigation Co. Ltd; Adelaide–Renmark (140 miles) and Adelaide–Mt Gambier (246 miles) by Commercial Aviation Co., Adelaide; Adelaide–Eyre Peninsula, Streaky Bay (310 miles) and Adelaide–Broken Hill (260 miles) by Eyre Peninsula Airways Ltd, Adelaide; and Brisbane–Toowoomba (75 miles) by Aircrafts Pty Ltd, Brisbane. They were successful enough, despite an emerging economic depression, to prompt two great Australian aviators to launch Australia's first major domestic airline.

What promised a new era in the development of Australian domestic air services began on the first day of 1930. Sir Charles Kingsford Smith and C. T. P. Ulm, known around the world for their pioneering transoceanic flights, formed Australian National Airways Limited and inaugurated a daily return service between Sydney and Brisbane. Although they received a government subsidy of eight shillings a pound, under a postal contract for mail carriage, air mail between capital cities at the time was almost negligible and the subsidy provided little financial help. Nevertheless the service was initially so successful that the company established a daily service between Sydney and Melbourne on 1 June 1930 and a Melbourne–Launceston–Hobart service from 16 January 1931.

From 1922 to 1930 route mileage flown by regular Australian air transport services had grown more than four-fold from 1,788 miles to 8,101 miles. But passenger miles flown increased a hundredfold, from 54,334 to 5,427,236.

The Great Depression, however, had a severe impact on civil aviation. Kingsford Smith and Ulm, operating by far the most ambitious services, were hit hard. At the same time their financial difficulties were compounded by the tragic loss of their airliner *Southern Cloud* on 21 March 1931 on a flight between Sydney and Melbourne. That blow finally forced the company to suspend all its operations on 26 June 1931.

The Larkin services, which had little public support, ceased when contracts expired in June 1930 and subsidies were withdrawn. A Brisbane–Lismore service established in 1930 by New England Airways Ltd was extended to Sydney in July 1931. Queensland Air Navigation Ltd closed down their Brisbane–Grafton service on 28 November 1930 and their Brisbane–Townsville route on 27 January 1931. (Qantas re-opened the unsubsidised Brisbane–Townsville service on 7 May 1931 but discontinued it four months later.) The years that followed were, for civil aviation, very lean ones, although there was growing activity on a number of Bass Strait services.

Government subsidy was the key to survival. During 1932–33 the government, with the prospect of an England–Australia service now a very real one, tackled the reorganisation and extension of the subsidised air transport system, with tenders advertised for an aggregate route mileage of 8,090 (including Darwin–Singapore, Darwin–Brisbane, Charleville–Cootamundra, Katherine–Perth and Tasmanian services connecting Melbourne and Launceston). The basis of payment was a fixed price per mile with the Commonwealth retaining money earned from the existing airmail surcharge.

Qantas Empire Airways Limited, a company formed jointly

by Queensland and Northern Territory Aerial Services Ltd and Britain's Imperial Airways in January 1934, was the successful tenderer for the Brisbane–Darwin–Singapore service (4,361 miles), connecting at Singapore with Imperial Airways, which flew the London–Singapore route. For QEA the five-year contract, commencing in December 1934 and using DH86 aircraft, saved the Qantas company 'from virtual extinction'.[5] It was to prove the basis for the airline's prewar growth and great subsequent expansion in the years after World War II. The government subsidy received averaged £63,685 per annum over the period of the contract. (Qantas, as it continued to be generally known, was also the successful tenderer for the Cloncurry–Normanton route [216 miles], receiving an average subsidy over the five-year contract of £2,557, or two shillings and 2.7 pence per mile.)

Other names of consequence in Australian civil aviation that benefited from the government reorganisation of subsidies and routes were C. A. Butler (later Butler Air Transport Company), who won Charleville–Cootamundra (629 miles; average annual subsidy over five years £6,255); MacRobertson Miller Aviation Co. Ltd, which took Perth–Daly Waters (2,252 miles; £17,565); and Tasmanian Aerial Services Ltd (later Holyman's Airways Pty Ltd), which received Melbourne–Hobart (460 miles; £12,199).

Government policy determined where these pioneer airlines would fly; public money sustained their operations.

The government's imprint was evident even in the choice of aircraft available. Until 1935 only aircraft made in countries that were members of the International Convention for Civil Aviation were allowed into Australia. That excluded the United States (which was not a member), where, although great new aircraft were being produced, the airlines were not governed by the airworthiness requirements provided under the Convention. That prohibition became increasingly untenable. Following a report to the government by the controller of civil aviation, Captain Edgar Johnston, in November 1935, it was decided to remove the ban. The first company to import an American airliner was Australian National Airways Pty

Ltd (not related to the original Kingsford Smith–Ulm ANA), which introduced a Douglas DC2 into service in June 1936, followed in 1937 by the larger DC3.

Australian National Airways Pty Ltd was formed in 1936 and was controlled by British and Australian shipping interests. It took over the equipment, establishments and services previously controlled by Holyman's Airways and Adelaide Airways. These services embraced the Melbourne–Hobart and Tasmanian Islands and the Perth–Adelaide subsidised services as well as the Melbourne–Sydney, Adelaide–Mt Gambier–Melbourne, Adelaide–Broken Hill–Melbourne, Adelaide–Kangaroo Island and Adelaide–Port Lincoln unsubsidised routes. Other important developments at the time were the establishment on 22 February 1937 of the Adelaide–Darwin services (through Central Australia) by Guinea Airways Ltd and the start, on 17 February 1936, of the Melbourne–Adelaide service by Ansett Airways Ltd. On 30 May 1938 W. R. Carpenter & Co. Ltd, following a successful tender for a service to Rabaul, New Guinea (2,522 miles; £13,114 annual subsidy), began operations using DH86B aircraft. This service operated once weekly in each direction along the eastern Australian coast through Rockhampton, Townsville, Cairns and Cooktown to Port Moresby, Salamaua and Rabaul.

From now until the outbreak of war air transport operations developed rapidly, particularly the unsubsidised services, most of which were used by the Post Office for the carriage of surcharged airmails at poundage rates. These included the services operated by Australian National Airways other than Melbourne–Tasmania and Melbourne–Perth and those of Airlines of Australia Ltd (which had grown out of New England Airways Ltd). The ANA Melbourne–Sydney and Airlines of Australia services between Sydney and North Queensland were subsidised from July 1939 on the basis of payment for miles flown.

At the outbreak of World War II fifteen companies operated a network of services throughout Australia — Adastra Airways Pty Ltd, Aircrafts Pty Ltd, Airlines of Australia Ltd (which incorporated with ANA in 1943), Ansett Airways Ltd, Airlines (WA) Ltd, Air Taxis Pty Ltd, Australian National Airways Pty Ltd, Butler Air Transport Co., E.J. Connellan, Guinea Airways Ltd, McRobertson Miller Aviation Co. Ltd, Qantas Empire Airways Ltd, South Queensland Airways Pty Ltd, Victorian and Interstate Airways Ltd and W.R. Carpenter & Co. Ltd.

This was an extraordinary level of activity for a country with such a small population. From 1930 air route mileage had increased from 8,101 to 30,475 and passenger miles flown from 5,427,236 to 42,901,209. At the beginning of World War II Australian companies were flying more than 9 million miles each year and employing over 370 commercial pilots. Australian airline, freighter and charter aircraft numbered well over 100 and there were some 200 private aircraft.[6]

There had been no government control over civil flying in Australia before December 1920, when the Commonwealth Parliament passed the Air Navigation Act. Its objects were to apply the provisions of the International Convention on Air Navigation (signed in Paris on 13 October 1919) to international and internal aviation in Australia. By proclamation the Act came into force on 28 March 1921. It was administered by the minister for defence. (The Air Navigation Regulations instituted under the Act were declared invalid by the High Court in 1936. A conference between Commonwealth and State ministers in early 1937 agreed that each State would determine what Commonwealth regulations on air navigation and aircraft should be imposed within the jurisdiction of the State. State powers — and State politics — were to be a force in aviation matters.)

The first controller of civil aviation in Australia was Colonel H. C. Brinsmead, OBE, MC, who was appointed on 16 December, 1920 and assisted by a small technical staff, all functioning as a branch of the Defence Department. Brinsmead was severely incapacitated in late 1931 when the KLM aircraft in which he was a passenger crashed on take-off from Bangkok. He died in 1934. His successor, Captain Edgar Johnston, previously deputy controller of civil aviation, was appointed controller on 4 May 1933. An infantryman at Gallipoli, a member of the 10th Light Horse in Egypt, an artilleryman in France, Johnston was finally a pilot in the Royal Flying Corps. He was an outstanding public servant and a major contributor to the development of Australian civil aviation over a period of more than thirty years. In those early times he was responsible for the acquisition and development of landing grounds. As early as 1926 he had supervised the acquisition or lease of 133 landing grounds and prepared them for civil aviation purposes.

As Australian aviation developed rapidly the overseeing government organisation also changed. In April 1936 a Civil Aviation Board was appointed with responsibility for the administration of the Air Navigation Regulations and 'for giving effect to the Government's policy for the further development of civil flying in the Commonwealth'.[7] It consisted of Edgar Johnston, as controller-general, a controller of operations, a controller of ground organisation and a finance member, while remaining under the overall control of the minister for defence. The Board continued until, on 9 January 1939, the Department of Civil Aviation and the post of director-general of civil aviation were created. Australia's first minister for civil aviation was H. V. C. Thorby. The prime minister announced: 'The Controller-General of Civil Aviation, Captain Johnston, will no longer be in complete control but will have charge of one of the three branches of the Department'.[8] Sixty-two-year-old A. B. Corbett, 'a lean, well-preserved man in excellent physical and mental mettle',[9] was appointed director-general on 3 April 1939 over Johnston — unfairly in the judgment of most of Johnston's peers. In June 1939 the Department of Civil Aviation had a total staff of 251 — 107 of them at head office; by December 1944 the total had grown to 758 — with 540 of these at outstations as technical and inspection officers for the growing number of aerodromes and radio stations established throughout the Commonwealth.

Britain's declaration of war on Germany on 3 September 1939 signified, for an Australia that was part of the British Empire, an automatic corresponding declaration by Australia. The air transport and aero club organisations and their ground facilities, built up over the years, were now of considerable strategic value. The Department of Air immediately took over four Douglas DC3 aircraft to form an RAAF Reconnaissance Unit. Pilots and ground engineers were called up for duty with the RAAF. (These four aircraft were returned to their companies in 1940.) Qantas flying boats (a total of five by 1940) were taken over to serve as reconnaissance and transport units. (Three were lost in service.) Heavy and light multi-engined aircraft were impressed and many aero clubs and flying training schools played an important part in the early expansion of RAAF flying training. The regular air transport services were used extensively during the war for the transport of troops and key personnel.

When Japan entered the war in December 1941 and Japanese forces penetrated swiftly southwards into South-East Asia and the Pacific civil air transport organisations were quickly mobilised for special operations of many kinds. American transport and combat air forces and army personnel moved into Australia in vast numbers. Reginald Miles Ansett, a man who was to dominate postwar Australian domestic aviation, saw an opportunity to be seized. Ansett Airways Ltd was permitted to relinquish its airline licences for the regular services Melbourne–Broken Hill, Sydney–Adelaide and (once weekly) Melbourne–Sydney so that the company's aircraft could operate under charter to the Transportation Branch of the United States forces. (From May 1944 these operations were conducted under contract to the Commonwealth as a service under Reciprocal Lend-Lease.) Ansett, who was always to personify the virtues of the private enterprise entrepreneur in Australian domestic aviation, had in fact received large government subsidies. Indeed, at the beginning of the 1939–45 war, more than half of the total passenger miles and freight ton–miles performed in Australia were subsidised by the federal government.

To ensure the fullest war use of civil aviation organisations and relieve service personnel for operations, the Directorate of Air Transport, Allied Air Forces made available in November 1942 twelve transport aircraft. They were allocated to Australian National Airways, Qantas and Guinea Airways.

For Australia's regular air services the task, between 1939 and 1944, was overwhelmingly the carriage of passengers and freight for the armed services (including the United States and other Allied services). Passenger miles flown increased from 49 million in 1939–40 to 100 million in 1943–44. But achieving these figures meant greatly increasing flying hours for the ageing aircraft. In mid 1943 the opinionated and authoritative A.B. Corbett reported to his minister, Arthur Drakeford: 'On present prospects Australia may have twelve obsolete and over-age transport aircraft with no organisation capable of national expansion to meet immediate postwar needs and no accepted plans for either national or international expansion. Civil aviation in Australia is expiring month by month.' He estimated that by year's end some 452 United States-owned military transport aircraft and twelve Australian-owned civil aircraft would be operating in Australia.[10] Australia had not secured from any source any new aircraft for civil aviation since 1939.

Australia's wartime prime minister John Curtin put Corbett's report before the War Cabinet, commenting: 'In the postwar period the Government is determined that Civil Aviation will be highly developed ... Australia must seek to organise its war effort in the air to obtain the greatest residual value that is possible in the postwar period.'[11]

Corbett, in 1943, had prepared an outline plan 'involving post-war problems of manpower and re-establishment, economic welfare, external relations, general economic, social and political policy and finance in relation to civl aviation' which had its origins, he wrote, 'in the need for forward planning of a new Department concerned with a new form of transport involving many new problems'. Probably no other war expenditure, said Corbett, 'produces so much of value to peace time use as does the expenditure on wartime aviation, both direct and indirect ... A nation which refuses to use flying in its national life must necessarily today be a backward and defenceless nation.'[12]

Australian air transport had met the competition of surface transport — on unequal terms — and built up in a very short period of time and with comparatively little assistance, said the Corbett Report, a reputation for safe, fast and comfortable passenger transport. All its essential needs, it said, had to be met by a country with limited resources. 'As a matter of fact the capital expenditure in Australia for every civil aircraft, aerodrome, navigation facility, lighting, fencing and buildings from the beginning of civil aviation to date is less than £5 million (assuming half has been provided by private enterprise). The United States has spent far more on one single aerodrome.' Corbett predicted that the wartime techniques of mass production would reduce the capital cost of civil aircraft, while pilots and ground engineers in very large numbers would be demobilised and seek employment in civil capacities. 'Aerodromes and navigation facilities have been improved for war purposes and are available for civil use. A long record of accident free transport in Australia has largely removed the older fears of flying.' Commercially, said Corbett, 'Air transport is now reaching a stage where it can produce reasonable returns for the capital invested'.

With more than a little self-confidence Corbett set down in one sentence the basis for attaining this goal. 'The secret of financial success is in heavy loading, maximum daily hours of plant operation, safety control, real economy in operating costs, and revenue based on cost of operating plus such profit as may be determined to enable charges to compete with surface transport.'

His outline plan for postwar civil aviation was just as succinct. Corbett proposed the ultimate provision of twenty-two distribution centres throughout Australia, each having a radius of some 300 miles, thus placing 'any place in inhabited Australia — mainland and Tasmania — within 300 miles of one of these distribution centres'. Each centre was to be located at the largest centre of population in its area 'and each has an aerodrome'. All first class mails were to be carried by air between the centres to specific timetables with a minimum of one daily service (and up to four times daily between the largest centres). The longest flying time between the two most distant centres (Perth, Western Australia, and Cooktown, Queensland) would be just under twenty-four hours. Between adjacent centres it would be from two to four hours. Distribution from each centre locally would be by train or car. His proposal, he said, 'involves the setting up of some entirely new air routes requiring new aircraft, personnel and air navigation facilities'.

His scheme, of course, also provided for the carriage of passengers on this national network. 'In terms of surface transport at 25 miles per hour,' he commented, 'it reduces Australia to an area having a radius of about 300 miles'. His report promised an important national role for its author. Corbett submitted that 'the Department of Civil Aviation is best equipped to prepare such plans'.

'Air transport is a means of communication and as such it must always involve a form of national service, at least in conveyance of mails ... eminently a public service in which the community shares the benefits. There are at least two great instrumentalities, the Post Office [Corbett had previously been deputy director of posts and telegraphs for Queensland] and the Railways, which perform services for the community on similar lines.'

His most relevant comment, in the light of immediate postwar developments in the structure of Australian interstate air transport, brought high politics into the aviation policy mix. 'The question of whether the capital invested in providing air transport in Australia should be provided by private enterprise or by the State is a matter for higher policy.'[13]

That issue was to divide the two major Australian political parties. The Labor Party course had been set in the very year that Australia's first aviation legislation, the Air Navigation Bill, became law. Arthur Calwell (a later Labor leader) recalled that at a meeting of the Federal Executive of the party in 1921 'they felt [Labor's] objective no longer adequately expressed the hopes and purposes of the party'. It was decided to convene a national Trades Union Congress. From that Congress, in June 1921, emerged the new objective of the

Labor Party — 'the socialisation of industry, production, distribution and exchange'.[14]

Corbett's reputation as a thinker and administrator was not, however, high. Hudson Fysh, at Qantas, in a letter to his chairman, Fergus McMaster, described the Department of Civil Aviation in August 1944 as 'chaotic'.[15] Corbett's plan was never seriously considered; the Labor Government had its own agenda. On 22 November 1944 the acting prime minister, F.M. Forde, told Parliament: 'The Government has decided that a wholly government-owned statutory authority will be formed to take over, operate and maintain all interstate airlines.' There was, in Cabinet, strong support for nationalisation of the airlines, mainly to protect the railways from competition. Both Ben Chifley (prime minister from mid 1945), and his life-long friend Arthur Drakeford were veteran members of the Australian Federated Union of Locomotive Enginemen. Corbett, who opposed nationalisation, had conveniently reached retiring age. He was succeeded, on 17 February 1944, by Dan McVey. (McVey immediately left for visits to the United Kingdom and North America; Corbett acted as director-general in his absence and finally ceased duty in August 1944.)

As a result of a series of mergers there were, as the war ended, only nine airline companies. Australian National Airways Pty Ltd was the principal domestic airline operator, with virtually no opposition on the main trunk routes and provincial feeder lines. Apart from the Labor Party's policy on socialisation, the government considered that the only alternative, if public ownership of the airlines were not introduced, was a virtual private monopoly exercised by the five shipping companies that owned Australian National Airways. It regarded air transport as a public utility that the government sustained by underwriting the airline operators through heavy subsidies. Its view was that the public was entitled to some control of the public monies involved and that private enterprise could not be relied on to open up non-paying but desirable developmental routes.

Prime Minister John Curtin died in Canberra on 5 July

1945, only two weeks before the Australian National Airlines Bill was brought down, on 18 July. Ben Chifley succeeded him as prime minister on 13 July. The Bill was passed by both Houses of Parliament on 14 August, two days after Japan surrendered and World War II ended. It conferred on the ANA Commission the power to operate between states and territories or within any territory of the Commonwealth. It also provided that licences to private operators should cease to be operative as long as adequate services were provided by the Commission. It was in essence an Act to create a monopoly of air services operated by a public corporation. In his second reading speech Drakeford made much of the ownership of Australian National Airways, listing the shipping interests of the shareholders. 'The list', he said, 'might well have come from Lloyds Register ... But where are the great pioneers of aviation? — the pioneers in whose names there has been so much sentimental appeal in the propaganda opposing this Bill? ... We discover that one by one the small pioneer enterprises are disappearing from the register. It is the inevitable process of absorption by a monopoly.' He listed the names 'of eight such enterprises which became merged — perhaps I should say sub-merged — in this monopoly'. They were Tasmanian Aerial Services Pty Limited, Holyman Airways Pty Limited, Adelaide Airways Limited, West Australian Airways Limited, Airlines of Australia Limited, New England Airways Limited, Rockhampton Aerial Services Limited and North Queensland Airways Pty Limited. 'Whereas in 1938', said Drakeford, 'sixteen companies were operating, in 1944 only nine remained, though the passenger miles flown were more than doubled in this period ... Between 1940 and 1944 a total of £1,900,000 was paid to all airline companies in subsidies and mail poundage fees ... Out of that total Australian National Airways received £1,350,000, or 70 per cent.' Figures for the twelve months ending 31 March, 1945 showed, he said, that ANA received 85 per cent of the total payments in subsidies and mail poundage fees.[16]

In that second reading debate Prime Minister Chifley made his views plain. 'I have supported no other Bill so strongly and warmly as I support this one ... my only regret is that the Constitution confines the Government to inter-State airlines; but I do not despair about the prospect of our controlling intra-State airlines. The proper monopoly, if there is to be one, is a government monopoly. That is our purpose.' [17]

When the Bill was passed, Chifley announced that Parliament would adjourn. Edgar Johnston wrote to Dan McVey: 'This announcement, made on a very cold, bleak day, was a great incentive to Members to curtail their remarks and get home.'[18] Great secrecy had been maintained on the contents of the Bill until its actual introduction and there had been no leaks. Even ministers, other than the prime minister, did not receive copies before it went to Parliament.[19] Almost every newspaper without exception, Johnston told McVey, attacked the Bill — mainly on the grounds that Prime Minister Curtin had pledged not to nationalise any industry while the war lasted.[20]

Qantas now also feared nationalisation. Hudson Fysh wrote to British Overseas Airways Corporation chairman Lord Knollys: 'It is proposed that I should go ahead with the Australian Government and make every endeavour to effect the best compromise possible to prevent complete nationalisation, which none of us here feel would be a good thing'.[21] Fysh saw Chifley in Canberra where he was told that a memorandum was in preparation for submission to Cabinet for the Australian government to acquire the Qantas Empire Airways shares held by BOAC — but not those of the Australian shareholders of the original Qantas. (Britain's Imperial Airways, which owned half of Qantas Empire Airways, was absorbed into Britain's new, government-owned corporation, British Overseas Airways Corporation in legislation that received Royal Assent on 4 August 1939. BOAC officially took over from Imperial Airways on 1 April 1940. Nationalisation of airlines was by no means only an Australian phenomenon.)

McVey had warned his minister, Arthur Drakeford, as early as May that the main argument of the Opposition would concentrate on 'the question of the constitutionality of certain provisions in the Bill'. There was no doubt, he said, that the

Commonwealth could, if it chose, establish and operate interstate civil air services. 'The doubt lies in whether the Government can claim a monopoly in this field.'[22] The legislation was soon challenged in the High Court; McVey was proved correct. On 15 December 1945 the *Sydney Morning Herald* reported:

> The attempt of the Commonwealth Government to legislate for the nationalisation of the interstate airlines met its not unexpected nemesis at the hands of the High Court yesterday. Time and study will be needed to digest all the implications of a set of judgments which are likely to become historic, but their effect as regards the airlines legislation was plainly set out in a short explanatory statement by the Chief Justice. By unanimous decision the Court has ruled that the Australian National Airlines Act, passed earlier this year by the Federal Parliament, is invalid in so far as it would prevent the issue of an airline licence for interstate services to anyone but the proposed Government Commission, or would bring to an end existing airline licences. In other words the Commonwealth is not entitled under its existing Constitution to establish a Government monopoly in respect of the internal airlines.[23]

The Act was amended to remove the monopoly provision and the Government went ahead promptly to establish, under the Australian National Airlines Commission, the government-owned Trans-Australia Airlines. It was a venture without precedent; the Commission, operating as Trans-Australia Airlines, was a business functioning within Federal Government. Unlike government departments, which operated through cash accounting, the Commission, though funded by government, was to provide annual balance sheets in the manner of private business enterprises. Its first chairman, A. W. Coles, was a symbol of private enterprise achievement. His credentials with the Labor Government were, however, impeccable. He had been one of two independent members of Parliament who had voted against the previous coalition government and helped bring Labor to power. Coles, nevertheless, had previously made it clear to Chifley that he would not accept the chairmanship of a government monopoly. It was his opinion that 'a monopoly of any kind, whether a private one or a government one, does fall down on its service. I am,' he said, 'a great believer in competition for business.'[24]

(In April 1946 Chifley also appointed Arthur Coles chairman of another new and wholly government-owned airline, British Commonwealth Pacific Airlines. BCPA was jointly owned by Australia, contributing 50 per cent of its capital, New Zealand, 30 per cent, and the United Kingdom, 20 per cent. BCPA was to operate internationally, between Sydney and Vancouver.)

On 7 February 1946 the minister for air, Arthur Drakeford, announced the names of the Commissioners who were to serve under Coles' chairmanship. His vice-chairman was W. C. Taylor, a Sydney solicitor, and friend and adviser to Ben Chifley, who had been a member of the Commonwealth Bank Board from 1941 until the Board's abolition in 1945. He had had a close personal association with Chifley since the 1930s. At the time of his appointment he had been vice-president of the New South Wales branch of the Australian Labor Party for five years. Dan McVey held three positions — director-general of civil aviation, posts and telegraphs (since 1939), and aircraft production (since 1942). Captain Edgar Johnston, deputy director of civil aviation, and A. C. Joyce, who, as senior assistant secretary to the Treasury, represented the federal treasury, were the other two members. (McVey resigned his government positions in mid-1946 and his place on the Commisssion to become managing director of Standard Telephones and Cables Pty Ltd, a position he had been offered during the war years but had refused on patriotic grounds.[25] He was succeeded as director-general of civil aviation by Air Marshal Richard [Dicky] Williams.) Joyce also resigned on his appointment as auditor-general. Their places were taken by G. P. N. Watt, assistant secretary of the Treasury and L. B. Fanning, the new director-general of posts and telegraphs, who attended their first Commission meeting on 30 June.

The Commission, formally established on 12 February, held its first preliminary but unofficial meeting at the Commonwealth Treasury Offices, Melbourne, on 13 February 1946, with Drakeford in attendance to explain the terms of the Commission's charter. (The meeting was unofficial because its members' appointments had not yet been formally confirmed by the Executive Council.) The Commission, said Drakeford, 'had been entrusted with a task of very considerable magnitude in providing air services for the people of Australia on a nationwide basis, not only to meet present requirements but also those which were likely to develop in the future'. Coles responded that the Commission was charged with the operation of services on a competitive basis and that 'the presence of a virile competitor in the operation of Australia's air services was all to the good'. (Coles also acknowledged that 'in some respects, notably the carriage of mails, the Commission would not be competing on an equal basis with private enterprise' but that 'in other respects the services would be fully competitive'. The prime minister had told Coles that it was the government's desire that TAA services should be used to the fullest extent for the carriage of airmails.)[26] It was agreed that an application be submitted to the Treasurer for an initial advance of £10,000 'to meet immediate requirements'.[27] The Department of Civil Aviation was asked to furnish a statement giving full particulars of all existing airlines services, including types of aircraft employed, timetables and subsidies provided by the Commonwealth.[28]

General press reaction to the establishment of the Commission was hostile. The *Sydney Morning Herald* response was typical. It commented on 9 February: 'On the principle that half a loaf is better than no socialist bread, the Government is going ahead with its plans — perhaps with an eye to the possibility that the half denied by the Constitution may be engorged by other means. In plain words, if the private airlines cannot be legally expropiated they may be squeezed out of the field by special pressures available to the Government.'[29]

At the Commission's meeting on 14 March in an old warehouse, Reliance House in Flinders Lane, members learned for the first time of the aircraft that might be available to launch its airline. There were eleven DC3s owned by the Commonwealth and leased to private operators and two C47s, acquired by private operators on the condition that the Commonwealth could, if it required, repossess them. They also were advised that there had been 53 applications for the position of general manager of TAA, 166 for secretary and 357 for other positions. The name of the airline was not yet established. The meeting agreed that 'the Minister should be informed that the intention of the Government that the name "Australian National Airlines" should be used by the Commission is, in the circumstances, impossible of achievement at present'. It noted that preliminary steps had been taken to protect the name 'Trans-Australia Airlines' but that registration of this name should not proceed without the minister's approval.[30] (The name 'Trans-Australia Airlines', generally attributed to McVey, was first suggested at the Commission meeting on 13 February.[31] Drakeford's approval of the name was noted at the Commission meeting on 10 April. On 30 July the Commission 'agreed that the business name "Trans-Australia Airlines" be used in all the Commission's activities and publicity apart from the actual meetings and announcements of the Commission in its corporate capacity'.)[32]

Of some historical note was a letter received from R.M. Ansett on 13 March proposing that he sell his own airline to the Commission. He wrote:

> A great deal of expense and valuable time could be saved by the Commission by taking over an existing organisation immediately available and to ensure continuity of operation my company would, in addition, should the Commission so desire, be prepared to act as Managing Agents at a fee to be mutually agreed until such time as the Commission could set up its executive organisation to take over the management. Our staff numbering approximately 200 is recognised to be experienced and capable in handling their respective functions, and this has been born out by the Company's successful operation over the past nine years.

An accompanying statement showed assets of Ansett Airways Limited as worth £102,476. They included three 21-passenger C47 aircraft (being converted to standard DC3s), six small six-passenger Airspeed Envoys, a two-passenger Porterfield aircraft and hangars at Essendon and Hamilton.[33] Two months later, after receiving an independent report assessing the Ansett offer, the Commission decided that it was not sufficiently attractive. Coles and Brain talked with Ansett and offered to buy his airline's assets at adjusted book values and without establishment costs, or at valuation with goodwill subject to arbitration. On 12 June Ansett declined their proposal. That outcome was, in the years ahead, to have immense significance for domestic aviation in Australia and for the fortunes of Reg Ansett.

In December 1945 McVey had advised his minister that 'for the position of General Manager [of TAA] there is only one man among the Australian airline operators who, in my opinion, is at all outstanding in his management of air transport and that is Captain Holyman but he has refused, I understand, to consider an appointment'. He suggested recruiting a senior man from Trans-Canada Airlines.[34]

Holyman was again approached in early 1946, this time to consider not only the position of chief executive officer of the Commission (at what, for the time, was the extraordinarily high salary of £10,000 per annum) but also the sale of his airline, ANA, to the Commission. That initiative was taken only after Coles and his vice-chairman, Taylor, had discussed the matter with the prime minister.[35] Holyman wrote to Coles, who was on friendly terms with him, on 24 April.

> I have given much consideration to our discussion the other day when you enquired whether the shareholders of A.N.A. would agree to dispose of their undertaking to the Airlines Commission for cash and I, myself, agree to become the chief executive of the Commission. Let me say at the outset that I am quite definite that I will not offer my services on such a basis. I know that if I have, as you were kind enough to suggest, rendered services of value to the development of aviation, it is attributable to the freedom and ability to create, direct and control which is afforded to me in an organisation such as A.N.A.
>
> I could never function as a public servant in a government corporation nor could my services be effective in such an organisation, for the very conditions essential to the proper carrying out of my functions would be absent, and so it would be a bad bargain for both of us. My shareholders are not prepared to sell out their undertaking for cash. A.N.A. has achieved much in the development of civil aviation in Australia and hopes to achieve still more.[36]

Holyman had, however, viewed with favour the concept of what he described to Coles as 'a composite company'. 'Upon any proposition combining the drive of free enterprise with Government interest you will always find A.N.A. willing to negotiate.' The concept was not precisely defined, though Holyman explained that 'the type of corporation which would be visualised is one that includes all those present operating interests which are willing to come in. I would think it unfair that a Government airline, either alone or together with any other operating company, should eventually destroy the assets of the various companies which, by their pioneering, have done so much to build up civil aviation. I am concerned, not so much with the companies themselves, as with the effect on the persons who put their money into aviation ventures and cannot afford to lose it.' Holyman seemed unaware or unwilling to come to grips with the commercial realities that lay ahead. He ended his letter saying that 'it is apparent that the Commission and A.N.A. may be to some extent competitive, although I am, of course, mindful of the government's statements in the High Court that the intention of the Commission was to supplement existing services, not to compete with them.' He hoped Coles would agree with him that 'it would be proper for the Commission, which will no doubt shortly be seeking staff, to undertake not to recruit staff from A.N.A'.[37]

Coles replied: 'In reference to staff, I do not know whether a Government instrumentality can refuse to consider applications from persons eligible ...' He reminded Holyman of his expressed opinion 'that competition with the Government Airline will result in your Company operating at a loss'. He made it clear that the Commission had no power to act along the lines of the suggested composite company and that 'in carrying out its duties under the provisions of the Act it will inevitably be operating in direct competition with other operators on interstate routes'.[38] That was polite language for head-to-head confrontation with ANA.

Hudson Fysh was also worried about possible loss of valuable Qantas staff to the new government airline. 'For all I know,' he wrote to his chairman on 3 April, 'we may be left denuded of seniors unless we can prevent the Commission taking them. The Commission is advertising for an Operations Manager at a minimum salary of £2,250 per annum, about £1,000 per year more than we can give.'[39]

His fears were realised when Qantas flying operations manager Lester Brain wrote to him on 10 April: 'I should like to apply for this position [TAA operations manager] and feel that I should have a good chance of selection. I have given practically the whole of my life since leaving school to flying and Australian air transport, twenty-two years of that time with Qantas. I have served the Company conscientiously and loyally through much of its history in peace and war.' Brain, more than any other individual, had been responsible for the operational excellence of the airline. After discussions with his chairman, McMaster, Fysh told Brain that he would be released and there would be no ill will.[40] (Another renowned Qantas pilot, G. U. (Scotty) Allan, was also to apply to join TAA.)

Brain was more successful in his application than he had expected. With the Holyman option now ruled out, Brain was offered the position of general manager of Trans-Australia Airlines and took up his post on 3 June. He wrote in his diary: 'Commenced duties with the Australian National Airlines Commission. A. W. Coles chairman of the board. W. R. Harrison acting secretary, J. W. A. McLeod personnel manager, John Borthwick — ex Qantas — Personal Assistant. Temporary offices in Chart House, 372 Little Bourke Street. Total staff today 22. No aircrew yet engaged.'[41] (John Borthwick, a former gunner in the AIF, had been Brain's personal assistant at Qantas. He moved with him to TAA and was later appointed Sydney manager.)

The new airline had acquired a man of great distinction. Brain had joined the original Queensland and Northern Territory Aerial Services (Q.A.N.T.A.S.) in 1924, became chief flying instructor of Qantas's Brisbane Flying School when it opened on 26 March 1927, rose to the position of chief pilot and flew the first of the Qantas Empire Airways DH86 aircraft (with which Australia began international airline operations) from England to Australia in 1934. It was under Brain that QEA and its pilots had mastered the new techniques necessary for long transoceanic flights in the flimsy, fabric-covered DH86 biplanes. He had presided over the introduction of the majestic Empire flying boats as flying operations manager until, in 1939, that romantic era of peacetime flying boat services came to an end. In 1944, after twenty years of flying, he became QEA's operations manager. (Brain saw no future for further promotion in QEA; Hudson Fysh was well established and only seven years his senior.)

Fysh, evidently confused as to Brain's new job, wrote to Lord Knollys: 'This will serve to confirm that Capt. Brain has got the position of Director General [*sic*] of the Australian National Airlines Commission. The salary is £3,000 to start, with ample expenses, and a five year contract. Brain leaves with mutual good will, and he could hardly be denied his chance seeing the greatly advanced salary and status to that which my Board felt unable to extend to him.' (That salary, though far less than the amount offered to Holyman, was higher than was paid to the most senior public servant in Australia at the time.) He was, in addition, promised increments at the discretion of the Commission to take it to £5,000 a year. The prime minister himself demonstrated his involvement in such matters. 'I desire to inform you,' Drakeford told Coles, 'that the Prime Minister has approved the terms of your letter of 3rd May, 1946 in which you advised L. J. Brain Esq. that the Government is agreeable to the Commission granting increments during his term as General Manager in the Commission's service, commensurable with the growth and success of the Commission's undertaking, to a top salary limit of £5,000 per annum.'[42]

The position of operations manager was offered to K.M. Hampshire. Other senior appointments went to S.H. Crawford (a member of the AIF in the 1914–18 war and former assistant secretary to the Department of Army) as secretary; R. E. Pope as chief accountant and J. L. Watkins as technical superintendent. (Hampshire, however, did not take up his appointment and on 16 July his position was filled by Group

Captain J. P. Ryland.) Pope was to prove a brilliant financial executive and Ryland was to follow Brain as general manager. But it was the appointment of John Watkins and his profound influence on the selection of aircraft for the new airline over the years that was to be of crucial importance to the success and worldwide reputation for excellence of the new Trans-Australia Airlines.

Almost eight hundred applications poured in for positions on the airline's flying staff. Aircraft, however, were somewhat scarcer. Coles wrote to the director-general of civil aviation on 23 May 1946: 'The Commission at its meeting on Tuesday, 21 May, 1946 decided to ask for the release of two [DC3] Dakota aircraft to its control as from 18 June, 1946 and one further Dakota as from 2 July, 1946.'

On 14 June, after eleven days in his new post, Brain reported: 'Apart from the considerable initial work done by the Chairman and members of the Board, the past fortnight covers the first two weeks of activity of the embryo organisation and much of the time has been given to the basic problem of establishing a nucleus of seniors, and the getting into motion of an integrated organisation. I feel that progress in this fundamental task has been satisfactory and will gather momentum rapidly as it develops.' Very satisfactory progress had been made, he said, in the arrangements with the RAAF and the obtaining of the essential instructors, maintenance engineers and other staff required. The takeover of three C47 Douglas aircraft had been followed up with the Department of Civil Aviation and arrangements completed to take delivery of two of them from Australian National Airways at Essendon on 18 June, with the third coming on 2 July. 'It is noted that each of the three aircraft will have at least nine months of normal operation available before becoming due for major overhaul for renewal of Certificate of Airworthiness.' Brain also noted that a message had been received from Edgar Johnston in America advising that 'a cable was sent on 12 June to Captain G. U. Allan in London advising him of the acceptance of his application for the position of Operations Manager.' Group Captain J. P. Ryland, he reported, had been appointed Manager, National Airlines School. 'Mr. Ryland is a very experienced commercial airline operations executive and at present holds the position of Manager, Airline Division of Ansett's. Prior to the war he was Senior Captain and later Operations Manager for Ansett Airways.'[43]

Captain G. U. (Scotty) Allan had flown with both Kingsford Smith and Ulm and been a key member of the flying team that had so successfully operated both the DH86 overseas services and the big flying boats. Both Hudson Fysh and Lester Brain had a great admiration for his abilities. Captain Edgar Johnston had strongly supported his appointment to TAA as operations manager. But Scotty Allan had had second thoughts. The Commission meeting of 14 June noted: 'A cable was received from Mr. Allan declining the offer of appointment as Operations Manager due to renewal of his agreement with Qantas'.[44] (Scotty Allan went on to become assistant general manager of Qantas.)

Brain and Ryland moved swiftly to establish the pilot training school through which, at Brain's direction, all pilots, regardless of their background or experience, had to pass. Barracks, classrooms, mess and hangar facilities were taken over at the RAAF base at Point Cook. (John Chapman, later assistant general manager, took over as manager of the school when Ryland, in mid July, was promoted to the position of operations manager.)[45]

On 2 July, the day the third ANA aircraft was delivered, the Treasury arranged for the transfer of £350,000 to the Commission to pay for four DC4 four-engined airliners, ordered on the Commission's behalf from the Douglas Aircraft Corporation. The DC4s were scheduled for delivery in October and November. (The DC3 carried twenty-one passengers at an average speed of 150 miles an hour and had a range of 450 miles. The DC4 had an optimum range with maximum load of 1,800 miles and carried forty-four passengers at an average speed of 185 miles an hour.) At that time the RAAF had a fleet of 109 DC3s, bought by the Commonwealth under Lend-Lease. Brain was advised that twenty-two of them would be available progressively for civil use and recommended that the Commission take twelve. Brain's overall plan was to have twenty aircraft operating passenger services after conversion plus three unconverted aircraft for use at the training school, and for special freight and other flights.

By August it had been agreed that pilots would wear a merchant marine type uniform of navy blue double-breasted jackets and merchant marine style caps with soft white tops. In mid July Helen Somerville was appointed air hostess superintendent. The starting age for hostesses was set at between twenty-two and twenty-eight years and their training period was six weeks. Like the pilots they were to wear navy blue. Brain advised the Commission: 'Based on the expected intake of pilots and the output through the school, we should be in a position to staff and operate full passenger and mail services between Melbourne and Sydney on a basis of four services daily each way at the beginning of October, and within a further two weeks we should be able to operate regular services on a lesser frequency from Sydney to Brisbane, or Melbourne–Tasmania or Melbourne–Adelaide, as may be decided'.[46]

TAA was fortunate to have access to American aircraft. As early as May 1944 McVey had briefed Prime Minister Curtin, then in London, on the pre-eminence of American civil aircraft design. In 1943, on a visit to the United States, McVey had seen at first hand American progress. Donald Douglas, president of Douglas Aircraft Corporation, had informed him that their DC4 type would begin production in September 1944 and that there were plans for a DC7, an aircraft of 155,000 pounds carrying sixty-four passengers and with a range of 2,500 miles. At Lockheed, corporation president Courtland Grose let him see a mock-up of Lockheed Model 89 (which was to develop into the Constellation), 'a very large ship of 185,000 pounds all-up weight and a range of 5,000 miles with accommodation for 96 passengers'. The Consolidated Vultee Aircraft Corporation, at San Diego, showed him a prototype of their Model 39, using the complete wing of the B24 Liberator bomber, and designed to carry thirty-four passengers.

'There is no corresponding activity in Great Britain', wrote

McVey, 'since the whole of the engineering and productive capacity of Britain (except for some preliminary design work on the *Brabazon* civil type) is being devoted exclusively to military and naval operational aircraft'. The situation was, he said, 'a serious one for the Empire, because it would appear that only American aircraft will be available to civil airline operators immediately after the war ... it will be most difficult later to effect a change over to British types'.[47] In a later letter McVey wrote that under an arrangement between the British prime minister and the United States president

> it was agreed that Britain would continue the manufacture of operational aircraft and that the United States would not only supplement Britain's production of combat types but would, in addition, also build transport types. As a result, Britain has no transport types in production suitable for civil aviation purposes except one machine, the 'York', which is a converted Lancaster bomber ... Even British Overseas Aircraft Corporation, Britain's chosen instrument, is now using a large number of American aircraft ... Much as we deplore the fact that British civil types are not available we must, as true Britishers, applaud the reason ... War needs come first.[48]

Of the three US corporations visited by McVey, Consolidated Vultee would soon influence the fortunes of the infant TAA. Consolidated was to provide the aircraft type that helped TAA to early dominance over its only competitor, Australian National Airways Pty Limited.

Brain's office in Chart House had second-hand furniture, no carpet and, in a bitter Melbourne winter, no heating. (Electricity was rationed.) He worked until after midnight day after day. (In the meantime the Commission had negotiated with the Department of Interior for the lease of the basement, ground floor and two upper floors of the Manchester Unity Building, at 339 Swanston Street. It became TAA's head office on 1 July.)

Brain's single most important task of the many he faced was the appointment of key executives and flying staff. It was Brain who brought in R. Edelsten (Dick) Pope as chief accountant. (Pope had served on convoys to Russia in World War II, done anti-submarine and minesweeping duties, served in

'E' boats and earned the Distinguished Service Cross.) For the crucial position of Chief Engineer Brain told Coles there was no single person with the high technical qualifications required plus the practical experience of aircraft maintenance and engineering. Coles agreed to his proposition that two men were needed.

'On the highly technical side', said Brain, 'there was John Watkins who had applied and who was, in my opinion, the best in Australia in the field of aircraft design, performance, analysis and so forth. Then there was Jack Davies, at that time chief engineer for Ansett. I considered him to be one of the best of the administrative chief maintenance engineers, with much practical experience.' Watkins, acting superintendent of airworthiness and aeronautical engineering in the Department of Civil Aviation, was appointed technical superintendent and Jack Davies chief maintenance engineer.[49] (Davies' background included service with the RAAF, Qantas, Larkins Airways and Holden's Air Transport, New Guinea.)

Watkins had great intellectual capacity and a rich aviation background. He had started his university course in mechanical engineering in Adelaide when his engineeer father, in the course of buying heavy equipment from the British Vickers Group, mentioned to its Australian representative that his son was passionately interested in aviation. That representative was Sir Keith Smith, who with his brother, Ross, had made the historic first-ever flight from England to Australia in the Vickers *Vimy* in 1919. Keith Smith gave him a letter of introduction to Vickers. In 1931, as the Great Depression was deepening, Watkins went to England and completed the course of advanced studies in aeronautics at Imperial College. Helped by his letter from Keith Smith he was then employed at Vickers, Weybridge, in Surrey in a junior capacity, soon becoming a stress calculator in the Barnes Wallis team that was working on the first geodetic wing. He returned to Australia in 1934 and was employed initially by the Defence Department as a stress analysis engineer before moving to the Department of Civil Aviation. In the following years he was intimately involved in the study and assessment of civil aircraft of many types.[50]

Aircraft magazine later summarised his qualities: 'John Watkins has a most distinguished name internationally as an aeronautical engineer — noted not only for his equipment selection foresight for TAA and the organisation of its engineering structure, but also as an informed and original thinker on aviation development and a skilled analytical writer and lecturer on the subject'.[51] It was Davies, however, who in 1946 had the more immediately important task within TAA of creating from scratch its maintenance and overhaul organisation. Under Davies, that group set the high standards that from the start assured TAA's operational and safety record. (Davies rejoined Ansett in the mid-1950s but was killed in an accident in Melbourne in 1960.)

The Commission made early use of John Watkins. At its meeting on 30 July 1946 it agreed that he head an advance party to the United States via England on 8 August. His primary task was to supervise acceptance and delivery of TAA's Douglas DC4 aircraft. But Coles had an additional agenda for him that would prove of profound importance. Watkins later wrote:

> To my utter astonishment Arthur Coles, after the expected pep-talk about the DC4 assignment, said he was relying on me to find out what new equipment was being developed that would enable us to offer our passengers a better product than our established rival, at a competitive price ... What a challenge, and what a marvellous opportunity! Clearly I was going to be glad of every bit of knowledge of a very wide range of aircraft, and their operational limitations within safe airworthiness parameters, that my fourteen years of work as a jack-of-all-trades in aeronautical engineering had given me.[52]

Watkins' brief was nothing less than to advise Coles on the best aircraft available to trounce Australian National Airways. It was a measure of Coles' foresight that, though without experience in aviation matters, he recognised that choosing the right aircraft was fundamental to TAA's success. He set John Watkins this task a month before TAA made its first scheduled flight.

The four DC4s, it was agreed, were to be named after major Australian explorers, using full given names and surnames.

TAA's DC3s were to be named after other Australian explorers using surnames only. (*John Eyre* was proposed for the first DC4; *Hawdon* for the first DC3.)[53]

Brain's early senior flying staff appointments were Ryland and Chapman. Ryland, then thirty-five, had joined Ansett Airways as a junior pilot in 1937. He enlisted in the RAAF when World War II began (with 4,500 hours flying hours already accumulated) and during his six years of war service earned the Distinguished Flying Cross. At war's end he held the rank of Group Captain. He had rejoined Ansett after demobilisation in 1945 and came from Ansett to TAA. His long flying experience was one of two great assets he brought to the task of creating the disciplined structure needed to sustain airline flying operations. The other was character. Ryland had great personal strengths and a complete disregard for popularity. A disciplinarian, he was formal to those above and below him. (He would never allow himself to address Brain by his given name; it was always 'Sir' or 'G.M.' Only years later, when Brain resigned, did he use 'Lester'.)[54] John Chapman, who took over management of the flying training school at Point Cook when Ryland became operations manager, had been chief pilot for Guinea Airways, with ten years' experience flying in the Northern Territory and South Australia.

Brain's key appointment in the all-important role of traffic management came from Qantas. Doug Laurie was recruited as traffic superintendent. Brain knew the man and his qualities well. Laurie was QEA station superintendent at Darwin when, on 19 February 1942, the Japanese launched their first and heaviest air attack on Darwin in bright sunlight. (The attack was commanded by Admiral Nagumo, who had been in charge of the spectacularly successful raid on Pearl Harbor that brought the United States into World War II.) On that same day the Japanese landed at Dili, in East Timor. The Supreme Command was now evacuating Java and an improvised shuttle service was started between Tjilajap and Broome, on Australia's northwest coast, using American, Dutch and QEA civil aircraft as well as military transports. Brain arrived in Broome on 21 February and was met by

Laurie, who had come from Darwin. In all, QEA operated ten trips from Tjilajap carrying eighty-eight passengers and much cargo. (The QEA flying boat *Circe* was lost during these operations on 28 February.)

When Laurie applied for the position with TAA (advertised as traffic manager) on 15 July 1946 Brain was generous in his comments but unwilling to antagonise Qantas. 'Your present employers', he wrote to him, 'regard you as being one of the brightest and most promising and energetic of its commercial-traffic seniors ... If you were unemployed or otherwise employed I should be willing to offer you a position immediately, but knowing the value placed on you by your present employers I would not consider taking you away at this stage.'[55] That situation changed when Laurie, who was Qantas manager for Queensland and enjoyed much autonomy, faced an unwelcome transfer to Qantas's head office in Sydney. Brain wrote to him a second time on 10 July. 'In view of happenings in the meantime, I am not so sure that we would not consider an application from you if you felt disposed and considered yourself morally free to do so. We still have our complete Traffic Department to set up ... I should be interested to hear further from you.'[56] Laurie responded and was formally offered a position on 31 July. He was required to take up his position 'not later than Monday, 2 September, 1946' and was, as a result, present at the tense meeting at 9.30 a.m. on 2 September when Coles gave his executives just one week to get TAA services under way.[57]

Coles' deadline was politically driven. Prime Minister Chifley wanted Trans-Australia Airlines in place and operating scheduled services by election day, 28 September. An established airline had a reasonable chance of survival if Labor were defeated; a paper airline, seen by many as a floundering bureaucracy, was doomed. Coles was a natural leader, already regarded with respect by his new executives. He quietly dominated that 2 September meeting, communicating the political urgency that now required an extraordinary response from them.

A Melbourne–Sydney flight was scheduled for the following Monday. Coles' retailing instincts determined the fare to be set. Australian National Airways' fare was six pounds ten shillings but a 15 per cent discount was common. Coles decided on 'one fare for all — the lowest'. He set the standard TAA fare at five pounds ten shillings and sixpence, 15 per cent less than the official ANA fare. He was insistent that, from the start, the new airline should have a slogan to distinguish it. Laurie reminded the meeting that ANA, with its monopoly on the eastern coast, had 'a lousy reputation for service'. Coles listened and pronounced that the TAA service should be seen as friendly. A slogan that was to identify TAA for decades came from publicity manager Ian Sabey: 'TAA the friendly way.'[58] The meeting was over by 10.30.

'Nobody', said Laurie later, 'slept much in the week that followed. The engineers even had to make passenger steps and baggage barrows. We cajoled and bullied suppliers and printers. Staff were hired and instructed. We had to advertise and make arrangements for ticket sales. [A temporary traffic office was secured in the Myer Emporium Building in Londsdale Street.] Traffic manuals and staff instructions were out in three days, plus passenger manifests, aircraft load sheets and tickets. Essendon airport was closed because heavy rain had softened the grass landing areas and all civil flying was transferred to the big RAAF station at Laverton [fifteen miles southwest of Melbourne]. We had to dolly up an old shed there. At Mascot we took over premises from ANA.'[59]

It was dark, bitterly cold and drizzling at 5.45 a.m. on Monday, 9 September 1946, when Captain J. A. Hepburn and his first officer, Captain J. A. Nickels, lined up TAA DC3 *Hawdon* for take-off. There had been only one pre-departure crisis; the bar for the dignitaries and press members had been forgotten. It was heaved into the aircraft as it taxied out.

The flight to Sydney took three hours five minutes and arrived at 8.50 a.m. There was (apart from Coles' wife and two children) only one paying passenger on board. Arthur Coles gave him his money back as he boarded the aircraft.[60]

CHAPTER 1

1946

Not the planned inauguration

September was what Brain described as a 'running in period' for the airline. 'The operation of this interim service', Brain reported in mid-September, 'is affording our ground organisation and staff the desired opportunity to settle down to smooth operation without heavy pressure from the public, pending completion of our offices and passenger amenities at each terminal'. The frequency of the service between Melbourne and Sydney was increased from once to twice daily on 23 September. Brain reported:

> Considering the fact that we announced this service as an interim one without complete passenger amenities at aerodromes or city terminals and that there has as yet been no full publicity or advertising, patronage from the paying public has been greater than expected.
>
> It is obvious that our policy of stating the earliest possible date for development of operations and then bending every endeavour towards meeting those dates has enabled us to … develop operations several months earlier than would have been the case had we waited for confirmation of completion and availability of buildings and facilities.[1]

By mid September the No. 1 pilots' course at Point Cook had been completed and all personnel from the course had been posted to route duties. No. 3 course, comprising twenty-five pilots, had begun on 9 September, and there were then fifty pilots under instruction plus a special course for ground engineer trainees. The engineers were to prove the backbone of the new airline. While the major source of pilots was the RAAF, TAA's engineering strength was founded on the experience of a nucleus of men who had served with the Commonwealth Aircraft Corporation.

Lawrence Wackett became the first manager of CAC in 1936 and built up a powerful organisation that set the highest standards of technical precision in design, materials control and manufacturing quality. The Corporation not only contributed greatly to Australian aviation during and beyond the war years but was also the source for a flood of expertise into the industry. In particular its influence on the technical standards of TAA was marked. John Watkins brought to TAA Tom Savige as chief draftsman and Herb Maley as aircraft and equipment engineer, both from CAC. Savige, in turn, brought with him five draftsmen and a tracer while Maley recruited two other TAA engineering stalwarts, Alan McKeown and B. G. (Bart) Woodgate. (Between them, Woodgate later wrote, in a Lawrence Wackett memorial lecture delivered to the Royal Aeronautical Society, 'Savige and Maley, drawing on their experience at CAC, set up a standard of precision in definition and rigor of demonstration which had a great part in leading to the high regard for TAA technical standards'.)[2]

It was Brain who set in train the agenda that determined the quality and expertise of TAA pilots. 'During the next twelve months', wrote Brain, 'our intake of pilots through our School must include a proportion of experienced civil airline Captains, since even a first class and very experienced Air Force pilot requires a period of approximately 12 months experience as Second Pilot on civil airlines in order to become throughly familiar and competent to assume command on scheduled passenger services'.[3]

Three additional fully converted aircraft owned by the Commonwealth were taken over by mid September — two from ANA and one from QEA. Agreement was also reached for the transfer of twelve C47s from the RAAF to TAA. 'Of the remaining nine aircraft to be transferred to us by the RAAF', wrote Brain on 17 September, 'seven are located at Amberley in Queensland and two at Laverton in Victoria. It is expected that delivery will be taken of these aircraft during the next ten days.'[4] The new airline was rapidly expanding its resources in pilots, engineers and aircraft. It services, too, were increasing.

But Federal politicians were concerned with issues more fundamental to their well-being than aviation as the election approached. It was an election that had great import for TAA management and staff, still in doubt as to the intentions of the federal Opposition. TAA was, however, now an operating airline. To the great relief of the airline's employees the Labor government was re-elected on 28 September for another three-year term and Drakeford continued as minister for civil aviation. (TAA was not, for long, to remain the only airline owned by the Australian government.)

The Melbourne–Sydney afternoon flight on 1 October, Brain told the Commission, 'carried a full load of 21 passengers, of whom 20 were public paying passengers'. The Melbourne–Sydney service was increased to four times daily on 7 October (including one scheduled call at Canberra southbound and northbound) and a once-daily service was started between Sydney and Brisbane. 'As from Monday [7 October]', Brain wrote, 'all our scheduled services are declared fully open to the public'.[5]

The industry magazine *Aircraft* commented on TAA's beginnings:

> It was not the inauguration that the Government initially planned — the taking over of all private interstate airline interests and their running as a Government instrumentality — but it was a start. Against the single return trip of the TAA airliner could be balanced the eight return trips over the same route of Australian National Airways' well-established service, and Ansett Airways' ... single return trip. It would have seemed a highly dangerous business undertaking were it not that that single trip represented the initial thrust of the most powerful airline organisation Australia could devise, backed with political determination and £3 million of Government funds.[6]

The private airlines, it wrote, showed no trepidation but

planned additional services and a strong front of competitive development. 'Interesting, too, will be the attitude of smaller airline organisations, particularly Aircrafts Pty Ltd (APL) of Brisbane, which stepped boldly out of the intrastate field with the inauguration of a direct non-stop service between Melbourne and Brisbane, and Ansett Airways, which have been running an excellent service between Adelaide, Melbourne and Sydney for some time.' The private airlines, it wrote, based their future hopes on the defeat of the government and a further challenge to the validity of the Airlines Act expressed in the Privy Council appeal now pending.[7]

For the private airlines the attitude to TAA of the major opposition parties was not absolutely clear. 'In his first published reference to the question at a Hobart meeting,' wrote *Aircraft*, 'Mr Menzies said the Liberal Party opposed the establishment of the Government airline and would ensure that TAA competed fairly. But he did not say the venture would be abandoned.'[8]

The Labor government soon made it clear that competition against TAA would have bounds. The acting deputy secretary of the Department of the Treasurer circulated a memo to all permanent heads of departments on 11 September 1946, which read:

> As the Australian National Airlines Commission has been set up by Commonwealth legislation to operate interstate air services on behalf of the Government, it is required that this service and other services to be established by Trans-Australia Airlines be used, wherever possible, when it is necessary for officers of Commonwealth Departments and authorities to travel by air on official business. I shall be glad if you will arrange for officers concerned in your Department and for authorities under your control to be instructed accordingly.[9]

(TAA increased its Melbourne–Sydney service to five flights daily from 4 October and routed two services via Canberra, noting that 'these added facilities should provide a substantial TAA passenger potential to and from the Federal Capital if the existing rail travel entitlement of the Gold Passes of Members of Parliament were extended to cover travel on the Government's airlines services'.)[10]

By the beginning of October TAA had taken over eleven of the twelve RAAF C47 aircraft due. The route development plan called for six DC3s to be in service with commencement of a Sydney–Brisbane service on 1 October, seven DC3s by 1 November (when Melbourne–Hobart was scheduled) and two DC4s by mid-November — with Melbourne–Launceston now added and the long Melbourne–Perth service inaugurated by the big DC4s. By early December the plan was for eight DC3s and three DC4s to be flying on passenger services.[11]

On 4 October, TAA's first DC4 Skymaster, VH-TAA — christened *John Eyre* — arrived at Laverton on schedule; on board the second, *Thomas Mitchell*, which arrrived on 15 October, was John Watkins, returning from his critical assignment in the United States. Watkins had arrived at the Douglas plant at Santa Monica on 21 August, and on 7 September left on a crowded schedule of visits to US airline operators, aircraft manufacturers and the civil aviation administration in Washington. His sole objective was to choose TAA's next airliner. Watkins had already eliminated Britain's Airspeed Ambassador and now rejected in turn Lockheed's Saturn, Boeing's 417 and a Douglas design commonly known as the 'eggbeater'. He was left with two contenders — the unpressurised Martin 202 (and its planned pressurised successors) and the pressurised Model 240 development of Consolidated Vultee's Convair 110 prototype. It was the Convair's size, performance and passenger cabin pressurisation that won his enthusiastic approval. But Convair's order book, at some three hundred aircraft, was full and the waiting time for deliveries a matter of years. On his return, Watkins had time to ponder what he knew would be his recommendation.

On Saturday, 23 November 1946, Watkins was in his office in Melbourne tackling the mountain of work that had accumulated in his three months' absence when a telephone call came through from Convair's Australian agents. He was told that Western Airlines, which had ordered twenty Convair 240s, had financial troubles and had reduced their order to ten. Convair was willing to hold the Western position on their production line for any new buyer if a commitment was made within one week. It was an extraordinary opportunity.

That deadline seemed an impossible one but Watkins reacted immediately. He left the office and went home, where he completed a draft submission for Brain by late Sunday night. But when he took it to Brain next day his general manager told him he had more immediate problems. Watkins tried again on the Tuesday, with the same result, and again on the Wednesday. Time was running out. But Brain promised to take the submission home and read it that night. On Thursday morning he had Brain's endorsement. Brain took Watkins' submission to his chairman and Coles summoned Watkins. What followed in the next twenty-six hours was a whirlwind demonstration of Coles' decisiveness and influence, and a defining moment in the airline's history.

Barely an hour later Watkins (with a staff member, Rod Noble) was in Coles' car on his way to Laverton and a waiting TAA DC4. Coles had tracked down his minister, Arthur Drakeford, to Adelaide, where Drakeford was addressing a Trades and Labour Council meeting. On the flight Coles asked Watkins the minimum number of Convairs that TAA could operate efficiently. 'Four', said Watkins. Coles, allowing for the possibility of an accident, told Watkins to cost five aircraft and spares. The aircraft was on its descent into Adelaide's Parafield airport when Watkins came up with a figure — £750,000. That amount was needed, of course, in US dollars, at a time when Australia's dollar reserves were very low.

Coles put his proposition to Drakeford over dinner at the South Australian Hotel, with Watkins and Noble strategically placed at a nearby table. Watkins was called over to brief the minister on the Convair and the technicalities of pressurisation. Drakeford was as decisive as Coles. A call was placed after dinner from the Federal Members Rooms in South Australia's Parliament House to the prime minister in Canberra, where Chifley was due to speak in the House of Representatives. Coles and Watkins listened as Drakeford, for some twenty minutes, eloquently described the merits of the

Convair and the comforts of pressurisation. When he replaced the telephone he told them that the prime minister had given his support. There was a proviso. Chifley would not rule on whether the dollars necessary could be made available. That decision, he said, had to come from the Treasury secretary (and member of the Australian National Airlines Commission), Norman Watt. Coles rang Watt to outline the situation, but Watt could not give him an immediate decision.

They flew back to Melbourne, where Coles rang Watt a second time. There was still no decision. Next morning, Friday, 29 November, Coles rang Watt at hourly intervals. At midday Coles rang Watkins to tell him that approval for the necessary dollars had been given. He told Watkins he had still to see the director-general of civil aviation, Air Vice-Marshal Williams, to get final clearance, via Williams, from Drakeford. 'Get Frank Learman (Convair General Sales Manager in San Diego) on the phone for me when I get back', said Coles. A ministerial memo to Williams provided final and formal approval. Learman was called from his bed to accept TAA's order for five Convairs. Just under twenty-six hours had passed since Brain had put Watkins' proposal on Coles' desk.[12] 'Without the Convair', wrote Watkins later, 'in the critical years 1948–1950 it is doubtful whether the new airline would have survived'.[13] TAA, he said, was 'buying off the drawing board'.[14] Although the Convair 110, from which the 240 was developed, had been flying on its test programme since July 1946 and had made over forty flights, accumulating over ninety flying hours, the first flight of the production Convair 240 was not scheduled until January 1947.

The aircraft TAA was buying was a twin-engine, 40-passenger presssurised aircraft with a 300 miles per hour cruising speed. Deliveries were to begin in July 1947. Its builder, Consolidated Vultee Aircraft Corporation, was the only aircraft manufacturer experienced in operating an air transport service. During World War II Consolidated had operated Liberators between California and Australia. In an outstanding record across the Pacific their aircraft had averaged fourteen hours' flying a day, a tribute to the concentrated effort put into maintenance.

An internal Consolidated memo circulated by Frank Learman on 29 November 1946, read: 'Mr Adley, of Brown & Dureau, our Australian representatives, and Lester Brain, Manager [*sic*] of Trans-Australia Airlines ... telephoned Thursday evening, 29 November, from Melbourne to advise that TAA would buy five Convair 240s identical to Western's at a fixed price of $290,000 each (in lieu of $263,000 plus escalation) plus radio and automatic pilot, with delivery schedule one in June, two in July, and two in August, 1947.'[15] It was Coles who had made the decision to buy at the fixed price. The decision was taken without any hesitation on his part and was to save TAA some hundreds of thousands of dollars.[16]

The Convair had been selected, said a TAA briefing report, 'to provide passenger services of the highest possible standard on its heavy-traffic routes in Victoria, South Australia, Tasmania, New South Wales and Queensland. The heaviest traffic in this region exists on the non-stop flights between capital cities, representing a maximum stage distance of about 450 miles.' Equipment available to TAA at the inception of its services, said the report, consisted of Douglas DC3 and DC4 aircraft, 'the former of limited capacity and speed, and the latter at its best only on long stage operations. Although both these aircraft have given and will continue to give TAA most useful service ... the need was felt for thoroughly up-to-date equipment ... TAA felt that it was essential to specify the inclusion of cabin pressurisation. Although the terrain traversed by the scheduled airlines is not high enough to make pressurisation an operational necessity, nevertheless it represents the only significant advance in airline travelling comfort to be developed in the last twelve years.' The direct operating cost of the Convair, 'thanks to its 40-passenger capacity and its high speed, is expected to work out at a figure at least 15 per cent below that for the DC4 and 20 per cent below the DC3'.

The hand of the federal government was never far from the

reins of civil aviation. Long used to a priority system during the war years for air travel by people it deemed important, the government did not want to relinquish totally its special access to the air services. The formal wartime priority system, administered by the director-general of civil aviation, had ended in January 1946. Cabinet had then decided that airline operators give priority to accommodating the travel needs of a substantial cross-section of public sector dignitaries on official duties. These included members of Cabinet, heads and senior officers of consulates and legations, the President of the Senate and Speaker of the House of Representatives, judges of the High Court and their associates, members of Parliament travelling to and from Canberra in connection with each sitting period, heads and senior officers of Commonwealth departments and private secretaries to ministers, when instructed.

The Department of Civil Aviation had received assurances from all operators on the basis of a number of seats being held until six hours before scheduled departure times — with a proviso that very important passengers would be accommodated at less than six hours' notice 'in circumstances of great emergency and high importance'.[17] That list of privileged travellers grew. The leaders of the Opposition and the Country Party were added. So were the Premiers of each State and their private secretaries, plus judges of the Arbitration Court, Federal Bankruptcy Court and the Australian Capital Territory.

They made, in all, a body of people eligible for special treatment sufficient to threaten considerable inconvenience to ordinary passengers who might have to forgo their seats. Lester Brain was disturbed and wrote to the Department of Civil Aviation in October 1946: 'The Australian National Airlines Commission is, by Section 24 of its Act, deemed to be a Common Carrier of passengers. The Commission would probably hesitate to adopt any procedures involving in effect the institution of travel priorities if such procedure were to involve it in breaches of its statutory duty as a Common Carrier.' The government airline was raising its voice against its owners on behalf of its ordinary customers. The Department's reply, however, did little more than reiterate the existing arrangements, adding that 'in practice, much more than six hours notice can be given so that occasions when another passenger must be put off to make way for a priority passenger would surely be rare indeed'.[18]

As 1946 ended TAA had become an airline of substance. In the three months since Coles had refunded the fare of the only paying passenger on the airline's first service, it had grown with extraordinary rapidity. December 2 had seen the start of the Melbourne–Adelaide DC3 service and the Melbourne–Perth DC4 Skymaster service (which called, each way, at Adelaide). By December TAA could boast that it was carrying 16,000 passengers a month and was serving every Australian capital city.

CHAPTER 2

1947

This socialised means of transport

In December 1946, immediately following the elections, the Bill for government acquisition of the shares of BOAC in Qantas Empire Airways was passed by both Houses of Parliament.

Traffic statistics at 1 December 1946 showed that TAA had carried 15,781 passengers to that date. Brain wrote:

> In the last week of the period we carried 2,000 paying passengers. With the addition of our Melbourne and Perth services from December 2 this weekly paying passenger figure will increase and will rise steeply during the Christmas and New Year period with the increased usage of Skymasters ... The highest percentage average passenger load factors are experienced on the Melbourne–Sydney route on which we and other operators are now running an aggregate of sixteen services daily in each direction, including several Skymaster schedules.[1]

On 9 December he reported:

> It is expected that Essendon airport will be reopened to civil airlines next Wednesday, 11th December, and that ANA and other operators will return to Essendon on that date ... It is now confidently expected that the tarmac area in front of our new temporary passenger terminal building at Essendon will be completed for 15th December and we have therefore made tentative arrangements to transfer the operation of our services to Essendon from 16 December. Since we have not previously operated from Essendon this will involve a complete transfer of staff and facilities from Laverton to new quarters at Essendon. It is in-

> tended that our DC3 and DC4 services will commence operating from Essendon on 16 December and that the normal engineering servicing of both types of aircraft will also be carried out at Essendon ... Major maintenance on DC4 aircraft will be carried out at Laverton until such time as our steel igloo hangar is erected and complete at Essendon.[2]

There was extraordinary camaraderie in this formative period of TAA, both at the most senior levels and amongst all staff. This intense loyalty and departmental cooperation within the airline was greatly stiffened by the widespread critical attitude of an overwhelmingly free enterprise press. TAA was seen as the child of socialism — a business strongly funded and politically supported by government. *Aircraft*, commenting on the heavy charges imposed for airmail by the Post Office, wrote: 'So far as we can see the attitude of the authorities has been dictated not by the idea of service to the public but by plans to bolster the Government airline with airmail contracts'.[3]

'Australian air transport', it wrote, 'has again broken records — and broken them astoundingly. The statistics for 1946 released ... by the Department of Civil Aviation, show the industry to be in a most flourishing condition.' Route mileage went up 11.1 per cent, miles flown by 13 per cent and the number of paying passengers (633,537) by 43.9 per cent. Passenger miles flown rose by 44.8 per cent. (Average load factor was a healthy 73.5 per cent.) The jump in the carriage of freight was over 150 per cent — with ANA carrying 85 per cent of the total.

'It is difficult to draw any real conclusions from a comparison of the operations of the Government airline in the initial stages of its "war" with ANA', wrote *Aircraft*. TAA's (paying passenger) load factor, it noted, was 69.7 per cent compared with ANA's 69.4 per cent. It commented generously that 'the Government airline did extremely well to record those statistics against its long-established rival'. From a general transport angle, it wrote, there was 'one notable feature of this "fight" '. What TAA had gained, said *Aircraft*, was largely new business. 'ANA gained some of it too. It might have gained more without competition but it didn't lose any.'[4]

If the press saw TAA favoured by the government, Lester Brain had cause to believe that its rival was the darling of the oil companies. Two days before Christmas 1946 he had a conference with representatives of the Vacuum Oil Company and Shell on the question of petrol prices. Between August and December, Brain told the companies, petrol prices to TAA had dropped by twopence a gallon; in the same period prices charged to ANA had fallen 6.5 pence. It was a fact, however, that after these adjustments both airlines were left paying the same price for their petrol (two shillings and fourpence a gallon). Brain's argument was that there had been for some years 'differential prices between the Government contract rate and that paid by ANA or, for that matter, most other commercial users'. This differential, he wrote, 'had been upset as from 1st October, 1946 when the oil companies granted ANA the benefit of the Government contract price'. Brain's contention of favouritism rested on the charge that 'the oil companies had voluntarily made this reduction in price to ANA and had thereby foregone the increased profit which might be expected to be made'. The inference that could reasonably be made, he told the oil companies, was that they 'had decided to support ANA in its competition with TAA by fourpence a gallon discount'.

Both oil companies' representatives, Brain reported, 'assured me that they had no desire to support either Government or private enterprise in the competition for airline business and that they had adopted the policy set out with the object of placing the companies concerned upon an equal competitive basis'.

Aircraft had, by its use of words like 'war' and 'battle', introduced terminology that would for decades to come colour descriptions of the competitive activities of the government and private airline. The oil companies reflected what was to be a general attitude in many Australian boardrooms: private enterprise intended to support private enterprise. 'ANA', Brain told the Commission, 'had purely by reason of TAA's operation, a fund which must approximate something like £50,000 per year presented to them by the oil companies which could be used for the purpose of combating TAA competition'.[5]

The broader battle lines for TAA and its competitor were in fact to be greatly influenced by the general political views that Australians expressed through the ballot box. Australians were not unique in their left-versus-right attitude to airline ownership. David Corbett, in his *Politics and the Airlines*, studied the politics governing commercial airlines in Australia, Britain, Canada, India and the United States, and found a close relationship between their political and administrative systems and the ownership structure of their airline industries. Corbett's study was concerned 'with the usual notion that a belief in public ownership is the distinguishing mark of leftness in politics, and that believers in public ownership are to be found in Labour parties; while rightness is identified with belief in private ownership and opposition to public ownership, and this is the characteristic of Conservative parties'.[6] In Australia these defining political attitudes were always to set parameters for public debate and passenger preference as the airline industry rapidly expanded to become the preferred means of interstate travel. From private enterprise supporters the attitude to TAA was bitter. 'It is probably quite difficult today', wrote Eric Allen in *Australian Aviation* in 1986, 'for many people to imagine the depth of hostility which was directed at TAA during its first few years of operation'.[7]

While *Aircraft* had acknowledged the remarkable competitive achievement of the infant TAA in its first months, the airline had by no means been successful when measured by the critical private enterprise yardstick of profit. Arthur Coles was dismayed to learn, as the March 1947 quarter ended, that there was 'a serious disparity between present earnings and expenditure'. The earning rate achieved in the first six months of operations was £1,641,000 a year. Coles had initially considered £2,000,000 a year an appropriate initial target. But the expenditure rate disclosed was some £2,370,000 a year, and this excluded interest on Treasury advances. That expenditure rate, the Commission noted at its meeting at the end of March 1947, 'was so much in excess of the revenue rate as to preclude any probability of equating the two rates by the end of this calendar year'. The airline's financial position called for immediate review of expenditure in three broad categories — direct operating costs, indirect charges and administrative charges. Administrative charges were seen as 'particularly out of proportion to the volume of the present operations'. While this sombre assessment of financial matters was recorded, the Commission nevertheless acknowledged 'the extraordinary achievement on the part of the Management, executives and staff of TAA in establishing a new inter-capital airline organisation which, within such a short period of active operations, had established an excellent record of services'.[8]

Lester Brain's confidence was not shaken by these initial adverse financial outcomes. It was his view that management had been required to set up and operate as a large internal airline network in the face of competition with a long-established airline 'which had achieved a monopoly on all our major intercity routes, and had a volume of established business reckoned to be one of the largest in the world'. It had been his aim, he told Coles, 'to break in and develop a volume of business at least equal to that of our formidable competitor over the routes on which we would be in competition, and desirably a greater volume over all services. In the intervening period it was considered that losses would be inevitable.' Brain argued that 'these establishment costs would be less in the aggregate if the building up of an economic volume of traffic were pursued ruthlessly than if the build up were carried forward timidly and extended over a long period'.[9]

In the six months of TAA's operations, public demand for air travel had been greater on most of the main intercity routes than the space available to meet it. Brain had judged that ANA could, within eight months, have satisfied that demand. He had gone forward on the basis of achieving TAA entry on a 'sellers' market' and securing 'some measure of approval for satisfying the existing public requirement' while, at the same time, 'avoiding the higher cost and public odium that would have accompanied our forced entry after the demand for air transport had been adequately met'.

To achieve TAA's extraordinary build-up, which Brain saw as 'without parallel in airline history', it had been necessary, in circumstances of general shortage of experienced, specialised and versatile airline staff in all branches, to secure a small nucleus of competent seniors, 'associating them with a sufficient number of inexperienced or quickly trained staff or men qualified in only one function'. That, said Brain, had inevitably resulted in an excessive number of staff in TAA when compared with a long-established organisation. 'In all this development', he wrote, 'one firm policy limit was directed and that was that speed must be completely subject to safety'. He acknowledged that the high rate of growth in staff numbers was behind them but rejected suggestions that TAA should now draw a line on expansion and concentrate on achieving a profitable outcome as soon as possible. 'It has also been questioned as to whether we can now justify our fares and rates on our costs. The answer ... is that our fares and freight rates are not based on our costs. The freight rates are generally the same as our competitors and our fares are the same as their discount fares, granted to the majority of their customers.' If TAA was to become a successful profitable undertaking in the face of strong competition, he concluded, 'we must continue to develop and expand'.[10]

TAA pilot training at Point Cook terminated on 21 March 1947 (at the conclusion of the No. 7 DC3 course), having trained 150 pilots and 180 engineers. With the transfer of the National Airlines School to Essendon the engineering and maintenance group also transferred there for general duties. TAA had news from San Diego of progress on the aircraft that would be its main counter to ANA competition. Consolidated Vultee cabled that the first test flight of its production Convair 240 had been carried out successfully in mid March.[11]

In mid April Australian National Airways responded to the TAA competition with a nationwide publicity drive, coupled with an announcement of fare reductions. Their initiative came as TAA carried its 100,000th passenger. ANA's passenger load factor over all their services had, month by month, declined and was now below 60 per cent. In fact the publicised ANA fare reduction was a discontinuation of their discounts and a faithful adoption of the fares schedules set by TAA, but the advertising campaign was framed to suggest that the new scale of ANA fares was the lowest in Australia. In general the press, disposed as it was to private enterprise, lent credence and support to this ANA manoeuvre. The ANA load factor rose again. (Within TAA it was calculated that a 1 per cent improvement in TAA's load factor was worth an additional £1,000 a month.)

On 5 May TAA expanded operations with a new service from Adelaide to Sydney via Mildura and Canberra. While the leading townspeople of Mildura who attended the airline's luncheon held to mark the service indicated that they would be prepared to judge competitive services on their merits, they did not, Brain reported, 'conceal their feeling of doubts in regard to a Government-owned enterprise'.[12] It was yet another indication that in the broader public relations battle TAA carried much political baggage. The *Sydney Morning Herald*, when the government announced its intention to assume complete control of Qantas Empire Airways with the acquisition of the shares held by Q.A.N.T.A.S., took the opportunity to reinforce what was a general media view. 'The Prime Minister', it wrote, 'has strong leanings towards the socialisation of air transport and hopes for the day when all Australian airlines "will be under government control". Realisation of this aim would be contrary to the healthy development of air transportation.'[13]

That Qantas shareholding was acquired by the Australian government in mid 1947, making it the sole owner of both Qantas Empire Airways Limited and Trans-Australia Airlines. 'Whatever political or strategic reasons may be advanced for nationalising external airlines,' wrote the *Herald*, 'there are no sound arguments for Government usurpation of the private operators' place in the internal field'.[14]

All the head office departments of TAA in the airline's temporary quarters at Chart House moved by the end of May to TAA's new headquarters at 339 Swanston Street (opposite the National Gallery). TAA occupied the ground floor, basement and floors nine, ten and eleven. (The finance and publicity departments were already well established there.) That move coincided with the beginning of scheduled freighter operations on 27 May, with weekly services between Melbourne and Sydney and Melbourne, Launceston and Hobart.

Australia's new airline was already attracting the attention of British aircraft manufacturers. In May Melbourne received visits by two new British aircraft types, the Vickers Viking and Bristol Freighter. Both had been critically assessed by John Watkins and his team, neither had impressed. The Commission was told: 'Whilst the Viking is an improvement in safety and performance on the DC3 it is not considered comparable or competitive with the Convair for our requirements in Australia. On our assessment the Bristol Freighter also is not considered attractive for possible passenger handling due to its relatively high noise level and riding qualities in rough air.'[15]

There were developments of consequence in civil aviation other than in aircraft. In June 1947 the first trials in Australia of the Instrument Landing System (ILS) were carried out. The TAA freighter *Giles* tested the Department of Civil Aviation's mobile ground equipment (a surplus military set) at Essendon. Radar, developed during the war years, had already provided pilots with Distance Measuring Equipment (DME). The ILS had been developed by the US Civil Aeronautics Authority in 1940, was taken over by the US Army and became the standard instrument landing system used by both US and British forces. In November 1946 it had been adopted as the standard system for installation at international airports. ILS provided a radio 'rail' down which an aircraft made its descent to the runway. This 'rail' was defined by two ground systems — the Localiser, at the end of the runway, established a course to fly along, while an associated installation called the Glide Path Set, situated near the part of the runway used for touchdown, provided an indication of the proper glide path for the aircraft. (The standard glide angle was 2.5 degrees.)

Australia's Department of Civil Aviation planned local manufacture of the ground sets and their installation at principal airports.[16]

Aircraft was again generous to TAA in its comments in July. 'Trans-Australia Airlines', it wrote, 'has been forging steadily ahead in consolidation of services and its traffic figures for the first three months of this year's operations are a credit to it. It has been enterprising in many ways and has merited success.' The surprising thing, it noted, was that ANA had not lost ground in the process. 'Its total traffic figures on the routes in which it is competing with TAA are well ahead (89,610 as compared with 54,418) though it has, of course, more services on these routes. Over all routes ANA (like TAA) is establishing monthly records with monotonous regularity.' On 12 July TAA inaugurated a weekly service originating in Melbourne each Saturday to Cairns, in northern Queensland (via Sydney, Brisbane, Rockhampton and Townsville).[17] There was, reported Brain, a 'definite warmth of welcome apparent among the public and business community', which had not, at the northern ports, seen a scheduled service before using DC4 aircraft.[18]

The TAA operational record was, for so short a period, an extraordinary one. Since 2 July 1946 TAA pilots had flown 4 million miles and carried 150,000 passengers. TAA captains had averaged five thousand flying hours.[19]

The Australian government now took steps to secure public revenue from the robust civil aviation industry. The minister for civil aviation, Arthur Drakeford, announced a system of charges by the Commonwealth for the use of its aviation facilities. (A DC4 Skymaster, for example, was to pay £13 15s and 6d on a trip from Melbourne to Sydney.) The reaction from ANA was anger. ANA general manager H.F. Walsh described the government announcement as a bombshell. It was obvious, he said, that the charges were not assessed payment for use of Commonwealth aviation facilities 'but were a straight-out imposition designed to put private operators out of business'. Drakeford made it clear that the government-owned QEA and TAA would pay on the same basis as other airlines.

Walsh responded that for Qantas and TAA the charges involved only a book entry. Revenue from the charges, said Drakeford, would total some £300,000 a year but would recoup only a small proportion of annual expenditure on airports.[20] The *Sydney Morning Herald* took up ANA's charge. 'Coming at the present time,' it wrote in its leading editorial, 'the stiff new imposts are bound to be regarded as a further move in the Government's plans to achieve by indirect methods what it has been prevented from accomplishing by Act of Parliament. By hook or by crook the private airlines are to be put out of business.'[21]

TAA estimated that the government decision to impose route charges from 1 August (which covered use of ground facilities, aeradio and navigation aids and meteorological services) would cost it £125,000 a year. Consideration of a general increase in passenger fares and freight rates to absorb this cost was deferrred pending the likely early gazetting of regulations empowering the director-general of civil aviation to approve rates charged, 'making it possible for the Director-General on his own initiative or at the request of the Commission to call a conference of airline operators to discuss this question'.[22]

The government also now exercised its power over actual TAA operations. The airline was directed to operate a service between Adelaide and Darwin commencing on 1 November.[23] (TAA accepted the direction and added a weekly Adelaide–Alice Springs service.) The *Sydney Morning Herald* commented: 'Mr Drakeford indicated that the Government was preparing to substitute a TAA service for the privately operated line between Adelaide and Darwin. Guinea Airways developed this route but private enterprise pioneers cannot expect any consideration from a Government bent on occupying the whole air transport field. Darwin, of course, is in Federal territory and the Government can do as it pleases there.'[24]

Guinea Airways continued to operate their service between Adelaide and Darwin on the same days and to the same timetable as TAA's for three return trips, terminating on 7

November. That termination followed a negotiated settlement with the Commonwealth government and formal recognition that TAA was operating an adequate service on the route. Under the terms of settlement between Guinea Airways and the government the airline handed over to TAA all their plant and equipment at Darwin and route stations, excluding Adelaide.[25] According to *Aircraft*, this 'demonstrates clearly what little part ethics play in the game of politics and how crushingly the Government is prepared to use its weight when invested with the necessary power'.[26]

That government move, while it undoubtedly reflected an agenda to shape Australian domestic aviation in the public interest, was just as clearly driven by Labor's political principles. The government wish to control all domestic operations, within States as well as interstate, was still a priority. It now sought from the States a further allocation of controlling powers by a voluntary handing over of State authority. *Aircraft* wrote: 'Not long ago that surrender [of powers] was defeated in a referendum of the people and in the light of events we must concede that the people were right. Were it again put forward as a referendum question we would vigorously urge its defeat — as we now urge that State Governments should hold tight to their powers.' Existing controlling authorities from the Commonwealth down, it said, 'are no longer above suspicion. They are interested parties, not now as governors of the people (the democratic tradition) but as seekers after profit ... Their paramount purpose is to advance the interests of a single airline ... arbitrarily imposed upon the nation at financial risk to taxpayers.'[27]

The Queensland government acceded to the federal government's request for a transfer of State powers and the Queensland Commissioner for Transport requested that TAA submit by 1 November applications for licences to operate air services within Queensland. The Commonwealth, for its part, announced plans for the early introduction of a Bill to amend the Australian National Airlines Act 1945 to permit TAA to engage in intrastate operations in Queensland.[28]

The original date for delivery of TAA's Convair aircraft had now passed. It was expected (in September) that the first two aircraft would not arrive until January 1948, with one more in February and the final two in March. Management decided, in view of the high quotation given by Consolidated Vultee for delivery flights to Melbourne, to use TAA crews for the flights. The bad news was mitigated by record traffic figures. In the week ending 5 September, TAA carried 6,007 paying passengers, and on 15 September they carried their 200,000th paying passenger. Staff employed by the airline at 31 August now totalled 2,534. In January, with the staff level at 2,316, the airline's aircraft had flown 2,705 hours in the month; in August the hours flown had increased to 4,263.[29] By November the news from San Diego had again worsened. TAA's five Convairs, they were informed, would not arrive before April, May and June. John Watkins was sent to the United States on 15 November to try to expedite the delivery dates and to make final and detailed inspections of standards of workmanship and compliance with contract specifications.[30]

Aircraft tempered its views on government charges for aviation facilities when it wrote, in August: 'In itself, the decision of the DCA to impose charges on the airlines was both inevitable and fair ... In the next five years ... it will spend more than £30 million in airport and airways improvements. The money has to come from somewhere.' But it attacked what it called plans to aid the finances of TAA by removing from some private operators a valuable source of revenue. All intercapital airmail, following a new government decision, was to be carried by TAA. This, it said, 'was a pill with a bitter taste'. The sugar coating 'belongs entirely to Trans-Australia Airlines, fortune's child of Government instrumentalities'. TAA, it estimated, would make a yearly financial gain of from £300,000 to £450,000. 'The Government has only one genuine airline concern at the moment, and that is to make TAA successful — at no matter what cost.'[31]

The political agenda of the Labor government in Canberra both intensified public criticism of TAA and directly affected operations. The Commission was told on 24 November that the aggregate number of passsengers of both TAA and ANA had increased steadily until 7 September, with TAA to that date gaining an increased proportion of the total volume of air travellers. After that date the total carried by TAA declined steadily while the total carried by ANA continued to increase in proportion to TAA's decline. 'There can be little doubt', wrote Brain, 'but that this trend since 7th September is attributable directly to political propaganda in the Press and public reaction to the [Commonwealth government's] proposal for nationalisation of banking'. There was a widespread public feeling, he said, that the introduction of control and standardisation of air fares and travel conditions in the industry had eliminated any perception that to travel by TAA was to their competitive advantage. 'This effect has been accentuated during recent weeks by the considerable publicity gained by Ansett in his claim to charge lower fares and to represent himself to the public as a private operator and public benefactor battling with an unreasonable Government. In his published statements Ansett has vigorously attacked TAA and omitted reference to ANA.'[32] He urged that instead of the prevailing policy of cooperation and friendly competition with ANA under controlled fares and conditions there should be a vigorous plan adopted 'which should avoid as far as possible Party political issues' but should openly proclaim the detemination 'to firmly establish TAA as the major national airline organisation ... The overall policy and intentions of the Government have never been clearly stated and should be stated.'[33]

For TAA staff the flood of adverse press comment that government ownership provoked left many wondering why their chairman and general manager did not respond publicly. That issue was raised by management itself in TAA's staff magazine. Under the headline 'That Propaganda Blitz' it wrote in December 1947: 'For the past month and more the staff has watched in the Press an outpouring of propaganda and criticism against TAA, the volume and intensity of which has been almost without precedent'. Almost none of the criticism, it said, had been against TAA as an airline, or of its facilities, efficiency, standard of service or staff. 'The whole propaganda campaign has been political ... Let us all be clear on this — TAA is a national undertaking and is owned by the people of Australia. TAA is non-political and will continue to serve the people of Australia ... irrespective of the party politics of the day ... TAA will maintain solid support and emerge triumphant as Australia's finest airline and one of the greatest public utilities ever established in the name of the people.' Coming from a non-political organisation the concluding rhetoric was both passionate and politically tinged.

TAA's critics, however, had all the ammunition they wanted when the airline's annual report for the year to 30 June 1947 was tabled in the House of Representatives on 3 December. The report in the *Sydney Morning Herald* gave the general flavour of its public reception. 'Huge Loss by TAA.' The annual report (the second) showed a loss of £505,927 which with the £5,528 loss from the previous part-year brought TAA's total losses to date to £511,455 During the year revenue had been £1,038,071; expenses (training and operations) were £1,339,689 plus administrative, advertising and publicity costs of £204,310. Treasury advances were £1,800,000, making the total since the airline's establishment £2,170,000. 'Interest on advances will not be chargeable during the year', wrote the *Herald*, 'because under the National Airlines Act interest may only be paid out of profits derived from the Commission's operations'. The annual report noted that in the space of one year the Commission had established a major airline and had achieved, by 12 December 1946, its immediate objective of daily air services between Australia's capital cities. In that year staff numbers had increased from 55 (at the end of June 1946) to 2,392.

The leader of the Country Party, Arthur Fadden, commented in Parliament that 'this socialised means of transport will not please the taxpayer who must make good the loss'. H.F. Walsh, ANA's general manager, described the TAA loss as 'incredible'. It meant, he said, 'that 46,000 basic wage earners with two children have had a very ill-spared four shillings and threepence a week deducted from their hard-earned wages to foot TAA's nine-months loss — for TAA was operating for only nine months of the year'.[34] The political battle lines were clearly defined. Drakeford told the House that TAA was now being instructed to 'enter the field of developmental services'.[35]

Though ANA and TAA, as the two major airline entities, were at the forefront of public and political consciousness there had also been great development during the year in the Department of Civil Aviation. It had been, wrote the director-general, Dicky Williams, 'expanding fast, trying to build up the essential organisation needed to encompass its growing responsibilities'. An interdepartmental committee was sifting through 'hundreds of applications from would-be airline owners'. There had been, he said, a record expansion of civil airports, new chains of radio navigational aids and communications equipment were planned, and air traffic control 'became a branch in its own right'. Between 1939 and July 1947 the Department's staff had grown from 251 to 2,030. During 1947 permission was given for the establishment of services by five new operators, including New England Airways and East-West Airlines.[36]

Lester Brain's last report to the Commission for 1947 ended: 'I would again urge the desirability of a clear and firm Government statement of the position and policy in relation to the Commission, that the Government should give us all possible support during this difficult period, and that the Commission should exercise its fullest powers in fixing a nationwide policy that would appeal to a big majority of the public'.[37] The airline's last initiative for the year was in its country services. One of the first of these, between Melbourne and Corowa, was inaugurated on 29 December (and later extended to link Corowa and Narrandera with Canberra and Sydney, and Narrandera, directly, with Mildura and Adelaide).

More public debate ensued in the new year. 'In quest of powers to govern aviation as it wishes', wrote *Aircraft* in January 1948, 'the Federal Government ... has introduced yet another Bill — designed this time to give it power to operate the Government airline, TAA, on intrastate services coincident with its interstate network'. Simultaneously, it said, 'it took power to implement the decisions of the 1942 conference at which, in wartime conditions, some of the States agreed to surrender of their Constitutional powers over air transport for periods ending at various times after the war. If the Commonwealth Government attempts to force its ideas further by trying to seize powers which the States were willing to transfer as a war measure — and as a war measure only — it will raise further antipathy to its general ideas in this direction.' Time, said *Aircraft*, would be against the government. 'Victoria and Tasmania did not grant any [wartime powers] and — except in the case of Western Australia — the others expire too soon to be of much use. Western Australia's can be made effective until 1950.' Drakeford, it said, 'had been granted power by the government to deny Commonwealth airport and other facilities to those who do not obey his fares rulings, but has not yet tried to apply it'. Ansett and ANA were resisting the minister passively by non-payment of air route fees. 'The question that arises from all this is — where are we heading? At the moment it looks like complete anarchy in the airline field.'[38] (At much the same time notice of intention was given by the Commonwealth government to acquire compulsorily all freehold land and buildings owned by Australian National Airways at Essendon airport.)

TAA now moved to expand within Queensland. At its meeting on 27 January 1948 the Commission decided to inform Qantas Empire Airways that its objective was to take over as early as practicable in the 1948–49 financial year the operation of existing QEA internal services, plus three additional services for which State Transport Licences had recently been issued.[39] Arrangements were completed for the start, on 16 February, of DC3 services from Townsville to Charters Towers, Julia Creek, Cloncurry and Mount Isa. (The aircraft used operated through Brisbane, thus increasing TAA's coastal service between Brisbane and Townsville.) Fares on the new route were based on threepence halfpenny per passenger mile (with a loading for short stages). Qantas, which cooperated fully with the federal government throughout, agreed to TAA's request to hire, rather than purchase outright, the DC3 aircraft required from them. TAA also took pains to arrive at an amicable arrangement with the small operator Townsville and Country Airlines, which operated Anson services between Townsville and Mount Isa, Townsville and Charters Towers, and Townsville and Burketown. The TCA airline used ANA as managing agents. 'We indicated', wrote Brain, 'that we had no desire to force them out of existence'.[40]

There were continuing problems with the Convair deliveries. The airliner had not yet been fully cleared by the US Civil Aeronautics Administration, although the main hurdles had been surmounted. Modifications were still being made to de-icing and pressurisation equipment, with the CAA indicating that a full licence, permitting export, would not be granted until all difficulties were overcome. (American Airlines, with 100 Convairs on order, was taking deliveries under a restricted licence.) For TAA the delays meant that instead of having an aircraft delivered to them that had been tested in three months of actual operations, their aircraft would be amongst the first delivered. The delays were becoming critical. Two TAA Skymaster aircraft were due to be taken over (by direction of the Commonwealth government) by the government-owned British Commonwealth Pacific Airlines in April.

The price of the Convair, Brain reported, had been increased by the Consolidated Corporation and replacement aircraft were, in the event of loss by TAA during delivery or early operations, likely to cost some $US500,000 each. He recommended, in view of the existing dollar stringency and the difficulty that might arise in providing dollars for replacement aircraft, that the Convairs be insured in dollars.[41] Plans were well advanced for TAA aircrew to make the delivery flight of the first Convair early in May. The chosen route from California was via Canada, Labrador, Greenland, Iceland, Scotland and London, and thence through Marseilles, North Africa, Iraq, India, Malaya and the Dutch East Indies to

Australia. It was to be the first time that a commercial aircraft would be flown from the United States through England on a delivery flight to Australia. (The circuitous route was chosen to save the precious dollars that would have been involved by the installation of overload fuel tank equipment necessary for a Pacific flight; even the saving of the dollar cost of petrol between London and Australia had been a factor.)

Recommendations were now put to the Commission for the purchase of another, smaller aircraft type. This time there was good news for the emerging British aircraft industry. It was decided that the De Havilland company be requested to grant TAA an option to purchase the first six of its Drover aircraft from the production line.[42] The Drover, costing £14,000, could carry six passengers with baggage and a small quantity of freight. It had a cruising speed of 135 miles per hour, carried one pilot and was fitted with a lavatory. 'Within a few months', Brain wrote in April 1948, 'we expect to take over the internal services operated in Queensland by Qantas, who at present include four Dragons and two Fox Moths on these services. Since both the Dragon and Fox Moth are obsolete and unsafe by present day standards it is felt they should be replaced as soon as practicable.' Deliveries were possible from 31 January 1949.[43]

The Australian domestic aviation industry continued its rapid growth. In 1947 civil airlines in Australia carried over a million passengers on regular internal routes for the first time. Australia, according to figures released by the Department of Civil Aviation, was now 'at least the third — may even be competing for second place with Great Britain — aviation country in the world'.[44] TAA now flew over a route network of almost 8,000 miles, its fleet covering over 30,000 miles a day. More than 350,000 passengers had been carried.

TAA continued to probe aggressively the limits of its charter, carefully keeping its most powerful supporter informed. In March 1948 it was decided 'that the Minister be advised, for the information of the Prime Minister' that Newcastle, NSW, had been included as a scheduled stopping place on the

TAA network 'for the express purpose of facilitating *interstate* travel to and from that city'. No standing allotment of seats was authorised for intrastate travel between Sydney and Newcastle.[45]

In mid April, as the all-important date for delivery of the first Convair approached, the Australian National Airlines Commission indicated that all was not well with Consolidated's technical acceptance programme. 'Acceptance of the first and subsequent TAA Convair–Liner ex-factory', it noted, 'is a matter for decision by the Commission after consideration of a full report by its senior technical representative at San Diego (Mr. J.L. Watkins) covering the nature and extent of all material variations from the contract specification as affecting suitability of the aircraft for TAA operations in Australia, e.g. in respect of such matters as weight, performance and range, load capacity, pressurisation and de-icing systems, noise level etc.'. Further, it concluded: 'All other considerations apart, delivery ex-factory of the first or any aircraft will not be accepted by the Commission until that aircraft is fully certificated by the USA Civil Aeronautics Authority [*sic*] at the new maximum take-off weight of 40,500 pounds'. Yet another delay in the delivery date for the first Convair was advised from Consolidated. The scheduled 5 May date was put back two to three weeks.[46]

The delays and the continuing reports from America of Convair certification problems gave ANA, which had suffered at government hands by withdrawal of earlier approval of a dollar purchase by ANA for DC6 aircraft, powerful propaganda material. The Australian press embarked on an enthusiastic scare campaign against the aircraft. 'Papers all over Australia', said John Watkins, 'claimed the Convair was a failure and that it would not have the range to fly from Melbourne to Sydney with more than half its payload ... that it was of unsound design in every respect'.[47]

Prime Minister Chifley warned his Commission representative, Bill Taylor, that the government could not take risks with the Convair. Unless Taylor could satisfy himself that the scare stories were unfounded he was, said Chifley, to vote for cancellation of the order. 'Taylor, hitherto a staunch supporter of the Convair,' said Watkins, 'decided to play safe and vote against it'.[48] At the same time Commissioner Norman Watt, as Treasury representative, had taken the view that there were now more urgent calls on Australia's dwindling dollar resources. Commissioner L.B. Fanning, with responsibilities as director-general of post and telegraphs, wanted dollars for specific telephone equipment while the deputy director-general of civil aviation, Edgar Johnston, had a need for some of Australia's dollar allocation to buy air navigation equipment.[49]

John Watkins, who had worked hard on the Convair problems for six months at San Diego, received a cable from Coles on 17 May 1948 instructing him to return to Melbourne immediately. He was met at Mascot by both Coles and Brain. It looked certain, he was told, that the Convair contract would be cancelled. Coles told him that he was the only one of the five Commissioners to favour continuing with the Convair procurement. A special meeting of the Australian National Airlines Commission had been called for 26 May, said Coles. Watkins had five days to prepare his case in favour of the Convair.[50]

It took Watkins two hours to read his report to the Commission when it met on 26 May. When Coles put the matter to the vote the report was accepted unanimously. 'It was a close shave', said Watkins. 'I firmly believe that if the Convairs had been cancelled, TAA would not have lasted much longer.'[51]

The Commission decided that the Watkins report go to the minister 'with advice that after full consideration and discussion of its contents ... the Commission fully endorses the report as providing a comprehensive survey of the Convair–Liner CV 240–5, and that the minister be informed that the Commission is satisfied that the CV 240–5, when certified by the US Civil Aeronautics Administration at the increased maximum take-off weight of £40,500, will comply substantially with the requirements under the Purchase contract ... that it be recommended to the Minister that he endorse the

Commission's proposal to authorise acceptance of five Convair–Liners as and when the aircraft are offered for delivery ex-factory with CAA certification at 40,500 pounds maximum take-off weight'.[52] 'Throughout the American aviation industry', Watkins wrote, 'the Convair is now regarded as not only the best but actually the only thoroughly modern replacement aircraft for short-range operations'.[53] (The Convair was finally granted approval by the Civil Aviation Administration for a maximum gross take-off weight of 40,500 pounds on 27 July.)

Watkins had again played a pivotal role in assuring the survival of TAA. It was hardly an exaggeration to write, as Ian Sabey did later, that if Watkins had failed to persuade the Commission on 26 May, then 'the uproar over what would have become the "Government Convair Fiasco' would almost certainly have put TAA out of business'.[54]

CHAPTER 3

1948

The brink of remarkable developments

While the Convair drama was unfolding private meetings in Canberra at prime ministerial level also had profound implications for the survival of TAA. Chifley was asked in Parliament whether it was true that he had had discussions with Captain Ivan Holyman on the merger of TAA with ANA in a new company in which the government would hold 51 per cent of the shares. Both Chifley, in his answer in the House, and Holyman, when questioned by the press, were evasive. But ANA general manager H. F. Walsh, in an address to a business organisation in mid-year, admitted that ANA still favoured the concept (put forward before the government introduced its plan to nationalise all domestic airlines) for the creation of a big national airline in which the government and private airlines would have financial interest. Walsh, however, denied any recent approach to the government about such a merger.[1]

Other powerful influences were affecting Australia's civil aviation industry in the second half of 1948 as the sterling area's shortage of dollars reached crisis point. Dollars for the purchase of aircraft and spares were scarce. National conservation of petrol was imperative. For both TAA and ANA these pressures meant reining in development. The director-general of civil aviation requested both airlines to make an immediate reduction of 5 per cent in their use of aviation spirit. (Both announced cuts in services to achieve a yearly saving of some 700,000 gallons.)[2]

TAA carried its half millionth passenger on 1 July 1948, and while *Aircraft* acknowledged that it had 'as fine a record as any other Australian airline', it returned to the charge that TAA was not free from political control.

> When a Government rewards a politician who, as a former independent MHR used his Parliamentary balance of power on several vital occasions to aid the present Government, by making him chairman of the Airlines Commission; when it appoints a prominent party member as vice-chairman, and selects as members three executive officers of three Government departments, it does not free that Commission from political influence and control ... And when we regard the representatives of the Civil Aviation, Treasury and Postmaster-General's Departments on the Commission, can we dissociate our thoughts from the amazing ease with which TAA obtains new route permits; from the ready availability of dollars for the Convair purchase; and from the recent grant of a £325,000 airmail susbidy? How it will end is for the future. But we are not forgetting that as yet there has been no outright denial of an approach by Mr Chifley to ANA offering that airline control in a merger arrangement.[3]

Beyond that particular uncertainty, the issue of TAA's survival was threatened more fundamentally by the opposing political philosophies of Government and Opposition. A federal election was now only eighteen months away.

The prime minister had a different recollection of events when the issue of a TAA–ANA merger was again raised publicly some months later. 'Mr Chifley', wrote *Aircraft*, 'said that no merger was likely at present. He had been approached about such a proposal some months ago and had promised to give it consideration.' It was the first admission by Chifley that there had been talks on such a major issue. Holyman now also confirmed that talks had taken place. 'In the earlier part of the year', he said, 'at the request of the Prime Minister, some discussions took place regarding the possibilities of a merger of ANA and TAA on the basis of the formation of a joint Government–Private Enterprise Corporation. The discussion terminated fruitlessly in June last and no revival of the matter has since taken place.' ANA, he said, had not initiated any approach to the prime minister at any time. ANA's hopes, it was clear, were based on the defeat of the Labor government.

In purely operational terms TAA's competitive prospects were assured when delivery of its Convairs finally began. The first Convair, VH-TAQ, was flown by TAA operations manager John Chapman, with Frank Fischer as co-pilot. It left San Diego on its delivery flight on 26 August, arriving in London forty-seven hours later (with an actual flying time of 29.5 hours). It was Consolidated's first Convair to be seen overseas (and the forty-fifth to be delivered) and was demonstrated to the British aviation industry before it left London on 1 September. The longest leg flown was from Basra to Karachi — 1,302 miles. The delivery flight put beyond doubt the capabilities of the Convair. It touched down at Essendon on 7 September.[4] The aircraft had covered 17,729 miles in a flying time of 78 hours 32 minutes.

At Essendon Drakeford and Air Marshal Dicky Williams went on board for a demonstration flight. Chapman climbed away steeply, reaching 3,000 feet in 97 seconds. He feathered one propeller and flew for twenty minutes on one engine at 210 miles per hour on half throttle. When he landed he demonstrated the reverse thrust of the propellers.[5] Aviation journalist Stanley Brogden, who flew on the delivery flight, commented: 'I believe the Convair will force ANA to buy some pressurised aircraft within twelve months'.[6]

The euphoria that accompanied the aircraft's arrival was tempered by the knowledge that serious manpower problems at Consolidated's factory would now further delay deliveries of subsequent aircraft. Brain advised that dates could not be accurately reckoned but he estimated that the second and third Convairs would be ready for departure from San Diego towards the end of September while delivery of the fourth and fifth aircraft was not expected before late November. There were other constraining factors for TAA. 'We have not yet received any detailed official advices ... on the decision to peg and restrict petrol supplies to airlines', Brain wrote. 'In view of our plans and commitments, including the new Convairs and Drovers, the effect on our planned development and economy could be very serious.'[7]

During the year ended June 1948 Australia's scheduled internal airline services carried 1,217,178 paying passengers, an increase of 39 per cent on the previous year. ANA was still the leading carrier with 584,140 passengers, compared with TAA's 343,811. Its load factor, at 70.6 per cent, was better than its rival's 62.5 per cent. Between these two airlines and the fourteen other domestic operators there was a wide gap. Butler Air Transport carried 72,749 passengers; Ansett Airways, 64,187; Guinea Airways, 44,947. The smallest, Connellan Airways, operating around the Centre from Alice Springs, carried 564.[8]

'By 30th June, 1948', said the Department of Civil Aviation annual report, 'Australian civil aviation had not only established itself in a peace-time economy, but had expanded and improved its services faster than in almost any other country in the world.' By far the most pressing problem 'was to bring Australia's aerodromes up to post-war standards'. In Sydney, light aircraft were to be moved to Bankstown. 'Mascot', said the report, 'was being developed into Sydney's international terminal'.[9] An American organisation, Aviation Research Institute, ranked Australian National Airways first in the world for passenger load factor and seventh overall among the world's airlines; Trans-Australia Airlines, wrote *Aircraft*, 'is not far behind. It already rates tenth position.'[10] (In the last three months of 1948 TAA's paying load factor rose to 70.1 per cent and was the best of all Australian airlines.)[11]

TAA introduced its first Convair on regular, scheduled operations on 21 October 1948 between Melbourne, Sydney and Brisbane, and on 13 November added services to Launceston and Hobart. There were teething troubles and delays, mostly the result of faulty assembly of hydraulic connections in San Diego, with some delays caused by the use of Australian-made spark plugs (as used in the Skymasters). There were also some failures in the much-publicised cabin pressurisation. But passenger reaction was overwhelmingly favourable.[12] TAA had its heaviest ever concentrated volume of traffic over the 1948 Christmas and New Year holiday period. Passengers carried for the 1948 year were 55 per cent up on 1947, freight was up 150 per cent and mail up 60 per cent. The passenger load factor for the year, at 68.3 per cent, compared with 60.7 per cent for 1947. TAA's increased popularity was also boosted by three ANA DC3 crashes during 1948, one resulting in loss of life.[13]

By mid January 1949 the fourth Convair had been delivered. But TAA now had its first major setback. The fifth Convair was seriously damaged when landing at Keflavik, Iceland, on 10 January, on its delivery flight from America. A report from the captain, J. Groves, stated that 'there was a severe snowstorm and that wind gusts caused the aircraft to run off the ice-covered runway and collide with solid obstructions'. The aircraft was considered repairable but preliminary estimates of the delay in delivery were from four to six months.[14]

On 27 January 1949 TAA was advised of the minister's decision that it should now proceed with the takeover of the internal Queensland services of Qantas, the Brisbane–Darwin service, and the Flying Doctor operations centred on Cloncurry and Charleville. The date for the start of these TAA operations was 'amicably agreed' with Qantas for 2 April. 'It was apparent', wrote Brain, 'that hostility to TAA in Queensland has very considerably abated'.[15] Hay, in New South Wales, was added to the TAA network on 4 March. A week later a daily 'Cannon-ball' service between Adelaide and Sydney began, using Convairs. It cut the scheduled DC3 time for the 725-mile route by three hours to two hours fifty-five minutes. That initiative made it possible for passengers departing from Brisbane to reach Perth, on the other side of the continent (via Adelaide) on the same day. The addition of the Qantas routes dramatically added to TAA's reach. As at 11 March the airline provided capacity passenger miles at the rate of 279 million a year; from 2 April, with the takeover of the Qantas operations, that figure rose to 339 million.[16] TAA route miles increased from 8,603 on 31 August 1947 to 13,652 twelve months later — largely through the addition of the Qantas routes.

The Convair, though popular, continued to have problems with pressurisation, and Sabey's publicity department was instructed 'to concentrate on the speed and modern comfort of the Convair and to omit publicising pressurisation'.[17] There were also unexpected costs (equivalent to six pounds per flying hour) from abrasion wear on the aircraft's metal propeller blades, which had to be replaced after each 800 hours of flying. The aircraft's performance was also disappointing; it had not given either the expected speed or agreed power output. (At the same time de Havilland reported technical problems with the Drovers. Brain wrote: 'Delivery dates are at present obscure'.)[18] Despite the Convair's technical problems, TAA was well satisfied with its operation and economics, claiming a higher utilisation — 8.5 hours a day — than any other company (except possibly KLM). TAA's chief pilot, F.H. Cooper, left Melbourne on 20 May for London and Iceland. In England he inspected the new British airliner, the Vickers Viscount, and test flew the Armstrong–Whitworth Apollo.[19] A new aircraft type appeared on TAA's Sydney–Perth route on 12 June when a DC6 was hired from BCPA to operate a weekly service. Two days later the fifth Convair, its repairs completed, left Iceland, arriving at Essendon on 23 June. It went into service a week later. (Four of the five Convairs were, by the end of July, equipped with modified pressurisation equipment developed by TAA engineers that provided, said Brain, 'entirely reliable results'.)[20]

Drakeford now made another important decision affecting all airlines. TAA was advised of government policy that 'all buildings at airports be provided and owned by the Commonwealth government and leased to operators'.[21] The government also appointed a new member to the Australian National Airlines Commission, G. T. Chippindall, to succeed L. B. Fanning. Chippindall had been a career public servant with the Post Office since 1908, was director-general of war organisation of industry from 1940 and had acted as chief executive officer of the Economic Cabinet. At the end of World War II he was appointed head of the Department of Supply and Development, and chairman of the Australian Shipping Board and the Disposals Commission. He had returned to the Post Office in 1946 and, in 1949, became director-general.[22]

TAA carried its millionth passenger on 9 August 1949. Australian National Airways now responded to TAA's Convair challenge with what *Aircraft* reported as a 'provisional priority order' for ten Vickers Viscount airliners, with deliveries beginning in 1952. Though that initiative was never to be followed through the move was seen as a bold one. The 40-passenger Viscount was powered by the Rolls-Royce Dart turbine engine and, with no reciprocating parts to provide the normal vibration and noise associated with civil aircraft power plants, was remarkably smooth and quiet in performance. It also promised operations at 25,000 feet — 'above the weather'. It was, like the Convair, pressurised.[23]

TAA's airmail contracts were attacked when its annual grant was increased from £325,000 to £400,000. Even the lower figure, wrote *Aircraft*, had been unwarranted by the service rendered. 'An increase of 20 per cent in that payment', it said, 'makes it even more blatantly a subsidy'.[24] That charge was true or false according to one's political leanings. It was a fact, however, that government subsidy underpinned almost the entire world international airline industry.

The director-general of the world's International Air Transport Association, Sir William Hildred, told the Association's thirtieth anniversary meeting that the wage earners of the world presented for all airlines an incredible new market. 'Once we get into this mass market', said Hildred, 'our troubles will tend to disappear. But because of our inability to keep reducing fares in a time of rising costs, this mass market appears for the moment tantalisingly out of reach. We must continue to be dependent upon government help and government subsidy for a long time to come.'[25] The culture of government subsidy was embedded in the system.

Australia was among the leaders in the world's airline industry and that industry was, in 1949, on the brink of remarkable developments. 'In England, in Canada and elsewhere', wrote *Aircraft* in October 1949, 'aircraft manufacturers are developing radically new aircraft — bigger, faster and more comfortable than any that have yet flown on the airlines of the world. Throughout the world, too, scientists and engineers are producing new navigation aids and streamlining air traffic control systems so that air transport will, in the years to come, be safer, more regular and on a more economic basis than ever before.' But, it commented, airlines worldwide 'have been developed on an uneconomic basis at the expense of national exchequers ... a large part of the international aviation system is made up of airlines that are entirely national instruments ... air travel is still too dear for anything but narrow patronage'.[26]

John Watkins provided Brain with an overview of the new aircraft under construction by the world's manufacturers after a visit, with Coles, to the annual display and exhibition in England of the Society of British Aircraft Constructors — and subsequent visits to Canada and the United States. The significant theme at the SBAC display was the emerging concentration on gas turbine engines for commercial aircraft, used as either straight jet engines or to drive propellers as 'turboprops'. Both flew in the Vickers Viscount (fitted with four Rolls-Royce Dart turboprops) and the Armstrong Whitworth Apollo (with four Armstrong Siddeley Mamba turboprops) as well as in a C47 fitted with two Mambas and an Avro Lancastrian, using two Rolls-Royce Avon jets. They witnessed flying displays of the Avro C102 Jetliner (powered by four Rolls-Royce Derwent jets), the de Havilland 106 Comet (four de Havilland Ghost jets), the Handley Page Hermes V (four Bristol Theseus turboprops) and the Handley Page Miles Marathon II (two Mambas). Watkins reported: 'The main conclusion drawn from all this experience is that the gas turbine engine has now arrived at a state of development which justifies its being considered as a practical alternative to the piston engine for commercial use.' The dilemma for airlines, he said, was whether to embrace the pure jet engine, or 'to add reduction gearing and a propeller, with its associated complex mechanism including pitch controls, in order to obtain satisfactory economy for medium range commercial operation'.[27]

Watkins thought the Comet 'a very beautiful aeroplane', though designed primarily for long range and carrying only thirty-six passengers. It was doubtful, he said, 'whether internal services within Australia will justify the use of such a large unit'. The cruising speed of the Comet was expected to be 480 to 500 miles per hour at 30,000 feet. It was the Viscount, however, that most impressed him. 'In the field of intercity transports employing the propeller turbine, the Vickers Viscount Model 700 appears to be considerably superior to anything else in its class.' It had, he said, 'exceptionally fine flying qualities and is a most comfortable vehicle in which to travel. There is an almost complete lack of vibration in the cabin.' The Viscount 700 promised a cruising speed of at least 300 miles per hour at 20,000 feet and, said Watkins, 'would be able to save some fifteen minutes on the typical Melbourne–Sydney stage as compared with our present Convair operations'.[28]

Despite Lester Brain's misgivings about the restrictive effect of petrol rationing on TAA's performance, the 1948–49 year (to 30 June 1949) was one of growth. Route mileage for domestic airlines increased by 6.8 per cent and passenger miles by 12.4 per cent. For both TAA and ANA it was a remarkable year. Between them they carried over a million passengers, with good load factors (TAA's was 67.9 per cent; ANA's 68.2 per cent). TAA earned record revenue of just under £4 million and its annual loss fell to £94,886. Drakeford attributed the loss to the fact that TAA had paid £159,173 in landing fees to the government. (Qantas, for the nine months ending December 1948 — the first period in which the company was fully government-owned — reported a profit of £104,384.)

Overshadowing TAA's operational achievements as 1949 closed was apprehension. The federal elections were due on 10 December and all indications were that the Chifley government would be defeated. Brain and his senior executives feared that a hostile Liberal–Country Party government under Robert Menzies would act swiftly to reverse what they had long criticised as a socialist measure by disbanding TAA. At best they expected harsh treatment. Country Party leader Arthur Fadden, in an address to an election meeting at Wangaratta on 22 November, declared that a Liberal–Country Party government would sack Arthur Coles.[29]

When election day came Australians voted to end the eight-year-old Labor regime. TAA's strongest supporters, Chifley and Drakeford, lost office. Instead, TAA had as political controller Robert Menzies, long an advocate for the private airline operators, Arthur Fadden, whose bitterness towards Coles and the airline he had founded was deep, and a new minister for air, Thomas White, a vociferous opponent of TAA. The airline waited for the axe.

The first to feel the blast of change was Chifley's close friend W. C. Taylor. Taylor's four-year term as Commissioner had expired; he was replaced by Gerald Packer, a consultant accountant of Melbourne and former RAAF group captain. The usual courtesies were not observed. Coles was not advised that Taylor would be replaced. Brain, who had known Packer since he joined the RAAF in 1924 and admired his financial skills, read of his appointment in the press. (Though a Liberal supporter and appointed on the recommendation of Thomas White, Packer was to prove a staunch friend to TAA.)

There were, however, indications that the new government might have to move with caution. A gallup poll in early 1950 showed that 52 per cent of Australians considered that TAA should continue to compete with the private airlines. Only 35 per cent wanted the airline sold to private operators or merged with them. Even support among Liberal–Country Party voters had risen; in the preceding twelve months it grew from 32 to 43 per cent.[30]

The Menzies government marked time on the airlines issue in the opening months of 1950, appointing a Cabinet subcommittee to inquire into Australia's aviation facilities and organisation. Speculation continued, however, that the old idea of a merger of the two major airlines would take place, on the grounds that duplication of services was uneconomic.

It was well known that Arthur Coles had been appointed for a five-year term that did not expire until February 1951. On 24 April 1950, however, in another defining moment in the history of Trans-Australia Airlines, Arthur Coles wrote to the Governor-General, W. J. McKell (whom he had met at Mascot when McKell was New South Wales premier on 9 September 1946, when TAA's DC3 *Hawdon* had made the airline's inaugural flight). 'I respectfully beg to submit my resignation as a member and Chairman of the Australian National Airlines Commission.'

Coles' public reasons for resigning were undramatic. The development of both TAA and BCPA, he said, had reached the stage where his constant attendance in the capacity of chairman was no longer required. 'In view of this position, I feel that there can no longer be justification for my retention of the post in the status of a full-time executive chairman.' Coles denied that any pressure had been brought to bear by Menzies. Menzies was publicly gracious. 'Mr Coles has done extraordinary good work', said Menzies. 'The progress shown by TAA reflects great credit on Mr Coles and those working with him.' Coles' resignation was announced on 22 May. (Some years later Lester Brain made it known that Coles, in his years with the Commission, had donated his annual salary of £3,500 to the trustees of Geelong College. His work had been done on an honorary basis.) [31]

'This news', wrote *Aircraft*, 'might have had sensational implications, in view of the rumours that a merger of government and private airline interests is under consideration by Federal Cabinet. In fact, it hadn't. Mr Coles pointed out that his relations with the Prime Minister were most amicable and that he had resigned merely because he considered a full-time chairman no longer necessary.' Despite the widely diverse views of the industry and the public on government airline operations, it wrote, 'there will be few who will deny the vital, personal impact which Mr Coles has had on the Australian air transport picture ... What will always be remembered about Mr Coles is that his direction, and his choice of a highly competent team of executives, created two airlines, one domestic and one international, which bear comparison in operational efficiency with any in the world.'[32] G.P.N. (Norman) Watt, who had been secretary of the Treasury, was appointed acting chairman of the Australian National Airlines Commission from 23 May 1950 (and was confirmed as chairman in March 1951). Dr (later Sir) Roland Wilson succeeded Watt at the Treasury.

Arthur Coles had led the airline through its most difficult period. From its beginnings it had been bitterly criticised as a subsidised spoilt child of government, owing its survival to the contributions of the Australian taxpayer. When he left, however, the airline was operating profitably. Lester Brain told staff: 'It is with very real pleasure that I am able to tell you that from the interim figures available for the financial year ending 30 June [1950] TAA will have shown a profit for that year. TAA is paying its way — it can no longer be claimed that we are a burden on the taxpayer.'[33]

Brain wrote to Coles, acknowleding his own great debt to him.

> More than any other person you were responsible for framing and directing the policy which has enabled TAA in the face of public criticism and powerful, well-established competition to win through to popular public acceptance and to profitable operation ... More than anyone else I realise that during those vital years of establishment and development you acted not only as Chairman of the commissioners but took an active part in top management ... Your great business experience and knowledge of public affairs, and your directions on policy, some of which were contrary to my thinking at the time, have been the major factor in establishing the character of the organisation and steering it through its existence. I have learned a great deal from you and am deeply grateful.[34]

The reputation of TAA was by now also firmly established in other countries. TAA was uniquely honoured, reported *This Air Age* in April 1950, when John Watkins was selected by the Indian government as an airlines expert to advise on air transport in India. 'The authority responsible for the appointment', it wrote, 'had unrestricted choice from world airlines'.[35]

Ansett had moved on 13 April 1950 to increase competitive pressures by the introduction of what it called air coach services, by 28-passenger DC3s, as inter-capital economy flights at fares 15 per cent lower than those of other airlines. The TAA response was swift, the Commission deciding on 17 April that competitive action was necessary to safeguard revenue. Second class, or 'tourist services', using high-density 28-seater DC3s, were organised. (TAA had actually prepared for such a service two years earlier by converting two DC3s to the 28-seat arrangement.)[36]

Traffic management was a key function in the airline. In May 1950 Lloyd Hargraves, who was to have a long and successsful career in TAA, was transferred from his position as airport manager at Essendon to the role of assistant traffic manager, under Doug Laurie. (Hargraves, then thirty-two, had joined TAA in 1946 as station manager, Launceston. He had served — on loan — with the Royal Navy during the war and took part in the invasion of Normandy.)

By 30 June 1950 the TAA network served 56 ports — Queensland 32, New South Wales 6, Victoria 2, Tasmania 4, South Australia 4, Western Australia 1, Northern Territory 6, Australian Capital Territory 1. Its accepted policy was that profits arising from trunk routes were available to carry developmental and uneconomic services in outback areas 'so that people who need the benefits of air transport are not deprived of the facility simply because an individual route cannot generate sufficient traffic to cover costs'.[37] Under the Airlines Act the Commission was reimbursed for losses incurred on services that it was directed to operate by the minister and on developmental services for the years 1947–48 and 1948–49. No request was made for reimbursement of losses in 1949–50 when the Commission made an overall profit.

In 1946 TAA had operated 1.4 million revenue-ton-miles; by 1949 that had risen to 27.8 million. In the same period ANA's figures had risen from 23.7 million (1946) to 34.1 million. The total for all other airlines combined was 5.9 million (1946) and 11.4 million (1949). Total Australian domestic traffic had grown from 30 million in 1946 to 73.3 million in 1949.[38] Total TAA staff at 30 June 1950 was 3,188.

In addition to the development of its own services TAA had played a major part in assisting the operations of BCPA, carrying out all engineering maintenance and major overhauls and acting as technical engineering consultant in operational matters and in the selection of new aircraft types. The Commission, subject to a statutory prohibition from borrowing moneys except in the form of advances from the Treasury, had received total advances to 1948–49 of £4,370,000. No advances were required in 1949–50 or 1950–51. From its inception TAA had incurred total operating expenditures of £13.506 million and earned revenue of £12.841 million, so that the accumulated deficit to 30 June 1950 was £0.665 million.[39] The relationship between overall revenue and expenditure had improved progressively from 64 per cent in 1946–47 to 94 per cent in 1949–50, clearly demonstrating that the airline's financial achievement could not be attributed to increasing mail payments. Over £9.5 million had been received in passenger fares in less than four years of operation.

TAA now had a fleet of thirty-five aircraft — nineteen DC3 passenger aircraft and four DC3 freighters, three DC4s, five Convair 240s and four DH84s.[40] Nevertheless, as the heavy traffic season from Christmas 1950 to Easter 1951 approached, Brain reported that the airline was embarrassed by shortage of aircraft availability of all types, including DC3s.[41] (Brain also reported that he had advised Vickers' representative in Australia, Sir Keith Smith, that TAA was 'keenly interested in the Viscount as a possible replacement aircraft but considerations would depend on knowing firm delivery dates and prices'. Nonetheless he told the Commission: 'Future replacement by more modern types of aircraft is a most difficult problem to decide at this juncture and is dependent on so many factors, including the actions of our major competitors'.)[42]

The Convairs, despite their teething troubles, were now performing well. On 23 October 1950 a daily non-stop Convair 'Rocket' service was inaugurated between Melbourne and Brisbane. Figures provided by Consolidated for Convair operations by the eleven commercial fleets now using them showed that TAA led all operators (with a healthy and increasing margin) in terms of the highest time flown by any single aircraft and the highest fleet average flying time. *Aircraft* commented: 'Since American Airlines put the Convairs into operation six months earlier than TAA, and practically operates from the doorstep of the factory, it is certainly an achievement that TAA has been able to use this new equipment so effectively'.[43]

That achievement was reflected in TAA's balance sheet. In November 1950 TAA's harshest former critic, Thomas White, rose to tell the House — as minister for civil aviation — that TAA, for the year ending 30 June 1950, had made a profit of £214,818, representing 4.9 per cent on capital. Of more significance to TAA, in a press statement that evening, White indicated that when a government-owned airline was not a drain on the taxpayer and paid interest on capital it had every reason to continue. The government's main concern, said White, was to achieve efficiency through controlled competition.[44] It was a statement that encapsulated a government dilemma and a political ambivalence. The staunchly private-enterprise Menzies government, though opposed to the socialist notion of government ownership, did not rule out the principle of government control.

Nevertheless Cabinet remained divided on the issue of TAA's future as Holyman, fortified by the change in government, exterted pressure for the merger of ANA and TAA by threats that his airline would go into liquidation.[45] His argument was simple. No private airline could survive against one backed by the resources of government; no investor would commit funds to an airline that could be wiped out by the return of a future Labor government.[46] The new government gave ANA a financial boost by not insisting on the collection from it of air navigation charges for the airline's use of government-owned airports and air navigation facilities (while TAA continued to pay these charges).[47]

Those in Cabinet who rejected Holyman's arguments were political pragmatists, noting the ever growing public support for TAA's retention. Holyman's case in favour of amalgamation was turned against him. Such a merger had dangers. It could facilitate the nationalisation of the merged airline if Labor again gained government. Uncertainty ruled through 1951 as TAA continued to prosper. At the beginning of the year the Commission moved to further reduce costs and increase efficiency. It was decided 'that the service of the Commission be established on the basis of a total permanent staff establishment of not more than 2,500 officers ... having regard to the availability of temporary employees to augment the permanent service'.[48]

New equipment was seen as critical to future performance. In a Cabinet agendum Thomas White wrote: 'In a letter to me dated 14th February, 1951 ... the Australian National Airlines Commission seeks approval to the immediate placement of an order for six Vickers Viscount aircraft plus spares, for delivery in 1953, subject to an undertstanding that the Government is not contemplating a new tax on kerosene used as aviation fuel. The Commission points out that its existing fleet of aircraft is becoming obsolete and that it is essential that replacements be made during the next few years. Present plans of the Commission call for the retirement of twelve DC3 aircraft during 1953.' Technical officers of the Commission, he wrote, had reported that of all commercial aircraft currently being developed, the British Vickers Viscount, fitted with Rolls-Royce Dart turbo-prop power units, was most suited to Australian requirements and would be economically competitive with current aircraft 'provided that kerosene remains free of import duties'. The Commission, said White, 'is conscious of the frequently expressed policy — with which I am in full accord — that Australia should support the British Aircraft Industry ... and in the light of studies and reports available to it [he attached John Watkin's report on the Viscount] has reached the conclusion that the acknowledged supremacy of the British Aircraft Industry in the field of turbine powered aircraft now justifies practical support of the policy on the understanding that the Government is not contemplating a new tax on kerosene as aviation fuel.' Cabinet was told that the Commission had been offered six Viscounts by Vickers with spares for a total firm price of approximately £1,934,000, with deliveries from February to June 1953.[49]

TAA also required two additional 'heavy aircraft' for its fleet during 1951–52 for anticipated increased traffic requirements — either Convairs, DC4s or DC6s. These, it noted, could be financed from the Commission's resources while the Viscounts would require capital advances by the Treasury. The Perth service posed particular problems as it was not considered that Viscounts could operate the route economically. 'The popularity of the DC6 leads us to believe this machine would adequately fill the need', the Commission was told.[50]

The Perth service, because of the long distance from Adelaide, the difference in time zone and the strong headwinds that could be experienced, was the problem route for both TAA and ANA. Brain and Walsh argued forcefully about it when, in early 1951, they discussed rationalisation possibilities for operations on the two airlines' networks. Those discussions were driven by the government policy of efficiency and controlled competition.

Brain wrote to Walsh:

> In my conference with you at your office it was made clear that the aim was to explore possibilities of mutual rationalisation of services with a view to achieving joint economies and maintaining collectively the best service to the public and minimising increases in fares and freight rates becoming necessary because of steeply rising trends in all operating costs. It was contemplated that the economy of both operators should benefit from any mutual rationalisation, avoiding overlapping and sharing seat availability at a planned level to suit seasonal traffic demands ... Your letter suggests only that TAA should completely change the timetable of its Perth service which we commenced on 3rd February, 1947 ... The new timetable which you suggest is not one which I would consider acceptable.

TAA, he said, 'had worked out and reviewed our timetables from a study of public demand and convenience associated with the economic necessity of obtaining maximum utilisation of available aircraft, effecting connections with our other services at junction points, and the operational necessity in certain cases of getting aircraft into position for subsequent scheduled flights'. Brain then pointed out the inherent logic that was, over decades, to determine the course of the operations of the two major Australian domestic airlines — a course that was to lead inevitably to parallel scheduling and much public criticism. 'I understood you to agree that it would be strange if two commercial airlines, after studying the same facts, data, and associated requirements, did not frequently arrive at a very similar answers to the same problems.'[51]

Walsh responded: 'I must confess that for our part we are finding that a theory of rationalisation is much easier to express than to fit into the economics of our industry ... It seems absurd to have two daily services each leaving within half an hour of each other.'[52] Walsh wanted TAA to operate morning services while ANA retained its established night services. Brain was adamant: 'We cannot accept your thesis that ANA should have preference in scheduling on competitive routes on the grounds that the operator who first operates a particular schedule should have an exclusive right to that schedule thereafter'.[53] He reported to the Commission:

> Mr Walsh again raises the subject of Perth schedules but with no thought of collaboration or sharing with TAA towards some possibly desirable objective but only to advance a one-sided principle that ANA should enjoy priority and protection in scheduling routes on which it operated prior to TAA coming into being. Such a principle, if accepted, could mean the economic elimination of TAA ... In neither their correspondence nor their actions to date have ANA given any indication of acceptance of TAA as a continuing competitive operator in the domestic airline field or any willingness to confer and agree with us on rationalisation proposals unless they are weighted heavily in ANA's favour.[54]

ANA was relying, in its stand, on political solutions to its problems. That was not, in mid 1951, something that in TAA's view any longer posed a threat to its survival. The Commission chairman, Norman Watt, told staff: 'TAA is no longer a controversial issue in the political sphere'.[55] Nevertheless, despite a government policy that emphasised cooperation, ANA redoubled its competitive efforts. 'ANA', Brain told the Commission, 'are maintaining and have intensified their competition and in many respects with an apparently reckless regard for costs ... In general they are setting such a pace in competition which we may not be able to ignore if it affects our business proportions but which, if we follow and do likewise in order to maintain our share of the traffic, will have inflated both our costs considerably and is the complete antithesis of economic rationalisation.'[56]

While the government was formulating aviation policy, ministerial approval for major developmental projects was delayed pending the outcome of Cabinet consideration of its domestic airline policy. In particular, TAA's application for approval to purchase Viscounts in February 1951 was deferred by Cabinet in April. Though subsequently approved, the original refusal of TAA's request resulted in the dates for delivery of Viscounts being delayed from February–August 1953 to July–December 1954.[57]

Aircraft capacity was now an overriding preoccupation for TAA as passenger demand continued to increase. The airline lost one of its DC3 aircraft in August when a freighter crashed shortly after take-off at Hobart, killing the two pilots. (Watkins advised Brain that snow had fallen and, in the extreme cold, it was likely that a thin layer of ice had accumulated on the aircraft's wings and control surfaces before and during take-off.)[58] In that same month the Senate was told that the Commission could not buy Viscount airliners 'because the Government could not guarantee continuation of the present policy on kerosene imports'. It was an issue of policy 'which could not be determined at this stage'.[59] (TAA, however, took delivery of its fourth Drover aircraft in December 1951, with the fifth aircraft due for delivery in February 1952, and the sixth and last one in April.)

Despite Norman Watt's assertion that TAA's survival was no longer a political issue, the public argument continued. Walsh put the case for total private enterprise airlines in *Aircraft* in September 1951. If TAA continued, he wrote, four things would inevitably follow: '(a) A period of steep increases in fares and freight rates. (b) The establishment of socialised airways with the disappearance from the scene of ANA and the other 14 private enterprise airlines (c) With that disappearance the great development of airways in Australia will come to a halt. (d) The policy of socialisation will have received such a fillip, and such a bitter lesson will have been taught to private enterprise that with a change of Government wholesale socialisation will be the order of the day.'[60] The Commission noted as late as October 1951: 'The appearance in the press during recent weeks of large news paragraphs reviving the possibility of TAA being sold or merged has had a widespread disturbing effect among our staff ... It is not possible for Management to remove the anxieties caused by articles and official statements published in the press. This is a real disadvantage which we are specially subject to.'[61]

Holyman still believed that the Liberal–Country Party government would solve his airline's financial problems by forcing a merger of the two airlines. Both faced huge rises in costs. Brain told Edgar Johnston in mid October that TAA estimated that costs of fuel, labour and supplies had risen by almost a million pounds a year since October 1950. ANA, he said, had similar estimates. Holyman had agreed with him 'that an increase in the fare and rate structure of approximately 15 per cent would be required for the balance of the financial year to avoid finishing with a loss'. Significantly, however, he wrote: 'Captain Holyman stated quite definitely ... that he did not propose and would not be agreeable to implement the increases until proposals which he had made to the Government for a merger of TAA and ANA had been considered and decided. He stated that he had informed the Government that if his proposal for a merger were agreed, then consideration of fare and rate increases could be deferred and he estimated that any increase then necessary would be much smaller.'[62] TAA, said Brain, had done an analysis of the savings that might be achieved by a merger and had concluded 'that, theoretically such savings would be of the order of 4.2 per cent and that this theoretical saving might easily be lost through lack of stimulus of competition which could be expected to occur as the result of a practical monopoly'.[63]

When TAA tabled its annual report in Parliament on 31 October, reporting its second trading profit, one of its most trenchant critics, the *Melbourne Herald*, wrote:

> Whether the latest balance sheet of TAA will influence the Federal Government's de-socialisation policy remains to be seen. But it will certainly harden the average citizen in his conviction that all round good has resulted from competition in air transport. TAA has completed a record year, covering more miles, serving more places and carrying considerably more passengers and freight than last year ... Having regard to this impressive record and to the staff unrest that may result from rumours of a possible change of ownership, Mr Menzies should clarify the Government's attitude towards TAA.[64]

Menzies at last revealed his policy. He told Parliament on 21 November 1951 that his government's policy was equal competition between the publicly owned airline and its major privately owned competitor. 'TAA, having been successfully and efficiently established — and having secured a substantial share of the public goodwill — we consider it desirable that its competition should continue, so long as that competition is fair. Quite frankly,' said Menzies, 'the Government would regard it as unfortunate if either Trans-Australia Airlines or Australian National Airways Proprietory Limited, its major competitor, disappeared from the airline business, since such an event would create either a straight-out government monopoly or a private monopoly, to each of which this Government and, we believe, the public are in principle opposed'. A Cabinet Committee, he said, would 'work out promptly ways and means of securing fair competition'.[65] TAA would continue as a government-owned airline operating under conditions of full and fair competition with private airlines. There was to be an immediate review of fares and freight rates and their subsequent regulation.[66] Norman Watt told the Commission that White 'looked to the Commission for the fullest co-operation in giving effect to the Government's policy, and that this would involve some sharing of Government travel (Members of Parliament and Commonwealth Officers to have the option of electing to travel by TAA or by a private airline according to their personal wishes) and the allocation to ANA of a larger amount of air mail than they carry at present'.[67]

Implementation of that policy was not, however, a simple matter. ANA was by now in severe financial difficulties, though the extent of its troubles was difficult to assess since (as a proprietory company) it had never published its balance sheets. ANA had been persuaded to agree to an investigation by a private auditor (Sir Edwin Nixon), who recommended that the government form a public holding company to buy TAA, ANA and any other airlines considered necessary — a proposal urged in 1943 by Corbett and long favoured by Holyman. (Holyman was to urge a plan for the merger not only of TAA and ANA but of all Australian overseas and domestic operators.)[68]

Despite the government's announced decision on policy for civil aviation in Australia, TAA management and staff continued to operate in an atmosphere of uncertainty. Norman Watt wrote to the prime minister on 11 February 1952 pointing out that 'from press announcements there have been discussions between the Government and ANA but little progress has been made along the lines of the government's policy [and] there have been press statements that ANA have notified the Government of their unwillingness to carry on under the Government's plan and that the Government is contemplating a review of the policy announced last November'. The staff of TAA, he said, was concerned and uneasy at this revival of uncertainty. 'Meanwhile the Commission is unable to reply publicly to the statements which are being made on behalf of ANA.'[69] (The Commission lost Captain Edgar Johnston on 11 February 1952 when his term as Commissioner expired. He had served two full terms dating from the constitution of the Commission on 12 February 1946. W.D. McDonald, with a background of successful engineering and business experience, as well as a fine military record, was appointed to the Commission in August.)

On 22 March Watt submitted a paper for consideration by the Cabinet subcommittee. One thrust of that paper related to the financial and operational disadvantages suffered by

TAA because of its inability to operate intrastate services except in Queensland. 'The fact that most of the intra-state airlines are controlled by or affiliated with ANA', he said, 'has only recently been revealed. In the past most of these ANA interests have been held by nominees, but more recently the trend is for these shares to be transferred into the name of Bungana Investments Pty Limited.' Bungana was, said Watt, a holding company for ANA interests. 'It is owned by the same shareholders and in the same proportions as is ANA itself.' The known financial interests or affiliations of ANA and Bungana were Butler Air Transport Pty Limited of New South Wales (60 per cent held by Bungana); Queensland Airlines (over 90 per cent owned by Butler); Townsville & Country Airlines Pty Limited (50 per cent owned by ANA, 100 per cent operated by ANA aircraft); Guinea Airways, South Australia, which, said Watt, 'exists only on paper as an independent airline ... Guinea Airways' operations are dominated and almost completely integrated with ANA'; Airlines (WA) Limited, Perth (with Bungana as the largest shareholder); and Air Beef Pty Limited (north Western Australia — jointly owned by ANA and MacRobertson Miller Aviation but staffed and run by ANA with ANA aircraft). In addition, said Watt, ANA or Bungana operated Air Ceylon and owned their DC4 aircraft; part-owned Cathay Pacific Airlines of Hong Kong; mainly owned Australian National Hotels Pty Limited; and owned the Aviation and Engineering Supply Company and National Instrument Company.[70]

Menzies had made it clear to Holyman that his proposal to form a holding company that would buy both ANA and TAA was not an acceptable solution. Instead the government offered ANA financial assistance. Menzies wrote to Captain Holyman on 28 March 1952:

> Cabinet yesterday gave long and close consideration to the problems of the structure of the major airlines and, in particular, discussed the proposals relating to your services in Australia advanced by your Company ... We are opposed to monopoly and will seek to avoid it wherever we can. We believe that competition between your own Company and TAA has produced advantages to the travelling public and has assisted in the creation of a

> remarkable technical efficiency of operation all-round. In these circumstances the Government's strong desire is to retain both your own Company and TAA as major operators. I will go further and say that we would all regard it as a grave misfortune if ANA, whose long service to civil aviation is well known and appreciated, went out of business. But a merger as proposed by you would produce a monopoly. We have therefore decided to reject it.[71]

'In the light of that decision', Menzies wrote, 'we have most earnestly sought for ways and means of meeting what we recognise to be your current financial problems and prospective capital difficulties ... if competition is to be maintained your particular difficulty has to be recognised and, if possible, solved'. Cabinet had, he said, 'discussed the future of the airlines in terms of two major operators because while we recognise and value the place of the smaller airlines, we believe that all experience indicates that in our present state of development there is no room for more than two major national operators if the necessary standards of efficiency are to be maintained'.[72] He put to Holyman proposals adopted by the government 'for ensuring that each of the major operators shall be in a position to operate on a basis of solvency and that your Company should have as much security of tenure as will enable it to plan its finance and development for the future ... We believe the agreement should be a long-term one. We propose a period of ten or fifteen years.'[73]

The Menzies proposals to rescue Holyman included provisions relating to rationalisation of routes and timetables that were in conflict with the powers and discretions of the Australian National Airlines Commission and required amendment of the Australian National Airlines Act to compel the Commission's compliance. Its general provisions related to matters involving undertakings on the part of the Commonwealth to assist ANA, but placing no obligations on TAA. 'Accordingly', Norman Watt wrote to Doug Anthony (senior) on 4 July 1952, 'the Commission feels that it is proper that it should not be a party to the Agreement'.[74] He pointed out, however, that TAA was materially affected by the agreement. He asked that the contemplated reduction of 25 per cent in air route charges should be reviewed. 'The industry is still in a developmental stage and is not geared financially to make a substantial contribution to Consolidated Revenue. Nevertheless it is very heavily taxed.' Customs and excise on petroleum products, imposed originally on petrol used in ground transport had, he said, 'also applied to aviation fuel, the consumption of which was insignificant at the time the tax was originated'. (Aviation fuel represented over 45 per cent of TAA's direct operating costs.) No similar tax on fuel was imposed on the aviation's industry's competitors by rail or sea.

The agreement with ANA, ensuring it a share of airmail substantially equal to TAA's, meant a substantial reduction in TAA's revenues. Watt pointed out that 'over the past two years the annual sum of £540,000 has been payable to TAA for the carriage of air mail [which] also assisted TAA to operate extensive developmental services in out back areas'. The loss of airmail revenue, said Watt, necessitated the provision of separate finance to cover losses in operating developmental services. He asked the minister to consider the relative competitive advantages enjoyed by ANA through 'the powerful shipping and commercial interests which own and control it'. 'The concessions given to ANA by the agreement are in the main at the expense of TAA's present revenues to such an extent that unless some compensatory adjustments are made in TAA's favour, the financial stability of the Commission will be jeopardised and permanent deficit will be difficult to avoid.'[75]

Only days later, in obvious anger, Watt wrote again to his minister reporting the issue of a High Court writ on behalf of Queensland Airlines Pty Limited challenging the Commission's intrastate operations in Queensland. 'It is incomprehensible', he wrote, 'that ANA, whilst seeking and accepting assistance from the Commonwealth Government designed to enable it to operate on a competitive basis with TAA, should permit the issue of the writ ... which if successful would result in serious damage to TAA'.[76]

ANA was not the only private enterprise operator in financial difficulties. A third player, Ansett (soon to play a critical role in the survival of the two-airline system), was fighting against competition and rising costs. Ansett Transport Industries Limited, wrote the *Australian Financial Review*, was facing a prolonged struggle 'in which the directors will require all the support from shareholders they can win'. The Ansett group involved not only airline operations but also hotels and passenger road transport. 'Ansett Transport Industries', commented the *Review*, 'present consolidated accounts. Unfortunately these omit some material required for a full discussion of the financial position of the group.'[77] That lament was to be much repeated in future years whenever the affairs of Ansett were debated in the press.

While Norman Watt and the government discussed matters of high policy, the Commission, in July 1952, provided John Watkins with a letter of instruction authorising him to bring outstanding matters regarding the purchase of Viscount aircraft to finality with the makers, Vickers-Armstrongs Limited (a Vickers Limited subsidiary). On 20 August Watkins signed the contract for the purchase of six Viscounts at a base price of £217,000 (with an escalation formula). Nine days later approval was given to complete the purchase contract for twenty-four Rolls-Royce Dart engines and spares.[78] Watkins' signature on the Commission's contract was, with the commitment by TAA to the Viscount, to have effects on Australia's domestic airline system every bit as profound as the government's ingenious scheme for what it hoped (in the event wrongly) would be the survival of ANA. A Commission paper on 29 September 1952 noted that the first TAA Viscount would be delivered at least two months ahead of the first ANA Viscount, 'the contract for which has not been signed'.[79] (ANA was never to sign that contract; the decision not to do so was to prove catastrophic.)

After final negotiations with ANA the Civil Aviation Agreement Act was introduced and passed in October 1952. Its express intent, stated in the preamble, was 'to ensure the continued existence of the company as well as the Commission and the maintenance of competition between them, and for the efficient and economic operation of air services within Australia'.[80] Under it, each operator was to receive a substantial share of airmail and have equal access to government business. As well, both airlines were to receive government assistance to pay for new aircraft. A government guarantee was given to ANA under which it could borrow on overdraft up to £3 million to buy six Vickers Viscounts. (TAA was to receive capital from Treasury for the same purpose.) Any future purchases of heavy aircraft by TAA could be matched by ANA under government-guaranteed loans up to an overall limit of £4 million. The agreement gave ANA security for fifteen years.[81]

The final government agreement with ANA provided that air route charges would be halved and both operators would pay them. ANA and TAA were required to consult on sharing routes, timetables, freight rates and fares. In the event of disagreement an impartial chairman, appointed by the government, would have the power to make binding decisions. (Sir John Latham, former Chief Justice of the High Court, was to become the first such chairman.)[82] The independent chairman, said Menzies in his earlier letter to Holyman, would have the power 'to settle finally any difficulties in relation to what I have called "rationalisation" '.[83] Private enterprise was to be government-backed. Cooperation was to moderate competition.

'In so far as these benefits to ANA were likely to adversely affect TAA', the Commission recorded, 'the Commission used its utmost endeavours to protect its undertaking. The Commission, however, was not a party to any of the negotiations.'[84]

'The Government relied on its financial power, and on the private airline's financial weakness, to force it to cooperate since it could not be compelled by law', wrote David Corbett in his *Politics and the Airlines*. 'It was an ingenious solution, worthy of the mind of Mr. Menzies, a constitutional lawyer of repute. It amounted to a complete circumvention of Section 92 of the Constitution.'[85]

ANA, the House was told in the second reading speech by the minister on the civil aviation Agreement Bill on 24 October 1952, had made a loss in 1949–50 of £216,682 (while TAA had made a profit of £214,818); in 1950–51 ANA had lost

£10,221 (while TAA's profit was £205,799); for the six months to 31 December 1951 ANA had lost £201,775.[86] TAA itself reported, in its annual accounts for 1951–52, a trading loss of £74,438. (It listed cost increases of £220,000 from a rise in the basic wage, and aviation fuel price rises worth £148,000 as major causes.) ANA's financial difficulties were not solely the result of telling competition from TAA. Both airlines faced competition from other private operators, led by Ansett Airways and Butler Air Transport.

Section 92 of the Australian Constitution prevented the federal government from direct intervention to keep these other competitors out of interstate operations. The government did, however, have powers to stop Ansett and Butler from importing new aircraft with which to compete. In choosing not to use them, it sowed the seeds for the future downfall of its cleverly devised two-airline system.

CHAPTER 4

1953

Opposing political philosophies

Holyman was not satisfied by the concessions and generous benefits given ANA. In January 1953 *Aviation Report* commented: 'ANA's persistent opposition to the Menzies Government insistence on maintaining domestic airline competition with TAA is worrying Canberra seriously ... ANA has already threatened to pull out of the airline business altogether, a reflection probably of the feeling of the five shipping companies (Orient Steam Navigation Co., Adelaide Steamship Co., Union Steamship Co. of New Zealand, William Holyman and Sons, and Huddart Parker Ltd) which own ANA ... ANA has a history of monopoly mindedness not unlike that of Pan American. Before the Labor government came to power ANA was well on the way to acquiring every important element of the domestic network.'[1] *Aircraft* reported suggestions that 'Australian National Airways, dissatisfied with the degree of security offered by the existing Agreement, had urged that all Australian trunk airlines, international and domestic, should be merged into one operating unit'. Holyman, it wrote, had admitted that the proposed merger scheme came from 'a lengthy confidential report made by him personally to the Government'.[2]

Holyman had cause for concern. 'The future of ANA', wrote *Aircraft*, 'is at present the major puzzle of the Australian airline picture. It is known that the private airline is far from happy with the 15-year Agreement, particularly in view of the positive statements of Labor leaders, including Dr Evatt and Mr Calwell, that it would be abrogated as soon as a Labor Government came again to the Treasury benches.'[3]

Norman Watt wrote to his minister on 3 February: 'I believe Captain Holyman, managing director of ANA, has put it around that the Civil Aviation Agreement is not working satisfactorily and attributes the fault to TAA for non-cooperation in that section of the Agreement which relates to rationalisation.' He listed matters on which agreement with ANA had been reached, commenting that 'very real progress has been made and that the advice tendered to the Government by the Commission that rationalisation would be to the mutual advantage of both airlines has proved correct ... savings which have already been effected by the two airlines are estimated at the rate of £352,000 per annum'. Holyman's criticisms, he said, seemed part of a definite plan of action. All that had been agreed between ANA and the government 'seems now to be viewed by Captain Holyman as the beginning and not the settlement of the matter'. The agreement was being attacked in two ways, said Watt. 'Firstly by an attempt to have the basic arrangements reviewed and in their place an entirely new set-up of Australian Airlines, both domestic and overseas. Secondly, through the build-up at the expense of TAA of certain subsidiary airline companies — Queensland Airlines and Butlers — which are under the financial control of the shipping companies which own ANA.'

He reminded Anthony that Holyman had refused to increase fares and freight rates in August 1951 and that the loss of revenue to ANA during the year ended June 1952 by reason of this decision was of the order of £525,000. (Fares were subsequently increased in April 1952.) Holyman was, he said, again refusing a fare increase despite a further upward movement in costs. 'The loss of revenue to ANA in the current year by refusal to increase fares by 6 per cent as from 1 October last will amount to £215,000.' During the current year, said Watt, ANA would reap the full benefit of the substantial air mail business transferred from TAA of some

£230,000 and from the reduction in air route charges by 50 per cent — some £110,000. 'I would remind you that ANA's policy, put into practical effect throughout its history prior to the advent of TAA and propounded since TAA was established, is that of monopoly.'[4]

The government was well aware of Holyman's monopolistic policy. As early as 1951 he had put a firm proposal to Government (considered by Cabinet in November 1951) that a new company be formed to acquire the whole of the assets of TAA for £3 million and the assets of ANA for £4.5 million, which, with a further £500,000 cash, would provide a paid up capital of £8 million. It was claimed, said a summary of events prepared for the minister by the director-general of civil aviation in January 1955, that 'the unified control and rationalisation of services would best serve the national interest and effect substantial economies to enable the undertaking to return a net profit after taxation of £500,000 per annum'. Cabinet had, of course, favoured the retention of the two major airlines. 'A few months later,' said the director-general's report, 'Captain Holyman submitted ... a further proposal for amalgamation, this time of QEA, BCPA, TAA and ANA. The matter was brought before Cabinet on 22 January 1953.' Cabinet decided that in view of the passing of the legislation for the agreement made with ANA, 'it would be inappropriate for the Minister to discuss with ANA the proposals for the amalgamation of the four airlines'.[5]

Holyman was now formally proposing regional monopolies within Australia. He described them as 'zoning areas of operation'. He wrote to Watt in February 1953: 'I am firmly convinced that rationalisation of present services between ANA and TAA in the form of zoning areas of operation will eliminate duplication of services, with consequent savings in costs ... After making a close study of traffic requirements and operating costs I consider zoning of Queensland and Tasmanian services would effect savings in the vicinity of £350,000 per annum each to TAA and ANA.' In summary he proposed that from 13 April ANA abandon all its Queensland operations north of Brisbane and that these be taken over by

TAA, while TAA should abandon its direct services from Victoria and New South Wales to Tasmania (and its services within Tasmania), with ANA extending operations to take them over. Not content with this move to cut competition, Holyman also wanted TAA to abandon its Sydney–Adelaide direct service while ANA dropped Riverina and Townsville–Mt Isa services. He considered the matter, he said, 'one of extreme urgency'.

Watt, with some understatement, replied that 'your zoning proposals constitute a radical departure from any previous basis of discussion'.[6] Lester Brain advised his chairman that 'ANA's proposals are in sharp conflict with the announced policy decisions of the Government, the letter and spirit of the Civil Aviation Agreement and the provisions of the Australian National Airlines Act'.[7] A detailed analysis of the Holyman plan put before the Commission on 3 March commented: 'Apart altogether from any legal and political considerations there can be no possible doubt that the public almost without exception would resent and protest against the absence of competition and that the esteem and goodwill of TAA would suffer greatly'.[8] If zoning on Holyman's basis were applied to a sufficiently substantial area or areas, said a Commission report, 'competition would be eliminated in favour of areas of monopoly'.[9] Watt told Holyman that the Commission was unable to accept his proposals.[10]

Holyman had also made a decision on new aircraft that would, in retrospect, have effects on his airline of far more consequence than his efforts to exclude competition on non-trunk routes. *Aircraft* reported in January 1953: 'Australian National Airways threw a spanner into the apparently well arranged future equipment picture of the Commonwealth's domestic airline last month with the decision to cancel its provisional order for six Vickers Viscount turboprop airliners. No reason for the cancellation was given.'[11]

While Holyman was attempting to bend the Civil Aviation Agreement towards a regional monopolies structure (expressing the view that only trunk services should be competitive), the ebullient Arthur Butler was, in January 1953, suggesting that Butler Air Transport and Queensland Airlines should operate the services in Queensland taken over from Qantas Empire Airways by TAA.[12] When TAA firmly rejected his plan Butler responded with proposals to sell Butler Air Transport's interest in Queensland Airlines to TAA and, in return, that TAA should relinquish the services it operated in the Channel Country to Butler. TAA was not impressed.[13] (Butler was granted special government assistance at the rate of £23,000 a year from 16 February.) Butler's alternative proposal was that he be licensed to operate services between Sydney, Melbourne and Brisbane at much reduced fares.[14] (Butler was advised by Anthony that 'he was perfectly free to make his decision' on interstate routes.)[15]

The TAA–ANA disagreement (following further proposals on rationalisation by TAA) was brought before Sir John Latham in a preliminary meeting, on 28 May 1953, with Latham stating that he proposed to treat the meeting as a conference rather than act on the basis of arbitration. At a later meeting (on 5 June) Holyman made the telling statement that ANA had never competed with any airline except on inter-capital routes. There had, in fact, been prior rationalisation agreements made on 18 August 1952 with Holyman, affecting Melbourne–Tasmania, Melbourne–Adelaide–Perth, the Riverina, Sydney–Brisbane, Sydney–Hobart, Brisbane–Cairns and Townsville–Mount Isa. Holyman was now, however, changing the agenda for rationalisation policy.

TAA's year had started with a review of its organisation. The Commission was told that the airline had passed through two phases — first, 'the phase of establishment, with full support of the Government of the day'; second, 'the phase of uncertainty, where the ultimate fate of the airline had been in the balance'. It was now, said the report, entering the third phase 'on the basis of a permanent existence but subject to the conditions arising out of the Government–ANA agreement'. The submission proposed a general manager, an assistant general manager and five divisions — commercial, operations, finance, engineering maintenance and technical development. The old atmosphere of improvisation, collaboration across specialised functions and a general non-territorial approach by management was changing. Over the decades a creeping rigidity, redolent of public service structures, would take its place. Watt proposed to the minister an increase in salary for Brain of £400 a year to £4,500. The public service connotations for TAA were evident in Anthony's reply. 'The highest salary paid to Permanent Heads of Commonwealth Departments is £4,100 per annum and approval of any salary in excess of that amount could produce unending reprecussions throughout the Public Service. The salary of Mr. Brain is already the equal of that of the highest paid officer of the Public Service and I do not feel able to recommend any further increase at the present time.'[16] Recommendations for other senior salary levels were put forward 'in the knowledge of the salaries now payable to senior positions in the Civil Aviation Department'.[17]

This Air Age announced that administrative changes approved by the Commission divided responsibilities under Brain, as general manager, and Ryland, as assistant general manager, among the five directorates of commerce (J. Borthwick), finance (R. E. Pope), operations (J. Chapman), technical development (J. Watkins) and engineering (J. J. Davies). G. M. Sheppard (who had joined TAA in January 1947) was appointed from Victoria to the position of manager for New South Wales.[18] (Davies resigned from TAA soon afterwards and E. J. Brunckhurst was appointed chief maintenance engineer on 4 April 1953. Brunckhurst had started his career with Qantas in 1929 and won his pilot's licence. Following a distinguished air force career, he had joined TAA in July 1946.) Ian Sabey resigned from his position as chief public relations officer in September and was placed on a retainer as public relations consultant.

TAA noted with some smugness in mid 1953 that ANA had been negotiating in London with BOAC for the purchase of six Hermes aircraft. The Hermes was a four-engined modern, pressurised aircraft slightly larger than the DC4 Skymaster with a cruising speed similar to the Convair's. 'The history of the Hermes', the Commission was told, 'has not been encouraging'. It had had many teething problems and was not popular with pilots.[19] Watkins reminded TAA staff that the airline's selection of the Viscount turned primarily on its better economy, 'which reflects the basic simplicity of the medium-powered turbine engine as compared with the modern piston engine'. It was expected, he said, to prove economically superior to the Convair, would cruise some fifty miles per hour faster and would fly higher, in smoother air.[20] (ANA dropped the Hermes idea in August because of the flying qualities of the aircraft and its inability to meet the safety standards of ICAO. It began negotiating for the purchase of DC6 aircraft.)[21]

Lester Brain told TAA staff in September of the outcome of the many meetings held before Sir John Latham to discuss rationalisation of services with ANA. Agreement had eventually been reached between the two airlines without the necessity for a formal arbitration decision. 'Conclusions were reached', said Brain, 'which have now been announced by Sir John Latham. The decision that both operators remain active in competition between Tasmania and the mainland and over the main trunk routes from Perth to Cairns means the rejection of zoning proposals so far as concerns the main trunk routes.' ANA and TAA, he said, had 'agreed to an exchange of services under which TAA will relinquish Riverina services in New South Wales now operated in competition with ANA. TAA will in return operate services between Townsville and Mt Isa now operated by ANA ... TAA will continue to operate the service Melbourne–Sydney via Corowa.'[22]

In June ANA, in what was to prove a disastrous decision, sought government approval to buy four DC6 aircraft and spares for $6,750,000. A Cabinet agendum in October noted: 'As the Company's request was in accordance with the provisions of the Agreement ... approval was given for the necessary dollar allocation and for the guaranteeing by the Commonwealth of a loan of £1,500,000 for the purchase of two of these Douglas aircraft (DC6 types, second-hand) and spares. The remaining two aircraft of the Douglas DC6B type, to be delivered new from the Douglas factory, are being financed from the Company's own resources. The two DC6s are due for delivery by the end of this calendar year and the two DC6Bs in early 1955.'[23]

TAA responded to the ANA purchase by requesting government approval for the immediate purchase of one DC6 'for competitive operation on the route to Perth'.[24] The minister for civil aviation was not sympathetic. The effective capacity of TAA's existing fleet of four DC4s and five Convairs was, he told Cabinet, 'considerably in excess of ANA's fleet of eight DC4s'. Although ANA would, he said, 'have a small advantage in passenger capacity after the arrrival of their two DC6s, this capacity advantage will pass heavily to TAA when their Viscounts arrive about next August and this advantage will not be overtaken by ANA on the arrival of ANA's two DC6Bs in 1955'. There was no evidence, Anthony commented, 'that ANA intends to use the DC6s on the Melbourne–Adelaide–Perth route'. With somewhat more prescience he noted the importance of the relative passenger appeal of the two fleets. 'On a cost per seat mile basis the Viscount appears to have a distinct advantage of the DC6 and DC6B and only by securing a large volume of freight can the economy of these aircraft be made to approach that of the Viscounts. Having examined the matter most carefully and having personally heard the views of both operators I feel that the TAA request to purchase immediately a DC6 aircraft at a cost of up to $1,400,000 should not be approved and I recommend accordingly.'[25]

There was, however, a significant boost to TAA morale when a Viscount of British European Airways recorded the fastest time in the transport section of an air race held in October 1953 from London to Christchurch, New Zealand. A report to the Commission commented that the most impressive feature of the Viscount was 'not so much the speed or the fact that with additional cabin fuel tanks [it] was able to make the 12,000-mile trip with only four intermediate stops, but rather the demonstration of the reliability of the aircraft and its turbine engines'. The BEA Viscount spent six days in Australia before its homeward flight, received widespread publicity and was seen by thousands. 'The visit and demonstrations of the Viscount', said the report, 'were of exceptional value to us at this juncture'.[26]

Despite the Civil Aviation Agreement (between the government and ANA) and the subsequent rationalisation agreement (between TAA and ANA) there were still, as 1954 began, substantial grounds for conflict. Watt recorded, in a note to Brain, that since the conclusion of the Agreement there had been a pronounced and significant change of re-equipment policy on the part of ANA. Instead of ordering Viscounts they had made a quick purchase of two DC6s, with two DC6Bs to follow. 'The fleets of TAA and ANA', he wrote, ' thus become far from comparable (from the point of view of seat capacity at least) and the difficulties attendant on the production of a rationalisation formula which will be both practical of operation and equitable in its application and effects become correspondingly greater.' Brain had already pointed out to Watt that it was current ANA policy to 'avoid being bound by a rationalisation formula' and that ANA desired 'complete freedom of action in the matter of scheduling'. That threatened an opportunity for ANA to attract significant passenger traffic from TAA, at least during the nine months before the Viscounts could be introduced'. The ANA DC6 purchase, wrote Brain, 'has provided the first real challenge to TAA's equipment superiority since the Convairs were introduced.'[27] TAA favoured a rationalisation formula of some kind that would take into account the differences in fleet types.[28]

There was a non-commercial diversion for the airline as it prepared for a royal tour of Australia. 'We have been advised by the Director-General of Civil Aviation', said a Commission report in mid January 1954, 'that TAA Convairs will carry Her Majesty the Queen and the Royal Party on three separate occasions, making a total of six flight stages, during the forthcoming Tour ... The Royal Aircraft was completely overhauled in December, 1953 and between 2nd and 7th of February the cabin interior will be modified in accordance with the detailed specifications as prepared by the Director of Engineering, Mr Watkins, to meet the requirements officially indicated to us.' In addition to carriage of the royal party TAA was also committed to thirty-six additional charter and special flights to carry official parties and servicemen throughout the royal tour.[29]

For the 1953–54 year TAA estimated revenue from all sources, calculated on an increase of 5 per cent in aggregate passenger miles and a paying passenger load factor of 71 per cent, of £7.75 million. Freight growth was put at 4 per cent and expenditure calculated at £7.762 million. On those figures a reduced profit before tax of £110,000 (down from £137,000) was estimated. That figure was below the £300,000 profit needed to pay a dividend on capital at a proper rate and taxation. Rationalisation savings, however, promised to help reduce the gap, as did the relief expected by the 50 per cent reduction in air route charges. Nevertheless TAA also planned for a modest increase in fares.[30] Revenue, however, was threatened on two counts. The Department of Civil Aviation proposed that to achieve departmental economies, there should be a curtailment by the airlines of night schedules that would cost TAA some £175,000 per annum.[31] As well, a merger by the government of Qantas and BCPA meant loss of income; TAA had carried out all the maintenance and overhaul requirements of BCPA and provided medical and technical consultant services. 'The cessation of TAA's arrangement with BCPA', the Commission was told, 'accordingly adversely affects TAA's organisation and finances'.[32]

Competitively, TAA received backing against its rival from an unusual quarter. ANA had been supported fully by the Australian government in a proposal that it should operate its DC6s on the Tasman route to New Zealand. That proposal was firmly rejected by New Zealand. 'ANA's entry to trans-Tasman or any other overseas service', said a Commission paper, 'would have been completely opposed to the spirit of the Civil Aviation Agreement and the Commonwealth Government support of ANA in this matter showed a complete indifference to the Agreement. This position was only averted by the opposition of the New Zealand government.'[33] TAA was under competitive pressures of another kind that it could not avoid. Ryland reported in April 1954 that of its nine heavy aircraft (five Convairs and four DC4s), one would be out of service undergoing periodical complete overhaul throughout the period until March 1955. 'This means', he wrote, 'that until the arrival of our Viscounts we will have only eight heavy aircraft available compared with ANA's ten heavy aircraft'.[34]

While these matters of higher policy were decided Lester Brain remained restless over the ministerial decision to cap his salary. He wrote to the Commission in mid 1954 pointing out that at the time of his initial appointment 'there was no suggestion .... nor did I have any desire to seek the security of Government employment or that the position should be in any way tied to the Public Service ... I agreed that a letter to me from the chairman specially endorsed with the approval of the Prime Minister would be acceptable.'[35] Chippindall wrote a personal letter to Anthony (who was succeeded as minister for civil aviation by Athol Townley) supporting Brain, commenting: 'It does not seem to me that any question of relativity with Public Service salaries can possibly be raised and any failure to advance Mr Brain ... could be regarded as a breach of agreement by the Government. There is another serious difficulty, and that is that both the General Manager and the Assistant General Manager have received offers by other organisations with salaries much higher than those now being paid to them ... By present-day standards and any sound method of assessment their salaries are too low.'[36] Watt also wrote to Townley: 'In accordance with Section 17 of the Airlines Act the rate of salary payable to the General Manager is subject to the approval of the Governor-General. I would be glad, therefore, if you could see your way clear to authorising a submission to the Governor-General of a Minute.' He pressed for a salary of £5,000 a year for Brain.[37] At the end of September Watt was advised officially by Townley that a recommendation would be submitted to the Executive Council seeking the Governor-General's approval of his request.[38]

While ANA remained unsatisfied by the Civil Aviation Agreement, TAA saw pressure mounting from other operators in 1954, despite the clear government policy on domestic aviation. That policy required two major operators concentrating on the trunk routes, with certain other areas supporting those routes, and subsidiary operators feeding into the trunk routes. (Those subsidiary operators were Butler and East-West in New South Wales; Queensland Airlines in southern Queensland; Guinea Airways, in South Australia; Connellan in Central Australia; MacRobertson Miller between Perth and the northwest of Western Australia; and Airlines of West Australia, in the southwest of Western Australia.)

Ansett did not fit into either category, while Butler now showed signs of intruding on the trunk routes in competition with Ansett. 'Government policy', said a Commission report, 'will be frustrated if Ansett or Butler are permitted to develop into a major competitor on any of the main trunk systems'.[39]

Ansett's air services had been operating with the now outmoded DC3 and with flying boats, but Reginald Ansett had embarked on a policy of re-equipping with the Convair 340. His style was to offer cut fares, advertising that his service was the equal of TAA/ANA in all respects. TAA saw it as a duty not only to provide services to those who could pay higher fares but also to meet any demand for low-cost services, provided it could do so without loss. It recognised, as the Commission was told in August 1954, that 'Ansett's business has developed significantly since he introduced cut fares in 1949, in large measure at the expense of TAA and ANA. As he is now re-equipping with modern aircraft he can no longer be ignored.' Low fare operation was now on the TAA agenda. ANA policy also, it recognised, in order to meet competition from TAA Viscounts, would 'almost certainly move in the direction of high-density seating in their DC6s, with lower fares'. Ansett, however, was the immediate threat. It was proposed that in conjunction with ANA there should be DC4 services to compete on a fare basis with Ansett. 'This line of action should prevent Ansett making any serious inroads on our passenger business.' There were clear indications, the Commission was warned, 'that if Ansett is not curbed, Butler will endeavour to meet his competition. Butler may become a

east coast dominance by TAA which was hoped for'. On the Perth route, said the report, 'the competitive prospect is far less satisfactory. In competing with the DC6B the Viscount is matched against an aircraft of greater capacity, greater load flexibility and greater range — including the ability to fly non-stop Melbourne–Perth or Sydney–Perth if desired'.[52] (The Viscount had not been designed for operation over distances like Perth–Adelaide against the strong headwinds encountered.) Overall, the Commission was advised, 'the immediate problem is to hold our business. We can do this with one DC6B and six Viscounts and at the same time dispose of one DC4 and six DC3s.'[53]

As early as January 1954 a report to TAA's general manager had boldly recommended the purchase of two Comet II aircraft for use on the Perth route, with the period until delivery covered by DC6 charter.[54] That recommendation had been followed immediately by the the crash of a Comet at Elba. On 10 January BOAC Comet G–ALYP, flying from Rome to London, disintegrated over the Mediterranean ten miles south of the island of Elba. It was not the first Comet crash. On 26 October 1952, BOAC Comet ALYZ had crashed on take-off from Rome, though there were no fatalities. On 2 May 1953, BOAC Comet G-ALYV had crashed near Calcutta, killing all forty-three people on board. The recommendation that TAA should buy the Comet was not proceeded with.

On 22 January 1955 TAA's fourth Viscount arrived in Melbourne, carrying twenty German migrants from Hamburg on the delivery flight. TAA had now completed its sixth week of scheduled Viscount operations. Public response had been all that was hoped. The average load factor for the period was 89.5 per cent. It was planned to more than double Viscount utilisation by the addition of two daily flights on the Melbourne–Sydney route and one extra Sydney–Brisbane flight. TAA's competitive future seemed assured.

There was, however, shock news for the Commisssion and TAA staff. On 3 February 1955 Lester Brain wrote to Norman Watt: 'Herewith I beg to tender my resignation from the Service of the Commission with effect from 17th March'.[55]

CHAPTER 5

1955

Imminent collapse

'My prospective new employers,' Brain told Watt, 'are naturally desirous of announcing my appointment. However I have asked them to abstain until after this week's Commission meeting because I feel that it is really most important to TAA that any announcement ... should cover in the one item the fact of my new appointment and at the same time of my successor in TAA. This would prevent newspaper speculation and humbug.'[1]

On 6 February 1955 Norman Watt officially announced that John Ryland, who had been TAA's assistant general manager for eight years, would succeed Brain as general manager. He was forty-three. Brain, said the announcement, had resigned from TAA to become managing director of De Havilland Aircraft (Aust.) Pty Ltd.

'I had no inkling of Mr Brain's intention to resign,' Watt wrote to Harold Holt (who was temporarily acting minister for civil aviation), 'until the evening of Thursday 3rd February'. Brain's surprise departure was seen as evidence of the government-enforced linking of the salary level of the airline's general manager to the salaries paid to senior public servants. It had already been made clear to government that the Commission itself regarded Brain's treatment as a breach of the agreement reached with him, an agreement endorsed by Chifley as prime minister of the day. There was some apprehension that Lester Brain might now take legal action to recover monies that should properly have been paid to him. Brain sent Watt an extract from an opinion on his situation from R. M. Eggleston QC, which stated: 'It is clear that Mr Brain's remuneration over the period during which he has been employed by the Commission has been considerably less than would have been warranted by the underlying spirit of the agreement [with him] taken in conjunction with the remarkably successful development of the undertaking'. The growth and success of the Commission's undertaking, he said, 'substantially exceeded the expectations entertained when the agreement was entered into'. It would not have been unreasonable to find Mr Brain's salary rising to £5,000 before the expiration of the five-year term of the agreement, that is to say by June 1951. In fact his salary from July 1950 to January 1953 was only £4,000 and from January 1953 to July 1954, £4,500. Eggleston commented: 'The normal remedy of an executive who considers that he is underpaid but who has no legally enforceable right to a higher salary from his employer is to seek more remunerative employment elsewhere'.[2]

Brain believed that the issue of his salary level was so sensitive that to have confronted the government on it might well have put at risk TAA's future as an independent entity. He had taken no action to bring the question before the Commission in 1950–51 because, he wrote to Watt, 'I was convinced at that date when competition between TAA and ANA was still warm and the Government of the day's domestic policy undecided that an appropriate decision by my Commission [on his salary level] when referred to Government channels could be embarrassing and even influence the Government towards deciding on a merger'. Brain, however, dismissed the notion of litigation. 'Nothing is further from my thoughts on the eve of my relinquishment of my present post than to raise anything litigious or contentious between me and my Commission.'[3]

It had been a demonstration that the interests of government, in managing public service salary levels, were directly at odds with the interests of TAA as an airline competing in a commercial environment. TAA senior management were, in effect, to be treated as public servants but expected to act as corporate executives in a business enterprise.

The matter of government influence went beyond salary levels. Holt wrote to Norman Watt criticising the Commission's announcement that Ryland would succeed as general manager. 'I should have thought that, in an appointment of this importance, the Minister would have been consulted beforehand', he wrote. He acknowledged, however, that the Commission had the responsibility to make the appointment.[4] From the government's point of view there was yet a further complication, which Holt raised with Watt. 'You are aware, of course', he wrote, 'that it has been the practice to keep the salary of the senior executive officers of Trans-Australia Airlines and Qantas Empire Airways Limited in line and that Mr Townley has been directly concerned with these matters since he took office as Minister for Civil Aviation'.

Government determination of the conditions of employment for the senior executives charged with running the two government airlines was always to inhibit both TAA (as a Commission) and Qantas (as a company with all its shares owned by the government). Cabinet had only recently approved a salary of £5,000 a year for the general manager of Qantas. Townley advised Watt that he proposed to recommend a similar salary level for TAA's new general manager, John Ryland.[5]

The bureaucratic chains that bound airline administration consumed the time of the highest officers of the public service. Watt's efforts to provide a gratuity for Lester Brain involved in ensuing months Roland Wilson, as secretary to the Treasury, Sir Richard Williams, as director-general of civil aviation, Athol Townley as minister, the office of the Commonwealth solicitor-general and Cabinet itself. It was finally decided that an 'act of grace payment' of £6,250 to Brain would be less costly than a payment based on contingent financial liability in respect of his eight years with TAA plus furlough payment in respect of his twenty-two years with Qantas (a total of £6,874). It was not until November 1955 that Watt was able to write to Brain: 'Confirming the telegram which I sent you yesterday, I have the greatest pleasure, personally and on behalf of the Commission, in informing you that, following cabinet consideration of the matter, I am now in receipt of advice from the minister of civil aviation which has enabled the Commission to authorise an ex gratia payment to you in the amount of £6,250 in recognition of the special circumstances of your long and distinguished service to civil aviation in Australia.'[6]

Aircraft made an informed guess that Brain's salary at de Havilland's was £7,500 a year. He went to a company that now had less work at Bankstown than at any time since 1939. The company was making parts for the CA22 Winjeel trainer, producing a small order of DH115 two-seater Vampire trainers for the RAAF and a small Sea Venom order for the RAN. Over the de Havilland company hung the shadow of the Comet disasters.[7]

Ryland took up his position in a critical year for Australian domestic aviation. Ahead lay a period of competitive challenge for three distinct aircraft — the DC6B, the Vickers Viscount and the Convair 340. On 8 March TAA noted that their request for dollars to purchase a DC6B (for the Perth route) had been refused 'in view of the Commonwealth's straightened dollar resources'. On the same date the Commisssion confirmed that Vickers-Armstrongs had been advised of a firm TAA requirement for three additional Viscounts.[8] Up to 3 March TAA Viscounts had carried almost 30,000 passengers at an average passenger load factor of 86.1 per cent.[9] The airline's future rested on the performance of its Viscount fleet. All the signs were that it would do well.

The final aircraft in TAA's initial Viscount order, TVF, delivered on 9 April, was the first to be factory equipped with the Rolls-Royce Dart 506 engine, which represented a considerable advance in efficiency on the Dart 505. TAA had thirty-six Dart engines (sixteen installed in aircraft and twenty spare engines) requiring conversion to the 506 standard. TVF was also fitted with additional wing tanks, and it was planned to install these on TVE to ready it for the Perth service with

TVF. (They began operations on the route, using sleeper chairs, on 19 April.) John Watkins, director of engineering, reported: 'Not only is the Dart 506 engine essential to effective operation of the Viscount on the Perth service, but it has other important benefits in our normal inter-city operations'. The engine provided increased power output as well as a lower specific fuel consumption and enabled an increase of speed at 18,000 feet from 306 to 321 miles an hour. That meant, with each Viscount making some 1,750 inter-capital trips a year, a saving each year for each aircraft of 28,000 gallons of kerosene and 89 hours' flying time.

Engines were not only key elements in operating economics. Watkins commented: 'Having regard to the present intensely competitive situation as between Viscounts and ANA's DC6 and DC6B aircraft ... the improvement in cruising performance by the change to the Dart 506 engines should be brought into effect on all our Viscount aircraft at the earliest possible moment.'[10]

For both political and procurement reasons TAA was not able to hire a DC6 or DC6B for its Perth route. Although it was possible to operate the medium-range Viscounts to Perth with a stop at Forrest, they were not considered competitive with ANA's DC6Bs on that route nor was it considered sensible to deplete the east coast Viscount fleet. The decision was made to accept the situation and use DC4s with sleeper chairs and reduced seating capacity until the long-range Viscounts were ready. Nevertheless the Commission decided that pressure to obtain a DC6B should be maintained 'and that the view should be pressed both to the minister and treasurer, and to the prime minister, that it is the *only* satisfactory solution available for TAA's needs'. From September 1955, it noted, 'a DC6B is vital to TAA's maintenance of its position on the Perth route'.[11] ANA operated their first DC6B on the Sydney–Adelaide–Perth route on 9 March, with TAA responding with the DC4 fitted with sleeper chairs.

There were problems on the ground for TAA at Mascot airport, Sydney. Existing terminal facilities occupied the bulk of the ground floor of the old DCA Control Tower and overflowed into two adjacent terminal huts. Even during normal periods facilities for passengers and staff were overtaxed. In peak periods the public areas were crammed. ANA's facilities were vastly superior. DCA, however, had advised that because of their financial commitments on new airports they could not provide funds for improvements. There was, though, no objection raised to extensions if TAA provided the capital. Plans were put to the Commission in March 1955 to extend and upgrade the TAA Mascot terminal.

Though ANA was still the main preoccupation for TAA, Reginald Ansett was steadily increasing his share of domestic traffic. 'He appears confident,' said a Commission report in April 1955, 'that it will cost the major airlines more to force him out of business than to bear with his selective cut-price tactics. There seems no ultimate alternative to the operation of Air Coach Services in opposition to Ansett if our traffic is to be protected.'[12] Ansett had introduced his lower fare policy in April 1950. From 1949–50 to 1953–54 his traffic had increased by 126 per cent. In the same period TAA's passenger traffic had grown by 25 per cent. Ominously for ANA, their traffic had actually decreased by 3 per cent. The addition of two Convair 340s to the Ansett fleet had substantially increased his passenger business potential. As well, he planned to introduce air coach operations on the Perth route. TAA calculated that in 1955–56 Ansett would have some 10 per cent of the Australian domestic traffic. Ansett was emerging as a force to be reckoned with.

Ryland's conclusion on air coach directly affected fleet planning. He reported: 'TAA's fleet is not suitable for Air Coach on a wide scale. The Viscount, DC4 and proposed DC6B are suitable, but the Convair 240s are not. ANA are at present in a better position with their DC4s, DC6s and DC6Bs. TAA should therefore dispose of their Convair 240s and replace them with Viscounts. A fleet of 11 Viscounts and one DC6B (plus DC4s and DC3s as necessary) is recommended.'[13]

John Ryland made only modest changes to TAA's organisation following his appointment. To fill the position he had vacated Captain John Chapman, director of operations, was appointed assistant general manager. The supply department was placed within the directorate of engineering and John Watkins' position as director of engineering was 'elevated above other directorial staff' with a higher salary. (Watkins was elected a Fellow of the Royal Aeronautical Society in mid-year, one of only fourteen Fellows in Australia.) Captain R. E. (Reg) Bailey, formerly manager flying operations, succeeded Chapman as acting director of operations. In other senior appointments Frank Austin was promoted to the position of technical superintendent, G.J. Dailey became senior planning engineer and B.G. Woodgate senior aeronautical engineer.[14]

There was another notable aviation appointment in Australia in mid 1955. Donald George Anderson, thirty-seven, succeeded Air Marshal Sir Richard Williams as director-general of civil aviation. A flight lieutenant in the RAAF in World War II, with 3,000 hours' experience as a military transport pilot and RAAF Ferry Command test pilot, Anderson had joined the Department of Civil Aviation after the war as an examiner of airmen.[15] He was to prove an able, influential and powerful administrator in a period of turmoil and great change for Australian domestic aviation.

Arthur Butler, Reginald Ansett and Ivan Holyman, all men of independent mind, were now increasingly in conflict. Holyman's ANA was in trouble. As TAA reported a record number of paying passengers carrried for the year to 30 June 1955 (at 685,121), ANA's result for the period was the worst in its history, promising a trading loss of £150,000.[16] TAA, by contrast, reported a profit of £221,059 — almost double that for the previous year. Revenue had risen 11 per cent to almost £12 million.[17]

At the same time Arthur Butler was poised to compete on the Sydney–Melbourne trunk route. Butler told John Ryland on 26 August 1955 that he would operate Viscount services daily into Melbourne from Sydney from late October at the same fares as Ansett, as well as flights to Coolangatta in Queensland.[18] Ansett competition, he said, had seriously affected his business. He also revealed that he believed there was no future for small airlines in Australia; the situation would develop, he said, into two major airlines only. Butler told Ryland that he was now independent of Holyman and that the ANA's interest in Butler Air Transport (through Bungana) was less than 50 per cent. Butler revealed an initiative that surprised but did not ruffle Ryland. He confided he had proposed to the government that with the aid of a £4 million capital guarantee and further capital available as required, he should purchase TAA. He would then, he said, compete as a non-government enterprise against ANA.

In fact, Butler was in trouble. Shareholders in Butler Air Transport were divided into two camps, each seeking control of the airline. In one camp were ANA interests, in the other employee shareholders and other supporters of Arthur Butler. The *Financial Review* reported on 20 October 1955 that Butler had offered a half interest in the airline to the government of New South Wales. (The offer was refused.) Arthur Butler, said the report, had been instructed not to operate his Viscount in competition with ANA. 'The two companies — Bungana Investments Pty Ltd and Holyman Bros Pty Ltd', it wrote, 'hold more than half the shares in Butler Air Transport Limited but not a majority voting right'. Holyman told the *Review* that he had voted against Butler's proposed expansion plans. (Holyman interests commanded 4,489 votes, Butler and employee shareholders 3,056 votes and outside shareholders 2,835 votes.[19] Ryland told the Commission that 'ANA's real role and attitude as the major financial interest in Butler/Queensland Air Lines is obscure and complicates evaluation and action by TAA'.)[20] Arthur Butler's board, however, backed his plans for Viscount operations. He began twice daily return Melbourne–Sydney flights on 12 December (one via Dubbo) and, competing with Ansett's Convair 340, services to Coolangatta. ANA, despite Holyman's attitude to the Butler initiative, carried out ground handling for him in Melbourne.[21]

Butler did not get far with his proposal to the federal government to buy TAA. The *Argus* newspaper in Melbourne wrote on 9 September 1955: 'A brief news item yesterday threw thousands of Australians into alarm. It said that the rejected offer by Butler Air Transport to purchase Trans-Australia Airlines for £5 million had spotlighted renewed pressure by Australian National Airlines for amalgamation with TAA ... Has the Government a plan to hand TAA over to private control? If so, we offer the Government two words of warning. FORGET IT. TAA has been a model of efficiency since it was born nine years ago today.'

While the conflict between Holyman and Butler continued, Ansett Transport Industries reported a record year and a profit of £175,761 on revenue of £5,370,445. Ansett's fleet expansion, in Ryland's view, was 'limited only by import licence problems, at least for a time'. He told the Commission: 'He is now diversifying his operations and strengthening his organisation by developing road passenger and freight business ... Ansett must be regarded as a potentially serious competitive threat.'[22] Butler, by contrast, was considered a nuisance, but never a threat.

TAA ended the 1955 calendar year with a trading profit for the final six months of £206,951 compared with £134,720 for the same period in the previous year.[23] Though the Viscounts were so strongly demonstrating their competitive appeal (the seventh Viscount, VH-TVG, was delivered on 29 January 1956), there was a worrying development for Watkins and the airline. TAA had been advised by British European Airways in November that cracks had been found in the wing spar booms of one of BEA's oldest Viscounts, which had flown 4,600 hours. Subsequent inspections showed a number of similar stress corrosion cracks in ten other early aircraft with flying times varying from 1,840 to 4,600 hours. TAA, on Vickers' advice, had at once purchased an industrial X-ray machine and begun its own inspections. By the end of January some 80 per cent of the areas where cracking could occur had been examined on all TAA Viscounts without detecting any defects in the wings. TAA was advised that the spar booms of their aircraft embodied an improved type of surface protection, but Watkins, while not believing the airline would be faced with withdrawing any Viscount from service in the immediate future, thought it likely that in the longer term there would be problems. He arranged with Vickers for a complete set of inner and outer wings to be sent to Australia, to be available as replacements if needed, to avoid grounding an aircraft for repairs.[24] (Two Viscounts were withdrawn from service for spar boom replacements in late 1957.)

The Rolls-Royce Dart turbine engine was at the heart of the Viscount's commercial and competitive success. (The progressive Viscount load factor since entering service with TAA was 86.7 per cent.) TAA now moved to procure for its fleet the smaller, twin-engined airliner with the same power plant, the Fokker Friendship, that John Watkins had always supported. The F27 prototype had made its first flight on 24 November 1955 but in early 1956 Ryland wrote: 'There appears to be growing general agreement with our opinion that the Friendship will be a successful and significant aeroplane ... Our very satisfactory experience over twelve months with Rolls-Royce Dart engines operated in our Viscounts makes the twin-Dart 265 m.p.h. Friendship a most logical selection for the DC3 replacement in our fleet.'[25] An order was placed in April with Fokker for six Friendships for delivery in 1959. At the same time TAA ordered from Vickers two of the larger 810 series Viscounts, with delivery in 1958. (The Viscount had been a major success for Vickers; by May 1956 orders worldwide totalled 306.) TAA's eighth and ninth Viscounts (TVH and TVI) were delivered in June 1956 and the tenth, TVJ, in July. In June 1956 TAA sold one of its Convairs, VH-TAP, to Pakistan International Airlines, following nearly eight years of successful operation with its four sister aircraft in Australia. As the Viscount fleet grew it was also planned to dispose of four DC3 aircraft.

The first six Viscounts delivered to TAA had been the V720 series, the last three the V756. A programme was devised to convert all the Viscount fleet to V756s over a two-year period, involving cockpit changes, a stronger undercarriage, changing all narrow-bladed propellers to the new square-ended pattern and conversion of all Dart 506 engines to Dart 510s (with a significant increase in cruising speed). Viscount VH-

TVD was undergoing a complete overhaul which, Ryland reported, 'is of major significance as the highest time between overhauls yet conducted anywhere in the world.'[26]

TAA had also taken a position on the French Sud-Est Caravelle aircraft (for use on the Perth route) with an option for two aircraft. That option (for May–June 1960 delivery) had expired in September 1956 but Sud-Est had agreed to an extension to March, 1957. Active technical evaluation of the Caravelle and other possible alternative aircraft was continuing.[27]

As these fleet decisions were made TAA prepared for the task of carrying competitors, officials and visitors to Melbourne for the Olympic Games, due to begin on 22 November 1956. The number of flights into Melbourne was expected to double. TAA's Essendon terminal was decorated with a huge boomerang on the tarmac frontage while a giant kangaroo, holding an Olympic torch, stood above the terminal building. Bookings were heavy. Forty additional special flights were scheduled for the day before the Games opened.

In October 1956 TAA celebrated the tenth anniversary of the start of scheduled services. It did so as its annual report, tabled in Parliament, showed a profit for the financial year to 30 June of £302,945 (up from £221,059 in the previous year). For the first time in its history TAA now showed in the accumulated profit and loss account, for all its operations over the years, a credit balance. The Viscounts had averaged the very high utilisation rate in their aggregate operation of almost ten hours a day, and their Dart engines had flown a total of 94,000 engine hours without a single in-flight failure. The airline now had a total staff of 3,687.[28]

As Butler's second Viscount began operations towards the end of the year Ansett, on 16 November, introduced direct Sydney–Melbourne services using Convair 340 aircraft. (All previous Ansett services had called at Wagga en route to Melbourne.)[29] On 12 December 1956, R. M. Ansett announced at the annual meeting of Ansett Transport Industries that profits after tax had increased to £258,700. From 1953 to 1956 he said, reserves had increased from £102,994 to £415,520.

Ansett Airways revenue in the year had grown by £400,000 to £2,100,000. He told shareholders: 'The number of passengers carried by TAA rose 9 per cent. ANA carried 4.33 per cent fewer passengers. The number of passengers carried by Ansett Airways increased by 21.17 per cent.'[30]

There was another sign, as 1956 ended, that Australian civil aviation was undergoing radical change. In November 1956 the government borrowed $US27 million in New York to finance the purchase by Qantas of seven Boeing 707–138 airliners, powered by J57 Pratt & Whitney pure jet engines. The aircraft were due for delivery in 1959.

For the two main domestic airlines in Australia change was to come through crisis. It was plain by now that Holyman's choice of the DC6B aircraft had been disastrous. Their poor passenger appeal and low load factors had weakened the airline as TAA's Viscounts, with far higher load factors, went from strength to strength. Over the same period ANA was losing money at the rate of £350,000 a year from its DC3 operations. When Senator Shane Paltridge was appointed minister of civil aviation, shipping and transport in October 1956 he faced the imminent demise of ANA. One-half of the carefully constructed government two-airline structure was close to collapse.

Holyman's long contribution to Australian aviation was recognised in the 1957 New Year honours list by a knighthood. On 18 January 1957, without warning, while on holiday in Honolulu, Holyman collapsed and died.[31]

CHAPTER 6

1957

Inherent industry instability

The dominant figure in Australian civil aviation as 1957 began was Don Anderson. He was, wrote Stanley Brogden in his *Australia's Two-Airline Policy*, 'immensely able, steeped in departmental policy and ruthless when it was needed ... Knowing nothing of aviation the new Minister had to rely on his Director-General to a degree unusual in federal departments. This vested Anderson with enormous power and it is fortunate for all concerned that Anderson was a man of the utmost integrity and amenable to subordinates' advice.'[1] Shane Paltridge was himself a man of great ability. Both were to be tested.

There had been no rigorous study of Australia's civil aviation industry since Corbett's attempt, during the war, to come to grips with its needs and possibilities. Following his appointment, Anderson immersed himself in such a study. His conclusions were to bring about new legislation that would remove the inherent instability of the industry and set its course for decades to come. In an address to the Royal Aeronautical Society in Victoria, Anderson summarised his views.

> What impressed us most was the fact that on a turnover of something like £25,000,000 for the year 1955–56, our airlines had a net profit of £648,000, which is something like 2.6 per cent on turnover and about 9 per cent on capital. By any commercial standard this is a very marginal, in fact a poor return, especially

> if that £648,000 included some element of subsidy. As we saw the position the trunk route part of the domestic airline system was quite capable of being profitable. There was some duplication of services and of facilities but we were sure that if the trunk route services were rationalised ... there was no reason why the trunk route system should not be self-sufficient and pay its way. *This was assuming, of course, that the capacity provided was not excessive and, in particular, that there should not be more than two major operators.*[2]

Capacity control was the key. 'If there were three such operators and the capacity was excessive,' said Anderson, 'the load factors for the aircraft used would be so low that everybody would lose'. The position with the feeder services to the trunk routes, he said, was also far from good. It was estimated that in 1955–56 DC3 operations had lost the industry some £800,000. (ANA had lost £350,000, TAA £180,000 and Butler £60,000.) Some of these losses, of course, had been made on developmental routes, but the underlying cause was that with rising costs, the DC3s now needed an 80 per cent load factor on some routes simply to break even.[3]

At ANA Holyman's successor was P.W. Haddy, chairman of the Adelaide Steamship Company Limited, who was appointed ANA chairman on 6 February 1957. (He was joined on the board of ANA by Ian Holyman, representing the Holyman family interests.) One day later Warren McDonald, formerly vice-chairman of the Australian National Airlines Commission, was appointed Commission chairman. Norman Watt's extended term as chairman had expired. McDonald, a Tasmanian, a company director and grazier, had served with the AIF from 1939 to 1945, rising from private to brigadier, was chief engineer of the Second Australian Corps, had served with the 6th and 7th Australian Divisions and been mentioned in despatches. He had been a member of the Commission since July 1952.[4]

Haddy and McDonald at once faced new Ansett initiatives. The *Financial Review*, on 21 February, wrote: 'There is some good, old-fashioned competition in the air ... In celebration of its 21st birthday Ansett Airways Pty Ltd has challenged both the railways and competitive airlines TAA and ANA, and

Butler Air Transport, by introducing from tomorrow a daily tourist flight Sydney–Melbourne at only six pounds, or just two shillings more than the first class train fare ... The move by Ansett was in answer to last week's announcement by TAA that it would increase the number of its tourist flights, costing seven pounds two shillings and sixpence between the two major capitals.' To emphasise his competitiveness Ansett was using the pressurised Convair while both TAA and ANA continued to use unpressurised DC4s and DC3s.[5]

While Don Anderson had been studying the volatile and expanding aviation industry, TAA had undertaken an analysis of yet further proposals made by ANA. Again they argued for, first, a merger of all domestic airlines in Australia in a holding company and, second, an alternative plan for the merger of only ANA and TAA. Both proposals, said TAA, were completely opposed to existing Commonwealth government policy and both were unrealistic as the Commonwealth had no legal power to impose such a change. 'It would be found impossible to preserve the existing airlines as separate organisations competing amongst themselves under the control of a holding company. Major decisions all having a direct bearing on profit or loss, such as purchase of existing aircraft, fare levels, development of new routes, conditions of service, salaries of top executives etc. would necessarily be made by the holding company. The economies resulting from integration of staff would not be achieved.' The Commission, said the TAA analysis, 'has furnished its views as to the reasons why the [government] policy has not proved a success as far as ANA is concerned. They relate directly to matters within the control of ANA and, indirectly, to the effect of the development of Ansett ... The results for both TAA and ANA would have been more favourable if Ansett had not meanwhile been developing as a competitive third operator with modern equipment.'[6]

TAA now envisaged the collapse of ANA. It set down the action necessary should ANA be permitted to withdraw from operations in Australia under the Civil Airlines Agreement Act. The policy favouring competition, it said, should be maintained. 'Ansett (and possibly other operators) should be consulted as to the part they wish to play. TAA should be made responsible for the maintenance of essential air services now provided by ANA subject to directions from the government in respect of services to be allotted to any other airlines. The Government will support TAA as required for additional finance and for rights from the State Governments to operate intra-state services.'[7]

Haddy, meanwhile, had learned in talks with the new chairman of the Commission, Warren McDonald, that TAA would not agree to the latest merger proposals put forward by ANA, which was also informed that the Commission regarded further development of its tourist class operations as a matter of prime importance in the light of the growing competition from Ansett Airways. It told ANA it would no longer defer measures to meet Ansett until ANA was agreeable and that it was firm in its intention to increase the frequency of its tourist class schedules on the Sydney–Melbourne–Brisbane route from three to six times weekly at an early date, as well as on the possible introduction of such services between Melbourne, Adelaide, Perth and Tasmania 'without necessarily awaiting similar action on the part of ANA'.[8]

In the meantime, as TAA profits greatly exceeded budget estimates, ANA incurred steadily increasing losses. On 10 May 1957 Haddy told the government that ANA could not meet its payments on aircraft under the loan agreement that had enabled their purchase.[9] For the Government this was both a challenge and an ultimatum. The financial collapse of ANA meant the collapse of the Government policy under which two major airlines, one private enterprise and one government-owned, would compete to provide Australia's trunk route services. It was a dilemma brought about in part by the government itself. By allowing Ansett and Butler to import heavy aircraft, and with no legal power to prevent them operating on interstate routes, its two-airline policy had failed to prevent the emergence of a multi-operator system.

Both Butler and Ansett had plans for further expansion.

Butler, on 13 December 1956, had announced an order for six Fokker F27 Friendships for delivery in 1959 — to be financed by a proposed huge share issue. At the same time the dispute concerning ANA control over Butler Air Transport continued. Ansett's first-line aircraft now consisted of one Convair 340, one Convair 440 and an additional Convair 340 on charter from Hawaiian Airlines. He had two Convair 440s on order, one for delivery in June 1957 and one in early 1959. In addition he had an option on four Viscount 840 aircraft for delivery in 1958–59 when the Convairs were to be retired. He was flying three Convair flights daily (with extra flights on Friday and Sunday evenings) Melbourne–Sydney, two Convair flights daily through Coolangatta to Brisbane and two daily between Melbourne and Hobart. 'Ansett's activities', the Commission noted, 'are becoming a stronger threat to the major airlines'.[10] In April 1957 the irrepressible Reginald Ansett applied for a licence to operate from Cairns to Port Moresby, New Guinea, in competition with Qantas Empire Airways.[11]

TAA's financial strength was, of course, not in doubt. Nevertheless its ability to expand always depended on the government's willingness to provide the necessary capital. At the beginning of 1957 it was clear that considerable government advances would be needed over the next five years. Replacement aircraft — Viscounts for Convairs and DC4s and Friendships for DC3s — as well as long-range jets or turboprops for the Perth route — all involved far greater initial cost than the aircraft of TAA's original fleet. Where the investment in the existing fleet (which in March 1957 included eleven Viscounts) represented a capital cost of £12.3 per 1,000 seat-miles annually, the fleet programmed for 1961–62 represented a capital cost of £20.4 a year per 1,000 seat-miles. In addition TAA needed capital for new buildings at airports, which, under existing departmental policy, had to be provided by the operators. TAA calculated that total capital requirements for 1957–58 were some £7 million, of which the additional capital needed from Treasury would not exceeed £2.5 million.[12]

While the Menzies government, and in particular Shane Paltridge as the responsible minister, faced the deepening ANA crisis, supporters of private enterprise for Australian civil aviation raised their voices again. The *Financial Review* on 13 June 1957 carried an article urging that TAA be sold. 'What a good opportunity to sell TAA and the Government's interest in overseas air services ... Australian Governments are chronically short of cash for works they must retain — roads, schools, aerodromes, hospitals. Sell the [airlines] that can be run every bit as efficiently under private ownership as under public ownership. Then taxation needn't be so high and business would have more money to finance its own necessary expansion.'[13]

TAA now made it plain to the minister that it believed Ansett should replace ANA as the private operator. Giles Chippindall, as Commission vice-chairman (and acting chairman while McDonald was overseas), wrote to Paltridge in June 1957 forwarding a memorandum criticising the suggested ANA holding company and suggesting the merits of Ansett as their future major competitor. It was a paper arguing, in effect, that ANA's implicit ultimatum to withdraw from airline operations was an empty threat; that Ansett could emerge as the necessary second half of a two-airline system and so safeguard government policy.

> You will see that the Commission is strongly of the opinion that the proposed holding company embracing TAA and ANA has most of the objections expressed in respect of the larger proposition of a holding company embracing all airlines. It will also be seen that Ansett is already a significant competitor on the main eastern trunk routes and that his expansion in recent years has been quite remarkable. He is a good operator and with up-to-date aircraft in hand and on order is in an entirely different position to that occupied by him in 1952.
>
> I feel that with Ansett as the main competitor he would be agreeable to a reasonable degree of rationalisation with the Commission for the general benefit of airline finances. Unfortunately that has not been easily achievable with ANA which, we believe, has never in its thinking reconciled itself to the continued long-term existence of TAA.[14]

The memorandum was high in its praise of Ansett. Ansett,

it said, 'is a virile and imaginative competitor at present operating on all TAA/ANA routes except Adelaide–Perth'. Ansett's percentage share of traffic in passenger miles had increased between 1950–51 and 1956 from 10.5 to 16.7. In the same period ANA's share had fallen from 44.7 per cent to 37.5 per cent. (TAA's share had increased only marginally, from 44.8 per cent to 45.8 per cent. 'His [Ansett's] actual increase in business', said the memorandum, 'was almost three times that of ANA and only 13 million passenger miles less than that of TAA ... He unquestionably possesses the organisation and the operating skill to develop into a much larger operator ... in the event of ANA withdrawing from the field.'[15]

Addressing directly the implications of ANA's withdrawal from operations the paper asked: 'What transfer of ANA's assets could be involved to enable continuity of domestic services? What distribution of ANA's aircraft would be required and where would the aircraft be used by TAA and Ansett if Ansett were to become TAA's competitor ...?' TAA proposed a distribution of aircraft in the proportion of 70 to 100 in favour of TAA (with an initial 55 to 100 ratio 'as a more realistic and practical approach and more likely to permit Ansett to make an orderly absorption of the increased responsibilities entailed'.) The total aircraft fleet required from ANA, it said, was four DC6Bs, eight DC4s, three DC3s and three Bristol Freighters. It acknowledged that Ansett might wish to acquire his additional fleet units from overseas sources rather than from ANA.[16]

Ansett, meanwhile, had indicated to the government that he was willing to expand and replace ANA as the second major Australian operator. At the same time the government moved to prevent the immediate collapse of ANA by agreeing to an extension of time for its loan repayments. Ansett indicated that he would agree to buy ANA's DC6s and DC6Bs but that he also wished to buy four Lockheed Electra turboprop airliners from the United States. He also announced that, irrespective of his success or otherwise in acquiring ANA, he intended to purchase eight Convair 440 aircraft for early delivery.[17]

While these matters of moment developed, the Commission chairman, Warren McDonald, was still overseas. In Paris, on 5 July, he had discussions with Sud Aviation, securing an extension of an option to buy two Model 210 Caravelles for delivery in May–June 1960. Earlier, on a visit to the Lockheed factory in the United States on 3 June, he had inspected the Electra mock-up. He reported on his return: 'The great advantage of both the Electra and the Caravelle on the Australian domestic services will be in the vastly improved service that can be rendered on the Sydney–Melbourne–Perth route. With either plane ... the whole of the difficulties and inconveniences of this route can be completely eliminated.'[18]

On 30 July 1957 Reginald Ansett made an offer of £3,300,000 for the issued share capital of ANA with the condition that Ansett Transport Industries be given an option on all the Bungana Investments shares in Butler Air Transport. It was an important proviso. Control of Butler Air Transport would achieve for Ansett what TAA and ANA had been unable to achieve (in relation to both Butler and Ansett Airways) — it would remove competition by a third operator on the trunk routes. ANA refused the Ansett offer. On 8 August the *Financial Review* commented:

> With the rejection of the Ansett offer to take over ANA it now appears that the shipping companies which control the private airline have definitely overplayed their hand ... On the showing of recent weeks the Government is determined to provide no further assistance to private operators above what has already been made through the provisions of the 1952 Civil Aviation Agreement ... If Mr Ansett sticks to his announced plans to become the biggest single private operator the implications for ANA are obvious indeed. The performance of ANA throughout this difficult and protracted affair has been in the most grotesque tradition of high-handed business. One of the most extraordinary features of the ANA retreat from the unprofitable position into which its business has deteriorated has been the extent to which it has been carried out in secret. If public relations is of any value to a company involved in a highly political issue which carries very embarrassing overtones for a Liberal Government then ANA has denied itself almost completely what could be a valuable weapon. How different has been the approach of Mr Ansett, who has managed to cast himself in the public role of the sort of

> 'battler' whom most Australians have come to admire ... ANA has failed because of sheer inability to compete, an inability which stems principally from the lack of public attraction of the DC6 aircraft.[19]

The failure of ANA was emphasised by McDonald's announcement in early August that TAA, for the year to 30 June 1957, had carried a record 793,946 paying passengers — an increase on the previous year of 43,078, or nearly 6 per cent. Over the previous three years there had been an overall increase in passengers of 20 per cent. It meant a satisfactory financial result for the airline despite steep increases in almost all costs.[20]

The end came for ANA on 23 August. On the recommendation of its directors the shareholders of Australian National Airways Pty Ltd decided to accept the offer of Ansett Transport Industries Ltd of £3,300,000 for the purchase of the airline with all its assets.[21] On the following day Reginald Ansett announced that his offer for all of ANA's issued capital had been accepted. He was, the Commission was told, to pay £1,000,000 in cash immediately, £1,250,000 in cash in twelve months and £1,050,000 in cash in twenty-four months. 'A condition of the deal', said the report to the Commission, 'was the sale to Ansett of Bungana Investment Ltd's controlling interest in Butler Air Transport Ltd for £120,000'.[22] The *Financial Review* commented: 'Ansett Transport Industries Ltd has emerged from this week's deal with ANA as Australia's biggest aviation force. With the combined Ansett–ANA fleet and the 40 per cent interest in Butler Air Transport Ltd, Ansett now has virtual control of all the major private airlines ... ANA offered its assets to the Government for £12 million but the Government rejected the offer. On 25 June, at a Cabinet meeting in Brisbane ... Cabinet rejected a proposal by ANA for a merger of all Australian airlines.'[23]

It was, as contemporary aviation commentator D. N. Gillison wrote, the end of the maritime phase of Australian commercial air transport. Its beginning, said Gillison, 'was in the concept of shipowners who, stimulated by the enterprise and vision of two Tasmanian brothers, Victor and Ivan Holyman, and perhaps quickened in their reaction by the prospect of competition between air and sea transport, provided the principal funds for the company's [ANA's] formation. Thereafter the destiny of the company, which was developed under the pervading influence of the late Sir Ivan Holyman, who was its chief architect, builder and controller, was in the hands of shipping executives and it was they who guided shareholders in their decision this week.'[24]

Ansett Airways had been founded by Reginald Ansett in 1936, the same year that saw the birth of ANA. Born in 1909, Ansett began his career working in his father's bicycle shop in Inglewood, Victoria. During the economic depression of the early thirties he worked as an axeman in the Northern Territory but, at twenty-two, as owner of an old motor car, he began a road service between Maryborough, Queensland, and Ballarat, Victoria. It failed, but the young Ansett showed the temperament he was always to exhibit. He staked all he had on a new motor car and operated a road service in Victoria between Hamilton and Ballarat. That soon led to a garage in Hamilton, a growing staff, and buses operating a growing road transport service.

Ansett's interest in aviation preceded the Hamilton initiative. He had learned to fly when he was twenty-one. In 1936 he bought an aircraft, a Fokker Universal, and started a Hamilton–Melbourne air service on 17 February. It was the birth of Ansett Airways Pty Ltd. After extraordinary difficulties Ansett's company, by the end of the 1939–40 year, paid its first dividend. In 1944 he bought the Pioneer tourist bus service, began bus building and started on an impressive programme of building and buying a chain of tourist hotels that reached from Tasmania to North Queensland.

The Ansett organisation, TAA's new and formidable competitor, had grown by 1957 to a group with capital assets valued at £5 million.[25] With the purchase of ANA, it had increased its airline revenue from £2.5 to £15 million. (TAA revenue was £11 million). The total combined revenue of Ansett Transport Industries had risen, with the ANA purchase, from £7 million to £20 million. TAA had forty-one aircraft and Ansett Transport Industries fifty-three aircraft.

Ryland told the Commisssion: 'It is obvious that the size of the combine and its flexibility makes it a very real threat to TAA's continued satisfactory trading activities. Ansett's policy ... contemplates expansion wherever possible, which could further increase the disparity with TAA.'

He noted that at the time of the introduction of the Civil Aviation Agreement Act in 1952 the fleets of ANA and TAA were approximately equal in terms of heavy aircraft and that the total revenues of the two airlines were much the same. By the end of November 1957, however, he reported that TAA would have thirteen heavy pressurised aircraft while Ansett would have twenty-one. In addition, Ansett would have eight DC4s to TAA's four. In total, the Ansett fleet would comprise twenty-nine aircraft, the TAA fleet seventeen.[26] TAA's competitive position had been weakened.

In a major statement on Australian civil aviation policy to the Senate on 6 September Shane Paltridge said that the financial crisis in ANA was symptomatic of the condition of the entire air transport industry. TAA was the exception. 'Most airlines,' he said, 'other than TAA, have been incurring deficits or operating under extremely marginal conditions and even TAA's profit was relatively small judged by normal commercial standards'. The general crisis had been due, said Paltridge, to two unrelated causes. 'The first has been the inability of airlines to make profitable returns on DC3 aircraft which still comprise in numbers the main element of the Australian aircraft fleet ... The second is that overlapping and duplicated services on certain trunk routes has reduced load factors to uneconomic levels.'[27] The government, he said, considered it necessary to eliminate these causes of instability in the industry and had made a number of decisions towards that end.

> In the case of feeder services it is willing to extend subsidy assistance to the operators of essential air services in rural areas. It is also prepared to help selected operators obtain suitable replacement aircraft for the DC3 ... The policy adopted in the case of trunk route operations is basically the same in concept as that embodied in the 1952 Civil Aviation Agreement Act — that of providing fair and equal conditions of competition for two

> major operators. The private airline concerned will be given continued access to Government mail and business and assistance for re-equipment purposes. It will, however, be necessary to eliminate the wasteful effects of uneconomic competition on trunk routes by strengthening the rationalisation provisions of the Civil Aviation Agreement Act. Under these conditions the Government believes that the trunk route operators should be able to make reasonable profits and yet provide at the same time the highly competitive type of service for which Australian airlines are noted.[28]

The government's requirements and intentions were set out in the Supplementary Civil Aviation Agreement 1957, which Ansett signed in late September. It was proposed that the Agreement be annexed to a short Bill providing for parliamentary ratification of the Agreement as a supplement to the 1952 Agreement (and containing parliamentary approval to the execution of the Agreement by the Commission). One notable provision was for the appointment of a Rationalisation Committee comprising the minister's nominee, as chairman, to be known as the Co-ordinator, plus a nominee of TAA and Ansett. The director-general of civil aviation, Don Anderson, was to become this Co-ordinator, further increasing his already considerable power and influence. If, after consideration of any matter brought before the Committee the two operators' representatives could not agree, the Co-ordinator was given power to make a decision that would be final and binding.

At its meeting on 26 September the Commission noted: 'The Civil Aviation Agreement of 1952 required that reasonable fleet equality in heavy aircraft should exist between TAA and ANA. There will be a substantial departure from the intention of that Agreement if reasonable equality in heavy aircraft is not maintained between TAA and the joint ANA–Ansett fleet.'[29]

This time of defining change in Australian domestic civil aviation was occurring against a background of even more dramatic change for the world's airlines. Operators, said the director-general of the International Air Transport Association, Sir William Hildred, were seeking unprecedented capital to finance their entry into the jet age while their overall financial position was deteriorating. In 1956, he said, airlines had operated on a margin of only 1.5 per cent of revenue.[30]

While TAA had achieved dominance on Australia's trunk routes with its turboprop Viscounts it, too, had plans to equip with pure jet aircraft. It prepared a submission for the minister in late 1957 seeking approval to buy two Model SE120 Caravelles fitted with Rolls-Royce Series 200 Avon engines, at an estimated cost of £3,167,424. It wanted them to meet the demands of airline traffic between Perth and the eastern States.

The Viscount had proved popular on the Perth route and had been able to operate at a modest profit, but the capacity it offered when carrying the necessary fuel load was already inadequate as 1957 ended. Technical development of the Viscount beyond initial expectations had permitted safe non-stop operations for the previous two and a half years with acceptable regularity, but loads had been severely restricted. The existing TAA turbine-engined fleet consisted of eleven Viscounts, with two on order for delivery in mid-1958. To these were to be added six F27 Friendships, due for delivery in February–May 1959, and a further six Friendships in the second half of that year. It was planned that all piston-engined equipment (the DC3, DC4 and Convair 240) would be disposed of as early as practicable. The resultant fleet, TAA told their minister, would then possess the requisite degree of balance in comparison with equipment in service or ordered by Ansett–ANA — excluding, however, Ansett's publicised plans for the addition of Lockheed Electras. The introduction of Electras by Ansett, said TAA, 'would introduce a seriously unbalanced situation'.[31]

The Commission had considered two types for the Perth route, the L118A Electra, manufactured by Lockheed Aircraft Corporation, California, and the SE210 Caravelle, built by Sud Aviation, Toulouse. It had concluded that the total cost of procurement and introduction into service of a minimum fleet of two aircraft, together with necessary spares, would be £400,000 less for the Caravelle than for the Electra. The Caravelle's direct operating cost per mile, it was estimated, was 15 per cent lower than the Electra's. The superior speed for the pure jet Caravelle (the Electra was a turboprop) gave it a block flying time for Sydney–Adelaide–Perth-return of 11 hours 49 minutes compared with 13 hours for the Electra. 'Perth can, accordingly,' said the proposal, 'be brought substantially closer to the eastern States and served on a basis that can eliminate all-night flying and the unsuitable early morning arrival at Adelaide on the east-bound flights'. The Caravelle already had 2,000 flying hours to its credit, including a tour of the United States; the prototype of the Electra had not yet flown. No dollar requirement would be involved in buying the Caravelle.

'Taking all the foregoing matters into account, it is the opinion of the Commission that significantly more profitable and successful operation would be assured with a fleet of two Caravelles than with two Electra aircraft.' Formal approval was sought from Paltridge to enter into a contract with Sud Aviation for the purchase and delivery during 1959 of two Caravelle aircraft.[32] The minister advised that it was doubtful if Cabinet approval would be possible before the end of January 1958.[33] TAA nevertheless had also obtained an option with Lockheed for two Electras for delivery in July–August 1959. By December 1957 the Electra prototype had successfully flown.

TAA's official option with Sud-Aviation called for delivery of two Caravelles in June–July 1960. Ansett's Electra delivery schedule, under that timetable, gave him a clear eighteen months of unchallenged leadership in equipment. Ryland told the Commission on 4 November 1957, however, that there was a very good chance of negotiating a much earlier delivery time for the Caravelles.[34]

In its November 1957 issue *This Air Age* reported a profit by TAA for the 1956–57 year of £308,829 on a record revenue of more than £10 million. A 5 per cent dividend of £218,500 was paid to the Commonwealth Treasury.[35] The same issue reported the resignation from TAA of its commercial director, John Borthwick. L.L. (Lyn) McKenzie, TAA's Queensland manager, was appointed to succeed him.[36] On 28 November the *Financial Review* reported on Ansett's position. 'He has taken over ANA at a time when the combined losses of ANA and Ansett Airways were, in 1956–57, running at a rate of about £370,000 a year.' It thought, however, that a combination of increased fares, coming into operation in early December, and economies achieved through amalgamation, gave good grounds for thinking he could move to a solid profit in 1957–58.[37]

When Ansett Transport Industries had assumed control of Australian National Airways as a party to the Civil Aviation Agreement Act 1957 the two companies remained separate legal entities. The heavy debt burden taken over by ATI, representing ANA's re-equipment loan money, amounted to £3 million. Ansett undertook to repay this debt at the rate of £400,000 each six months. By 23 October 1957 the Ansett and ANA aviation activities were completely integrated under the name Ansett–ANA.

In December 1959 *Aircraft* magazine commented with prescience:

> The Civil Aviation Agreement Act has always been a paradox as the creation of a Government to protect a private industry from unfair Government competition. It becomes even more so in the signature to the amended Act of Mr R. M. Ansett. The late Sir Ivan Holyman gave away some of his competitive independence in the original Act to gain some competitive respite plus a share of Government business and financial sponsorship. Mr Ansett gives away a large part of his independence to aim at a larger commercial goal, with some added gains promised (DC3 route subsidisation and re-equipment assistance) and Government policy protection from the same type of private enterprise which he himself formerly offered. It seems inevitable now that he will become the controlling influence in Butler Air Transport — and any airline he controls becomes subject to the rationalisation provisions of the Act.[38]

The government, it said, had created a cartel. Its policy to achieve two and only two trunk route operators had now been achieved through 'the contractual obligation' entered into by Ansett Transport Industries. 'There is a clear intention by the Government to overcome the disabilities imposed by the Constitution by an extension of these contractual obligations to all Australian domestic airlines.'[39] (Throughout this period of upheaval a number of smaller intrastate airlines, apart from Butler and Queensland Air Lines, continued to expand their areas of operation. They included Airlines (WA) Ltd and MacRobertson Miller Aviation Company in Western Australia; Guinea Airways in South Australia; Connellan Airways in the Northern Territory; East-West Airlines in New South Wales; Southern Airlines in Victoria; and Qantas, Mandated, Gibbes Sepik, Papuan Air Transport and Carsair Air Services in Papua and New Guinea.)

There was great irony, politically and philosophically, in the Ansett acquisition of ANA and his ready acceptance of the revised two-airline structure. The private enterprise government and the private enterprise entrepreneur had collaborated to produce a legislative framework under which risk was removed from the entrepreneur and profits guaranteed. The central thrust of the government was to create stability. That intent made it paramount for the government to ensure the commercial survival of Ansett. The implications for the public, as users of the system, were immediately evident. TAA had been operating profitably as the government airline; only the private airline was losing money. And yet on 6 December 1957 fares and freight rates for both airlines were increased by an average of 5 per cent. Ansett had much to look forward to.

CHAPTER 7

1958

TAA's new competitor

Arthur Butler had his own agenda for the future of Butler Air Transport, and it did not include acquiescence in Ansett's vision. At the time of the Ansett–ANA negotiations it was announced that Ansett had an option to buy the Bungana interest in the Butler airline. Subsequently, however, it was disclosed that a Butler issue of employee shares (paid up to one twentieth of their value) had left Bungana without control. Ansett responded by buying BAT shares on the open market.

Ansett made two other moves. He offered Arthur Butler a seat on the board of Ansett Transport Industries and secured an injunction preventing the allocation of voting power to the employee shares that Butler had issued. In a spectacular initiative he carried hundreds of Ansett nominee shareholders from Melbourne, Brisbane and Adelaide on nine special flights in his aircraft to attend a general meeting of Butler Air Transport in Sydney on 21 January 1958. 'This meeting', wrote Stanley Brogden, 'was ... adjourned on the grounds that the existing ballot papers were invalid, and five minutes before new ballot papers arrived. This prevented the election of a new board but did not prevent Ansett securing approval for instructions to the old board preventing any attempt to dispose of assets or to make fresh capital issues without the approval of a shareholders' meeting.'[1]

After legal moves in the New South Wales Equity Court the battle for control was resolved in Ansett's favour. A new board was elected on which Ansett had four directors, including himself; Arthur Butler was the sole Butler nominee. Ansett was elected chairman. Butler now refused to take his seat on the BAT board and declined Ansett's offer of a seat on the board of Ansett Transport Industries. Butler's pioneering role in Australian domestic aviation was at an end.[2]

Ansett had won two airlines. Butler Air Transport (subsequently renamed Airlines of New South Wales), with a route mileage of 7,000 in New South Wales and southern Queensland, carried more than 200,000 passengers a year. Queensland Air Lines, BAT's subsidiary, operated 2,000 route miles and carried 50,000 passengers annually. Both would in future feed their interstate passengers into the Ansett system.

In his managing director's address to shareholders at the annual general meeting of Ansett Transport Industries on 17 December 1957, Ansett had made clear his plans for both BAT and QAL. 'We do not intend to amalgamate or absorb Butler Air Transport into the Ansett–ANA airline but to maintain its present, separate identity ... Our attitude to Butler's subsidiary airline — Queensland Air Lines Pty Ltd — is just the same. We will do everything to assist that company to expand its activities as a Queensland intrastate operator.'[3] The threat of a third airline operating on the interstate routes had been removed.

In February 1958 TAA's new competitor, Ansett–ANA, showed the aggressive style that would characterise its competition. It began advertising a new weekly service on the Brisbane–Longreach–Mount Isa route despite the fact that no licence had yet been issued by the Queensland State Transport Commission. TAA reacted by expressing its strong opposition to the Transport Commission, the Queensland minister for transport and the director-general of civil aviation.

TAA also noted breaches of the Supplementary Civil Aviation Agreement by Ansett–ANA. Package tours had been offered at rates lower than those agreed by the two operators;

western route tourist flights were being operated with aircraft in first class configuration (forty-four seats against TAA's fifty-six); free travel for agents in excess of the agreed amount was being provided and first class meals were offered on tourist services.[4] Ansett applied further pressure by applying to operate on a number of routes on which TAA was the sole operator — an extension of his existing Melbourne–Broken Hill route to Alice Springs, a Sydney–Brisbane–Mount Isa–Darwin service and a service between Melbourne–Adelaide and Alice Spings (with a weekly Darwin extension). In yet another competitive move Ansett withdrew all coastal Queensland DC3 services (except his Townsville–Cairns shuttle) and introduced Convair 440s to Rockhampton and Mackay. Northbound from Brisbane Ansett was now providing 1,092 pressurised seats compared with TAA's 308 pressurised and 273 DC3 seats.[5]

TAA responded to Ansett's Mount Isa initiatives. John Ryland, visiting Mount Isa, announced plans for the introduction of fully pressurised Viscount and Fokker Friendship aircraft to Northern Territory routes. Two Viscount services each week were to operated from June — Brisbane–Mount Isa–Darwin and Sydney–Mount Isa–Darwin. (The Friendship deliveries to TAA were expected in early 1959, with their introduction on Territory routes planned for later in that year.)[6] The *Northern Territory News* recorded that TAA made no profits from its northern services but operated them at heavy loss as a contribution to the development of that vast, underpopulated region.[7]

In late 1957, the government had announced its policy with respect to developmental and feeder routes. Its first step was to be the payment of subsidies on essential air services in rural areas as from 1 July 1958. In its response TAA advised the minister that the major operators could, within reason, support some degree of loss from feeder lines and developmental routes out of the profits from the main trunk routes. Those feeder and developmental routes, it said, need not necessarily break even to make a valuable contribution to a large-scale operator by providing greater scope for the spread of overheads and increased on-carriage traffic. 'TAA's past policy', it noted in an internal Commission report, 'has been to reduce subsidy claims as far as possible and to regard these unprofitable routes as a national responsibility ... There is some advantage in continuing our present policy to reduce and eventually eliminate claims for subsidy. Such a policy would strengthen our hand in resisting the intrusion of other operators ... where we operate with sole rights.' It was decided to inform the Department of Civil Aviation that in 1958–59 subsidy would be claimed only for the Channel and Gulf Country services — some £36,000 — and that there would be no claims for subsidy on other DC3 routes.[8]

Again prodded by Ansett initiatives — this time by Ansett's application to fly to New Guinea — TAA's chairman and general manager had discussions in March 1958 with Qantas vice-chairman W. C. (Bill) Taylor on the future of the New Guinea services. 'It was agreed', wrote Warren McDonald, 'that our best efforts at the moment should be directed towards the retention of the New Guinea services entirely by Qantas. At a later date, it was suggested, Qantas might be willing to vacate the field in its entirety.'[9] At the inaugural meeting of the new Rationalisation Committee on 20 March 1958, when discussion took place on Ansett's claim to operate between mainland Australia and New Guinea, TAA formally announced its opposition to the granting of a licence to Ansett–ANA. In its submission it pointed out that in 1957 the combined operations of Ansett–ANA, Butler Air Transport and Queensland Air Lines produced a total capacity seat mile availability of 776 million — 37 per cent more than TAA. The Ansett Group carried 448 million passenger miles compared with TAA's 393 million; and the combined turnover of Ansett–ANA airline operations (quoted in an Ansett press statement of 24 August 1957) was, following the Butler merger, £15 million as against TAA's £10 million. These disparities would be worsened, the airline said, if Ansett were allowed additional advantage over TAA from the mainland–New Guinea route.[10] 'The basis of the Commission's objection', Ryland wrote to Don Anderson, 'is that should there be any change in the present policy affecting operations to and from New Guinea, the Commission would consider that TAA should be allowed to enter that sphere of operations.'[11]

The formidable Qantas chief executive, C.O. Turner, also entered the fray. He wrote to the director-general of civil aviation on 18 April 1958 in response to a letter from Anderson signifying that an application by Ansett Airways to operate to New Guinea was being considered. Turner pointed out that the defined areas of responsibility laid down by the government for the operation of Qantas services were recorded in a departmental letter of 31 March, 1948. 'We have no knowledge', said Turner with typical acerbity, 'of any alteration of the Government's policy ...' The Qantas board, said Turner, was concerned that 'if permission is granted to Ansett–ANA to operate a service to New Guinea it would develop into a service to the Far East by connecting at Port Moresby with Cathay Pacific Airways. Ansett–ANA has inherited a capital interest in Cathay Pacific [which] has already obtained rights to operate into New Guinea.'[12] Qantas chairman Hudson Fysh wrote in similar terms, though less brusquely, to Paltridge.

The Ansett vigour came at a bad time for TAA. On 25 January 1958 twenty-four early model Viscount aircraft in the fleets of Air France, Aer Lingus and British European Airways were grounded as a result of fatigue cracking in the inner wing spar booms. On 28 January TAA began examining the spar booms in its six V720 Viscounts. Work was started on a spar boom replacement programme. It meant the nonavailability of Viscount aircraft in varying numbers over a period extending to October. 'This withdrawal from service', said an internal report, 'will seriously affect route capacity'.[13] John Watkins warned: 'It is not possible to say with any degree of confidence that there may not be other unpleasant operational limitations arising ... as the situation affecting outer wings, the upper booms of inner wings, and centre section spar booms is still actively under examination'.[14] (Tests by Vickers, however, were to raise the life limit of TAA's spar booms and limit the number of aircraft continually out of commission until October to one.)[15]

This diminution of TAA's fleet capacity was accompanied by a dramatic government announcement that rejected the future fleet re-equipment plans of both TAA and Ansett–ANA. *Aircraft* wrote: 'Federal Cabinet, in an extraordinary decision made in the early morning hours of March 28, rejected the application of Ansett–ANA to import four Lockheed Electra turboprops and the application of Trans-Australia Airlines to buy two Sud-Aviation Caravelle jet airliners.'

The minister's statement announced:

> Noting that the 800 Series Viscount will carry a greater number of passengers than the 700 Series now in service and will fly at speeds of up to 400 miles per hour, Cabinet indicated that it would be prepared to approve the extended purchase of these aircraft as replacements.' The domestic system, said Paltridge, was passing through 'a grave economic crisis'. There was an 'urgent need for a period of stability [which] could not be achieved if both airlines were pioneering the operation of two entirely new aircraft types ... The purchase of larger and faster turbine aircraft at this stage would stimulate a competitive race for other new turbine types which could be disastrous to economic stability.[16]

The assumption by the government, wrote *Aircraft*, that the amended Airlines Agreement Act gave it the right

> to carry rationalisation to the stage of arbitrarily deciding what equipment each domestic airline shall buy, far from aiding the airlines to achieve stability may very well have reactions that are entirely contrary to that aim ... The decision made is extremely doubtful in its practical wisdom; it is open to the strongest criticism in its economic and technical basis ... It writes an abrupt cancellation to a signed contract with an overseas supplier, Lockheed ... and it is taken against competent managerial and technical advice, a retrograde and bad decision which dismays every member of the airline industry who now sees the Government's earlier declaration to maintain the two main airlines' competitive structure as meaningless political veneeer and, incidentally, unfairly hurts the private operator, Ansett–ANA.[17]

At the meeting of the Australian National Airlines Commission on 28 March 1958 Ryland said: 'We have no reason whatever to withdraw from our judgement that the Caravelle is the most appropriate purchase for operation of the Perth route. In the belief that it is unlikely that the Government decision can be immediately upset it is considered that we should negotiate without delay with Sud-Aviation the best possible alternative delivery positions for those which we must forego ... We should take this action in the hope that there may be a relatively early possibility of the whole question being re-opened and new decisions taken.'[18]

Warren McDonald, who was himself greatly upset by the government's refusal to allow the Caravelle purchase, wrote to Paltridge on 29 April: 'The Commission is most anxious to dispel any impression that it accepts the decision without further reference, as might be inferred from your statement in the Senate ... The Commission is very seriously concerned at the effects of the rejection ... and notes, furthermore, that fresh reconsideration will be given to a restatement of the case now being put forward by Ansett–ANA in support of their request ... to buy a fleet of Lockheed Electra aircraft.' The Commisssion's decision on the correctness of the Caravelle, he wrote, remained unchanged.[19]

One TAA concern was that Ansett had scheduled the introduction of the faster and bigger Viscount 832 aircraft for the end of 1958, giving him a competitive advantage of 30 miles per hour in speed, a more modern interior and the capacity to carry fifty-two passengers. TAA had exerted pressure on Vickers for more favourable Viscount delivery dates but had learned there was no possibility of securing aircraft similar to Ansett's without a five-month time gap. Of some consolation, TAA regarded the Viscount 832 as seriously inflexible by reason of limitations on disposable load — restricting its effective operation to use as a first class passenger aircraft. Vickers indicated that an improved version with structural provisions that removed the limitations on load involved an additional delivery delay of three months. TAA decided to accept the extra delay in exchange for what it deemed a more economic aircraft. 'It is concluded', wrote Ryland, 'that we should, without prejudice to the Caravelle project, order four of these Viscount 810 Mark II aircraft in replacement for our two remaining Convair 240 aircraft and two of our DC4s, which can then be regarded as surplus to requirements'.[20]

On 3 April the *Financial Review* wrote: 'Has the Government's intervention in the re-equipment programs of Australia's big domestic airlines really done much to restore the stability for which it has been striving so earnestly? Judging by the outcry which followed its action, public opionion is not so sure. In any case, what set out to be a flat rejection of proposals by TAA and Ansett–ANA to buy foreign aircraft has now been broken down a little. The Minister for Civil Aviation, Senator Paltridge, is to reconsider at least the Ansett proposal to import American Lockheed Electras.'[21]

Airline enterprise had been replaced by government fiat. For Ansett the Paltridge decision meant that he would not have a first line turboprop aircraft until 1959 — a full five years after TAA had brought its first Viscount to Australia. Even then he would have only four Viscounts to match against TAA's fifteen (plus twelve Friendships soon to follow). In his favour, his four Viscount 800 series aircraft would be in service well before TAA had comparable equipment, together with the two Viscounts inherited from Butler Air Transport.

Ansett, for his part, faced a threat to his continuing ability to make equipment decisions as an independent operator. The government, however, saw an emerging equipment race as potentially destabilising for the industry and a scenario that might either end with the unavoidable nationalisation of Ansett–ANA or the provision of big subsidies to keep it in being — both politically disastrous. These matters were discussed by Ansett and Paltridge in early April. The minister issued a statement promising to give further consideration to the Ansett case. 'During the course of the discussions', said the statement, 'it was made clear and accepted on both sides that no guarantee had been given to Mr Ansett that the Government would issue licences for the Electras'.[22]

At the heart of the government's dilemma was the attempt to reconcile two opposing objectives. Its central political aim, since first resisting the creation of Labor's TAA, had always been the survival of private enterprise in Australian civil aviation. Private versus public ownership was the overriding political issue. It had, however, already seen the collapse of Holyman's privately-owned ANA. The fear was that Ansett, a newcomer to the big league, would go the same way if the Government allowed a hugely expensive re-equipment race. What it had now done, however, with the objective of industry stability — and for the survival of private enterprise — was to forbid the exercise of such enterprise by the private operator.

There were, though, powerful forces at work that were to favour Ansett's choice of equipment. Qantas had put forward proposals to Paltridge for the purchase of five Lockheed Electras at an estimated cost of £8.035 million. The minister considered them ideal for use on QEA's secondary routes. Their early delivery (they were available from 1959) made possible an advantageous resale of almost the entire Qantas Super Constellation fleet. Such a purchase had additional attractions for the minister. It made practicable the installation of special engine overhaul facilities for their Allison engines — engines that were used in the RAAF's C130 transport aircraft.[23]

On 12 May Warren McDonald told a Commission meeting that three days earlier he and Reginald Ansett had been called into conference with the prime minister and minister for civil aviation, following resubmissions by both the Commission and Ansett for their equipment purchases. At no time during the discussions, said McDonald, had there been any criticism of the Caravelle on technical or other grounds. At the conclusion of the meeting the prime minister had directed that TAA and Ansett–ANA were to discuss with each other the problem of future equipment 'with a view to avoiding undue multiplicity of types'.

It was clear, following the prime minister's intervention, that TAA had to contemplate an alternative to the preferrred Caravelles. It was formally decided 'that every endeavour be made to reach agreement with Ansett–ANA with a view to a joint submission for approval for Caravelle equipment. Failing agreement on Caravelles, the Commission would advise the Government of its willingness to accept Electras as an interim type on a basis of equal numbers (two each) and equal deliveries, and on the understanding that the Commission would not be precluded from seeking approval later for the purchase of Caravelles.' It was this Electra alternative that formed the basis of the final government decision on 23 May. Ansett and TAA were each given approval to buy two Electras. Neither airline was satisfied. Two Electras hardly made an economic fleet. Ansett's planning had been made on the basis of four Electras. TAA faced a severe downturn in staff morale at all levels. The airline had been forced to accept the the Ansett choice of aircraft. Overall, Ansett came out well ahead. While both airlines also ordered four Viscount 800s, Ansett had earlier delivery dates for his as well as an advantage in his Electra deliveries.[24]

In public and political terms the outcome was generally perceived as a complete government surrender to Ansett. TAA, which had pioneered the introduction to Australia of the pressurised Convair and the turboprop Viscount, had been both snubbed and humiliated by the government's refusal to allow it the pure jet aircraft of its choice, the Caravelle. The reputation of Reginal Ansett as a political persuader of influence was greatly enhanced. There was a deep irony to it all. Walled round with government support, Ansett emerged as the white knight and saviour of private enterprise.

McDonald, publicly, made the best of the situation. Unlike Ansett he could not, as chairman of the Australian National Airlines Commission, ever confront the government publicly. He issued a statement at the end of May saying that immediate approval would be sought for the purchase of two Electras, with delivery expected early in 1959. 'The Commission', he said, 'has not abandoned its confidence in the Caravelle jet, but is deferring its application to buy two of these aircraft in accordance with the Government's decision ... It still hopes to bring the benefits of jet transport to the Australian public as soon as the Commonwealth Government feels this can be done without endangering the stable development of the airline industry of this country.' (Delivery was not, as McDonald stated, to be 'early in 1959'. TAA was subsequently forced to accept the third and fourth deliveries for the four Electras approved. Ansett was to receive his two aircraft in March and April 1959; TAA was to get its Electras in June and July 1959.)

With the introduction of the Electra, said McDonald, TAA's turboprop fleet would total twenty-seven aircraft. 'This fleet will consist of eleven Viscounts now in service, the two Super Viscounts [Viscount 800s] due to arrive shortly [they were delivered in July 1958] and the 12 Fokker Friendship airliners which have been ordered as replacements for the DC3 fleet.'[25]

TAA's disappointed staff were told in the June 1958 issue of *This Air Age*: 'TAA will next year become the first airline in the world to operate an all-turbine-powered fleet. This will follow the delivery of two Lockheed Electra prop-jet airliners and twelve Friendships to join our thirteen Viscounts.'[26] (The Electra, pressurised and air-conditioned, had sixty-eight first class seats and a rear lounge with six seats. Its cruising speed was 400 miles an hour, its take-off weight 113,000 pounds.)

Although this politically driven drama was resolved, both TAA and Ansett–ANA, in subsequent months, expressed uncertainty about the merits of the Electra. Warren McDonald, when he visited Lockheed Aircraft Corporation during an overseas tour between 28 May and 23 July, was not able to get approval to fly in the aircraft. This, he reported, was 'no doubt by design, as at the time Lockheed were unwilling to allow possible customers to fly in the aircraft on account of noise level and vibration ... Concern was shown by quite a number of interested parties (including Allison and American Airlines) about this problem.'[27]

McDonald also had discussions with Ansett while in London. Ansett, he said, 'was concerned ... and proposed to return to Australia via the US for the purpose of flying in the Electra'. He indicated 'that if there were any problems with the Electras and both airlines did not purchase these aircraft he would be willing to dispose of two DC6Bs to TAA and would,

I believe, order more Viscount 810s … It is quite obvious … that he intends to model his fleet on the same types as TAA … It is no secret that he hopes to absorb TAA at some time or other.' Ansett expressed his confidence to McDonald that he would be able to withdraw from his Electra contracts.[28]

TAA saw advantages in withdrawing from the Electra commitment. The Commission was advised that 'cancellation of the Electra project and acquisition of two DC6Bs would result in considerable capital savings to both operators' and that fleet operating costs would be lowered. 'TAA', said the report, 'would be freed from the possible need to retain turbo-prop aircraft until, possibly, 1966. Introduction of jets at an appropriate time would be more easily accomplished. There would be a greater degree of stability within the domestic industry.'[29] Both airlines were also strongly influenced by the increasingly competitive trading conditions they faced.

Ansett's Electra doubts seemed firm when he discussed the matter in August with TAA. Ryland reported: 'Ansett … raised the question of who should meet any financial obligation that may arise from the cancellation of his Electra contract. It was agreed that this matter … should be put to the Minister for representation to Cabinet [and that] the Minister should ask for an appointment with the Prime Minister on August 14th to … ask his Government's assistance or good offices in regard to Ansett's withdrawal from the contracts. With this understanding the meeting broke up and the Chairman [McDonald] departed for Canberra.'[30]

That meeting had also included discussion of an acceptable scheme of rationalisation as an integral part of an overall agreement between Ansett and TAA. Both agreed immediately to set up a Rationalisation Committee to 'determine and plan the operation of a sound system of rationalisation on all competitive routes, with rationalisation to commence forthwith and be completed not later than 1 December 1958. Rationalisation, TAA proposed, was 'to confer equal benefits on both operators'. The 'general basis' was 'that each company would carry half of the pre-determined traffic for any period at an average overall load factor of 65 per cent'. Ansett argued for an average load factor of 70 per cent. A figure of 68 per cent was finally agreed on.[31]

Reginald Ansett now demonstrated both his wilfulness and his unpredicability. At 9.45 p.m. on that same day he rang McDonald and withdrew from all agreements despite the fact that Paltridge in the meantime had contacted Canberra and put in process arrangements for a prime ministerial meeting on the last possible day before the deadline expired for withdrawal from the Lockheed contracts. 'Ansett's course of action', wrote Ryland, 'in withdrawing from these negotiations after accepting the terms is inexplicable'.[32]

The result was that on 14 August 1958, with the minister's approval, TAA entered into an agreement with Lockheed to secure its delivery positions for Electras pending clarification of finance. On 30 September Paltridge introduced into the Senate the Airlines Equipment Bill and two associated loan bills. The Bills passed through all stages and were approved. On the following day the legislation passed through the House of Representatives. They authorised, among other provisions, loans for four Electras for Qantas and two TAA Electras. TAA was further provided with perpetual borrowing power of up to £3 million under government guarantee. Ansett also benefited from the legislation by the authorisation of government guarantees covering specific loans totalling £5 million, including £3 million to buy two Electras for Ansett–ANA and £2 million to buy six Friendships for the Ansett subsidiaries, Butler and Queensland Air Lines.

Of longer-term significance, the Airlines Equipment Act bound the two major domestic airlines in specific detail to a contractual obligation giving the minister power to determine the types of aircraft to be used by the two airlines and the capacity to be provided on the routes on which they operated in competition. What emerged during the parliamentary debate, however, was the still firmly entrenched political attitudes to the two airlines by the opposing parties. The Liberal–Country Party reaffirmed the coexistence policy of private and government operators, with the implicit need to back the private operator; the Labor Party was clear that it preferred outright backing of the government-owned airline.

When the annual report of the Australian National Airlines Commission was tabled in Parliament it revealed that the year 1957–58 had seen record traffic figures and big extensions of TAA services, producing a profit for the year of £282,702. Ansett was also doing well. The *Financial Review* reported on 2 October 1958: 'He is believed to have converted an ANA loss of the order of £400,000 in 1956–57 to a profit around £150,000 in the financial year just ended. Much of this huge gain in profitability stems from the staff economies he has achieved.'[33]

November brought a blow to TAA profitability in the current financial year. For eleven days from 19 November the airline was subjected to a series of rolling strikes by pilots, essentially because the Australian Air Pilots' Association was opposed to arbitration of its claims before the Full Arbitration Commission. The Association had first volunteered to submit salary claims to arbitration before the Public Service Arbitrator as early as 1952. In that year also the Association took part in a hearing before the Full Arbitration Court. From the pilots' point of view that hearing had been rendered pointless by the Court's decisions that its function was not to create standards but simply to recognise such accepted standards as are not shown to it to be unjust, extravagant or inadequate. The Court also expressed the view that the functions of airline pilots were of such a nature that this could not be compared with any other occupation and, as a result, the normal method of comparative age justice could not be applied. The Association summarised its experience with arbitration in 1958, stating that it 'has been constantly led into the most restricted application of the Arbitration Act'.[34] The complexities of the arguments put forward by pilots and operators in their disputes over the years is not covered in detail in this TAA history, except for the general effect on the airline and its relations with its pilots. (Those seeking more detail are referred to the excellent account provided by Nicholas Blain in his *Industrial Relations in the Air*, University of Queensland

Press, 1984.) The 1958 strike ended on 29 November, with TAA net losses estimated by Ryland at £55,000.[35] (In mid 1959 the Australian Air Pilots Federation was dissolved and replaced by the Australian Federation of Air Pilots.)

The *Review* did not see any diminution in competition coming as a result of the government's rationalisation proposals. It quoted the minister's second reading speech: 'Although the airlines will provide on an equal basis the capacity necessary to carry [the] traffic at a specified optimum revenue load factor — it will probably be in the vicinity of 70 per cent — they are each free to carry as much of the business as their authorised capacity permits. A shift of only 1 per cent in the traffic is equivalent to a revenue increase (without significant extra cost) of £190,000, so that there will be a great incentive to attract an extra percentage of the market and at the same time to reduce costs.'[36]

It was a shallow comment. Competition, in the accepted sense of enterprise and manoeuvre across the whole spectrum of capital investment in equipment and the battle for domination in the market by autonomous entities, was no longer possible. The structure devised for Australian domestic civil aviation left room for competition only at the margin. It would have been more accurate for the *Review* to conclude that competition had been reduced to one per cent of the possible prize offered by the market. That emasculated competition, moreover, was to take place within the cocoon of the strictest regulatory control.

The consolidated net profit after tax of Ansett Transport Industries as a whole for the year to 28 June 1958 was almost double the reported TAA profit. Ansett, however, did not reveal the quantum of the contribution from aviation activities. His managing director's report, published in the *Financial Review* on 18 December 1958, noted, however, that the combined airline staffs had been reduced by some 800 employees. 'Private enterprise through your company', he said, 'now controls an airline system larger than the Government-owned internal airline and is in a position to withstand competition from that organisation despite the many privileges our competitor enjoys. There is no doubt that the rapid progress of the Government-owned airline towards a complete monopoly of internal services has not only been halted — but the balance is slowly swinging back in our favour.'[37]

A more accurate appraisal would have concluded that 'private ownership', not 'private enterprise' controlled the large Ansett–ANA airline system. The initiatives that had made possible the emergence of Ansett as a major force had not resulted from the virtues of private enterprise but from the Government's political imperatives. The element of enterprise, such as it was, had been political enterprise. The clear-headed Reginald Ansett had recognised the financial security offered. He had moved into a politically protected commercial environment, underwritten by Commonwealth legislation and financial guarantees.

CHAPTER 8

1959

A political football

As 1959 began, a noticeable but not sharp falling off in passenger air traffic on Australian domestic operations had emerged, together with a much more pronounced drop in freight carriage. That trend had come as new aircraft — Electras, Viscount 800s and Friendships — were about to arrive. Since the month by month rate of growth in passenger traffic had reached its peak of 10 per cent in March 1956, there had been a steady downward trend in the rate of growth despite the overall achievement each year of record total figures and a generally buoyant economy.

One area of substantial decrease had been the Sydney–Melbourne route, the highest density route in Australia. Contributing causes had been the raising of standard air fares late in 1957 (though this move had increased revenue returns for both airlines) and the cessation by Ansett Airways, following its integration with ANA, of its low-cost coach services. There had, nevertheless, been a huge increase in airline revenue for the integrated Ansett air services. Passenger revenue in 1956–57 for Ansett Airways had been £1,862,112. In the 1957–58 annual report of Ansett Transport Industries the combined revenue from all Ansett airline operations had almost quadrupled to £7,067,972. First class passenger returns had dropped some 15 per cent, but had been more than compensated for by an increase of about 25 per cent from tourist class services. The big market for tourist class travel was set to become an overwhelming influence in the airline business.

TAA's figures showed a different picture from the overall domestic aviation one. Far from showing any decline in passenger traffic, its figures for the September, 1958 quarter showed the airline held 55 per cent of the interstate market compared with 51.7 per cent for the same quarter in the year before. The long haul to Perth had shown an overall year-to-year increase of more than 17 per cent. TAA had not lost first class traffic. Because of its fleet composition, it offered separate first and second class aircraft. Ansett, on its big DC6s and DC6Bs, offered mixed class services.

As 1959 started TAA had the initial major advantage, from its turboprop fleet, in attracting passengers. Ahead lay an Ansett–ANA advantage from its lead in Electra and Viscount 832 operations, with the possibility then of providing completely tourist operations with its DC6Bs. If competition had its financial limits under the new regime it was nevertheless unlimited in its stimulation of corporate pride. Neither airline wanted to run second.

Restraint still ran the agenda of the government. In February the *Sydney Morning Herald* reported that Cabinet would reject applications by TAA and Ansett–ANA to import additional Electras. Senator Paltridge, it said, would advise Cabinet that to grant permission might lead to uneconomic competition between the two airlines, 'causing another economic crisis in the industry'.[1] *Aircraft* commented: 'Enterprise, public or private, is under a severe handicap when it becomes subject to political considerations. This has been proved once again in the refusal of the Government to grant Ansett–ANA an import licence which would have allowed them to take up a December 1959 delivery date for a third Lockheed Electra ... On this ocasion there was no question of dollar grants or loan guarantees. Ansett had arranged his finance privately. All he sought was the right to choose his own equipment ... Rationalisation must not be allowed to become stultification of enterprise.'[2]

Again the government caution had been politically inspired. The National Airlines Act was before Parliament for amendment — with the removal of clauses giving TAA monopoly rights to serve the Northern Territory. At the same time Ansett's application to operate into Port Moresby from Cairns was a sensitive issue. Opposition Labor members were proclaiming that Ansett was being favoured at the expense of TAA.

It was nevertheless a time of excitement for Ansett–ANA. On 18 March its first Electra, able to carry seventy-eight passengers at more than 400 miles an hour, started operations on the Melbourne–Sydney service. Two days later it was joined by Ansett's first Viscount 832, a 52-passenger version of the Viscount with a higher speed than TAA's Viscount 700s. That advantage was demonstrated when on 25 March an Ansett Viscount 832 took off from Sydney five minutes behind a TAA Viscount 700, passed it at Yass, and arrived at Melbourne ten minutes ahead of it.[3] For the first time since the Ansett acquisition of ANA, Ansett–ANA had first-line equipment that was more advanced technically and had greater public appeal than its rival's aircraft.

The Ansett Electra publicity was spectacular. Packaged as the 'Golden Jet Service', the Sydney–Melbourne Electra featured gold carpets, gold-corded handrails on aircraft stairways and, for the 10 p.m. service, a special lobster, spatchcock and champagne menu. Appropriate glamour was provided by hostesses who exchanged their grey and blue uniforms for wraparound gold lamé short evening frocks.

TAA morale was sustained by a prized international accolade. On 8 April the airline won what the international airline industry regarded as the world's most prestigious award — the Cumberbatch Trophy of the Guild of Air Pilots and Air Navigators — awarded for the best airline contribution to reliability in aircraft operation. The assessment committee had been unanimous, TAA was told, in selecting TAA as the winning airline for 1958.[4] In the twelve years since its first service with a lone DC3, TAA had achieved recognition as a world leader.

To counter the Ansett advantage in equipment, TAA switched emphasis in their competitive campaigning to the frequency of turboprop services they could offer. That was to be an increasingly effective move as their own new equipment came into operation. Their two Electras were due in June and July and the first of their two Viscount 816s at the end of April. The first of twelve Fokker Friendships was due in mid April. In addition, the minister had given approval in March to import two further Viscount 816s. These aircraft were to give TAA a total fleet of thirty-one turboprops and a long-term advantage in equipment over Ansett–ANA. (In a remarkable, quite unplanned coincidence, the first Electra, the second Viscount 816 and a Fokker Friendship arrived on their delivery flights at Melbourne on the same day, 24 June.)

A significant move affecting TAA Viscount and Friendship engine overhauls, and adding appreciably to TAA's engineering capabilities, was the agreement by Rolls-Royce in February 1959 that they would withdraw previous objections to Australian domestic airline operators undertaking their own overhaul of Dart engines. Rolls-Royce decided to close down Dart engine overhaul facilities in Australia and offer to TAA all overhaul tooling and equipment at the company's Mascot establishment, as well as maximum technical assistance to ensure a smooth changeover.[5] TAA expected 'to effect very substantial economies' from the change.[6] (TAA took over Dart overhaul from Rolls-Royce in April 1960 following the completion of overhaul and engine test facilities at Melbourne airport.)

TAA, of course, resented the removal of its legislated right to a monopoly of Northern Territory operations while its rights to operate purely intrastate operations, unlike Ansett's, were limited to Queensland and Tasmania. That restriction gave Ansett the lion's share of on-carriage from within the States. TAA strategy to counter this weakness was to strengthen links with the rapidly developing East-West Airlines in New South Wales and MacRobertson Miller in Western Australia. It planned to hire out some of its Friendships to these two airlines and to the South Australian airline,

Guinea Airways, with which TAA had a five-year agreement. In July, as Ansett Transport Industries chairman and managing director Reg Ansett announced record ATI revenue of £22 million and a record profit, the Guinea Airways board rejected an Ansett bid for its shares.[7] Guinea shareholders, however, in turn rejected their board's decision and Ansett acquired the airline. (Its name was changed in 1960 to Airlines of South Australia.)

The explosive development of tourist class air services had by now considerably changed the pattern of domestic airline operations in Australia. The change was no surprise but its rapidity was. Since the introduction of tourist services in the United States in 1948 the share of tourist traffic on domestic trunklines had risen from 11 to 40 per cent (by June, 1958). In Europe, where the major intra-Europe routes were short haul, virtually all flights were converted to tourist class following its introduction in 1953. By 1959 less than 10 per cent of traffic was carried at first class fares.

TAA and ANA had introduced tourist services on 2 October 1955 on the Melbourne–Sydney–Brisbane route, using DC4 aircraft, but frequencies were low and the fare differential small. They did not attract the volume of traffic anticipated — in fact, in the first nine months the TAA load factor was only 39 per cent. (ANA load factors were similar.) Subsequently, however, as frequencies were increased and the fare differential increased to almost 30 per cent (after a general fare increase that was not applied to tourist class), load factors rose until, in 1957–58, they averaged 65 per cent. Melbourne–Adelaide–Perth tourist services were commenced jointly by TAA and Ansett–ANA in December 1957 with one DC4 service a week. In May 1958 TAA added a further Viscount service and Ansett–ANA a DC6. In November 1958 Ansett–ANA began a daily mixed class DC6B service (concurrently operating it on Melbourne–Sydney–Brisbane), with TAA adding a weekly Viscount service.

Ansett–ANA's introduction of Electra aircraft, however, and the subsequent relegation of DC6Bs to secondary routes brought a substantial capacity increase, particularly on the

Queensland coast. To stimulate new business Ansett–ANA announced tourist service from 18 March 1959 to Townsville and Cairns at fares 30 to 35 per cent below first class. TAA had to face the fact that its equipment was less suitable for mixed class operations, but it neverthless introduced mixed class aircraft to both Queensland and Tasmania on 15 March.

Despite the introduction of tourist class services there was no significant overall change in the total traffic carried by Australian domestic operators in 1958, though TAA's total traffic increased. TAA judged, however, that without their introduction, particularly to Perth, there would have been an overall decline in traffic. The growth in tourist traffic carried by TAA, in proportion to its total market, had steadily increased — from 1.4 per cent in 1955–56 to 15 per cent in 1958–59. After the increase in tourist frequences in November 1958, however, almost 20 per cent of TAA's traffic had been carried on tourist flights — with that proportion still rising. The Ansett–ANA experience was similar.

The general effect for both airlines was clearly recognisable. It was expected that the stagnation experienced in Australian domestic airline traffic growth would give way to a steady rate of increase as tourist services developed. 'It seems evident', Ryland told the Commission in April 1959, 'that this is the area from which expansion of Australian air traffic must come.'[8] Statistics confirmed his view. Figures from the Department of Civil Aviation in mid 1959 indicated a steady upswing in overall traffic following the extension of tourist services. (Air freight provided 15 per cent of TAA revenue in 1958; for Ansett–ANA it was over 25 per cent — both airlines had experienced a percentage decline on the previous year. One of Ansett's first actions was to cut back the ANA all-freighter services.)

The effect of the introduction of the first Ansett–ANA Electra, said *Aircraft*, 'was most dramatic'. At the end of the first fifteen days of operation Ansett–ANA, in full-page newspaper advertisements, told the public that the 78-seat Electra had already carried 7,099 passengers with a load factor of 80 per cent on a break-even load factor of 50 per cent. In that period the airliner had earned £69,650 and cost £45,680 to operate. That left a profit for fifteen days of £23,970. (The Electra carried sixty first class and eighteen tourist class seats; average first class load factor was 80.5 per cent; in the tourist section it was 90 per cent.)

For Ansett–ANA there was a welcome wash-off effect, building the load factors of the former BAT Viscount 700 and the DC6Bs that were backing up the Electra on the Sydney–Melbourne route as well as lifting totals on connecting services. That meant that TAA was losing traffic to provide this Ansett boost. In the interim period of three months between the introduction of Ansett–ANA's Electra and the start of TAA Electra services TAA was resigned to a decline in its competitive traffic share to 45 per cent, or even less. That meant a loss of at least 7 per cent of the market, or 14 million passenger miles for the quarter.[9]

A month after the start of Ansett–ANA Electra services TAA, on 16 April, received the first of its own new equipment with the arrival of the first Fokker Friendship to reach Australia. By May it was in regular operation between Burnie (Tasmania), Melbourne, Canberra, Corowa (New South Wales) and Sydney. The second TAA Friendship and first Viscount 800 series arrived in May and the second in June. The Friendship was soon to become a familiar sight. Eighteen were on order for Australian feeder routes — twelve for TAA and three each for Butler Air Transport and Queensland Air Lines. (TAA's initial Friendships could carry a maximum of thirty-six passengers. The last four carried forty.)

June 1959 was the critical month for TAA, however. Though more Friendships arrived, the important event was the delivery of the first TAA Electra. It made its inaugural flight on a Perth service on 4 July and went into regular scheduled operations on 8 July. The second TAA Electra was delivered in mid July. Both TAA Electras had an advantage over Ansett–ANA's. The initial TAA Electra was the first in the world to incorporate a major nacelle-tilt modification which, with other changes, made it a much quieter aircraft with noticeably less vibration. (Following much adverse comment to

Lockheed on the excessive vibration experienced in the forward cabin area the company had undertaken to correct the fault by tilting all engine nacelles upward by three degrees. Despite this major modification the Electra had given Lockheed its best year ever in the field of commercial transports, both in earnings and the number of aircraft sold. Delivery of 112 Electras was scheduled for 1959 with production continuing at the rate of two a week.)[10]

Important commercially as all these events were in 1959 the underlying competitive reality was made clear when the minister, under the Airlines Equipment Act, made his 'Determination No. 1', operative from 1 June to 31 December 1959. Its primary object was to specify the capacity required by both major operators and to limit their capacity within the total determined and the period specified. The effect of the minister's determination on aircraft fleets was that TAA would be permitted two Electras, four Viscount 816s, ten Viscount 756s and nine F27s. The ATI Group was permitted two Electras, four Viscount 832s, two Viscount 747s, six F27s, four DC6Bs, six Convair 440s, one DC4 and two DC3s plus capacity equivalent to an extra Viscount 832.[11] In general terms TAA had a qualitative advantage from its concentration of turbine-powered aircraft.

Aircraft was not enthusiastic about this first 'determination' of capacity. It wrote: 'The unrealistic proposition that a Government or a Government Department can contrive to make two competitive airlines operate in a finely balanced state of financial stability neither having, or being permitted to have any competitive advantage, merely by legislating to this end and by applying under this legislation a mathematical formula of "rationalisation" is now being put to the test in Australia ... Whatever way the situation is handled the result will have its political repercussions ... Under the present rationalisation proposal the end could be two Government-controlled airlines who might as well be one ... It is high time the airline business ceased to be a political football.'[12] Ansett strongly attacked the government's rationalisation decision, claiming that the application of the minister's determination protected the government airline and held back development of the private airlines.[13]

Despite the early introduction of Ansett's Electra services, there was a pronounced traffic swing back to TAA by early July 1959, with the airline carrying half of the competitive passenger market before the arrival of its own first Electra. (It had fallen to a low point of 46.7 per cent traffic share in April from 54.2 per cent in January following Ansett's introduction of the Electra.) For the eighth successive year TAA set an Australian record for the number of passengers carried by a single domestic operator — 870,811.[14] TAA profit for 1958–59, however, at £253,911, was lower by £28,792 than for the previous year — partly as a result of the pilots' strike. More dramatic were the official DCA figures on the explosion in tourist traffic. Compared with the same period in the previous year it was up 150 per cent in January 1959 and 400 per cent by June 1959.[15]

For TAA the demand for tourist seats caused problems. Ryland told Don Anderson in April 1960: 'The idea of carrying tourist class passengers in first class cabins commenced with the introduction of Electra aircraft into regular domestic service. The mixture of first class and tourist seats did not match the demand and surplus first class seats were used for the carriage of tourist passengers when the small tourist cabin was fully sold ... It has been customary for both operators to book tourist passengers in first class cabins providing this could be done without turning away first class traffic ... Empty first class seats return no revenue.'[16] Ansett–ANA, however, now strongly opposed the practice. The airline's general manager, Frank Pascoe, wrote to Ryland: 'The current practice has very quickly resulted in the situation where a large proportion of the travelling public have become aware of the fact that late reservations made for tourist accommodation will result in obtaining travel in the first class compartment. This has led to an ever increasing number of first class seats being availed at tourist fares.' He wanted a firm policy whereby neither airline would allow tourist class passengers to travel in first class seats.[17]

Both airlines now found they were having troubles with their Electras. Regularity of operations had suffered substantially because of a high rate of mechanical and electrical malfunction. By mid September TAA had recorded seven premature engine changes; Ansett had twelve. Both TAA and Ansett had, by contrast, experienced excellent mechanical dependability with their new 800 series Viscounts (and with all their Dart-powered aircraft).[18]

In November 1959 TAA announced the sale of its last two Convair 240 piston-engined aircraft. On 10 November, Cabinet announced approval at last for Ansett to buy an additional Electra. Ministerial approval had at least in part been forced by a vigorous TAA advertising campaign stressing that it could provide double the turboprop services of its competitor. TAA had twenty-six turboprops, Ansett–ANA fourteen. That seemingly huge disparity, however, did not apply to the competitive routes. Nine of TAA's turboprops were Friendships (compared to Ansett's six Friendships). These aircraft were not mainline equipment. TAA was far ahead on Viscounts, with fifteen (Ansett had six). The issue of fleet parity between the two major carriers remained a major problem for the government and the smooth operation of the rationalisation formula.

The implications for TAA from the addition of a third Electra to the Ansett fleet were nevertheless unwelcome. 'Approval of Cabinet for Ansett to acquire a third Electra', the Commission was told, 'makes it extraordinarily difficult for the possible successful application by TAA to purchase or charter jet aircraft in the immediate future'. TAA had been told by the Department of Civil Aviation that no domestic jet operation could be contemplated before 1963. 'The competitive implications if Ansett obtains early delivery of an Electra are serious and we could expect a traffic volume drop with corresponding downward effect on trading profits', said the Commission report. 'Under the circumstances it is believed there is no alternative to TAA other than to seek immediate approval from the Minister to purchase a third Electra aircraft.'[19]

As the decade ended, exciting new jet-powered airliners were emerging from the world's manufacturers. McDonald, on an overseas tour that included the Soviet Union as well as England and the United States, was briefed on Boeing's 720 airliner, the Douglas DC9, Convair's 660 and both the British De Havilland 121 and Vickers VC10. He also flew in the Soviets' TU104. His general impressions were not, however, of great prescience. McDonald thought that the Boeing aircraft was having more than its share of teething troubles and that 'at this stage it appears that the British jets from 1963 onwards could be as successful as the Vickers turboprops proved in 1954'.[20] On 7 December 1959 Warren McDonald informed the Commission that his term of office terminated that day, following his resignation from the Commission. He was succeeded as chairman by Sir Giles Chippindall.[21]

Ansett, meanwhile, with his usual vigour, had persuaded Lockheed to let him have early delivery of his third Electra. It went into service in February 1960 as the whole industry faced a shortage of equipment resulting from the rapid traffic expansion in late 1959. Paltridge was forced to issue a revised 'determination' that took into account the sudden jump in the growth rate from the original 7 per cent envisaged when the first determination was made to an astonishing 27 per cent. In February 1960 Paltridge also resolved to a great extent the dilemma of fleet parity between the two major airlines (and prevented what he told Parliament would have been 'an equipment rat-race involving millions of pounds in further capital outlay') by imposing on the Australian National Airlines Commission a cross-charter 'agreement' under which TAA was forced to exchange three of its Viscount 700 series aircraft for two of Ansett's four DC6Bs. This unprecedented step took from both airlines the ability to shape their aircraft fleets as they saw appropriate. In effect the government had taken control, treating the two airlines as a single entity in terms of equipment needs.

Ansett was further helped when TAA, as an unwilling party, agreed in January 1960 to rationalisation of the Perth route. 'Our share on the Perth routes', said an internal TAA analysis prepared for Ryland, 'dropped from a high of over 59 per cent and eventually [April 1961] settled at the current figure of about 51.5 per cent — partly due to the rationalisation and partly due to restrictive results of the Cross Charter Agreement'.[22]

The cross-charter agreement was sealed on 26 February 1960 and the contract for TAA's third Electra was signed on the same day. Government control was further evident when Don Anderson (as the Co-ordinator under the rationalisation provisions) determined that for the four weeks beginning 19 March an overall passenger load factor of 68 per cent was necessary 'to provide for the profitability of the total airline services of TAA and other airline operators as defined in the Agreement and generally to provide for the stability of the domestic air transport industry with due regard for the interest of the public'.[23] Once again the irony of the central issue in the ongoing and stormy party political debate — private enterprise versus government enterprise — was emphasised. Government action had provided the private operator, Ansett, with assured profits.

The cross-charter agreeement (to which TAA was again an unwilling party) had a twofold affect on the airline. First, it suffered a net loss of one aircraft, which had been used with a great deal of success to provide special flights at peak times and seasons and maintain a significant traffic advantage over Ansett–ANA; second, the rationalisation of aircraft capacity under the agreement restricted TAA's capacity so that traffic flowed over to Ansett–ANA. The result was to increase Ansett–ANA's load factor by some six to seven points on main trunk routes while TAA's load factor remained almost static. 'The full effect of the Cross Charter Agreement', Ryland was advised, 'was a loss to TAA of 2 per cent of the passenger market which, together with the Perth route rationalisation, cause our market share to drop from about 55 to 52 per cent … The airlines of Ansett Transport Industries are now significantly larger than TAA and in better competitive and financial shape.'[24]

The cross-charter agreement, however logical from the

government's point of view, provoked political uproar. Labor saw it as a deliberate weakening of TAA and a boost for Ansett. Ansett, on his part, insisted that his own preference had been to sell the DC6Bs and buy a fourth Electra. To provide TAA with a third Electra, Paltridge approved the immediate charter by TAA of an Electra from Qantas, and gave permission for TAA to place an order for its own third Electra. The agreement was to last for three years. Under its terms neither airline could order turboprop aircraft heavier than the Electra, nor could they introduce low fare services. (That provision precluded Ansett from introducing DC6B coach services.)

TAA staff reacted with anger. Meetings held in Brisbane, Sydney, Melbourne and Hobart saw vigorous protests. From the point of view of staff, Ryland told the Commission, the cross-charter meant that TAA was being further hampered by government directives and that job security was at stake.[25] For Ansett the cross-charter was a major financial and competitive boost. The world market price for his four DC6B aircraft and spares was below the amount still owing on them so that their sale into the market would have involved a substantial capital loss. Simply to retain them in the Ansett–ANA fleet would also have been financially embarrassing. They had proved incapable of attracting passenger traffic in competition with TAA's turbine-powered fleet so that, with TAA obtaining some 55 per cent of the total competitive passenger market, there had been serious concern within Ansett–ANA about the airline's overall operating economy.

The cross-charter agreement was a brutal acknowledgment that TAA had proved the superior airline, a superiority achieved by careful and efficient evaluation and selection of aircraft over a long period. TAA fleet superiority had been evident since the introduction of its pressurised Convairs.

Publicly Sir Giles Chippindall had no option but to support the agreement. In a statement to the press he said: 'An exchange of aircraft between TAA and Ansett–ANA as set out by the Prime Minister, Mr Menzies, receives the full approval of the Australian National Airlines Commission, which operates TAA ... The cross-charter proposal provides a quick and inexpensive way of achieving fleet parity between the two operators which will, in the view of the Commission, have long term benefits for the industry.'[26]

Chippindall gave TAA staff, through *This Air Age*, a reassuring message: 'It will be seen', he said, 'that nothing has been done that will place TAA at a disadvantage to Ansett–ANA in the matter of their respective fleets, the major units of which will now comprise ... TAA, three Electras, twelve Viscounts, two DC6Bs — a total of seventeen aircraft; Ansett–ANA, three Electras, nine Viscounts, two DC6Bs — a total of fourteen aircraft.'[27] In a personal visit to address Brisbane staff he rejected the widespread newspaper stories that the government was 'trying to kill TAA'. The government's policy, he said, 'is to maintain TAA in the airline business, with competition from a private airline ... Nothing has been done and nothing is likely to be done which will cause TAA to have a fleet inferior to that of any other operator.'[28] The Paltridge cross-charter decision set the pattern for the years ahead. No more Electras were to be ordered by either airline.

Though the Electras were proving themselves in economic terms they were again faced with unpleasant technical problems. Since going into service in the United States in January 1959 there had been three fatal crashes killing a total of 294 passengers and crew. All told, 121 Electras were now in service with thirteen airlines.

The first fatal Electra accident occurred on 3 February 1959 when an American Airlines aircraft, making an instrument approach to La Guardia, New York, crashed into the East River. The cause, it was agreed, was pilot error. The following two crashes were different. A Braniff Electra crashed near Buffalo, Texas, with no survivors on 29 September; the next, in March 1960, was a North West aircraft, which crashed in Indiana killing all aboard. No one knew the causes of the accidents. As a result the US Federal Aviation Agency (FAA) placed precautionary performance restrictions on Electras, limiting their cruising speed — a restriction adopted at once by Australia. The main effect for TAA and Ansett–ANA was to restrict descent speeds at certain altitudes by a modest 23 miles per hour. Schedules were not greatly affected (on the Sydney–Melbourne route flight times increased by about seven minutes; on the Perth route the difference was some twenty minutes).[29] There was no significant adverse public reaction.

By May 1960 Lockheed had found the source of the trouble that had caused the crashes. They were, it said, due to 'dynamic coupling at high speed of oscillatory movements of the outboard power package nacelle and the wing'. Company tests had shown that 'prior damage to the nacelles plus the immense external forces added by the flight through clear-air turbulence at high speed set off oscillations which built up forces to the breaking point'. Modifications to the aircraft were to be made by August 1960. In the meantime Electras were to operate under existing speed restrictions.[30]

John Watkins told Ryland: 'The ingenious and highly complex hypothesis is advanced that "gyro-whirl" of the outboard nacelle may have become coupled with the natural frequencies of the wing and built up a type of divergent flutter rapidly leading to loads at the wing root great enough to cause failure of a hitherto undamaged wing structure. The finer points of this hypothesis and its simulation in the wind tunnel could only be properly understood and critically evaluated by a specialist experienced in the study of flutter problems. We have no one on our staff with this background of experience.'[31] Short of independent grounding of the TAA Electras, said Watkins, 'we can only respect the thoroughness and impartiality of the Federal Aviation Agency in the United States and accept their conclusion that a real margin of safety is in fact preserved against the destructive effects of this phenomenon while flying the Electra is strictly limited to an indicated airspeed of 225 knots ... We should concur in the present opinion of the Department of Civil Aviation that continued operation under present speed and other restrictions is justified.'

Ansett's pressure on the government to allow services to

New Guinea was rewarded in April 1960. Shane Paltridge told Qantas vice-chairman W.C. Taylor: It has been decided that Ansett–ANA and TAA will be authorised to operate between the mainland and New Guinea and that Qantas will restrict its activities within Papua–New Guinea to the operation of its Far East services'. For TAA there was an additional benefit. It had also been decided, wrote Paltridge, that 'TAA will assume responsibility for the Papua–New Guinea internal and regional services which have been operated by Qantas and purchase Qantas' Papua–New Guinea assets necessary for this purpose in accordance with financial arrangements approved by the Treasurer.'[32]

Qantas, which had begun operating in New Guinea in 1944 by buying out W.R. Carpenter and Company, did not welcome the change. Qantas chairman, Hudson Fysh, told Paltridge that the financial consequences for Qantas as a result of withdrawal would amount to more than £3 million over a five-year period.[33] Giles Chippindall made it clear to Fysh that there had been no TAA pressure for the change. He had first learned of the government decision in the press, he said. 'I can well understand your feelings,' he wrote, 'and those of your executive officers regarding this decision. Qantas has pioneered the services on this route and carried them out with conspicuous efficiency and is now in the position of seeing the route pass to other hands. I would like to assure you that TAA neither directly nor indirectly did anything to influence the Government's decision. The only move taken by this organisation was to lodge an application for a licence some months ago when we were advised that Ansett–ANA had applied for such a licence. Our move was a protective one only.'[34]

'We naturally feel rather sad at having to give up this whole operation,' Fysh responded, 'but from the practical side we are going to feel it most owing to the loss of contribution to our overhead and the loss of an invaluable training ground for young pilots. I am very happy to say there has been no suggestion whatever here that TAA have "undermined" us in any way.'[35]

The *Financial Review* commented on 14 April: 'The revenue to be taken from the New Guinea service — both the Sydney–Moresby run and the internal routes previously operated by Qantas — is valued at about £1.4 to £1.5 million a year, including freight ... The New Guinea route should ... add something like 4 per cent to total revenue of TAA and Ansett–ANA.' The greatest benefit, it said, 'may well go to TAA, now taking over the entire Qantas internal route structure, which carried the lion's share of the passenger traffic considered likely to be available for on-carriage to the mainland.'[36] Ryland, however, after a preliminary survey of Qantas's New Guinea operations, concluded that the internal New Guinea network was likely to be a drain on the Commission's finances. Qantas had valued their assets available for transfer at £827,000, but Ryland concluded that 'the final capital investment of TAA in the area may be of the order of £1,000,000 to £1,250,000'.[37]

TAA and Ansett–ANA began operations on the Australia–New Guinea trunk route on 9 July 1960 using DC6B aircraft. TAA operated the first flight.

The *Review,* on 12 May, commented on the results for passengers of the 'new era' in domestic aviation since the Ansett takeover of ANA. 'Between the September quarter of 1957 and the March quarter this year retail prices in Australia ... have risen by only 6.5 per cent. In the same period first class air fares have risen approximately two and a half times as fast. Tourist fares have risen even faster.'[38] A week later the Australian National Airlines Commission was told that agreement had been reached with Ansett–ANA for further fare increases of 7.5 per cent first class and 10 per cent tourist class on competitive routes. An increase in revenue of some £850,000 was estimated, with no resultant loss of traffic. An additional £90,000 revenue was expected from smaller increases on the noncompetitive routes.[39]

In June 1960 TAA had its first fatal airliner crash. A Fokker Friendship arrived over Mackay, Queensland, at 8.40 p.m. on 10 June but went into a holding pattern because ground mist was thickening at the airport. When the captain and the Mackay tower agreed that the mist was dispersing the

Friendship was cleared for a visual approach. Just after 10 p.m. the aircraft crashed into the sea. Conditions were stated to be fine with bright moonlight. There were no survivors. Ten bodies, including those of the captain and first officer, were recovered. Paltridge announced that a public inquiry into the causes of the accident would be held.[40]

On 19 July a second serious incident for TAA placed in jeopardy a Viscount and the fifty people aboard when it prepared for a normal descent from 20,000 feet into Brisbane just after 9 p.m. A hostess reported to the captain that a passenger armed with a pistol wanted to speak to him. Captain Benton sent Flight Engineer McDonald to assess the seriousness of the situation. When McDonald returned he reported that in addition to the firearm the passenger had two sticks of gelignite to which leads were attached and a battery placed in an ashtray on the arm of the seat. The first officer, T.R. Bennett, went to the cabin.

The passenger threatened to explode the gelignite if there was any attempt to land at Brisbane. He demanded that he be flown to Singapore. On board, flying supernumerary, was another TAA captain, D. R. Lawrence, who was summoned to the cockpit. Captain Benton, convinced that the passenger must be disarmed at all costs, instructed Lawrence to arm himself with a fire axe located in the cockpit and return to the cabin. Bennett was trying to convince the passenger that the aircraft did not have the fuel to fly to Singapore when Lawrence (who was not in uniform and had the axe hidden under a topcoat) leaned over from the seat behind to confirm the statement about fuel. It was at this moment that Lawrence reached in his coat for the axe. The movement sufficiently distracted the passenger to allow Bennett to seize the hand that was holding the gelignite leads and at the same time knock away the gun which fired once and fell to the floor. Bennett started punching vigorously while Lawrence struck the passenger several times with the axe handle. (Lawrence, during the struggle, found himself seated on the gelignite.) The passenger was subdued. The incident had lasted some thirteen minutes. When the aircraft landed the passenger was taken into custody and charged at the city watchhouse. First Officer Bennett was later awarded the George Medal for his actions and Lawrence was commended.[41]

The loss of the Friendship, coupled with the use of a DC6B on the Sydney–Moresby–Lae route (and the possibility of the need to withdraw a Friendship from normal services to operate on internal New Guinea routes) called for an urgent examination by TAA of its fleet planning requirements. These pressures were compounded by the need to return all TAA Electras to the Lockheed factory in California for structural modifications. The immediate capacity solution proposed in July 1960 was the purchase of a second-hand Viscount 800 series aircraft from Continental Airlines, Denver. (New Viscounts were not available for delivery before April 1961.)[42]

The Electra chartered from Qantas was returned on 7 September, following the delivery of TAA's new Mk II Electra from Lockheed at the end of August. It did not incorporate the modifications that were to be effected in all Electras flying worldwide — that would have meant a five-month delay in delivery. The first TAA aircraft to return to Lockheed for modification was scheduled to leave Australia at the end of January 1961, the second in late March and the third in early June, with each spending about a month with the manufacturer. (The modifications allowed a lifting of all speed restrictions on the aircraft. TAA had strong doubts that Lockheed would meet this timetable.)

Despite all the drama of the year the financial outcome for both TAA and Ansett was healthy. TAA reported a 1959–60 record trading profit of £352,938, while Ansett Transport Industries announced a group record profit of £671,881. (Ansett did not separately disclose the profit of Ansett–ANA's aviation activities.) It had been a year of exceptionally buoyant traffic, stemming in part from the general national prosperity and in part from both the introduction of new aircraft and the expansion of tourist class traffic. TAA's traffic overall increased by 24.1 per cent with tourist traffic 40.9 per cent of the total. *Aircraft* was effusive. 'Congratulations are due to both airlines', it wrote, 'but they must also go to the Government — particularly to Senator Paltridge and to his department head, Mr D. G. Anderson — on a situation that must be attributed at least in part to successful application of the two-airline competitive policy'.[43]

Ongoing stability in the aviation industry, however, was never to be easy to achieve. Technological progress in airframe and engine design was rapid and the world environment for manufacturers competitive. As the Electras settled into the Australian scene new aircraft were promised from the United States, Britain and France. In December 1960 the Boeing Company announced a huge order from United and Eastern Airlines for 80 Boeing 727 short-haul airliners. That launch order made it possible for Boeing to commit to production of the 727. (Its fuselage was Electra size but its cruising speed was some 550 miles per hour.)

The announcement clearing the way for 727 production was a blow to the British, whose 727 competitor was the de Havilland Trident, due for delivery in 1963 — the same year scheduled for first deliveries of the 727. France was competing with the smaller Caravelle 8. All three aircraft had their three jet engines in the tail. Both TAA and Ansett–ANA had now to evaluate these aircraft and make decisions for the future. Frontrunner for both was the Boeing 727.

CHAPTER 9

1961

Boundaries of competition

Though the domestic aviation market was still sound as 1961 began and the differing equipment ambitions of both airlines had been resolved by government edict, the political or commercial pressures and complexities continued to test the boundaries of opportunity and competition under the two-airline policy. The year was to see yet more major legislation, from both the federal Liberal-Country Party government and the Labor government of New South Wales. Ansett pressed to diminish what he saw as unfair TAA financial advantages, and TAA sought to bring more equality to a system that gave Ansett superiority in intrastate operations.

The core Ansett argument was that Ansett Transport Industries' Ansett–ANA had a fundamentally different structure from the Australian National Airlines Commission's TAA. H. W. (Harold) Poulton, a lawyer and policy maker (who had joined the Department of Civil Aviation in 1955, succeeding Edgar Johnston in his post as first assistant director-general, policy, and who was in 1964 to join Ansett Transport Industries as executive director, policy), wrote in his *Law, History and Politics of the Australian Two Airline System*: 'TAA had advantages which the private airline did not enjoy, such as low capitalisation, ready access to cheap government money, use of staff superannuation funds in its business and its retention of a major share of government business'. TAA, for its part, he said, 'was irked by the restrictions imposed on it'. TAA wanted greater freedom to compete with Ansett by operating intrastate services from which it was excluded, particularly in South Australia and Western Australia. Quoting Sir Giles Chippindall, Poulton wrote: 'He considered that intensive rationalisation controls over the deployment of available aircraft capacity put an unnecessary fetter on competition. He suggested that within the limits of general control over capacity deployed over the whole system each airline should be free to deploy its fleet as it thought best. TAA also wanted greater freedom to expand into associated activities such as promotion of tourism, general aviation and engineering.'[1]

Ansett's first move in 1961 was to finalise, on 12 January, the purchase of the major Papua New Guinea airline, Mandated Air Lines (owned by the trading company W.R. Carpenter), which operated eight DC3s and carried some 23,000 passengers each year. The purpose, of course, was to secure its on-traffic for the profitable mainland route. The price paid by ATI — two million ATI shares and £450,000 cash — matched the price paid by TAA of approximately £1 million to Qantas for its New Guinea aircraft and other assets.[2]

While this move protected the Ansett on-carriage from New Guinea, he retained his great advantage in on-carriage from intrastate operations. ATI subsidiaries carried 446,078 passengers and 4,609 tons of freight in 1961–62; the three independent intrastate operators, MacRobertson Miller, East-West and Connellan, carried 194,208 passengers and 4,434 tons of freight. (In January 1961 TAA's founding general manager, Lester Brain, was appointed a consultant to the board of East-West Airlines.)

Though TAA welcomed the new involvement in New Guinea it had inherited internal services on which Qantas had operated at a loss. Commission member G. Packer reported to Chipppindall: 'The conclusion is inescapable that the whole New Guinea operation must be re-examined critically without delay. I assume that our minimum objective would be to break even on the combined Mainland–New

Guinea and Internal services after meeting interest on capital. It would be necessary to reduce current rate of loss by £50,000 per annum to do so.'[3] (In April TAA moved to buy two Bristol Freighters — from the Pakistani air force — for use in New Guinea for freight carriage on the route between Madang and the Highlands.)

What Ansett lacked, as 1961 began, was access to the Adelaide–Alice Springs–Darwin route (in Ansett's view a rapidly emerging trunk route), despite the fact that TAA's monopoly rights to fly within and to federal territories had been withdrawn in 1959.

When the minister made his formal report to Parliament for 1960–61 he noted: 'In recent years the civil airline fleets of the Commonwealth, both domestic and international, have been almost wholly converted from piston-engined to turbine-powered operation at a cost of approximately £80 million ... Because of the national value of civil aviation the Australian public has traditionally made greater per capita use of its air transport services than the people of most other countries of the world.'

On Australian international aviation he said:

> This has resulted, over the last forty years, in the development of our international flag carrier, the wholly Government-owned Qantas Empire Airways Ltd., from a small bush airline operating in outback Queensland and the Northern Territory, into one of the world's great airlines, operating a subsonic jet fleet on a 'round-the-world' route through the USA and the United Kingdom. Qantas now provides services to five continents and twenty-seven countries, and official statistics show that on the basis of revenue-ton-miles performed in 1960 it was the seventh largest air carrier in the world ... One particular development is that during the year arrangements were made for the New Zealand Government to assume complete ownership and control of Tasman Empire Airways Limited. After a period of more than twenty years in which it has shared ownership of TEAL, first with the United Kingdom and Australia and, since 1954, equally with Australia, the New Zealand Government now becomes the sole owner of its own international air carrier.'

That development of TEAL, he said, paralleled closely the development of Qantas. 'Qantas was for many years partly owned by United Kingdom interests but is now wholly owned by the Australian Government and operated in pool-partnership with the United Kingdom and India.'[4]

There were other changes in New Zealand of closer interest to TAA. Ansett Transport Industries acquired a 49 per cent interest in the internal Airlines of New Zealand, giving Ansett–ANA a modest competitive edge in the carriage of tourist traffic originating in that country.

When TAA's third Electra returned from the United States on 18 June 1961 with the necessary modifications to allow it to fly at higher speeds, the airline became the first domestic airline to have the modifications incorporated into its entire fleet. It also, as staff were told, marked 'the end of TAA's part in one of the most massive research and modification programmes in civil aviation history'. (The modifications involved opening the wing structure and adding strengthening metal weighing some 1,400 pounds.) Restrictions limiting Electra operating speeds were lifted by the Department of Civil Aviation on 10 June, allowing the aircraft to fly at cruising speeds up to 405 miles an hour.

TAA results at the end of the 1960–61 financial year reflected ongoing difficulties experienced by Australian industry and a general economic squeeze. There was a drop of 3.5 per cent in traffic for the twelve months compared with the previous year (by far the largest fall occurring in the last six months of the year) — the first decline in passenger traffic since 1952–53. Ansett was similarly affected. The *Financial Review* wrote: 'The recent decline in airline traffic, rising costs, including sharp increases in Federal Government air route charges and the very heavy burden of capital servicing costs assumed by Ansett–ANA have combined to increase the difficulties of the private airline to earn a sufficient level of profits safely to cover its capital servicing commitment. The present situation has been described by responsible industry observers as "very threatening to the future of the present two-airlines system".'[5]

Ansett sent a letter to all members of Parliament to protest his difficulties, at the same time taking out full-page newspaper advertisments across the country to publish its contents. 'Mr Ansett', wrote the *Review*, 'raised a number of fundamental issues of principle concerning the ground rules for the conduct of a two-airline system in Australia'.

> Of these issues, including those of the fair sharing of Government business between two airlines, recent Government moves to increase air route charges and the need for both operators to begin within three years the re-equipment of their fleets with front-line pure-jet aircraft, the one which Mr Ansett clearly regards as being the most important is the question of the correct principles which should guide TAA in the calculation of its capital costs. Mr Ansett feels that TAA is getting away with capital costs which, because of its preferred position as a Government airline [makes] it much easier for TAA to disregard the urgent pressure under which Mr Ansett undoubtedly finds himself ... He wants the Government to oblige TAA to change its methods of accounting so that it will be obliged to treat its present payments of interest on money borrowed from the Government not as a dividend from its operations each year, but as a cost which must be reckoned before a profit is struck ... The Government clearly does not want to 'sell out' TAA. And it simply cannot afford to see Mr Ansett driven to the wall.

There can be no denying, wrote the *Review*, 'the grave difficulties being met in the effort to establish a workable equilibrium in an industry where the private operator has assumed heroic capital burdens and must meet the exigencies of the capital market on normal profitability criteria.'[6]

'As if in automatic response to [Ansett's newspaper advertisements]', wrote David Corbett in his *Politics and the Airlines*,

> the Government obtained legislation in October 1961 requiring TAA to earn a rate of return, or profit target, to be set in advance each year by the Minister with the concurrence of the Treasurer and after consultation with TAA. Furthermore, TAA which in the past had always provided and administered its own insurance and staff superannuation funds instead of insuring with a commercial insurance firm, would no longer be allowed to draw on these funds for investment in its own business but would have to invest them in Commonwealth securities. Both of these new financial requirements deprived TAA of competitive advantages ... and seemed to confirm a trend of policy against the Government-owned airline.[7]

This policy trend — a clear one — was driven by the government's overriding political imperative that required, for the continuity of its two-airline system, the commercial survival of Ansett–ANA. That government anxiety was well understood and exploited by Reginald Ansett, who had behind him, in his relentless application of political pressure, the most able and informed intellect in the field in Australia. Harold Poulton, as former assistant director-general (policy) for the Department of Civil Aviation, combined his legal and policy expertise with an intimate knowledge of the interplay between bureaucracy and Cabinet.

One major issue raised by Ansett was his exclusion from the Darwin route. He soon had his way. Don Anderson, as rationalisation Co-ordinator, formally recognised Darwin as the administrative centre of the Northern Territory and an important international airport and, on that basis, approved Ansett's application to serve Darwin from Sydney, Brisbane and Adelaide from 15 October 1961. Only the Perth–Darwin run now remained a monopoly route, served by MacRobertson Miller.[8] The favourable Ansett decision by Anderson on Darwin established for all except TAA supporters his impartiality and detachment as Co-ordinator. Though he was responsible to the same minister as the Australian National Airlines Commission in his role as director-general of civil aviation, it was seen that as judge and jury in rationalisation disputes, his decisions were not influenced by the ties that linked TAA, through the Commission, to the government. (Nevertheless Ansett was denied the right to operate local F27 and DC3 services between Adelaide and intermediate points on the Darwin route.) In fact, of course, Anderson's decision reflected the pressing government need to strengthen Ansett's profitability.

For TAA the decision had direct effects on profits as its growth rate declined from some 6 per cent in January to almost zero in May. (In fact airlines worldwide were now passing through a difficult period. The eighty-three airlines belonging to the International Civil Aviation Organisation (IACO) had, in the previous year, average profits of little more than half a million dollars each (less than half the preceding year's). Operating costs were rising faster than revenues — a trend that had been evident since the introduction of the big, long-range pure-jet airliners. The worldwide surge in the purchase of these airliners had increased seat capacity by 50 per cent or more on many routes, while passenger traffic had grown at a much slower rate. The Commission decided on 15 September 1961 that 'the Minister be informed by letter of the dire effects of the Darwin decision on the Commission's revenues and profit and of the overall effects on its economy'.[9]

The *Financial Review* reported: 'Sir Giles Chippindall, chairman of the Australian National Airlines Commission, said last week it was time Mr Ansett stopped bleating about his hard luck and counted his blessings'. On the issue of comparative profitability it wrote: 'The industry is now so closely interwoven with the fabric of overall government high policy that the issue of TAA profits needs to be thoroughly clarified. The same could be said for Ansett–ANA profits which are presently hidden, at least from the public gaze, within the ATI accounts ... The position is that Ansett–ANA has had to pay more for its fleet than TAA and that it must pay substantially more to service the capital involved in owning the fleet than does TAA ... Ansett–ANA has been engaged in a period of swift expansion, perhaps too swift, which has left the company with very large capital obligations much of which is financed by short-term debt.'[10]

The public Ansett campaign to redress what it saw as the wrongs committed against it was, as David Corbett noted, immediately successful. On 28 September 1961 the *Financial Review* reported: 'Radical new civil aviation legislation to be introduced into the Senate today by the Minister for Civil Aviation, Senator Paltridge, makes major concessions designed to provide great strength to the financial structure of Ansett–ANA. The legislation will also provide for the purchase by TAA and Ansett–ANA of two pure-jet aircraft each, to be delivered not before July, 1964.'[11] The legislation provided for a ten-year extension of the 1952–57 Civil Aviation Agreement Acts. Under it the Commonwealth government agreed to guarantee the repayment by Ansett–ANA of loans for the purchase of jet aircraft up to an amount not exceeding £6 million at any one time. That provision fundamentally underpinned the strength of the capital structure of Ansett Transport Industries. The Commonwealth also required the two airlines to extend the existing cross-charter arrangement of two Ansett DC6Bs for three TAA Viscounts until the start of the first pure-jet services. In a major concession the Government undertook not to increase air navigation charges by more than 10 per cent in any twelve months and not to increase taxes on aviation fuel more than any corresponding increase in motor-vehicle tax. TAA, under the legislation, was obliged for the first time to seek to achieve a profit target specified by the minister, while its self-insurance scheme, then backed by the full resources of government, was to be put on a separate statutory basis. Combined with the decision allowing Ansett into Darwin, the new legislation was widely recognised as a major breakthrough for Ansett.

Not all went Ansett's way. In New South Wales in October the State government, under a policy designed to bring to intrastate operations a similar rationalisation system to that imposed federally, reallocated intrastate air services by granting East-West Airlines a far greater share of rural airline routes. (East-West had resisted an Ansett takeover bid.) The Heffron Labor government cut the share of air traffic operated by Airlines of New South Wales (an Ansett–ANA subsidiary) from 70 to 51 per cent and increased the East-West share from 30 to 49 per cent. Ansett responded with threats of all-out competition against East-West.

A backlash now emerged against the stridency and political clout of Reginald Ansett. The conservative *Age* newspaper in Melbourne wrote:

> The chairman of Ansett Transport Industries, Mr R. M. Ansett, is setting some strange precedents in his zeal to promote his enterprise. There is an air of pressure about his voluble addresses to Governments which many must find difficult to understand. It is clear that TAA has been compelled to make sacrificies in the interests of Ansett–ANA to maintain the two-airline policy to which the Government is committed. Ansett–ANA has been given

> access to the New Guinea network and to the Darwin route at considerable expense to TAA. Controls over load factors on main internal routes have also cost TAA traffic to its competitor ... In New South Wales it seems that all that is happening is that East-West Airlines is to receive no more than a benefit already enjoyed by Ansett–ANA in a wider sphere. There is some evidence to suggest that Ansett–ANA is gradually manoeuvring to a position of superiority in the name of rationalisation which could seriously affect the future of TAA. Many people are convinced that eventually Australia will have only one airline because it will not be possible to justify the two-airlines system for much longer because of high costs. If that position arises the Government airline should be the survivor.[12]

It had been a turbulent year for Australian domestic civil aviation. TAA was now fifteen years old and had 4,848 staff members. In 1961 it provided scheduled flights to 140 ports on more than 40,000 miles of routes across Australia and the Territory of Papua–New Guinea. Its services ranged from Electra flights between Melbourne and Sydney to DC3 calls to cattle stations in far west Queensland and Otter flights through the New Guinea mountains to otherwise inaccessible highland towns. TAA pilots also flew flying doctor services to remote parts of Queensland and the Northern Territory. Within Australia alone the airline now carried more than a million passengers a year. For the 1960–61 year it reported a record profit of £383,444 on a record revenue of £17,093,011 (up from £14,622,213 in the previous year). Those results were achieved despite general economic conditions that had resulted in a decline in the number of passengers carried on all airlines within Australia. The annual report noted: 'With the granting of Darwin routes to its competitor TAA was left with a non-competitive network only one sixth the size of its competitor's. This operational imbalance must have a marked effect on TAA's financial situation.'[13]

Both TAA and Ansett–ANA were given permission in February 1962 to each buy one Viscount 800 aircraft, following an application by Ansett in December to buy a Viscount to replace one that had crashed into Botany Bay, Sydney (one of the three he had received from TAA under the cross-charter arrangement). TAA currently had two Viscount 800s to

Ansett's five, while Ansett had five Viscount 700s to TAA's nine (two of which were cross-chartered to Ansett).

In mid-1962, when Commission member Gerald Packer died and was replaced by Robert Law-Smith, a TAA link with Qantas was made. Law-Smith was vice-chairman of Qantas and had been a board member of the airline since 1956. A grazier and company director, he had served in the RAAF from 1940 to 1946.

On 10 September 1962 the minister, following a review of the Commission's powers in the field of aerial and charter work (a field in which the Commission relied on 'incidental powers'), formally advised the Commission that no steps would be taken by the government to obtain intrastate powers for TAA 'until the Government considers that the need arises and the Government takes the view that there is no need at this time'.[14] That meant, said a Commission report, 'that the Commission will remain barred from any intrastate services in which it wished to engage within New South Wales, Victoria, South Australia and Western Australia; and that Ansett–ANA or other subsidiaries of Ansett Transport Industries will continue to enjoy a virtual monopoly of intrastate operations in New South Wales, Victoria and South Australia and MacRobertson-Miller will retain its monopoly of intrastate services in Western Australia. The more significant result is that Ansett–ANA through its affiliated carriers has access to the bulk of the on-carriage over interstate routes which originates on the intrastate routes.'[15]

The Government also did not consider it appropriate 'to amend the Airlines Act to give the Commission a specific power in the charter and aerial work fields'. The continuing lack of this power meant that charters could not be operated in the States in which TAA had no intrastate rights, though these had taken place to a limited extent previously (under the Commission's 'incidental' powers).[16] Outside the Territories, Queensland and Tasmania, the Commission was told, 'TAA now cannot operate charters either directly or indirectly'. On the matter of aerial work it was the Government's belief that aerial work with helicopters 'should more appropriately be left to private operators'. That meant that TAA was now limited to the operation of helicopters on regular public transport services only (airport to city heliport operations).

(The 'incidental powers' under the Australian National Airlines Act allowed the Commission to do 'all that is necessary or convenient to be done for or as incidental to ... or in connection with the establishment, maintenance or operation by the Commission of airline services'. The minister's review now made clear that ministerial approval would from now on be necessary before engaging in any activity that relied on the Commission's incidental powers.)

Both airlines were actively engaged in 1962 in evaluating their aircraft choices for the future. Chippindall, Ryland and Watkins all left for Europe and the United States in September to visit aircraft manufacturers. Under consideration were a modernised Caravelle from France (an outsider), the British BAC One-Eleven and Hawker-Siddeley Trident (a de Havilland design, the DH121, before de Havilland became part of the Hawker-Siddeley group), and the American Boeing 727, all powered by tail-mounted jet engines. Under government legislation TAA and Ansett–ANA were not bound to choose the same aircraft type, but they were required to choose aircraft that were comparable in size and performance. The Trident had been designed to meet the requirements of British European Airlines on their routes in Europe, the Boeing 727 to meet the needs of American Airlines and Eastern Airlines (with the first aircraft expected to fly in January 1963). The developed Caravelle 10A was the only contender that had no restrictions on operating out of Essendon airport, while the British Aircraft Corporation's BAC One-Eleven — slightly larger than the Viscount 800 — had been designed for the short-haul market and was available at about half the price of the Boeing 727. (The first BAC One-Eleven flew in August 1963.)[17] TAA's assistant general manager, John Chapman, reported that 'the choice [for a heavy aircraft] appears to lie between the Trident and the Boeing 727'.[18] For the second, smaller aircraft type, for introduction in 1966–67 as a Viscount replacement, Chapman thought the BAC One-Eleven, which carried some sixty-six passengers, the most suitable contender.

Reginald Ansett had already made the Ansett–ANA choice. He wanted the Boeing 727. TAA, on technical and operational grounds, had favoured the British Trident and was also under considerable pressure to buy British. But it was recognised at top management levels that the commercial risk involved in choosing different equipment from its competitor was considerable. The safer decision, which was taken after some deliberation, was to follow Ansett and order the 727. Both airlines were also swayed by the fact that the 727 was not only the biggest and fastest of the contenders, but was built by the world's largest airliner manufacturer and was assured of selling in massive numbers. (More than six hundred were eventually in service.) On 19 November 1962 Paltridge announced government approval for the airlines each to order two Boeing 727s. The aircraft's performance was impressive. In full-page advertisements in November TAA announced: 'In performance and size the 727 is tailored to Australian routes and their future development. The 727 has a maximum cruising speed of 600 miles per hour, with a maximum range of 3,000 miles, and will carry up to 112 passengers. It has three rear-mounted pure jet engines'. The Boeing 727 was yet to fly; the first aircraft was rolled off the Boeing assembly line at Renton on 28 November. The aircraft's introduction in Australia was scheduled for late 1964 or early 1965.

While the 727's speed was the attraction for air travellers, it was the aircraft's promised productivity that attracted the airlines. There were, though, benefits for government, which had to plan and finance airport development, from the decision to order common equipment. As Stanley Brogden commented in the *Financial Review* on 27 November 1962: 'There was a desire, for the first time in aviation history in Australia, to make simultaneous provision for the introduction of new aircraft and for the introduction of airports and other facilities such as the permanent way and signalling system of the airline network'.[19] (Ansett made a demonstration of independence to his private enterprise supporters by deciding to finance the purchase of his two 727s without using his government guarantee.)

In December 1962 Prime Minister Menzies announced the government's £30 million airport development programme. It included a new international terminal for Sydney and major improvements at Adelaide, Hobart, Mount Isa, Kalgoorlie, Townsville, Lae and Coolangatta. Melbourne, however, was the main beneficiary. The programme included the creation of a new airport on a 5,000-acre site at Tullamarine at a cost of £10 million. (Tullamarine was to begin operations in 1967.) Important technical changes were also planned for the airways system. A new type of radio range (the Visual Omni-Directional or VOR) was to be installed at twenty-two locations, and increasing use of modern, long-range radar equipment was planned for the main traffic centres.

Aircraft described the twin announcements on equipment and airport development as 'a red letter period for Australian aviation'. The industry, it wrote, 'has been left in a state of slightly dazed excitement ... The step forward to jets is a major milestone for the industry and for Australia.'[20]

When the annual report of the Australian National Airlines Commission was tabled in Parliament it showed that TAA for the 1960–61 year had exceeded its previous record profit and returned a new after tax record profit of £463,333. From that profit a dividend of 5 per cent, or £375,000, on its capital of £7.5 million was paid to the government. The result had been achieved in a difficult trading period when the slow recovery in the national economy had dampened the industry's traffic volumes. (Total TAA payroll of just over £6 million, for a staff of 4,665, accounted for 36 per cent of all expenditure.) Revenue for the year was just over £17 million, paying passengers carried over a million, and hours flown over 100,000. The Australia–New Guinea services had operated at a profit during the year but scheduled operations within the Territory incurred substantial losses. In other activities of substance the Engineering School at Melbourne Airport provided courses to 458 engineers and apprentices. TAA continued to maintain and operate aircraft for the Queensland branch of the Royal Flying Doctor Service and for Northern Territory Aerial Medical Services. (Total flying time for the two organisations was 3,034 hours.)[21] While the airline profits of its competitor Ansett–ANA (and the Ansett subsidiaries in New South Wales, South Australia, Queensland and New Guinea) were not revealed for the year, the parent company, Ansett Transport Industries, announced a profit of £1,066,256 before tax and a dividend total for the year of 10 per cent.

In tabling the annual report of the Department of Civil Aviation, Paltridge told the Parliament: 'These results provide clear proof of the success of the Government's rationalisation policies, for they show that the major domestic airlines were able to declare satisfactory profits in a year when total air traffic was slightly less than in the previous year and costs were generally higher. The control of aircraft capacity under the provisions of the Airlines Agreement Act 1961 and the associated Airlines Equipment Act 1958 had the most important single effect, resulting as it did in the maintenance of profitable load factors in a year of static traffic growth.'

TAA signed the contract for the purchase of its two Boeing 727s in early January 1963, with delivery promised for October and November 1964. There was already disagreement with Ansett on the starting date for their introduction into service. Ansett wanted a delay until mid 1965; TAA wanted their aircraft in service before the Christmas period of 1964. (The issue was resolved by March, both airlines agreeing to have the aircraft in service for the Christmas peak.)

In early 1963 a TAA comparison of the capital structures of TAA and Ansett Transport Industries showed that for TAA, issued capital (£7.5 million) represented 40 per cent of capital (interest-bearing funds — £7.29 million — represented 39 per cent, and non-interest-bearing funds — £3.894 million — 21 per cent). For ATI issued capital (£6.565 million) represented 18.3 per cent of capital (interest-bearing funds — £23.81 million — represented 66.7 per cent, and non-interest bearing funds — £5.388 million — 15 per cent). This meant, the

Commission was advised, that 'while 40 per cent of TAA's funds is subject to dividend only 18.3 per cent of ATI's funds is so subject'. The gearing ratio of borrowed funds to fixed capital had an obvious and significant effect on the relative profitability of the two airlines as the cost of interest-bearing funds was a charge against income before profit and tax were determined. For ATI, however, the high gearing ratio carried a penalty in relation to financial stability. For TAA it was clear that 'if TAA could increase the proportion of borrowed funds to Treasury advances this would be to its advantage'. The Commission was told: 'So long as an adequate return on Treasury advances is being achieved it is probably undesirable for the airline industry to be making large profits. Pressures to reduce fares and provide free or uneconomical services and concessions would build up.'[22] That philosophy — antipathetic to large profits — was not the basis of private enterprise thinking.

Both TAA and Ansett–ANA were approached in early 1963 by the Douglas Aircraft Company requesting letters of intent for their small Douglas DC9 jet airliner, then in the design stage. For once there was agreement by the two. No commitment was given, though both needed to decide within eighteen months whether to opt for the DC9 or the British BAC One-Eleven. (The One-Eleven was already in quantity production with plenty of orders.) The decision was a major one, involving far greater expenditure than for the 727s. Each airline needed nine or ten of the smaller jets for an outlay of some £20 million each. Ansett nevertheless indicated that he preferred the DC9 while TAA now expressed firm interest. (No airline in the world had yet placed orders for the DC9.) It was known that the Department of Civil Aviation wanted Australian orders for British aircraft and that the RAAF wanted One-Elevens for its VIP flight. (Within TAA, E. J. Brunckhurst, chief engineer for maintenance and overhaul, was appointed in March to supervise engineering arrangements for the introduction of jet aircraft, as well as moving the airline's engineering base from Essendon to Tullamarine. He was given the title of chief engineer, project planning.)[23]

As decisions on these major changes to Australian civil airline operation were made, in April 1963 construction began on a large, new head office building for TAA in Franklin Street, Melbourne. With the impending introduction of jet aircraft and the planned move to Melbourne's new airport at Tullamarine the three projects, all huge, were to transform the airline.

Internationally there was also a dramatic development. The world's first order for a supersonic civil airliner was won by the Concorde, produced jointly by British Aircraft Corporation and Sud Aviation, France. It was designed to fly at Mach 2.2, more than twice the speed of sound, cruising at some 1,450 miles an hour at almost 60,000 feet. Pan American Airways ordered six Concordes for delivery in the early 1970s.

At the end of April 1963 Ansett added to his airline acquisitions when he bought a controlling interest in the Western Australian airline MacRobertson Miller. On 2 May the *Financial Review* front page led with the headline 'TAA swamped. Ansett Growth Menaces Dual Airline System'. The Ansett acquisition was a sound intrastate airline that had operated for some thirty years, had a modest aircraft fleet and fine pilots and engineers. It had one Fokker Friendship (with a second on order), six DC3s and a Dove. In 1961–62 it had carried 66,855 passengers and earned gross revenue of £1,542,813. Apart from the gain in Perth on-traffic from the purchase, Ansett planned to expand tourist operations in the State's northwest. The Ansett takeover, the *Review* commented, 'underlines and increases the predominance of the Ansett airline network over Trans–Australia Airlines. It may also prove to be the beginning of the undoing of the two-airline policy in Australia.' The total Ansett airliner fleet, including all subsidiaries, was now ninety aircraft; the TAA fleet totalled fifty-nine. The Ansett group subsidiaries were now Airlines of New South Wales (formerly Butler), Airlines of South Australia (formerly Guinea Airways), Ansett Mandated (formerly Mandated Airlines) in New Guinea, Airlines of New Zealand, Queensland Air Lines, MacRobertson Miller Airlines, and Ansett Flying-boat Services. TAA was still forbidden from entering intrastate operations, except in Queensland and New Guinea. 'It would be idle to deny', wrote the *Review*, 'the large hand which a benevolent Commonwealth Government has played in the emerging power of Ansett'.[24] To further emphasise Ansett's ability to diversify, Ansett Transport Industries also received a commercial television licence in Melbourne for operation by its wholly owned subsidiary Austarama Pty Ltd.

A report to the Australian National Airlines Commission on 23 May lamented the effects of the Ansett reach in tourist travel: 'TAA suffers a major competitive disadvantage through the diversified activities of Ansett Transport Industries. The co-operative effort of the ATI group, comprising hotels, air and road transport, holiday resorts, motels etc. produces an integrated organisation which TAA, due to retricted powers, is unable to match in the marketing of holiday travel.' Apart from expanding its own holiday travel section and continuing to seek closer identification with non-Ansett resort proprietors there was little TAA could do except, said the report, seek 'ultimate extension of powers to enable TAA to participate financially both in its own right or jointly with existing owners'.[25]

John Ryland, reviewing the pattern of development of the two-airline policy over the years, told the Commission: 'Having regard to the inordinate growth of the ATI complex and the degree to which the balance between the two operators has moved in ATI's favour since it replaced ANA, it appears necessary to again bring to the Minister's notice the imbalance that now exists in favour of ATI. It is also understood that ATI is again negotiating with East-West Airlines with a view to acquisition, and also is in contact with Patair, the Papuan private operator. These are the only two remaining operators of any consequence. The danger of the growing imbalance is very real and could be expected to become more apparent in its effect in, say, twelve months time.'[26] (Ansett had also approached the smaller Connellan Airways Ltd, of Alice Springs. E. J. Connellan, the airline's governing director, told the *Financial Review* in June: 'We did not sell because we sincerely believe that we give a better developmental service than would either Ansett–ANA or TAA if they took over from us.')[27]

On 24 July 1963 Chippindall wrote a strong and significant letter to Paltridge:

> Recent developments which must greatly enhance the strength of Ansett Transport Industries and the competitive position of Ansett–ANA in comparison with TAA have been reviewed by the Commission as further factors in the increasing imbalance between the two operators, to the detriment of TAA's position. In particular, the purchase of a controlling interest in MacRobertson-Miller Airlines by Ansett Transport Industries and the granting of a commercial TV licence at Melbourne to one of its subsidiaries must, in the Commision's view, produce marked advantages to ATI and, in particular, Ansett–ANA ... The Commission considers that ATI's overall traffic uplift of the order of 1,870,000 as against TAA's overall uplift of 1,236,000 for 1962–63 provides a much more realistic commercial consideration than is obtained from a comparison of Ansett–ANA's uplift with that of TAA.
>
> The Commission also considers that the acquisition of MacRobertson-Miller, in giving ATI the Perth–Darwin route and thus completing its round-Australia coverage, has greatly enhanced ATI from a prestige point of view ... [It] understands that accession to the MacRobertson-Miller routes carries a Commonwealth Government guaranteed subsidy which ensures the operator a reasonable profit ... The projected US radio installation at North West Cape, the progressive development of the Ord River scheme and the growing interest in the exploitation of the natural resources of Western Australia appear certain to give ATI a rich field for the expansion of its operations ... In its competitive situation the Commission finds it impossible to treat Ansett–ANA in isolation. ATI has now become a complex of over 80 subsidiaries ... Its further growth can seriously inhibit the activities of the Commission, excluded as it is from fields of operation which are open to its competitors ... The increasing strength of the ATI Group and its overall assistance to Ansett–ANA cannot be controlled by rationalisation alone ... The Commission views with apprehension the position where every possibility of expansion is open to the Ansett Group. The Commission takes the view that an early extension of its powers is essential unless it is to be relegated to a secondary role in Australian domestic airline operation.[28]

That TAA apprehension was reflected in the *Financial*

Review when, in its main editorial comment on 29 August, it wrote: 'One source of great interest in the administration of the industry in recent times has been the position of Ansett Transport Industries. With the widening of ATI interests into intrastate operations, into road transport, tourism and television diffusion the question is bound to be asked whether the preservation of the two-airlines system really demands a social commitment to financial success of the whole range of Ansett enterprises. Could not the community commitment to the Ansett group be more narrowly confined to its aviation interests?'

Despite the competitive vitality and enterprise of Reginald Ansett, when the Civil Aviation Report (1962–63) was presented to both houses of Federal Parliament by Paltridge, TAA showed a record year, paying a dividend of 7 per cent to the Commonwealth Treasury for the financial year (1 per cent above the 6 per cent set by Paltridge as a minimum requirement). The dividend, also a record, represented a payment of £525,000. TAA revenue exceeded £18 million and passenger traffic rose to 1,272,774.[29]

On 22 October 1963 a tragic accident to the BAC One-Eleven prototype airliner, on a test flight over Wiltshire, southern England, raised major concern over the safe operation of all airliners with rear-mounted engines and tailplanes mounted high on the rudder. Under the command of test pilot Mike Lithgow, the One-Eleven went into a stall. Its behaviour was more violent than predicted or anticipated. A rapid and pronounced pitch-up of the nose of the aircraft occurred, which Lithgow could not reverse. Within three seconds the aircraft was in a deep stall, not previously attempted on test flights. In fine flying conditions the aircraft assumed a completely stable but unalterable very rapid rate of descent, with the fuselage remaining level and horizontal. The airflow over the stalled wing passed over the high tailplane, making the horizontal tail controls completely ineffective. Lithgow pushed the engines to full throttle and they responded, but with no effect on the aircraft's speed (because of its high drag attitude). The crew used all control and power settings without avail. In a continuing stable attitude the aircraft rapidly lost height and hit the ground, the fuselage still horizontal, killing all on board. Severe fire after impact destroyed most of the aircraft except the tail assembly, but flight recorders were recovered. The time from entering the stall to impact was some ninety seconds. Ryland advised the Commission on 18 November that TAA would seek 'a convincing argument from Boeing in regard to the 727 and from Douglas in regard to the DC9 — both of which aircraft have the high tail geometry which appears to be the basic reason for the flat fall characteristic — as to why a [similar] situation cannot occur with tail designs similar to that which has arisen in the case of the One-Eleven'.[30] (TAA later learned that the Boeing 727 had twice during its flight tests been taken — unintentionally — into the deep stall condition and held there for a considerable period of time. In both instances it had regained normal flying speed by forward movement of the control column, although considerable height was lost.)[31]

Domestic traffic growth now taxed the capacity of both trunkline operators. In the calender year 1963 Australian domestic airlines for the first time carried more than three million passengers. TAA and Ansett were each forced to buy an additional DC6B aircraft to cope with the 1963 traffic rush. Both predicted that 1964 would see a further traffic increase of 10 per cent.

It was at the local level, however, that innovation began for TAA in 1964. On 28 January a supplemental service was started in Tasmania to serve the Hobart–Devonport–Wynyard–Smithton route. Although it began with DC3s, these were soon replaced by Beechcraft Queen Air aircraft, seating eight passengers. It was the first of such regular services on country routes by the two major airlines using light twin-engined aircraft where the traffic available was insufficient to justify the use of DC3s or F27s. When the Department of Civil Aviation had given the industry notice of its intentions to introduce supplemental services there was wide controversy over whether they should be operated by the major airlines or by charter companies. The Department decided that the major airlines, because of their extensive operational facilities, their capacity to absorb sectional operating losses and their public transport experience, should be given the responsiblity for their introduction. They were to be regular airline services. (By 30 June 1964 services with light-twins were operating eight such routes, two from Adelaide to Millicent–Naracoorte and to Renmark–Mildura and one from Brisbane to Kingaroy–Gayndah using Italian Piaggio Portofino aircraft; the others — in Tasmania — using Queen Airs.)

The market for air freight in Australia, though it had declined over the years, was now strengthening, prompting competitive moves between TAA and Ansett–ANA in 1964. In March, as TAA cargo sales and development manager Doug Laurie introduced standardised trans-shipment and freight-collect rates throughout the country (and free pick-up of cargo in Melbourne and Sydney), Ansett–ANA launched a campaign to use more freighter aircraft and offer rate reductions. Both airlines were describing air cargo as the 'sleeping giant' because of its undeveloped potential.

Reginald Ansett captured the high ground on fleet re-equipment with an announcement in mid March that he would send a letter of intent to the Douglas Aircraft Company for two DC9 jets for delivery in late 1966. 'Subject only to the approval of the Minister for Civil Aviation,' said Ansett, 'we will certainly buy them. We think they are the right aircraft with the right engine.'[32] (He could not place a formal order. The federal government required TAA to make its own evaluation of the DC9 and BAC One-Eleven before this could be done so that both airlines could place simultaneous orders for similar delivery dates.) TAA responded with an announcement from Sir Giles Chippindall that it planned to purchase a third Boeing 727 for delivery in mid 1965. The choice of a smaller jet, he said, was still under close study.[33]

Paltridge approved the TAA 727 order in May. It was to be one of his last acts as minister. On 10 June 1964 he was succeeded as minister for civil aviation by Senator Denham Henty. (A senator for Tasmania, Norman Henry Denham

Henty, sixty-two, had been minister for customs and excise since 1955.)

Both airlines, as well as the government's policy, received high praise in mid-year from the respected British journal *Flight International*. Its air transport editor, Mike Ramsden, commenting on Australian air transport, wrote: 'It has successfully and completely mastered the problem of competition, which makes the passenger more important than anybody or anything else'. In a second comment he said: 'It [Australian air transport] is the safest in the world by any measure of safety'.[34] Nevertheless the intensity of the private versus public ownership debate continued when federal Labor member Clyde Cameron, in debate in Parliament, attacked what he described as 'the preferential treatment given by the Government to the Ansett group of companies'. *Aircraft* asked: 'Why is it that when the operations of the Ansett airline organisation — and now his TV activities — come under scrutiny in Federal Parliament there is much more evidence of hate than of anything else in the opinions of the most vocal Opposition members? ... Remembering the heavily preferential treatment of TAA in its formative years and the other ruthless methods used by the last Labor Government to break the private airlines Mr Ansett would be well advised to protect his business flank against the future.'[35]

The *Financial Review*, commenting on the parliamentary debate, was less emotional. It wrote: 'It was not quite clear from this week's debate on the Ansett group of companies whether the Government was more concerned to defend the two-airlines policy or to defend Mr R. M. Ansett personally. If it had not been apparent before the debate began it certainly became apparent as the debate progressed that Ansett Transport Industries is in fact an integral part of government policy ... The rights or wrongs of Mr Ansett's activities aside, this obligation on Government members tended to expose them to some very effective reasoning from the opposition benches.' The paper quoted Labor member Dr Jim Cairns. 'If the Government is concerned to do something about competition in the airlines business [said Cairns] why is it not prepared to do something to prevent Ansett gobbling up every other private airline in Australia?'[36]

Although the expansion of air freight had not kept pace with increases in passenger traffic it was now showing healthy growth on the main routes, prompting TAA assistant general manager John Chapman to recommend in June 1964 the purchase of an additional DC4 freighter aircraft. TAA still had three DC4s in service, with only one used on passenger operations; the other two carried freight. (It also had three DC3 freighters.) The DC4 was still proving an economic freighter. (Ansett had applied for approval to buy an additional DC4 to make a total fleet of six DC4 aircraft — with two used on passenger services. Ansett also had three DC3s.)[37] Indicative of the growing interest in the freight market by both airlines was a decision by Ansett–ANA to convert two of its DC4s to Carvairs (designed for speedier handling of cargo) and TAA's conversion of DC4s to provide large cargo doors and a special floor-roller system to handle palletised cargo.

In July 1964 Ansett suffered his first major reversal in his intrastate operations. After three years of litigation a decision of the Privy Council in London, where Ansett had challenged the law passed by the New South Wales government to hand over routes within the State to East-West Airlines, went against him. Although the Commonwealth government, because it was financially involved with East-West through the grant of subsidies, had the power to refuse licences to East-West for routes given it by the State government, that option seemed a political impossibility.[38] The federal government, however, began a study of the Privy Council decision to see to what extent the Commonwealth could control intrastate air services. The decision, Paltridge told Parliament, 'suggested that the Commonwealth had not exercised to the fullest extent the constitutional powers it possessed in relation to air navigation'.[39]

Both airlines had their schedules disrupted on 24 July when the Department of Civil Aviation grounded all Electra aircraft operated by Australian airlines. The order followed the discovery of what appeared to be a crack in the upper wing section of a TAA Electra. Ten Electras (three each for TAA and Ansett and four Qantas aircraft) were grounded for four days while tests took place. The scare proved unwarranted; the cracks were harmless corrosion specks that did not affect airworthiness.[40]

Both airlines were also jolted when a road transport company, Interstate Parcels Express Company (IPEC), moved in August to enter the air freight business. IPEC director Gordon Barton applied for permission to import five DC4 aircraft for use as air freighters. IPEC was by no means without expertise. Its negotiations with the Commonwealth government were in the hands of former TAA general manager Lester Brain.[41] To further unsettle both the Commonwealth government and the two major airlines, IPEC bought five thousand shares in East-West, with the blessing of East-West's directors. The company was already using excess capacity of the small freighter firm Brown and Brain, which operated with two DC3s across Bass Strait. Gordon Barton was indicating that he might make similar moves to use any excess East-West capacity for freight carriage.[42]

In December the federal government rejected the IPEC application (and an application by a second road transport company, Comet Pty Ltd, a subsidiary of Thomas Nationwide Transport) to operate air freight services between Australian capital cities. (IPEC's application to import five DC4 aircraft and for an air freight operator's licence was also refused.) At the same time Mr Justice Spicer, in his capacity as Arbitrator for the Airlines Rationalisation Committee, supported an Ansett–ANA appeal for equality with TAA on the Adelaide–Darwin trunk route at TAA's expense. Both airlines, he ruled, were to provide equal passenger capacity on the Adelaide–Darwin route. It established the principle that on declared competitive trunk routes competition must be equal in relation to capacity and frequency of service. The decision was a significant one for D.G. Anderson in his role as the airlines' Co-ordinator. It was the first successful challenge by Ansett to an Anderson ruling.

Important differences in the manner in which Ansett

Transport Industries and TAA structured their accounts emerged when, on 28 September, ATI announced a record profit of £1.5 million for the year to 30 June 1964. That record profit was only possible because of the large depreciation provision of £3,215,734 and the resulting small tax provision of £61,736. The treatment of tax provision differed from TAA's, an unusual state of affairs that flowed from the high depreciation rates on aircraft allowed for tax purpose to both airlines. The Income Tax Act allowed for the writing off of aircraft over four years but, in their accounts when calculating profit, both Ansett and TAA allowed between eight and ten years for writing off an aircraft's cost.

Because of the large-scale re-equipment over past years both organisations, from the Tax Commissioner's point of view, had earned much lower profits than publicly shown from airline operations as a result of the large tax-deductible depreciation allowances. The net effect was that for the first half of an aircraft's life depreciation for tax purposes was about double that allowed for profit calculation, while for the second half of an aircraft's life no depreciation could be claimed for tax purposes.

TAA provided for tax on the basis that taxable profit came after depreciation, based on the life of its aircraft. When no actual tax was payable TAA's provision for tax was transferred to the provision for future income tax liability. Ansett, in contrast, did not make allowances for any deferred tax before arriving at its profit though it had, since 1959–60, been appropriating from its profit a reserve for future income tax. To compare Ansett's result with TAA's his provision for future income tax had to be increased and taken from the disclosed profit. For the bemused commentator the best basis for any comparison between Ansett and TAA was to use Ansett's stated profit and TAA's before-tax profit.[43] It remained a difficulty for outsiders to make judgments on the comparative profit performances of the two organisations. When TAA's results for the 1963–64 year were tabled in Parliament on 28 October they showed a record net profit after tax of £640,691. (A dividend of 7 per cent was paid, absorbing £525,000.)

Profit figures were only one element in the continuing public relations battle between Ansett and TAA. In September 1964 Ansett won a significant skirmish for prestige with the toss of a coin.

Negotiations to decide which of the two airlines should be first into Australia with their 727s became deadlocked in Melbourne on 25 September. It was agreed that the matter should be decided by tossing a coin. Ansett tossed, and won. That outcome meant that Ansett's first 727 would land at Essendon airport at 2.45 p.m. on October 16 — minutes ahead of TAA's first 727.

The arrival of the first two Boeing 727s had a significance far more profound for Australian aviation than any passing contest for prestige. It marked a technical watershed, introducing a new generation of high productivity jet aircraft that would, over the years ahead, transform air travel into a new form of mass public transport. Combined with later dramatic changes in the technology of communications and computers, the jets, as they developed, would also change the culture and practices of airline management. Politics would continue to shape the aviation environment, but political parameters would themselves be refashioned by global changes in the way the world did business.

CHAPTER 10

1965

Ansett's golden franchise

The two-airline system in Australia, always a political issue and always a subject of wide public and media interest, came under increasingly detailed analysis in the press as 1965 began. Writing in the *Australian*, Stanley Brogden commented: We fly on a kindly, two-way monopoly'. The Australian domestic aviation system, he wrote, was unique in the world. 'A public utility and a privately owned company are vested by the Government with almost exclusive rights to operate regular commercial air transport within the Commonwealth and its territories ... Is this in fact a monopoly? The Government's airline policy for thirteen years has been built on the principle of preventing any form of competition for the major operators, so the word is justified.' But, he concluded, the two-airline policy was a sensible solution to a very difficult problem. 'Both operators are keen to maintain the two-airline policy, though they want to alter some of its aspects. Mr Ansett would naturally like to see TAA sold to private enterprise but he is firm he wants two airlines. TAA frankly says that with a monopoly by one airline, either privately owned or publicly owned, there would not be the same quality of service or equipment.'[1]

The *Financial Review*, quoting Reginald Ansett, explained the reason for Ansett's enthusiastic support of government policy. It gave his large, privately owned company legislated access to assured profits over a long time period. 'The value of this franchise', said Ansett, 'cannot be calculated. Nowhere else in the world is there such an arrangement which ensures civil aviation economic stability for such a period. Operating within this situation with efficient management controlling costs, reasonable profits are assured for fifteen years ... No trunk aviation competitor will be permitted, other than TAA, and industry re-equipment with full-jet aircraft will be gradual and over a period long enough to enable financial and economic digestion to take place without disruption to the industry.'[2] The *Financial Review* aviation writer commented: 'There is growing public uneasiness, and even mistrust, about the politics of aviation, the administration of equivocal legislation, and the link between private enterprise and public patronage ... We have a policy restricting operations on interstate air routes to two competing airlines. Because some of its end results have proved beneficial it has become something of a sacred cow.'[3]

TAA's competitor was now an impressive organisation under an able leader. When Ansett Transport Industries came into being in 1946 total yearly revenue was under £1 million. By 1951 it had climbed to £5 million, but this substantial achievement was puny when compared with the years following ATI's acquisition of ANA in 1957. In nine years, with Ansett's further acquisitions, revenue rose to £39.2 million. Although the group, in 1965, had many and varied interests, airline operations were still dominant. Airline assets were worth £25.2 million and provided 64 per cent of the ATI group revenue. Although Ansett–ANA and TAA were much the same size, the Ansett subsidiary airlines made the group 25 per cent bigger in aviation operations than TAA. Department of Civil Aviation figures showed that unduplicated route mileage of the ATI airlines was double that of TAA (65 per cent of all Australian routes) — a total of 54,130 miles against TAA's 28,319 miles.

The TAA competition was efficient. Measured in capacity-ton-miles and revenue per employee produced, however, Ansett was 12 per cent better in the former and 14 per cent better in the latter. From the published ATI accounts it was not possible to calculate the profit of ATI airline companies. Ansett had repaid all monies on which Commonwealth guarantees were necessary and had arranged his own finance without government guarantee for the purchase of his three Boeing 727s. Although he had been criticised for preferring loan funds rather than equity capital he was, in fact, following widespread airline industry practice. His group profit for the twelve months to 30 June 1964 was almost £3 million, exclusive of interest, which covered his total interest bill some 2.12 times. There were, indeed, government subsidies paid to Ansett airlines but they were relatively small — some £300,000 yearly (compared with the group's total airline revenue of £25 million). In short, government assistance to the ATI group lay in the indirect but powerful government commitment to its profitability. Ansett, already 25 per cent bigger than TAA, was growing faster and had far more freedom to manoeuvre to increase his rate of growth. 'By 1977, unless there are radical changes', wrote the *Review*, 'our two-airline system will comprise one big operator — Ansett — and one relatively small one — TAA, if current growth rates continue'.[4]

What troubled the *Financial Review* was the blurred financial boundary between the Ansett aviation operations and the non-aviation activities of the Ansett Transport Industries group. It asked, in a heading on 9 March 1965: 'Do Ansett's TV losses keep up air fares?' Those losses, it estimated, had been close to £1 million for the first half of 1964–65. It was more than a rhetorical question. Under the Australian National Airlines Act the minister, Senator Henty, was required to take into account the profits of private enterprise airlines — and the conduct of non-aviation enterprises associated with them — when setting the TAA profit target. Ansett Transport Industries was accepted as 'a privately owned air transport undertaking'. The *Review* wrote: 'The individual responsible for accepting such a definition must be a close relation to Humpty Dumpty of "Through the Looking Glass" fame. "When I use a word," Humpty said scornfully to Alice, "it means just what I choose it to mean." Should Ansett's aviation profits, it asked, help him absorb his television losses? 'Is it not ridiculous that we can trace a direct link between non-aviation losses by ATI and air fare levels required by TAA? Should TAA fares be sensitive to Ansett's non-aviation costs? Is it not a matter of public concern that air fares rose by 6 per cent in a period that enabled ATI to absorb its large television losses?'[5]

Growth rates for TAA were nevertheless high. For the twelve months to January 1965 passenger traffic was 17.2 per cent up on the previous year. In the first week of January there had been an extraordinary traffic increase, compared to the previous January, of 28 per cent. There had been a 28 per cent annual increase in air express cargo carried and a 13 per cent increase in ordinary air cargo.[6] The Boeing 727s were in place but even with their contribution it was clear that growth would outstrip capacity.

'Until recently', said a Commission report in March 1965, 'it was thought there was no urgency associated with introduction of our secondary jet equipment, and that the fourth Boeing 727 to enter service in July–August 1966 would ensure sufficient total fleet capacity to carry through to 1968. Current examination of the traffic growth trend, in the light of continued significant increases beyond our expectations, now clearly shows the essential need of substantial additional fleet capacity beyond the fourth Boeing 727.'[7] There were three possibilities to meet this need — purchase or lease of at least one additional Electra, purchase or lease of a fifth and possibly sixth 727, or selection of secondary jet equipment for introduction in late 1966. It was the third alternative that TAA favoured. 'Since the Boeing 737 cannot be available until 1968,' said the report, 'it must be eliminated. The choice lies between the most suitable versions of the BAC One-Eleven and the Douglas DC9.'[8]

In the first two weeks of March there had been a spectacular increase in orders for the DC9 from major airlines including Eastern, KLM and Continental, bringing firm orders to 114. Nevertheless Douglas had offered TAA delivery of two aircraft in November and December 1966. Firm sales of the DC9's competitor, the BAC One-Eleven, were seventy-four at 23 March, when British Aircraft Corporation offered TAA a version of the One-Eleven known as the 500 series (rejected by Eastern Air Lines). It did not, like the DC9, have leading-edge high-lift devices on the wings and the version was subject to engine development by Rolls-Royce. BAC offered delivery in March 1967 but with 300 series One-Elevens available for lease in the second half of 1966. Both the One-Eleven and the DC9 were highly regarded by John Watkins' engineering group but, the Commission was told, 'Careful evaluation of commercial and operational factors indicate the desirability of the DC9, even though first cost is higher'. Its seat capacity was greater, its high-lift airfield performance markedly better and its power plant was the same as the 727's. (The Douglas solution to the deep stall problem — an increased tail span coupled with careful development of wing characteristics — was seen to provide a sound and simple way to avoid the problem. The One-Eleven, though it had modifications to the wing stall characteristics, used a 'stick-pusher' to warn of the approach of the stall and a triplicated elevator power control system, which were seen as effective but more complex.)

Economic arguments also favoured the DC9. John Watkins wrote: 'The BAC One-Eleven 500 would be cheaper to buy per aircraft than the DC9B but the DC9B will go into airline service in Australia with at least ten more seats (and up to sixteen more in some layouts)'. On a fleet basis the extra seats provided far greater earning potential. Further, the DC9B's operating costs including fuel were, on TAA's calculations, at least 4 per cent lower than the BAC One-Eleven 500's on a seat-mile basis.[9] John Ryland recommended that a letter of intent be sent to Douglas for six of the twin-jet DC9s, with delivery of two in 1966 and four in 1967.[10] (The cost of the six aircraft was £13.7 million.) The longer-range DC9-30 was now favoured over the previously selected DC9-20. It cruised at up to 550 miles an hour and carried ninety-one passengers in two-class layout. Its Pratt & Whitney JT8D-7 jet engines were interchangeable with the JT8D-1 engines used in the 727s.

Ansett, while favouring the DC9, pressed for later deliveries of the last two aircraft, citing a less optimistic view of growth. Behind that stance was a concern about the capital loss involved in the sale of his Electras. As was usual with the government his view prevailed, and TAA was forced to agree to delivery of the last two DC9s in late 1968 and 1969. That outcome, commented Brogden in his *Australia's Two Airline Policy*, was 'vital proof of the TAA desire to be more competitive and the difficulties of Ansett in this context'.[11] (Ansett, unwillingly, had to seek government guarantees for the purchase of his six DC9s. Changes in American financial regulations required Australia to use the US Export–Import Bank for the loan monies involved. The Bank required government guarantees.)

The DC9 choice was a further blow for the British aircraft industry. Its Trident 1E — the only Trident version that was potentially suitable for use on Australian routes — had been rejected by TAA in favour of the Boeing 727 and was not yet in airline service, while more than 110 Boeing 727s had already flown more than 80 million miles on scheduled passenger operations — including TAA's two 727s, which had carried some 200,000 passengers in the preceding five months.

Britain had applied the strongest possible pressure to have its aircraft accepted. One move, bitterly resented by the airlines, had been a campaign to force the Australian government, under the preference clauses of Australia's trade agreement with the United Kingdom, to impose a 7.5 per cent punitive Customs duty on the US-built 727s bought by Ansett and TAA, following their rejection of the Trident. Within the Menzies government were powerful pro-British forces. (D.J. Killen told Parliament that the airlines should be compelled to buy British.) In April they had their way. The federal government announced that duty would be charged on the 727s.

The decision was an absurdity, merely putting funds into

the Commonwealth Treasury at the expense of the airlines. (Brogden commented: 'As the whole aim of the present two airline policy is to ensure the existence of the private-enterprise segment of the industry, and this presupposes an adequate earning rate on capital, the ... situation is ridiculous'.)[12] What was still undecided was whether duty would be imposed on the DC9 purchases. The minister had the power, under the trade agreement, to waive the duty if he decided that British aircraft were not 'reasonably available' or 'suitably equivalent'.

Watkins was keen to phase out all Electras in favour of more 727 capacity following wing corrosion problems. He told John Ryland on 13 September 1965: 'While ... the Electra wing corrosion situation is clearly under control it is equally clear that a lot of work is going to be involved in keeping it so ... When viewed in conjunction with all the technical, maintenance, supply, operational and commercial penalties we are paying for mixed heavy fleet operation, I can only once more urge that every feasible step be taken towards the earliest consolidation of our heavy fleet in the minimum number of Boeing 727s that will adequately serve the scheduling requirements of our longer stages, plus the maximum number of DC9–30s that our traffic growth will support ... We must accelerate the elimination from our fleet of all DC6B and Electra equipment.'[13]

TAA's new 16-storey head office building in Franklin Street was nearing completion when results for the financial year to 30 June 1965 were announced. Once again TAA had carried a record number of passengers and record volumes of cargo. Traffic growth had been almost double that anticipated, with a total of 1,678,647 passengers carried in Australia and Papua New Guinea — an increase of 17.3 per cent on the previous year.[14] The results had been achieved despite a year in which three important rationalisation decisions had curtailed TAA operations — on the Adelaide–Alice Springs–Darwin route, on Brisbane–Longreach–Mount Isa and on the Melbourne–Canberra–Sydney route. The airline industry, Ryland told staff, 'is enjoying a period of financial stability and rapid expansion brought about in part by the elimination of wasteful competition, the economics imposed on the industry in the amount of capacity each airline may deploy, as well as the restrictions placed on the purchase of new equipment'. The airline now had 5,500 employees.[15] Australian domestic aviation had experienced overall growth in passenger traffic of 20 per cent in 1964–65. In this heady atmosphere of expansion TAA's third 727 was delivered at the end of August and plans were drawn up to place major emphasis on the use of the airline's jet airliner fleet in air freighting. (The 727 had the same freight capacity as a DC3.)

If traffic was increasing, so too were costs. The Commonwealth Treasurer, in his budget speech, had announced increased rates of customs duties on aviation fuel and increased air route charges. The Arbitration Court had made decisions increasing wages costs. Pilots were negotiating new agreements and engineers and transport workers had new logs of claims before the Court. Chippindall, on behalf of the Commission, sought ministerial approval for an increase in passenger fares and cargo rates of 5 per cent, to apply from 15 October 1965.

On 10 November TAA signed a £6 million contract with Douglas for three DC9-30 airliners. The first two were scheduled for delivery in November 1966 and the third in March 1967. The government also gave approval for the order of a fourth Boeing 727 for mid-1966 delivery. Ansett placed similar orders for similar delivery times.

By the end of November 1965 all TAA staff members previously at 339 Swanston Street had moved into the new, 16-storey Franklin Street head office. It had taken seventy-five weeks to complete and was finished sixteen weeks ahead of schedule. The minister for civil aviation, Senator Denham Henty, officially opened the building. Among the guests attending were the first chairman of the Australian National Airlines Commission, Sir Arthur Coles, and TAA's first general manager, Lester Brain.

The Civil Aviation Agreement had been in operation for twelve years and, as it was due to expire in 1977, was now at its mid-point. Both TAA and ATI airlines had reached financial maturity, returning dividends to the public purse and to ATI's private shareholders. Chippindall prepared a review for the minister of all that had transpired since the Agreement had come into force, commenting: 'It ... seems an appropriate time to take stock and consider what changes may be necessary'. There had been, he said, public comment that the operation of the two-airline policy had resulted in a weakening of real competition; that there had been an emergence of restrictive practices limiting service to the public, and there had been criticism of the growing strength of Ansett Transport Industries. 'In the Commission's view,' he wrote, 'the operation of the two airline policy needs to be altered for the future so as to gain greater public acceptance and reflect a better public image. This could be achieved if equal size and equality of opportunity for the airline activities of the public and private airline could be restored. In this way each would then be capable of effective competition with the other.'

Among the main proposals put to the minister by Chippindall as 1965 ended were equal access on major routes; the support of the Commonwealth in negotiating rights for the Commission to engage in intrastate operations; power to engage in charter and aerial work; power to provide tourist accommodation; repeal of the profit target provisions until such time as a true comparison could be made of the financial operations of Ansett–ANA; a policy in respect of the issue of route licences that would achieve equality of size and opportunity between TAA and Ansett–ANA; and a review of existing rationalisation controls to ensure that within the capacity limits fixed by the Airlines Equipment Act, both operators would be free to deploy their respective capacity to best advantage to meet public requirements.[16] It was an ambitious shopping list.

Though very large sums of money were now committed to the purchase of new jet airliners, investment in land and buildings had grown at a far faster rate than investment in aircraft. The cost to both TAA and Ansett–ANA of facilities necessary for Melbourne's new Tullamarine Airport was some

£5 million. Both TAA and Ansett had upgraded their headquarters at great cost. (The TAA building had cost some £2 million.) The expensive buildings they erected on airport land, however, could never become their property. All airport land was leased from the government. Formerly it had been government policy to erect the buildings and then lease them to the airlines. Now they had to provide the buildings from their own resources. The passenger terminals were built by government and leased, but administration buildings, hangars, workshops and catering buildings were provided by the airlines.

On 26 January 1966, still firmly in control of the Liberal–Country Party government that he headed, and still by far the most dominant figure in Australian political life, Robert Gordon Menzies surprised all political commentators and his closest colleagues by retiring as prime minister after a record term in office. He was succeeded as prime minister by Harold Holt. Menzies left after a year that saw two initiatives of fundamental importance to Australia, one from each side of federal politics. On 28 April 1965 the Menzies government had committed combat troops to Vietnam. Of profound significance for the other side of politics, the Labor Party in August dropped the 'White Australia' policy from its platform.

The first major public aviation issue for debate, as 1966 began, which flowed directly from the government's need to manage the competitive capacity of the two domestic airlines, was parallel scheduling of services. That issue reflected the widely held conviction that TAA and Ansett–ANA were not competitors but, as the *Financial Review* wrote, 'grew together with the affectionate antagonism of identical twins'. Henty promised a public inquiry into the possibility of staggering airline timetables.[17]

The problem had become systemic, emerging from the fact that morning and evening peak period traffic between Melbourne and Sydney required the combined capacity of both TAA and Ansett–ANA. Those peak needs set the scheduling patterns throughout Australia for the day. Both airlines were insistent that even with only slightly staggered departure times, one airline would find itself favoured. The irony was that any government intervention in scheduling would destroy the last remnants of competition. From the introduction of the Civil Aviation Agreement Act in 1952 each had been under an obligation to 'co-operate rather than compete to the limit of their strength'. Rationalisation had been enforced on fare levels, routes and flight frequencies. Loopholes had been closed in the ensuing Civil Aviation Agreement Acts of 1957 and 1961. The Airlines Equipment Acts had extended rationalisation to the purchase of airliners. Further, in 1964, a ruling by Mr Justice Spicer changed and tightened the machinery of rationalisation. Where previously the Co-ordinator (Don Anderson) had attempted to assess the broad national route picture in reaching decisions on specific route conflicts, Spicer had introduced a new principle. Under it, on the declared competitive trunk routes, competition between the two airlines had to be equal in relation to capacity and frequency of service, with each route regarded separately. The areas for possible competition and for the exercise of independent judgment had shrunk. These consequences had flowed from the opposing philosophies of the political parties on private versus public ownership as manifested in TAA and Ansett–ANA. The notion that private ownership provided 'private enterprise' had, in the process, become a mockery. Ansett–ANA was as much a creature of government as was TAA. For both airlines the general concept of 'free enterprise' was a myth. (TAA's financial shackles were far tighter than Ansett's. The Commission was increasingly concerned that it had not been permitted to retain profits and build up its general reserve to guard against future contingencies.)[18]

Within the labyrinth of regulation and control, competitive initative was chained. The 1965 year started with a refusal by the director-general of civil aviation to grant TAA a licence to operate a Perth–Darwin service. Although it was clear that Perth–Darwin was a trunk route airline service and, on that basis, fair game for TAA, the licence applied for involved a government 'territory', not a State, and the granting of the licence was entirely within the discretion of the director-general. The decision was not subject to appeal.[19]

There was a slowing in the high passenger growth rate in 1966, partly from a fall-off in the stimulus that had come from the introduction of the 727s, partly from the effect on the general economy of a prolonged drought and partly from the introduction to Australia in February 1966 of decimal currency. 'During the changeover period', said the Department of Civil Aviation in its annual report, 'many businessmen were reportedly too busy with conversion problems to travel and staff holidays were also restricted'.[20] The new currency of dollars and cents was accompanied by a new technology. TAA, now carrying traffic at the rate of two million passengers a year, signed a contract for a computer to fully automate its reservation system and supersede the existing manual and punched-card methods. (Some weeks later, reinforcing the public perception of mirror-image airlines, Ansett announced that it, too, would introduce a computer reservations system.) The industry also now had a new minister, with Queenslander R.W.C. Swartz succeeding Denham Henty.

The changing face of aviation was marked in a diffferent way at Samarai, an island settlement on the eastern tip of Papua, when a TAA Catalina flying boat made its last trip on 3 January. The aircraft was the last surviving Catalina on the Australian register and had operated since 1962. New airports in the area had removed the need for flying boats. A twin-engined Beechcraft A80 was now operating many of the old Catalina services in the Territory.[21]

Far more dramatic was a change that would reshape the international airline industry of the world. Boeing announced that Pan American Airlines had contracted to buy twenty-five huge Boeing 747 aircraft, and taken an option on an additional ten. The 747, Ryland told the Commission, could seat up to 490 passengers and provide passenger-mile costs some 35 per cent below those of existing jet airliners. The total value of the Pan American order was $525 million.[22]

On 1 July 1966 Air Chief Marshal Sir Frederick Scherger, formerly Chairman of the Chiefs of Staff Committee, became the new chairman of the Australian National Airlines Commission, succeeding Sir Giles Chippindall. Scherger had had a distinguished career in service aviation both as a pilot and as an administrator. In World War II he had held various senior front-line positions including that of Allied air force task commander. He had been Air Officer Commanding the Royal Air Force in Malaya from 1953 to 1955 and was the RAAF's first air chief marshal.

Immediately on his retirement, Chippindall publicly criticised the two-airline policy. Australian airlines, he said, were in danger of becoming too coddled, with too much government control over schedules and restrictions on the deployment of aircraft. The policy had resulted, he said, in benefits for Ansett–ANA that had not been given to TAA. The effect was gradually to convert the two-airline system into a one-airline system divided into two parts. 'We ... have a picture of steady expansion of the share of the aviation market power accruing to the Company [Ansett Transport Industries] over recent years and a growing imbalance.' The position since 1952, said Chippindall, 'when the private airlines and the Commission had parity of route licences [is that] the Commission has received no airline licences of consequence whereas the Company has acquired many new licences by acquisition of independent operators'. For Ansett Transport Industries, 'only 78 per cent of its airline traffic is obtained from its competitive routes, with the remaining 22 per cent being obtained in areas where it possesses the sole licence — in other words where it has a monopoly'. Unless the two-airline system was made more competitive, he concluded, 'the great gains that system has brought to Australia are likely gradually to be frittered away in a pattern of controls and restrictions which must eventually destroy the two airline system as we have known it.'[23]

The media saw Chippindall's criticisms as valid. The *Australian*, in its main editorial on 14 July, wrote:

> Even on the operational side its [the two-airline policy's] inequities are becoming staggering. Lopsided route allocation has led to Ansett control of about 130 per cent more mileage in continental Australia than is allocated to TAA. The Ansett group's share

> of domestic traffic is higher than 54 per cent, compared with TAA's slightly less than 46 per cent. Apart from this, the official insistence that the two airlines consult and co-operate on everything from the highest to the most fiddling junior level means that the whole industry is practically one airline not quite split into two divisons ... Nobody benefits under a system in which the introduction of DC9 aircraft is delayed because, while TAA was ready and willing to go ahead with it in late 1967, the Ansett group preferred to wait until late 1969 ... The blame lies with the Government which professes to favour balanced development of the industry but fails to ensure it occurs in fact.[24]

The *Age* wrote: 'All is not well with the two airline policy. The chief cause for dissatisfaction is that the public is just not told what is going on, what the problems are and what the Government intends to do.'[25]

R.M. Ansett responded with typical vigour. The government, he said, should sell TAA to private enterprise. The only airline in a cocoon was TAA, which had its capital subscribed by the Commonwealth, its loans negotiated by the Commonwealth at noncommercial rates, its board appointed by the Commonwealth, its modest dividend target set by the Commonwealth and its future negotiated by the Commonwealth.[26] But it was the Commonwealth, too, that gave financial comfort to Ansett by a ministerial decision that delayed the introduction to the Australian public of all-jet air travel on trunk airline routes. Original delivery dates agreed for the introduction of the second batch of three DC9s to both airlines had been August, October and November 1967. Swartz now consented to delays so that the first aircraft in the second batch was scheduled for delivery in November 1967, the second in November 1968 and the third in August 1969. (Ansett had requested even later dates.)

The TAA position was clear and public. 'TAA had intended, during the next eighteen months, to import into Australia a total of six DC9 jet aircraft', Chippindall had told *Aircraft*. 'These aircraft are urgently needed to meet the requirements of traffic growth, allow for a more economical range of operations and the retirement of older aircraft ... I cannot stress too strongly the importance of bringing these DC9 machines into service at the earliest date. TAA is fully prepared for [their] early introduction ... However, ATI took the view that the second group of three DC9s should be delayed by spreading deliveries through to the second half of 1969, and at the moment this view has been adopted by the authorities.'[27]

Ansett's need for delay was driven by the depreciation policy of Ansett Transport Industries for its three Electras. The company followed a pattern of depreciation over a ten-year period. Their sale in 1967 would have brought an appreciable book loss. TAA, by contrast, depreciated their Electras on the basis of hours flown. Their aircraft had been written down to a residual value of 20 per cent of their cost and TAA expected to sell them without loss.[28] Publicly Ansett argued that its decision on delivery dates had been driven by its estimate of traffic growth rates — which was lower than TAA's estimate. (In the event TAA was right. Ansett had used a 7 per cent rate; actual growth in 1967 was some 10 per cent and increasing.)

Ansett Transport Industries was now adopting a new policy that would even more effectively obscure from public view the financial results of its airline subsidiaries. It had never been possible to accurately compare Ansett–ANA's results with TAA's. ATI's separate airline subsidiaries lodged financial statements with State registrars. There was, even under these arrangements, no way in which assessment could be made of Ansett–ANA's financial results insofar as they were affected by inter-company transfers and charges. The new ATI policy was to wind up the subsidiary companies and conduct them under trade names as operating divisions. Scherger wrote to Swartz on 29 July with updated figures to indicate 'the increasing disparity between ATI and TAA to the latter's disadvantage'. Non-airline activities of the ATI group, he said, now accounted for 40 per cent of its total assets. 'The financial success of this sector of ATI can strengthen the Company and increase the imbalance between it and TAA ... The spread of diversified interests of the ATI group in itself gives that Company a great advantage over TAA in spreading overhead costs, particularly in regard to advertising and other services, a much greater cash flow and great flexibility in inter-subsidiary transfers and charges.'[29]

One of the most contentious government actions in Australian domestic aviation, the Cross-Charter Agreement of 1960, came to an end on 29 August when the four DC6Bs still operated by the two airlines made their last revenue flights. (That agreement required TAA to charter three of its Viscount 700s to Ansett–ANA while Ansett–ANA, in return, chartered two of its DC6Bs to TAA.) Though now outdated, the DC6Bs had been good money earners for both airlines. TAA was left with one DC6B to sell, Ansett with five. The compulsory 1960 agreement had been the government tool to achieve fleet parity for the two airlines. That ongoing requirement was now accomplished under the terms of the 1961 Civil Aviation Agreement Act. 'Wingtip to wingtip', wrote the *Financial Review* on 24 August, 'TAA and Ansett–ANA now fly along together with great precision in matters of equipment disposal and delivery'.[30]

TAA's fourth Boeing 727 arrived in Melbourne on 11 August. The first Douglas DC9-30 had made its first flight early in the month. A total of 237 DC9-30s had been ordered, and orders for DC9s in all its versions now approached 400.

When TAA's twenty-first annual report was tabled in Parliament on 18 October 1966 TAA again attacked elements of the two-airline system. 'Of the airports in Australia which handled more than 5,000 passengers in 1965,' it said, 'TAA operated into only 27 and its competitor into 56'. The system of noncompetitive routes, said the report, gave Ansett–ANA almost 20 per cent more traffic than TAA. There were, however, hopes for change. Minister Swartz revealed that the government was to review the two-airline system. It also announced that there were no policy restrictions preventing TAA from tendering for defence contracts — a source of revenue previously not pursued because of clauses in the Australian National Airlines Act. (The TAA net operating profit for the year to 30 June was $1,202,357. Payroll and staff charges made up the largest single cost item. TAA staff numbers had grown to 6,263.)[31]

Towards the end of 1966, and at the request of the Commission, a review of TAA's fleet re-equipment programme was presented with the aim of achieving 'the highest possible standards of engineering and operational safety'. Although TAA operations, it said, 'have always been maintained at a very high level of safety there is ample evidence that an increasing strain is being thrown on all levels of the organisation because of the proliferation of types of equipment'. The TAA fleet now contained eighteen 'quite different types of aircraft with sub-types or variants existing within several of these groups, and 15 quite different types of powerplant, again with several variants within types'. Apart from diversification of types, said the review, 'we are also forced to recognise that some of the aircraft on which we are at present dependent are amongst the oldest and most heavily used of their type in the world'.

The Electras posed a special problem. The normally expected increase in structural problems had been aggravated by special material problems. The rework of the wing plank joints carried out in the United States had done nothing to reduce the observed trend to an increasing incidence of other types of structural problems that had called, in some cases, for elaborate and time-consuming repairs. The Viscount 700s, too, had problems with life limitations that not only affected wing and tailplane spars but also the basic fuselage shell structure — influenced by pressurisation fatigue. (There had been a dramatic and tragic illustration of problems in the Viscount when an Ansett–ANA Viscount 832 aircraft crashed near Winton, Queensland, on 22 September. The aircraft disintegrated in the air at some 5,000 feet. Examination of the wreckage suggested that there had been a vapour explosion in the port wing between the engines.)

The review, looking five years ahead and based on traffic growth averaging 8 per cent a year, suggested a fleet composition that involved only five aircraft types and four engine types. It envisaged four Boeing 727s, fourteen DC9s, eight Fokker F28s, twenty Fokker F27s and nineteen DH6 Twin Otters. That fleet goal involved the elimination from the existing fleet of two earlier-type Otters, four Viscount 720Cs, three Electras, seven Viscount 756s, four Fokker F27-102s, five Douglas DC4s, two Bristol 170s, twenty DC3s and three Viscount 816s (as well as miscellaneous light aircraft and helicopters). 'Realisation of this plan', the review concluded, 'would for the first time give TAA groups of contemporary aircraft sufficiently large to show real benefits in relatively standardised work scheduling [and] would vastly simplify the problem of crew rostering and positioning'.[32]

CHAPTER 11

1967

A monopoly with two shareholders

On 5 January 1967 the *Financial Review*, in its main editorial, wrote: 'The parallel scheduling [of the two airlines] has been a focal point for general public dissatisfaction with the rigidities of the two airline system and the special consideration Ansett Transport Industries appeared to be getting from the Federal Government'. Obession with this issue, it said, obscured the real bases for dissatisfaction. 'These include declining standards of service, frequent postponements of departure times, dirty aircraft, poor terminal facilities, threadbare services on country air routes where one airline has a monopoly and the steady rise in air fares despite the great efficiencies in new equipment ... Such are the rewards of monopoly.'

New schedules had been proposed by the two airlines to head off criticism but these, wrote the *Review*, are the results as much of the new equipment now coming or soon to come into operation as of any basic concern to break the parallel scheduling'. The journal recognised that there were optimum traffic demands clustered round specific times, writing: 'If both airlines independently arrive at similar schedules based on on-the-hour flights, but demands for half-hourly staggered departures are to be met, which airline is to take on the half-past schedules? Do they draw straws? If the half-past flier loses as a result will it be subsidised? Should they stagger the schedules but pool the revenues? If they did, wouldn't this crack the facade of the two airline system?'

The heart of the matter, the *Review* concluded, was the rigidities of the two-airline system 'governed largely by the need to preserve balance between the two in a market of very limited size'.[1] Closer attention to the revised schedules of both airlines, it said, 'reduces optimism about possible real competition'.[2] The new timetables of both operators were almost exactly alike. There was other evidence that competition was not the highest item on the agenda. TAA agreed to charter one of its Viscounts to Ansett–ANA, a move that was helpful to TAA's competitor in rearrangement of its new schedules to better match TAA's. The *Sydney Morning Herald* expressed the general public's perception. 'Excessive Government fears of a return to TAA control of domestic airline services have produced virtual monopoly conditions in which there are two shareholders — Ansett–ANA and TAA.'[3]

Ansett–ANA, however, as 1967 began, was bleeding financially from an event for which no legislation could offer protection. The downhill slide had started the previous September when its Viscount crashed near Winton. The airline had been completely blameless but the effect on Ansett–ANA traffic share was immediate and prolonged.

The fire that brought the Viscount down had not occurred in the engine, as many suspected, but started because a driveshaft between the auxiliary gearbox and cabin air-pressurisation unit, designed to break and stop driving when overloaded, did not do so. The intense heat that resulted, plus a leak from an affected oil-metering valve, started the fire. It was a one-in-a-million risk. Although the Department of Civil Aviation announced modifications to weaken the shaft in Viscount 800s, no other Viscount users in the world thought it worthwhile to modify their aircraft, so remote was the chance of such a failure.

Before the Winton disaster Ansett–ANA had enjoyed its usual 49 per cent share of the traffic on competitive routes. By 30 September, eight days after the crash, this share had dropped by 2 per cent. By early December the decline reached its lowest point. Ansett–ANA was getting less than 46 per cent of the traffic. Each one point drop in traffic, in a total market worth some $86 million a year, meant an annual loss for Ansett–ANA of $860,000. A three per cent drop, therefore, threatened a $2.5 million loss.[4] At the same time, independent of this single event, domestic traffic growth had been falling. In the twelve months to December 1965 the traffic growth rate had been 15 per cent. In the twelve months to December 1966 the growth rate in passenger miles performed was down to 7.4 per cent and in passengers embarked to 5.9 per cent.[5]

Both airlines were also facing huge costs imposed on them by the need to move their Melbourne operations from Essendon to the new Tullamarine airport. The distinguished Australian journalist Maxwell Newton, writing in *Nation* in February 1967, commented: 'Each domestic operator is currently conducting anxious investigations into the ultimate cost that it will have to bear for moving ... each currently believes that the cost of the move will amount to some $10 million in the early stages, rising in a relatively short time to some $15–$17 million each ... the vast costs of the Tullamarine project will bring sharp new pressures to bear on the already straitened fabric of the Government's shaky two airline policy'. (Both Ansett–ANA and TAA also faced substantial revenue loss as international carriers began operations to Tullamarine. On-carriage from the international airlines from Sydney to Melbourne — previously carried on domestic services — would be lost.) Tullamarine was not, Newton wrote, the only cost-raising pressure. Five other major Commonwealth decisions had been taken to make domestic aviation pay its share of infrastructure costs. There had been steady increases of 10 per cent a year in air navigation charges levied by the Commonwealth; a rise in aviation fuel tax; a decision to force both operators to pay import duty on both the DC9s and Boeing 727s; disallowance for tax purposes of costs involved in improving leasehold property; and a doubling of the period over which aircraft were depreciated for tax purposes. Additionally, wrote Newton, 'both domestic operators have had to find recently some $50 million each to finance the purchase of four Boeing and six DC9s [and] each is going to have to find the money for yet another six DC9s each [costing] about $22 million'.[6]

On 13 April 1967 the first of each airline's DC9s completed their delivery flights and landed at Essendon. Once again the decision on which was to land first was decided by a toss of the coin. This time it was Sir Frederick Scherger who won on behalf of TAA. Their arrival followed a welcome Government announcement that the DC9s would be permitted duty-free entry — a decision that ensured that the DC9 would for the foreseeable future become the major short-haul jet used by Australia's two domestic airlines. TAA's first DC9 went into scheduled operations early on 17 April. (The aircraft carried 105 passengers in all-economy layout, 80 in all-first class. TAA configuration generally used was for 91 passengers. Cruising speed was 560 miles an hour. Each DC9 could do the work of two Viscounts.)[7] The second DC9 for each airline was introduced into service on 11 May.

The arrival of the DC9s was followed by the retirement from the TAA fleet of four V720C Viscounts, which were offered for sale. Some fifty similar V700s were available for sale in the United Kingdom, Europe and North America at the time. TAA estimated the total market value of the four aircraft at just over one million dollars and their total book value at $721,000.[8] (The minister's consent to sell aircraft worth more than $100,000 was necessary.)

The DC9 was the second new aircraft type introduced by TAA in four months. In December, in Papua and New Guinea, it began operating two Twin Otter turboprops, the smallest turbine-powered units in the TAA fleet. The Twin Otter, the only twin-engined aircraft approved for category 'C' airstrips, had access to some 134 New Guinea airfields and had remarkable short-strip performace. (In a demonstration in Australia it had landed with nineteen passengers and stopped in 300 feet.)[9]

TAA was approaching its twenty-first birthday. It now served, over a network of 43,000 miles, 149 cities, towns and stations throughout the Commonwealth and places as far apart as Perth and the Solomon Islands. On average it operated 230 aircraft movements each day, with about half of these on the main trunk routes. It was, wrote *Aircraft*, 'a strong and exceedingly virile organisation with a reputation among world airlines that is both high and well earned. It is noted for its technical integrity, for its record of safety and for its keen and perceptive judgment.' In 1946–47 TAA had carried 146,588 passengers and lost nearly $1 million. In the year to 30 June 1967 it carried two million passengers, returned a net profit of $1,193,472 and paid a 7.5 dividend of $1,125,000 on its capital of $15 million. It now operated a fleet of sixty-nine aircraft. In its twenty-one years it had paid to the Commonwealth in taxes and other charges some $9 million.

The technical achievement of the airline under John Watkins and his team had been remarkable in its reach. It had been the first airline to bring a pressurised airliner into service in Australia with the Convair, and the first airline outside Europe to operate turbine-powered aircraft, with the Viscount. TAA had played a major role in the development of the hugely successful Fokker F27 almost from its inception as a design project through suggestions and negotiations with the manufacturer. In its negotiations with Boeing on configuring the 727 for Australian operation, it had a key influence in bringing to Boeing the realisation that overseas domestic sales required a new concept in the specification and engineering of the aircraft type. It had been at TAA's instigation that a mission representing airline engineering organisations, aerodynamic research and the Department of Civil Aviation visited the world's major commercial aircraft manufacturers and airworthiness authorities to investigate the nature of the problem of the so-called 'deep stall' in tail-engined aircraft. TAA was the first airline ever to specify an 'airspeed hold' capability in a commercial autopilot and the first to sponsor a system of monitoring engine performance by fuel flow techniques (subsequently adopted by Rolls-Royce as a primary basis for jet powerplant control). It also had claim to first place in the development of a truly reliable technique for the inspection of stress corrosion cracking in the plank joints of Electra wing panels.[10]

TAA's coming of age, as *Aircraft* noted, had been reached at a time that marked the beginning of a new era in Australian air transport organisation. The arrival of the first DC9-30s had begun a process of consolidation in the two domestic airline fleets that was to bring increasing benefits to the public in speed and comfort of travel and, for the airlines themselves, eliminate operational problems and effect direct cost savings. At the same time the development of Australia's airport and airways systems, coupled with major changes from the re-equipment of the international airlines and its effect on tourist traffic, promised additional stimulation.[11]

It was also a time for reassessment at government level, domestically and internationally. Domestically, the federal government was reviewing its two-airline policy and already had before it the views of the two airlines. At the international level, on 25 July Qantas submitted a formal proposal to the government that the airline buy four of the big Boeing 747s for delivery in 1971 and take out options on a further two. With spares and other necessary new equipment the 747 project was costed at $134.5 million, plus an additional $48 million for the two aircraft on option. At the other end of the aviation spectrum there was a significant development for the domestic charter operators. The government approved the introduction of what it called 'commuter services' in country areas. They were not airline services but regular flights by charter firms with small single- and twin-engined aircraft, operating to published timetables. TAA was continuously reviewing its own fleet planning. In mid 1967 it saw its future main fleet embodying only four aircraft types — two mainline jet types, a medium turboprop type and a light turboprop for subsidiary services. There was, at the same time, a new initiative in pilot training. TAA's first intake of eleven cadet pilots began training in June on an 81-week course that would take them through to airline pilot licence standard. (That intake was equal to about half the airline's average annual pilot replacement rate.)

TAA also had to plan for a variety of aircraft for other agencies with which it operated, including the Royal Queensland Flying Doctor Service and the Northern Territory Aerial Medical Service — at the time four Drovers and four Doves — plus a DC3 each for the Bureau of Mineral Resources and South Australian Department of Lands. (Mid-1967 marked the fortieth anniversay of the Royal Flying Doctor Service, which was launched in June 1927 when Dr George Simpson flew from Cloncurry, Queensland, to treat an injured Mount Isa miner and bring him back to Cloncurry. It also marked the arrival of its latest aircraft, a twin, turbo-charged Beagle 206S, to operate from Broken Hill in New South Wales.)

In its twenty-first year TAA was looking even farther ahead. The Commission was told as 1967 ended that traffic volumes on its main trunk routes would justify, after 1972, the use of aircraft approximately twice the size of the Boeing 727. John Watkins wrote: 'It is undoubtedly the grave problem of congestion at major North American and European airports that has led to the phenomenal success of the Boeing 747 jumbo-jet programme, reflected in sales of about 140 aircraft already at some $US25 million each — twelve months before the prototype is due to fly ... The size of the Boeing 747 itself is clearly quite out of scale in relation to the foreseeable needs of TAA but it should be possible to gain most of the economic benefits expected of the jumbo jet by careful design of an airliner of approximately half the size, powered by similar big, advanced technology engines. This has been the philosophy behind the so-called European Air Bus project. We expect a visit from the combined Franco-British Air Bus team early next year.'[12]

It was a year that ended with pressure from the government on both Ansett–ANA and TAA to find ways of improving the overall finances of the industry. One suggestion involving fundamental change came from the director-general of civil aviation. Anderson proposed revenue pooling. The TAA reaction was unequivocal: 'could not be entertained'.[13]

While an eventful year in aviation, 1967 had also seen the beginnings of great politico-military initiatives in the world at large. In July Britain had announced its policy of withdrawal from East of Suez and, a month later the Association of South-East Asian Nations (ASEAN) was established. That diminution of British influence was accompanied in Australia by the abolition of appeals to the British Privy Council on Australian federal jurisdiction. More directly, Australian aviation reflected the long attenuation of imperial links and sentiments between Britain and Australia. On 1 August Qantas Empire Airways dropped the word 'Empire' from its name to become Qantas Airways Limited.

The year also ended in tragedy. Australia's prime minister, Harold Holt — whose government had been re-elected on 26 November, died in a drowning accident in December. An interim government under the Country Party's John McEwen took office on 19 December. On 10 January 1968 it was replaced and John Gorton became prime minister.

In January 1968 TAA's chairman, Sir Frederick Scherger, and general manager John Ryland met the minister for civil aviation, R.W. Swartz, to hear from him government decisions that were to affect the operation of the two-airline policy. The calendar year 1967 had seen TAA, on the Australian domestic routes where it competed with Ansett–ANA, achieve a passenger market share of 52.7 per cent. On the Australia–New Guinea route the TAA share was 51.3 per cent and on internal New Guinea routes 56.6 per cent. Where TAA competed with Ansett–ANA it was leader. But Ansett received much more traffic from the many routes he served on which there was no competition. TAA's share on noncompetitive mainland routes was only 11.9 per cent. That meant that in total over all passenger traffic carried for the 1967 year, the TAA share was reduced to 48.3 per cent.[14]

The government decisions advised by Swartz were by no means critical ones, but they were welcome. Swartz informed them, first, that the duty paid on Boeing 727 aircraft would be removed retrospectively and, second, that further subsidies for developmental routes and rural services would be available for those that qualified.[15] Other issues raised at that meeting were not so welcome. The government, under pressure from Reginald Ansett, whose ATI was in financial difficulties, was considering proposals for an increase in the dividend requirement of TAA and a change in the Australian National Airlines Commission policy affecting provisions for the payment of the Commission's eventual liability for superannuation to its staff, placing such provisions outside the TAA business (with capital to be employed in lieu). Both Ansett proposals were aimed at increasing TAA's costs, an outcome which, in turn, would make TAA more amenable to another proposal initiated by Ansett — that tariffs should increase by 5 per cent from 1 February.

Scherger met Reginald Ansett and his finance director, Ralph Cooper, on 19 January. Reporting the meeting to Swartz, Scherger wrote: 'At this meeting Mr Ansett informed me that ATI could only remain viable if it paid a 10 per cent dividend on its capital and that the airline component of ATI was only supporting a 6 per cent dividend ... Mr Ansett said his situation was caused by the failure of the Government to interpret correctly the Australian National Airlines Act (Section 32) which requires that the Minister, amongst other things, take into account the profits that have been and are expected to be made by privately owned air transport undertakings when fixing the dividend for TAA.'

It was Mr Ansett's opinion '(a) [that] TAA had Government backed and arranged borrowings which were made at a substantially lower interest rate than could be achieved by ATI, (b) that TAA's use of superannuation provisions gave TAA an advantage over ATI of $700,000 to $800,000 annually; (c) that TAA's share of Government business amounted to 70 per cent of the total, (d) that TAA's ration of equity capital to total funds employed is more advantageous than ATI's [and ...] (e) that with these financial advantages an additional and overwhelming advantage was given to TAA by setting its dividend target at 7.5 per cent'.

Scherger had not been impressed. He told Swartz: 'I accept without reservation Mr Ansett's views that his current profitability level may well involve far reaching implications for ATI but I reject the proposition that the causes of this situation are due to the factors he enumerates'. Ansett, he said, did not seek the Government guarantees available to it when buying Electras (and the lower interest rates that went with them); its DC9 fleet of six aircraft was financed by such government guarantees; its Boeing 727 interest rates, on a ten-year fleet life, involved an interest differential of only $86,000 per annum. On superannuation, he pointed out that the cost of ground staff superannuation to TAA was $1.2 million a year greater than for ATI (because of the benefits laid down in the Commonwealth Superannuation Acts). While he conceded that the TAA share of government business was greater, he commented: 'We believe it is matched by an imbalance in the private sector in favour of ATI'. On the ratio of equity capital to total funds employed in the business he wrote: 'Both organisations' ratio of equity capital to borrowed funds (counting the superannuation provisions not separately invested as borrowed funds) are identical for practical purposes'.

Overall, he wrote, 'there are no [ATI] financial advantages of a magnitude to outweigh the very considerable increased superannuation costs of TAA. If these were weighted correctly they would justify ... a dividend target less than the current 7.5 per cent.' Scherger rejected any need on TAA's part for a tariff increase.[16] 'The question remains then', he told the minister, 'of the threat to the continued operation of the two airline policy (which is supported by the Commission) and the means to cure the present ATI financial difficulties which pose this threat'. Their causes, he said, were twofold — a too rapid expansion by ATI at too high cost in unrewarding areas such as intrastate operations, hotels, television and helicopters, 'causing cash losses of considerable magnitude of funds borrowed on the security of the airline operations' and 'the operation of the competitive airline element on a basis of services which its revenue cannot support sufficiently profitably'.

TAA suggested, he concluded, that the cure for ATI was to adjust the capacity provided on its routes to the revenues available to support it, to withdraw from unrewarding areas and to continue collaboration with TAA to seek mutual benefits from the rationalisation of schedules and other expenditures, and to share facilities. 'These alternatives, singly or in combination, however unpalatable, will produce a profitable competitive airline and are sound business decisions.'[17]

At a Commission meeting on 21 February, when these matters were discussed, it was recorded: 'Historically ATI has moved from one crisis to another at fairly frequent intervals and the steps now proposed [by Ansett] can be no more than a temporary solution to a regularly occurring problem. The present financial crisis in which ATI now finds itself is to a large extent self-inflicted — for example, since 1961 when extensive legislation was passed to achieve what was regarded at that time as comparability between the airlines, ATI has embarked upon some singularly unrewarding ventures such as the acquisition of the third commercial television licence in Melbourne, the purchase at highly inflated values of very substantial holdings in interstate television companies, and the taking over of a subsidiary airline (MacRobertson-Miller), the earnings of which could not service the dividend requirement of the capital invested in the project by ATI.'

The financial policies followed by the board of ATI, said the minutes, 'have been unsound, ill-advised and imprudent, and in many respects are parallel to those followed with such disastrous consequences by a number of public companies in the early 1960s. The cost structure of the industry is already inflated by ATI's inability to withstand industrial pressures (the consequences of the pilots' threatened stoppages are enormous) and the imposition of higher than commercial rates of interest upon the Commission would be a further and unjustifiable burden on the travelling public. The proposed substantial addition to the capital of the Commission at this time would be financially imprudent.'[18]

The *Australian* quoted from Stanley Brogden's just-published *Australia's Two Airline Policy*: 'It is generally believed in informed circles that ATI airlines provide most of the [group] profit. This gives rise to criticism that the Government is merely subsidising the ATI non-aviation interests such as TV ... another view is that without its protected aviation interests, ATI would not last long.'[19]

The pilots' threatened stoppages mentioned at the Commission meeting were to have drastic consequences. The dispute had its first formal airing on 28 February 1968, when both TAA and Ansett–ANA notified the Flight Crew Officers Industrial Tribunal of an industrial dispute with the Australian Federation of Air Pilots (AFAP) over the crewing of the DC9. That Tribunal had been only recently created when the Conciliation and Arbitration Bill 1967 was introduced into Parliament on 19 October 1967. It was, wrote Nicholas Blain in his *Industrial Relations in the Air*, a 'new, special statutory tribunal ... designed to deal with industrial disputes involving pilots, navigators and flight engineers in the airline industry'.[20] The legislation brought pilots, who previously had operated with unique and extraordinary power in industrial matters outside Australia's conciliation and arbitration system, under the jurisdiction of the system. On 4 February 1968, Professor J. E. Isaac had been appointed as the inaugural Tribunal.

The AFAP requirement was that DC9s should be crewed by two pilots and a flight engineer. The position of the airlines and of the director-general of civil aviation was that the minimum crew should be only two pilots. They were notified by the AFAP that existing two-crew operation of the DC9s would cease on 1 March. The DC9s in Australia had been flown with two-pilot crews since their introduction. Worldwide there were then 244 DC9s flying with 38 airlines. All were licensed for two-pilot operation. Nevertheless the AFAP was adamant in its demands.

The inability of Ansett–ANA to withstand industrial pressure was immediately evident. Ansett had agreed with TAA that both would adhere to the principle of a two-pilot crew for DC9s, but following the threat of direct action he immediately yielded and decided to continue with three-crew operation. TAA (which now had three DC9s) remained firm on the issue of two-crew operations and its DC9s were grounded from 1

March. (That blow was compounded on 5 March when flight engineers further disrupted services by grounding all TAA's Boeing 727 and Electra aircraft for two days.)

Emotions ran high during the DC9 dispute. Ansett, for sound economic reasons, did not welcome the necessity to operate his DC9s with a crew of three. On 7 March he tried to persuade all his pilots to withdraw from the AFAP. Among the pilots themselves there was dissension. The AFAP's Victorian Branch, influenced by the voting of Ansett pilots, announced in mid-March its preference for two-crew operations. That decision brought hard words from the Federation. It wrote to its members: 'In Ansett–ANA there appears to be a group [that] comprises two sections ... In the main there are the "hard-core" Management pilots and those influenced by them ... You've heard them say many times "We can't afford trouble — We are the private enterprise airline — We'll go under if there's any strife". One is driven to wonder whether it is their own position at the top of the Management tree they seek to protect because, let's face it Gentlemen, the pilots, the aircraft and the industry will still be here regardless of who sits in the Board chairs, and the old-fashioned whine "We must protect Reg" is so much hogwash ... We certainly do not need or want people who act only to sabotage the Federation, who give every appearance of acting in collusion with Management against their fellows.'[21] It was intimidating stuff, far from elegantly expressed.

Ansett exploited the commercial situation with his usual pragmatism. While TAA's DC9s were grounded, TAA and Ansett–ANA each received delivery of their fourth DC9. Although the minister, under the Airlines Equipment Act, had ruled that these aircraft should be introduced into airline service on the same day, Ansett began using his fourth DC9 while TAA's DC9s were grounded. TAA, of course, protested vigorously, and on 26 March Swartz sent a telegram to Reginald Ansett that read: '... I require Ansett–ANA to abide by the terms of the certificate issued in respect of [DC9] VH CZD and not use this aircraft in regular public transport services until the comparable DC9 of TAA is introduced'.[22]

Following legal action in the High Court not directly concerned with the crewing issue, the AFAP lifted its ban on the operation of TAA's DC9s and pilots returned to duty on 9 April — in time to meet expected heavy Easter traffic. The DC9 fleet had been grounded for thirty-nine days. (The formal crewing dispute before the Tribunal was not resolved until much later. On 6 August 1969 Isaac rejected the AFAP's demands.) For thirty-nine days TAA had had no revenue from DC9 operations, and for two of those days no heavy aircraft in the TAA fleet had operated at all. There had been countless interruptions to schedules and aircraft type substitutions. By extraordinary effort staff had been able, nevertheless, to maintain in the air an equivalent 47 per cent of the competitive capacity. The drop in market share, however, had had significant financial consequences, estimated by Ryland in mid-April at $1.25 million. But there had also been gains, he told a staff meeting. The AFAP strike, he said, 'demonstrated that the Commission was prepared to stand its ground on a serious issue which could affect its future ... It showed, so far as our competitor is concerned, that we are not tied to him in policy matters. It produced substantial press and public support.'[23]

Salary claims and industrial relations generally had always been complicated by the Ansett vulnerability to strike action. Within the industry two consultative groups were created to provide a forum for consultation and discussion. The Airline Operators Group, in existence for many years, was concerned mainly with flight crew industrial matters but it had no powers. A report prepared for TAA's vice-chairman, R. R. Law-Smith, noted: 'It is felt that both TAA and Qantas endeavour to use this group for high level discussions and policy shaping [but] experience has shown that the Ansett organisation does not appear to use the group — evidenced by the Ansett level of representation and contribution'.

A Ground Staff Industrial Group was formed in February 1969, at the instigation of TAA and Qantas, 'to foster better inter-company communication ... [but] Ansett informed TAA that ATI would not be represented and the meeting lapsed'.

There was a blunt description of the dominance of Reginald Ansett personally. 'The Ansett representatives', said the report, 'invariably make it clear that irrespective of how desirable a certain course of action may appear to be, and irrespective of the industrial or even Management views on the matter, they must reserve their position as the final decision must rest with Sir Reginald Ansett'.

Ansett had been a critical influence in the negotiations with pilots in 1966. Following protracted negotiations between Ansett–ANA, TAA and the Pilots' Federation in 1966, the two sides had reached an impasse when the pilots refused to accept a recommendation from Professsor Isaac for a 15 per cent increase in salaries. 'A strike was called by the Pilots' Federation', said the report, 'but at the eleventh hour Ansett decided to grant additional increases to pilots plus further increases in 1967 and 1968 which gave total increases of approximately 27.5 per cent — and which it is believed have been responsible for a lot of the industrial unrest in other areas within the industry since that date. The Commission's best endeavours to enlist Governmental pressures that might have deterred Ansett from offering these increases were to no avail. TAA had no alternative but to go along with the agreement made by Ansett.'

There had been other such instances of Ansett's readiness to avoid strikes at any cost. The TAA report concluded: 'The Ansett organisation is not prepared to face the consequences of industrial action. The employee organisations know that to be the case and exploit it. Ansett negotiators have no real authority. There is only one real authority — Sir Reginald Ansett himself.'[24]

On 4 June 1968 TAA signed a purchase agreement with Boeing for its fifth 727 aircraft, for delivery in November 1969. With the DC9 dispute behind it, the airline looked forward to expansion in a buoyant domestic economy with rising interline traffic on a world scene in which international airlines were experiencing substantial growth. In its annual report for the financial year to 30 June 1968 it recorded revenue passengers totalling 2,169,562 on a passenger load factor of 67.4 per cent. Revenue earned for the year was $71,052,195 and net profit $1,133,384.

The moves towards fleet consolidation and standardisation were now well under way. All DC6B aircraft had been eliminated from the fleet. Five Viscount 700s had been retired (with a further two going in 1968 and the remaining four in the first half of 1969). The DC3 fleet had been reduced from twenty to fourteen (with only nine remaining at the end of 1968). Disposal of the DC4 fleet was scheduled for December to January with the delivery of four Quick Change Fokker Friendships, marking the end of operations for DC3 and DC4 freighters. (The Quick Change Friendships had been bought primarily for freight work but could be used for passengers by a simple conversion. TAA already had eleven Friendships in service.) Six new Twin Otters had been added to the TAA fleet in 1968, operating along the Queensland coast and essential rural and developmental services previously serviced by DC3s in parts of Queensland, New South Wales, the Northern Territory and South Australia. (One went to New Guinea, where two others had been operating for some two years.) The fifth DC9 was delivered in early November. There was, though, one drag on progress. The potential gains in efficiency and cost from fleet consolidation remained limited until the technically obsolescent Electras could be retired. They had already been in service for ten years. Planned retirement of the Electras and their replacement by DC9 capacity had been set back to 1970 to accommodate Ansett's financial needs.

The DC9 strike had profited Ansett–ANA, which achieved a sharp increase in load factor during the six weeks' grounding of TAA's DC9s, at last reversing the severe effects of the Winton Viscount crash. In the second half of the 1966–67 financial year pre-tax profit for Ansett was only $1,415,014; in the second half it jumped to $3,672,416.[25] Ansett Transport Industries was, however, now facing what the *Financial Review,* commenting on the ATI results, described in November 1968 as 'a high tax era'. Ansett, it said, 'has been paying nominal taxation for many years, partly because of past subsidiary losses, but also by depreciating its aircraft over eight years or longer in its books but over only four years for the Taxation Commissioner ... Partly reflecting the new write-off situation Ansett's taxation provision jumped from $214,039 to $2,228,090'. The ATI annual report acknowledged that '[a]s a result of temporary advantages arising from tax depreciation, taxable income may be in excess of book profits in some future years and disproportionate provisions for income tax will then be required'. Notes to the accounts said that the reserve for future tax did not represent total deferred tax at current rates. Despite the assistance provided by the TAA strike, the company's load factor over the twelve months declined for the fourth successive year (down from 64.5 per cent in 1963–64 to 62.1 per cent in 1967–68).[26] (TAA, in the preceding four years, had paid about $1.5 million more to the Government in income tax than had ATI.)[27]

The 1968 year had a tragic ending for ATI. Viscount VH-RMQ, operated by MacRobertson Miller Airlines, lost a wing at 7,000 feet on descent at Port Hedland, Western Australia, on 31 December and crashed with the loss of twenty-six people. It was the fourth Viscount loss in Australia. The first, TAA's VH-TVA, crashed on take-off on a training flight in October 1954 at Mangalore, Victoria. The second, Ansett's VH-TVC (operated on cross-charter), was lost after experiencing thunderstorm turbulence over Botany Bay in November 1961. The third, Ansett's VH-RMI, crashed at Winton in September 1966 following fire and the loss of a wing.

A report to the Australian National Airlines Commission in February 1969 commented: 'Apart from the VH-TVA accident [a training accident] it can be said that the last three Viscount crashes have, to a significant extent, been influenced by the fast-disappearing non-redundant design philosophy employed in the Viscount structure [i.e., non-'fail-safe' philosophy; the Twin Otters, also, were not designed to be 'fail-safe']. The Port Hedland accident is particularly significant as it was quickly and quite conclusively established that the sudden loss of the starboard wing in good flying conditions resulted from a classical example of fatigue failure of the main spar lower boom, adjacent to the outboard side of the No. 3 engine nacelle ... This is the first case of a Viscount wing failure by fatigue. The fact that it occurred when 29 per cent of the then prescribed maximum service life still remained and without any discernible extraneous aggravating conditions is naturally most disturbing.'[28]

TAA started the 1969 year with an industrial dispute (involving the dismissal of a member of the Transport Workers' Union) that seriously disrupted operations on all routes for thirteen days in January, costing the airline more than $1 million and 50,000 passengers.[29] The last year of the decade was, however, marked by a change that looked to the future. The TAA fleet was to appear in new colours — announced as 'the Look of the Seventies' — replacing the traditional red, white and blue. On 1 April the first freshly painted aircraft, DC9 VH-TJK, rolled out of the hangar at Essendon carrying the new TAA colours of Australian ochre, white and 'starlight' blue. The kangaroo symbol, previously in red, reappeared in Australian ochre. The two main colours, Ryland told staff, were 'truly indigenous Australian'. The ochre was 'the colour of the great Australian desert', the blue of 'the starry stillness of our night skies'.[30]

Also of significance for the future, TAA's first group of cadet pilots graduated at a special ceremony at Essendon airport on 27 February. The eleven graduates had been trained from the elementary flying stage to airline standards in the first course of its kind run by an Australian domestic airline. All were posted as first officers on Fokker Friendships.

Reflecting the great surge in international air travel in the second half of the decade TAA brought representatives of its major general sales agents throughout the world to Melbourne in March for a conference. Commercial director Lyn McKenzie told staff that in 1968 some 430,000 passengers flew into Australia from abroad — an increase of some 20 per cent on the previous year. Assuming that half continued beyond their point of entry the revenue available domestically, he said, was well over $10 million and, with the impending entry of Boeing 747 jumbo jets, was likely to continue to grow strongly.[31]

That great changes in international aviation were imminent was evident at the 1969 Paris Air Show. Of greatest technical significance was the first public appearance in flight of the prototype Sud Aviation–British Aircraft Corporation's supersonic airliner, the Concorde. Next was the first public appearance abroad of the definitive Pan American version of the Boeing 747 jumbo jet. But there were also other exhibits that were to shape the future. The twin-jet Fokker F28 was demonstrated in flight displays while both Lockheed and Douglas had models of their big new tri-jet aircraft, already in production — the Lockheed 1011 and the Douglas DC10 (with a capacity of more than 250 passengers). Sud Aviation also gave a full presentation of their A300B — better known as the European Airbus.

In Australia in June 1969 the future of domestic aviation to 1972 was settled by a government decision to allow the purchase of fourteen new jet aircraft worth some $80 million. Both airlines were allowed an additional 727 and six more DC9s. (TAA's existing heavy aircraft fleet comprised four 727s, with a fifth due in November 1969, and five DC9s, with a sixth arriving in August. All Viscounts and Electras were to be progressively phased out by March 1971.)

In that same month Reginald Ansett won his argument for an increase in the TAA dividend rate. The minister formally advised the Commission that the dividend required from it would rise from 7.5 to 8.5 per cent for 1969–70. That advice came as TAA faced various wage claims of substance. The Commission was told: 'If these all occur at the rate now expected we would be $805,000 short of the dividend requirement of 8.5 per cent. If this proves to be so then it will be necessary to increase revenue either by achievement of higher growth rates or increase in tariffs if the Ministerial determination is to be achieved.'[32] That advice to the Commission came from its director of administration, R. E. Pope, who had been, since the airline's formation, its able guide in all financial matters. At the end of 1969 Dick Pope reached retirement age and formally concluded his service with TAA.

The decade also ended with the appointment of a new Australian minister for civil aviation. Senator Robert Cotton succeeded Reginald Swartz.

CHAPTER 12

1970

The affectionate antagonism of identical twins

In January 1970 TAA's director of operations, R.E. (Reg) Bailey, wrote: 'A situation of almost complete parity has now developed between TAA and its main competitor, with both airlines operating an almost identical fleet of jet and prop-jet aircraft, and planning to introduce three additional jets during 1970. Allowing for operational and scheduling factors, and aircraft maintenance requirements, seating capacities which can be made available by each airline become very similar, with neither organisation able to achieve any significant advantage over its competitor on the main competitive routes.'[1] The two-airline system was now a twin-airline system, competing, as the *Financial Review* put it, 'with the affectionate antagonism of identical twins'.

The year did not start well operationally for TAA. On 5 January the airline's first 300 series DHC6 Twin Otter ran out of fuel on the second leg of its delivery flight from the United States, and made a forced landing on a steeply shelving coral beach on the island of Ta'u (in the Manua group of Western Samoa), some seventy miles short of its intended destination of Pago Pago on Tutuila Island. Following normal practice, the delivery flight had been subcontracted to the ferrying organisation Air Capital International, which had previously conducted the acceptance and delivery flights of six of TAA's existing fleet of Twin Otters. The US Federal

Aviation Administration exonerated the captain (who was flying solo) on the grounds that the forecast winds had been highly inaccurate. (Reg Bailey was not so generous. It was his view that the pilot either had a faulty compass or had applied the drift due to wind incorrectly. He recommended that Air Capital be asked not to use this captain for future TAA deliveries.)[2] Salvage was not possible, but the aircraft was fully insured. Scherger told his new minister, Robert Cotton, that TAA's fleet strength in Papua New Guinea would not be seriously affected by the delay in obtaining a replacement aircraft.[3]

That non-fatal Twin Otter incident was followed by a far more serious one. On 28 April Twin Otter VH-TGR, operating a scheduled regular public transport flight in the eastern highlands of New Guinea that had originated at Mt Hagen, crashed into a mountain ridge near Kianantu airstrip in conditions of fog, drizzle and low cloud. Of the eleven people on board five were killed instantly and three died subsequently.[4]

The new minister for civil aviation, Robert Cotton, reviewed the government's aviation policy in broad terms in an interview for the *Financial Review*. One important issue that was increasingly affecting airline finances was the steady increase in government charges. Growth in demand for aviation services in Australia, said the minister, was much higher than in most sectors of the Australian economy, placing immense strains on the provision of infrastructure. At the same time technological developments had brought with them increasingly sophisticated equipment requirements. 'The total expenditure on civil aviation in the year 1968–69, he said, 'amounted to $39 million'. The current value of Australian facilities was some $200 million and the annual cost of operating this infrastructure was $65 million. Asked why landing fees in Australia were so high that they had provoked an open and organised revolt by foreign airlines in 1969, Cotton responded that it was government policy to move gradually towards a position where costs attributable to commercial aviation were being fully recovered. 'At present annual departmental costs exceed $70 million while revenues comparable with these costs would be about $20 million. Even with fuel tax of some $10 million added you will see that our recovery rate is less than 50 per cent.'[5] The issues of 'cost recovery' and 'user pays' were to remain on the aviation agenda for long into the future.

Another aviation issue with long-term political implications occupied Parliament in 1970. John Watkins provided a TAA submission to the House of Representatives Select Committee on Aircraft Noise. The first two types of jet airliners brought into service domestically in Australia, the Boeing 727–100 (in November 1964) and the Douglas DC9-30 (in April 1967), used the American Pratt & Whitney JT8D fan-jet engines, with a by-pass ratio of 1:1. This fan-jet directly mixed the relatively low-velocity airstream from the engine's 'fan' with the very high-velocity jet exhaust stream to reduce noise (and provide better economy). It was an advance, in terms of noise, on the unsilenced earlier pure-jet engines, though the fan itself produced a piercing whistling tone with a nuisance value at least equal to the noise of the pure-jet engine itself.

In the six years since 1963, when the JT8D had been developed, all the western world's major aero engine manufacturers and the aeronautical laboratories of their countries had devoted substantial resources to noise suppression studies, largely because of the great thrust requirements of the bigger engines needed to power the larger and heavier international jet airliners. For domestic Australian operations, however, there was little likelihood of reducing existing aircraft noise. The costs involved were high. Watkins wrote:

> The domestic jet fleet by 1972 will comprise 12 Boeing 727s plus 24 Douglas DC9s ... the overseas funds needed [for noise suppression through nacelle modification], in addition to the normal purchase price of the aircraft as in use today would amount to $7,200,000. If the net result were to be an increase of 5 per cent in the direct operating cost of this jet fleet — and assuming as would inevitably be the case that such an increase had to be passed on to the public through increased fares — the amount to be added to the already high internal Australian expenditure on transport costs would be in excess of $8,000,000 per annum.[6]

The future was just as unpromising, despite new noise standards set by the US Federal Aviation Administration for new aircraft types.

> This is because, wrote Watkins, the authorities have accepted the basic fact that more thrust in jet propulsion means more noise, other things being equal. Each Rolls-Royce RB211 engine of the Lockheed L1011 tri-motor airliner, with its gross weight of 409,000 lb, will have to produce about 3.5 times as much thrust as today's JT8D in the 160,000 lb Boeing 727. Even after applying the best techniques available in the current state-of-the-art it would not be possible to keep the noise level down to that of the lower-powered engine ... In our view it would be quite unrealistic to believe that Australia could unilaterally impose some far more stringent certification requirement in respect of noise than that now being written into the airworthiness code of the government of the country [the US] which has supplied the vast preponderance of airliner capacity on which our air transport system has been built.

With some prescience Watkins concluded his submission: 'These circumstances all tend to reinforce our belief that the most urgent problem calling for a solution is the working out of practical and effective machinery for land-use zoning control in the neighbourhood of airports'.[7]

Despite Reg Bailey's accurate observation that TAA and Ansett–ANA had comparable capacity on the main competitive routes, that situation was always influenced by the additional aircraft available to Ansett from his noncompetitive operations. Scherger was concerned enough to write to Cotton in April 1970 when Ansett applied for permission to import two additional twin-jet Fokker F28 aircraft (to increase his F28 fleet to four). 'Approval of these applications', said Scherger, 'would increase further the Company's advantage in jet equipment which arises from a severe inequality of access on the part of the Commission to substantial air transport markets. A fleet disadvantage of four modern jet aircraft threatens the competitive position of the Commission and poses problems for the future of the Government's policy.'[8]

Government acquiscence in the Ansett application, he said, would mean that by the end of 1970 the comparative fleets would be fourteen jet aircraft for TAA and eighteen for ATI plus sixteen prop-jet F27 Friendships for TAA and twenty-two for ATI — a total of thirty aircraft for TAA and forty for ATI. 'The Commission's fleet disadvantage in jets and F27 units arises because the Company [ATI] has an extensive network of high-density non-competitive routes whereas the Commission has a minor non-competitive network only. Your last capacity determination under the Airlines Equipment Act shows that the Company has a non-competitive capacity need over eight times that of the Commission. This disparity occurs because of the non-competitive operations conducted by the Company, primarily in Western Australia and the Northern Territory and also in New South Wales. These are areas where traffic has built to a level capable of sustaining profitable jet operations and yet the Commission has not so far been authorised to operate.' (TAA had more Twin Otter aircraft than ATI, but Ansett operated a fleet of all-cargo aircraft while TAA's cargo needs were provided by F27s. Both had equal Electras and supporting Viscounts.) The solution, wrote Scherger, 'appears to lie in providing the Commission with authority to acquire jet aircraft on equal terms with the Company'.[9]

Following agreement with Ansett Airlines of Australia (the renamed Ansett–ANA) on delivery dates for the remaining jet aircraft on order through to November 1971, TAA was carefully reviewing the relationship between its future capacity and forecast traffic demand. 'The results', said a Commission report, 'are disquieting. A conservative interpretation of the recent trend of traffic growth has led to the adoption of 13 per cent per annum as a figure for forward planning. Projections based on this clearly indicate that there will be a shortfall of available capacity even before the completion of deliveries of current orders ... equivalent to the capacity of an additional DC9-31 plus at least three further F27 aircraft. Presumably either public demand will not be met in this period or some recourse may be had to chartered activity.'

There were conclusions of much greater significance for TAA's future. The report continued: 'Careful trial assessments of feasible network operations with a hypothetical new aircraft of 250 seat capacity, employed as a B727 replacement, have shown that the traffic volumes and frequency requirements on the more heavily-travelled routes would enable the practical introduction of limited numbers of such 250 seat equipment as from the second half of 1972. The confidently expected reduction in seat-mile operating costs of large advanced-technology aircraft will be a potent factor in avoiding the need for excessive fare increases.' To minimise the total requirement for additional capital funds, it said, 'every effort should be made to avoid the procurement of any aircraft which represent merely a temporary stop-gap in the desired orderly progression towards an efficient and well designed fleet composition for the future'. The airline saw 'substantial economic merit in moving as rapidly as possible towards the selection and introduction into the TAA fleet of large jet equipment of approximately 250 seat capacity'.[10]

While these studies on the future composition of the TAA fleet were in progress TAA was disposing of the aircraft that had sustained it in earlier years. Negotiations were in progress with a Singapore company, Air Saber, for the sale of the first TAA Electra to be retired (in mid-1971). Most of TAA's five Viscount 756 aircraft had been stripped of worthwhile component parts and negotiations were in hand with scrap dealers for the sale of the fuselages. The only remaining TAA DC4 (and the residue of the aircraft's DC4 spares inventory) was sold by mid May. TAA's sixth Boeing 727 was delivered to Essendon on 18 July. On Wednesday, 19 August, TAA Viscount VH-TVP carried the airline's last Viscount passengers, and the airliner on which TAA's early dominance had depended was retired from the fleet.

For civil aviation, 1970–71, said the DCA annual report, was to be 'a most complex year'. Domestically the financial year began on an optimistic note, with growth of 10 to 15 per cent predicated. Those expectations were not to be realised. (Growth was 8.6 per cent, compared with 16.3 per cent in 1969–70.) The progressive development of economic pressures as the country experienced a recession, said the DCA, were to have 'a severe effect on all sectors of the nation's civil air transport industry'.[11] TAA was given an additional financial challenge by its new minister, Robert Cotton. The Commission noted in June 1970: 'The Minister has notified a dividend target for 1970–71 of 10 per cent, as compared with 8.5 per cent for 1969–70, raised from 7.5 per cent which applied over the previous five years. In accordance with usual practice no reason has been given for the increase.'[12] The Ansett wish to see TAA pay a dividend rate equal to that which it saw as necessary for its own commercial survival had been granted.

A 10 per cent dividend required a payment to Treasury of $1.5 million — an increase of $225,000 compared with an 8.5 per cent dividend. To provide that dividend required from TAA an increase in gross profit of $410,000. To earn that profit level meant the imposition of a 6 per cent increase in fares and freight rates, an increase granted by the minister in July.[13] (The last increase — of 5 per cent — had been imposed in August 1967. Since that time heavy traffic growth and the increasing efficiency obtained from the introduction of more jet aircraft, as well as the reduction in the number of aircraft types in service, had allowed rising costs to be absorbed, but the point had now been reached at which further absorption of increased costs was not possible.)

There were strong grounds for believing that Ansett had found a sympathetic listener in Cotton. In July the Commission was advised by their minister that Cabinet intended to amend the Australian National Airlines Act so that the Commission's ground staff superannuation funds should become a loan and — or advance from the Treasury, bearing interest. That outcome, further increasing TAA's costs, had also been an Ansett goal.

In 1970–71 many of the world's biggest and strongest airlines were to be hit by an economic slump unprecedented in the history of international civil aviation. The director-general of the International Air Transport Association described the situation as a decline from 'a situation of profitless prosperity to one of profitless growth'.[14] There were, however, two spectacular infrastructure developments in Australia in 1970 — the opening by Queen Elizabeth of the new international passenger terminal building at Sydney's Kingsford Smith Airport in May 1970, and the opening on 1 July of Melbourne's $50-million Tullamarine Airport. (The target date set for the transfer of domestic operations to Tullamarine was, however, mid-April 1971.) The new Melbourne airport reinstated Melbourne as an international stop-over after a period of five years during which the old Essendon airport had been unable to handle aircraft of the size of the Boeing 707 and the DC8.

These two considerable projects had been part of a national airports plan approved initially by the federal government in 1963–64 that included the extension of the runway into Botany Bay, Sydney to 9,100 feet (with a further extension to 13,000 feet by 1972), runway development and a new terminal building at Launceston, a new terminal building at Canberra, and extensive runway improvements at Perth, Brisbane and other centres. That airports plan had made possible regular international services to Brisbane, Perth and Darwin as well as Sydney and Melbourne. (Since 1938 Sydney's airport had grown from 161 to 1,600 acres, spreading over two golf courses, a polo field, a gun club, a race course and part of Botany Bay.)

Australia's domestic airlines in 1970 ranked as the fourth busiest among all the International Civil Aviation Organisation's member states, behind only the United States, Canada and Japan. In 1969–70 the domestic airlines had carried 6,393,000 passengers, a 14.5 per cent increase on the previous year. At 30 June 1970 there were, besides the two trunkline operators and the intrastate airlines, 18 commuter operators operating to 238 ports in Australia and Papua New Guinea. Passenger miles performed by all the mainland airlines in 1969–70 were 17.1 per cent above the level of the previous year — the biggest rise in any one year since 1947–48.[15]

The opening of the new Melbourne airport was to divert a large volume of domestic traffic on the Melbourne–Sydney route to international operators. For TAA, which had previously won more than 60 per cent of international on-carriage on the route (one of its strongest markets), the outcome was to weaken its competitive position. That traffic loss was one of several influences that, in the second half of 1970, saw TAA getting a significantly smaller share of the total competitive market than it had won for a number of years. Scherger told Cotton in October: 'In the Commission's view its deteriorating competitive position results from a number of factors involving domestic and international on-carriage and a gradual weakening position in traditional markets arising mainly from Government action in the past aimed at assisting the Company [Ansett] to obtain a higher proportion of passenger traffic'.[16]

Ansett expanded further in Papua New Guinea with the takeover of Patair, the third internal New Guinea airline. The purchase and ATI control was confirmed on 27 July 1970. Ansett Airlines of Papua New Guinea and TAA were now the only two airline operators in the Territory. TAA operations there, after ten years, were marginally profitable and traffic growth was buoyant. The gross value of the Commission's assets in Papua New Guinea was $8.8 million.

Political change lay ahead for both airlines as the Territory moved towards self-government. TAA saw in this progress towards independence an opportunity to diminish Ansett's influence. Scherger wrote to Cotton on 25 November 1970: 'The Commission has formed the view that the native population would most likely support a single government-owned airline operating domestic (and most probably international) air services [and that] preparatory steps should be taken now to prepare the way for such development'. He recommended that the Commission be empowered to set up a subsidiary airline in the Territory, renaming TAA's operations there 'Airlines of New Guinea'. The local administration, he said, would be given the opportunity of acquiring either total equity or a controlling financial interest in 'Airlines of New Guinea' at any time and so establish the nucleus from which the new Territory government could form its own internal airline.[17]

A more pressing issue for TAA was its aircraft equipment requirements for 1972 and beyond, after the delivery of its twelfth DC9 in November 1971. Scherger told Cotton in

November: 'The Commission is anxious not to delay in moving towards the introduction of large wide-bodied jet equipment of 250–280 seat capacity so as to achieve the lower seat mile cost and greater efficiency which these large aircraft provide. A suitable introductory date for such aircraft would be in the second half of 1974 ... The Commission has considered what aircraft type would be most suitable to meet traffic demands from the beginning of 1972 to the middle of 1974 and has concluded that the Boeing 727–200 series aircraft would be the most suitable equipment.' He sought approval to acquire four 727–200s.[18]

Ansett had a different view. *Aircraft* commented: 'TAA wants to introduce a wide-bodied type ... into service in 1974. Ansett Airlines of Australia does not believe the growth factor merits the introduction of a wide-bodied type until as late as 1976–77, with emphasis on the later date.' To carry Ansett through until at least 1975, it wrote, the airline's preference was the stretched version of the Boeing 727–200.[19] A compromise agreement was reached for the introduction of the first domestic wide-bodied types in late 1975 or early 1976 with, in the meantime, orders by each airline for six Boeing stretched 727–200s. Ansett also made plain that he required a major government undertaking before he would commit to the re-equipment programme. In its December 1970 issue, *Aircraft* wrote: 'Sir Reginald has asked the Commonwealth Government for an assurance that it is prepared to legislate for an extension of the Airlines Agreement Act beyond its present terminating date in 1977 and he has made it clear that he is not prepared to enter into any long term commitment for the purchase of new equipment until the policy situation is clarified. "I must know where we are going in regard to Government policy before I commit my shareholders to the most expensive equipment expansion programme in the history of the company", he told *Aircraft*.'[20] (Ansett ended the 1970 year by introducing, in December, Fokker F28 twin-jet Fellowship aircraft on intrastate routes in New South Wales. That initiative was short-lived. They were withdrawn in April 1971 when the routes proved uneconomic for jet operations.)

There was drama and near tragedy on the dark and wet evening of 29 January 1971 at Sydney airport. TAA's Boeing 727 VH-TJA, taking off on runway 16 just after 9.30 p.m., struck the tail fin of a Canadian Pacific Airlines DC8, which had just landed on the same runway to complete a flight from Vancouver. Some 8.5 feet of the fin and rudder were sheared off from the taxiing DC8 and there was considerable damage to the undersurfaces of the TAA aircraft. The 727, already airborne, continued its take-off and remained airborne for some forty minutes, dumping excess fuel, before landing without further incident.

The subsequent accident investigation report attributed the collision to a conjunction of errors made on the flight decks of both aircraft and in the Sydney control tower. The tower had given the DC8 the instruction 'take taxiway right', which was misheard as 'backtrack if you like', but the controller did not subsequently verify the DC8's position as still on the runway. The TAA captain did see the DC8 ahead but made the decision that it would be avoided using normal take-off techniques. The investigation report concluded that had the 727's take-off been abandoned when the captain sighted the DC8 ahead it could have been brought to a halt some 2,000 feet short of the Canadian aircraft. Alternatively, if the 727 captain had elected to climb out more steeply the collision would have been avoided. Though both aircraft were damaged there were no injuries to passengers or crew.

TAA received good news from Western Australia as the year began. The State's minister for transport, R.O'Connor, advised Sir Frederick Scherger that the government of Western Australia would welcome TAA's entry on the Perth–Darwin route. Scherger wrote to Cotton at once, reminding him that TAA had applied many times for a licence to operate the service 'but had been refused on the grounds that a monopoly for this service had been granted to MacRobertson Miller Airlines until 1 September 1971'. That date was now fast approaching and TAA needed time to acquire suitable aircraft. He formally requested that TAA be licensed 'to operate the service from Perth to Darwin and return, landing at Port Hedland, with the rights to pick up and put down traffic at Port Hedland'.[21]

Overall, however, domestic aviation growth had stalled. Ryland told TAA staff in April: 'Our present difficulties followed steps earlier this year aimed at dampening inflation in the Australian economy. These moves led to a dramatic downturn in domestic airline traffic which eliminated industry growth. This happened suddenly and to a greater extent than expected. In terms of gross revenue loss the decline of 10 per cent in passenger volume represents about $7.75 million per annum ... Cutting costs has been the only effective means by which the decline in revenue could be contained.'[22] Scherger wrote to his minister: 'Restrictions on Government departmental spending and a downward turn in business in the private sector of the economy as a result of Government warnings on inflationary trends indicate that traffic growth for the ensuing financial year will be at a lower rate than that experienced over the past few years'.[23] (Cotton approved a 6.5 per cent increase in fares and cargo rates for the two major domestic airlines in August.)

The 1971 year brought a milestone of note in the changing composition of the TAA fleet. On 30 April the airline's two remaining Electras, VH-TLA and VH-TLB, were retired from service. Both had been introduced into service in July 1959, and between them they had accumulated some 68,000 hours in the air. (TAA's first Electra, VH-TLA, entered service on 8 July. Its third Electra, VH-TLC, had been retired on 1 November 1970.) The Electra was the first 'heavy' aircraft purchased by TAA under the terms of the two-airline policy and the first aircraft operated with a maximum gross weight in excess of 100,000 pounds. It was also, at the time of its introduction, the most costly (at $2.2 million per aircraft) and the fastest (cruising at 405 miles per hour) and had the longest range (2,900 miles). Except for a few DC3s operating in Papua New Guinea the TAA fleet had now been streamlined to four types — the 727, the DC9, the Friendship and the Twin Otter.

There were also significant administrative changes at the most senior levels in TAA. John Chapman, deputy general manager since April 1968, retired on 23 July 1971 after a long career that began in September 1946, when he took up the position of manager and chief flying instructor of the National Airlines School. John Watkins, who had played such a pivotal part in the equipment choices that had established both TAA's worldwide reputation and its commercial competitiveness, retired on 16 July after eighteen years as director of engineering. No new deputy general manager was appointed to replace Chapman. Instead, Reg Bailey and Lyn McKenzie were appointed assistant general managers. Bailey was made responsible for engineering and operations, McKenzie for commercial activities. (F. W. [Frank] Austin directly headed TAA engineering as engineering manager.) Earlier in the year, on 6 February, Lyle Byrne, secretary to the Commission, had retired after more than twenty-three years of service, twelve of them as secretary, and was succeeded by L.J. Fitzgerald.

On 20 June the Commission noted, 'The transfer of operations from Essendon to the new Tullamarine Airport proceeded smoothly ... TAA achieved the first domestic airline arrival and departure on the first day of operations.'[24] The new airport, as expected, diluted revenues for both TAA and Ansett. The domestic passenger loss from the Melbourne–Sydney route in 1970–71, the first year of Tullamarine operations, totalled 138,766 passengers, worth $3.7 million in revenue. TAA lost 61 per cent of this traffic (worth $2.25 million). The loss of international traffic reduced growth in domestic traffic volumes over the Melbourne–Sydney route from 12.4 to 2.8 per cent. (TAA's loss was 10.2 per cent, Ansett's 6.9 per cent.)[25]

While all these matters occupied the Commission and TAA management, Scherger had also to press his minister, as TAA's twenty-fifth anniversary approached, on strategic issues of longer-term significance. He wrote to Cotton again in August 1971 to remind him that from 1 October the agreement between MacRobertson Miller Airlines and the Commonwealth would cease and that any claim that may have existed for exclusive rights on the Perth–Darwin route by Ansett Transport Industries would disappear. 'A Commonwealth licence to TAA to operate between Perth and Darwin', he wrote, 'would be the first necessary step in extending the two airlines system to Western Australia'.[26] The Commission, he said, opposed the granting to ATI of an application to introduce a sixth Fokker F28 jet for use by MacRobertson Miller. ATI's high-density noncompetitive network, he reminded Cotton, produced 18 per cent of the ATI airline revenue ton miles in 1970 compared to only 1.5 per cent of total TAA revenue provided by its much smaller noncompetitive network. (Both TAA and Ansett, as the Western Australia route issue was debated hotly and publicly, produced booklets setting out their opposing views.)

Only a week later he wrote to restate the Commission's view of the existing two-airlines system in the light of the possibility that the government might extend the term of the Airlines Agreements. 'Since 1957', said Scherger, 'the Commission has moved from a pre-eminent position as the leading airline within the government policy to a position secondary in importance behind ATI. This has occurred because, firstly, ATI has over a period absorbed a number of independent airlines and, secondly, has obtained competitive licences through the rationalisation machinery and expanded into areas where previously TAA was the sole operator. The position has now been reached where the ATI airline group is pre-eminent with a significantly larger and stronger airline operation.'[27] (Ansett, for his part, renewed his criticism of TAA's use of superannuation funds in its trading operations and suggested to the government that TAA should become a public company.)[28]

Scherger's third area of concern was Papua New Guinea and the airline's position there when internal self-government was reached. 'It appears to the Commission', he said, 'that this matter is becoming increasingly urgent and that, in the interests of both Australia and the Territory, now is the time to put the future civil aviation policy for the Territory on a sound basis'. He reiterated the Commission's request for powers to set up a subsidiary airline, 'Airlines of New Guinea', to allow the Administration to acquire an equity in the airline.[29] All three issues, of course, had been raised before. All had political significance for the government as all directly affected Ansett. The minister had not indicated a willingness to listen as attentively as he had in the past to protestations from Ansett.

For TAA staff, however, September 1971 was a time to celebrate the survival and rapid expansion of the airline. TAA's twenty-fifth birthday was marked by a re-enactment, on 9 September, of the airline's first flight in 1946. The 28-eight-year old DC3 *Hawdon*, which had made that inaugural flight, took off from Laverton with twenty-one passengers, thirteen of whom had travelled on the initial flight.

Financially, despite the many problems of the industry, the 1970–71 year was a satsifactory one for TAA, and it was able to meet its first 10 per cent dividend target ($1.5 million) despite the heavy fall-off in business in the final six months. When Cotton tabled the TAA annual report in the federal parliament on 9 November it disclosed a record profit of $1,887,423 after tax.

The approval sought by TAA to buy four Boeing 727–200s was received in January 1972. Ansett, however, had not committed to his four aircraft. Cotton told Scherger on 8 February 1972: 'I have had some correspondence with Sir Reginald Ansett regarding the company's desire to have the extension of the Airlines Agreements considered by the Government as a prelude to the company confirming its orders for four of these aircraft. On 28 January I ... indicated to Sir Reginald that I hoped to submit the two-airline policy question to the Government early this year.' Cotton said that his task would be made easier if he could report positive achievements by the airlines 'in certain major problem areas which are a source of irritation and criticism and provide grounds for objections to the extension of this policy'. He listed parallel scheduling, the cessation of air services in many country areas, claims that insufficient attention was given to air freight and the need for greater initiatives from experimental cheaper fares.[30]

There was a great deal of internal reflection within TAA on the changing balance of strength between the ATI group and the Commission. A memorandum from the Commission to its minister on 20 March 1972 said: 'At the present time the Commission is operating relative to the Company [ATI] with financial penalties estimated to be at an annual rate of $5.6 million. Some estimation has been necessary as the Company does not publish airline financial information but, if these estimates are seriously inaccurate, the Commission would like to know what the Government accepts as the true comparative position.' To date, said the report, TAA had been able to operate profitably over the years despite the growing imbalance because it had achieved higher load factors. 'Up to two years ago on the main (specified) competitive routes the passenger load factor achieved by the Commission was consistently 3 percentage points higher than the Company — equivalent at current levels of trading to an advantage in profitability of $1.5 million per annum. In 1970–71 this load factor difference fell to 2 percentage points and in this financial year, 1971–72, the difference in favour of the Commission is 1.5 percentage points and falling. In recent months both load factors have been equivalent and the profitability advantage possessed by the Commission has disappeared. The financial balance can be restored only by alleviating the financial penalties affecting the Commission.' Government action, said the memorandum, had worsened the imbalance. Scherger reiterated the by now familiar list of actions proposed by the Commission to restore balance. Chief amongst them were the setting of a lower profit target to recognise the cost imbalance of $5.6 million per annum, deferment of the decision on divestment of superannuation funds, and TAA access to Western Australia's Perth–Darwin route.[31] TAA asked that Cotton pass a copy of the memorandum to the prime minister.

As this memorandum went to the minister there was a dramatic change at Ansett Transport Industries. Australia's largest road and rail transport group, Thomas Nationwide Transport (managing director Sir Peter Abeles, chairman Ken Thomas), announced that it had purchased a significant shareholding (23.5 per cent) in the Ansett group. On 7 April it announced a takeover offer for the remainder of the ATI shareholding. The initiative was widely discussed in the press and treated as a matter of national importance. The *Australian* commented: 'The whole purpose of Australia's two-airline policy will be negated unless TAA is allowed to diversify to meet competition from the new combination of Ansett Airlines and Thomas Nationwide Transport. No one at the moment can tell precisely what practical effects the new grouping is likely to have but it must be inevitable that an alliance with a joint turnover of $300 million a year and interests ranging through hotels, television, tourism, sea, land and air transport must be better equipped to cope with the fluctuating fortunes of the airline business than a corporation restricted to flying planes.'[32] The *Age* wrote that the takeover offer was 'the most serious challenge to Sir Reginald Ansett's sovereignty of Australia's turbulent transport industry'.[33]

The TNT move provoked political action at both State and Federal level. In Canberra the Senate, on 13 April, directed its standing committee on primary and secondary industry and trade to investigate the matter. In Victoria (under Premier Henry Bolte) the Victorian Parliament acted to protect Ansett by passing the Select Committee (Ansett Transport Industries) Act 1972 restricting, until 30 November 1972, the rights of substantial shareholders in any takeover offers for ATI.

That move to protect Ansett, Lyn McKenzie told the Commission, provoked 'a considerable backlash against ATI'.[34] (In a move significant for the future of both McKenzie and TAA itself he was appointed acting general manager for the period 29 April to 22 May during Ryland's absence.) *Finance Week* wrote: 'Some people who ought to know better seem to think the protection of Sir Reginald Ansett is a public duty'.[35] Journalist Maxwell Newton said: 'His [Ansett's] whole business is built on Government favours of one kind or another ... Nor should it be surprising that it was a Victorian Premier, Henry Bolte, who bailed Reg out of his biggest trouble ... Reg has taken the traditions of political patronage as the path to profit to even greater heights than yet attained.'[36]

The Senate committee looked at the degree of non-Australian ownership of TNT and ATI and 'the financial participation of non-Australian financial interests in the attempted takeover operation'. It was unable to determine the extent of non-Australian participation but concluded that the evidence did not indicate any concentration of overseas shareholdings in TNT and ATI of an order that might be regarded as control. It also considered 'the extent to which the proposed takeover might be prejudicial to the Australian aviation industry and how this might be minimised'. That concern was partly driven by the Commonwealth's financial involvement in the domestic aviation industry in airports and facilities. Among its recommendations was a requirement that ATI should publish separate airline accounts.[37]

One significant reaction to the TNT move was an indication by TNT competitors Brambles, Mayne Nickless and IPEC that they would like closer ties with TAA. For its part, TAA already had close associations with TNT subsidiaries Rudders, Kwik-As-Air, Hawthorn Taxi Trucks, TNT Courier Service and All-Trans, and revenue from the TNT group of some $265,000 per year. In addition, TNT owned or was associated with travel agents for TAA that wrote annual travel business for the airline of $790,000. TAA's attitude, McKenzie advised the Commission, was to continue existing arrangements with these businesses.[38]

On 27 April TNT announced that it would not proceed with the takeover, but by June agreement had been reached between ATI and TNT whereby ATI would register the 23.5 per cent shareholding acquired by TNT but ATI's articles of association would be amended to limit the voting rights of any shareholder to a maximum of 10 per cent. TNT was invited to nominate a representative to the ATI board. Scherger commented publicly: 'With this development it's hard to see how we will survive unless we're allowed to diversify'.[39] To Senator Cotton he wrote: 'Ansett's association with TNT strengthens further the stronger arm of the two airline policy — TAA is too small and too restricted to compete. If TNT eventually took over ATI the combined enterprise would be three times as large as TAA.'[40]

The annual report of the Australian National Airlines Commission for 1971–72, despite a demanding year, recorded a 10.6 per cent increase in revenue (to $120,072,287), but costs increased at a greater rate (10.9 per cent), resulting in a $252,537 fall in net operating profit after provision for tax. A 10 per cent dividend of $1,500,000 was paid to the Commonwealth. (Ansett, meanwhile, as part of the price paid to retain control of ATI when he was resisting the TNT takeover bid, had lifted the ATI dividend to 15 per cent.)

On 29 August 1972 the minister for civil aviation formally notified Sir Frederick Scherger of the government's decisions on the future of the two-airline policy. 'The Commonwealth', said Cotton, 'is prepared to negotiate an appropriate agreement with the Australian National Airlines Commission and with Ansett Transport Industries having the effect that the two airline policy is not to expire on 18 November, 1977 but is to be determinable by the Commonwealth or the Company on five years' notice, any such notice not to be given before the end of 1977'. As a prerequisite to this extension, he said, TAA and ATI would be required to abide by provisions in the agreement to accept ministerial direction to reduce parallel services, maintain and encourage the operation of rural air services, actively pursue the introduction of additional promotional fares and stimulate the growth of air freight. (In recent years ATI had withdrawn services from more than a hundred country airports. The government also required both airlines to keep operations within curfew periods to an absolute minimum, to accept the validity of the government's cost-recovery policy and to recognise the desirability of the minister's permitting limited expansion of other established and smaller operators (such as East-West Airlines, Connair,

Bush Pilots and Business Jets) within the framework of an economic two-airline policy.[41]

There was an additional requirement for Ansett Transport Industries. 'As a further prerequisite', wrote Cotton, 'Ansett Transport Industries Ltd is required to enter into an undertaking to furnish an annual statement of its airline results to the Minister for presentation to Parliament'. From TAA it required a change to 'its accounting arrangements relevant to the operation of its Staff superannuation schemes'. With this impost came a government undertaking 'to permit TAA to exercise its "incidental powers" so far as is legally possible so as to undertake Government contracts, outside engineering work and to enter into mutually beneficial arrangements with surface transport carriers and hotel/motel operators, the specific approval of the Minister for Civil Aviation to be required in each case.'

Of great significance, however, for TAA was a decision on the most valuable single ATI privilege by far — its complete monopoly of air routes within Western Australia. These provided Ansett with an annual profit of about $1 million and on-carriage worth some $2 million a year. 'The Government', wrote Cotton, 'has decided in accordance with the principles of the two airline policy TAA should be licenced to operate on the Perth–Darwin route via Port Hedland. Operations will not commence before June 1973 and future expansion on the route will be phased in such a way as not to give TAA equal access before June 1975.' (TAA was also to be licensed immediately to operate over the Darwin–Gove sector and on the Cairns–Weipa, Thursday Island route.)[42]

Cotton elaborated on the required changes to TAA superannuation arrangements. 'The Commission', he said, 'is to remove from TAA's business the accrued and accruing superannuation funds now employed in financing a substantial part of its activities ... The Commonwealth will assume responsibility for the eventual pension liability in respect of TAA's non-flying staff.' To provide the funds necessary for that Commonwealth responsibility, TAA was to pay to the Treasury employer contributions under arrangements similar to those applying to Commonwealth authorities generally. 'The funds required to replace superannuation provisions now used in TAA's business', said Cotton, 'will be provided as loans from the Commonwealth [with interest on the replacement funds to be related to rates applicable to first-class commercial borrowers]'. (For flying staff the Commission was required to set up a trust.)[43]

When Cotton outlined the government changes to its civil aviation policy to Parliament he summarised the place of civil aviation in Australian business life. 'Civil aviation', he said, 'is one of Australia's major industries. The Commonwealth itself has approximately $425 million invested in a wide network of airports and airways facilities, while the value of aircraft and other assets of airlines and general aviation operators exceeds $680 million. Total employment in the industry is more than 50,000 people. Last financial year our airlines carried 8 million passengers. Our aviation policies are, therefore, of utmost concern to the nation.'

Changes were also imminent in Papua New Guinea aviation. On 5 September 1972 Senator Cotton and the Papua New Guinea chief minister, Michael Somare, announced that the Territory was to have a major role in shaping its own future aviation policy. 'A single national airline with Papua New Guinea Government involvement would', said Somare, 'be best for Papua New Guinea'. It was proposed, he said, to offer shareholdings in the airline to Ansett Airlines of Papua New Guinea, Trans-Australia Airlines and Qantas. 'This national flag carrier in the field of civil aviation', said the joint statement, 'would be a symbol of unity within Papua New Guinea'.[44]

Ryland told the Commission that 'until the new internal airline is formed we aim to continue operations, maintain separate identity and avoid any appearance of running down, both for business and staff morale reasons'. (TAA's fleet in Papua New Guinea comprised five F27 Friendships, seven DC3s and four DHC6 Twin Otters. Total staff was 377.)[45]

By far the most significant change in 1972 for both TAA and Ansett came on 2 December when the nation went to the

Arrival at Mascot of the first official TAA flight (Skyliner "Hawdon") from Melbourne, 9 September 1946, after touchdown, 8.35 am. It had left Laverton RAAF base at 5.45 am.

Essendon Airport not long after TAA commenced operations. The low building facing the tarmac in the centre of the picture was the original TAA passenger terminal. The road at left is now Tullamarine Freeway.

The DC3 Hawdon – formerly a wartime C47 with the USAF known as “Shanghai Lil” – took three hours to fly TAA’s first service from Melbourne to Sydney.

The Convair 240, under development at San Diego in 1946, caught the attention of TAA. It saw in this revolutionary new aircraft the opportunity to take the lead by becoming the first airline with a pressurised airliner on its main routes.

TAA's first general manager, Lester Brain (right), with John Ryland who succeeded Brain as general manager in February 1955.

Safety demonstrations were a much cosier affair in the cabin of a DC3 during TAA's early operations.

The Douglas DC4 was popular with pilots, and it enabled TAA to commence trans-continental services to Perth on an equal footing with its competitors.

The Convair played a pivotal role in the survival of TAA from 1948.

TAA bought five De Havilland Dragon DH84 aircraft when in April 1949 it took over the 3,760 miles of internal network operated by Qantas. The DH84s were used on services in the Gulf and Channel country, for Royal Flying Doctor Services flights and for dingo baiting.

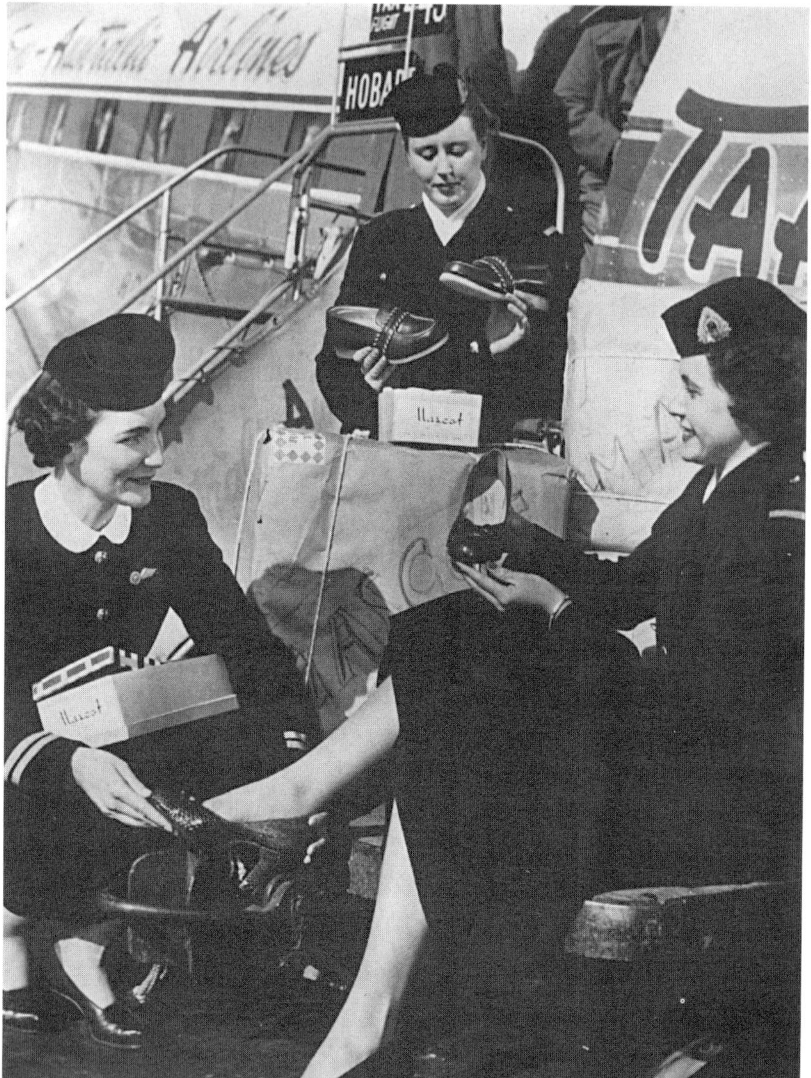

Elaine Smith (left), who later became Air Hostess Superintendent, and her colleagues are taking part in an early promotional photographic shoot for new air hostess uniforms.

TAA's first Viscount aircraft arrived in Melbourne in October 1954, the second and third in mid-December, and the fourth later in the month. The Viscount gave TAA dominance on Australia's trunk routes.

The Melbourne maintenance base for TAA aircraft in 1955 was at Essendon Airport. Aircraft on the tarmac include DC3s, a DC4, a Viscount and Convair 240s. The low building in the centre was the passenger terminal.

TAA training and development manager Captain Frank Fischer, on a pre-flight check.

A 1958 Australian National Airlines Commission meeting. Left to right: J. Chapman (assistant general manager), J. E. V. Murdoch, Sir Giles Chippindall (vice-chairman), S. H. Crawford (secretary), W. D. McDonald (chairman), J. P. Ryland (general manager), Brigadier A. S. Blackburn and K. H. Vial.

As its rural network continued to expand, TAA bought the tri-motored De Havilland Drover for its Gulf and Channel and Royal Flying Doctor services. The Australian-built Drover, seen here refuelling at Mitchell River homestead in 1959, could carry seven passengers.

TAA placed an order for six Fokker F27 Friendships for delivery in 1959. The F27, like the Viscount, used Rolls-Royce Dart engines.

A unique day for TAA. Three new aircraft arrived at Essendon Airport near Melbourne together on 24 June 1959. In front, a Lockheed Electra, followed by a Vickers Viscount and a Fokker F27 Friendship.

One of the Douglas DC6Bs operated by TAA under the cross-charter agreement that led to it exchanging turbo-prop Viscounts with Ansett Airlines of Australia for DC6Bs.

Described by an Australian aviation writer as "the last of the gracious aeroplanes", the TAA Lockheed Electra had a comfortable lounge area at the tail of the aircraft.

The single-engine Otter saw service with TAA in Papua New Guinea.

The Douglas DC9's self-operating stairs increased the aircraft's flexibility. The DC9, fitted with special low-pressure tyres, was used to operate proving flights by TAA into airports in the north-west of Western Australia during a period when the airline was seeking access through Western Australia from Perth to Darwin.

Australian National Airlines Commission, 10 December 1960. Left to right: L. G. Packer, Ken Vial (vice-chairman), Lyle Byrne, Sir Giles Chppindall (chairman), John Ryland (general manager), J. E. V. Murdoch, E. C. Wackett and John Chapman (assistant general manager).

TAA operated helicopters as an extension of interstate air services into Melbourne. This TAA helicab flew passengers between Essendon Airport and the helipad on the Yarra River, opposite the present-day site of Southbank and Crown Casino.

Hiller helicopters in TAA livery.

Signing the contract for the Boeing 727. Standing (left to right): Dick Pope (finance director), Reg Bailey (flight operations director) and Les Fitzgerald (legal officer). Seated (left to right): Two Boeing representatives, Sir Giles Chippindall (chairman), John Ryland (general manager) and John Watkins (engineering director).

A TAA Boeing 727-100 rolls out of the Boeing factory at Renton. In November 1962 the government gave its approval for the purchase of the first Boeing 727. It arrived in 1964.

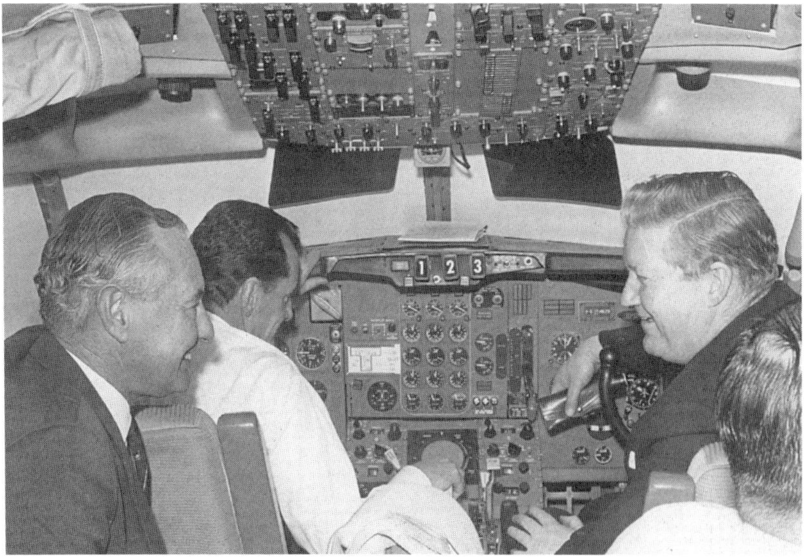

An early visitor to see the first TAA Boeing 727 flight simulator was Director of Civil Aviation Don (later Sir Donald) Anderson. Anderson was later appointed chairman of Qantas. He is sitting in the right-hand seat alongside TAA flight training and development manager Captain Frank Fischer with TAA general manager John Ryland looking on.

Flying boats are not usually associated with TAA, but in the early days of operators in Papua New Guinea the airline operated amphibious Catalina aircraft on their Sunbird services, after taking over operations from Qantas. The last Catalina service was in 1965.

This Bristol freighter saw service with TAA in Papua New Guinea.

Before computers, reservations staff kept track of flight bookings on paper records and maintained a large board to enable staff, when answering phones, to check flights with seats available. Reservations rooms were maintained in all capital cities and in many regional centres before the advent of modern telephone services that permitted regionalisation of reservation centres. TAA ordered a computer to automate its reservation system in 1966.

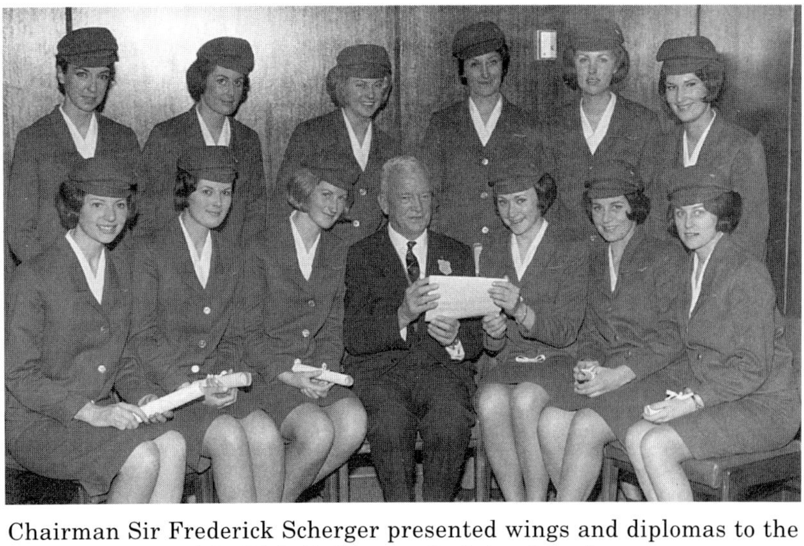

Chairman Sir Frederick Scherger presented wings and diplomas to the 1966 graduates of the TAA Air Hostess Training School.

The Douglas DC9 was the second pure jet aircraft in the TAA fleet. The airline's fleet of DC9s was grounded for six weeks while TAA fought and won a significant industrial battle over the planned use of just two pilots in the cockpit.

Gathered around the "Chart Room" table at TAA head office at 50 Franklin Street, Melbourne, on the airline's 21st anniversary on 9 September 1967 were the chairman, Sir Frederick Scherger, and the airline's management committee. From left: schedules planning manager Tony Dignam, finance director Dick Pope, engineering director John Watkins, assistant general manager Captain John Chapman, Sir Frederick Scherger, general manager John Ryland, commercial director Lyndon McKenzie, operations director Captain Reg Bailey and Commission secretary Lyle Byrne.

One of several De Havilland Twin Otters which TAA used initially in Papua New Guinea and later on flights into outback Queensland and for services between Queensland coastal cities and island resorts.

Left to right: Lyn McKenzie, commercial director, John Ryland, general manager, Stanley Brogden, aviation journalist, and John Watkins, engineering director.

TAA vice-chairman, Air Vice Marshall Wackett, shakes hands with a Boeing executive at the delivery in Seattle of a Boeing 727. Looking on are flight operations director Captain Frank Ball and chief maintenance engineer Jim Brunkhurst.

A TAA DC3 prepares to taxi at Mt Hagen in the Papua New Guinea highlands.

Captain Frank Ball as manager flight operations presents a diploma to a graduate of the TAA Air Hostess Training School. Captain Ball later became the airline's fourth general manager.

Hawdon was the centre of attention in 1971 when passengers prepared to board the aircraft for a flight to re-enact the airline's first service.

Sir Arthur Coles, TAA's first chairman, was congratulated on his 72nd birthday by some of his former colleagues from the airline's formative years. From left: Captain Reg Bailey, Captain John Chapman, former commercial director John Broderick, first public relations manager Ian Sabey, Sir Arthur Coles, Lester Brain, Dick Pope, John Watkins and New South Wales manager Geoff Sheppard.

Air hostess uniforms reflected the changing fashions through the decades.

Management information services manager, Bill Chatham (left) explains a new reservation computer installation to general manager Lyndon McKenzie, chairman Ken Vial and assistant general manager Tony Dignam.

The contract for the purchase of four European Airbus A300B4 jets was signed by TAA and Airbus Industrie on 10 December 1979. From left: Hugh Tansley, regional sales manager, Airbus Industrie, George A. Warde, vice-president, Airbus Industrie, Sir Robert Law-Smith, chairman of TAA, Lyndon McKenzie, TAA general manager.

TAA chairman Sir Robert Law-Smith, 1979.

TAA chairman Sir Robert Law-Smith addresses guests at the official welcoming ceremony of TAA's second Airbus A300B, VH TAB, at Brisbane. The aircraft was later christened the *John Oxley*, after the Australian explorer, by the Governor of Queensland, Sir James Ramsey.

In September 1979 Robert Law-Smith advised the government that its choice for a wide-bodied aircraft would be the Airbus A300B4. Delivery of the first Airbus was in mid-1981.

Experts gather at the TAA Catering Centre in Melbourne which provided catering for TAA and most of the international airlines operating in and out of Melbourne International Airport during the 1980s.

Australian Airlines flight attendants show off the flexible combinations introduced during the 1980s.

Flight attendants modelling new uniforms introduced during the 1980s.

Australian National Airlines chairman Neil Smith, who joined TAA in 1983.

Frank Ball, general manager, 1973.

James Strong joined TAA as general manager in December 1985.

Ted Harris became Australian Airlines chairman in November 1987.

John Schaap joined Australian Airlines as general manager in July 1989.

Passengers and crew from this Boeing 737-300 got together on 31 October 1990 to welcome in deregulation of the Australian domestic airline industry.

polls in a federal election. The long reign of the Liberal–Country Party coalition ended with the return of a Labor government. The new prime minister, Gough Whitlam, took office on 5 December. It was not until 19 December, however, that the full Whitlam ministry was sworn in. The new minister for civil aviation was C. K. (Charlie) Jones.

CHAPTER 13

1973

At risk

Although the Labor victory on 5 December 1972 was unambiguous, the precise composition of the House of Representatives remained uncertain because the results in some closely contested seats were not known until Friday, 15 December. So it was not until Monday, 18 December, that the Federal Parliamentary Labor Party — the Caucus — assembled to elect those who would form the full ministry. Between 5 December and 19 December, when the full ministry was sworn in, the Whitlam government operated as a duumvirate with Gough Whitlam and Lance Barnard, the deputy prime minister, holding between them all twenty-seven portfolios. For those two weeks the prime minister was minister for transport and civil aviation. Charlie Jones formally became minister for transport and civil aviation on 19 December, but TAA was made aware of his authority on the first day of the Whitlam–Barnard duumvirate. The *Sydney Morning Herald*, on 5 December, reported: 'Mr Jones (Transport) says TAA will be directed to lower fares'.[1]

Two days after Jones took office Scherger wrote to him with congratulations and a Commission brief. Matters of major concern to the Commission, he said, were the pending divestment of its superannuation funds; TAA entry to the Perth–Darwin service; amendments to the Commission's Act to permit diversification of activities; and TAA's part in future airline operations in Papua New Guinea.[2]

Despite these strategic concerns TAA was able to report encouraging competitive results on the trunk routes for the calendar year that had ended. Ryland told staff that DCA figures for 1972 showed that TAA had carried just over three million passengers while Ansett Airlines of Australia had carried 2,846,249. TAA growth during the year had been 8 per cent, Ansett's 4.7 per cent. In mid December the first of the airline's four Boeing 727–200s was delivered. (Twenty feet longer than the existing TAA 727s, it carried up to thirty more passengers — giving it a maximum of 151 seats — and had 67 per cent more cargo space. It went into regular service on 1 March.) TAA confidence was obvious. It was announced that more than $3 million would be spent in 1973 on construction of new passenger and cargo terminals at Sydney airport.[3]

TAA made a swift response to the new minister's edict on fares. On 22 February 1973 Scherger told Jones that the airline proposed to introduce 'two new creative fares — off-peak fares and advance purchase excursion fares (APEX)'. They would, he said, 'bring air travel within reach of more people and improve revenues'.[4] (Off-peak fares, providing a 15 per cent reduction on return fares, were introduced in June 1973.)

Jones also wanted to see closer cooperation between Qantas and TAA, and a meeting was held between Ryland and Qantas managing director Captain Bert Ritchie in Sydney on 15 February to advance this agenda. The new minister indicated his willingness to allow existing superannuation fund provisions to stand pending clarification of government policy. In fact, the Commission had accepted divestment in principle but had opposed the terms under which it was to take place. ((The Cotton plan for divestment had imposed terms that would have increased TAA costs by $600,000 in the first year, rising with each subsequent year. The previous government had prepared the way for divestment by including in the federal budget an amount of $25 million for loans to the Commission and by amending the Australian National Airlines Act in respect to borrowing limits and profit targets.) TAA had been investigating the establishment of independent trusts for both ground and flying staff funds. The aim had been to achieve a scheme of divestment that would not increase TAA's costs and would minimise the outflow of funds.[5]

The funds involved were considerable. The cost of superannuation for TAA ground staff was estimated to be $1 million per annum more than the cost of superannuation for Ansett. Under existing arrangements employee contributions were paid to the Commonwealth Superannuation Fund, but TAA's superannuation contributions were used in the business. They totalled some $22.5 million (in mid-1973), for which TAA charged itself an interest rate of 5.5 per cent. In the flying staff fund the pilots' contributions were paid over to a trust and invested outside the business while TAA's contributions were, in the main, used in the business. (The principle of TAA's using superannuation funds in the business as approved by Treasury in 1957 rested on the broad base that cash outgoings for pensions year by year were matched by cash inflow, leaving a large frozen cash fund to be permanently invested in trustee securities — mainly Commonwealth Bonds.)

On 20 February 1973 Charlie Jones issued a statement that was to set the overall agenda for TAA's future. He announced that 'the Australian National Airlines Bill would be amended to honour an undertaking by the previous Minister for Civil Aviation in the Liberal government (Senator Cotton) when the Two Airline Agreement was re-negotiated on October 17, 1972. Senator Cotton then assured the Chairman of the Commission, Sir Frederick Scherger', said the Jones statement, 'that the ANA Bill would be amended to permit TAA to enter fields such as hotels and motels, road transport, aviation engineering work for outside organisations; to operate within Papua New Guinea after independence if permitted by the PNG Government; and to operate services in any State where the State government enacted legislation referring sufficient powers to the Commonwealth to enable the Commission to provide such services'.[6]

Not all was sunshine and light for TAA. No diminution in the profit target set was contemplated. Jones told Scherger on 28 March that traffic growth rates should better place the Commission 'to meet the profit target determined by my predecessor'.[7] Ryland reported to the Commission: 'Since the Labor Government came into power there has been an increase in activity in Industrial Relations, especially from the point of view of directives being issued by the Government to TAA and Qantas in certain areas. These include an additional week's leave, advice that long service leave provisions would be improved substantially, a 35-hour week to be introduced during the life of the present Government and in all probability within the next eighteen months, and an increase in the annual leave loading from 17.5 to 30 per cent. The general approach is that TAA as an instrumentality will have to apply whatever is decided by the Government but it will be up to Ansett as to whether or not it wishes to fall in line.'[8]

The future of airline operations in Papua New Guinea was decided in May 1973. The Territory was to have its own new airline — Air Niugini — (though not in the manner envisaged by the Commission) and was to acquire without payment some $24.5 million worth of airfields, navigation aids and other assets belonging to the Department of Civil Aviation. A new airport for Port Moresby and a second new airfield near Lae were promised. Papua New Guinea was to have a 60 per cent equity in the new airline, giving it control, and the right to buy out a planned 24 per cent TAA and Qantas shareholding as well as a planned 16 per cent Ansett holding. Under the agreement all staff employed by TAA and Ansett Airlines of Papua New Guinea were, if they wished, to get jobs with the new airline. At independence Papua New Guinea was to negotiate a bilateral agreement with Australia for air services between the two nations.[9]

Jones introduced the Australian National Airlines Bill 1973 in the House of Representatives on 3 May 1973. As drafted it would have given TAA more than had been promised by Cotton, but it was amended by agreement between the government and opposition parties — which controlled the Senate — removing all reference to the 'Corporations Power' in the Constitution. (This power would have enabled the Commonwealth to give TAA as prime movers the ability to engage in land and air services on an interstate and territorial basis, as well as intrastate, without legal requirement for reference of power by the States concerned. It also would have given TAA a prime power to enter the hotel and accommodation industry independently of any other part of its business.) The amendments to the Bill also removed the prime power for TAA to engage in interstate road transport.

In effect the changes meant that any operation involving the provision by TAA of road transport, hotels, accommodation, engineering work and aerial work had to be 'incidental' to the provision by TAA of airline and charter services. The Bill as amended did give TAA power to provide for the Commonwealth and its instrumentalities aviation, land transport and engineering services as well as other services from its own resources; to acquire or establish subsidiaries; to invest moneys not immediately required for the purposes of the Act in any manner approved by the Treasurer; and to operate in Papua New Guinea in accordance with arrangements between the governments of Australia and that country. Ryland told the Commission: 'The Bill substantially fulfils the undertakings given by the previous Government last year'.[10] The proposed legislation was passed by the House of Representatives but the Senate further amended the Bill to compel TAA to change its staff superannuation arrangements so that accrued employer superannuation funds could not be used in its business. The amended legislation was returned to the House of Representatives for further consideration and was passed by both Houses on 21 August. The Act provided that divestment should take place four weeks after the Bill received Royal Assent — on 21 September. (On that day, as required under the Act, the accumulated superannuation funds were passed to a Trustee and an initial amount of $29.4 million was lent by the Trustee to the Commission.)[11]

Sir Reginald Ansett was concerned by the initiatives of the Labor government, writing to Ryland on 7 June that costs in the industry had risen dramatically as a result of industrial decisions. 'The effects of the National Wage case', he said, 'and the granting of four weeks annual leave were alarming and these, combined with an abnormally large number of known Award changes which will take place during the fiscal year 1973–74, indicate a need to adjust current fares and freight rates.'[12] The government's vigorous industrial relations agenda sat awkwardly with the minister for civil aviation's agenda for lower fares. Ansett had objected to the TAA proposal for APEX fares. Scherger told Jones on 14 June that 'we have reached the conclusion that the APEX fare should be held in abeyance for the present'.[13]

The 1972–73 annual report of the Australian National Airlines Commission for the year to 30 June 1973 showed that TAA had increased its total revenue by 10.9 per cent over the previous year but that total costs had risen by 11.4 per cent. Net profit after tax was $1,966,327. The payment to the Commonwealth in the nature of a dividend was $1.5 million, or 10 per cent on a capital of $15 million. TAA was now serving 153 ports within Australia and Papua New Guinea as well as operating regular scheduled services to Cocos Island and to five external ports — Bacau (Portuguese Timor) under charter to Transportes Timor, and, on behalf of Qantas, Jayapura (Irian Jaya) and the British Solomon Island ports of Munda, Yandina and Honiara. Flying staff totalled 1,252. The airline's fleet comprised one Boeing B727–276, six Boeing B727–76s, twelve Douglas DC9s, 18 F27 Fokker Friendships, ten De Havilland Twin Otters (DHC6s) and nine Douglas DC3s. On order were three Boeing B727–276s.

TAA also provided flight crews and engineering support for the six DH Dove aircraft operated by the Northern Territory Aerial Medical Service, which provided emergency aerial ambulance and medical services to isolated outback stations as well as regular medical inspection tours for preventitive medical and dental treatment. The Royal Flying Doctor Service (Queensland Division) provided a similar emergency service to people living in remote areas of Queensland. TAA had been closely associated with this service since 1946 and provided complete engineering support for its three Beechcraft A80 aircraft.[14]

The outlook for the 1973–74 financial year was bright. After two years of reasonable growth the rapid rise in national economic activity had been reflected in a surge in traffic, evident from March but accelerating sharply in May and June. Both TAA and Ansett forecast an annual growth rate for 1973–74 of 14 per cent.

In the Budget speech of the Labor government on 21 August 1973 the Treasurer, however, had some unpleasant items for the airline industry. (Both airlines were bound by the 1973 Airlines Agreement to achieve the cost recovery objectives set by the government for the use of its facilities. The government objective was to recover 80 per cent of the annual cost of these facilities by 30 June 1978.) The Treasurer announced increased lease rentals on government-owned airport properties, five cents a gallon fuel excise, and adjustments to charges for postal and telephone services. In all they added $3.29 million to TAA's costs for the remainder of the financial year. On 22 August Scherger wrote bluntly to his minister advising him that these extra costs would require a fare and freight increase of 3.5 per cent. In previous correspondence TAA had advised that the cost increases already in train for the industry required an 8 per cent increase in rates. He requested approval from Jones from 1 September of a 10 per cent increase in economy class fares, a 16 per cent increase in first class fares and an 11.5 per cent increase in cargo rates.[15] (Jones approved the increases, which came into effect on 20 October.)

On 30 August Scherger made a major announcement. 'TAA, for a period of years, has sought the opportunity to provide competitive services in Western Australia, the Northern Territory and Cape York Peninsula', he said. 'We are pleased that the Government has now recognised these claims. TAA will immediately undertake planning and discussion where necessary which will enable these competitive services to be commenced at the earliest possible date.' The statement also confirmed that the airline was 'studying the government's policy decision to give TAA greater opportunity to diversify its activities including the possibilities of entering into beneficial arrangements with surface transport carriers and hotel/motel operators'. It was TAA's intention, said Scherger, 'to enter into arrangements mainly with existing businesses which will stimulate the tourist industry generally'.[16] (One of the first initiatives, in November 1973, was the Commission's joint participation with Mayne Nickless Ltd in the formation and operation of a limited liability company, TAA–Mayne Travel Industries Pty Ltd, to operate in the hotel and coach tour business.)

While Western Australia had for long been seen as a valuable addition to TAA's network, South Australia, where ATI operated, was not coveted. The premier of South Australia had indicated to Cotton in October 1972 that his government would like to see TAA operate in his State — though TAA had not seen this correspondence at the time. In September 1973 Scherger advised Jones that this correspondence had now come to his attention. His response, he said, was that while the Commission would like to expand its operations within South Australia it was apparent that this would not be in the best interests either of the State or TAA until traffic volumes increased sufficiently to justify a second airline. TAA, he said, 'would not have an economically viable operation by sharing equally the intrastate services with Ansett Airlines of South Australia'. The Commission, he said, would reconsider the matter in twelve months.[17] In a further review of its overall operations TAA made the decision to withdraw from all Twin Otter operations in the Gulf and Channel areas of Queensland and the Northern Territory by 31 December 1973, as well as from the Mount Isa–Tennant Creek route.[18] It planned to encourage commuter operators to replace these services while at the same time introducing a weekly F27 service between Brisbane and Alice Springs calling at Charleville, Quilpie, Windorah and Birdsville in each direction (which placed more than forty homesteads and fifteen previous ports of call within a 100-mile drive of an airport operating the new service).

TAA's general manager, John Ryland, had not been well. *This Air Age* reported in its September–October 1973 issue: 'General Manager John Ryland, absent on sick leave for some weeks, is home from hospital and making excellent progress towards recovery. Through acting general manager Lyn Mckenzie he asked that the following message be passed to all staff: "I have left hospital to convalesce and now expect to make a rapid recovery'.[19] Only weeks later, on 20 October, he died.

John Ryland, CBE, DFC, was sixty-two and had been general manager of TAA for more than eighteen years. An airline pilot with Ansett Airways in 1939, he was called from the Reserve as a flying officer with the RAAF and during World War II rose to the rank of Group Captain. He had joined the newly formed TAA as its operations manager in 1946 and became general manager on 28 March 1955. Throughout the airline's formative and turbulent years he had played a decisive part in shaping the airline and leading its ever increasing staff. The Commission met on 26 October and unanimously decided to appoint assistant general manager Lyndon Lloyd McKenzie to succeed Ryland as general manager and chief executive officer for a period of five years commencing Monday, 29 October.

Lyn McKenzie, a South Australian, had begun his career in local government, studied accountancy and developed an accounting practice before serving as aircrew in the RAAF from 1940 to 1946. In the closing months of the war he was taken prisoner by the Japanese when his aircraft was forced down. His career at TAA began on 1 July 1946 in the finance department. After serving as manager in Victoria and in Queensland, he was appointed commercial director in 1957. He had been assistant general manager for two years and acting general manager since 6 August. His appointment was followed in 1974 by a number of senior postings. The two positions of assistant general manager were replaced by the establishment for two deputy general managers — Captain

Reg Bailey filling one, with the other left vacant. Operations manager Captain F. J. (Frank) Ball became operations director, engineering manager F. W. (Frank) Austin became engineering director. T. C. (Trevor) Fenton was appointed personnel director and A. L. (Lloyd) Hargraves became commercial Director. A. B. (Tony) Dignam, manager, administration and policy, became administration and policy director.[20]

Lyn McKenzie took up his position as TAA moved towards a generational change in aircraft. Growth rates of air traffic, which had declined in 1971 and 1972, took an upward turn at the end of 1972 and continued at a high level. It was anticipated in October 1973 that TAA's existing fleet plus the three additional Boeing 727–276s on order (and scheduled for delivery in November 1973 and April and July 1974) could handle forecast traffic until November 1974. From that date additional units would be needed. Although TAA wanted to move as quickly as possible to the use of wide-bodied aircraft of 250–280 seat capacity it was now accepted that the earliest practical date for the introduction of these aircraft was late 1976 or early 1977. (Three wide-bodied aircraft were under consideration — the Lockheed 1011, the Douglas DC10-10 and the European Airbus A300B4.) Scherger asked Jones for his approval to order four more Boeing 727-276s for the period 1974–1977 at a cost of $30.679 million, and a letter of intent was sent to Boeing. (Funds from internal sources covered most of this cost. TAA needed loan funds totalling $7.75 million in addition to its internal resources.)[21] The minister, however, advised approval of only two additional aircraft 'on the basis that future capacity needs could best be satisfied by the early introduction of wide-bodied aircraft'.[22]

Aircraft commented: 'A challenging new element in Australia's two airline trunk route rivalry — the marketing of services operated by two competing aircraft types — may develop this year and come to a real testing point in 1975–76, the thirtieth year of that contest. It rests on the respective timing by TAA and Ansett for the introduction here of wide-bodied jets and (to a degree) it owes some of its quickened interest to last month's intervention by Transport Minister

Jones on the question of airline equipment programming ... When Mr Jones returned to Australia in December from an overseas tour he made it plain from his first airport comments that (a) he had been impressed with the A300 European Airbus which he had seen at Toulouse and (b) that he thought our two domestic airlines should be introducing wide-bodied jets instead of further 727s.' Lyn McKenzie told *Aircraft* that the minister's comments were entirely in accord with TAA's thinking and planning, and though they had earlier joined with Ansett in seeking ministerial approval for four more Boeing 727s to meet equipment needs through to 1976, it was now by no means certain that TAA would seek the additional two 727s.[23] (Ansett planning was still based on 1977 as the earliest introductory date for its choice of a wide-bodied type.)

TAA finalised its staff participation in Papua New Guinea on 1 November 1973. Twenty TAA staff elected for secondment to Air Niugini, providing a nucleus of people experienced in New Guinea operations. Contracts of sale were signed for aircraft, buildings and equipment. TAA's capital contribution to Air Niugini was $480,000 and a pooling agreement was prepared covering the Brisbane–Port Moresby route. On 1 November the first aircraft to operate for Air Niugini — a former TAA F27 Friendship — took off from Port Moresby on the first flight of the new airline. The general manager of Air Niugini was Ralph Conley, formerly TAA's manager, Papua New Guinea. TAA had made its first flight into New Guinea in July 1960 with a DC6B, the first scheduled flight between the mainland and Papua New Guinea by an Australian domestic airline. That was followed by the introduction of Bristol freighters by TAA in 1961, the F27 in 1968 and the Boeing 727 on the mainland route in May 1967. Air Niugini's fleet consisted of eight Fokker F27 Friendships and twelve DC3s, all from the original TAA and Ansett fleets.

The 1973 year did not end well for TAA. In November an industrial dispute with TAA pilots (a seven-day strike in the eyes of the Commission but a 'lockout' as described by Nicholas Blain in his *Industrial Relations in the Air*) took place following TAA's dismissal of a pilot for allegedly breaching government regulations by flying an aircraft too low on a flight from Melbourne to Tasmania. To pressure TAA to reconsider its action the pilots stopped flying on 19 November and for a subsequent twelve-hour period. The TAA response was a powerful one. It refused the pilots' demands and as a result there was no flying for a week. On the issue of safety TAA would not budge. The cost to the airline was significant. TAA suffered a loss of profit of $1.5 million during the stoppage and a further profit loss in the ensuing two weeks of more than $1.1 million.[24] (The pilot concerned was offered re-employment in June 1974 but only as a permanent first officer.)

A setback of a different kind involved the ongoing politics of the two-airline system. Ansett had powerful political friends in Western Australia to help him defend his monopoly within the State. On 6 December legislation that would have enabled TAA to operate within Western Australia was defeated in the Western Australia Legislative Council. The Opposition in the Council denied the Commonwealth Powers (Air Transport) Bill a second reading. The Labor premier (Tonkin) commented that the result 'showed the power behind the Ansett lobby'.[25]

TAA responded with a proposal to the federal government that it operate direct flights between Perth and Darwin on a territorial licence. The response of the Department of Transport Air Transport Group (which replaced the Department of Civil Aviation in the Labor government's reorganisation of departments) was rapid. On 15 February 1974 C.J. (Chris) Smith, first assistant director-general air transport policy, wrote to Lyn McKenzie enclosing 'Territorial Airline Licence No. 2 which has been amended to authorise operations between Darwin and Perth'.[26] (Following the government's departmental reorganisation Charles Halton was appointed Secretary to the Department of Transport and director-general of civil aviation.) The territorial licence for the direct Perth–Darwin route did not, of course, permit operations within Western Australia, which required enabling legislation by the State Parliament.

The monopoly in Western Australia was the jewel in the Ansett crown. The unduplicated route length of its subsidiary MacRobertson Miller Airline Services was almost 20,000 kilometres, the number of passengers embarked annually almost 300,000. Over the period 1960–1973 the average rate of growth in passenger kilometres performed by MMA was 17.38 per cent, reflecting the rapid growth in the Western Australian economy. That compared with a cumulative rate of growth over all Australian domestic airlines of only 10.9 per cent. In 1974 future growth was assured. There was a huge backlog of work to be done to service existing communites in the Pilbara, Kimberleys and Eastern Goldfields areas based on projects already completed or under construction. Major investment projects were expected in the State for 1975–76. The stakes for both TAA and Ansett in Western Australia were substantial. Ansett, as a consequence, responded with great vigour to the Air Transport Group decision by a succession of challenges.

First, he referred the proposal to the rationalisation machinery provided under the Airlines Agreement Act. The Co-ordinator (Charles Halton) made his decision on 23 April, allowing the TAA Perth–Darwin operation without restrictions on TAA's right to Port Hedland traffic. Next Ansett appealed, under the procedures allowed, to the Arbitrator, Sir John Spicer. On 7 June the Arbitrator also decided in TAA's favour. Unbowed, Ansett then announced that he would institute proceedings in the High Court to block TAA's right to pick up incidental traffic in Port Hedland. On 21 June TAA was forced to announce that it had postponed the starting date of its first DC9 service on the route because of the Ansett court action. 'We see an Ansett appeal to the High Court', said McKenzie, 'as a desperate last bid stand to delay TAA's entry to the route'.[27]

The Ansett–TAA confrontation continued within Western Australia. In July 1974 Sir Reginald Sholl was appointed Royal Commissioner 'to enquire into the proposal for two commercial airlines to operate intra-state routes in Western Australia'. Public proceedings began on 26 August 1974.[28] (Sir

Reginald was to conclude that there should be a delay of three years before the State government decided on whether or not TAA should be allowed to operate intrastate routes in Western Australia.)

Scherger appealed to the minister on 19 July.

> In the light of the hold-up in rationalisation proceedings before the Arbitrator, caused by ATI's threat to undertake a High Court test of the Commission's incidental powers to carry intrastate traffic, the Commission seeks your approval to introduce the once weekly DC9 services Brisbane–Mount Isa–Gove–Darwin and Perth–Port Hedland–Darwin which were awarded to TAA in the Co-ordinator's decision which ATI has appealed to the Arbitrator. As matters now stand both the Co-ordinator and the Arbitrator have decided that TAA should be approved to operate these services but, as a result of ATI claims that the incidental provisions of the Australian National Airlines Act are ultra-vires the Australian Government's powers, the proceedings before the Arbitrator will be draw out to an extent that it is unlikely they will be completed before the end of the year. If ATI does undertake a High Court test of the Commission's incidental powers it will not be heard before the latter half of October and, even then, the matter may not be resolved because the High Court may decide that the issue is hypothetical.
>
> The Commission sees only one way of overcoming the problem of extensive delay in this matter and that is by introducing the services awarded by the Co-ordinator and endorsed by the Arbitrator. Accordingly the Commission seeks your permission to introduce [the services] from Tuesday 27th August, 1974 ... It is intended to carry a reasonable amount of incidental intrastate traffic on the Perth–Port Hedland–Darwin route until such time as it may become necessary to refrain from so doing because of High Court proceedings.[29]

Charlie Jones gave his approval, but Ansett reacted immediately. He instituted proceedings in the Supreme Court of Victoria on 12 August, successfully seeking an injunction, to operate until Sir John Spicer made his final decision on the rationalisation matters still before him. Sir John declined to make this decision until judgment was given by the High Court in the proceedings instituted by Ansett to test the validity of the Commission's right to carry incidental intrastate traffic between Perth and Port Hedland. TAA still had a long wait ahead before the matter was to be resolved.

Of far greater significance to TAA's future financial strength than any other single matter had been amendments introduced by the government in 1973 to the Superannuation Act 1922–1973. These provided for automatic annual adjustments of pensions of retired TAA employees in line with cost-of-living increases and imposed a new and extremely severe financial burden on the airline estimated by the Australian Government Actuary at $14 million in respect of past liability plus a large recurring and increasing annual charge.[30] Scherger wrote to Jones on 5 March, commenting: 'These amendments have resulted in the [Commonwealth Superannuation] scheme now being the most expensive retirement benefit scheme in Australia'. It was, he said, a burden not shared by TAA's competitor. The 1973 amendments, said Scherger, had 'increased the Commission's costs in this year by $3.8 million with similar increases in future years. The cost of ground staff superannuation to the Commission is now approximately $5 million per annum in excess of the matching cost for Ansett Airlines of Australia. An even-handed two airline policy is not possible with such financial imbalance'. The sums of money involved, he said, were too great to be offset by changes to the dividend target. 'The implications are so serious that it is important for a way to be found to relieve the Commission of this new financial burden.'[31]

By March 1974 TAA confirmed to the minister its assessment of the earliest suitable date for the introduction of a wide-bodied aircraft type. All three manufacturers of the types under consideration had advised TAA that for aircraft optimised for Australian conditions, a period of two years should be allowed from signing of any contract to delivery. That meant that for mid-1976 delivery a contract would have to be signed by July 1974. Such an early commitment, in TAA's view, would not allow the A300B sufficient in-service operational experience for proper evaluation. Only a small number of A300s had been sold (sixteen firm orders).

There were more serious problems with both the McDonnell Douglas DC10 (which had 202 firm orders and 125 aircraft in service) and the Lockheed L1011. In a National

Airlines aircraft in the US, fan blades of a DC10 engine had sheared and penetrated the fuselage, resulting in the ejection from the cabin of a passenger in flight. There had also been a disastrous accident involving a DC10 operated by Turkish Airlines. (The DC10 engine problem also applied to the A300B.) The Lockheed L1011 aircraft (138 firm orders, 61 in service) was under a cloud because of reservations about the long-term financial viability of both Lockheed Aircraft Corporation and its engine-makers, Rolls-Royce.

Scherger told Jones on 15 March 1974: 'In view of the reservations about all three aircraft types and the large financial commitment involved — to the order of $85 million for four aircraft, spares and associated set up costs — adequate time should be allowed to assess in depth the merits of the three alternative aircraft types available'. He recommended a timetable for selection of aircraft type by November 1974, contract signing by March 1975 and introduction into service of the first aircraft two years later, in March 1977.[32]

The Commission made further progress with its diversification initiatives in May 1974 in its second business venture outside normal airline operations. It bought a controlling interest in the Great Barrier Reef area tourist resort of Great Keppel by acquiring a 51 per cent interest in a company that owned in perpetuity the resort lease on Great Keppel Island, ten miles offshore from Rockhampton in Queensland's tropical north. (The company was Parkview [Keppel] Pty Ltd.) The resort embraced more than eight acres of beach frontage and a grazing or business lease over the remaining area of the island. TAA planned to increase the size of the resort from its existing thirty-five guest units to a minimum of one hundred units, with major improvements in the entertainment and service areas.

The Ansett–TAA duopoly in Australian domestic airline operations aroused both wonder and amusement in the *Wall Street Journal*. A reporter, William D. Hartley, wrote in June 1974: 'They fly the same types of aircraft to the same places. They own the same numbers of planes, which leave at the same times. They provide essentially the same services and food and even share information with each other. Daily, messengers carry Ansett traffic reports to Trans-Australia officials and vice-versa — not a difficult trip since their headquarters are only a block apart in downtown Melbourne. Their symbiotic relationship is so pervasive it even reaches into their separate restaurants in Tullamarine Airport here with each having the same number of tables and chairs.' Nonetheless Hartley expressed somewhat bewildered admiration for the system. 'And yet', he wrote, 'there must be something to it because at a time when airlines around the world complain about falling profits and many more seats than passengers — some American carriers have mothballed jumbo jets because they can't fill them — Ansett and Trans-Australia are happily wealthy and fill their aircraft to near capacity. The two average around 65 per cent full on their competitive routes, which are the major trunk routes, while [aircraft on] the most important route between here [Melbourne] and Sydney are filled to over 70 per cent. In comparison, major trunk routes in America were filled to only 52 per cent capacity during 1973 ... The homogenised concept under which the two work is called "controlled capacity" and, simply, it prevents either airline going wild and trying to buy too many airplanes to force the other under.'[33]

That the system worked was evident in the annual report of the Department of Transport for 1973–74. Australia's domestic airlines during the year carried more than nine million passengers on scheduled services — an increase of nearly 20 per cent on 1972–73. Capital city airports handled 76 per cent of all airline passengers. The domestic airlines employed 17,320 people (at 30 June 1974). For TAA total revenue increased by 15.8 per cent to $154,230,680. That picture of substantial growth was not matched by profit performance, however. Total revenue was up 15.8 per cent to $154,231,000, but total costs increased by 19.1 per cent. TAA's net profit declined from $1,966,327 in 1972–73 to a marginal $99,681 in 1973–74, a decrease of 94.9 per cent. Scherger, in the Commission's annual report, attributed the poor financial results to strikes both within and outside the industry and abnormal and continuing increases in wages and salaries. All the $99,681 profit went to the Treasury by way of dividend. 'At the end of the financial year', said the report, 'it was clear that costs of operation for 1974–75 would continue to rise as a result of industrial awards and increases in fuel and superannuation costs, payroll tax and prices for spare parts and supplies used by the airline'. The Commission, it said, had not yet made any provision in its accounts for its increasing and recurring superannuation costs. An overall increase of 12.5 per cent in passenger and cargo rates on 12 August 1974, said the report, 'may be insufficient to cover all presently known increased costs of operation and will not meet any part of the additional cost of ground staff superannuation'.

The seriousness of the financial implications arising from the superannuation commitments imposed on TAA was of fundamental concern to Scherger. On 15 November 1974 he wrote to his minister that 'the additional cost is of such magnitude that the Two Airline Policy is now gravely endangered and that the Government's airline, TAA, is at risk'. The $5 million difference in annual cost between TAA and Ansett was now, he said, 'of such magnitude that the Commission cannot hope to compete effectively against the radically lower costs of its competitor'. If fares were to be increased to cover the Commission's increased superannuation costs, said Scherger, 'ATI's profits would simply rise by some $5 million per annum'. If fares were not increased, 'the Commission would be faced with permanent trading losses and with no prospect of paying a dividend'.[34]

Jones appeared more concerned with the disappearance of the Commission dividend, proposing that the dividend could be paid from the Commission's realisation reserve. Scherger stood up to his minister, pointing out in a letter on 12 November that such a proposal to pay a dividend from non-trading profits was 'a major concern to the Commission and a serious departure from sound commercial practice'. The realisation reserve, which stood at just over $3 million, was specifically provided to meet possible future losses on the disposal of major assets. An examination of past records of the gains and losses when major assets had been sold, Scherger wrote, demonstrated the wisdom of maintaining the reserve.[35] The financial position of TAA was not helped by a four day pilots' strike on 19 November in support of a pay rise. Scherger told Jones on 5 December that the airline had been completely grounded by the strike, and there had been a consequent revenue loss exceeding $2 million and an estimated loss of profit of $1.3 million.

Yet another government pronouncement, as 1974 ended, threatened TAA's 'sound commercial practice' and finances. Scherger told Jones on 9 December: 'I was gravely concerned to learn last week from the Department of Transport the full impact of the Cabinet decision to place procurement functions of all statutory authorities, including those engaged in competing with private enterprise, under the control of the Australian Government Purchasing Commission. We were advised that the decision means that all our procurement of goods and services from one cent upwards would be controlled by the new Commission ... It is clear that if the Cabinet decision is implemented, TAA's efficiency and viability will be seriously affected. It may well be that this would be sufficient in the current economic climate to affect TAA's business standing to an extent that it may never recover its former competitive position ... In our view this matter is of vital importance if the Airlines Agreement is to continue, as we shall not be able to compete successfully with Ansett Transport Industries if we are subjected to the delays, added costs, and commercial limitations inherent in the proposed Purchasing Commission procedures.'[36]

Gough Whitlam was later to write in *The Whitlam Government, 1972–75*: 'My Government set out to improve the services and finances of the two government airlines' in order to 'compete more fairly with Ansett Airlines in accordance with the Government's two-airline policy'.[37] Those good intentions were not immediately evident to TAA in 1974.

It had not been a happy year for the airline and it closed with a downturn in traffic and doubts about future growth in the light of both international and domestic economic conditions. That gloomy outlook prompted Scherger to advise his minister in December that it was 'desirable to delay the introduction into service of a wide-bodied jet aircraft until early 1978'.[38]

Nature contributed to TAA's problems when, in the final days of 1974, Cyclone Tracy hit Darwin, isolating the city and causing unprecedented damage. TAA's city office was completely destroyed. All staff housing in Darwin was severely damaged and many TAA staff lost their homes. The airline nevertheless played its part in what was to be the greatest airlift in Australia's history. From Boxing Day through to 31 December TAA staff worked from 5 a.m. to 8 p.m. at the airport supervising, loading and turning round the evacuation flights. When normal services were at last resumed TAA operated from the Qantas Darwin office.

The front page headline for the December issue of *This Air Age* summarised the prevailing TAA mood. 'It's been a hard year', said the airline's staff magazine. Lyn McKenzie (who had been appointed a member of the Australian National Airlines Commission in November) told staff: 'Recent industrial unrest, rising costs and the generally poor economic climate all contributed to making 1974 one of the most difficult years in TAA's history'.[39] The actions of the government, which McKenzie was not at liberty to criticise, had hardly helped.

CHAPTER 14

1975

The harsh winds of worldwide economic downturn

Charlie Jones was prepared to be helpful. He attended a special meeting of the Australian National Airlines Commission on 23 January 1975 at which, in Scherger's words, 'several very important matters' were discussed, including the Australian Government Purchasing Commission. 'It was encouraging to learn', Scherger wrote to him after the meeting, 'that you are in agreement with the approach of the Government airlines on this matter and that you would be prepared to allow them to put their case [for exemption] to the Prime Minister'.[1]

TAA had also to cope with demands for sensitive information from a Royal Commission on Government Administration. Scherger responded strongly, pointing out that the ANAC was a business undertaking engaged in direct competition with private enterprise. He wrote to the Royal Commissioner:

> The internal workings of our major competitor, Ansett Transport Industries Ltd and its subsidiaries, will not be made available to your Commission or the public. Quite apart from the fact that we feel that the relationship between the Minister and the Commission ought to be treated as confidential to your Commission, it is considered that the competitive aspect should be taken into account ... It may assist your understanding of the Commission's approach in this matter to know that our competitor has always endeavoured to obtain information as to our relations with the

> Minister and the internal workings of TAA. A recent example of this was a full scale cross examination of one of our directors by Counsel appearing for Ansett Transport Industries at the Royal Commission into Airline Services in Western Australia.[2]

Jones was not as helpful on the critical superannuation issue. He told the Commission that, yes, he felt that each statutory authority should be treated separately from the Australian Public Service, as the authorities had different roles to play. Ideally, said Jones, if industry could afford to give employees high wages and better conditions then that was an industry matter and the Australian Public Service should not be a pacesetter in this regard. However, said the minister, the disparity in superannuation costs between TAA and Ansett had to be faced. There was, he said, the prospect that industrial pressure would, in time, bring Ansett's superannuation benefits into line with those of TAA. Like Scherger, he was opposed to a fare increase to cover TAA's increased superannuation costs as this would only raise Ansett's profits.[3]

One proposal at the meeting with Jones offered a hope of resolution. It was suggested that TAA charge its accounts, for ground staff superannuation, an amount per employee equivalent to that contributed by the ATI Group and pay that sum to Consolidated Revenue or to the superannuation Trustee handling the Commission's contributions. 'This', said the ANAC meeting minutes, 'would bring the cost structure for the Commission's staff superannuation into line with Ansett Airlines of Australia ... Under such a proposal the Government would need to meet the difference between the reduced contribution by the Commission and the actual cost of the superannuation scheme.' A working group was proposed of staff from the Treasury, the Government Actuary and the Commission to implement this proposal.[4]

Intervention in TAA administrative matters by Charlie Jones seemed boundless. He told the Commisssion in February 1995 that in line with the government's actions 'to restrain the over-concentration of both population and business interests in a relatively small number of cities within Australia', he questioned the Commission's initiatives to concentrate its operational staff in Melbourne, Sydney and Brisbane. 'I wonder', he said, 'whether these theoretical savings are in fact achieved when the need to provide more frequent overnight accommodation and back-up staff for the late running of aircraft are properly taken into account'. There were 'intangible benefits', said Jones, to society at large when crews were domiciled in towns where TAA aircraft made night stops.[5]

When the report of the Royal Commission into Airline Services in Western Australia was made known in May 1975, Scherger wrote to Jones to make clear the Commission's reaction. The general effect of the findings of the report, he said, would 'if accepted by your Government ... lead to a continuation of ATI's Western Australian monopoly for years to come'. Holding this belief, he said, and in the event of the High Court ruling in the Commission's favour on the proposed Perth–Port Hedland–Darwin operation, 'we would institute such a service as soon as possible'.[6]

It was never easy for TAA to quantify accurately the financial contribution of the airline activities of the Ansett Transport Industries group. 'The ATI report for the year ended 30 June, 1974 does not', said a report to the Commision in May 1975, 'give separate accounts for the airline operations. Airline accounts, unaudited ... were provided to the Minister and tabled at the same time as the Commission's annual report.' These showed that the ATI airline division contributed $188.6 million, or 68.8 per cent of Ansett's total revenue of $274 million. The ATI group operating profit before tax of $13.851 million was an increase of $3.227 million on the previous year.[7] That ATI profit compared with the dismal Commission profit for the year of $99,681. Lyn McKenzie told *Aircraft*: 'The biggest effect on TAA profit was a strike that amounted to a complete stoppage. That strike cost us probably $2 million. It probably made more than that for Ansett because ... he was filling every seat he had available. Each additional ticket almost became net profit.'[8]

Using information from a submission made to the Royal Commission in Western Australia, TAA estimated that MacRobertson Miller Airline Services contributed $19.705 million of the total $188.6 million 1973–74 revenue from all ATI airline activities — or some 10 per cent.[9] From the Ansett point of view Western Australia was a prize worth fighting for. The premier of Western Australia was now, with the defeat of the State Labor government there on 30 March 1974, Charles Court, heading a Liberal–Country Party government. He wrote to Scherger on 26 June, 1975 advising him that his Government proposed 'to act along the lines recommended by Sir Reginald Sholl'. He did not, he said, see the issue as simply being one of whether or not Ansett Transport Industries had a monopoly in Western Australia. 'I am therefore concerned that, resting on the concept of monopoly as opposed to the balance of benefit and disadvantage you propose instituting a Perth–Port Hedland–Darwin operation should the High Court rule in your favour.' That, he thought, was 'quite contrary to the main thrust of the Royal Commissioner's findings'.[10]

With the worst year in TAA's history barely over, the retirement on 30 June 1975 of its respected chairman, Sir Frederick Scherger, was announced, ending his nine years' service as chairman. The former chairman of the Australian Chiefs of Staff Committee and the RAAF's first Air Chief Marshal had been a strong and popular Commission chairman during a challenging and difficult period in the airline's history. His energy and realism in his confrontation of both commercial and political problems was widely respected in Canberra and the community generally. Within TAA his unfailing good humour had been a mark of his leadership. It was no mere form of words to record that his departure was a considerable loss.

Scherger was succeeded as chairman of the Australian National Airlines Commission by K. H. (Kenneth) Vial, a chartered accountant and company director, who had been vice-chairman since February 1960. (Vial was acting chairman from 30 June 1975 and chairman from 15 October.) He had been a Commission member since 1956. Richard Robert Law-Smith, CBE, AFC, a Commissioner since 1961 (and a director of BHP, CIG and the Commonwealth Aircraft Corporation), was appointed vice-chairman.

Scherger departed as Australia's combined domestic airlines recorded for the 1974–75 year the carriage of more than 9.5 million passengers on scheduled services — but the annual growth rate had fallen dramatically from the 20 per cent achieved in the 1973–74 year to only 7 per cent. The hours flown by the domestic airlines fell by 5.5 per cent. During this slowdown Ansett Airlines of Australia and Trans-Australia Airlines had each introduced three additional Boeing 727-200 series aircraft to their fleets (bringing to six the total per airline). The year had also seen a government-initiated change to fare structures under which the airlines now based their fares on a 'flag fall' charge plus a standard rate per kilometre flown. The rationale behind this innovation was the introduction of a system in which passengers were to pay the same fare anywhere in Australia for journeys of similar distances and class of travel. (It also reflected a downward tapering of fares in favour of long-distance passengers.) [11]

During the 1974–75 year Jones had approved increased fares and freight rates to provide the airlines with an overall 12.5 per cent increase in revenue. That boost, combined with good traffic growth in the second half of the financial year and a stringent cost reduction programme by TAA, lifted net profit after tax to $2,217,904. The Commission made a payment in the nature of a dividend to the Commonwealth of $1,275,000, or 8.5 per cent on its $15 million capital. Once again, however, no provision was made for the airline's greatly increased superannuation costs.[12] The federal government's Budget, introduced into Parliament on 19 August 1975, again brought cost increases for the airlines. Additional costs included a fuel levy of $2 per barrel, higher postal and telecommunications charges, the effect of wage indexation decisions and increased agents' commissions. Revenue expectations were modified, following a government decision that all government travel should be economy class from 1 September. TAA requested immediate increases in tariffs.

Competitively, however, TAA had bounced back. *Aircraft* reported that the Air Transport Group's provisional statistics for domestic airlines for the quarter ended 30 June 'show that

TAA has regained its clear passenger traffic lead over Ansett Airlines of Australia', following three months of almost level pegging. There was, though, 'little in the passenger growth rates to make the domestic airlines happy'.[13] Inflation was now a major factor. It had continued at the unprecedented rate of 17.6 per cent to March 1975 while, during the same period, average weekly earnings had increased by 27.8 per cent. Company profits had declined and major corporations such as BHP, ACI, ICI and Western Mining had announced deferment or abandonment of expansion plans. A report from the Commission for the Department of Transport noted that a $2,500 million budget deficit would be recorded by the Australian government and that it would therefore be likely to pursue tight credit policies and maintain high interest rates. 'Under these circumstances it is unlikely', said the report, 'that there will be any rapid and early expansion in the private sector, particularly if business confidence remains low'. The report concluded that it was already necessary to provide for 'very heavy cost increases in the 1975–76 financial year requiring substantial tariff increases'. That, it said, held out the prospect of 'a contraction in frequency and standards of service and employment opportunities and a serious deterioration in cost–revenue ratios, possibly leading to trading losses'.[14]

Charlie Jones continued to torment the government airline with the need to respond to ministerial initiatives. One of these was that TAA, Qantas, the Australian National Line and Australian National Rail should all use a common logo. It was an unworldly, even ridiculous proposal for TAA and Qantas in particular, both of which had spent decades and much money in establishing their commercial indentities. Vial courteously and firmly rejected the idea.[15] Early in September Jones telephoned Lyn McKenzie to suggest that the domestic airlines might consider switching to a one-class service 'so as to lessen the problems already arising from the decision that all government travel would be economy class'. That suggestion, to alter fundamentally the economics of the Australian domestic aviation industry merely to relieve the government of an embarrassing reaction by its public servants, was clearly driven by the most naked political self-interest. Ken Vial responded: 'In my view the domestic airlines could not voluntarily switch to one class service on all routes'. The industry, he said, would be seriously disrupted, there would be a net loss of revenue of about $7 million and some four jet aircraft would be surplus to requirements. 'Such disruption', wrote Vial, 'would occur during a year when the domestic airlines are fighting for survival. Government policies relating to cost of fuel, Government travel and the cost recovery policy [for government aviation facilities provided] must result in heavy fare increases at a time when air travel is depressed. Estimates [attached] show the airlines facing probable fare increases as high as 49 per cent this financial year which must depress air traffic further. The cost of a switch to one class service would increase these estimates and require further fare increases.' [16]

The 1975 Budget speech by the Treasurer had stated that the government's policy of a 70 per cent recovery of attributable costs for providing aviation facilities to the airlines should be achieved in 1975–76, with 80 per cent by 1977–78. In October 1975 TAA was asked to formally state its views on the government policy of cost recovery. Vial did so in uncompromising terms. The Treasurer's statement, said his report to Jones, 'was made without prior consultation with the domestic airlines as to its consequences'. To meet the 70 per cent recovery this year, it said, 'would add millions of dollars to costs and result in further large fare increases. These would be at ruinous levels ... Decline in traffic would accelerate.'[17]

The minister responded on 10 October 1975 that the government believed it was 'reasonable to balance any difficulties in the industry against its own problems in meeting the rising costs of operating these facilities ... The Government looks on the provision, operation and maintenance of the air transport infrastructure as a form of commercial enterprise and it quite properly regards an element of interest on its capital investment in the infrastructure as a legitimate commercial return.'[18] He did, however, indicate that he would propose to the Government that it 'modify the future course of its cost recovery policy'.[19]

Jones formally approved a 7.5 increase in air fares and a 5 per cent increase in air freight rates to take effect at midnight on 26 September, 1975. 'This approval', said a Department of Transport letter, 'effectively compensates TAA for all cost increases to date ... together with the anticipated fuel increase from 1 October, 1975 and the drop in revenue resulting from the transfer of Australian Government travel to economy class'.[20] Lyn McKenzie replied with alacrity that this statement was incorrect and that the increase approved did not compensate for the revenue loss from the government economy class travel decision.[21]

Both TAA and Ansett had always to fight ongoing political as well as commercial battles. TAA's prospects in Western Australia had dimmed with the election of the Court Liberal-Country Party Government. Now, federally, there was to be a similar political shift, though it was to come about after a drama unparalleled in Australian federal political history.

The climax approached when Malcolm Fraser (who had defeated Billy Snedden on 21 March to become leader of the Liberal Party) announced on 15 October 1975 that the Government Appropriation Bills would be blocked in the LCP-controlled Senate until the Government agreed to an election. The Senate did not directly reject the Budget or defeat the Appropriation Bills. The Opposition tactic was to refuse passage by returning the Bills to the House of Representatives. That meant, nevertheless, the effective denial of supply and the paralysis of government. On 16 October the Senate carried out the Fraser threat, deferred the Appropriation Bills and brought on a political crisis. On 11 November at 10 a.m. the prime minister, Gough Whitlam, telephoned the Governor-General, Sir John Kerr, to make an appointment to advise a half Senate election. At 1.10 p.m. Kerr, who saw it as his role to end the crisis arising from the effective denial of supply by bringing on a federal election for both Houses, dismissed Whitlam from office. Some twenty minutes later he appointed Fraser as caretaker Prime Minister on the condition that he advised dissolution of both Houses of Parliament. Just after 2 p.m. the Senate passed the Appropriation Bills. At 3.14 p.m. the House of Representatives (where Labor still had its majority) voted no confidence in the Fraser government. At 4.45 p.m. a double dissolution was proclaimed.

On 13 December 1975, following a federal election, Malcolm Fraser's Liberal–Country Party Government came to power. The new minister for transport was P. J. (Peter) Nixon.

Aircraft, which had been no friend to TAA at its birth, commented: 'It is to be hoped that TAA does not suffer like in those dark days of the past when under successive Liberal–Country Party Governments TAA — in the words of a senior TAA man — "couldn't take a trick". While there is no reason to believe Peter Nixon will be anything but entirely even-handed in his handling of the finely balanced two-airline system it is worth pointing out that it would be disastrous if the LCP Government in any way favoured Ansett — that flagship of private enterprise! — against TAA. Even if Australia has been under what some people describe as three years of creeping socialism there is no reason to throw into jeopardy the fine balance between TAA and Ansett ... The airline may be Government-owned but the senior management is free enterprise oriented.'[22]

For TAA, however, the immediate implications of the change in government were not as pressing as the realities of the market as 1976 began. In the whole of 1975 traffic growth had slumped to just 3 per cent. In January 1976 it was nearer 1 per cent. Vial told *Aircraft*: 'It [growth] is worse than ever and very disappointing because we exist on growth. The airline's ability to absorb ever-increasing costs is influenced tremendously by growth ... The traffic downturn was perhaps hastened by the election and the uncertainty.' There was some hope that the new government would look more sympathetically at the effects on the airlines of the Labor government's cost recovery programme. 'We hope', said Vial, 'that Mr Nixon will be seeking some formula making it more acceptable to the airlines while still having what he regards as a reasonable recovery programme after taking into account the effects it will have on the industry'.

Aircraft asked Vial bluntly: 'Do you think you suffered traffic-wise from Labor being in power?' It was a hard question to ask about the political party that had brought TAA into being thirty years before. 'Some Labor Ministers', said Vial, 'were quite outspoken and I think on occasions riled some sections of the business community. Ansett got a lot of sympathy traffic from that. Our traffic did diminish but there were other factors. The west coast of Australia is a matter which gravely concerns us — Ansett's (through MMA) exclusive operation up the north-west coast. It's the long hauls where you generate a lot of revenue and you build up your business. It is the on-carriage to and from Perth linking the north-west coast where we believe we are suffering. This is why we are trying very hard to get rights to operate in that area.' Vial admitted that the industry might well have an excess of capacity.[23] (TAA told Nixon that Ansett's MMA operations produced a pre-tax profit of half a million dollars while on-traffic to eastern ports was valued at some $3 million per annum. The total airline revenue produced for ATI by its monopoly operations in Western Australia, Queensland, South Australia and New South Wales was some $40 million higher than TAA's revenue from its own monopoly operations, which were, said TAA, small and just covered direct operating costs.)[24]

TAA's commercial director, Lloyd Hargraves, gave *Aircraft* a longer-term perspective. The airline's friendliness and fighting spirit, he said, had 'propelled TAA to the position which it holds today — that of an airline which in the last [1975] calendar year carried four million passengers. TAA was the first Australian airline to break the four million passenger barrier in a year.' Since 1973, he said, TAA had taken equity participation in four companies — TAA-Mayne Travel Industries (operating as AAT — Australian Accommodation and Tours), Great Keppel Island, Wanderers' Paradise Tourist Park (at Airlie Beach, Queensland) and Dunk Island. (TAA and P&O Australia Ltd jointly purchased the Dunk Island tourist resort at the beginning of 1976 from Avis Rent-a-Car Systems Pty Ltd.) *Aircraft* commented: 'As TAA moves into its thirtieth year since its foundation it is facing probably the most difficult economic circumstances it has ever faced ... The fact is that TAA — like most of the world's airlines and not because of anything which could be described as bad management — is feeling the harsh winds of the worldwide economic downturn.'[25]

TAA set another precedent as 1976 began. For the first time since Australian National Airways had been taken over by Ansett Transport Industries, TAA had ordered a new major aircraft for its fleet without a similar order from Ansett. TAA confirmed with Boeing that it would take delivery of an additional 727–276 aircraft in November. A Bill was introduced into federal Parliament on 19 February authorising the Commission to undertake borrowing of $7.4 million to buy the aircraft. (Total cost of the 727 with spares was some $9.3 million.) The purchase meant that TAA would have seven of the larger 200 series 727s compared with Ansett's six. (It followed the withdrawal by each airline of a 100 series 727 — both of which were taken out of service after Air Niugini began operating its own Australia–New Guinea services.) Since the Ansett takeover of ANA in 1957 both airlines had introduced major aircraft into service on the same day.

Ken Vial had an encouraging meeting with his new minister on the question of infrastructure costs, and Nixon accepted the TAA proposal that the working group set up by the previous government to inquire into the cost of superannuation for the Commission's ground staff should be directed to commence its inquiry. Vial was also able to express with some vehemence the TAA reaction to Charlie Jones's instruction that Commission staff must adhere to the government policy for its public servants that they travel economy class. Such travel by TAA staff, he told Nixon, was not a measure of expenditure restraint and not travel at government expense. Staff reaction, he said, had been very unfavourable, based on the belief that the order was unreasonable and lacked a logical basis. It was also, said Vial, inconsistent with the autonomy given the Commission to manage its own affairs, and the issue was becoming a major industrial one.[26]

Vial also pressed Nixon to allow TAA to take over the operation of the Sydney–Norfolk Island air service, which Qantas had operated for many years but from which it now intended to withdraw. Traffic on the route, he said, was not heavy and was insufficient for competitive operations.[27] Nixon, however, reversed the decision of the Labor government to give TAA a monopoly of the services provided to Cocos and Christmas Islands and ordered that the services be shared with Ansett. It was a specifically political decision as Nixon made clear in a letter to TAA on 1 March 1976. 'It is my understanding that the decision of the previous Government to give TAA a monopoly of this service was part of an aim to direct as much Government business as possible towards TAA. You will appreciate that, as a matter of political philosophy, I could not normally find such an arrangement acceptable ...'[28]

On the central issue threatening TAA's finances — ground staff superannuation — the new Government brought no relief. At its meeting on 17 March 1976 the Commission was advised that the government had decided to introduce a new superannuation scheme for Commonwealth public servants and staff of government authorities. TAA was automatically embraced by the new scheme. It provided for a 5 per cent contribution by employees with a pension of 50 per cent of final salary at age sixty-five together with a refund of employees' contributions plus interest. But it also provided that the pension be updated annually in line with the Consumer Price Index so that, the Commission was told, 'the new scheme continues the financial burden already flowing from the updating arrangements in the present scheme'.[29] Vial wrote to Nixon reminding him that under the Australian National Airlines Act 1945–75 the Commission was empowered to determine its own terms and conditions of employment. 'It is therefore proposed', he wrote on 5 March, 'that with the advent of the new Commonwealth scheme the Commission should institute a new superannuation scheme for its ground staff which would be less costly than the Commonwealth scheme but which would provide comparable benefits to those available to equivalent staff in Ansett Transport Industries Limited'.[30]

Ansett had also seized on a new LCP minister to make proposals of his own. Nixon advised the Commission on 8 April that ATI had made representations that the Commission should pay an increased dividend, that its capital should be restructured and that a payment of $2 million should be paid from its reserves to the Commonwealth.

TAA's reserves at June 1975 totalled $18.23 million, but included in this figure were insurance provisions of $5.849 million and a future income tax benefit of $3.673 million — a total of $9.522 million. These amounts merited exclusion from the reserve total as the funds were not available for use in the business. Their exclusion gave TAA a reserve figure totalling $8.708 million, it compared with ATI airline reserves of $17.269 million. The suggestion of a $2 million payment from the TAA reserve further worsened this comparison. The gearing ratio of debt to equity of TAA and Ansett Airlines' accounts at 30 June 1975 was TAA 258.5, Ansett Airlines 290.7. TAA's percentage of debt to net worth was more favourable. A payment from its reserves without a corresponding increase in capital meant a less favourable gearing ratio. Any increase in capital, however, had the effect of compelling a higher dividend payment in future years. TAA calculated that in order to pay a 12 per cent dividend after tax required profit to be earned on capital at the rate of 20.8 per cent.[31]

It was clear that Nixon was listening to Reginald Ansett. He told Vial on 17 March:

> In general terms we believe that the Commission should be aiming for a higher return from its annual operations than has been achieved in the past. While it is reasonable to take into account the profitability of Ansett Transport Industries Limited in setting the dividend target this is only one aspect of the matter. We recognise that the airline industry is subject to varying fortunes from year to year and it would be unrealistic to expect that good profits will be earned every year. However it seems to us that TAA should have as an annual goal a return on the Commonwealth's investment which is commensurate with the

risk involved and is designed to provide a satisfactory average dividend over a number of years.

He had noted, he said, that the level of shareholders' funds in the ATI airline subsidiaries was of the order of $50 million and the average profitability over the past two years had been some $5 million, representing a return of about 10 per cent on shareholders' funds. 'Applying this to TAA — and leaving aside the amount in insurance reserves — the comparable figure would be approximately $2.7 million. On a revenue basis and using the 1974–75 results as a guide, ATI airline profitability is about 1.8 cents in the dollar and, if this were applied to TAA's revenue for the same year, its profits should have been $3.4 million.'[32]

Nixon set a 12 per cent return on capital for TAA for the 1975–76 year. Vial, however, replied to the Nixon TAA–Ansett comparison by pointing out that there was a difference of 1.5 cents per revenue tonne/kilometre in ATI's favour over its whole airline operations and that this was a most significant financial advantage for ATI. 'As ATI's yield from competitive services should be the same as TAA's,' he wrote, 'the revenue yield from the ATI monopoly airline services which supply only 15 per cent of ATI traffic must be at a very high level to raise the overall revenue yield so far above TAA's'.[33]

The new Treasurer in the LCP government now expressed the view that the dividend targets set previously for TAA had been too low and he was looking to the Commission to make an additional retrospective payment. In a letter to Nixon on 30 April 1976, Vial argued that to attempt to raise these dividend targets retrospectively would put TAA in the position of never being certain if it had discharged its liabilities to the Commonwealth in respect of any past financial year. He pointed out that the percentage of profit retained by TAA and ATI over the five-year period just concluded (excluding 1973–74, when the unilateral pilots' strike seriously eroded TAA's profit and benefited ATI) was approximately the same — TAA retained 49.1 per cent, ATI 50.1 per cent.[34]

Both TAA and Ansett agreed on a joint request to Nixon for an increase in fares and rates of 3 per cent, pointing out, however, that this modest increase would not cover all cost increases and that a further request would come when market conditions improved. In its estimates in May 1976 for the 1976–77 year TAA forecast no growth in passenger traffic and only marginal growth in air cargo, with costs inflating at the rate of some 15 per cent. That promised a heavy loss for the year close to $15 million.

This prospect did not reduce the Government appetite for extracting more revenue from the domestic airlines. In May the Department of Transport requested that the domestic airlines suggest an acceptable method or providing an additional $10 million towards government revenue in addition to the revenue forthcoming from an announced rise of 15 per cent in air navigation charges from 1 December 1976. TAA could only respond by reaffirming that declining traffic trends and slow revenue growth, set against costs estimated to rise by some 15 per cent per annum, provided financial forecasts of 'a very heavy loss'. The problem for the domestic airlines in the coming financial year, it said, 'will be surviving and attempting to achieve profitable operations. The industry will be in no position to meet heavier taxes or additional Government imposts.'[35] The depressed domestic traffic levels led TAA to lease one of its 727s for twelve months to Iran Air until July, 1977. Ansett had sold two 727–100s and TAA had sold one. Both agreed to maintain their 10-aircraft 727 fleet when their seventh B727-200 was delivered in November–December by each withdrawing from service another B727-100. Both had options for an eighth 727–200 for delivery in April 1978. The prospects of only modest traffic growth brought a deferral of the decision to select a specific wide-body aircraft.

Ansett saw in the new government an opportunity to further a long-held ambition. In a letter to Lyn McKenzie from Charles Halton, TAA was told: 'You are aware that the Minister has received representations from Ansett Transport Industries Limited suggesting that the Commonwealth Government should give prior attention to reviewing Government policy in such a way that the rigid distinction that has previously prevailed in relation to authority to operate international services to and from Australia on the one hand and domestic services with Australia on the other should no longer prevail. Ansett Transport Industries Limited has submitted that policy should provide for the allocation of services on the basis of suitable equipment and development of an integrated Australian air transport system.' Ansett proposed, said Halton, that both Ansett and TAA should be licensed on an equal basis to provide, instead of Qantas, the Australian entitlement to operate on the Brisbane– Port Moresby and Cairns–Port Moresby routes.

He also had wider ambitions. The allocation of all regional air routes, he proposed, required a complete reappraisal to ensure that Australian transport resources were properly employed. He wanted Australian domestic carriers to be permitted to develop a substructure of regional services. Specifically he asked that the routes to Auckland, Christchurch, Wellington, Fiji and Bali be considered. Ansett was taking on Qantas. (He also wanted an investigation of the considerable on-traffic carried by Qantas from its international operations on the Australian domestic network.) 'The Department', wrote Halton, 'will be carrying out studies of the various issued raised by Ansett Transport Industries'.[36]

TAA had itself long held the view that there had been over many years a growing intrusion by international airlines into the domestic sphere, helped by the proliferation of international airports in Australia. 'Australia', McKenzie wrote to Halton on 9 June 1976, 'now has five major international airports, not counting Cairns and Townsville. The result has been that international airlines call at these five ports to pick up and set down traffic, causing serious erosion of domestic revenues.' He instanced a Qantas timetable headed 'Australian Domestic Services' as demonstrating the extent of intrusion by international airlines into domestic operations. If these international operations could not be more tightly defined and controlled, said McKenzie, then there was 'a stronger case for the Ansett proposal to allow the domestic airlines to enter the sphere of international operations'. There was, though, an evident danger. 'If the wider Ansett proposal to allow domestic airlines to operate internationally is successful, Qantas could press for even more freedom to operate within the domestic market.' He thought there was a strong case for the domestic airlines to replace Qantas on the New Guinea route and 'to operate some flights between Australia and New Zealand because of suitability of equipment'.[37] (These issues were raised as the government of Papua New Guinea indicated that it wished to acquire the shares of Qantas and TAA in Air Niugini 'to avoid potential areas of conflict of interest'.[38] For TAA that eventuality promised a privileged access for Ansett to on-carriage from Air Niugini worth some $6 million a year. In October 1976 Air Niugini was given approval to extend its services to Sydney, resulting in a combined loss for Australia's two domestic operators of more than $1 million in annual revenue.)

Ansett also urged the minister as a matter of priority to review the Commission's financial structure. 'We have emphasised many times', he told Nixon, 'that it is not the percentage dividend which TAA is set that is really critical. The critical issue is the amount TAA pays to the Commonwealth by way of dividend and this, of course, is governed by the amount of issued capital.'Evidence indicated, he said, 'that its capital should be significantly increased'. The Commission should also, said Ansett, 'make a supplementary payment in the forthcoming budget to the Commonwealth from accumulated operating profits'. Urgent action was needed, said Ansett 'to require TAA to disgorge accumulated profits to the Commonwealth and also to restructure its capital'.[39]

The government was obviously listening. In June 1976 it announced that a Committee of Inquiry under the chairmanship of the managing director of Broken Hill Proprietary Company Ltd (BHP), J. C. McNeill, would be established to examine the activities and form of management of the four Commonwealth transport business undertakings — Qantas, TAA, the Australian Shipping Commission and the Australian National Railways Commission. It had one strong political directive — to inquire 'whether the financial and other arrangements under which the instrumentalities operate are conducive to the efficient conduct of their business and whether such arrangements confer advantages or disadvantages on the instrumentalities which are not normally available to the private business undertakings'.[40]

TAA canvassed the notion of a threat to its existence from these moves when Ken Vial sent a brief to J. C. McNeill.

> 'Disposal of TAA to a party other than Ansett Transport Industries Limited would justifiably be resisted by ATI on the ground that it would destroy the two airline policy in its present form. It is clear that ATI's sustained position as one of the two airlines in the two airline system depends on the continued existence of TAA as the other. It appears that ATI is dependent upon the two airline policy and the protection it affords for its operation. This is reflected in the views expressed by its Chairman [Ansett] in his report to shareholders for 1961–62: 'Last year's Directors' report [said Ansett] referred to the 1961 Civil Aviation Agreement Act which extended the existing two airline system until 1977. The year has shown how little understood by the public is the significance of this legislation to the civil aviation industry and to this Company in particular. It gives the Company an Australia-wide aviation franchise of about 50 per cent of the industry revenue, which totals approximately $36 million per annum. This franchise is for another fifteen years and its value cannot be calculated. Nowhere else in the world is there such an arrangement which ensures civil aviation stability for such a period.'
>
> There is no reason to believe [Vial continued] that the views of the ATI Chairman have changed since that time ... If the two airline policy were to be scrapped and TAA disposed of, the ability of the Commonwealth to regulate the conduct of domestic airline services would be seriously eroded, if not lost for practical purposes. It is difficult to understand why the Government would wish to single out TAA from other Government instrumentalities and dispose of it in view of its long, unbroken record of profitability, standards of efficiency, significant contributions to Government revenue and the high esteem in which it is held by the Australian public. TAA's contribution to Government revenues through income tax, aviation fuel tax, air route charges and dividend is in excess of $30 million per annum and increasing ... Withdrawal by the Government from active participation in the domestic airline operations would, without controls similar to those which presently exist, lead to a private monopoly.[41]

There was to be no way out for TAA on the serious matter of its superannuation costs. The proposal that TAA implement its own fund and leave the Commonwealth scheme was so strongly resisted by ground staff that it could not be further considered. Vial acknowledged the situation in a letter to Nixon on 6 October 1976. 'The Commission', he said, 'believes it has no alternative but to permit eligible staff to become contributors to the current Commonwealth Superannuation Scheme and intends to do so even though no decision has yet been made by the Department or Treasury as to how the increasing liability so arising is to be funded'.[42] (Vial gave an estimate of just how large the TAA liability was. He told J. C. McNeill that in the event of the disposal of TAA a liability to the order of $60 million would arise in respect of staff entitlements for superannuation, furlough and recreation leave.)[43]

There seemed no end to the financial pressures on TAA. On 28 November 1976 the government announced a 17.5 per cent devaluation of the Australian dollar. For the airline the consequence was an increase in capital outlays and operating costs. The purchase cost of its eighth Boeing 727-200 increased by $2.27 million and the outlay for aircraft spares for the financial year rose by almost a million dollars. Additional fuel costs for the full year were estimated at $700,000. Nevertheless the strict capacity control that had been exercised by the airline gave promise that the dividend target set by the government could be met.

The 1976 year ended with two significant events. Papua New Guinea's minister for transport, B. R. Jephcott, advised TAA that Air Niugini was to repay, on 31 December, the total shareholding of Qantas and TAA in the PNG National Airline Commission. 'The Papua New Guinea Government', he wrote, 'is aware of the outstanding contribution made by the Australian Government airlines in the formation of Air Niugini and before'. He advised that the Ansett shareholding would be reduced from 16 to 12 per cent.[44]

On 2 December the Committee of Inquiry into the Commonwealth's Transport Business Undertakings made its report. There was, it concluded, no case for the disposal by the government of its shareholding in Qantas. 'Although for somewhat different reasons', said the report, 'the Committee also came to the view that there is not a convincing case to sell TAA ... The case for merger of Qantas and TAA has some appeal which, however, does not stand close analysis.'[45]

CHAPTER 15

1977

Arguments for change

In December 1976 the High Court gave its judgment in the proceedings instituted by Ansett to test the validity of the Commission's right to carry incidental intrastate traffic between Perth and Port Hedland in Western Australia. The Court found in favour of the Commission, but this welcome news was tempered by the effect of the retirement as Arbitrator of Sir John Spicer. It meant further delay for TAA. His successor, Sir Nigel Bowen, was not appointed until April 1977, and it would not be until July 1977 that the two parties appeared before him so that he could complete the hearing part heard by the former Arbitrator. The Ansett monopoly in Western Australia dragged on.

There were, though, government initiatives in train that signalled change for the domestic aviation industry. In May 1977 Nixon advised that the Department of Transport was to undertake a review of domestic air transport policy, to be directed by a high-level Steering Committee.[1] It was a timely move. The Airlines Agreement Act of 1952/72 provided that ATI or the Commonwealth could terminate the Agreement at any time after 31 December 1977, giving not less than five years' notice; the Airlines Agreement Act of 1973 expired in June 1978. Chairman of the Steering Committee was C. W. Freeland, first assistant secretary, Air Transport Policy

Division, who was required to report to the minister by 1 December 1977.

A modest addition to the competitive routes of the two-airline system was made when, in February 1977, both TAA and Ansett began regular jet flights between Cairns and Alice Springs via Mount Isa and between Sydney and Alice Springs in March. Both airlines also introduced their first scheduled jet service between Adelaide and Canberra.

In TAA itself there had been changes. Captain Reg Bailey, assistant general manager (who had begun his career in the airline as a trainee captain in October 1946), took early retirement on medical grounds in mid 1977.[2] Lloyd Hargraves had retired from his position as commercial director because of ill health as 1976 ended, after thirty years with the airline. Doug Laurie, general cargo manager, also ended thirty years of service in 1976 and retired. Neil Murray, a consultant with international airline experience, took up the newly created position of commercial services and development director.

The 1977 government review of air transport policy promised to be the most important event of the year for TAA. It gave the Commission the opportunity to set out for the minister its radical recommendation for change. In its submission, forwarded to the Department in September 1977, it identified the inherent weakness of the existing system when it dismissed the suggestion that Australia should have a three or more airline policy operating on the trunk routes. That alternative, it wrote, 'would merely increase costs and compound the inefficiencies of the present system'. The two-airline system, TAA acknowledged, was fundamentally inefficient.

The direction for Australian domestic aviation that TAA favoured was a dramatic one, rejecting completely the carefully constructed two-airline system. 'The Commission', said its submission, 'recommends that the Government open negotiations with ATI with a view to the amalgamation of the two existing airlines as soon as practicable'. It recommended 'a Government-owned single airline operating the trunk route airline system'.[3] That, of course, had been the goal of the 1946 Labor government.

The Commission set out what it saw as the central weakness of the existing policy. 'The economic arguments which can be mounted in favour of this alternative', said the Commission, 'are beyond dispute'. Immediate savings in costs, it said, could be passed on to the travelling public in lower fares. 'But it is the longer term where the greatest benefits would become evident. The economies of scale permitting the early introduction of wide-bodied aircraft, the better use of facilites, the separation of schedules and the settlement of industrial disputes ... can be secured with confidence in the long term with a one airline system. If low cost air transport is to be provided for the benefit of all Australians then this is the best way to achieve it.'[4] With understatement that was little short of irony the Commission conceded: 'The main objection to this would be of a philosophical and policy nature and the problem of maintaining satisfactory standards of service in the absence of direct competition'. What the Commission did not concede was that the proposal was a political impossibility. The argument was rational, the attitude hopelessly nostalgic.

'The two airline policy', it said with accuracy, 'no longer applies to two airlines'. Since becoming a party to the Agreements in 1967, it said, 'ATI has invested millions of dollars in industries far removed from its original and traditional airline and tourist activities'. It listed ATI's road freight and furniture removal businesses; general aviation aircraft sales; insurance; pastoral properties; manufacturing; credit cards; television; hire purchase and finance; road construction; and plastics interests. 'There can be no doubt', it said, 'that the two airline policy, despite its critics, has worked as efficiently as possible within its constraints, and has enabled both operators to earn profits. However the system has been an increasingly costly one because of the inefficiencies which result from the splitting in half of the small market.' The users of air transport, said the submission, had been 'denied the full benefits flowing from the increased productivity of larger and more efficient aircraft ... because the industry has had to meet the high costs of providing duplicated services and facilities made necessary by the two airline system'.

'The question to be asked', it said (underlining its conclusion for emphasis), 'is whether Australia can continue to afford the increasingly costly luxury of a two airline system'.

The submission set out the commercial paradoxes of a system in which a government airline, owned by the nation's taxpayers, gave away financial benefits to assure the profits of its privately owned competitor. ATI, it said, had 'inadequate regard for community standards in making [industrial] settlements. It was always prepared, in particular circumstances, despite agreement with TAA to the contrary, to enter into separate and private negotiations and settlements. 'The plain facts are that under the Airlines Agreements ATI has a guaranteed existence and a number of benefits conferred and yet it cannot be restrained from ignoring Government policy if it chooses to do so.' In a normal commercial situation, it said, 'the Government [as sole TAA shareholder] would direct its own traffic in passengers, freight and mail away from ATI and withdraw other benefits which ATI enjoys. The Government, however, has given away whatever bargaining power it had in this area by the Airlines Agreements. It may be necessary for the Government to give, or threaten to give, notice of termination of the Airlines Agreements to restrain ATI from continuing to make settlements in this manner in the future.' It listed separate settlements where ATI had made arrangements outside government guidelines. 'The list starts in 1966 when ATI agreed to grant the Airline Pilots a 27 per cent pay increase instead of the 15 per cent awarded by the Flight Crew Officers Industrial Tribunal. Since that time there have been a further seven instances of negotiations with the Airline Pilots Association where ATI has made separate agreements. The sums involved run into millions of dollars and the cost is increasing each year with wage escalation.' The cost to the industry, it said, was of the order of $16 million per annum in 1977 dollars, requiring an increase in tariffs of at least 3.5 per cent to cover the additional costs.

Parallel scheduling, said the Commission, was a focal point

of criticism of the two-airline policy. 'In recognition of this the Commission [believes] that any new agreement must contain a requirement to un-parallel schedules.'

The two-airline system, the Commission submitted, had become a duopoly in which competition was principally in marketing effort. 'It is not clear to airline users that effective competition has been achieved and is producing benefits for them.' While the real benefits of customer choice, safe operations and a stable and viable industry existed these benefits, it said, 'have been achieved at considerable cost'. The existing policy 'is regarded as creating a cartel, with the price of the product being set by agreement on a cost-plus basis ... at a level to recover costs and guarantee profitability'. By world standards, it concluded, 'the Australian trunk route market is too small to allow efficient operation by two airlines in open competition'.[5]

(The cosiness of the two-airline system, when the duopoly's interests overrode the imperatives of competition, was evident in a draft mutual aid agreement in late 1977 to provide defence against leap-frogging tactics by unions when negotiating with the airlines. The draft proposed that in the event of one airline being unable to operate because of industrial action the profit from the other airline would be shared so that the airline unable to operate would have some income to meet the costs that continued after operations ceased.[6] It was an initiative proposed by the Department of Employment and Industrial Relations.)[7]

Far removed from matters of high policy was the modest addition to the TAA fleet on 24 October 1977 of an aircraft built in its home city of Melbourne. TAA took delivery of an Australian-built Nomad aircraft on behalf of the Northern Territory Medical Service. That service, part of the Australian Department of Health, operated flying doctor services in the Northern Territory, visiting cattle stations, missions and Aboriginal settlements on a regular basis. (The aircraft was the first of six Nomads ordered by the Department of Health for the NTMS.) TAA was technical adviser to the Department on the Nomad purchase and had, since 1952, provided the pilots and engineers for the NTMS aircraft based in the Northern Territory. The Nomads were ordered to replace Twin Otter and Dove aircraft operating from bases at Darwin, Alice Springs and Gove.[8]

The Commission was increasingly concerned with fundamental issues of future government aviation policy and future government attitudes to TAA that threatened to further weaken its financial strength. The Labor government, despite its political philosophy favouring government ownership of TAA, had by its more general social and industrial policies imposed additional burdens on its airline. The Liberal–Country Party government, as Nixon had made clear, was driven by a philosophy that was more sympathetic to TAA's private enterprise competitor than to the State-owned airline. Neither government had smoothed the path of the government airline.

That political environment had not changed. The LCP government made it plain that in assessing TAA's financial position it judged that if the airline could finance major capital assets such as aircraft using internal resources then there was a case for insisting on a better dividend return for the government from its investment in TAA. That was no easy ask. Over recent years the dividend paid by TAA had, in the aggregate, roughly equated with the profit after tax. Not only was there nothing there to provide a higher return; there were no funds available from profits for the Commission to build up its reserves to equal Ansett's.

When TAA first started operating jet aircraft and acquired its fleet of six Boeing 727–76s and twelve DC9s these units were 80 per cent financed by loans arranged by the Commonwealth government. It was the amortisation of the initial fleet units and the later 200 series 727s that had provided sufficient funds for the repayment of the loans involved as they fell due (as well as the recoupment of the funds provided from internal sources). The amortisation of the assets of any business, of course, provides for replacement of those assets. In airline operations the write-off period for aircraft was significantly less than for other fixed assets. As a result funds for the replacement of aircraft were generated more quickly. What the Treasurer was now suggesting was that funds from this source — meant for the replacement of fleet units — were fair game when he looked to a better return from dividends.

That Treasury pressure came as TAA advised Nixon in October 1977 on its continuing evaluation of the various wide-bodied jet aircraft types for its routes. It was still studying the method to fund their very high launch cost of more than $100 million for a small fleet of only three aircraft. Earlier hopes for an inherent economy of operation from these larger units were now not as rosy. The direct operating costs per seat-kilometre of the three wide-bodied types under consideration were no better, Nixon was told, than those of a new DC9-30 aircraft at current acquisition costs. The improved fuel efficiency of the bigger aircraft was offset by their high capital cost (some 40 per cent higher than for narrow-bodied jets), as well as higher air navigation charges per seat.[9] The Treasurer had also suggested that TAA might lease, rather than buy, its aircraft. Vial responded: 'Leasing is not as an attractive proposition as purchase from self generated funds or from funds acquired under loan arrangements'.[10]

On 4 November Nixon authorised the acquisition by the Commission of its ninth Boeing 727-200. The current fleets of both TAA and Anset Airlines of Australia as 1977 ended comprised four Boeing 727-100s, seven 727-200s and twelve DC9-30s. Both airlines had an eighth and ninth 727-200 on order for delivery in 1978 plus an option on a tenth for delivery in May 1979.

While the government wanted more in dividends from TAA, Treasury revenues were continually boosted by the airline's contribution from other imposts. Duty paid on aviation fuel was a heavy cost burden (and was not paid by the international airlines). Vial told his minister on 24 November 1977 that 'the effect of the 1977 Federal Budget provisions relating to crude oil pricing will, in the current financial year, add $5.471 million to our aviation fuel costs'. A recent increase of 6.4 per cent in the duty component on Avtur raised duty to 55.8 per cent of the cost of the product. TAA calculated that its commitment to meet duty alone for the 1977–81 period would be more than $90 million.[11] Such costs were, of course, eventually met by the airlines' customers in higher fares and freight rates.

Ansett continued to provoke the indignation of its trunk-line competitor by additional diversification of its business interests — diversifications, as Vial told Nixon on 19 December 1977, that 'have been assisted by cash funds built up in the main from the ATI airline operations which benefit from an agreement requiring the Government to protect the continued existence of the Company as an operator of *airline services* within Australia'. ATI had announced the purchase of all the shares in Avis Rent-a-Car System's which, said Vial, was a 'threat to the Commission's competitive position and commercial progress' that was 'particularly serious'.

'This latest acquisition', he wrote, 'reported to be worth $10 million, comes shortly after the Government has agreed to ATI's request to guarantee the repayment of principal and interest of a loan to acquire a Boeing 727-200 aircraft. TAA was able, through its normal cash flow generated by its airline activities, to finance internally its intended purchase of its eighth Boeing 727-200 aircraft. It now appears likely that the request from ATI for a Government guarantee was made at a time when that company had sufficient funds in hand to acquire their comparable aircraft without such assistance.' It could be argued, he said, that as the government guarantee enabled ATI to obtain loan funds at a preferred rate of interest, 'the cost of funds to purchase Avis has really been reduced with Government assistance.' TAA was placed in the position, he said, 'where the more it promotes airport car rental services [where Avis had a monopoly] to its passengers the more it contributes to the commercial and financial well-being of its competitor'.[12]

Despite the imposts made on it by government and the vigorous competition of Ansett, the 1977 year had been a successful one for TAA commercially. In the 1976–77 financial year, with only a marginal increase in traffic and ever increasing costs, the airline had made a record after-tax operating profit of $6.973 million — a dramatic increase of 195 per cent on the previous year's result — on a revenue increase of only 10 per cent. By effective application of aircraft capacity, the passenger load factor had risen from 64.3 per cent in the previous year to 67.7 per cent. (Operating profit represented 46.5 per cent on average capital.) That high operating profit had been reduced, in the final profit figure, to $2.260 million after a provision of $5.666 million for long-service leave and other lesser charges. The Commission had made a dividend payment of 15 per cent ($2.25 million) to the Commonwealth. (In the previous year the dividend of $2.7 million exceeded the profit for the year by 65 per cent, or $1.063 million, reducing the amount of internally generated funds retained.) During the year TAA had itself further, if modestly, diversified by acquiring a 33.33 interest in Tara Holiday Village Pty Ltd, which operated a resort on the Gold Coast.[13]

Although industry traffic growth in the new financial year had been buoyant at 10 per cent, the Commission thought it prudent to base long-term fleet planning on a more conservative 5 to 7 per cent. Even on this basis, however, the existing jet fleet plus the two B727-200s on order were not sufficient to satisfy traffic demands to the year 1981. Approval was sought as 1977 ended to purchase a tenth Boeing 727-200 for delivery in May 1979. Neither government funds nor overseas borrowings were needed — the Commission planned to finance the purchase by borrowing from the superannuation trustees the difference between the purchase price of $A12.6 million and internally generated cash funds.[14] (This was followed in July 1978 by a request for approval to purchase two further B727s.)

Of more immediate substance as the year drew to a close was the finding by Sir Nigel Bowen, as Arbitrator under the rationalisation provisions of the Airlines Agreements, on TAA's application to operate the Perth–Port Hedland–Darwin route. Sir Nigel found in favour of the Commission and TAA was able, at long last, to begin services on the route on 17 November 1977.

While 1977 had seen the announcement by Nixon of a

major review of domestic aviation, his standing as minister, as well as that of the head of his Transport Department, Charles Halton, was low. In January 1977, *Aircraft* wrote:

> Mr Nixon and ... Charles Halton have a poor reputation with the industry ... Something is wrong when major industry reports, like those of the McNeill committee and the industry review committee, continue to lay hidden in the files of the Department, preventing any Parliamentary and public scutiny and discussion ... Something is wrong when the senior executive of a major airline [said publicly] that what Australia really needed was a separate civil aviation administration. And something is certainly wrong when transport administration in this country begins to take on all the appearances of a continuous seminar with a mass of study groups and think tanks but damn little decision making and action ... It all points to the need for the Government to reconsider the idea of a separate civil aviation administration.[15]

That there was substance in these criticisms was evident in a letter from Nixon to Vial. The minister wrote: 'Despite the regular day to day contact which takes place between the Aviation Industry and my Department, and the meetings which are arranged from time to time on a variety of issues, there appears to be no formal machinery within which the Industry and the Department interact'. Nixon proposed the establishment of an Aviation Industry Consultative Council under the chairmanship of the permanent head of his department comprising the general managers of ATI, East-West, Qantas and TAA and representatives of general aviation commercial and private operators.[16] The proposal, however, had all the appearances of yet another talk group, with no capacity for decision making. Ansett did not like the idea and said so bluntly. 'I dislike the title', he told Nixon, 'and I see very little value in the proposed Committee'.[17] (The outcome was a revised proposal for a body to be known as the Aviation Industry Advisory Council under the chairmanship of the minister.)

The *Financial Review* commented on 11 January: 'Australia's two-airline policy, which this year is coming under stronger pressure than for a generation, is an example of one of the most controlled business environments in the free-enterprise world ... The unfortunate side has been the

Tweedledum and Tweedledee effect. This has been the weakness most noticed and criticised over the years. It is time for a much more critical look ... The tradition of cosy, mutually convenient arrangements between the airlines and the Public Service and Governments which regulate them must not be allowed to prevent a thorough public debate in the coming months.'[18]

John Watkins, now speaking in the role of former TAA director of engineering, contributed to that public debate. He told the Royal Aeronautical Society in Canberra that the federal government might be deliberately clamping down on Australian air transport. 'I suggest that it is not just by coincidence that the marked falling-off in air transport growth has happened since the industry began to feel the bite of a deliberate selective government policy of cost-recovery through taxes and charges levied on air transport operators.' Airline managements, he said, worked on a very fine margin of profit after tax, with TAA running between 0.5 and 1.5 per cent of gross revenue. 'So the Government's arbitrarily decided cost increases are unavoidably passed on to the air traveller.' It was ironic, said Watkins, that the suppression of air traffic through discriminatory and short-sighted application of a government cost-recovery program 'may well be the major reason why the domestic airlines have lacked adequate incentives to maintain their progressive fleet planning policies. One can only hope that much wisdom will be distilled from the deliberations of the Departmental Committee which is reviewing the Government's air transport policy.'[19]

The broad outline of Australia's scheduled domestic aviation operations was a clear one, with three categories of operators providing services across the continent. The two major operators, TAA and Ansett Airlines of Australia, competed on the trunk routes with B727s and DC9s (with Ansett also using Electras for freight). Regional airlines operated, in the main, F27s and F28s in specified geographical areas, mostly intrastate. Apart from East-West Airlines Limited, which mainly served New South Wales, and Connair Pty Ltd, which operated in central and northern Australia, the other regional operators were owned and operated by Ansett as divisions of Ansett Transport Industries (Operations) Pty Ltd. They were Ansett Airlines of New South Wales, Ansett Airlines of South Australia and MacRobertson Miller Airline Services, operating in Western Australia and the Northern Territory. The third category providing air services comprised commuter operators (introduced in 1967) flying where aircraft such as F27s or larger could not land and using light aircraft. Between them the domestic airlines (excluding Connair) employed 18,047 people, including 1,375 pilots.[20]

For TAA and Ansett the competitive network expanded in October 1977 when they began direct jet services between Sydney and Townsville and onward to Cairns and, in January 1978, when direct Sydney–Launceston services started. Capital city airports, however, accounted for 64 per cent of all passenger movements on scheduled domestic services.

At its meeting in mid May 1978 there was a brief pause in the proceedings of the Commission to express sadness at the death of R. (Dick) Pope, who died on 18 April, 1978 after a prolonged illness following a severe heart attack. Dick Pope had been a pioneer in the administration of the airline from its beginnings and at the centre of its financial management from the time he joined the airline in May 1946.

TAA's senior management structure was changed in mid 1978. Effective on 3 July Frank Ball and Tony Dignam were appointed assistant general managers, controlling the airline's two main elements. Ball headed engineering, flight operations, marketing, public relations and other operational functions; Dignam was responsible for commercial services and development, finance, data processing and property. Captain Len Morey was appointed flight operations director. Below the two assistant general managers were Trevor Fenton, as personnel director; Frank Austin, who remained engineering director, and Neil Murray as commercial services and development director. Ken Kennett was appointed to the new position of marketing director. Bryan Palmer replaced Kennett as manager Victoria while Ralph Conley became manager Queensland, replacing Ben Cochrane. Geoff Beames replaced Conley as manager associated companies. At the head of the Commission the chairman, Kenneth Vial, was awarded the KBE in the Queen's Birthday honours list. *Travel Trade* commented: 'We are beginning to see the creation of a depth of management in TAA ... But Ansett flies far behind. Sir Reginald still makes the major decisions at Ansett. And he makes the right ones, as the success of the company shows.'[21]

The first part of the government review of domestic air transport policy, dealing mainly with two-airline policy matters, was completed on 31 March 1978, but it was not made available to the Commission (as the Commission tartly pointed out in its 1977–78 annual report) until the end of July — when it was also made available to the public.

'The general thrust of the Report's recommendations', said Nixon, 'is to retain the principle of two major airlines operating over the trunk route network in Australia but to make a number of significant changes to the present Agreements between the Government and the airlines with the object of fostering competition'. The two most significant changes recommended were the removal of the rationalisation arrangements in the Airlines Agreement, which called for continuing consultation between TAA and Ansett, and the complete removal from the two-airline policy of the carriage of freight. It also recommended that some competition from the regional airlines be allowed on segments of the trunk routes. Not surprisingly, the Report 'expressed concern' at the narrow range of fares available within Australia and the extent of parallel scheduling.[22]

The Report brought no shocks for TAA. It could hardly have expected the acceptance of its own proposed radical changes. It had no objections to the broad thrust of the recommendations. But despite its concern about parallel scheduling, it offered no solutions for the intrinsic inefficiencies of the system. The *Financial Review* commented: 'Although proclaimed as a major overhaul of the two airline policy the review represents little more than a tinkering with the controls'. It had, wrote the *Review*, 'shunned the worldwide trend of stripping away the mass of regulations governing competition between domestic airline carriers'. The Committee's recommendations to encourage more innovation in fare structures 'can be viewed as window dressing while the basis of the two airline policy remains intact'. Australian airline users could, it said, expect more of the same 'and the airlines can plan on a pretty comfortable existence with a guarantee against competition, either domestic or foreign'.[23]

(The whole edifice of the two-airline system depended on the Customs (Prohibited Imports) Regulations under which the importation of aircraft was prohibited except with the consent in writing of the Secretary of the Department of Transport. In 1977, however, the High Court had found that the grant of import permits to the freight carriers IPEC — Interstate Parcel Express Company Pty Ltd — and Air Express was not in breach of the Commonwealth's obligations as set out in the Airlines Agreements Act. IPEC operated two Argosy freighters between the mainland and Launceston, Tasmania.)

In July Australian air travellers were again called on to meet the rising cost of the two-airline system. Nixon approved a tariff increase for the airlines of 6 per cent. He did, however, tell both TAA and Ansett that he wanted consultation between them 'with a view to *quickly* bringing forward firm proposals involving the reduced incidence of parallel scheduling'.[24] The tariff increase had been urged by Ansett when he detailed to the minister cost increases in the twelve months to June 1978 of some $26 million, much of which, he allowed, would be absorbed by predicted growth of about 10 per cent. But, said Ansett to Nixon on 18 August: 'In delivering the 1978–1979 Federal Budget on Tuesday this week the Treasurer has announced several measures which will raise the costs of the Company enormously'. The first of these, he said, was 'the introduction of world parity pricing of Australian indigenous crude oil', which on existing usage would 'result in a cost increase to the Company of approximately $13 million per annum for this commodity alone'. It was clear, said Ansett, that the Company could not possibly absorb these increases but 'must immediately increase both passenger and freight tariffs'. The dilemma for Ansett, and for TAA, was that such an increase, following so closely on the July increase of 6 per cent, would cause further contraction of traffic growth. 'It is with considerable regret', he concluded, 'that we hereby seek your urgent approval to apply a 5 per cent increase to all passenger and freight rates.'[25]

TAA's operating profit for the 1978–79 year, at $7.128 million, was down 23 per cent on the preceding year, but the government took a dividend from the airline of $6 million, or 40 per cent of the government-subscribed capital. That dividend absorbed 80 per cent of the year's profit and, said the Commission's annual report, was 'clearly in excess of the dividend level that could be recommended on commercial considerations'. It did not, said the report, allow for a proper level of profit retention and it increased the already excessive reliance on loan finance. 'The Commission', it said, '... is, of course, bound by the Government's direction to pay $6 million'.[26]

The considerable additional costs arising from the Budget announcement looked small when compared with the likely costs flowing from compliance with the minister's wish that parallel schedules should be minimised. The Commission, which in its submission had advocated abandonment of parallel scheduling, now advised Nixon on 30 August: 'Deparallel schedules over the trunk network would add significantly to industry costs because of decreased flexibility in aircraft utilisation and lower load factors. Our estimates put these costs in the area of $30 million per year for the industry which would need to be recovered from airline users who may not recognise any great increase in consumer benefits.'[27] The matter, the Commission noted when it met in August, 'had become an emotional issue'.[28] According to a report to the Commission, the review of domestic aviation had recommended both de-paralleling of schedules and more competition within the industry. It commented: 'These two recommendations are in conflict as de-paralleling would entail more rigid scheduling controls than those applying at present and the virtual elimination of competition in scheduling'.[29]

Because of Section 92 of the Australian Constitution dealing with trade between the States, changes to the two-airline system could not be imposed by the federal government. Legislation could only be enacted with the agreement of the two airlines. TAA, of course, was bound to follow the wishes of its shareholder as expressed by the minister. Ansett, who was not bound, held the key to change. And Ansett was protected under the existing Agreement from change, if he did not welcome it, by the clause which stated that the Agreements made prior to 1973 could only be terminated by giving five years' notice. (The 1973 Agreement had terminated on 30 June 1978.) 'The key to the whole affair', wrote the *Australian*, 'is Sir Reginald Ansett who wears the unchallenged crown as Australia's toughest businessman. He is not afraid to stand up for his rights in any court of law and he is surrounded in his Melbourne headquarters by some of the country's best legal brains.'[30]

Ansett put his position in his usual forthright way at a meeting in August with Charles Halton and other departmental officials. Minutes of that meeting recorded: 'Sir Reginald Ansett said that he saw the Airlines Agreements in a historical perspective. The Company [he said] had inherited the 1952 Airlines Agreement which the late Sir Robert Menzies had "written in one weekend". Mr Menzies had told Ansett to accept responsibilities arising under the Agreement. It had prevented him [he said] from being free to act. He couldn't use the subsidiary airlines to upset the Agreement. He had to behave himself.' That, said Ansett, had been the position over the years. 'In short, whilst the Company had accepted the benefits, it had also honoured the responsibilities imposed by the Agreement.' (Halton commented that 'whatever everyone thought they were agreeing when they negotiated the Agreements, High Court decisions had now thrown doubt on what protection was provided. The import control', he said, 'was the real power'.)[31]

For the travelling public it was difficult to sympathise with airlines that continued to raise both fares and profits. That the 1977–78 financial year had been a good one for both airlines was evident in the thirty-third annual report of the Australian National Airlines Commission. TAA operating profit after tax rose 42.7 per cent to $3,378,012, achieved on revenue that had increased 15.5 per cent (to $270,581,640) on the previous year. A dividend of $2.25 million was paid to the Commonwealth.[32] The 'cartel' that the Commission had described in its submission to the government review, operating on a 'cost-plus' basis, continued to provide a comfortable commercial environment. 'A notable omission from the Commission's accounts', reported the *Sydney Morning Herald*, 'was any provision for employees' superannuation under the Government's Commonwealth Superannuation Scheme'.[33] In the meantime the government assessment of TAA's superannuation liabilities continued. McKenzie advised the Commission of their extent in August 1978. Three separate trusts were maintained (all with the Commonwealth Trading Bank) for ground staff, pilots and hostesses. 'Total funds of all trusts', he wrote, 'held by the trustees at 30 June, 1978 were $93,210,663 and annual net earnings were $7,195,377. The return on average funds was 8.3 per cent against 7.9 per cent in the previous year.' During the year TAA had repaid $10 million in loans from the trusts. The value of TAA loans stood at $19.4 million. Fund assets for which market values were available totalled $66.97 million at book value and $72.757 million at market value.[34]

At the margin of these fundamental issues of airline operations were TAA's tourist and other subsidiaries and property purchases. TAA announced in September 1978 that following acquisition by the airline of the 50 per cent interest in Dunk Island holiday resort and its associated operation, Bingil Bay Cruises, held by P&O Australia Limited, both had now become wholly owned TAA subsidiaries.[35] It had also completed negotiations to purchase Phillip House, Elizabeth Street, Sydney (its Sydney city office), and had advanced negotiations to take a fifteen-year lease on land next to it.[36]

On 3 November 1978 TAA–Mayne Travel Industries Pty

Ltd signed an agreement for the purchase of a majority holding in Kay Rent-a-Car Pty Ltd, the Hertz licensee in Australia. That move prompted the minister to reconsider arrangements for rental cars at Commonwealth airports. Nixon had proposed contracts based on one national operator and one operator on an airport-to-airport basis (selected from unsuccessful tenderers for the national contract). 'I have since been considering the desirability of a change in these arrangements, particularly in the light of the now established links between two of the national operators and the two domestic airlines.' He now wished to call 'open tenders for these contracts so that all rental car operators can have an equal opportunity to be the successful bidder'. He asked for agreement from both TAA and Ansett on 6 December 'to the successful tenderer being provided with space in your airline-owned terminals at Commonwealth airports on reasonable terms and conditions'.[37] Vial told him that the matter was a contentious one and the Commission could not accede to his request. It believed, he said, that 'the public interest is best served by limiting the concession to two national operators'.[38]

The 1978 year had seen widespread media discussion of Australian domestic aviation, most of it critical. That gloomy and inward-looking view was given a brighter, international dimension by the authoritative British journal *Flight International*. John Watkins referred to it in a letter to the *Age*, writing:

> It was refreshing indeed to see ... *Flight International*'s ranking of Australia's airlines as the world's safest. Recent denigration of our air services in comparison with those elsewhere gives far too little recognition to unique Australian problems. An area as large as the USA and about twice the size of Europe, with but a fraction of their population, is served with a huge mileage of routes. Our operators are consequently denied the overseas benefits of large fleet economy and, at many ports, of uniform workload. Distance from the manufacturer necessitates technical self-sufficiency, recognised world-wide as outstandingly competent.
>
> Australia is the world's most air-dependent nation ... The sooner the Government recognises this fact and gives the airlines encouragement and cost relief instead of discriminating against the air transport mode with ever-increasing imposts and charges

> the better the recovery of the nation's economic health ... The public can take comfort in the certainty that the airlines will not lessen their world-leading emphasis on safety. When the chips are down this has to be air transport's ultimate concern.[39]

When Lyn McKenzie wrote his Christmas message for staff in the December issue of *This Air Age*, he reported that traffic growth had fallen dramatically during the year and that the expected 10 per cent growth had shrunk to little more than 3 per cent. Public pressure had increased for lower fares, he said, but rising staff and other costs had made it necessary to raise fares first by 6 per cent and then by a further 5 per cent. No decision had yet been made on fleet development into a wide-bodied aircraft type.[40]

Financial pressures on TAA saw it, in December 1978, seek ministerial approval for a major change to its operations in Queensland. It asked Nixon for permission to abandon its F27 services on the Townsville–Mount Isa and Brisbane–Longreach routes and allow their replacement by services operated on behalf of TAA by Bush Pilot Airways (the major Queensland commuter airline) using smaller Metroliner aircraft. (At the end of a three-year period it was proposed that Bush Pilots should take over the services in their entirety.)[41] That TAA request was driven by heavy annual losses incurred by F27 operations on these routes (and on their F27 Albury–Canberra sector) of some $1.25 million. 'A tariff increase of 56 per cent would be needed', TAA told the Department of Transport, 'for operations for the whole year to merely break even against direct operating costs'.[42] The TAA initiative was to be resisted with vigour by Queensland but Nixon's response to the State was blunt. 'If the Queensland Government wishes me to direct TAA to maintain F27 services', he said, 'I would be prepared to look at this provided the State is prepared to subsidise the losses incurred on these services'.[43] (The Albury–Canberra service was taken over by Masling Commuter Services, making one TAA F27 surplus to requirements. The aircraft was sold.)

The mounting criticism of the Australian domestic aviation industry continued as 1979 began. Central to the perceived shortcomings of the two major airlines was the level of air fares. On 11 January the *Financial Review*, in its main editorial, wrote:

> There is a case for making available the considerable amount of spare capacity which exists on the international flights between Sydney and the other capitals ... But this suggestion leads into the tangled issue of whether competition should be allowed ... between international carriers and domestic carriers for normal domestic traffic. If this were to be conceded it would be difficult to argue against TAA and Ansett being allowed access to business out of Australia within the ranges appropriate to their aircraft. Both Qantas and the domestic airlines reject such proposals with horror, since they have the unpleasant smack of genuine competition and free enterprise ... Reports prepared for the Domestic Air Transport Review last July ... indicated TAA and Ansett are inefficient by world standards, that they are over-staffed and that the range of fare types was too narrow ... There is little doubt the two-airline policy as it operates now is strongly inimical to competition, cheaper air fares and cost efficiency in both the major airlines.[44]

Both airlines, however, advanced many initiatives to provide concessional lower fares. On 1 September 1978 TAA and Ansett each introduced standby fares with a discount of 40 per cent off the normal economy fare on some services and, in November, 30 per cent on some other routes. The Advance Purchase Excursion Fare (APEX) was extended to more routes, and in April 1979 a Super-APEX fare of 40 per cent off economy was introduced. In addition to the APEX and Standby fares there had been a proliferation of other concessional initiatives including Budget, Discover Australia, Holiday Package, Group Travel, See Australia and Special fares, as well as concessions for children and students.

An internal TAA study analysed fare levels in the United States and reported: 'Australian economy air fares are less than US economy fares under 1000 kilometres'. As the average Australian passenger travelled 814 kilometres on TAA flights the study thought it reasonable to claim that he paid less for economy travel than his counterpart in the United States. 'Despite the ... evidence', it concluded, 'it is likely the clamour will continue for decreased domestic fares'. The need, the Commission was told, was 'to simplify rather than extend our fare structures'.[45]

Utilisation of TAA and Ansett aircraft on services outside Australia was raised with the minister in February 1978. Both airlines had discussed the operation of B727 services between Hobart and Christchurch, New Zealand. It was considered a marginal economic proposition in the short term but with longer-term potential. TAA thought the route had particular attractions for United States tourists who could enter Australia at Sydney and leave via Hobart for New Zealand. A starting date in June 1979 was proposed.[46]

TAA saw its main problem, however, as its minister. The Commission was told by Lyn McKenzie in February 1979 that the airline wanted the minister to be better informed about the difficulties facing the industry in a period of pressure for fare reductions and rising costs — some coming from government action. He wanted ministerial help to reduce fuel tax and to modify the government policy for cost recovery. (The government target was now 100 per cent recovery of infrastructure and facilities costs.) On the airline's list for ministerial help was resolution of the superannuation problem in the current year; forcing a situation in which ATI had no greater flexibility than TAA in the settlement of industrial disputes; adoption of a policy of full support for TAA exemption from any legislation that was fundamentally designed for government departments; and provision of a stable dividend policy. (The Commission was advised that TAA faced a growing deficiency in its ground staff superannuation fund that might 'well exceed $50 million'.)[47]

Though the two-airline policy had resulted in financial stability for the two domestic airlines the Commission report recognised that 'greater cost efficiency is now being demanded'. But, it said, 'the major problem of cost duplication cannot be avoided under the present system'. Press comment, it noted, was 'almost unanimous in labelling the two-airline system as inefficient'.[48] (While fare levels always provoked the most criticism, it was never directed at those aspects of government policy that had forced fare rises. The government's policy on oil pricing alone had caused fares to rise by some 17 per cent between 1974 and 1979. The government move to achieve full cost recovery from its provision of infrastructure and facilities had also brought substantial cost increases.)

The influential weekly magazine the *Bulletin* put the prevailing media view in March 1979. 'Something is wrong, very wrong, with the Australian two-airline system.' Though public debate had focussed largely on high air fares and parallel scheduling, it said, the basic problem was 'lack of management enterprise at the head of both TAA and Ansett'. The years of regulation, the cosy sharing of an expanded market, said the weekly, had resulted in managements that administered rather than innovated. 'Control of the industry has passed from the airlines to the bureaucracy. It is a situation which clearly harms the public interest but it is not one that the Department of Transport, which has usurped power, is willing to change.' It quoted comments by Qantas planning director Jack Dawson to a seminar in Perth. 'TAA and Ansett were overdue in ordering wide-bodied jets which, worldwide, have resulted in huge cost savings, largely through fuel economy, and have made the low-fare revolution possible.' TAA and Ansett cost structures, said Dawson, reflected the costs of operating obsolescent narrow-bodied jets on transcontinental routes. (In an effort to reduce fuel costs TAA in 1979 progressively introduced new flying procedures for its 727s and DC9s, reducing climb, cruise and descent speeds.)

The Department of Transport review of domestic aviation had come down with a report, the *Bulletin* wrote, 'that largely recommends continuance of the status quo with, if anything, more governmental control'. In its earlier years, said the *Bulletin*, the two-airline system had worked well. The Department of Civil Aviation 'became intimately involved in the airline industry ... The specialist departmental officers and their opposite numbers on the airlines were of a similar age, had mostly served with one another in the wartime RAAF and had a genuine commitment towards innovation ... The system became unstuck during the days of the Labor Government which abolished the Department of Civil Aviation, incorporating it into an all-embracing Department of Transport.'

The people at the top of the airlines, it commented, had aged. 'Sir Reginald Ansett, for instance, has turned 70 and his top executives are mainly around 60 years of age ... At TAA the chairman, Kenneth Vial and the deputy chairman, Robert Law-Smith, are both due to retire this year. The general manager, Lyn McKenzie, will step down in May next year.' The article concluded with prescience: 'Eventually we would hope to see a deregulated airline industry in Australia with real competition spurring both organisations'.[49]

The Queensland premier, Joh Bjelke-Petersen, was adamant in his refusal to accept the TAA decision to discontinue its inland F27 services, forcing Vial to write to him on 2 March 1979: 'TAA accepts the wish of the Queensland Government that the inland F27 services should continue but this does mean that TAA must find some means of offsetting the heavy loss being incurred'.[50] The federal government was blunter. Nixon told Law-Smith on 16 April: 'The Prime Minister advised the Premier that there is no legal obligation on TAA to continue to operate inland services either under the Australian National Airlines Act or the Airlines Agreement. The Prime Minister has put the view that the Commonwealth would not support a direction being given to TAA to continue and expand uneconomic services within Queensland ... should the Queensland Government be willing to fully compensate TAA for the losses incurred in operating these services the Commonwealth Government would ensure that TAA maintained those inland services.'[51]

At the same time TAA wrote again to the minister stressing the intrinsic inefficiency of a two-airline system. 'I must ... raise with you', Vial wrote to him in April, 'the critical overall position of the major domestic airlines which really amounts to a question of survival. With the present cost problems facing the domestic airline industry, together with the public pressure for lower fares, it is timely to ask whether Australia can continue with the two-airline system, which was created to provide competition in too small a market — and still does.' Vial again advocated a single trunk route airline. He submitted an account of the cost savings that could be achieved by a merger of TAA and Ansett Airlines of Australia through the elimination of duplicated facilities. It totalled $40 million in direct operating costs. Parallel scheduling would be eliminated, he said. A single fleet would have fewer, bigger units. 'A single domestic operator would have 30 per cent less movements through Kingsford Smith Airport, Sydney, a major potential saving for the Government.' New aircraft types would be capable of servicing certain regional routes more efficiently than Qantas 747s. There would be fuel savings each year worth some $23 million. Labour disputes 'could be settled in accordance with established labour policies at less cost to the industry and ultimately to the public'. The Commission, wrote Vial, had concluded that the benefits to Australia from a single major domestic operator far outweighed the disadvantages associated with a government-controlled monopoly.[52]

The Ansett view did not contemplate such radical change. Ansett's respected director of engineering, J. M. Warner, in a wide-ranging survey of the Australian domestic airline industry (given in his 1979 Sir Geoffrey De Havilland Memorial Lecture), concluded: 'Following the recent review of the Two Airline Policy, it is unlikely that there will be substantial changes; there will be relaxation in some areas with a view to increasing competition; there will be greater flexibility in promotional fares. By and large, however, the recovery of the country's economy will be the greatest factor in improving the airlines' situation.' The government review of the industry, he said, 'came down heavily on the side of the two-airline system'.

A third scenario for the future of Australian domestic aviation was also emerging from within the Liberal Party. The influential senior Tasmanian Senator Peter Rae was pressing for the sale of TAA to private enterprise. In May 1979 political commentator Laurie Oakes wrote: 'He [Rae] has now managed to get the private enterprise versus public ownership debate off the ground in Australia, coincidentally in the same week that Britain's new Prime Minister, Mrs Margaret Thatcher, announced plans to sell off some Government-owned firms ... There is a growing mood among Liberals that it is about time the party showed it was serious about its free-enterprise philosophy.'[53] Peter Bowers, political correspondent for the *Sydney Morning Herald*, wrote on 16 May: 'The Federal Government is considering selling Trans-Australia Airlines, the Government-owned domestic airline, to the Australian public ... The proposal is limited to TAA. There is no question of Qantas being sold. The discussions have been so secret that not even departmental heads were consulted.'[54]

On 11 August 1979 Sir Kenneth Vial retired from the Australian National Airlines Commission after four years as chairman and twenty-three years Commission service (the longest-serving member of the Commission). (The new chairman was Robert Law-Smith, who had been a commissioner since May 1962 and vice-chairman from October 1975. He was also chairman of the National Bank and vice-chairman of Qantas.) Vial's last substantial letter to the minister, written on 3 August, responded to the public speculation on the possible sale to the public of equity shareholding in TAA. There were, he said, several significant matters that would need resolution before such a sale could be seriously contemplated. It was something of an understatement. Vial raised 'the effect upon the financial position of the airline of the losses incurred in the repayment during the financial year of Government-arranged Swiss loans'. 'As you know', he wrote, 'these repayment losses amount to $28 million — an amount which exceeds the total Commonwealth Government Advances and Reserves of the Commission as disclosed in the 1978 balance sheet'. On the superannuation issue he wrote:

> We have only just been advised that the recent actuarial evaluation of the deficiency in the funding of the Commission's liability under the Commonwealth Superannuation Act as at 1 July, 1976, is of such magnitude that there are no conceivable circumstances under which it could be financed from internal sources ... Furthermore the funding deficiency will continue to grow ... Should the government seriously contemplate disposal of all or some of

> its equity interest in the airline, the Trustee of TAA's Superannuation Funds may no longer consider it prudent to advance 75 per cent of its assets to TAA as non-Government guaranteed loans. As at 31 July, 1979 these borrowings totalled $65 million, the major share of which might have to be refinanced in the event of a disposal being contemplated.

Vial also drew attention to the highly geared finances of the industry. 'As a consequence our gearing ratio (borrowings to capital) is higher than would be acceptable to the investment market ... It may be necessary to inject further capital of perhaps $40 million.'

There was more. Vial wrote: 'Before a satisfactory sale price could be expected intending purchasers would have to perceive the investment as likely to offer dividend returns higher than those recently achieved ... which, of course, has direct implications in the provision of unprofitable services, the writing off of capitalised exchange losses so that these losses do not continue as a drain on profits in future years, and the alleviation of unbearable superannuation contributions.' There were also, he said, 'implications for the Government's Air Transport Policy, particularly in the areas of fare setting, because the Government control over its prices directly affects the profitability of TAA'.[55]

There were, it was evident, more than a few obstacles in the way for the achievement of Senator Rae's ambition to privatise the government airline.

The Government recognised them. It also recognised the political fact that TAA, as its market share had always shown, was well regarded publicly. On 9 August Nixon wrote to Vial: 'I can advise you that there is no intention to sell TAA'. Discussions were proceeding, said the minister, 'with a view to preparing a revised Airlines Agreement governing the Two Airline Policy which is predicated on a privately owned and government owned airline'.[56]

It was a future that had Ansett's support. After a major internal reappraisal of the two-airline policy it found, reported the *Financial Review*, 'that the policy is the only one under which competition can exist in the limited Australian air transport environment'. The thrust of the Ansett position, it said, was that Ansett believed the two-airline policy was necessary 'to protect a private enterprise operator against a government airline operator'. It quoted an Ansett paper presented in Canberra to parliamentarians on 11 October 1979, which said: 'It is naive in the extreme to suggest that with this type of competition normal free market policies can be operated without controlling regulations'.[57]

At the same time Ansett strongly criticised TAA for indicating that it might soon place an order for wide-bodied Airbus A300 B4 aircraft. The *Australian* reported: 'They [Ansett] are critical of TAA for apparently rushing ahead on a major acquisition program which Ansett Transport Industries General Manager (Policy) Mr Brian Grey openly says should be made in collusion between the two airlines'. Australia's route structure, said Ansett, was unsuitable for wide-bodied aircraft. It was Grey's view, wrote the *Australian*, that if the airlines chose different aircraft 'someone is going to be right and someone wrong. It will be very doubtful that both are right. God help the fellow who is wrong.'[58]

TAA had, in fact, indicated to Nixon in September that its choice for a wide-bodied aircraft would be the Airbus A300 B4. Law-Smith wrote to him advising that the earliest availability of the Airbus incorporating necessary TAA modifications was early 1983. (Airbus Industrie quickly offered TAA earlier delivery dates.) The *Age* reported on 10 October: 'A spokesman for TAA confirmed that it had paid a holding deposit on four of the wide-bodied airliners. The Transport Minister, Mr Nixon, allowed this to protect favourable positions guaranteed to TAA on the Airbus production line. By moving first, TAA has placed Ansett Airlines in a difficult position and there is considerable interest in how the rival airline will react.'[59] Two days later, in its lead editorial, it commented: 'The decision by TAA, endorsed by the Federal Government, to go it alone and order four wide-bodied 272-seat Airbus jets is being seen as the first evidence of a split in the cosy TAA–Ansett duopoly. TAA has taken a lead ... The fact that the Federal Government allowed TAA to place an

Airbus order ... is a sign that it is serious about making the industry more competitive and more consumer-oriented.'[60]

Frank Pascoe, general manager of Ansett Airlines of Australia, wrote immediately to Lyn McKenzie: 'We understand from press reports that the Commission has lodged an application to the Minister seeking approval to the introduction of two Airbus Industrie A300 B4 aircraft in October, 1981 and March, 1982 respectively. No industry discussions have been held in relation to the application and in view of the Airlines Equipment Act, 1958 we now request that discussions take place immediately and the outcome of these be communicated to the Minister.'[61]

TAA's jet fleet comprised twelve DC9-30s, ten B727-200s and one reserve B727-100. Two more B727-200s were on order for delivery in January and August 1980. In addition, Nixon had approved the acquisition of a thirteenth B727-200 by August 1981 (the option for which expired on 15 December 1979). There was a further option available from Boeing for a fourteenth B727-200 for delivery in September 1982. The thirteenth and fourteenth 727s were needed to service anticipated traffic growth demand up to late 1983. However, Airbus Industrie had now offered early delivery of four A300 B4 aircraft, two in October 1981 and one each in June 1982 and May 1983. These were the aircraft on which TAA had lodged a deposit, refundable only if a definitive purchase agreement was executed by 9 November 1979. The Commission, in its review of all new aircraft types available, had concluded that the two most suitable were the A300 and the Boeing 767. (The new generation narrow-bodied types, the DC9-80 and Boeing 757, were rejected as inadequate as long-term frontline types. The Lockheed L1011 and DC10-10 were considered too large and the Airbus A310 was not available until 1984.)

TAA considered the A300 B4 superior to the Boeing 767 because of its better size as a frontline aircraft over a life of fifteen to twenty years (272 seats compared with the 767's 229). TAA considered it more economical, with superior cargo capability. It had been well proven in service since May 1974. (The 767 was not available to TAA before November 1982, at which date its service life would have been only three months.) These were the major considerations that led to a unanimous Commission decision on 22 October to seek approval to buy four Airbus A300 B4s.[62] Acquisition of four Airbus aircraft, TAA calculated, would permit the disposal of up to six of its oldest DC9s. (Ansett's technical services director, John Bibo, told the *Age*: 'There is a big chance the competition could force us to go along [choosing the Airbus]'.[63] Airbus Industrie, however, had advised that it could not guarantee dates matching TAA's for delivery of similar aircraft for Ansett, though it had put proposals that it said 'would ease the pain'.)[64]

The TAA Airbus initiative was of sufficient substance to involve the prime minister, Malcolm Fraser. Nixon advised him that neither the existing two-airline policy nor changes proposed to it would affect the TAA proposal. Both operators, he said, were obliged to comply with his capacity determinations in accordance with the Airlines Equipment Act. He had no firm information on Ansett's future re-equipment plans, he told Fraser, but had taken the view that the government should not seek to interfere with either operator's commercial judgment — a decision that could conceivably lead to a situation where each operator acquired different equipment. That was not necessarily a bad thing, said Nixon, and, if it eventuated could have some beneficial effects on parallel scheduling.[65]

TAA had taken the decision to proceed with its costly re-equipment plan at the same time as its concern increased about the Commission's major financial problems. Its liability in relation to the Commonwealth Superannuation Scheme was a continuing and grave financial uncertainty needing urgent resolution. A report in late 1979 showed that the Commission's liability for contributions was in excess of provisions already made by more than $96 million as at July 1976 and had increased since that date to more than $100 million. 'It is clear', said the report, 'that it is totally beyond the financial capacity of the Commission to provide for this obligation'.

TAA's existing financial organisation was 'inconsistent with a commercial competitive financial structure'. The Commission, it said, was undercapitalised in that its capital and reserves represented less than 13 per cent of its total assets. (The matching figure for ATI was 27 per cent.) It was 'overly dependent on debt', with the result that it had to set aside 'a high proportion of its annual cash flow to meet interest payments and loan repayments'. Profitability was 'inadequate to finance future expansion and meet the Commission's obligation to pay a reasonable dividend to the Government'. Total assets at 30 June 1979 were $238 million; capital and reserves totalled $30 million. The Commission calculated that it needed an immediate capital injection of at least $25 million.[66]

On 5 December 1979 TAA was given federal government approval to purchase its four twin-engined Airbus A300 B4 aircraft. At some $200 million (including spares, ground equipment and bigger hangars), it represented the largest single investment ever by an Australian domestic airline. The first two aircraft were scheduled for delivery in October 1981 (when TAA planned the retirement of four DC9s).[67]

There were two other events of moment as the 1970s ended and the new decade began. One was political. Peter Nixon's term as minister ended and he was replaced in December as minister for transport by Ralph Hunt. The other was to bring to an end an unrivalled personal commitment to Australian domestic aviation. Sir Reginald Ansett was to lose control of Ansett Transport Industries and, in January 1980, leave the industry he had served since 1936.

CHAPTER 16

1980

The possible sale of TAA

Reginald Ansett's departure in January 1980 had followed a series of takeover bids and counterbids for ATI and a hard year for his company that had started with the collapse of the ATI finance subsidiary, Associated Securities Limited, and been followed by the loss of Avis Rent-a-Car's exclusive authority to serve Australia's fifty-eight major city and country airports. Four major groups had been involved in a battle for ATI shares that had ended with the company coming under the joint control of News Corporation and TNT. ATI now had, as joint chief executives, Sir Peter Abeles and Rupert Murdoch (whose particular interest was the ATI-owned Melbourne television station, Channel 10). Both were aggressive and entrepreneurial in style and both had powerful political connections.

The uncertainty surrounding the control of Ansett Transport Industries had forced the government to discontinue the negotiations necessary for a revision of the Airlines Agreement. The new minister, Ralph Hunt, announced on 20 December that with the ownership of ATI settled, a revised Airlines Agreement would be negotiated based on the recommendations of the Domestic Air Transport Policy Review. The *Bulletin* thought he would go further. It quoted Hunt in its 22 January issue: 'The whole purpose of re-writing the two airlines agreement is to try to break the airlines apart ... If you are going to persist with the present situation there is no justification ... for having two airlines as such. You might as well have one big airline system in Australia.'[1]

As the decade began, all the world's airlines were shocked when in January Saudi Arabia raised the price of crude oil by one-third. Concurrently there were increases in Australian crude and in the price demanded by other oil-producing countries. For TAA fuel costs (which had risen by almost 24 per cent in 1978–79) increased by 46.8 per cent in 1979–80, adding $25.688 million to costs. Further severe increases in the cost of fuel were expected for 1981–82.

On 31 January, following the rising costs of both wages and fuel, TAA and Ansett Airlines of Australia were granted yet another increase in fares and freight rates (8 per cent for fares, 8.5 per cent for freight). Lyn McKenzie pre-empted the announcement of this increase with a statement advocating that under any revised two-airline legislation there should be freedom for TAA to take the initiative on the level of air fares, that cargo rates be no longer controlled and that fares be excluded from the legislation. 'ATI's attitude on these matters is not yet clear', he said, 'but there does appear to be some concern about competition from TAA and its effect on the return from the new owners' investment in ATI. The real concern in the public interest is that fares and freight rates are not increased as a direct result of the final outcome of the long drawn out share battle for control of ATI.'[2]

Murdoch, however, told the minister that Ansett would be happy to see the two-airline policy torn up, provided the government sold TAA to private interests. Ansett Airlines, he said, would deregulate everything and compete vigorously if TAA were sold. 'I think', said Murdoch, 'TAA would like only one airline in Australia. ... We believe in the free enterprise system and in competition. We pointed out to the Minister that equal competition is very difficult between a private enterprise company and a government company.'

Hunt's response seemed firm enough. He told the *Australian* that the Murdoch proposal was not feasible and 'not Government policy'.[3] On 5 March he informed Sir Robert

Law-Smith (who was knighted in the New Year honours list) that 'he had advised ATI by letter that the government was not prepared to sell TAA'. He had also rejected an ATI proposal that TAA should be required to make a profit of 10 per cent of revenue and be the pacesetter for fare increases.[4] (They were proposals that would have guaranteed ATI high profits and ensured that TAA took all the criticism for fare increases.) The sale of TAA was nevertheless a policy still favoured by many government members. The informed and respected aviation commentator Stanley Brogden wrote: 'The alternative which is being sought by the right wing of the Liberal Party is for the Government to get right out of the airline industry and start a free-for-all which would end in a private enterprise monopoly by one airline'. He described an alternative possibility that involved the TAA purchase of Ansett and, beyond this, 'a vast government-owned airline embracing Qantas, TAA and Ansett'. One big airline, said Brogden, could secure reductions from the government across the whole field of taxation. 'This is the only country in the world which taxes aviation turbine fuel to any degree, and our user-pays system of recovering 100 per cent of the cost of government-supplied facilities is almost unique.'[5] The future structure of the aviation industry, as the eighties began, was an uncertain one even for those most closely involved.

Despite the new leadership at ATI and the ensuing rhetoric on competition, little changed for the travelling public. A TAA paper recorded on 8 January 1980: 'Ansett's new timetables are a carbon copy of the TAA timetables given to Ansett when the two airlines exchanged their March schedules on 14 December. They bear no resemblance to the timetables given to TAA by Ansett at that exchange or the final exchange on 31 December. The TAA timetables contained unique features designed to bring about de-paralleling of timetables and to suit our A300 introduction next year ... Ansett's latest announcement has put an end to those hopes.'[6]

While there was competition between the airlines in special discount fares it did not address the general public concern about the ever rising cost of air travel. In March the federal government responded to this concern by announcing a major public inquiry into Australia's air fare structure. At the same time Ansett announced its answer to the TAA Airbus purchase. The airline decision was a dramatic one. ATI was to buy twenty-one Boeing jets at a cost of some $400 million — five wide-bodied 767s, four additional 727s and twelve smaller 737s.

Time, however, was on the side of TAA. Airbus Industrie offered TAA better delivery dates for their four A300s over the twelve months beginning June 1981. The first TAA wide-bodied aircraft was now scheduled for airline operation in Australia two months before the first flight of the Boeing 767 and more than seventeen months before ATI could take delivery of a 767. (Ironically the ATI rejection of the Airbus had made possible this extended lead by TAA; the third TAA Airbus was one of the aircaft originally offered by Airbus Industrie to ATI.)

TAA had led Ansett competitively through 1979 and ended the year in a dominant position, mainly because of Ansett's industrial and financial problems and the general effect of the takeover battle. It had carried a record one-year uplift of almost five million passengers, an increase on the 1978 calendar year of 8.5 per cent. Load factor had been a high 71.9 per cent and market share on the competitive routes 50.6 per cent. It was in this strong position that Lyn McKenzie announced that his successor, on his retirement in May, would be assistant general manager Frank Ball, with Tony Dignam becoming deputy general manager.[7] Frank Ball had joined the airline on 9 September 1946, the day of its inaugural service. He had operated as pilot from Brisbane until his appointment as training captain in 1949. He became operations manager for the airline in 1957 and was commercial director before his appointment as assistant general manager in 1978. Tony Dignam, a bachelor of economics and a qualified accountant, had also joined TAA in 1946 after five years in the RAAF as a wireless operator.

While the competitive position was strong, the overall TAA financial position — resulting from previous edicts by its government shareholder — was now disastrous. A headline in the *Australian* on 26 March 1980 read: 'TAA Cries for Help; Millions Owed in Pension Commitments". TAA, said the story, 'is pressing the Federal government for several million dollars to avert technical bankruptcy ... Government sources said yesterday it [the sum needed] could be as high as $30 million.' The problem, it wrote, had 'plagued TAA since the Whitlam Government extended the provisions of the Commonwealth Superannuation Act to provide for the annual updating of pensions of retired ground staff in line with cost of living increases'.[8]

The campaign to force a government sale of TAA continued. On 24 March Ansett's general manager, Frank Pascoe, called on the federal government to sell the airline. It was difficult, he said, to create an artificial atmosphere of normal commercial operation in a government enterprise no matter what safeguards were written into the agreement. At the same time Liberal Senator Rae told a meeting of the Royal Institute of Public Administration that TAA should be restructured and operate as a private company.[9] Many other Liberals shared his view. On 12 April the Federal Liberal Party Council, at a meeting in Canberra, called on the Fraser government to sell TAA within five years.[10]

There were willing buyers. The IPEC transport group said it would bid $60 million for TAA, but the offer was mocked by Abeles and Murdoch. Both estimated that TAA was worth at least $150 million. Abeles stated: 'At $60 million we would be delighted to buy all its equipment tomorrow'. From Perth, West Australian businessman Robert Holmes a Court, head of the Bell Group, announced that his company would be interested in buying TAA. 'The decision by the Liberal Party Council', he said, 'is a very sensible policy'.[11]

Law-Smith acted to dispel growing uncertainty at TAA. In mid April he sent a message to all staff: 'It was widely reported at the weekend that the Liberal Party's Federal Council meeting in Canberra on Saturday passed a resolution urging the Government to sell TAA. I want you to know that I have a clear undertaking from the Government that it has no intention of selling ... I think we can take pride from the fact that outside companies are so interested in TAA. They obviously regard TAA as a successful and attractive business.'[12] The Labor Party reacted by declaring that it would reverse any decision by the Fraser government to sell the airline.[13]

At Ansett the new management pressed with vigour what had long been an ambition of Sir Reginald Ansett. The airline wanted rights to operate internationally by providing services between Townsville, Darwin and Singapore. Only twelve months before, in May 1979, Nixon had advised the Commission that Qantas would remain the sole Australian flag carrier until at least 1981. That, Law-Smith told Hunt, 'raised the possibility of the domestic airlines expanding into international operations from some time next year ... The Commission', he said, 'would wish to participate in these operations in the event that the Government decides to relax its policy reserving international operations to Qantas'.

TAA did not, however, want more than a limited role for domestic carriers in the international sphere, believing that a large-scale move by the domestic carriers into international operations would involve a move by Qantas into domestic operations — something that would be very damaging to the domestic operators. 'The Commission believes', Law-Smith told Hunt, 'that Qantas should remain as the sole Australian international flag carrier, with some participation by the domestic airlines in regional international operations under Qantas auspices'.[14]

The Commission had good reason to fear Qantas competition on the domestic routes. Qantas, on its sectors between Brisbane, Sydney, Melbourne, Perth and Darwin, had on average some 20,000 vacant seats each week. Use of those seats for domestic traffic would have diverted business worth more than $75 million a year. 'The immediate effect on the domestic airlines', said Law-Smith, 'would be catastrophic ... [and] create massive industrial problems through the resultant domestic airline staff surplus covering pilots, flight engineers, hostesses, maintenance engineers and airport personnel'.[15] That argument, of course, left unstated the needless waste of national resources involved, and the inescapable overall effect on industry costs and the level of air fares that came from flying with so many empty seats.

Instead of competition with Qantas, Lyn McKenzie advised closer cooperation. He told the Commission on 28 April 1980: 'With new ownership at ATI effective consultation between TAA and AAA [Ansett Airlines of Australia] has almost ceased. Matching the improved service initiatives of AAA will reduce our profitability so we must seek financial benefits in other directions. Qantas is also under attack from ATI with a solid campaign aimed at obtaining approval to operate international routes under the ATI flag. So a closer relationship between Qantas and TAA seems logical.' He wanted rationalisation of services for ground handling, catering and cabin servicing, joint use of freight facilities, special TAA flights to connect with Qantas flights and operation of 'thin' overseas routes on behalf of Qantas to New Guinea and Noumea. McKenzie acknowledged both the inherent absurdity and the political implications of insisting that Qantas deny its considerable unused capacity to domestic air travellers. Though both TAA and AAA were opposed to general operation by Qantas on domestic routes, he reported: 'It is inevitable that the empty seats will eventually be made available for sale'.

It was Lyn McKenzie's last submission to the Commission. 'Minutes of this, the last meeting to be attended by Mr McKenzie, should record', said the meeting on 28 April 1980, 'the Commission's heartfelt thanks for his devotion to duty over his long period of service'.[16]

Sir Peter Abeles was courting the Queensland government, asking the State premier for rights to fly between Townsville and Mount Isa. TAA's response was to inform Bjelke-Petersen that immediate action would be taken to provide more direct western route F27 flights to and from Brisbane and to introduce a direct jet service between Townsville and Mount Isa. TAA undertook to continue F27 operations at existing levels for a period of two years — provided TAA remained the only airline operator on the routes.[17]

On the main trunk routes Ansett had introduced new

competitive initiatives to regain market share, including a 20 per cent fare discount on night flights from Perth and unlimited free drinks and hot meals on evening flights. Each move had been introduced with heavy advertising. TAA estimated that between January and March 1980 Ansett had spent more than $2 million in media advertising compared with $1.2 million by TAA. AAA had also, TAA charged, failed to operate at the agreed load factor of 73 per cent and, as a consequence the load factors achieved by both airlines had dropped. Overall, the consequences for TAA had been a decrease in market share from 50.6 per cent at the beginning of the year to 49.2 per cent by the end of April. During March and April alone TAA's profitability had fallen behind budget by $1.5 million. It was forced to match all AAA's discount fares and introduce the same level of cabin service, which, it estimated, would add a minimum of $3.5 million to its annual costs. 'The severe financial effects of these moves', wrote Law-Smith, 'were a significant influence in the Commission deciding to agree with the ATI request to seek approval for a fare increase of 5 per cent'.[18] Once again it was the public who were to bear the costs of what, on the surface, looked like competition.

On 21 May 1980 the minister announced details of the promised public inquiry into domestic air fares. The chairman of the independent inquiry was W. J. Holcroft, chairman of the Transport Industries Advisory Council and the Manufacturing Industry Council. Hunt warned: 'No-one should be under any illusion that the Inquiry will automatically lead to an across-the-board reduction in fares. The rapidly rising cost of fuel will inevitably lead to fare rises. Three years ago fuel contributed some 15 per cent of airline costs but it is now of the order of 25 per cent.'[19]

Hunt also advised the Commission on proposed changes to the Australian National Airlines Act designed, he said, to enable TAA to operate in a manner that was closer to that enjoyed by commercial airlines. The intensified competitive attitude of ATI, Law-Smith replied, made it imperative that TAA was given capacity under its Act to respond to ATI. But Hunt's proposed changes were, Law-Smith told him, 'totally inadequate to allow TAA to act as a commercial enterprise'. All the old arguments that had to date fallen on deaf ears were restated. A prerequisite to commercial competitive operations was, he said, a solution to the ground staff superannuation problem. Further, TAA's low capitalisation made it overly dependent on debt, forcing it to set aside a high proportion of annual cash flow to meet interest and loan repayments. The proposed dividend payment policy did not embrace a profit retention safeguard and, further, allowed for dividends to be paid from reserves. 'In the Commission's view TAA can operate as a commercial enterprise and compete effectively only if it has a similar cost structure to ATI, which would require a similar capital gearing position and a similar policy on dividend payment and retained profits.'[20]

There was to be movement at last, however, on the superannuation issue. Hunt requested the Commission to 'establish a new ground staff superannuation scheme' and to 'terminate further entry to the Commonwealth Superannuation Scheme'. The Commission moved swiftly, advising him that a new scheme, to be known as 'The TAA General Superannuation Plan' and managed by the Australian Mutual Provident Society (AMP), was planned.[21] (The plan provided for a scheme almost identical to Ansett's, operating at an equivalent cost. It provided for a defined lump-sum benefit at retirement, eliminating the problem of pension indexation costs. While it would lead eventually to the total phasing out of Commonwealth superannuation for Commission employees, this was achievable only over a long period of time.)

Another movement, in mid 1980, exploded like a bombshell on a startled Qantas and TAA. The chairman of Qantas, Sir Lenox Hewitt, was now near the end of his term of office. Hewitt, however, was loath to go. He initiated an open, unprecedented and acrimonious dispute with the Government. On 13 June 1980 the *Age* reported: 'The chairman of Qantas, Sir Lenox Hewitt, is engaging in a public battle with the Federal Government to win a further five-year term as head of the airline'.[22] He gave the strong impression, wrote the *Sydney Morning* Herald, 'of trying to back Federal Cabinet into a corner and embarrass it into reappointing him'.[23] Hewitt lost his battle. The shock for Qantas and TAA came after the government removed him from his position as Qantas chairman. In early July Rupert Murdoch and Sir Peter Abeles announced that Sir Lenox would join Ansett Transport Industries as a consultant and would later be invited to join the board. The *Australian* quoted an unnamed TAA executive's comment: 'When Murdoch and Abeles took over Ansett there were tremors in the industry. If Hewitt makes up a threesome the tremors will turn into an earthquake.'[24]

Mid-1980 saw changes for the domestic aviation industry in the Northern Territory when economic regulatory authority over aviation passed from the Commonwealth to the Territory. A new airline, Northern Airlines, had been established there following the takeover of Connair by East-West Airlines. (As part of an agreement with the Territory government to establish the new airline, East-West had ordered an F28 medium-jet to operate on the intra-Territory network.)[25] Law-Smith wrote to the Territory chief minister, Paul Everingham: 'Next month [September] TAA will sever two long-standing associations with the Northern Territory. These are the provision of F27 services between Darwin–Katherine–Tennant Creek–Alice Springs and operations on behalf of the Northern Territory Aerial Medical Service ... TAA regrets the severing of these associations but does understand your Government's desire to foster the establishment of a new local territorial airline. TAA wishes the government and Northern Airlines well.'[26]

At TAA its new general manager, Frank Ball, announced the establishment of three new senior management positions. Personnel director T. C. Fenton was appointed airline operations director (controlling personnel, commercial services, catering services and operations control), D. G. Withers, management services manager (supply, data processing, property and facilities), and G. W. Beames administration manager (finance, associated companies and audit). The airline now had four directors — Ken Kennett, marketing director; Captain Len Morey, flight operations director; Frank Austin, engineering director, and Trevor Fenton, airline operations director.

TAA was gearing up for the introduction to its fleet in June 1981 of the Airbus. While it promised significant competitive and economic advantages, as well as enhanced profitability, the purchase of the four aircraft also meant a rapid expansion of borrowings, fixed interest and lease commitments by TAA. Frank Ball told the Commission on 25 August: 'The significance of this expansion of borrowings will be that TAA becomes locked into fixed interest debt which must be serviced despite the airline's profitability. This contrasts sharply with ATI's ability to dampen the effect of fluctuations in profitability through greater reliance on share capital, which is serviced according to profit result.'[27] TAA's debt–equity ratio had already deteriorated between 1974 and 30 June 1979 from 1.9:1 to 4.2:1. It was now expected to worsen rapidly and reach a level, by 1984–85, of 13:1. By comparison, the ATI debt-equity ratio at 30 June 1979 stood at 1.2:1. (The Qantas ratio at that date was 2.8:1.)

That federal government decisions affecting TAA were always subject to political imperatives was dramatically demonstrated in August 1980 when Federal Cabinet withheld approval for TAA's Airbus purchase while, at the same time, approving Ansett's purchase of Boeing aircraft. (The government also agreed to provide loan guarantees to ATI.) The decision — to withhold but not reject the TAA Airbus acquisition — was made at the insistence of the deputy prime minister, Doug Anthony, whose political power as a member of the Country Party came from rural Australia. Anthony argued that the Airbus purchase threat should be used as retaliation for the European Economic Community's policies against the importation of Australian primary industry products. More specifically, Anthony hoped that by delaying the government's Airbus decision the EEC would set more liberal trade rules on Australian sheep meat exports.[28]

The Anthony threat hit TAA hard in the middle of a major publicity campaign to promote the wide-bodied airliner. His action had been taken despite strong arguments from TAA and Hunt pointing out that while such a threat would have had leverage some years before, when Airbus orders were minimal, it now was nonexistent as Airbus Industrie had some 400 aircraft on firm order. TAA had made progress payments of some $25 million and had no doubt that Airbus Industrie would seek damages against TAA for noncompliance with their contract. TAA's business reputation, it was argued, was at stake. Further, the TAA initiative in ordering the Airbus had given it a lead over Ansett that it would lose if its contract was cancelled and it was forced to order Boeing aircraft. That lead, TAA estimated, was worth $2 million in market share; and resulting shortage of capacity if it did not receive the aircraft would bring an additional market share loss of 4 per cent worth, in 1981–82, some $32 million.[29]

Deputy Prime Minister Doug Anthony, following an overseas visit to Europe from which he returned with reassurances and promises from the EEC, withdrew his threat to cancel the TAA Airbus order. On 29 September Hunt announced that TAA could proceed with the purchase.

Hunt introduced the legislation to amend the Australian National Airline Act into Parliament on 17 September. The amendments, he said in his second reading speech, were the first in a series of legislative initiatives to give effect to domestic air transport policy changes and were central to them. The policy changes were to incorporate a new Airlines Agreement and amendments to the Airlines Equipment Act, Air Navigation Regulations and the Customs (Prohibited Imports) Regulations. 'Paramount ... was the need to place TAA on a more commercial basis ... on a similar basis to a privately owned airline. At the same time,' said the minister, 'the government is anxious to ensure that the Australian National Airlines Commission, as a statutory authority, is not advantaged over its competitors'.

Freight was removed from the two-airline policy. Existing and potential freight operators were to be able to acquire appropriate aircraft and provide freight services in unrestricted competition. Ansett and TAA were to be allowed, but no longer obliged, to consult on matters affecting passenger services. They were, however, required to consult and attempt to agree on industry load factors and to consult on core fares. There were changes to give TAA greater flexibility in staffing and in the process for determination of its dividend payment. For TAA these changes were to prove modest when compared with what lay ahead. A far more fundamental change to its structure was to come the following year. It was proposed, said Hunt, to legislate for the new Agreement in the next Parliament, together with a revised Airlines Equipment Act, and to reintroduce proposed amendments to the Australian National Airlines Act.[30]

On 19 September Hunt announced that TAA and Ansett had signed the new Two Airlines Agreement. Law-Smith had signed unwillingly. He told the Commission on 22 September that he had reiterated to the minister the Commission's view that he could not sign the agreement until the ground staff superannuation problem had been finalised. The minister, he said, understood the position but told him he 'could not, in the face of the coming election, bind a future Government'. (The Fraser Liberal–National Country Party government was re-elected on 18 October.) If he had refused to sign the agreement, said Law-Smith, the government could have introduced legislation requiring him to do so, 'and the assurances on ground staff superannuation given [in writing] ... by the Minister would not have been forthcoming'.[31] (In May the Commonwealth had agreed to accept responsibility for the unfunded TAA liability as at 30 June 1976. At that date it stood at $96.228 million.)

The Anthony intervention on TAA's Airbus order had not resulted in any delay to the TAA Airbus programme. The airline's first A300 was still on schedule to roll off the production line in January 1981 and arrived in Australia in mid year. There had been intense activity to prepare for it. TAA had committed $36 million for necessary capital works, including a new maintenance hangar at Tullamarine, extensions and new construction at the Tullamarine maintenance base, a new cargo terminal in Perth and renovations and alterations to the airline's Sydney and Melbourne terminals. Tools and equipment for the new type had cost $11 million, spare parts some $32 million, spare engines $12.5 million, with additional expenditure for ground support equipment and a new A300 simulator for pilot training. A new engine test cell was to be constructed at Tullamarine at a cost of $3.5 million. Overall, the actual cost of the four aircraft ordered constituted only some 60 per cent of the total contract price.

As these matters of high policy were resolved, a change in nomenclature for cabin crew reflected the changed public perception of the function of what had traditionally been 'air hostesses'. In October TAA's 700 hostesses became 'flight attendants'. At the same time TAA began training its first male flight attendants.[32]

TAA introduced a more public name change as part of a new corporate identity program planned for the lead-up to the introduction of the wide-bodied Airbus. From 12 November the airline name on TAA aircraft was changed from Trans-Australia Airlines to Trans Australia. The hyphen was dropped from the full airline name, which became Trans Australia Airlines. But the initials by which the airline was so widely known, TAA, remained unchanged. Far more substantial was the decision to change the livery of the entire fleet. In the new design, the blue and ochre stripe along the fuselage and the familiar 'T' on the tail of the aircraft, appropriate to the T-jet era, were abandoned. The kangaroo symbol vanished. The first aircraft to appear in the new TAA colours, on 12 November 1980, was the Boeing 727-276 VH-TBL. Royal blue and gold stripes ran along the fuselage and up into the tail, ending in a stylised TAA symbol. The first Airbus was to arrive in the new colours.

On 14 November the Australian and New Zealand governments gave TAA and Ansett approval to begin services between Hobart and Christchurch. On Saturday, 6 December 1980, TAA operated what was its first major international service, departing Hobart at 10.50 and arriving in Christchurch at 3.25 p.m. local time. The weekly service was operated by a 158-seat Boeing 727 — but under a Qantas flight number. (Ansett, which began a weekly service on Wednesdays, made it plain that it objected to operating under Qantas auspices; it wanted the route in its own right.)

Yet another suggestion from Canberra was put forward in early 1981 to reshape the Australian aviation industry. Democrat Senator Don Chipp called for a merger of TAA and Qantas. TAA did not respond officially but in off-the-record briefings it put forward its arguments why such a course lacked merit. Recent mergers in Britain and New Zealand, it said, had led to airline losses. In Australia TAA operated short-haul domestic routes, Qantas long-haul international routes; they were different tasks needing different equipment. These differences, said TAA, worked against the economy of scale theory. Maintenance practices of the two airlines were different; Qantas maintenance was centralised in Sydney, TAA's was spread to serve its domestic operations. Domestic marketing differed from the marketing of international services. Real economies of scale, it argued, could only be achieved by a merger of TAA and Ansett.[33]

In a climate of growing public uncertainty about the future of Australia's airlines, Hunt was forced to restate that the government had no intention to sell Qantas.[34] The Centre for Independent Studies (a policy research body favouring free market economics) produced a work by economist Michael G. Kirby, *Domestic Airline Regulation: the Australian Debate* (Australian National University, 1981). It gave solid, particularised argument that was severely critical of the two-airline policy. It was Kirby's conclusion that 'the many public interest arguments used in the Australian debate for rejecting market forces and for supporting detailed economic regulation of airlines do not stand close scrutiny'. The Australian air transport industry, he wrote, 'is marked by a substantial degree of economic inefficiency … The principal deficiency of the TAP [two-airline policy] is its failure to provide the major airlines with incentives encouraging them to operate efficiently.'[35] The *Bulletin* commented: 'It [Kirby's work] paints an unattractive picture of paternalistic bureaucrats and corporate commercial cowards running a cosy aviation system which enhances the power and prestige of the bureaucrats and provides absolute financial security for the businessmen, while removing normal commercial risks, producing inefficiency and ripping off the consumer through uncompetitive pricing and hidden subsidies for unprofitable routes.'[36]

It was a realistic and accurate picture. The much-trumpeted 'private enterprise' ethic of Ansett was not what business generally took to be 'free enterprise'; it had always been sustained by politically contrived protection. The two-airline system, which had served Australia well in the formative decades of postwar domestic aviation, had ossified. It was also increasingly the general perception that it was administered not for the benefit of the public but to sustain the two operators, guaranteeing them market share and profits. As TAA had acknowledged earlier in a submission to the government, the two-airline system was a cost-plus cartel. Profound change was inevitable.

Uncertainty on a smaller scale followed in January in the Northern Territory. TAA was advised by the Territory government that the recently constituted Northern Airlines, formed when East-West took over Connair and changed its name, was to close down. (It began flying in September 1980 but was now losing some $200,000 a month. Operations ceased in February 1981.) Frank Ball responded by proposing alternative TAA services.[37] Skywest Airlines, the largest air charter operator in Western Australia, was also interested, offering to buy Northern Airlines. It was Ansett, however, that subsequently took over the main Northern Airlines services.

The Holcroft Report on domestic air fares, also strongly critical of the two-airline system, was tabled in Parliament in February. The government's reaction was minuscule. It approved a revised air fare formula that decreased long distance fares but significantly increased short distance fares. (As most air journeys were over the shorter routes the result for most travellers was higher fares.) Publication of the report intensified public debate on the two-airline system as the government prepared to introduce into Parliament the new airlines agreement.

That new agreement, though it allowed the airlines to

introduce promotional air fares without consultation with each other, did not affect core fares (from which promotional fares were derived). 'The real control on air fares stays', wrote the *Financial Review* in March. 'Core fares will still require consultation between TAA and Ansett for any variation, and these must be submitted to the Department of Transport for approval.' That effectively removed core fare levels from competition.

The new agreement also increased regulation over the main routes by the definition it provided for 'trunk routes'. It described a trunk route as linking any two of the following centres: Alice Springs, Brisbane, Cairns, Canberra, Coolangatta, Darwin, Gove, Hobart, Launceston, Mackay, Melbourne, Mount Isa, Perth, Proserpine, Rockhampton, Sydney, Townsville 'and such other centres as the parties shall agree from time to time'. The *Financial Review* commented: 'To give TAA and Ansett (with Government consent) the ability to designate any town as part of the trunk route poses a big threat to any regional operator'.[38] Further, the new agreement made no change to the controls over airline capacity. The Holcroft Report acted as a catalyst to mobilise the growing number of federal government backbenchers who opposed the new airlines agreement. Led by West Australian Peter Shack, the group advocated the complete dismantling of the two-airline policy. Shack's closest ally, backbencher John Hyde, told the *Financial Review* that he believed eleven government members were prepared to cross the floor in the House of Representatives to reject the new two-airlines legislation.[39]

Hunt had other political problems. The major travel industry group, the Australian Federation of Travel Agents, also made a public statement saying it would object to the ratification by Parliament of the new agreement.[40] Ansett Transport Industries had already exerted pressure, proposing that the federal government consider the sale of TAA to private enterprise before consummating the agreement. The sale of TAA, reported the *Australian* (a Murdoch newspaper) on 12 March 1981, 'was one of the options put to the government ...

before committing Ansett to a $500 million aircraft re-equipment program'.[41]

On 13 March 1981 Hunt responded to all these growing pressures. He announced in Parliament that the government was to make a fundamental change to the structure of TAA, a change that cleared the way for its possible sale. The government intended to abolish the Australian National Airlines Commission. TAA would cease to be a statutory authority and become a public company. The Government, said Hunt, would 'initially hold 100 per cent of the shares in the new public company'. But, he said, 'the Government will commission private consultants to examine the practicalities of selling shares in TAA ... I emphasise, however, that the Government has made no decision to sell any part of TAA to the private sector. The Government will await the advice of the consultants before taking a decision on the matter.' The consultants were to report, he said, 'in about twelve months'. At the same time Hunt announced that the government would maintain the existing regulatory environment of the two-airline policy but would conduct an inquiry over the following five years into whether deregulation of domestic aviation was a desirable long-term objective.[42]

Law-Smith made a public statement on 21 April strongly opposing the sale to private interests of TAA. The government, he said, was faced with a dilemma. The Australian market for airline traffic was small by world standards. 'If a free market existed in Australian aviation', he said, 'it is almost certain that a monopoly or at least a dominant airline would emerge on the trunk routes. This is where the suggestion that TAA be sold runs into problems.' The government, said Law-Smith, wanted to safeguard 'against Ansett securing an interest in TAA and it may want to limit the nature and size of shareholdings in TAA'. Limits on shareholdings, he argued, were important to make sure that ownership was not concentrated. He invoked Ansett's recent history. 'In a very short space of time ATI changed from being a broadly based company owned by over 18,000 shareholders including many employees, into one that is now virtually owned by two large and powerful shareholders.' Regulation of the industry, he concluded, was necessary to ensure that monopoly operation did not eventuate, and such regulation inhibited investment potential and the opportunities normally found in the marketplace. He criticised the decision to make TAA a public company. 'When we first heard of this proposal we thought that a public company would provide us with the means of getting an injection of capital, relieving us of past burdens and freeing us from the constraints of a statutory authority in respect to our commercial activities. However, it must be recognised that there could be considerable cost and serious legal and administrative difficulties in making the change, and in addition it may not necessarily overcome our problems ... After thirty-four years TAA is still acknowledged as the industry leader.'[43]

The *Financial Review* commented: 'It is unprecedented for TAA to publicly put its position on Government policy issues, particularly when some are in limbo ... Showing an uncharacteristic lack of restraint TAA also took the opportunity to sideswipe Ansett Airlines.'[44] The *Age* editorial on 6 April carried the headline 'Aviation policies in turmoil'. The government, it wrote, had given little serious attention to the Holcroft Report and had, in the previous week, approved big rises in short-haul tariffs and small reductions in long-distance fares. Hunt's announcement that the government was considering selling all or part of TAA to private enterprise was 'a complete turnabout on previously stated policies'. It was, said the paper, a vague announcement, seemingly aimed only at quietening the increasingly vocal sections of the government parties that favoured less government involvement in commercial enterprises.[45]

Law-Smith wrote to Hunt: 'Merely converting TAA to a public company, fully owned by the Commonwealth, would put it in a position similar to Qantas, and would not of itself increase its freedom to operate competitively'. It would only be of significant benefit, he said, if there was a significant injection of capital, ground staff superannuation problems were resolved; TAA was freed from Loan Council control; a solution was found to the problem of unprofitable F27 services; and action was taken to achieve a significant reduction in involvement with government departments.[46]

Hunt's announcement came as TAA faced budget problems. Frank Ball advised staff: 'In the 1980–81 financial year to date we are behind budget and are going to find it very difficult to make our financial targets for the year'. The reasons, he said, were the continuing escalation of fuel prices and wages, and disruptions and losses suffered by the airlines as a result of external industrial disputes. Total costs since the September fare increase had risen at an annual rate of $34 million, with higher fuel prices and wage rates accounting for more than half that amount. The use of discount fares, said Ball, had been excessive, diverting normal full fare traffic instead of filling otherwise empty seats. Yield, as a consequence, had been eroded. Concurrently the airlines had experienced a decline in traffic growth. In November, before the onset of external industrial disputes, growth was running at above 10 per cent; over the Christmas period it had fallen to about 1 per cent. The challenge in the period before the first Airbus arrived, he said, was to increase profitability by raising revenues and minimising costs.[47]

TAA suffered a further financial setback when a strike in April by the Airline Hostesses' Association (seeking changes to their agreements with Ansett and TAA) grounded the airline. At the same time, Frank Ball reported a loss of more than $2 million for the financial year from TAA–Mayne Travel Industries operations. 'Hertz [which lost $2.2 million in the 1981 year] cannot be considered a valuable adjunct to the airline operation', he wrote, 'although AAT [which had incurred losses for two years] does generate air travel through air-coach tours ... the value of TAA/Mayne is presently nil'.[48]

On 28 May the government introduced into Parliament its package of airline Bills comprising the Airlines Agreement Bill 1981 (ratifying the agreement signed by the two domestic airlines); the Airlines Equipment Amendment Bill 1981 (which removed freight from the ambit of the two-airlines policy and revised policy controls over the import of aircraft by operators other than Ansett and TAA); the Independent Air Fares Committee Bill 1981 (which established an independent air fares committee to conduct reviews and determine domestic air fares); and the Australian National Airlines Repeal Bill 1981. No government backbencher opposed the Bills. They passed through the House of Representatives on 3 June and the Senate on 5 June. The first three affected the industry generally; the fourth, the most important for TAA staff, provided for the abolition of the Australian National Airlines Commission. TAA was to change its structure from statutory authority to public company on a future but as yet undetermined 'commencing day'. On that day the assets and liabilities of TAA were to transfer to the new company and every staff member of the Australian National Airlines Commission was to become an employee of the new company.

For TAA management the Bill removed the airline's obligations as a statutory authority to consult with government bodies. The powers of the government were to be restricted to the rights of shareholders to appoint directors. 'If', said Hunt in his second reading speech, 'the Government does decide to sell any portion of TAA to the private sector ... a full statement will be made to Parliament at that time'.

While these matters of policy occupied Parliament, TAA management and staff were preparing for the start of a new era in Australian domestic air travel. It came on 13 July 1981 when TAA took delivery of its first Airbus at Tullamarine. VH-TAA, named *James Cook*, became the first wide-bodied airliner to go into service on Australian domestic routes when it commenced scheduled services, after a period for final engineering checks and training, on 22 July, flying Melbourne–Sydney return. It was, wrote *Aircraft*, further proof that the government's own airline 'still has the leadership qualities it so spectacularly demonstrated in the early days of the TAA story'.[49]

It was also the beginning for TAA of fundamental change to its fleet structure. Government approval had already been given for a fifth TAA Airbus. The airline's remaining four firm orders were for deliveries in August and October 1981, and June and December 1982. Options were held for two further aircraft for delivery in August 1984 and August 1985. The new airliners could carry 269 passengers.

Airline operations in the financial year to 30 June 1981 had been drastically disrupted by industrial stoppages both within and outside the industry. Their effect on TAA's results for the year was profound, reducing profitability by an estimated $9 million. Operating profit before abnormal items and tax was a mere $46,000, compared with $5.077 million in the preceding year. (A consolidated profit after tax and extraordinary items of $2.52 million came almost entirely from the sale of surplus aircraft and income tax allowance benefits.) While total revenue increased 16.5 per cent, total expenses rose by 18.2 per cent.[50]

TAA had lost $3 million on its Mount Isa–Brisbane and Mount Isa–Townsville F27 services during the financial year.[51] Following Commonwealth government acceptance of the recommendations of the Holcroft inquiry, air fares now had to be cost-related. That meant that cross-subsidisation of the F27 services, which in the past had enabled TAA to operate the services at a considerable loss, was no longer possible. TAA was now examining closely all its F27 operations.

The introduction of the Airbus and the marketing thrust that accompanied the new TAA livery and corporate identity promised better financial results and competitive advantage for the new financial year. (Ansett, too, made changes, renaming and refurbishing its intrastate airlines and appointing local boards of directors. Ansett MMA was renamed Airlines of Western Australia, Ansett Airlines of New South Wales became Air New South Wales and Ansett Airlines of South Australia became Airlines of South Australia.)

Following the arrival of the second Airbus, regular flights to Perth commenced on 5 September and to Brisbane on 7 September. TAA's third Airbus entered service on 5 October and six days later TAA inaugurated a new transcontinental route, a Boeing 727 service operating weekly from Perth to Alice Springs and on to Townsville in northern Queensland.

(It formed part of a package of new routes planned for northern Australia.)

TAA, Ansett and East-West all introduced additional new services. TAA started direct Adelaide–Brisbane and Sydney–Perth flights. Ansett also began direct Sydney–Perth operations and re-introduced direct Brisbane–Canberra services. East-West began a number of new services with its F27 aircraft including routes from which TAA had decided to withdraw. Friendly cooperation had existed between TAA and East-West since it began operations in 1947, with the airlines exchanging on-carriage. Following TAA's decision to phase out F27 passenger operations, it negotiated with East-West a long-term agreement of friendship and cooperation. (Although the matter was pressed hard by TAA, East-West refused to contemplate TAA taking a shareholding in the airline — an objection based on government ownership of TAA.) In October 1981 East-West began operating Newcastle–Coolangatta–Brisbane, and in February 1982 took over TAA's Albury–Melbourne, Melbourne–Wynyard–Devonport and Melbourne–Devonport routes. (In December 1981 Noosa Air took over TAA's services between Maroochydore and Hervey Bay in Queensland. TAA, using F27s, and Noosa Air, using Bandeirante aircraft, also introduced a combined airline and commuter Brisbane–Maryborough–Bundaberg–Gladstone service.)

The Australian National Airlines Commission continued its opposition to the sale of TAA, or of any shares in the new public company, to private interests. Law-Smith told Hunt on 25 November:

> The Commission remains committed to its firm view that any sale of shares in the airline would not be in the best interests of TAA or the travelling public and, therefore, all the shares in TAA should be beneficially owned by the Commonwealth ... In April 1981 the Government, without prior consultation with the Commission, decided in principle to establish TAA as a public company, a change which in the Commission's view ... is in some respects less advantageous to the Commission than appropriate amendment of its enabling Act. We feel it is our duty as members of the Commission to bring to your attention the problems associated with the proposed change of status ... It is a great pity that

> the forthcoming change and the uncertainty which this is already producing are so damaging to the morale of the staff of the airline ... We are satisfied that the Government's two airline policy can be made to work in the best interests of all Australians if our representations on the status of TAA and the resolution of its problems are put into effect.[52]

Amidst all this uncertainty, several senior management changes at TAA took effect from 1 December following the retirement of Tony Dignam, deputy general manager, on 30 November. Frank Ball increased the number of divisions under him from four to six and grouped the three operational divisions under the new assistant general manager, Trevor Fenton (making him responsible for flight operations, airline operations, engineering and branch managers). Frank Austin remained as engineering director. Geoffrey Beames, as airline operations director, was responsible for commercial services, catering, schedules planning and operations control. Ken Kennett, as marketing director, controlled marketing, cargo and advertising. Jeffrey Pearce was personnel director, Don Withers planning and administration director.[53] Captain Len Morey, flight operations director, who had retired in October after thirty-five years flying with TAA, was succeeded by flight operations manager Captain Athol Fraser, fifty, who had joined TAA in 1957 and had flown most of the major aircraft types of the airline's fleet.

The reshaped management team was to face unprecedented challenges. The most disastrous years in TAA's history lay ahead.

CHAPTER 17

1982

The fruits of government fiat: technical insolvency

On 4 January 1982 the minister for transport, Ralph Hunt, announced that the government was inviting applications from private consultants to examine the practicalities of selling shares in TAA.[1] The announcement intensified media debate on the politics of aviation and the future structure of the industry.

'There is a difference between the two major domestic airlines', wrote the *Bulletin* in January 1982. 'And the difference is widening ... The change in ownership at Ansett has given the TNT–News Ltd subsidiary a new direction. And the new undercurrent of political and economic philosophies in Australia has liberated Trans Australia Airlines to a significant extent.

> The difference [it wrote] begins with their commercial objectives, for Ansett is unashamedly looking to maximise its return from every area of its activities and the airline is pitching for traffic which pays more. It is using a service and frequency bait to attract — some might say buy — this traffic. TAA, although undoubtedly profit-oriented, still has a service to the public and public service approach. It sees its role in the mass market, where the pickings are leaner but the reward for efficiency and volume is much higher. Ansett runs on motivated corporate entrepreneurs who happen to work for an airline. TAA's top people are mainly airline people first ... Trans Australia Airlines gives the impression of an immaculately tuned machine ... In many ways it's an airline's airline. It carefully maps out policies and detailed plans, then

> implements them. It has systematic layers of organisation and defined responsibilities.[2]

It was a polite way of saying that TAA, as a statutory body, was a bureaucracy.

The *Age* did not think TAA would be sold, basing its judgment on the political imperatives of the National Country Party. It quoted the words of the party's leader, Doug Anthony, in April 1981. 'If such a sale went ahead the realities of commercial competition would make it inevitable that the more costly and less profitable routes now operated by TAA would be dropped. This would mean great hardship for a great many Australians outside the major cities.' Those words, it said, represented the closest thing TAA would receive to a guarantee that it would remain in government hands, given the National Country Party's impeccable record in protecting the interests of its rural voters. 'The calling for a consultant's report', it wrote on 6 January, 'is part of a classical political trade between the competing interests of the [government] Dries and the pork-barrel policies of the NCP. For Australia's aviation industry and the travelling public it means the decision on what to do with TAA will have little to do with sound economics.'[3]

The *Financial Review*, in its editorial on 8 January, wrote: 'The continuing eagerness of some Government backbenchers to see TAA sold off to private enterprise has some curious parallels with the doctrinaire insistence by the Labor Party of the 1950s and 1960s on seeing Ansett nationalised. In both cases a practical question of the most desirable form of organising Australia's domestic air travel arrangements has been neglected in favour of ideological positions on public as against private enterprise.'[4]

On 12 January Law-Smith entered the rekindled debate, issuing a strong public statement opposing the sale of TAA to private interests.

> By any standard [he said] TAA has proven itself to be a successful and efficient airline operator. Each year, apart from its formative days, TAA has made a profit, despite limited capital and restrictions on the uses it can make of its profits compared with privately-owned businesses ... The public interest could be com-

> promised by two private airlines operating within the two airline policy and committed to maximising profits. Despite this danger there still are calls to sell TAA and de-regulate aviation in Australia. The arguments seem to be based on ideology and not practicality. The solution can be achieved without disposing of TAA ... In our thirty-four years of operation TAA has contributed some $458 million in revenue to the Australian Government.

He pressed for an increase in the airline's capital. (TAA's capital was $15 million — a figure which had not changed since 1960 and had increased only marginally since 1946.) Total shareholders' funds, he said, amounted to some $29 million. 'The two major shareholders in ATI — TNT and News Limited — have capital and reserves approaching $400 million. The lack of capital investment and the inability to retain development funds forces TAA to rely upon costly loan funds and reduces the ability to compete effectively in acquisition or diversification. With a small capital base TAA has a high debt-equity ratio, particularly since the purchase of new technology aircraft. (TAA's capital gearing ratio in 1981 was 7.8 per cent; ATI's was 67 per cent.)

It was a forceful statement for the head of a government statutory body, with political implications. Law-Smith made it clear that government initiatives had devastated the airline's financial position. The actuarial liability of the airline arising from the Commonwealth superannuation scheme, he revealed, now approached $140 million. 'The airline's large financial liability ... did not arise from any act of the airline nor was the airline consulted about the effect of changes to the scheme.' TAA had also, he said, written off capitalised exchange losses on Swiss franc borrowings amounting to $31.2 million. 'This loss was due to Government policy which prevents onshore borrowing by the Commission.'

He emphasised the social contribution TAA made in rural areas where profit was not, as in private enterprise institutions, the overriding goal. The airline, said its chairman, had continued to operate uneconomic Fokker Friendship routes to provide essential services for people living in rural areas, particularly in Queensland. 'TAA's Fokker Friendship operation in Western Queensland alone is costing the airline about

$3 million a year.' He concluded: 'It is difficult to see why the Government should wish to dispose of a profitable enterprise which plays such an important role in domestic civil aviation and pays all the normal taxes and charges as well as achieving a profit and providing a dividend each year to the government.'[5]

TAA gained some relief from its cross-subsidisation of F27 routes in Queensland. In March 1982 Ralph Hunt announced that Cabinet had agreed to match a Queensland government subsidy to TAA for its inland F27 routes, with each government contributing $1 million over the following two years.[6] The Queensland government also gave TAA approval to enter into a route-sharing arrangement between Brisbane and Gladstone with a new Queensland airline, Sunstate Airlines. Sunstate began operations in December, using Brazilian-designed 18-seat Bandeirante aircraft. TAA continued F27 operations but on a reduced basis.[7]

While Law-Smith confronted TAA's political masters, Frank Ball faced ominous developments in the marketplace. Worldwide, all airlines were now in trouble. The *Age* wrote: 'The crisis which has affected most of the big international operators, Qantas included, has its origins in accelerating fuel prices, higher fares, a slump in passengers and the economic recession'.[8] For TAA, with three large-capacity Airbus A300s in service, the anticipated growth in traffic for which they had been ordered had failed to materialise. The airline, geared for a 7 per cent growth in business in 1981–82, now estimated that it would fly much the same number of passengers as it had carried in 1978–79. All signs of growth had disappeared. Negative growth was forecast for 1981–82. Ball attributed the decline to the changed economic conditions coupled with the effect of higher fares now charged on short-haul routes as a result of the Holcroft inquiry. As revenue fell there were heavy cost increases, particularly in interest charges and salaries and wages. A strike by Licensed Aircraft Maintenance Engineers in August 1981 had reduced profit by a further $6 million.[9]

The decision to shed some of the airline's unprofitable F27

routes had already been taken in 1981. Capacity controls had been introduced to help bring costs down. The severity of the traffic slowdown now forced measures to reduce staff. Ball announced a policy of non-replacement of staff, a step towards getting staff numbers down as far as possible by attrition. That policy in itself, however, was not sufficiently effective. 'Our staff numbers', he said, 'are geared for growth but as growth is not present the numbers must be adjusted back to the level of business activity ... We are now inviting staff in some areas to consider taking leave without pay but to achieve the necessary reduction in staff numbers it may be necessary to retrench a small number of recently employed staff.'[10] (The airline had 9,003 employees, up from 8,632 twelve months earlier. Part of the growth in staff numbers had come from the introduction of the Airbus, part from refurbishment of TAA's DC9s and part from anticipated traffic growth.)

On 10 February Law-Smith announced that TAA needed a capital injection of $90 million and might have to lease its next Airbus aircraft to ride out its financial difficulties. He wrote to Hunt: 'I am writing to express my deep concern regarding TAA's deteriorating liquidity position and critical financial structure. At present TAA is operating with a bank overdraft of approximately $30 million and this is estimated to exceed $40 million by 1 March. Long term debt commitments exceed $250 million ... The existence of this critical financial situation is starting to affect TAA's creditability as a borrower in financial markets and is placing an extremely high interest burden on both cash resources and operating results.'[11] On the same day Frank Ball wrote to Charles Halton at the Department of Transport to inform him that there had been 'a firm decision to retrench somewhere between 200 and 250 TAA employees on the principle of early retirement, voluntary leave without pay and, as necessary, last-on first off'.[12] *Business Review Weekly* reported: 'TAA's overall market share has suffered because Ansett has won public support for frequency of service with its Boeing 737s against the wide-bodied comfort in TAA's Airbus'. Serious talk about selling the airline, it wrote, was likely to lose momentum. 'After all, who wants to buy a financially-strapped business?'[13]

At Ansett Sir Peter Abeles confirmed that he shared TAA's market assessment and that Ansett was embarking on its own review of the need to cut costs.[14] In a letter to Ansett staff on 19 February he wrote: 'There is no doubt that Ansett has been affected by the downturn in traffic in exactly the same way as other airlines within Australia ... However, Ansett Airlines of Australia is now firmly established as the market leader in the domestic aviation scene within this country and we are better placed to withhold from the necessity of taking any drastic action at this time. Accordingly I can advise that at this time Ansett Airlines of Australia will not be taking any action to retrench staff in any areas whatsoever.'[15]

Abeles informed Law-Smith on 19 February that Ansett intended withdrawing from the Hobart–Christchurch service from 3 March. TAA announced that it would take over sole operation of the route using Boeing 727s.[16] Over the fourteen months it had operated the service TAA had carried some 12,000 passengers between Tasmania and New Zealand at an average load factor of more than 60 per cent.[17] Ansett had plans for other overseas initiatives. The Ansett withdrawal from the New Zealand route followed advice to Hunt from Qantas chairman Jim Leslie on 27 January that Qantas had no objection to Ansett operating on the Australia–Vanuatu route.[18]

On 30 March 1982 the *Bulletin*'s John Stackhouse wrote: 'The general feeling is that TAA was trounced in the marketing battle with Ansett, is being harassed by industrial problems and by government interference and ... has dropped its bundle. [Ansett now had a 4 per cent market share margin.] The feeling is that fundamental changes will have to take place at TAA before it again achieves success. It is eventually in the management area that real change will have to come. The TAA-versus-Ansett story is not a simple commercial clash between roughly equal rivals. It is a clash of corporate cultures ... [TAA] will need a drastic infusion of strength, financially and spiritually, to be able to fight its way back.'[19]

The clash in cultures, however, was not simply one between those who favoured private enterprise in a free and unregulated market versus those who saw government ownership and regulation as providing necessary air services that did not all earn profits. Sir Peter Abeles was as aware as Reginald Ansett had been that the closely regulated two-airline policy guaranteed stability — and profits for ATI. He told *Executive News*: 'I've always been working in a completely free environment ... As the months and years are passing by I started to have my great doubts about deregulation. It has created a very bad aviation industry in the United States. Unfortunately for my private beliefs it is coming through very strongly now that some prophets of deregulation in America are changing their minds in the light of that experience. It could be that aviation is an area where because of the very high capital investments and the variety of markets plus the aspect of servicing the public that makes it impossible to operate in a truly deregulated market.'[20]

The Australian aviation industry was not unique in its deteriorating financial situation. Qantas Airways Limited's director of planning, Jack Dawson, told the Australian Transport Research Forum in Hobart on 17 March:

> The international airline industry's financial dilemma continues with every likelihood of becoming worse. According to reports quoting the International Air Transport Association last year's $2 billion loss by the IATA airlines will be surpassed in 1982 with an expected deficit of more than $3 billion. The top sixteen American airlines, the reports said, had accumulated $10 billion long term debts in 1981 and are expected to borrow at least $20 billion from external sources during the next ten years — that's twice as much as they borrowed during the decade of the 70s. IATA's latest estimate is that member airlines will need about $100 billion in order to re-equip their fleets in the next ten years, of which only $40 billion will be covered by internally-generated funds. ... The prospect of bankruptcies has become a reality.

Dawson, however, criticised Australia's domestic aviation industry. 'For the first time our two major domestic airlines appear to be in trouble, having a serious traffic slump on their hands and consequent over-capacity. But they themselves must bear most of the blame.' He told the forum he had some sympathy for TAA in the crisis because it was modernising its fleet with wide-bodied aircraft. But Ansett, he said, had been slow to provide the ingredients for stimulus and innovation in domestic air transport. 'They have so far played around with cosmetic issues like food service, a new paint job and hostesses' uniforms.' Ansett, he said, was pursuing through the back door ambitions to operate international services.[21]

The *Financial Review*, however, saw 'some disconcerting similarities between the disastrous performances of the international airline industry and the problems of Australia's domestic airlines, particularly TAA'.[22] (Abeles wrote to Qantas chairman Jim Leslie, formally complaining about Dawson's criticisms, and Dawson was called before his chairman. Leslie's message, however, was that he continue with such medicine. Qantas did not approve of moves made by Abeles to conclude arrangements with South Pacific governments to operate services on their behalf, viewing them as a back-door method of circumventing Australia's single-designation policy for international operations.)[23]

A new accord between TAA and East-West Airlines was signed by TAA in March 1982, replacing the original agreement signed in December 1972 for a term of ten years but similar in its terms. Ball told the Commission: 'In view of ATI's intention to tie up regional and commuter services throughout Australia the renewed expression of friendly co-operation is particularly valuable.'[24] (Ansett held a strong position in Queensland and New South Wales, was dominant in Western Australia and controlled both the Northern Territory and South Australia. Air Queensland, formerly Bush Pilots, directed most of its business to Ansett. In New South Wales TAA lost the on-traffic from Newcastle-based Masling/Aeropelican when it was acquired by ATI.) East-West itself, however, faced radical change. A syndicate headed by former Ansett executive Bryan Grey (of Skywest Airlines in Western Australia) made a bid to take over East-West. It was immediately rejected by East-West's chairman, John Riley, but on 23 August 1982, at an extraordinary meeting of shareholders, the offer was subsequently accepted. (Skywest formally acquired East-West in December.)

In May 1982 Law-Smith told *Business Review Weekly* that TAA had had an operating loss of $9 million for the first nine months of the financial year, the first operating loss for thirty years. 'While it is no surprise that TAA is facing an operating loss', the journal wrote, 'the size of the loss is a shock'. Factors contributing to the loss, it said, were 'the slump in domestic airline business, loss of market share to Ansett, the new air fare formula depressing short-haul traffic, the maintenance engineers' strike, losses by associate companies and the airline's interest rate and superannuation burdens'.[25] (TAA's Wanderers' Paradise Resort in Queensland was facing a serious financial crisis.) Frank Ball, in a management memo, thought the article helpful in reinforcing to staff why cost-cutting measures had been necessary. He advanced as additional factors for the losses the effects of Ansett's intrastate subsidiaries, losses on F27 routes and costs associated with the introduction of the Airbus.[26]

TAA was now to have a new minister. On 11 May Law-Smith wrote to Hunt expressing 'thanks and appreciation for the consideration and support you have given to the Commission while you were our Minister'. Hunt had been minister for transport and construction. The new minister, Wal Fife, was minister for aviation, following the removal of aviation from the Department of Transport and the creation of a separate Department of Aviation in May. Heading the new department was Colin Freeland. The creation of a Department of Aviation reflected both the turmoil in the industry and the concern of the government. It had been effected, said the prime minister, Malcolm Fraser, to give the industry 'undivided ministerial attention'.[27] One of Fife's first tasks was to inform the Commission of the government decision on 8 June that there would be no increase in TAA's capital base for the time being. Law-Smith advised him that, as a result, TAA would wish to borrow by 30 June the full $42 million of its Loan Council program for the financial year.[28] That meant more debt and an even higher interest burden.

That news came with Fife's announcement that the government had taken 'a further decision towards establishing TAA as a company'. Cabinet, he said, had decided to take over further responsibility for TAA's unfunded liability to the Commonwealth superannuation scheme of some $140 million in addition to the $96 million previously approved. 'TAA has established its own superannuation scheme for ground staff and TAA employees are no longer able to join the Commonwealth superannuation scheme ... These moves are designed to help place TAA on a more comparable basis to Ansett. Clearly, cost penalties such as those involved in current superannuation arrangements for TAA are difficult to reconcile with the government's two airline policy. The Government is moving to establish TAA as a company. I hope it will be possible to establish the company later this year. There has been no decision,' he said, 'on whether to sell any of the shareholding of TAA'. The decision on the need for further capital to improve TAA's gearing ratio would, said Fife, be made after consideration of the consultant's report on the feasibility study for the possible sale of all or part of TAA.[29] The government also decided that TAA would pay employer contributions to the Commonwealth at normal commercial rates for TAA employees who opted to remain in the Commonwealth superannuation scheme.

(In August, 1982 TAA's finance manager, Spencer Park, told the Senate Standing Committee on Finance that TAA would have collapsed if the federal government had not accepted responsibility for a $200 million deficiency in its staff superannuation fund. Park told the Committee that the airline's problems had begun in 1973 when indexation of pensions became automatic. At that stage, he said, the fund had a $2.5 million surplus. Following 1973 changes to the fund, he said, an actuary had recommended rates of contribution by TAA of approximately 58 per cent of relevant salaries — levels that were totally beyond TAA's capacity. TAA, however, continued to contributed at the rate of 20 per cent.)[30]

Ralph Hunt wrote a personal letter to Law-Smith on 18

June thanking him for expressing his appreciation 'for my helping to resolve the longstanding superannuation problem that has been a source of great embarrassment to both TAA and the Government. I was very pleased', wrote Hunt, 'that Wal Fife, as the new Minister, was successful in Cabinet in the final resolution of the problem'. He told Law-Smith that TAA's capital problem should be dealt with urgently. 'As you know, I am not one who supports the sale of TAA but I do believe it is absolutely essential for TAA to be given the right capital structure to enable it to compete in an unfettered manner with Ansett under the two airlines policy.'[31]

TAA had a surprising ally in its bid for additional capital. Sir Peter Abeles told the *Australian* on 12 June that the federal government 'should follow up its superannuation deal with TAA by investing in it another $150 million'. TAA, said Abeles, 'needs to be recapitalised in line with requirements in private enterprise'.[32] It was clear that Abeles recognised the necessity for a financially stable TAA if the two-airline policy, on which so much rested for ATI, were to survive. The mantra of the domestic aviation industry in mid 1982 was 'stability'. It was threatened by the economic recession, by yet more overcapacity from the impending arrival of the first of Ansett's Boeing 767s in December, by the stagnation of passenger traffic that followed the big increase in short-haul trunk route fares based on the Holcroft fare-setting formula and by the industry's aggressive discounting, which TAA had initiated to help fill its 269-seat Airbus A300s.

In July 1982 the *Financial Review* reported: 'Six months after announcing the terms of reference for a proposed consultant's report on the feasibility of selling TAA, the Government has finally appointed someone to do the job'.[33] Fife told Law-Smith: 'A consortium headed by Price Waterhouse has been appointed ... to investigate the practicalities of selling shares in TAA as a public company and measures to ensure the independent and separate ownership and management of Australia's trunk airlines. Price Waterhouse will be supported by Potter Partners and the legal firm of Blake and Riggall. The consultant is expected to commence work on 23

August and report to the government fourteen weeks later.'[34] He also advised: 'While acknowledging the Commission's commitment to total Government ownership, I must reiterate that the Government has decided that the company be established in a form most compatible with the possible sale of its shares at a later date. The inclusion of Stock Exchange listing requirements is therefore considered essential.'[35]

For the financial year to 30 June 1982 TAA reported an operating loss of $7,950,000 and a consolidated net loss after tax and abnormal and extraordinary items of $494,000. (Abnormal items were mainly profit from the sale of aircraft no longer needed; extraordinary items represented a provision for deferrred income tax.) No dividend was provided for and there were no transfers to reserves. 'The Airbus', said the annual report (which was not published until 26 April 1983), 'introduces significant advances in operating efficiency but its full benefit can only be realised with high utilisation, which has not been achievable under recent market conditions.'[36]

The overcapacity provided by the Airbus fleet was compounded when the fourth A300 was delivered in July 1982. At the same time Law-Smith advised Fife that he anticipated an industry passenger traffic decline for the 1982–83 year of some 5 per cent to a traffic level below that experienced in 1979–80. Prospects were abysmal. 'After several years of cost-cutting,' he said, 'we are approaching the limits beyond which further cuts will be detrimental to service standards ... TAA has recently been trailing Ansett in market share and even more severely in its share of high yield traffic. Of special concern is the belief that depressed trading is likely to continue not only through 1982–83 but at least through 1983–84. ... It is appropriate that you should be fully aware of TAA's critical financial situation.'[37]

In August 1982 Frank Ball announced the formation of a separate management centre for the cargo operations of TAA. The new division had its own set of books and its own dividend target. 'While cargo will still be part of the total TAA operation,' said Ball, 'it will be expected to stand on its own two feet and make a profit'. TAA cargo manager Ken Newman headed the new division. One of his first initiatives was to form a close association with the independent IPEC freight company, chartering capacity on IPEC's all-cargo DC9-30 and its Argosy freighters.[38] (Newman retired on 31 March and was succeeded by Col O'Brien.)

Another significant internal development saw the opening of a new, separate management centre. In September a new TAA $7 million catering complex was opened by Wal Fife at Melbourne's Tullamarine Airport. It was the biggest food production facility in Australia. As well as providing for the airline's needs the new centre gave TAA the capacity to increase its catering business with international carriers and provide services to hospitals, nursing homes and industrial organisations.[39]

By October 1982 TAA's finances were at crisis point. Law-Smith wrote to his minister in terms never before used: 'TAA faces a range of financial problems so critical and of such magnitude that they can only be overcome by assistance from the Government and an immediate injection of capital'. The forecast for the financial year was a massive operating loss of $43 million. 'The airline', said its chairman, 'is approaching technical insolvency'. Guaranteed borrowings, he said, were no answer to the problems facing the airline. 'We are unable to meet our current interest payments.' He listed the other elements of the approaching crisis. The 1982–83 cash forecasts indicated an estimated funds deficiency of $128 million by 30 June 1983. TAA was rapidly approaching the limit of its short-term borrowing capacity. The emerging financial crisis gave lenders under the Airbus Credit Agreement the right to declare a default and demand immediate repayment of outstanding funds guaranteed by the government. 'In the light of the rapidly emerging cash and trading position, the support of TAA's local bankers in the future is uncertain.'

'Many airlines may not be able to survive the next five years', wrote Law-Smith. 'With timely assistance from our shareholders in the form of a capital injection, the Government approval for leveraged leases of A300s and continuation of its current positive plan of action, TAA can avoid this fate and do its part in the preservation of the two airline system.' To overcome TAA's liquidity problems he asked for an immediate capital injection of $50 million with a further $100 million by 1 July 1983.[40]

As this letter was written Ansett deferred delivery of its four wide-bodied Boeing 767s from December to mid 1983. The comparable fleets now were: TAA — four A300s, 12 Boeing 727-276s, eight DC9-31s and eight F27s (a total of 32 aircraft); Ansett — 16 Boeing 727s-200s, 12 Boeing 737s and seven F27s (a total of 35 aircraft). TAA had known for some time, as Law-Smith told Fife, 'that Ansett's advantage in fleet numbers when translated into higher frequency is a major factor in TAA's poorer competitive performance in the current market'.[41] (TAA market share was now around 48 per cent of what was a reduced overall market. It had never fully recovered its market share following the August 1981 engineers' strike, which grounded TAA but not Ansett.) TAA's fleet disadvantage would have been mitigated to some extent if the Ansett 767s had been delivered in December. It was now to continue, in a period when TAA research forecast a continuing sharply downward trend in domestic air travel.

TAA was keen to move out of F27 services completely. Politics in Queensland, however, made this difficult. Despite the joint subsidies from the Commonwealth and Queensland governments of $2 million per year, TAA was still losing $4.56 million on its F27 services on the Queensland coast, through inland Queensland and on the Cairns–Gove–Darwin route. (In February 1983, following the agreement of the Queensland government, TAA's coastal city F27 services were replaced by Sunstate Airlines operations.)

It was a completely new environment for both TAA and Ansett. For three decades there had been relatively stable and strong industry growth, with passenger traffic increasing annually at an average 7.7 per cent. The forecast now was that demand for air travel would fall heavily until 1984–85. That decline flowed from an expected sharp downturn in the Australian economy, with falls in real gross domestic product, fixed capital expenditure and household incomes, as well as an increase in unemployment. A drought in the eastern States exacerbated the economic downturn. The depressed conditions were expected to create a critical watershed in the evolution of the Australian airline industry. The decline in real GDP, a major determinant of business travel, was to hit that segment of the business. At the same time the decline in the non-business segments was expected to be even greater. An internal TAA report commented: 'Current traffic levels are such that the appropriate industry fleet should be all narrow-body. However, it would be difficult for TAA to revert to an all narrow-body fleet given the capital already expended on the A300 aircraft and support facilities.'[42]

In mid December 1982 Fife (following a Cabinet decision on 13 November) advised Law-Smith that the government had agreed to make a capital injection of $25 million in TAA. That figure fell far short of TAA's needs. At its meeting on 13 December the Australian National Airlines Commission decided to sell eight TAA properties and dispose of resorts at Bedarra Island. It had also received ministerial approval to sell its main Sydney property, Phillip House. (Dunk Island and Keppel Island were retained as they were profitable in their own right and contributed to TAA traffic.)[43]

The government-owned Qantas also faced debt problems and wanted more capital. Chairman Jim Leslie attacked the government on 8 December, stating publicly that its was horrifying that the imbalance between the airline's debts and its capital worth was imposing an annual interest bill of $54 million. Unless the government gave Qantas a capital infusion, he said, the airline would face another loss for the year despite the sale of assets. 'If a small country like Singapore can suddenly put $200 million into its airline, as it did last year because it had a poor debt–equity ratio, Australia has to decide, if it is going to stay in the international airline business, to improve Qantas' debt–equity ratio.'[44]

The TAA financial situation, however, was far more serious. As it endured the worst-ever year in its history in 1982–83 it was, in December 1982, incurring losses of some $1 million a week. It had managed to obtain agreement from Airbus Industrie to delay delivery of its fifth Airbus, due in December 1982, for twelve months. But the aircraft was now considered to be surplus to requirements for at least four years. The manufacturer had refused to consider cancellation of the purchase agreement and had indicated that legal action would be taken to secure payment in full. The Commission decided, at its meeting on 13 December, to sell one of its earlier Airbuses 'on any reasonable offer'.[45]

The government was constrained, when considering the future of Australian domestic aviation, by the Airlines Agreement negotiated with Ansett and TAA in 1981. That agreement committed the government to maintain the two-airlines environment for at least eight years, until January 1990. Though the government might choose ultimately to dismantle the two-airline policy, it was not a decision that could be taken in 1982–83. The problem it faced was to maintain two viable airlines in the eight-year period ahead. To ensure that, the government's advisers considered that government control of one airline was essential.[46]

Options, however, were canvassed. One, put to the minister in January 1983, was to close down TAA by selling off its assets. That path, the minister was advised, meant either a monopoly of trunk route services by Ansett or designation of a successor to TAA under the two-airline policy — or, more radically, a move to deregulate the domestic airline environment. An Ansett monopoly had, he was told, significant political implications. Designating a successor for TAA was just as difficult. Only Qantas, and East-West Airlines in the longer term, were possibles for this role. A decision to dissolve TAA meant a decision by government on whether its creditors would be fully paid out or whether it would leave TAA in a situation of not being able to pay its debts. (The latter meant a situation in which lenders could call on Commonwealth guarantees.) It was an indication of the depth of the crisis in the domestic aviation industry that the option of the dissolution of TAA was even canvassed.[47] Other options put to the minister were the continuance of TAA as a 100 per cent

Commonwealth-owned entity, either as a statutory authority or a company; establishment of TAA as a company with 100 per cent Commonwealth ownership followed by the sale of all equity; retention of a minority Commonwealth shareholding; or a combination of Qantas and TAA operations in some way.[48]

The new year started dramatically when TAA's Queensland manager, on 5 January, received a typewritten letter demanding $A250,000, $US250,000 and the equivalent of $A500,000 in diamonds. The note indicated that failure to comply would result in the destruction of a TAA jet aircraft shortly after take-off, as well as detonation of a remotely controlled, highly explosive device in a car parked in a heavily populated public place. The letter was signed 'Survival Security Team Group 5'. TAA reported the matter immediately to the Federal Police and the Department of Aviation, as well as local authorities in Brisbane. The emergency ended on 12 January when another letter was received from the extortion group stating that it had never been their intention to harm the public or collect the ransom. Their objective, they said, was to demonstrate the potential danger that the public was subjected to because of 'ineffective flight path security'.[49]

It was an indication of the seriousness of TAA's commercial situation that the airline's pilots, not noted for their closeness to management, joined forces with TAA sales representatives throughout Australia in January and initiated calls with sales staff on TAA clients. Staff numbers were falling under the staff reduction programme. TAA staff numbers had peaked at 9,003 in November 1981; by 31 March 1983 they had fallen to 8,100. In February, to further cut costs, remaining F27 airline services were withdrawn from the Brisbane–Gladstone route (and replaced by Sunstate Airlines), and TAA began discussions with the Queensland government on transferring the State's inland services to a lower-cost operator. Overall, as a result of F27 route withdrawals to date, TAA had managed to reduce its F27 fleet from ten to five. Trunk route competitiveness improved when the airline extended its business class service in February to all its fleet. (Business class was introduced on Airbus services in October 1982 with a 15 per cent surcharge on economy fares. The business class service, a concept rejected by Ansett, was exclusive to TAA and was to prove effective in helping the airline regain market share.) Holiday package fares were cut by up to 25 per cent.

In this demanding environment Ken Kennett, TAA marketing director, retired and was succeeded by Bryan Palmer. Palmer's first message to staff was: 'This year will see us concentrating on the full fare passenger who is the mainstay of the industry'. Market share, he said, had now risen above 50 per cent. 'Our aim is to maintain this lead.'[50] There was a new opportunity in Western Australia. In February the State's Transport Commission announced: 'Following the Review of Internal Air Services and Policy the Western Australian Government has announced fundamental changes to its air transport policy with the objective of achieving a greater degree of competition on intrastate air services. The first stage of the new policy will involve the introduction of limited competition on selected air routes.' Submissions were invited to provided services on the routes from Perth to Geraldton, Kalgoorlie, Port Hedland and Karratha.[51]

A more fundamental change for both TAA and Ansett came when the Liberal–Country Party Government was defeated at the polls by the Labor Party, led by Robert Hawke. On 7 March 1983 Wal Fife wrote his last formal letter as minister for aviation to Law-Smith. Law-Smith responded: 'I believe that what you were able to accomplish as our Minister will be of lasting benefit to the airline industry and to Australia'.[52] On 11 March he wrote to congratulate K.C. (Kim) Beazley on his appointment as 'our Minister'.[53]

The main planks of the new government's aviation policy, as set out in official policy documents, were to establish separate departments of surface transport and aviation, responsible to the minister for transport; to establish a National Airports Authority; to abandon the second runway project at Sydney airport and instead build a second airport; and to retain Qantas as Australia's international flag carrier. It was also pledged to retain public ownership of TAA, review its capital structure and assist in obtaining for TAA intrastate rights in Western Australia. (Despite the recent election of the Burke Labor government in Western Australia in February the entry of TAA still required a referral of State powers to the federal government.) TAA saw the combination of ministerial responsibilities (for surface transport as well as aviation) as 'detracting from the general effectiveness of a Minister whose sole responsibility is aviation'.[54]

Geoff Beames, TAA's airline operations director, had resigned just before Christmas. Frank Ball took the opportunity to review the airline's management structure in an effort to cope better with the marked downturn in traffic (and forecasts of further decline), staff reductions and continued cost pressures, all allied with unprofitable operations. His aims were to strengthen the relationship between marketing and passenger sales, strengthen the ties between TAA and its associated companies, consolidate relations with commuter and regional international airlines and increase the identification of cargo as a separate profit entity. What followed was a reduction in the number of divisions in management from six to five and the elimination of some senior management positions. Ball recommended establishment of a commercial services department within the marketing division, transfer of cargo from the marketing division to the direct responsibility of the assistant general manager, establishment of a ground services department (within expanded personnel) and a ground services division and elimination of the three senior management positions — airline operations director, property and facilities manager and associated companies manager. These changes created an opening for the post of a second assistant general manager.[55] (Engineering director Frank Austin and flight operations director Athol Fraser retired on 29 April. Austin was succeeded by Frank McMullen and Fraser by Captain L. T. G. Heard.)

TAA also advised its new minister that as a result of the current and forecast decline in traffic TAA was anxious to reduce its wide-bodied capacity and was actively pursuing opportunites for sale or lease of Airbus aircraft — 'regrettably so far without success'.[56] (TAA acknowledged Ansett had clearly demonstrated that the efficiency of the wide-bodied Airbus in a regulated environment was outweighed by the higher frequency operations of its smaller aircraft.)[57] Law-Smith also told Beazley that the financial situation was so serious that 'while recognising the range of pressures confronting a newly elected Government, the Commission believes [a further injection of capital] must be given a very high priority in the Government's agenda'. TAA believed, he said, that the airline's total shareholders' funds including reserves and retained profits 'should equal at least 25 per cent of the balance sheet total or alternatively result in a debt-equity ratio of 60:40 as a commercially reasonable though not over generous standard'. TAA's lack of an adequate capital base, he wrote, 'has led to a situation where TAA can no longer be regarded as financially viable'.[58]

Beazley's response was prompt. On 3 May he advised Law-Smith that TAA would receive a further $90 million injection of capital before 30 June. 'It is requested', he wrote, 'that TAA meet the balance of its cash flow requirements by utilising the remaining $35 million from the approved Loan Council program for 1982–83'. The decision, he said, reflected 'the Government's strong commitment to TAA and will provide an appropriate long term capital structure consistent with a 100 per cent Government-owned airline'.[59] TAA was to remain in full government ownership. A Bill was introduced into Parliament on 4 May providing capital of $115 million for TAA (including the $25 million granted by the previous government) and $60 million for Qantas. That brought the total Government investment in TAA to $130 million and in Qantas to $149.4 million. It gave TAA a competitive debtequity ratio of some 70:30 and substantially relieved its interest burden and cash flow problems. (The interest saving for 1982–83 was only $2.6 million but for 1983–84 was estimated at $17.5 million.)[60]

Competitive pressures increased when, on 10 June 1983, Ansett Airlines introduced the Boeing 767 airliner into Australia. Ball told staff: 'If we continue to maintain the high level of efficient and friendly service to our passengers then I am confident we will continue to maintain market leadership. TAA's prime objective is to improve its share of the available high yield first class business. This is imperative if we are to achieve profitability in 1983–84.'[61] (Since the introduction into service by TAA of the Airbus there had been, as a result of the significant change in the composition of the Ansett and TAA fleets, a wider separation of flight time departures. One effect of the arrrival of the 767 was to drive both airlines back to closer parallel scheduling.) While both airlines fought for the high yield business, competition at the other end of the market was also intense. A 45 per cent discount on return economy fares was introduced in July.

There was another issue that concerned TAA, quite separate from the overcapacity of the two-airline system and their cost pressures, and unrelated to the economic downturn that had forced the general decline in traffic. The impact on the viability of the domestic airlines of international carriers operating over domestic routes was a serious concern. The increasing number of international gateways in Australia and the development of through fares by the internationals to these cities had reduced the traffic base of TAA and Ansett and considerably influenced their ability to trade profitably. Law-Smith told Beazley in October 1983 that TAA saw benefits for Australia in a new role for the domestic airlines. He wanted TAA and Ansett to operate regional international air services under charter to Qantas using surplus equipment in their fleets that Qantas was now proposing to duplicate. (Qantas had proposed buying six Boeing 767s.) Such services, he said, would counterbalance to some extent the increasing intrusion by the international operators on domestic routes.[62] (The opening of Adelaide to international flights had alone diverted traffic worth more than $9 million a year.) TAA argued that up to 85 per cent of the proposed use of the 767s sought by Qantas could be achieved with available domestic equipment, including the cornerstone of a new Qantas strategy — 'hubbing' arrangements on Singapore. By using Ansett 767s for these flights, said TAA, Airbus capacity could be shared by the two domestic operators and allow Qantas to begin 767 services some eighteen months earlier than the proposed date for their own 767 operations. (Qantas rejected the offers to use surplus 767 and A300 capacity as unsuitable to its needs.)[63]

Competition for the high yield business market had intensified. In Melbourne and Sydney Ansett had established Golden Wing lounges for the use of business travellers that were superior to TAA's Flight Deck Club lounges (which were in operation at Melbourne, Sydney, Brisbane and Adelaide). Ansett's Melbourne lounge was almost three times as big as TAA's, and Ansett had furnished and decorated it with seemingly little regard for cost. It had also provided a host of facilities for the use of members. In addition, for specially invited leaders of industry and commerce, cabinet ministers and civic dignitaries exclusive and luxurious private lounges had been developed. Ansett planned to double the size of its Sydney lounge and had prepared plans for a major development of their part of the Canberra terminal. TAA had no option but to respond. In October a plan was put forward involving more than $4 million expenditure to expand and upgrade its Flight Deck Club facilities.[64]

More serious was the competitive superiority of the Ansett fleet. Apart from the clear surplus of A300 aircraft the greatest drawback for TAA was at the bottom end of the fleet. Its nine DC9 aircraft competed with Ansett's twelve 737-200s, which were newer and had a better range and operational performance. Ansett had a resulting competitive edge in fleet numbers that translated operationally into better frequency and flexibility. TAA recognised that it would have to begin re-equipping, probably with Boeing 737s. Twelve to fifteen Boeing 737-300s were needed from 1985 to replace existing DC9-30s and some older Boeing 727s. (TAA's oldest DC9 would, by December 1985, be almost nineteen years old. Average DC9 fleet age would be just on sixteen years. The fleet average for its 727s would by then be just over nine years, with the oldest 727 thirteen years.)

Both airlines received a revenue boost from 3 October

when an average tariff increase of 6 per cent became effective. However, TAA's income was severely affected by a two-day domestic pilots' strike that began at midnight on 3 October. The strike was a protest against legislation introduced by the federal govenment affecting tax on lump-sum superannuation payments (a tax that affected not only pilots but a wide range of employees in Australia). TAA and Ansett revenue losses over the two days each amounted to more than $2 million.[65] (East-West and Qantas pilots continued to fly.)

In Western Australia Labor premier Brian Burke's government exerted additional pressure on the two-airline system. 'A major assault on the two-airline system has been launched by the West Australian Government', wrote the *Financial Review*, 'which has authorised another airline to compete with Ansett and TAA over several intrastate routes'.[66] That competition, however, was predominantly with the Ansett subsidiary, Airlines of Western Australia. Skywest Airlines had been authorised to compete on the busy routes from Perth to Port Hedland, Karratha, Kalgoorlie and Geraldton. (Skywest placed orders with British Aerospace for three Jetstream 31 commuter aircraft.) The decision ended the Ansett monopoly on the routes.[67]

On the east coast East-West Airlines was also increasing pressure on the two trunk operators. It was mounting a High Court challenge to the two-airlines agreement, had introduced discount fares on the rich Brisbane–Sydney–Melbourne trunk routes and, in November, introduced a cut-price return fare between Melbourne and Adelaide. The East-West ambition was to achieve deregulation of air services. (In December 1983 ownership of East-West Airlines again changed. West Australian Rick Stowe's Skywest Airlines Pty Ltd took over East-West Developments Pty Ltd and, as a consequence, acquired its controlling interest in East-West Airlines. Skywest and East-West, however, maintained their separate corporate identities.) Beazley told *Australian Business* that the government would fight further attempts by the airline to deregulate the industry. 'I don't believe in deregulation. It doesn't address market realities in Australia ... The

Independent Air Fares Committee and I', he said, 'feel there should be a greater capacity for public interest criteria in the decision-making process'.[68]

For TAA management and for the Australian National Airlines Commission itself there were changes as 1983 ended. Frank Ball advised the Commission at the end of November that the matter of executive succession planning and the restructuring of TAA's senior management organisation had been the focus of close and careful consideration. The aims had been to substantially upgrade management capability by appointing younger and better-qualified people to key positions, produce a clearer, simpler and more effective structure, and free up the decision-making process by enabling directors to devote more time to their primary responsibilities and by delegating authority and responsibility to departmental managers. In the new structure the primary elements of marketing, flight operations, engineering, airline operations and finance were clearly separated to achieve strong focus. J. W. Pearce was to be airline operations director, D. G. Withers personnel director, R. M. Winders finance director and B. W. Porter general marketing manager. D. F. Adams was to be planning and development manager.[69]

The Commission itself was to have a new chairman. Sir Robert Law-Smith advised that he intended to retire on 31 December. He had been closely involved with some of the airline's most difficult problems including recognition by government of TAA's ground staff superannuation problem, changes to the two-airlines legislation, the inquiry into the practicality of selling TAA and its proposed conversion to a public company, and the successful submissions to government for additional capital, as well as the introduction into service of the Airbus. It had been Law-Smith's task to guide TAA through the traumatic period when world economic conditions had led for the first time in the history of the industry in Australia to a substantial decline in traffic. His retirement ended twenty-one years of service that had begun with his appointment to the Commission in 1962.

The TAA annual report for 1982–83, tabled in Parliament

on 8 December, disclosed its worst ever result — a loss of $10.9 million. The loss on operations was far higher — $18.3 million — but it was offset by several abnormal items including the sale of aircraft and TAA's former terminal in Sydney. Total passengers carried had declined by more than 10 per cent to the level achieved in 1976–77. Though total revenue had risen for the year by 6.9 per cent the increase in costs had outstripped revenue by 8.8 per cent. Staff numbers had fallen to 7,874.[70]

The associated company AAT (Australian Accommodation and Tours) was sold in November, but the new owners had signed a long-term marketing agreement with TAA. There was to be no easing of the airline's capacity problem as the year ended. The fifth TAA Airbus left France on its delivery flight on 2 December. There were, though, some hopeful signs. East-West had withdrawn its High Court challenge to the two-airline system and the validity of the Independent Air Fares Committee Act.[71] The *Sydney Morning Herald* wrote: 'Economic recovery in Australia in 1983–84 should spell the end of the recession in the domestic airline industry'. TAA, it said, expected the good times to return in 1984–85.

CHAPTER 18

1984

The grip of uncertainty

The new chairman of the Australian National Airlines Commission was Neil Smith, who had joined the Commission in June 1983 and been appointed vice-chairman in October. Born in 1920, Smith was familiar with the airline business. His career had begun when he left school aged sixteen to become a clerical officer with the Victorian State Rivers and Water Supply Commission. His knowledge of the two-airline system derived from intimate involvement at the highest level with TAA's competitor, Ansett, over a period of seventeen years. From 1951 to 1958 he had been personal assistant to Sir Reginald Ansett. He was an executive director of Ansett Transport Industries from 1958 to 1968. He left Ansett to become general manager of the Gas and Fuel Corporation of Victoria, later becoming its chairman. Smith was a commissioner of the State Bank of Victoria, and had a reputation as a vigorous, no-nonsense pragmatist.

He took up his new position as the Australian economy, after two years of decline, began to grow strongly in 1983–84 with gross domestic product increasing at almost 6 per cent — the strongest growth in a decade — after a fall of 1.2 per cent in 1982–83. That surge in growth had been influenced by a large government fiscal stimulus, the breaking of the drought and greatly improved rural sector performance, plus healthy activity overseas, particularly in the United States.

Neil Smith's chairmanship started as the growth in the Australian economy broadened, in the second half of the financial year, with increases in private business fixed investment and non-farm stocks. Employment grew rapidly, unemployment declined and, with adherence to wage indexation under the Labor government's Prices and Incomes Accord, wage costs increased only moderately. Frank Ball told the *Bulletin* in January: 'We are trading profitably'.[1] He also told the Commission that in assessing future aircraft needs for the bottom end of the fleet the airline should now concentrate its attention on the Boeing 737-300.[2]

There were plenty of encouraging signs. TAA's cash flow was helped by the lease of two of its Airbus aircraft to Lufthansa's charter subsidiary, Condor, for six months. (In June TAA announced that Air Niugini would also lease a TAA Airbus, for a period of three years. To maintain appropriate capacity a Boeing 727 was leased from Ansett.) Lower staff numbers combined with lower interest bills from an improved capital base had also been major factors in reducing costs. For the first nine months of the 1983–84 year the airline had enjoyed an average market share of 50.3 per cent, reversing the Ansett dominance of the previous period. In March the Queensland government announced that TAA had been selected from five competing airlines to continue its operation of western Queensland routes under subsidy. In May Beazley gave approval for TAA to enter into an on-carriage agreement with East-West Airlines for a period of five years. A forecast TAA trading profit for the year boosted what had been sagging morale.

Lack of certainty for the industry and its overall structure under a future government remained. The Federal Opposition, in a policy statement released at the end of March, said it would, if in government, consider selling government bodies such as TAA, the Commonwealth Bank, OTC, Aussat, the Australian National Line and the Pipeline Authority. It was the first major announcement by the Opposition leader, Andrew Peacock, in the lead-up to to a federal election that the prime minister, Bob Hawke, had indicated on 26 March could be between December 1984 and May 1985. Peacock's statement re-ignited debate on the constraints and costs of the two-airline system and the possibilities of deregulation. 'Even the highly regulated broadcasting industry has multiple participants', wrote the *Financial Review*. 'Ansett and the Government-owned TAA can reap the benefits of a duopolistic market where each party is guaranteed access ... This market dominance makes people uneasy.' The proponents of the two-airline policy, in order of conviction, it wrote, were Ansett, TAA and the Australian Federation of Air Pilots. East-West, while not advocating total deregulation, wanted direct access to the profitable trunk routes. 'East-West', said the *Review*, 'will not concede that what it really wants is a three airline policy'.[3]

On 4 May 1984 Beazley introduced two Bills into the Parliament to allow TAA to be more competitive. One (the Australian National Airlines Retention Bill) repealed legislation passed by the former government (but not proclaimed) to make TAA a public company. 'It was clear', said Beazley in his second reading speech, 'that the aim of the whole strategy of transforming TAA into a public company was to sell it off to private interests ... What [our predecessors] left behind was an airline in the grip of uncertainty. I cannot over-emphasise the effect of this uncertainty on the management and staff of TAA.' The second (The Australian National Airlines Amendment Bill) lifted some government controls on TAA and provided that it would make the same (lower) contribution to the Commonwealth superannuation scheme that it made to its own private scheme. Its profit and dividend targets were to be based on commercial criteria. It also allowed the Australian National Airlines Commission the freedom to determine how the balance of profits, after the dividend had been paid, would be spent. Borrowing powers were expanded and more discretion was allowed for the purchase and sale of assets. (Both Bills were passed and received the assent of the Governor-General on 25 June.) Frank Ball told staff: 'These changes are aimed at giving us substantial financial independence and freedom from government control over our basic commercial activities and implement the Government's policy to retain TAA as a public authority'.[4]

Beazley announced another major change for the aviation industry in June. The government, he said, 'had taken an in-principle decision to proceed with the establishment of a national airports authority.' The authority, he said, was to take over from the Department of Aviation the operation of the six major capital city airports at Sydney, Melbourne, Brisbane, Perth, Adelaide and Hobart.[5]

For the year ended 30 June 1984 the Australian National Airlines Commission reported a consolidated operating profit (before tax and abnormal items) of $15.996 million. It was a dramatic turn around from the loss of $18.323 million in 1982–83. (That large operating profit was reduced to a net profit of $3.897 million by a significant change in accounting policies. There was a special write-off for exchange losses and a write-off in respect of interest charges capitalised in previous years.) On 9 July Sir Leslie Froggatt, who had been a Commissioner since 1981, was appointed vice-chairman. (Froggatt was a director of Shell, chairman of Ashton Mining Limited and vice chairman of Dunlop Olympic Limited. He had been chairman and chief executive of the Shell Group of companies in Australia from 1969 to December 1980.) Like Neil Smith, he knew the aviation industry well from former, enduring connections (through Shell) with Ansett. Neil Smith and Froggatt were to dominate the Commission.

Beazley wrote warmly to Smith on 4 September 1984: 'I am delighted to see that the Commission is forecasting a continuation of profitable operations during 1984–85 ... I believe the Commission's improved outlook reflects very creditably on the Commission's streamlining of operations and cost reduction measures and I congratulate the Commission on its results. It is also proof of the success of the Government's actions over the past eighteen months, in particular the significant injection of capital and the recent changes to the Australian National Airlines Act enabling additional flexibility.'[6]

In September 1984 the Commission prepared a comprehensive report to the minister on its operational targets, strategies and policies. Despite the encouraging 1983–84 results it was restrained in its predictions. The economic outlook, it said, suggested patchy traffic growth with another downturn in 1986 or 1987. Political and economic instabilities in the world's oil-producing regions indicated uncertainty in future fuel prices. Governments, it predicted, were likely to continue running deficit budgets, which, with money supply contols, suggested higher interest rates. As a consequence, said the report, 'the industry can look forward to "more of the same" of the last few years'. It concluded that 'the Government's decision to review the future of the two airline system could well lead to some measure of deregulation of both entry into the industry and pricing ... The probable adoption of both deregulation and the sale of TAA as official policy by the Liberal Opposition will ensure that the future ownership of TAA is a matter for continued debate.' The primary corporate objective of the Commission was 'to achieve a level of profitability equivalent to that of Ansett, given differences in structure'. (TAA was less profitable than Ansett because of a combination of lower yields and, in some areas, higher costs.) The operating environment was 'expected to be influenced by two major factors — the uncertain economic outlook and the debate on deregulation'.[7]

The existing Airlines Agreement Act ran for five years from 1981 with a three year notice period. The end of 1986, therefore, was the first opportunity for any of the parties to the Agreement (the Commonwealth, ATI or TAA) to give notice of termination. The Government's proposed review of the arrangements introduced in 1981 was considered by TAA to be timely.

The immediate operating environment of TAA was to suffer from action by its own flight engineers. Their future as flight crew members was threatened by advances in cockpit technology. That technology provided systems that made two-pilot operation of aircraft possible without the need for flight engineers. The Australian Airline Flight Engineers' Association approached both Ansett and TAA in November 1984 with a demand to guarantee employment for presently serving flight engineer officers for their normal career expectancy.

Ansett Transport Industries, recognising the industrial threat posed by the demand and the muscle of the Association, responded on 23 November, undertaking that its flight engineers would continue to be employed as technical crew members until normal retirement age and that 'a professional Flight Engineer Officer will be an integral part of the technical crew on every future aircraft introduced and operated by ATI configured to carry in excess of 120 passengers'.[8] Necessary or not, Ansett was willing to carry flight engineers and pass on the cost rather than face industrial action.

TAA's reponse was more principled. Ball wrote to the Association on 28 November: 'With the advanced technology built into the control, accessibility and monitoring systems contained in the aircraft under examination, two crew operation is considered by all relevant international authorities to achieve at least those standards existing in our current three crew environment. Therefore TAA is not prepared to create technical crew positions which cannot enhance operational standards nor provide meaningful work and job satisfaction.' He pointed out that major changes would not occur until late in the decade with the progressive retirement of the three-crew B727s. 'This gives us time in which to appraise the best way to handle the whole situation to meet your personal needs ...'[9]

TAA paid a heavy price for its rational approach. The airline's Airbus and Boeing 727 operations were grounded for twenty-four hours on 29 November and a further indefinite stoppage began on 6 December. The stoppage, said TAA, occurred 'because Ansett has given in to demands of the AAFEA which are contrary to world practice ... This has left TAA standing alone.' (It was not the first time TAA had had to stand alone. The airline was grounded for six weeks over the issue of crew complements on DC9 aircraft in 1968.)[10] Beazley condemned the flight engineers. 'There are today', he said, 'sixty-three airlines in the world that are operating or have ordered for operation eleven hundred and sixty-eight new technology aircraft, all of which are configured for two-pilot operation'.[11] (At the same time, in a separate industrial dispute, the Australian Flight Attendants Association held a series of half-day stoppages to discuss a log of claims. This dispute affected both airlines.)

On 17 December the Flight Engineers' Assocation accepted a TAA offer that while it operated aircraft requiring a three-man crew, flight engineers would be guaranteed the third position. There were other assurances on retraining, relocation and redundancy packages. The airline suffered heavy losses for eleven days. Its market share for the December quarter dropped from an expected 50.1 per cent to 46.3 per cent. The stoppage reduced profit by $9 million and seriously affected forward bookings by an estimated further $7 million. The strike had effectively negated the airline's hard-won trading recovery. Nevertheless the TAA effort to reduce costs and increase yield and market share had gathered momentum and it was anticipated that a sound operating profit for the financial year could still be achieved.

In an explicit pre-election commitment on aviation policy in November, the Opposition Liberal–National Party coalition (the renamed Liberal–Country Party coalition) said that, if elected, it would scrap the two-airline system and deregulate domestic air fares. TAA, it said, would be sold — as well as a minority interest in Qantas.

It was not given the opportunity to implement its policy. The federal election was held on 1 December and the Hawke Labor government returned. Kim Beazley ended his term as minister for aviation, was promoted to Cabinet and moved to defence. His successor, P. F. (Peter) Morris, announced on 13 December that the Department of Aviation would remain a completely separate entity and would continue to function in its own right 'in line with the Government's recognition of aviation as a major industry in Australia'.[12] He stressed, however, that the Department of Transport would also remain unchanged and that he would continue to administer the portfolio of Transport as well as Aviation.

On 6 February 1985 TAA launched a takeover bid to acquire Air Queensland. On the following day Ansett made a counter bid. For strategic reasons the Commission had adopted the policy that TAA should maintain an active role in the provision of Queensland regional services. The policy was implemented by TAA's operation of inland F27 services and its support of Sunstate Airlines in competition with Air Queensland in the State's southeast. It had become clear that the traffic in this region could not support two operators. Ansett's past and current policy was to achieve of an Air Queensland monopoly by weakening Sunstate's position. Air Queensland's main operations were conducted by leased Ansett F27 aircraft. It had six Metro-liners, but these had proved unsuitable and uneconomical and were grounded awaiting disposal. It planned to trade them in on the purchase of a newly developed turboprop, the ATR42 aircraft. On-carriage was the prize. Air Queensland's total on-carriage to Ansett was some $6 million a year, Sunstate's to TAA some $4 million.[13] TAA had a five-year commercial agreement with Sunstate. It now moved also to acquire a controlling interest in the airline. (To further strengthen its Queensland presence it was negotiating for a controlling interest in its Brampton Island Resort. With the sale of the Wanderers' Paradise Resort TAA no longer had a presence in the Whitsunday Coast area — one of the major tourism growth areas in Australia. Ansett, by contrast, had large investments in both Hayman Island and Hamilton Island, giving it a dominant position in the Whitsundays. Nevertheless TAA's holiday resorts at Dunk, Bedarra and Great Keppel — as well as Brampton — were now each profitable in their own right, as well as providing on-carriage passenger traffic of more than $10 million a year.)

The March 1985 issue of TAA's staff magazine jubilantly reported the outcome of the battle for Air Queensland. TAA was the winner. It had acquired a regional airline operating to forty ports in Queensland, serving isolated communities in the Gulf Country and Cape York, important coastal towns like Gladstone and inland areas including the Blackwater coal area. It also served TAA's three Queensland islands, Dunk, Great Keppel and Brampton, from Townsville, Rockhampton and Mackay respectively, using Twin Otter aircraft. Its fleet included four DC3s, five Twin Otters and a Nomad as well as its four F27s. *Business Review Weekly* commented: 'Not many people can give Ansett chief executive Sir Peter Abeles a lesson in how to run a takeover battle but in the past few weeks Sir Peter has felt the wrath of the Wizard. The Wizard, otherwise known as the mild-mannered TAA and Victorian Gas and Fuel Corporation chairman Neil Smith, had a score to settle with Abeles.' Smith, it wrote, had been 'pretty unhappy over the flight engineers' strike'.[14] *Aircraft* wrote: 'The swift raid by the beleaguered, Government-owned carrier was one of the most remarkable corporate moves in recent Australian aviation history; with surgical-like precision TAA comprehensively turned the tables on its arch rival'.[15]

The TAA euphoria was tempered by an announcement from Morris in April that the federal government would not renew its subsidy of airline services to western Queensland. 'It is our view', said Morris, 'that air services generally should operate on a commercial basis'.[16] The decision meant losses for TAA, but it advised the Queensland government in May that it intended to continue to operate the services. (Morris also dropped subsidies for Tasmanian routes.)

On 7 March Peter Morris announced an independent but comprehensive review of the two-airline policy. The inquiry head was Thomas May, a former head of the National Road Freight Inquiry, former deputy chairman of Telecom and vice-chairman of the Overseas Telecommunications Commission. (May was also chairman of Ibis Haulage Pty Ltd, a subsidiary of Thomas Nationwide Transport. Sir Peter Abeles was chief executive of TNT. That association came in for wide press criticism.) May's brief was to look at the role of East-West Airlines and other regionals, the import of aircraft, access by Qantas to domestic passengers, pricing control, air freight and constitutional powers on regulation — but not to comment on operational or safety matters. The review, said Morris, was 'intended to enable the Government to determine a framework for domestic aviation requirements into the 1990s'. The minister however, restated the government's commitment to retain TAA as a wholly Commonwealth-owned enterprise.[17]

TAA had firm views on the existing regulatory system. It saw its major long-term constraints as restrictions on fleet size and composition (provided by import controls) and the restriction of free access to air routes arising from States' rights and the Qantas role as the sole international carrier. 'The regulatory environment', the Commission was told, 'is complex and often misunderstood. It is not even clear exactly how much airline activity is shaped directly by the regulatory controls [but] the controls of the two-airline policy do not appear to constrain the major airlines on a day to day basis. In many respects the industry is self regulating.' It saw possible deregulation in the Australian context 'as an operating philosophy directed at reform whilst recognising possible need for some regulatory framework'.[18] Overall TAA rejected support for the status quo as unrealistic and argued not for deregulation but for a change in the nature of regulation to allow it to be more competitive.

In its most fundamental activity, the operation of aircraft, TAA was facing increasing pressure to reach decisions on the future mix of its fleet. There was an urgent need to add to its existing narrow-bodied fleet to improve competitiveness increased service through frequency. Its DC9 aircraft, first introduced in 1969, now had an average age of fifteen years. The early DC9s had accumulated 45,000 flying hours and were among the longest-serving aircraft ever operated in Australia. Their limited operational capability, especially in terms of range, made cost-effective scheduling difficult and often necessitated the use of the too large (but long-range) Boeing 727 to meet competition on low-density, long-haul routes. TAA's overall fleet size and mix was uncompetitive. It had five A300 Airbus aircraft, twelve 727-200s and nine DC9s, or a total of twenty-six aircraft. (With one Airbus still on lease this was reduced operationally to twenty-five.) Ansett, by contrast, had a total of twenty-nine jet units, including twelve

Boeing 737-200s in the all-important 100-seat size. (Ansett had an additional ten jet units in the fleets of its subsidiary airlines that were available to supplement the main fleet.) TAA's four-unit disadvantage translated into a serious service frequency handicap at peak traffic times. (There was potential unused TAA Airbus capacity but it was only available in large, discrete parcels and did not meet market needs.)

On 27 May 1985 TAA announced that it intended to buy twelve Boeing 737-300s to replace its DC9s.[19] (The 737-300 had transcontinental range, allowing it to operate directly from Sydney to Perth. It was quieter and larger than the old technology 737-200s of Ansett.) The first delivery was planned for July 1986, with monthly deliveries thereafter. Neil Smith wrote to his minister requesting approval for the purchase, which had a total project cost of $506 million. (To finance the project he asked for a further capital injection from government of $50 million. Smith rejected loan borrowings but provided for some $84 million from TAA internal funds plus the balance in lease financing. The request for additional capital was turned down.)[20] Publicly TAA announced its interest in the Airbus A320 as a possible replacement for its twelve-aircraft Boeing 727 fleet but said it had asked Airbus Industrie to stretch the A320 from its existing 142-seat configuration to 160 seats. (Ansett had ordered eight 140-seat Airbus A320s with options for a further nine and deliveries starting in late 1988. Ansett also proposed to replace its twelve 737-200s with twelve 737-300s.)

TAA had a minor victory over its competitor on 2 July when it resumed services to the Australian Indian Ocean Territories of Cocos and Christmas Islands. The contract for the services, previously with Ansett, passed to TAA because of the better load capacity of its Boeing 727. The daylight service operated weekly. (TAA had shared a service every three weeks to the two islands with Ansett from 1967 to 1984.)

The debate on the privatisation of government-owned organisations flared again in mid-1985 as the May Inquiry progressed. The Opposition campaign for selling large public enterprises had been led by the deputy leader of the Opposition, John Howard. He was to find that one of his staunchest opponents was the chief executive of Ansett, Sir Peter Abeles. Abeles (a close friend of the prime minister, Bob Hawke) told the *Financial Review* in July 1985: 'No-one will tell me why it should be sold or what magic will happen if it is sold ... There is no reason for selling it.' Privatisation, said Abeles, was not a panacea for any problems that TAA might be facing. Ownership did not necessarily make a difference to the way a large organisation would be run. Abeles also opposed deregulation. The Australian aviation industry, he said, was not conducive to further deregulation as it had to service a country the size of the United States but with a population of only fifteen million.[21] At the same time the minister for communications, Michael Duffy, attacked Howard's call to sell Telecom, saying it would lead to higher telephone charges in rural areas. But one of the leading voices of economic rationalism within the Liberal Party, federal member Jim Carlton, urged the Coalition to 'take up the cause of privatisation with a vengeance between now and the next election'.[22] A more measured and less ideological view was put by the Bureau of Transport Economics in its submission to the government's Independent Review of Economic Regulation of Domestic Aviation (the May Inquiry). It concluded: 'Economic theory suggests that promotion of competition by the removal of legislative barriers to entry into the domestic aviation market is the best way to achieve improved efficiency. The practical evidence also consistently suggests that movement towards this objective would result in airline services which better serve the public interest.'[23]

TAA, as a major participant in the industry, put its views to the May Inquiry in practical and pragmatic terms in August 1985. The challenge confronting the Review, it said, was to find an equitable package for domestic aviation that could translate the ideal of effective competition into a workable system that would maximise consumer benefits. TAA supported four policy elements to underpin a revised regulatory system. Regulation should be limited, it said, to that necessary to minimise market distortions and overcome institutional restraints. It wanted the maintenance of competition but with only two major operators on the trunk routes. Stability was seen as particularly important for a market that was small but required large investment and a substantial work force. Any changes to the regulatory system, it proposed, should be implemented only after consultation with the industry and over a long enough time scale so as not to needlessly disrupt the employment patterns and financial prospects of the industry.[24]

While such policy matters were ponderously considered by all affected parties, East-West Airlines was vigorously engaged in an ongoing strategy to bend the structure of the domestic aviation industry to serve its own ambitions. That it was succeeding was evident from the reaction of TAA. Neil Smith wrote to the minister on 8 August expressing the grave concern of the Commission about developments over the previous two years 'with respect to East West Airlines and its avowed intention to become the third major airline operator in Australia'. That concern, he said, stemmed from the effect of various decisions taken on behalf of the Commonwealth that were, collectively, damaging the Commission's business and undermining the stability of the industry, 'producing a result not intended by the parties to the Airlines Agreement 1981'. He instanced the issue of licences to East-West for operations over routes predominantly serving trunk route traffic; the approval of alleged specialist services by East-West that were not specialist in nature; the changed frequencies in East-West's Canberra–Sydney services; and the decision by the Independent Air Fares Committee to approve discount fares for these services. He complained that there had been lack of action under the Airlines Equipment Act to direct the disposal of East-West aircraft when capacity exceeded traffic requirements and that operational concessions that favoured East-West had been granted to the airline for the operation of F28 aircraft in uncontrolled air space. He concluded by making clear TAA's opposition to an East-West application to import a B737-200 aircraft.[25]

At a federal government seminar in Canberra on economic

regulation of aviation in Australia, Qantas joined East-West Airlines in asking for the immediate opening of domestic air routes to competition.[26] Frank Ball responded forcefully. TAA, he said, could tolerate East-West 'treading on its toes', but if it began 'jumping on them' it would face stiff competition.[27]

Ansett paid TAA the best of compliments in September. Frank Ball told staff on 9 September: 'Ansett have finally conceded — and announced they will be copying TAA's business class next week. TAA introduced business class in October, 1982. Now Ansett, by introducing business class, are admitting that TAA's competition is hurting them.'[28]

On the same day, the thirty-ninth anniversary of TAA's first ever service, chairman Neil Smith announced a net profit for the airline (after tax and abnormal and extraordinary items) for the year ended 30 June 1985 of $29.963 million (some seven times the profit of the preceding year). It was the highest bottom line profit in TAA's history.[29] Consolidated operating profit (before tax and abnormal and extraordinary items) was $29.476 million, compared with $15.996 million for 1983–84. The achievement was all the more significant because the year had included the costly — and unilateral — flight engineers' strike in December. During the year TAA had carried more than 4,800,000 passengers at an average load factor of 71.7 per cent (an 8.8 per cent increase on the preceding year).[30]

In September 1985 the airline moved to reshape its western Queensland services. Approval was sought to import three British Aerospace Jetstream 31 aircraft for introduction in May–June 1986 to replace F27 aircraft operating the rural services. The Jetstream 31 was a pressurised turboprop (already in service with Skywest in Western Australia). It was slightly faster than the F27 and, with fifteen seats, better sized for traffic demand and for the provision of increased service frequencies.[31]

In its broader, national perspective the Australian National Airlines Commission made public in October the specific changes it saw as necessary in the domestic aviation regulatory environment. It sought changes to allow it more equitable and effective competition through lessening of regulatory constraints. The main thrust of its submission to the Independent Review of Domestic Aviation, it said, was opposition to the maintenenance of the status quo. It argued that its competitors — Ansett, East-West and Qantas — each had substantial traffic bases denied to TAA. It accepted that Qantas be allowed continued access to domestic carriage of its own international passengers but, as a trade off, pressed for access by TAA to appropriate international routes. It also wanted the phasing out of aircraft utilisation and passenger load factor controls to allow individual airlines to determine on economic grounds the use and deployment of their fleets. It regarded deregulation of the domestic trunk network in isolation as unacceptable and only equitable if accompanied by deregulation of intrastate and international markets.[32]

In a separate submission to a review of New South Wales air services in October TAA pressed specifically for involvement in the State routes. Under existing arrangements two-airlines (Air New South Wales and East-West Airlines) operated separate monopoly bases in the major intrastate air passenger markets while TAA was excluded from operating within the State. East-West, however, responded with its usual vigour. The airline's managing director, Dennis Howe, said: 'Of more than sixty submissions to the government-ordered inquiry into domestic aviation only three advocated retention of the two-airline policy. Not suprisingly these advocates are Ansett, TAA and the ACTU. The two-airline policy, he said, had evolved into a highly protected, elitist system that only its beneficiaries could suggest was responsive to community expectations in 1985.[33]

For TAA the most significant change in 1985 was to come internally. Frank Ball, after four decades of service, retired as general manager. He had joined TAA as a pilot on 9 September 1946, the day the airline operated its first service. He was sixty-five and had spent forty-five years of his life in aviation, the first five in the RAAF. Ball's successor was a contrast in every way. James Strong, aged forty-one, had been two years old when Ball joined TAA. A lawyer by training, he came from his position as executive director of the Australian Mining Industry Council, based in Canberra, an organisation representing 160 companies that acted as a lobbying and research organisation. Before that he had been site manager for all Nabalco's operations at Gove (covering bauxite mining, alumina refining, engineering, accounting and export shipping). He had worked previously for the Australian Sugar Producers Association and had been an officer cadet at the Royal Military College, Duntroon. Though highly experienced in both management and high level government relations he had no background in the aviation industry (though he had had some twenty hours of flying training). He was TAA's first general manager to be appointed from outside the industry.

The change was both fundamental and generational. Strong's assistant general manager, appointed at the same time, was Jeff Pearce, who had joined TAA in 1961 under a cadet management scheme. He had been TAA's personnel director from 1981 and personnel and ground services director from 1983. Pearce was forty-two. (Frank Ball continued his association with TAA. He was appointed to the Australian National Airlines Commission — TAA's board — for two years. There was another senior retirement from TAA. Leslie Fitzgerald, who had served as secretary to successive Commissions for fifteen years, retired on 29 November.)

Strong had accepted a five-year contract on 14 October 1985. He commenced duties as general manager of TAA on Saturday, 14 December. (He had not applied for the position but had been approached by the Commission in mid year.) Finding a replacement for Ball had not been easy. Remuneration for the position of TAA general manager was tied to public service rates. That had not deterred Strong. He told *Aircraft*: 'While remuneration is important it is not the sole criterion. There is also the matter of personal satisfaction. It is a big challenge.'[34]

TAA's new general manager at once made his philosophy clear. 'An important priority', he said, 'will be the development of a new management team in an organised way'. There would be, he said, greater emphasis on offering a more commercially focussed service. Staff philosophy would be attuned to such a service. He told *Aircraft* that he fully subscribed to the business philosophy that selling airline seats was no different from selling oranges or shoes.[35] Ahead lay fundamental change to TAA's management structure and the introduction of a radically different corporate culture.

CHAPTER 19

1986

A new name, a new management

Strong saw his task as the revitalisation of the airline. Though he admitted with candour that he was a novice in the aviation industry it was clear from the start that he had briefed himself thoroughly. Underpinning a general philosophy of close concentration on commercial outcomes were specific management objectives. In the kind of measured and unambiguous terms that were to be the hallmark of his style, Strong made them known to both staff and public.

He aimed, he told the *Australian*, to lift the public profile of TAA with particular emphasis on style, competitiveness and level of service. The Ansett domination of the business market had to end. Among TAA employees he intended to encourage a more positive and enthusiastic attitude through improved industrial relations. TAA would be promoted as a vigorous, profit-oriented company. In his approach to government he would press for TAA operation on intrastate and limited regional international routes and the lifting of some of the restrictions on TAA's operations. He planned more aggressive competition on short-haul routes with East-West Airlines.

'I don't see total deregulation in Australia', he said. 'Because the effect would be a substantial falling off in the quality and level of service to the customer — except on the profitable routes ... The aim of any deregulation should be to look at specific areas of change with a deliberate aim to improve service to the customer rather than deregulation for its own sake.' The idea that total deregulation would lead to cheaper air fares was, he said, a mythical concept that should be resisted in serious discussions about the future of the industry. The two-airline policy was not, said Strong, designed to protect either TAA or Ansett but to guarantee a high level of service to the consumer.[1]

He told the *Bulletin* that the future environment would be one of greater competition and very aggressive marketing. 'I think this sort of atmosphere has arrived already. There's been a watershed change both in public and political opinion and tremendous importance is now being placed on the airline industry not only being competitive but having greater freedom to compete. But within a controlled environment ... One of the things that attracted me to the airline industry is this increasing competitiveness. I obviously did perceive in the talks I had with the board and the preliminary look I have had that there is this mood for change and the scope to be a catalyst.'[2]

The chief executive of his competitor, Ansett, shared Strong's conclusions on both deregulation and the value of the two-airline policy. Sir Peter Abeles outlined his views to a gathering in Perth. 'For the fifteen years from 1957', he said, 'civil aviation was undoubtedly the most debated subject in the Federal Parliament. In fact it attracted Parliamentary attention far beyond its true significance because aviation had become a battle ground for politicians of all colours.' On TAA he commented: 'For years TAA has never achieved the commercial result that would be expected by the most generous of shareholders, the Government. Only in the last few years have some Governments, particularly the present Government, decided they [TAA and Qantas] have to be run as commercial operations with independent Boards and act like commercial enterprises. The performance of both Government airlines has improved in recent years and hopefully will improve in years to come.'

The Abeles brief was always an ambiguous one when he

had to debate the merits of a regulated two-airline system as the representative of the free market culture. 'TNT,' he said, 'which operates in eighty countries and employs 52,000 people, and our partner in Ansett, Mr Rupert Murdoch — who has tackled the media everywhere in a free enterprise environment — would not prefer to stay in a regulated environment. We would much rather do our own thing and fight for our own thing ... Strange as the two-airline policy may seem to some [however] it is the only solution for Australia, other than having one large Government airline servicing the whole country.'

Both airlines were also at one in their attitude to East-West. (East-West's decision in December 1985 to challenge in the High Court the constitutional validity of the two-airline policy legislation added a further measure of uncertainty to the future shape of the regulatory environment.) 'When East-West decided to grow in the trunk route market', said Abeles, 'we were not prepared to just relinquish that market. East-West would like to be a third major domestic operator — but there is no question of deregulation involved in their pursuit of that ambition.'[3]

The thrust to reshape TAA as an organisation was accompanied, as 1985 ended, by a decision that would reshape its fleet. On 20 December Neil Smith announced that the airline would seek government approval (subsequently given) to purchase nine A320 twin-jet aircraft to replace its Boeing 727s and DC9s. The total cost of the A320 project (including spares, flight simulators, support equipment and training) was some $650 million. The first of the new aircraft was due for delivery in April 1989, with six entering service by September 1989 and the final three in 1990.[4] Together with its order for twelve Boeing 737-300s, TAA now faced an outlay of more than $1 billion (in 1986 dollars) for aircraft to be introduced into its fleet in the coming four years.

Strong told the Commission in January 1986 that he had commenced his review of the structure and functions of the existing TAA organisation, a review that would continue for several months. At the end of that time, he said, he would submit to the Commisioners a comprehensive proposal on both organisation and appointments. Strong planned change on a scale never before experienced by the airline both in the style and structure of management and in the appointment of people to carry it through. Much new blood was to be brought in and many who had made their careers in TAA were to go. At the same time he addressed an area of more immediate commercial concern — the problem of fare dilution from discounted fares. Strong advised that management systems for better control of traffic mix on a flight by flight basis would be investigated as a matter of priority.[5]

Strong's appointment to TAA was a clear indication that the Government wanted it to achieve goals that differed fundamentally from those that had long been accepted by the airline and, indeed, the industry. Over the lifetime of the various Airline Agreements legislation had, in differing ways, brought intervention to promote industry stability. The perception of stability, however, had varied throughout the history of domestic airline regulation. In the Australian National Airline Acts of 1945 and 1947 there had been implicit recognition of the need for industry stability as a goal, following government concern over the number of competing airlines and their ownership (and various bankruptcies). The 1952 Civil Aviation Agreement Act saw stability in a different light. While promoting fair competition, it had the central purpose of ensuring that, at a time when TAA showed every sign of putting its rival ANA out of business, both TAA and Australian National Airways could continue to operate. Stability meant the survival of ANA. (In 1952 the prime minister, Robert Menzies, spelt this out in a letter to ANA in which he wrote: 'The Government recognises that it is of the essence that you should feel some reasonable sense of stability'.)[6]

When Australian National Airways was in severe financial difficulties in 1957, with Reginald Ansett poised to acquire control, Menzies, on 3 September, announced the introduction of subsidies for essential services and financial assistance for fleet replacement, with the goal of eliminating 'instability in Australian civil aviation'. Ansett, like TAA, was given access to government-guaranteed loans. The government concern at the time, driven by its political philosophy of free enterprise, was that stability was necessary so that a private competitor to TAA should continue to exist. It was not until 1958, however, that the word 'stability' was used in legislation. The Airlines Equipment Act 1958 was designed specifically to prevent competitive overcommitment of financial resources to airliner purchases (more popularly described as the prevention of a re-equipment rat race). The purpose of the Act, said the then minister, Shane Paltridge, was to 'ensure the stability of the domestic air transport industry' and the continuance of 'the company' (Ansett) as well as the Commission. Under this Act stability was to be achieved by forcing equal capacity and passenger loads on both airlines with each operating similar airliners as a 'pre-requisite for stability'. (Stability was seen as the ability to survive financially.)[7]

That approach was broadened in the 1961 Airlines Agreement Act, which incorporated the goal of giving each airline similar cost structures as well as comparable fleets. In 1972, when the TNT takeover of Ansett was proposed, a Senate committee considered the two-airline policy in relation to the stability and development of the industry. It commented: 'The two-airlines policy has enabled competition to be maintained between the major airlines while ensuring the stability of the domestic air transport industry. By stability is not meant lack of change but rather a safe and orderly development of civil aviation in this country.' It also referred to the maintenance of safety standards and operational efficiency and 'proper growth ... without the financial crises experienced in prior years'.[8] (Ansett, of course, was eventually taken over by News Limited and TNT in 1979.) The Airlines Agreement Act 1972 provided for the introduction of other airline operators on routes that were not trunk routes as well as specialist freight and passenger services.

By 1977, responding to public and media disquiet over the cosiness of the two-airline policy, the government undertook a review of domestic aviation. Among the conclusions of the Domestic Air Transport Policy Review was that 'changes should be made to allow for greater competition'. The time had come, it said 'to allow a freeing up of entry to at least some of the trunk routes in the form of charter and specialist freight operators or a second level regional operator on routes associated with the regional network'. The 1980 Airlines Agreement 'strongly emphasised the need for increased competition'. A year later, in the 1981 Airlines Agreement, it was at last specifically recognised that significant changes in domestic operation made it 'appropriate that the provisions of the previous Agreements should cease to have force and effect'. It was designed to increase competition, allow other operators limited access to trunk routes and remove cargo from the two-airline policy. The momentum for change was increasing. The government, in 1981, announced an inquiry into the possible impact of deregulation — an inquiry that never eventuated since there was, in 1983, a change of government.[9]

James Strong came to TAA nine months after the Government announced the establishment of the Independent Review of Economic Regulation of Domestic Aviation (in March 1985). The Review was due to report by late 1986. It was of some significance that the current Government had made no public statements on the prime importance of airline industry stability. There were other forces stirring. The sacred cow of economic stability was no longer heading the priority list. Economic performance was emerging as the new yardstick. The Labor government's minister for finance, Peter Walsh, gave expression to a change in political philosophy that was permeating Labor itself. He told the *Financial Review* that he supported the privatisation of some public enterprises. 'It is my view,' he said, that 'what is important is not whether a business is public or private but whether it delivers the goods and services required by the public efficiently — at the lowest cost'.[10]

That the changes ahead for TAA were to be unprecedented and fundamental under its new general manager was given dramatic and symbolic expression on 3 March 1986. At a special meeting of the Australian National Airlines Commission it was agreed that Trans Australia Airlines, the name under which the airline had operated for forty years, would change. The new trading name of the Commission was to be Australian Airlines. With the name change a new livery was planned for the fleet, with the airline's new name abbreviated on the fuselage to the single word 'Australian'. The new livery also used the original kangaroo symbol of TAA. Neil Smith told his minister, Peter Morris: 'This major step is regarded as an important ingredient in a series of strategies to project the airline as being aggressive, competitive and commercial ... We see this dramatic change as being a very public statement that the airline is owned by the people of Australia at a time of great pride in our nation.' The name change, he said, would be implemented in July 1986 to coincide with the arrival of the first of the airline's Boeing 737-300 aircraft.[11]

There was drama of a different kind in April when TAA issued proceedings in the Federal Court in Melbourne against its sole shareholder, the Commonwealth, the minister for aviation, the Department of Aviation and East-West Airlines. That action was taken, however, after consultations with the minister and the department. It arose from an application by East-West to import three Boeing 737-300 aircraft to operate on new routes it had acquired in Queensland. East-West had gained the support of the Queensland Government in its public opposition to the two-airline policy. (Queensland retained the rights to issue licences to airlines operating flights within the State.) In December 1985 East-West had acquired the Lindeman Island resort from the State Government Insurance Office of Queensland and had appointed a friend and confidant of Queensland premier Sir Joh Bjelke-Petersen, Sir Edward Lyons, as chairman of its newly formed Queensland subsidiary, East-West Airlines (Queensland) Pty Ltd. It had applied to obtain State licences to operate services between Brisbane and Cairns and Brisbane and Proserpine. The purpose of the TAA action was to force adherence to the Airlines Agreement Act. TAA claimed that the issue of licences to East-West to operate in Queensland and the issue by the Commomwealth of a capacity determination or import permission for the aircraft would be breaches of the Agreement. It claimed also that East-West breached the Agreement by carrying passengers between trunk route ports in Queensland. In a more direct assault on East-West TAA gave the airline notice to vacate its terminal facilities in Perth and Brisbane and notice that it would no longer provide engineering assistance to East-West. (Ansett also took legal action.) The issue for TAA was not confined to Queensland. While the amended East-West licence permitted it to operate to a number of other trunk route centres in Queensland, it also gave it authority to provide services — via various intermediate ports — between Brisbane and the trunk route centres of Perth, Darwin, Launceston, Sydney and Melbourne.

In a press release on 17 April Strong stated that the aim of the legal action was to ensure that the current Airlines Agreement was observed by all parties. TAA, he said, had made major business investment decisions on the basis of the Agreement. 'These decisions could be put to risk by recent developments including a number of moves by East-West Airlines designed to rapidly expand its operations into areas outside New South Wales where it has a monopoly over a network of regional routes.'[12] The Federal Court, in June, rejected the applications by both Ansett and TAA for injunctions against East-West to prevent it beginning direct Brisbane–Mackay and Brisbane–Cairns services, but further action before the Court on other issues remained unresolved. (At 30 June 1986 six actions were still being heard concurrently in the Federal Court, involving Ansett, TAA, East-West and the Commonwealth government.)

Other litigation threatened, this time by Ansett against TAA, but it had its lighter side. Ansett's solicitors objected on behalf of their client to a TAA advertisement in Germany stating that the airline had 'the only true first class service which is offered in the whole of Australia'. Legal proceedings would be commenced, they said, unless agreement was reached for a retraction. TAA's director of legal services, Margaret M. Rush, responded. The TAA advertisement, she said, was no more extravagant than Ansett's that claimed 'No other airline offers such excellent fare. And yet they have the nerve to charge as much'. She hoped, she said, 'that any legal proceedings you may wish to commence will take place in the Federal Republic of Germany ... preferably at Munich during the Octoberfest'. Under her signature she wrote: 'TAA — die freundliche fluggesellschaft'.[13]

That politics more than anything else controlled the destiny of TAA was re-emphasised in May 1986 when the federal government released a leaked copy of the Opposition's aviation policy. A Coalition government, it confirmed, would sell TAA and a substantial part of Qantas. (The Opposition leader was now John Howard, who had replaced Andrew Peacock in September 1985.) It would also, said the document, terminate the two-airline agreement that gave Ansett and TAA the sole right to operate on trunk routes. The minister for aviation, Peter Morris, however, told the House of Representatives on 20 May: 'The Government's policy is that both Qantas and Trans Australia Airlines will remain in full government ownership. The Opposition's proposal is that they be sold off to a group of privileged Australians rather than that they should belong to all Australians ... The record shows that both organisations, given greater independence, responsibility and freedom by this government, have substantially improved their financial performance.'

Qantas now publicly attacked the two-airline policy, claiming that the 1979 government directive excluding Qantas from carrying international passengers on domestic routes was 'an unjustified, unfair directive issued to protect the domestic airlines'. More than 17,000 seats, it said, flew empty each week on the domestic legs of Qantas flights. (Until 1979 Qantas had been able to carry passengers domestically from other international airlines. Nixon withdrew this access.)[14] Qantas also rebuffed TAA and surprised the industry by entering into a commercial agreement with Ansett. Ansett retail offices were to become joint Ansett–Qantas sales outlets (with Ansett working in a similar way with Qantas outside Australia). It was a development that TAA judged could seriously affect its business. It estimated that a 25 per cent shift in Qantas traffic to Ansett would cost TAA some $7 million a year. (Qantas operated more than 50 per cent of the international capacity into Australia and carried more than 50 per cent of the total traffic.) The Qantas–Ansett agreement also meant an end to Qantas representation of TAA in North America, the United Kingdom, most of Europe and South-East Asia from 1 July 1986. TAA at once set out to conclude alternative arrangements with other airlines.[15] Because of the exclusivity of the Ansett–Qantas arrangement other airlines quickly expressed interest in working with TAA.

The beginning of July also saw the announcement by the Government of an aviation cost recovery policy plan for the use of its aviation facilities and services. It was aimed at achieving, over time, full cost recovery from the industry and thereby reducing the subsidy of some $170 million provided by taxpayers.

Conflict with TAA's six hundred pilots arose in mid-1986. TAA told the Australian Federation of Air Pilots (AFAP) that it could not meet the union's demands to make an agreement similar to one concluded with Ansett in the previous December. Ansett had agreed to extra payment for pilots on the basis of pilots being available, if required, for one extra day's work beyond their normal contract. TAA was willing to discuss additional payment for additional work that was actually performed. But it would not agree to increase pilots' salaries regardless of whether or not the extra work was done. (The AFAP had reached its agreement with Ansett without reference to TAA or the Arbitration Commission.) Strong wrote to all pilots: 'TAA is at the threshold of major change and development ... I recommend you consider carefully the impact which industrial action would have upon our success in the future.'[16] His appeal was successful. The AFAP cancelled a planned strike.

In July, in a move that surprised both East-West Airlines and the industry (and in the middle of the escalating battle between TAA and East-West), East-West's managing director, Dennis Howe, left the airline to join TAA's senior management as assistant general manager. 'The appointment of Mr

Dennis Howe, Strong told staff, 'is an injection of experience and fresh initiative into our company'. He forecast further injections. 'In general terms', said Strong, 'I believe there should be some further outside appointments in some specific areas, to complement, as distinct from detracting from, our current staff'. He warned: 'To be realistic not all of my news at all times will be happy news, but we must have a tough approach to performance'.[17]

Howe joined TAA as James Strong, in July, put his proposals for a new corporate structure and organisation to the Commission. He planned to divide management functions into three basic areas — operational, business and corporate. Corporate functions, under the general manager, included personnel, audit, legal and secretarial, flight security and safety, public relations, branch management, assistant general managers and cargo. Operational functions (under assistant general manager Jeff Pearce) covered flight operations, operations control, scheduling, ground services, catering and international contracts. Business functions (under assistant general manager Dennis Howe) involved marketing and advertising, finance, property, systems and data processing, reservations, planning and development, commercial services and commuter airlines. Much more detailed change lay ahead on revision of the management structure throughout the airline.[18] All senior management participated in a sample training course (based on a successful programme used by British Airways and SAS) to lift staff performance and motivation. (The course, presented by Time Management International, was directed towards individual reassessment by the attitudes towards work and personal life.) Strong addressed more than fifty meetings of staff throughout Australia to explain directly the business strategies that the airline was following. The *Age* commented: 'James Strong is casual and under-stated in manner and quiet in speech. His authority does not come from the trappings of office. When he recently addressed workers at Australian Airlines' workshops in Essendon it was noted approvingly that he arrived and departed alone. Initially, what most impresses you about James Strong is his ordinariness. With time it is his depth.'[19]

On 4 August 1986 the Australian National Airlines Commission operated for the first time as Australian Airlines. On the same day the airline took delivery of its first Boeing 737-300 aircraft. That boost to morale came as James Strong described 1985–86 as 'a vintage year for TAA'. The airline had one of its best market share leads over Ansett and growth was the most buoyant in ten years.[20] The preceding three years had seen a marked recovery from losses to profits. In its 1985–86 annual report TAA — now Australian Airlines — recorded a record consolidated net profit of $37.766 million, a profit achieved despite the fact that air fares rose by only 4.9 per cent — a figure well below the Consumer Price Index. Total revenue increased by 15.2 per cent to $811.281 million. Passenger revenue contributed $673.033 million (up 17.5 per cent), revenue from cargo and mail carriage $65.746 million. More than five million passengers were carried (at a load factor of 72.7 per cent).[21]

There were nonetheless reasons for caution in the year ahead. The high growth pattern of the broader national economy was slowing and the airline's fleet re-equipment meant new costs. 'We will have to cover a high increase in interest and depreciation charges resulting from the addition of twelve new Boeing 737-300s', said Strong.[22] There was no realistic expectation of any further injection of capital by the government, while at the same time government pressure for better performance by statutory authorities, including adequate dividends, was growing. East-West's encroachment was affecting market share.

Neither Australian nor Ansett had made significant changes to their fleets during the year. The Australian fleet comprised four A300-B4s (excluding one on lease to Air Niugini), twelve Boeing 727-276s, a Boeing 727 freighter (on lease), nine DC9-31s (one held on lease) and three Fokker F27s. (One A300 was sold to a Japanese domestic airline in October 1986.) Australian, however, was having second thoughts about its Airbus A320 order. Analysis had shown that the newer Boeing 737-400 was technically competitive with the A320 and would, because of benefits from commonality with the 737-300, prove a far superior economic investment. In August 1986 management proposed that negotiations start to terminate Australian's obligations to proceed with the A320 purchase.[23]

The political landscape was given sharp focus on 12 August 1986 when the Liberal and National Parties formally made public their aviation policy. Its cornerstone was 'the phased termination of the Two Airlines Agreement and the sale of Australian Airlines to the Australian public'. Australian Airlines, it said, would be formed into a public company and shares sold with safeguards in place to prevent monopolisation and promote competition. 'A clear and increasing majority of Australians', said the document, 'recognise that the consumer will benefit if Australian Airlines, along with all other companies providing airline services, is forced to compete in the market place without recourse to the Australian taxpayer'.[24] Aircraft described the policy as 'a grab-bag of ideological purity, sectional appeasement and genuine reform'.[25]

There was no doubt, in 1986, that a profound reappraisal of the broad working of the Australian economy itself was under way among economists, politicians, business and media. A series of five major articles in the *Financial Review* by the economist David Clarke began with the statement: 'We are standing at the most crucial cross-roads in our economic history'. Two particular features of the nation's history, he said, stood out — 'our close dependence on other economies and on Government intervention and regulation'. Australia, said Clarke, was falling further and further behind in the international economic race. 'We have failed to change as the world has changed around us.' Australians had believed they had traded the sheep's back for a train loaded with mineral wealth. 'Such attitudes enabled us to postpone the hard decisions and reforms.' Australia's debt burden, he said, was at its highest level since the Great Depression and its terms of trade had moved perilously against it. 'The great opening up of our economy in response to the internationalisation of the world economy over the past decade raises the vital question whether we should — indeed can — insulate our wage levels from the pressures this internationalisation has produced.'[26]

Within Australian Airlines this pressure for change was recognised. Strong told the Commission in September: 'It is essential for Australian Airlines to increase its revenue and reduce its relative cost levels. To make a major impact requires considerable managerial re-organisation and direction. The present management structure has excessive levels of control. It lacks incisive strategic thinking and ability to make decisions. Long-term service under stablised market conditions has resulted in a narrow span of vision and management within very restricted parameters of competition.' He summarised recent performance as a sequence of traffic growth leading to more scheduled flights leading to increased costs and rapid staff growth with an eventual larger turnover and lower profit levels. 'This trend is of concern to airlines around the world, including Ansett and Qantas. It affects other industries as well as aviation.'

To begin major organisational change and signal a new approach, said Strong, it was necessary to start at the top and work downwards 'with a determination to confront the difficulties and not merely re-arrange existing appointments'. Promotion of staff could not just be on the basis of a person available internally who had performed well in a previous task. He proposed the abolition of the position of 'directors', the early retirement of marketing director Bryan Palmer, the option for operations director Captain Len Heard to resume flying or take retirement and the early retirement of planning and development director Don Withers. 'In each case', said Strong, 'no replacement will be appointed'. The various deparments would report directly to the general manager or assistant general managers, 'removing an entire layer of management'.[27] Palmer, Heard and Withers retired in October. 'All three', said Strong, 'had given long and valuable service to the airline'.[28] Frank McMullen, engineering director, took early retirement at the end of 1986, following a period of sick leave. Doug Gillies was later appointed manager, engineering and maintenance.

There was change for the industry at government level too. On 22 October it was announced that the government intended to establish a Civil Aviation Corporation to operate the civil airways system in Australia. 'This', Strong told the Commission, 'appears to be a logical step to establish a matching facility to the Federal Airports Corporation which will assume responsibility for the major airports from the Department of Aviation on 1 April, 1987'.[29]

As the year ended Strong announced that two senior appointments to the airline were to be made, both reporting directly to himself. Mr R. (Dick) McIlwain, formerly of Utah Development Company Limited, was to become manager, human resources. Mr G. (Geoff) Dixon, formerly of Australian Mining Industry Council, was to be manager, corporate affairs. Both were appointed on five-year contracts after recommendation and selection by PA Management Consultants. McIlwain's areas were personnel and industrial relations. Dixon was to be responsible for all public relations and government relations with a major emphasis on communication within and outside the company.[30] Sir Leslie Froggatt, vice-chairman of the ANAC, retired on 22 February 1987.

Media comment and public opinion were matters of ongoing and daily concern to Strong. Public relations manager John Tilton told his staff on 8 January 1987 that Strong wanted a daily management meeting to discuss key issues and events. Press clippings from all major cities were to be provided each day. 'The general manager specifically mentioned letters to the editor as an area to be closely watched", he said. The daily meeting, said Tilton, 'will also enhance the cooperation we already receive from management and directors on public issues involving Australian by introducing an extra sense of urgency for everyone'.[31] Strong was meticulous in his requirements both internally and outside for the projection of the airline's identity. He had noticed, he said, that there was increasing use of 'TN' as an abbreviation for Australian Airlines. ('TN' was the two-letter code used as a prefix to flight numbers.) He instructed staff that 'Australian' was the preferred abbreviation for Australian Airlines. 'AA is not to be used under any circumstances.' The proper approved abbreviation was 'an important part of the image we are trying to achieve'.[32]

Neil Smith briefed his minister, Peter Morris, on an opportunity for the airline to operate externally. Australian had, in 1980, vied unsuccessfully with Ansett when the possibility of operating air services to Vanuatu was considered. Ansett subsequently provided flights on the route through an arrangement with Air Vanuatu and by contract under the licence held by Qantas. In 1986, following a breakdown in Ansett negotiations with the Vanuatu government, Ansett withdrew from its association with Air Vanuatu, leaving the island state with no direct air links with Australia from the end of January 1987. Smith told Morris that Australian now had 'an opportunity to expand its airline operation beyond the domestic Australian market'.[33] Vanuatu's Prime Minister, Walter Lini, advised Morris on 19 January 1987 that his government had decided to designate Australian Airlines to exercise the Vanuatu traffic rights on the Sydney–Port Vila route.[34] (By February 1987 Strong had come to the conclusion that because of Australian's inability to negotiate terms and conditions with its flight attendants for the Vanuatu operation it was, at least for the time being, 'a dead duck'.)[35]

The Independent Review of Economic Regulation of Domestic Aviation (the May Inquiry) reported its findings to the minister on 7 January 1987. May's report was critical of many aspects of the two-airline policy and generally sympathetic to East-West Airlines' attempts to operate in the trunk route market. He criticised the existing level of competition, fare-setting procedures and the inefficient use of fleet capacity — particularly the low number of seats offered per aircraft when compared with airline practice overseas — as well as restating public perceptions of the inadequacies of the system. The emphasis under existing arrangements, said his report, was on the preservation of the industry structure instead of the satisfaction of consumer needs. The system produced relatively low labour productivity combined with relatively high and stable profit levels. May had not been asked to comment on the question of ownership of Australian Airlines but he saw it as necessary to do so. His report listed the constraints that because of government ownership commercially disadvantaged it. Crucial areas were identified as Australian's high gearing ratio and inflexible salary structure, as well as the need for government approvals for borrowings and for the setting of profit and dividend targets. May also drew attention to the airline's limited opportunities to engage in intrastate operations.[36]

The May report was presented as Strong completed his first year with the airline. He told the Commission on 19 January: 'The release of the May Report confirms that the aviation industry in Australia is entering a period of major change. Australian Airlines is not well prepared for that change.' The disadvantages it suffered by lack of commercial autonomy, he said, would be even more significant in an increasingly competitive environment. There were many areas in the airline, he said, where action was needed. Fleet composition was a critical one. With eight types of aircraft in the Australian and Air Queensland fleets and a further major aircraft introduction programme scheduled, Australian was, said Strong, incurring very high costs and inefficiency in relation to crew training and allocation, inventory costs and maintenance. To improve cost control and as part of a programme to spread responsibility and accountability to area and branch management he advised that the system for compiling and monitoring budget performance required overhaul.

Revenue control was a major area where he saw superior performance by Ansett, which had for some years practised control over seat sales with an emphasis on knowledge of revenue and costs to ensure profitability. In the new Australian system he gave very high priority to improvement of yield and knowledge of individual flight profitability. 'The huge losses incurred in ancillary parts of the airline's business', he reported, 'must be stemmed. Following the sale of Hertz, the Air Queensland and Western Queensland losses must be curtailed.' (Australian Airlines' 50 per cent share in Hertz was sold in November 1986.) Australian should not enter into any new areas of business where a large airline could not match costs with second level operators. 'This should apply to New South Wales (if entry is gained), Western Australia and the Northern Territory. It raises difficult industrial issues which must be confronted. Persistence in areas where profits cannot be made will drag down the entire performance of the airline.' Personnel and staff was a major area of concern. While Strong recognised the value, through knowledge and experience, of long-serving staff he again pointed to the disadvantages 'through possible narrowness of vision and experience'. The introduction of some key staff to improve business performance, he said, would bring new perspectives and approaches. 'Staff attitudes are the key to our service performance and standards and must receive the highest priority.'

Australian had suffered losses by Air Queensland's ATR aircraft and from the Jetstream 31 aircraft operations in western Queensland. On 31 May Australian Airlines discontinued its scheduled Jetstream 31 services on western Queensland routes and also ceased operating all southeastern Air Queensland routes, including all flights from Brisbane. It maintained its north Queensland F27 services, based on Cairns. Air Queensland's ATR 42 aircraft were leased overseas and the Jetstreams, which had started operations in late August 1986, were withdrawn from service. (On 30 June 1987 the Air Queensland board agreed to recommend to the parent company that because of its financial position, it be wound up.)[37]

Australian saw the May Report as 'commercially naive and unduly influenced by economic theory rather than market reality'. It thought it heavily influenced by adverse public perceptions from its market surveys. 'It effectively suggests "loosening up" or "deregulating" only the interstate market — our market, sidesteps the intrastate regulatory issues and is silent on any quid pro quo's for proposed Qantas gains in interlining, domestic cargo carriage or even eventual domestic rights.' The underlying premise common to all May's options (other than the status quo and deregulation), said a report to the Commission, 'is opening up entry to the interstate market and protecting new entrants by imposing restrictions on Australian and Ansett'.[38] Nevertheless the release of the May Report, Strong concluded, 'coincides with the urgent need for Australian Airlines to set a detailed strategic programme for the next three to five years based on specific action in every area of corporate activity to bring about a more lean, efficient, commercially-oriented, better co-ordinated and integrated operation ... Unless this occurs the airline will not be able to compete or remain viable.' He planned a major 'lock-up' of management staff to examine all major policy issues.[39]

The critical issue of fleet composition was of immediate concern. Australian Airlines had committed to the A320 aircraft in late 1985 when the only new 140-passenger aircraft available were the A320 and the McDonnell Douglas MD80 (which it considered inferior). Australian Airlines saw the outcome of the May Inquiry as signalling significant change to domestic aviation policy and a need for the airline to again reassess the economics of the A320 in the light of the availability of the 138-passenger Boeing 737-400. Technological developments in aircraft had made older equipment obsolete. Strong told staff: 'Whilst the outward appearance of aircraft in terms of shape of the fuselage, wings and engines may not be altered dramatically, there are some very exciting and important developments in terms of control systems, weight reduction and power units on aircraft, all intended to produce greater efficiency and safety'.[40]

Comparable capacity to the nine A320s it had ordered was available from an equal number of 737-400s. The Boeing aircraft, however, came with a saving in capital costs of $US100–130 million in aircraft purchase price and infrastructure. There were further advantages in scheduling and staff efficiency from fleet commonality. The Commission was told: 'The economic penalties associated with the introduction of nine A320s between April 1989 and June 1990, which coincides with the termination of the present two-airline policy, are most serious. It is apparent that significant change will occur and we must position ourselves to have lower costs and more flexibility in our fleet.' Although the full impact of the May Inquiry was not to become clear until Government policy was established, management saw it as certain that there would be more competition and less regulation. It recommended that the sale or lease of Australian's nine A320s be vigorously pursued (while also attempting to reach a negotiated settlement with Airbus Industrie to terminate the A320 purchase contract).[41]

That dramatic changes for the aviation industry were coming was signalled in early March. Paul Kelly, in the *Australian*, wrote:

> The Hawke Government will examine the sale of transport bodies including airline terminals and the government carrier Australian Airlines ... as part of its cost savings exercise. Any sale of Australian Airlines will be coupled with deregulation ... a historic step for the Labor Party. The option of privatisation and deregulation in the air will cause profound heartburn within the Party ... but the message from the economic ministers to the Party is that some concessions from traditional ALP philosophy are needed this year to meet the Government's demands for public spending cuts ... If Cabinet proceeds it would be a classic case of stealing the Opposition's political garb. The Liberals are champions of selling Australian Airlines ... The economic ministers have a powerful lever. The alternative is welfare cuts or higher taxes.[42]

With a federal election pending the Labor government saw increasing merit in reassessing ideology. The *Financial Review* wrote: 'The Hawke Government has decided to pursue politically crucial reductions in interest rates by basing its election-year economic strategy on holding expenditure to at least zero real growth and achieving reductions in the deficit through a series of privatisation measures'.[43]

On 30 March 1987 the Australian National Airlines Commission sent its formal response to the May Inquiry report to the minister. Australian Airlines fully endorsed Morris's statement, in releasing the Review, that the Government's aims were to make aviation as safe as possible and to follow policies that would provide a long-term stable aviation industry to service Australia efficiently and economically. It proposed a transition to a flexible system of airline regulation, responsive to market forces and the changing public interest, while acknowledging both the size of the Australian market and the national advantages of a stable industry. Such a system, it said, would permit the entry of additional operators and allow more effective competition between Australian Airlines and Ansett. Within its proposed new system the Commission considered 'that major changes must be made to the policy and operating framework governing Australian Airlines'. Ideally, it said, 'these include the establishment of Australian Airlines as a company subject to the full range of legal and public scrutiny'.

Entry into public debate by Australian Airlines on its ownership, however, emerged as an issue between James Strong and his chairman, Neil Smith. On 28 May 1987 the *Financial Review* wrote:

> The chief general manager of Australian Airlines, Mr James Strong, yesterday refused to back calls made by the airline's chairman, Mr Neil Smith, to privatise the government-owned domestic carrier. Mr Strong, talking at the Aviation Club in Sydney, said Mr Smith's April 7 calls for the privatisation of Australian Airlines were 'his own personal comments'. Mr Strong said any decision to privatise Australian Airlines would be made by the Government on 'a political basis'. This conflicts with outspoken statements by Mr Smith when Australian Airlines released its submission to the Federal Government's review of the two-airline policy. Mr Smith said in April that Australian Airlines should be privatised, with a majority Federal Government shareholding so it could expand its capital base and be injected with 'a greater ingredient of efficiency and competition'.[44]

The respected international aviation journal, *Interavia*, commented on the consequences of government ownership of Australian Airlines. 'Notwithstanding improved profits in recent years,' it wrote, 'the fact is that, in pure commercial terms, Australian has consistently been out-performed by Ansett, and neither airline makes any bones about it being, in substantial part, a result of the Government's ownership and the restrictions that have gone with it.'[45]

In the financial year to 30 June 1987 Australian reported a consolidated net profit of $24.901 million. The airline carried a record 5.108 million passengers. Operating profit was, as forecast, down on the preceding year because of the initial cost of introducing the twelve Boeing 737-376 aircraft, but the reduction was substantially offset by the profit earned from the sale of six aircraft (two 727s, three DC9s and one Airbus) made surplus to requirements. 'We've now consolidated our recovery from a decade of recession that sapped the airline industry of growth', said Strong.[46] Unprofitable services, including those between Perth and Port Hedland and Hobart–Christchurch, were discontinued during the year. Strong commented in the annual report: 'There is a clear recipe for improving revenue in aviation provided by overseas experience. Proper revenue control, or "managing the seat auction" as it has been called, is now a necessity. Considerable time and investment is being devoted to this issue in Australian Airlines to lift its yield. It is already paying dividends.'[47]

The uncertain future shape of the industry was influenced by the imminent federal election set for 11 July 1987. The Opposition had promised that if elected it would immediately give notice of the end of the two-airline agreement and sell Australian Airlines and 49 per cent of Qantas. The Labor Government, however, was returned to office — but Labor itself had pledged during the campaign, on 5 June, that it would terminate the two-airline agreement in 1990.[48] That decision, wrote *Aircraft*, was 'a watershed in the Australian airline industry'.[49] (Change to the policy required three years' notice of intent.) The shape of the industry was, regardless of politics, to be changed substantially following a $150 million takeover of East-West Airlines by Ansett Transport Industries in August. That move, reported *Business Review Weekly*, gave Ansett 'an immediate edge in the $2 billion domestic airline market, lifting its share from 46 per cent to 54 per cent. It also snatched away from Australian Airlines feeder traffic worth about $40 million a year.' The Ansett move, Strong acknowledged, 'significantly increases the pressure on us'. It also, he said, would 'bring into sharp focus the issue of privatising Australian Airlines'. The Ansett coup gave it a tight grip on the New South Wales market — it had a monopoly on routes serviced by East-West and Ansett's Air NSW subsidiary.[50] The *Financial Review* wrote: 'Ansett's strategy has been to use the existing regulations to get to a position where it will be able to block out competition by the time the current regulatory regime is dismantled'.[51] It commented: 'To survive against a geared up and expanding Ansett in the foreshadowed deregulatory environment, Australian Airlines will require a massive capital injection'.[52] (The acquisition of the twelve Boeing 737 aircraft had increased the Commission's total assets by some $300 million. With this change the ratio of shareholders' funds to total assets had dropped from 21.2 per cent at June 1986 to 16.6 per cent at June 1987. The Ansett Transport Industries ratio was 28 per cent.)[53]

Ansett had also spread its wings in New Zealand. Ansett New Zealand, a consortium half owned by Ansett Australia in partnership with New Zealand interests, began scheduled flights on 25 July 1987, breaking the long-held monopoly of domestic services there by Air New Zealand.

The concentration of economic power in the industry by News Corporation–TNT posed a public relations problem for Australian. Geoff Dixon, manager, corporate affairs, reported in August: 'The problems Australian faces through having the largest press group in the country a major partner in Ansett [have] been emphasised by the East-West takeover. Discussions with politicians on the magnitude of Ansett's monopoly on NSW intrastate traffic and their almost total control of on-carriage met with sympathy but no action. The response was that with [another] election possible in December and likely by March nobody was prepared to criticise the action because of the possibility of an adverse reaction from the Murdoch press ... We are endeavouring to forge a closer relationship with the Fairfax press.'[54]

Dixon also reshaped overall public relations strategy, decentralising activities out of Melbourne, directing them more strongly towards the business travel market and developing a more formal liaison with marketing and other service departments. Internal communications were strengthened with a bi-monthly staff video and a revamped monthly newspaper (that halved printing costs). The airline's three customer-directed magazines (*The Australian Way*, *Flight Deck* and *Flying Start*) were used for more direct marketing (and all printed by an outside publishing house at no cost to Australian).[55]

The Labor government saw a major capital injection for Australian Airlines as a near impossibility, given the pressure it would place on the public sector borrowing requirement. Fiscal imperatives and the over-riding need to reduce the deficit were now at odds with traditional Labor ideology. Even the Australian Council of Trade Unions (ACTU), a traditional hard-line opponent of privatisation of government enterprises, saw the need to soften its stand. Its president, Simon Crean, stated that trade union support of asset sales would be relevant if 'the Government showed an inability to maintain the capital base of its commercial assets that in turn threatened that enterprise'.[56] The finance minister, Peter Walsh, conceded on 20 August that the government's two airlines, Australian and Qantas, would become an increasing burden to the public sector. 'Given that a reduction in the public sector borrowing requirement has been a major economic objective for some time there are obviously problems coping with that', said Walsh.[57] The prime minister himself entered the privatisation debate with vigour. Hawke, who had aggressively opposed the sale of government assets in mid 1985, now recognised the implications of inaction. He told the Victorian ALP conference that the new question in the debate about social progress and equity was whether public ownership made the best use of resources to achieve these goals.[58]

On 5 October 1987 Neil Smith announced that Australian Airlines would defer its order for nine A320 aircraft but that under a revised agreement with Airbus Industrie it would have a right to reschedule the delivery of the aircraft during the 1990s. That announcement followed approval by the

Minister on 30 September for the Commission to contract with Boeing for four 737-300s and eight 737-400s (plus a separate contract for a further three 737-400s subject to confirmation at a later date).[59] No mention was made in this public statement by Smith of the 737-400 purchases. The matter was a sensitive one for Airbus Industrie.

In the midst of these portents of major change both the chairman of the Australian National Airlines Commission and his minister moved on. Neil Smith retired on 31 October 1987. His retirement was an early one, since his term did not expire until 1988. In a public statement he said: 'It has become abundantly clear that the airline must have as its chairman a person who is able to devote an ever increasing proportion of his time and energy to the very onerous duties of office and, more particularly, is able to carry on uninterrupted through the next three years when major changes in the industry are inevitable. Deregulation is already certain and privatisation is now an issue of intense public debate, the determination of which could have a marked effect on the future viability of the airline. I regret I cannot meet either of the commitments that are needed.' Neil Smith was succeeded as chairman on 1 November by A. E. (Ted) Harris, AO, who had been appointed to the Commission on 30 April. (Harris retired as chief executive officer of Ampol Petroleum in November.) The new minister for Transport and Communications was Senator Gareth Evans.

In Australian Airlines there had also been changes to senior management. In June Strong had taken control of the finance division from assistant general manager Dennis Howe. Howe retired from the airline. In September Gary Toomey was appointed chief financial executive.

The airline's new chairman, Ted Harris, was a decisive, forthright and experienced businessman. He had already made his views on the future of Australian Airlines public. It must, he said, be either privatised or have government restrictions lifted to compete effectively.[60] The new minister, Gareth Evans, was preparing the way for a government decision. He announced an inquiry that could, reported the

Australian, 'lead to the national domestic carrier being fully or partly privatised by 1990 when a new "open skies" aviation policy will come into force'. A committee, Evans said, would advise the government on how the airline could meet its extensive capital requirements and how it could improve management and operating efficiency. The powerful five-man committee (which included ACTU secretary Bill Kelty) was to be chaired by Ted Harris.[61]

Evans told Parliament on 7 October 1987 that the government would phase out the two-airline agreement by October 1990. In a comprehensive public document he said: 'After 35 years of detailed economic regulation of interstate aviation by successive Australian Governments, I have today placed before the Parliament a motion which will bring the two-airlines policy to an end and open Australia's interstate services to free competition'. The government, he said, 'has decided to withdraw from aviation-specific economic regulation and to allow the market to operate within the constraints of the established competition policy controls applicable to industry generally'. Evans also announced that with effect from 1 July 1988 the government would restore Qantas's rights to carry passengers of other international airlines on the domestic sectors of its international services. 'The government', said the Evans document, 'has considered suggestions that Australian Airlines and Qantas should be amalgamated but has rejected this course of action ... Qantas will, for the foreseeable future, remain Australia's sole international airline and will not be permitted to operate scheduled domestic air services. If such a proposed merger were to take place it would be difficult for the Government to resist pressures from other domestic operators to be allowed to operate as designated international carriers, thereby placing the Government's single designation policy in jeopardy.'

Government intentions became even clearer when Senator Evans, in December 1987, introduced into Parliament the Australian Airlines (Conversion to Public Company) Bill. It was, he told the Senate, an important first step in the process of preparing Australian for its future role by establishing the airline as a public company, providing for its reorganisation into a more appropriate structure before incorporation and removing detailed government controls over its operations. It could not 'be expected to be fully competitive and efficient in the deregulated environment unless adequate capital is provided and controls affecting the airline's efficiency are removed'. He remained equivocal on the future ownership structure of the airline. 'Available estimates indicate that the capital injection required over the next three years is at least $250 million ... The capital injections could be spread out over the three year period if the Government is prepared to accept a lower level of dividends ... As an alternative to the Commonwealth having to find the funds from the Budget, given competing priorities, it would be possible to raise the necessary funds by an injection of private equity and still maintain majority Commonwealth ownership of the airline.' Australian Airlines, he said, had indicated that it wished to reorganise its activities into a holding company–subsidiary company structure as part of the changes necessary to establish it as a fully competitive public company.

'There are,' said Evans 'no aviation or competition policy reasons, as such, which require the public ownership of Australian Airlines'.[62]

CHAPTER 20

1988

No soft option

Evans was clearly signalling that it was the government's preferred option to privatise Australian Airlines. Australian's large capital injection needs could not be met from the Budget without making cuts in areas that had political costs. The government had no 'soft option'. Its dilemma was that the direct sale of the airline to private shareholders was anathema to Labor Party traditionalists. Labor's long distrust of market forces had entrenched the belief that government-owned enterprises brought a more socially responsible approach to commerce than possible under private enterprise. The Report of the Australian Airlines Advisory Group, under Harris's chairmanship, had further validated the privatisation option. The reasons traditionally advanced for government ownership of the airline, it said (that it was necessary to ensure competition, promote growth and better regulate the industry and maintain standards), no longer had the same force. The Report also concluded that reliance on borrowing or leasing (or statements of government backing) would not provide an appropriate financial structure for the airline or satisfactory accountability and discipline for management.

With impending public company status for Australian came even more intense pressure to cut the airline's operating costs. Strong put proposals to the Commission for reductions in staff numbers. He wanted 'to formally establish two methods of facilitating the termination of staff surplus to requirements through organisational change'. He planned to distinguish staff who would be encouraged to apply for selective voluntary severance from those nominated by management for termination on the grounds of redundancy. He 'recognised that a control process must be established to avoid payment to individuals who are not redundant in the true sense but simply inadequate performers'.[1]

While these fundamental changes faced Australian Airlines its competitor's strength in the transport field remained formidable. In a report on Ansett Airlines' joint owner, TNT, Bain & Company Limited summarised its position as 'one of the largest diversified transport and transport service companies in the world'. Transport, it said, 'is highly leveraged to world economic activity and the group has been involved in the higher growth sectors'. It had 'kept ahead of the pack' during its development period, but 'necessary development of the group's world-wide position will work against a reduction in expenditure outlays on both acquisition and major capital equipment in the next couple of years ... The group aims to build a substantial business in aircraft leasing and airline services; likewise, it stands to benefit substantially from deregulation in the Australian airline market.'[2]

Ansett's telling advantage from its acquisition of East-West Airlines, however, had been modified when the Trade Practices Commission (on 10 November 1987) demanded that Ansett divest itself of some aircraft and routes following its East-West takeover in July. Ansett was forced to agree to vacate all routes flown by East-West in New South Wales (except the major Tamworth and Albury routes), divest itself of East-West's interests in Eastern Airlines, a leading New South Wales supplementary airline, and relinquish control of Lloyd Aviation in Queensland. (Ansett had earlier agreed to divest itself of the Western Australian operations of East-West, incorporating Skywest.)

Australian's response was to plan for control or ownership of Eastern Airlines. Eastern was based in Tamworth, New

South Wales, and carried about 125,000 passengers annually on its commuter operations, generating revenue of some $10 million. It was the only New South Wales operator not owned by or aligned to the TNT–News Corporation group and it planned to apply for licences to acquire the former New South Wales East-West routes relinquished by Ansett. The intrastate market was though, still, dominated by the combined resources of TNT-News through Air New South Wales, East-West, Aeropelican and Hazelton, giving it 90 per cent of the market. (Ansett had offered for sale its East-West/Skywest operations in Western Australia and the divested East-West routes in New South Wales. Australian was not interested in buying either.)[3]

Australian had recently obtained the right to apply for licences to operate air services within New South Wales and Western Australia. The South Australian Government now offered assistance to enable Australian Airlines to operate within that State. (South Australia had long practised an open-skies policy, but Australian could not operate within the State without legislation by the government that either referred the matter of air transport to the federal government or adopted the appropriate section in the Australian National Airlines Act.) Strong's response, on 15 January 1988, was that 'specific legislation to enable Australian Airlines to operate within South Australia either directly or through a subsidiary may inadvertently raise expectations of imminent commencement of services ... You will appreciate that Australian Airlines will only seek to enter [South Australia] when it is able to identify opportunities which would give it an adequate return on its investment. The enabling legislation which we seek from your Government will permit the airline to respond more quickly to any opportunities which may arise in the regional aviation arena within South Australia.'[4]

Ted Harris briefed Evans in February 1988 on the form of corporate structure proposed for Australian Airlines. The Commission, he said, had determined that minimal restructuring should occur and that the Australian National Airlines Commission should become the transferring body, Australian

National Airlines Limited, without the creation of a holding company between the government and the new company. 'The Commission', he wrote, 'considers that it is important to keep the main business of the airline, its trunk route operations, within the parent company of the group. However, in both resorts and regional airlines businesses the Commission proposes to interpose two wholly owned subsidiaries — Australian Resorts Pty Ltd and Australian Regional Airlines Pty Ltd.'[5]

The Australian Airlines (Conversion to Public Company) Act was passed through both Houses of Parliament on 24 February 1988 and received royal assent on 9 March. The Commission was now deemed to have share capital of $130,000,000 divided into 260,000 shares of 50 cents each, fully paid up. It was required to issue these shares to the Commonwealth. The Commonwealth's total equity in its wholly owned airline was modest. At 30 June 1987 it was $190 million, made up of the $130 million capital subscribed and $60 million in reserves. (In its submission to the Advisory Group on Australian Airlines, management had advocated a future capital structure that would require equity injections totalling $250 million over three years and $450 million by 1995.)[6] The Act affected many people. The Commission, in February 1988, employed some 9,600 staff of which 8,900 were with the parent airline operation and the remainder employed by subsidiaries. The Australian Airlines fleet of thirty-eight aircraft now consisted of four A300s (including one on lease overseas), ten 727s, twelve Boeing 737-300s (with four more due in 1988–89), a 727 freighter on lease, five DC9s, three F27s and three Jetstream 31s.

In early April Senator Gareth Evans put forward a dramatic new scheme for resolving the problem of the dangerously low capital bases of both Australian Airlines and Qantas. Evans proposed the merger of Qantas, Air New Zealand and Australian Airlines into a single major Pacific carrier. (Implicit in the proposal was the sale of equity in the new entity.) Qantas's chairman, Jim Leslie, immediately gave his strong support for the scheme. 'I think this would be extraordinarily good for the airlines', he said. 'In simple economic terms it makes a lot of sense.' It would make, he said, 'one giant big bang step' towards improving the Closer Economic Relations pact between Australia and New Zealand.[7] Ted Harris's support was more restrained. Australian, he said, had 'a positive attitude to the suggested merger'. It was, though, he said, only one of a number of proposals aimed at improving Australian's depleted capital base.[8]

The Evans proposal had its origins in a strategic review by Qantas of the company's position in March 1988 in a dramatically changed aviation industry. Deregulation in the United States had fundamentally reshaped the market and brought the emergence of mega-carriers. Qantas was also driven by the enormous cost involved in the development of a global CRS (computer reservations) system. The Qantas preferred solution that emerged from the strategic review was the three-way merger between Qantas, Australian Airlines and Air New Zealand (known as 'the tricycle'), with the aim of creating a single international carrier with a domestic base in both countries.

The proposed Qantas strategy was endorsed by the Australian and New Zealand governments, Qantas, Australian Airlines and Air New Zealand. Gareth Evans, then minister for transport, saw it as a trigger to achieve endorsement of the privatisation of Qantas within the ALP political machine. This bold attempt at a three-way merger, the Qantas board was told, 'foundered solely on the opposition of Ansett'. The alternative of a Qantas–Air New Zealand merger (known as 'the bicycle') was blocked by the New Zealand Government's desire to maximise its cash receipts from the privatisation of Air New Zealand and by its opposition to any arrangement that denied the airline access to Australia's domestic markets.

For Ansett the implications of the Evans scheme were, of course, profound. A merger of Qantas, Australian and Air New Zealand meant the creation of a powerful regional carrier not only operating domestically in Australia and New Zealand but with a diverse international network. To compete against such an organisation meant entry for Ansett into the international market, which, though a long-held ambition, would require significant new investment in aircraft and services. Sir Peter Abeles made no immediate public comment, but an Ansett spokesman conceded that the company was concerned about the effect the proposed merger might have on its 10,000 employees and 30,000 shareholders.[9]

The federal Opposition strongly opposed the scheme as a device to take the heat out of the debate on privatisation within the ALP. It would, it said, do a great deal for New Zealand and little for Australia. It announced its own revised policy for wider privatisation of Qantas. One hundred per cent of Qantas, it said, would be sold.[10]

Abeles stated his views privately to the minister, reminding him of his acknowledgment in October that a merger of Qantas and Australian not only would be unfair to Ansett but would (with Ansett entry into overseas services) split Australia's international market. The domestic market, he said, had to be left out of any merger.[11] Evans informed the then Qantas chief executive, John Menadue, that Sir Peter Abeles had commented to him: 'Nothing will happen in Australian aviation unless Rupert [Murdoch] and I agree'. On 10 April Evans commented publicly that three days of talks with New Zealand had failed to resolve the 'formidable problems' of a three-way merger. Qantas was now left with little option but to seek a shareholding in Air New Zealand in order to protect its commercial interests and keep its wider strategic options open. (That course was a largely defensive strategy against its big and aggressive competitor, British Airways, which was also bidding for a shareholding in Air New Zealand — with considerable support from some political groups and also from Air New Zealand's management and board. The outcome was the achievement of a 19.9 per cent stake in Air New Zealand by Qantas.)[12]

On 30 April 1988 Australian Airlines commenced operations as an incorporated public company. The new board of the company comprised Ted Harris as chairman and seven of the other existing commissioners of the Australian National

Airlines Commission. James Strong was formally appointed chief executive officer. The change had been made, said Evans, to ensure that the airline would be 'strong, viable, efficient and able to provide effective competition in the deregulated environment that would prevail after the expiry of the Two-Airlines Agreement in 1990'. It would 'formally place responsibility for management of the airline squarely on the airline's board where it properly belongs'.[13] The minister's role was to act as the interface between the enterprise and government.

In a statement on 25 May 1988 headed 'Reshaping the Transport and Communications Government Business Enterprises', the government made public its plans for a fundamental review of the eight major transport and communications government business enterprises — Australian Airlines, Australian National Line, Australian National Railways, Telecom, Overseas Telecommunications Commission, Aussat, Australia Post and Qantas.

While the prospect of a major merger had occupied the minds of Australian it was also, at a less spectacular level of airline operations, setting policy for its involvement in domestic regional activities. Ansett was pursuing an increasingly vigorous strategy of varying ownership arrangements throughout Australia in regional networks to protect market share after deregulation. Australian's restricted presence in these markets had helped make viable the Ansett operations as a sole operator. Strong outlined Australian's policy to his board. It should, he said, establish a direct role in regional aviation by participation in a series of existing regional airlines and expansion of their operations where opportunity existed with, in each case, economic viability carefully assessed (to avoid the consequences of the purchase by TAA of Air Queensland). A central aim was to achieve the greatest possible commonality in terms of aircraft and integration of operations (though each regional airline would operate as a separate company). Viable parts of Air Queensland's operations were to be retained and, at an appropriate time, all operations would be linked under the name 'Australian Regional Airlines', with a common livery based on the Australian Airlines design. It was a strategy that, summarised, planned Australian's direct participation in a series of lower-cost airlines in the general aviation (GA) or supplementary airline licence (SAL) categories, as compared with the higher-cost regular passenger transport (RPT). In general, equipment was to be purchased by lease financing with little if any capital outlay (and with guarantees by Australian Airlines, using cash flow to service the lease costs). In addition, said Strong, close attention was being given to the separate question of the possible formation of a secondary network using smaller jet aircraft to link major tourism and holiday destinations throughout Australia, similar to the Ansett-owned East-West network.[14]

Actual ownership by Australian of these regional airlines had its problems. They were at best inherently marginal operations with thin levels of revenue in small markets facing escalating equipment costs and the entry into their deregulated environment of ever smaller, low-cost operators. Investment in them for Australian, as opposed to commercial links, carried risks. But Australian had not been able to build any permanent regional network by restricting itself to commercial links. The reality was that Ansett was buying up independent operators. Strong's view was that Australian's best course. if it spent money and time building up a regional airline, was to protect its investment by a strategic shareholding or effective control.

The existing regional situation for Australian in mid 1988 was that Air Queensland had ceased flying at the end of May. The F27 operations based in Cairns continued to service the Cape York area, with two aircraft integrated into Australian Airlines operationally. Twin Otter operations were to be separated and based in Townsville, trading as Australian Regional Airlines (Queensland) Limited under a general aviation licence. (The main routes were to Dunk, Lizard and Brampton islands.) Sunstate Airlines, effectively half owned by Australian, operated in southeast Queensland and operated up the coast to Cairns under a supplementary airline licence (mainly using Shorts and Bandeirante aircraft). Sunstate also had a company in Victoria linking Mildura, Broken Hill and Adelaide.

In New South Wales Australian Airlines had by now acquired 37.5 per cent of Eastern Airlines following the enforced Ansett divestment. It operated services from Sydney along the coast to Brisbane. Eastern had just gained new licences to five ports in the New England area (Taree, Kempsey, Grafton, Glen Innes and Inverell) and Australian had leased to it three Jetstream J31s (formerly used on routes in western Queensland). Eastern operated under supplementary airline licences. Australian was negotiating with Hazelton Air Services, which operated in western areas of New South Wales, to join its network. Australian had no direct intrastate operations in Western Australia and did not have suitable equipment to compete with Ansett for the exclusive licence to operate in the Northern Territory (where the premier route was between Alice Springs and Uluru (Ayers Rock).

Australian's conversion to public company status was only one of a series of major policy decisions taken by the government in an unprecedented programme of reform that was radically transforming the industry. They had significantly affected the corporate strategy of the airline presented to the minister in September 1987. The list of government initiatives was a long one and included the deregulation of the interstate aviation industry from October 1990; rejection of a merger between Australian and Qantas; restoration of Qantas interlining rights from July 1988; the inauguration of the Federal Airports Corporation (FAC); granting of long-term leases at FAC airports that entailed large future capital expenditure by Australian; and the formation of the Civil Aviation Authority (CAA) to regulate air safety and provide airways infrastructure. The government had also decided that Commonwealth enterprises should pay all state and local government taxes and charges, a decision that was to have an impact on the operating costs of the FAC and CAA. It was replacing the aviation turbine fuel excise duty with a specific en-route navigation fee to be collected by the CAA, and it was to put the government travel business out to tender as from 1 January 1988. Finally, a government decision had been made to remove from the credit to infrastructure costs the international airport departure tax and to deregulate the oil industry, with a consequent impact on the supply and cost of aviation fuel.

All these significant government changes to the environment of the aviation industry had occurred as Ansett had changed the nature and extent of the competition faced by Australian by its purchase of East-West Airlines (and had extended the Ansett monopoly on certain routes within the Northern Territory for a further five years). Meanwhile domestic aviation issues remained clouded by politics. The ALP's annual national conference voted to refer the contentious issue of the privatisation of Australian Airlines and Qantas to a committee, ensuring that a climate of uncertainty would continue for Australian's board, management and staff.

In this period of accelerating change to the regulatory and market environments, Australian Airlines had concentrated its attack on the high yield business in the business traffic triangle between Sydney, Melbourne and Adelaide, and achieved markedly increased revenue for each seat provided. By tight control over aircraft capacity and decentralisation of accountability and responsibility, costs and staffing levels had been held down. Benefits from closing down loss-making operations in Queensland were beginning to flow through to the bottom line. In New South Wales Australian Airlines, in its partnership with Eastern Australia Airlines, won the further rights to operate services between Sydney and the northern cities of Armidale and Port Macquarie. Two additional 36-passenger Dash 8 aircraft and a Super Jetstream 31 were ordered to service the new routes. (A large new Brisbane airport terminal had been opened for public use on 20 March.)

Major decisions by the airline had already been taken to meet the changing conditions. The A320 aircraft order had been deferred and an order for Boeing 737-400s substituted. Additional Boeing 737-300s had been ordered to allow the phasing out of DC9 aircraft. A development strategy had been determined for Australian at the eight major airports now under FAC control and strategic alliances developed with international airlines operating into Australia to combat the Qantas–Ansett commercial agreement. Ahead lay the necessity of heavy investment for new aircraft, airport terminal developments, computer reservation and distribution systems and feeder networks.

For the financial year to 30 June 1988 passenger demand had greatly exceeded expectations. Australian Airlines reported an increase in revenue of 16.8 per cent to over $1 billion and a massive increase of 56.1 per cent in operating profit before tax to $66,563,000. Consolidated profit (after tax and extraordinary items) rose by an extraordinary 88.1 per cent. It had been, said Strong in the airline's annual report, a watershed year, 'a turning point and beginning of a new era', marking the fruition of several years of planning and implementation of new strategies and service initiatives. It had also been the most successful financial year in the airline's history. (The airlines' total assets were now just over $1.5 billion. Shareholders' funds were only $217,634,000.) The strong passenger demand continued into the new financial year and, with falling oil prices, kept profits well in excess of budget.[15]

On 28 July Harris publicly announced the airline's order for Boeing 737-400 aircraft. *Aircraft* reported: 'Australian Airlines has ended months of informed speculation with an order for nine Boeing 737-400 airliners to take the total cost of its outstanding 737 family to about $600 million ... The package covers six 737-400s to be delivered in 1990 and three in 1991 plus four 737-300s ordered earlier. Australian has taken an option on five more 737-400s for delivery in 1992.' Strong told the journal that the overwhelming reason for standardising its mid-range fleet on the 737 family was 'to save significantly more than $100 million in typical start-up costs'.[16]

The reshaping of the aviation industry took place as the Australian economy, in Australia's bicentennial year, was dominated by the impact of major structural change. The nation was at last moving away from its reliance on agricultural and mineral exports towards strengthening its manufacturing and tourism industries. Government moves to discourage imports through taxes, interest rates and wages policy were slowing the economy (with gross domestic product estimated to grow by only 2 per cent in 1988–89). Inflation had fallen from 9.8 per cent in December 1986 to 7.1 per cent in December 1987 and was expected to decline further. That long-term outlook for the economy had direct repercussions on demand for air travel in Australia. The business market was not expected to increase, and minimal growth in domestic tourism was predicted.

Despite these impending economic constraints and the challenges and pressures on management and staff that rapid industry change had brought, the board of Australian Airlines Limited in mid 1988 called for a more agggressive approach to the utilisation of the airline's assets. It wanted a higher level of profit and the achievement of a more commercial capital gearing position, with the sale of up to 50 per cent of the company's resort properties. Management responded with a budget plan for an operating profit in 1988–89 of $127.5 million, the sale of half the resort properties for an estimated $80 million by 31 December 1988, a net profit (incorporating profits from the resort sales) of $165.5 million and a capital gearing by 30 June 1989 of 70.9 to 29.1. The board congratulated management on the airline's record profit for the month of July.[17]

Passenger traffic in September was unprecedented in the airline's history and a consolidated profit of $21.189 million recorded ($5.308 million above the budgeted $15.881 million). Growth in passenger-kilometres was up almost 20 per cent on the preceding year. Load factor, at 84.2 per cent, was the highest ever experienced during a prolonged period of operations and Australian's market share rose to 50.5 per cent. (Expo 88 in Brisbane, school holidays, business market strength and the Victorian Football League Grand Final all helped produce record demand for domestic air travel.) Profits continued to exceed expectations. A consolidated profit of

$28.381 million was recorded for October, $15.883 above budget, reflecting continuing strong demand on trunk routes. Load factor was an extraordinary 85.1 per cent. Industrial problems at Ansett gave Australian a market share in the new financial year to date of 54.4 per cent. On the high yield Melbourne–Sydney route it was 58 per cent.

Technology in other fields was also reshaping airline operations. In November 1988 Australian announced that it was jointly establishing with Ansett a new computer reservations system known as CRS supplied by Southern Cross Distribution Systems Pty Ltd. This amalgamation's ultimate aim was to deliver to Australian travel agents the giant European computer reservations system, Galileo. The development overseas of CRS (which provided high levels of automation to travel agency subscribers) had been prolific following the introduction of deregulation in the United States. In Australia CRS was initially to connect travel agency subscribers to the US-based Apollo CRS, with its major implementation in Australia planned for late 1990 (when Galileo came on stream). Travel agency automation to date had been provided by TIAS Pty Ltd (Travel Industry Automatic Systems), a company owned equally by Australian, Ansett and Qantas. (James Strong had recommended to the board that Australian Airlines join with Qantas and Air New Zealand in marketing a computer reservations system known as Sabre, with Qantas acting as the host airline for the system. That recommendation was made because of the need to achieve a critical mass of users for what was a very high-cost operation. Abeles, however, acted independently and persuaded Harrris to join Ansett in choosing the competing Galileo system. As a consequence both systems were developed in Australia and both lost large sums of money in what amounted to a financial disaster. They were eventually brought together under TIAS in a joint-venture arrangement with Ansett, Qantas, Air New Zealand and Australian Airlines.)

A $250 million redevelopment of Australian's airport terminals was well under way. Brisbane and Canberra were complete, redevelopment was under way in Melbourne and

Perth, and plans were in place for Adelaide, Hobart and Sydney. Australian was investing $134 million in the new Sydney terminal, providing eighteen aircraft gates (currently there were eight) and space to cater for an additional 1.5 million passengers by 1999.

Sydney airport was already suffering the effects of congestion. It was the major hub of Australian's operations, with 27 per cent of all passengers carried by the airline passing through Sydney. The capacity of an airport was established by determining the number of aircraft movements that could be processed in one hour. Sydney's capacity, the board was told in February 1989, was twenty-seven movements an hour but the industry's schedule requirements in major peak hours was thirty movements. Sydney's congestion problem was aggravated by the fact that some 40 per cent of all international flights to Sydney arrived in the five hours between 0600 and 1100. It was also influenced by the necessary link between commuter and airline operations, creating a simultaneous peak period for both. It was Australian's view that a third runway should be built at Sydney simultaneously with the establishment of a second airport at Badgery's Creek.[18]

Qantas now extended its influence in New Zealand. Though plans for a merger with Air New Zealand had failed, on 22 December 1988 Qantas signed an agreement for a strategic equity stake in the national carrier, as leader of a consortium that included Brierly Investments Limited, Japan Airlines and American Airlines. The New Zealand government had committed its international airline to privatisation.

On 30 March 1989 Ralph Willis, who had succeeded Gareth Evans as minister for transport and communications, advised Harris that the government had decided to develop a third runway at Sydney's Kingsford Smith Airport and was to begin development of a second airport at Badgery's Creek. Australian judged that the additional runway at Sydney would increase total capacity from 220,000 to 310,000 aircraft movements a year (an additional 40 per cent) and would provide for the airline's forecast passenger movements for at least the next twenty years.[19]

The half year to 30 December 1988 continued the heady growth of the previous financial year. The half year net trading result for Australian Airlines was a pre-tax operating profit of $80.8 million (more than $19 million better than budgeted and more than double the profit for the same period in the previous year).[20] The airline, said Harris, was 'performing better than at any time in its history'.[21] He revived the privatisation debate, saying in February 1989 that the result made Australian Airlines a very attractive proposition to potential investors and gave the Government a golden opportunity to sell the carrier for a good price. Australian, he said, needed maximum flexibility to meet new competition. Private ownership was the best way to achieve this. He suggested that a 30 per cent share in Australian be sold to strategic investors in transport or related industries, up to 15 per cent in a foreign airline, 10 per cent to Australian's pilots and staff and the remainder to the public.[22]

Harris had the prime minister, Bob Hawke, as an ally. In mid March Hawke surprised both his party and the media when he put privatisation back on the government's agenda. An extraordinary ALP national conference could be convened, he said, that could change the party's policy of full public ownership of government enterprises. His remarks were seen as putting pressure on the special ALP committee set up at the ALP conference in June 1988 to examine the investment needs and funding options for Australian and Qantas. The conference had reaffirmed that Australian Airlines would remain in full public ownership.[23] It was now clear that the government intended otherwise.

Hawke's view was strongly challenged in a paper prepared for the Public Sector Funding Review of the ALP by the Public Sector Research Centre of the University of New South Wales. Its author, Michael Johnson, concluded that 'its is essential for Australian airlines to be maintained as an independent state-owned airline if the domestic market is to operate as an effective competitive market. The costs of public ownership are lower than the cost of regulating a market comprised solely of one or more private carriers.' Priority in reform, he said, 'should be deregulation of the domestic airline market (including the regional market) and a reduction of controls over Australian Airlines and Qantas, not a dilution of public ownership'.[24] A paper putting the case for the retention of public ownership of Qantas and Australian, which was endorsed by the Administrative and Clerical Officers Association, the Amalgamated Metal Workers Union and nine other unions, was also submitted to the Funding Review. The government faced the considerable task of persuading rank and file Labor supporters that its policy was in the best interests of both the nation and the Party.

There was a shock for the management and staff of Australian Airlines as well as for the industry when, on 3 April 1989, James Strong announced his resignation. He would, he said, remain as chief executive until September. 'This has been one of the most difficult decisions in my life', said Strong, 'because of the degree of attachment I have formed with the airline and its staff'.[25] Strong was leaving (eighteen months before the end of his five-year contract) to become managing partner and chief executive of a new national law firm, Corrs (formed from the merger of Adelaide firm Mollison Litchfield, Melbourne's Corrs Pavey Whiting and Byrne, and Perth's Keall Brinsden). Corrs was one of the largest legal firms in Australia with more than 500 staff and 65 partners.[26]

Strong's resignation brought into sharp focus a fundamental weakness that flowed from government ownership. Ted Harris put the matter succinctly, stating that Strong's departure showed the inability of government business enterprises to hold top executives. Under government ownership, he said, Australian would never be able to compete effectively in the marketplace, in terms either of salaries or managerial flexibility. (In May 1988 the government had freed fifteen of its GBEs — Government Business Enterprises — to bid in the marketplace for top executives. It had approved an offer to Strong of a salary package of $225,000, more than double the $106,000 paid under his contract.) 'There is absolutely no way', said Harris, 'that the package we are able to offer even under the changed rules stacks up against what people with ability like James Strong can earn in the private sector'.[27] (There was a second pressure that influenced James Strong's departure. If Australian Airlines had gone to the marketplace for a chief executive on a market salary it would have been necessary for Strong, as with others similarly placed in GBEs, to resign and re-apply for his position. Harris had made it clear to the press that he could not publicly support Strong's reappointment without undermining the selection process. 'I think James took this as indicating that he did not have my support', said Harris subsequently. 'In fact I did support him. He had changed the public perception of the airline and was one of the best communicators I've ever seen. He represented Australian Airlines in an admirable way.'[28] There were, nevertheless, tensions between the two men. 'He might have thought I was too much a hands-on chairman', Harris acknowledged. 'And he might have been right about that.')[29] Harris could well have protested at his own chairman's fee in a period of unprecedented turmoil. 'I was paid the princely sum of about $24,000 a year', he said.[30]

He now pressed his argument for privatisation in even stronger terms than before. 'My feelings about privatisation are simple. I really don't care who owns the airline provided we are given an opportunity to compete. From what I can see, having been chairman for twelve months, government ownership of the airline cannot give us that opportunity ... For example, we may find we have to buy a secondary airline. Ansett could do that tomorrow morning — they did it by buying East-West. We could not do that. We'd have to go through all sorts of committees.' (Harris advised the minister in May 1989 that Australian would be moving to acquire full ownership of Sunstate Airlines, Queensland, Sunstate Mildura and Eastern Australia Airlines. It bought one-third of Sunstate Queensland in June.)[31] Harris said he anticipated it would take three or four months to find a new chief executive. He appreciated Strong's offer to stay on for up to six months, he said, 'at some cost to himself'. The airline under Strong, said Harris, had been transformed into a profitable and enterprising company 'and leads in overall market share, the all-important business market and in customer share'.[32] He left for New York and London with two other board members to interview applicants from North America and Europe for the position of Australian Airlines' managing director and chief executive. (A third board member, Gary Pemberton, was to divert from a visit to Brussels to attend the interviews.)[33]

On 4 June 1989 Ralph Willis strongly urged the sale of both Qantas and Australian Airlines, a move immediately condemned by the Labor Party's Left. He called for a total sale rather than maintenance of government control. Both the prime minister and the finance minister, Senator Walsh, backed his comments. The government was moving to confront those in the Party who were fighting for continued government ownership of the two-airlines. (Qantas directors had advised the government that if the airline were to remain in public ownership the airline needed a shareholders' equity injection of capital from the Commonwealth of $600 million in 1989–90 to bring its debit–equity ratio to 63:37 in that year and 65:35 in the following two years. Denial of capital, it said, would pose the real threat that Qantas would be forced out of business by mega airlines.)[34]

Australian had, in accordance with its corporate strategy, put its remaining five DC9 aircraft on the open market. In July it informed the minister that they had been sold to Australian Aircraft Sales (NSW) Pty Ltd for a total price of $US32 million for onward delivery to a purchaser at Long Beach, California. The first aircraft was delivered in July, the last of the DC9 fleet in November 1989.[35]

For the year to 30 June 1989 Australian Airlines Limited earned a pre-tax profit of $108 million, a 63 per cent increase on the previous year. It was a year in which the world economy had slowed in most countries, but not in Australia. Australian had established itself as the preferred carrier for domestic business travellers and carried more than six million passengers. The increased profit result was achieved despite a marked slowdown in the second six months. Air fares had increased during the year by 5.7 per cent but the general level of inflation was higher, at 7.6 per cent, reflecting a general increase in efficiency. Harris, in his chairman's report, wrote: 'On a personal note as Chairman, I wish to record my personal appreciation for the leadership given to the airline by Mr Strong. He will be greatly missed.'[36]

A 1989–90 budget for Australian Airlines Limited, covering both parent and subsidiary companies, was put to the board in July 1989. It aimed at a group trading net profit of $174 million. That considerable target was decided as the group moved from a year of unprecedented activity, characterised by a buoyant business market and record inbound tourist activity, to a year of great uncertainty. The government, through monetary policy, was trying to slow demand and the aviation industry was attempting to reach agreement on the difficult industrial relations issue of award restructuring. Airline industry deregulation lay ahead and both marketing initiatives and capital expenditures in preparation for deregulation had considerably increased costs. The planned introduction of the new Boeing 737-400s and new airport terminal developments also put pressure on funds well above internally generated levels to a degree that despite the planned sale of 50 per cent of the resorts, meant holding the capital gearing level static at 68:32 debt to equity. Capital injection, therefore, was required for the airline to achieve its desired debt to equity target of 60:40. (Extraordinary profits from the resort sales and sale of the headquarters building in Franklin Street, Melbourne, were expected to add $57 million to net profits.) The budget gave a return on shareholders' funds of 24.7 per cent, well above the board's targeted rate of 15 per cent.[37]

Australian's carefully crafted budget and the plans of all airlines and government for the entire domestic aviation industry were, in August, to be shattered by dramatic and unprecented industrial action from the nation's domestic airline pilots.

Pilot unrest had been evident as early as February, when

they stopped work to review their commitment to Australia's centralised wage-fixing system and an ACTU decision to pursue a $50 wage-tax package. That proposal, in their view, would not restore to them wage equity with comparable professions. In June the Australian Federation of Air Pilots (AFAP) advised pilots to prepare themselves financially for prolonged industrial action. On 7 August, sparking government fears of a general wage break-out, the pilots tabled a claim for a wage rise of 29.47 per cent, almost five times the federal government's proposal for a 6.5 per cent increase for the general work force. Acceptance of the pilots' claim by the government was a political impossibility. Both Australian and Ansett immediately rejected the claim.

Events now moved swiftly. On 11 August, in the first of a series of stopworks, pilots in Melbourne ceased flying to vote on a possible nationwide strike. The vote overwhelmingly authorised the Federation to take any industrial action it saw fit. On 15 August the federal government warned it would support any move by the airlines to end the dispute. In the Industrial Relations Commission pilots and employers reached a stalemate. Two days later the Federation announced an industrial campaign reducing pilots' working days to office hours. On 18 August the IRC met to determine a bid by the airlines to cancel the pilots' industrial awards and break the eight-hour-day action. On the following day the Commission set a 21 August deadline for pilots to lift their bans. On 21 August, the fifth day of industrial action, the pilots' awards were cancelled. The airlines announced a further deadline for the pilots — to return to a full flight schedule by the following night.

The stakes for both sides were dramatically high. The pilots, long acustomed to success from the exercise of their awesome industrial muscle, refused to compromise. The federal government began unprecedented negotiations for help from international carriers as Australia's domestic airline industry faced total shutdown. Ansett, Australian, East-West and IPEC began sacking pilots and issued writs against fifty individual pilots seeking damages for breach of contract. On

24 August 1989, in the worst crisis ever faced by the aviation industry, Australia's 1,647 domestic airline pilots resigned en masse.

CHAPTER 21

1989

High drama

In an atmosphere of high drama the minister for transport, Ralph Willis, announced that the Royal Australian Air Force would carry passengers on flights between Sydney, Perth and Melbourne, to the north Queensland coast and between Melbourne and Tasmania. Their aircraft, including Hercules transports and a Boeing 707, had to refuel at air force bases, following the refusal of the Transport Workers Union to refuel them. Qantas pilots refused to carry domestic passengers. The government also announced that fourteen overseas airlines flying domestic sectors had agreed to carry stranded passengers.

The president of the Australian Federation of Air Pilots, Captain Brian McCarthy, attempted to shift the basis of the strike from its wage claim to a broader issue. 'This dispute', he said, 'is not about the 29.47 per cent [claim]. The outcome would have been the same whatever the percentage. The dispute is about the right of employees, through their representative union, to directly negotiate with their employers. Pilots are being used by the Government and the ACTU to show Australia and the rest of the union movement what happens to any group which attempts to step out of line.'[1]

The *Financial Review* commented: 'Pressure is increasing on the government to provide financial support for the airlines ... The airlines can be expected to put a strong case to

Government that they are carrying huge losses to protect the government's wage policy, the integrity of which is vital to the government's political survival.' The prime minister, Bob Hawke, made his position on the strike plain, warning emotionally and dramatically that the pilots' action threatened not just the wage-fixing system but 'Australian life as we know it'. If they [the pilots] win, said Hawke, 'the whole wage system is dead and Australia is dead'. Hawke's fury and hyperbole worried Harris. He rang the prime minister to tell him that he was detracting from the main issue in the dispute and that his attack on the pilots was unhelpful.[2]

It was almost immediately apparent that the pilots' resignation strategy had made them vulnerable. By resigning they had ensured that when the dispute finally ended they had no right of re-employment. The airlines could choose who would and who would not be reinstated. They had left the way open for the airlines to recruit a new pilot body. Willis commented: 'They have resigned on absurd advice from their union. The organisation has virtually committed suicide. It is now a matter between individual pilots and their companies.'[3]

On 26 August the *Australian* reported: 'Productivity-based individual contracts, under which pilots would be paid more to do more flying, were offered last night in an attempt to end the domestic air dispute. The scheme, rejected by a pilots' spokesman, was offered by the chief executive of Australian Airlines, Mr James Strong, who has tacitly emerged as the public spokesman for Australian, Ansett Airlines, East-West Airlines and Ipec Aviation.' At the same time the airlines increased their pressure on pilots with a writ lodged in the Supreme Court of Victoria seeking unspecified damages from the Australian Federation of Air Pilots. (In the meantime the airlift by the RAAF and international airlines transported some 7,500 passengers, compared with a normal 40,000 for the day. The government had authorised all thirty-six international airlines operating in Australia to fly extra services between cities they traditionally serviced as well as to places they did not usually serve.) Strong said Australian would offer contracts to individual pilots but would not negotiate through the pilots' Federation. He differentiated the pilots from their Federation, saying that the union had deliberately engineered the dispute to bulldoze through the 29.47 per cent pay claim. In newspaper advertisements the airlines set out to attract pilots from Australia, the United States, United Kingdom, New Zealand, Singapore, Hong Kong, Fiji and Papua New Guinea.[4]

The pressure on the striking pilots was now as intense as the pressure they had applied to the airlines. The resources of the airlines, however, backed by the federal government, were far greater than those of the AFAP and its members. The *Australian*'s Paul Kelly commented: 'Bob Hawke sees the pilots dispute as the single most critical threat to his economic policy and political position in nearly seven years as prime minister — an issue, quite literally, he cannot afford to lose.' Hawke told the newspaper: 'There's nothing, to this point, which has threatened the economy and the future welfare of this country in the way that this has'.5 There was no softening of the pilots' stand; their Federation had, accurately, predicted a long period of industrial action.

As the strike passed into its fourth week the Federal government took an unprecedented step that, in its implications, showed there could be no pilots' victory. It approved financial assistance on a huge scale to the airlines to enable them to keep on their payrolls their idle staff. No direct payments were made but the Government decided to waive airport landing fees and other CAA and FAC charges for whatever period was necessary to recompense the airlines. Hawke declared the dispute a national emergency.

Australian operated its first flights with its own aircraft since the beginning of the strike on 13 September, when management crew flew some four stages daily. By mid September there were signs of a break in the pilots' ranks. Sir Peter Abeles announced that Ansett had negotiated individual contracts with fifty pilots.[6] Hawke, now staking his political career on the restoration of air services, wrote to each striking pilot individually appealing for an end to the strike. At the same time the airlines rejected a proposal from the

AFAP that a mediator be appointed. It was becoming apparent that, for the first time in the history of the industry, the airlines were in a position to challenge and crush the industrial power of the pilots. Ansett's general manager, Graeme McMahon, told the *Financial Review* on 17 September: 'A dispute doesn't exist so you don't need an arbitrator. The situation the airline industry finds itself in is that the pilots have all resigned. The challenge we face is to fill vacant situations and that process is under way.'[7] On 20 September both Australian and Ansett warned pilots that unless they applied for their old jobs under individual contracts within thirty-six hours they would lose all seniority and benefits. The airlines also advised the AFAP that they were prepared to offer contracts only to some 60 per cent of the pilots who had resigned. In newspaper advertisements the pilots were told: 'Pilots should be aware the airlines are resolute in their determination to rebuild their companies. We would prefer to do this with the majority of our former pilots. However, if the response to the employment offer is slow, the airlines will continue with widespread outside recruitment and training.'[8]

On Friday, 22 September, as the tide turned against the AFAP, James Strong spent his last day at Australian Airlines. He had, in just three and a half years, proved the catalyst he had hoped to be when he joined the airline. Strong's achievement had been, if at considerable cost to some who had served the old TAA loyally, to carry out the task implicitly set for him by the government. He had transformed the culture and commercial performance of the airline. Not even TAA's critics had ever argued that TAA had been other than a splendid airline, one that had set standards of technical and operational performance that were internationally acknowledged. Its record over decades showed that within the constraints of policies carefully contrived by successive governments to provide safe air travel for the nation in a stable industry, it had been been an airline that was competitive, popular and respected. But the two-airline policy that had evolved to accommodate the political realities of a nation equally divided on the fundamental issue of government versus private ownership no longer provided the industry structure necessary for economic survival. Strong's task had been to accommodate the new political and economic realities and carry through the harsh transformation of TAA into Australian Airlines.

As he departed he had no soft words for the striking pilots. He told the *Age* that the pilots' dispute had 'changed the face of aviation in Australia'. 'I get pilots ringing me or writing saying "How could you do this to us? What a terrible thing for all the loyalty we've given the airline." Not one of them ever stops to think that the airline has given them a wonderful career, the best training in the world, made them the pilots they are, given them very good salaries, wonderful superannuation schemes — and they have put the airline on the ground costing it millions and millions of dollars.' He was proud, he said, of his time at Australian. 'It's been the happiest period of my life.'[9]

The RAAF and the international airlines, which began airlifting passengers in late August, continued to operate throughout September. The introduction on 24 September by Australian of a 'wet-leased' 737-300 from the French airline Aeromaritime significantly increased capacity. But total uplift for the month for Australian was only 9.2 per cent of budgeted traffic. Total revenue for September was more than $97 million below budget.

On 4 October the AFAP, still seemingly blind to the full implications of the course it had taken, changed its strategy. It withdrew its huge salary claim and served a new log of claims based on existing awards, with salary and productivity savings. The airlines rejected the approach. The AFAP, they said, no longer represented the pilots they employed. On 13 October the formal industrial relations aspects of the dispute came to an end. The Industrial Relations Commission ratified awards for pilots who had rejoined the airlines. (The AFAP did not attend the final award determination proceedings.) On 30 October the prime minister told the ALP Caucus that the pilots' strike had effectively ended and that the pilots' position was impossible. He told Parliament that the only course to be followed now was the reconstruction of the airlines.[10] (The AFAP, following a further application to the Industrial Relations Commission, was told on 18 December that pilots were 'whistling in the wind' if they thought they could take up employment under better conditions than those covering pilots now working in the airlines. The Commission said the industrial relations between the Federation and the airlines could be restored only if the union became a party to the new pilots' awards and that if it rejected that action, it had no role to play in employment of pilots in the industry.)[11]

Reconstruction was a slow and difficult process. Pilots previously employed by Australian initially returned to the airline in a trickle — at only two a month. New pilots, however, were being hired at the rate of sixteen a month, with the rate limited only by the availability of training captains. Australian was providing capacity by a mix of aircraft flown by its own pilots, by foreign aircraft charters, by use of RAAF capacity and by capacity available from overseas airlines. An active programme of recruitment both locally and overseas was in progress. Australian, towards the end of October, had more than a hundred pilots from Australia and overseas awaiting interviews for positions of captain on A300, B727 and B737 aircraft.[12] They were all, however, in current employment and required to give notice. Significantly, the board of Australian Airlines, on 25 October, recorded 'that neither the board nor management had been given instructions by the Government with respect to any matter regarding the dispute and that the airline had never set out to destroy the AFAP'. The board, it noted, believed 'that pilots have an inherent right to be represented by whatever association the pilots deem appropriate or to act individually if a pilot so chooses'.[13] On 12 November both Ansett and Australian told the Australian Tourism Commission that scheduled air services would be back to normal by January.[14]

The airlines won their damages case against the pilots in the Supreme Court in Melbourne on 23 November. Damages were forecast to total $10 million. The court found that the airlines had not plotted to destroy the AFAP. The prime minister, however, urged the airlines not to pursue the matter of damages from the Federation.

For the industry the process of recovery and rebuilding continued. The RAAF operations were discontinued on 15 December. The airlines ceased making regular use of leased seats on scheduled international airline services on 31 December. From the public, their travel plans disrupted, demand remained low in the leisure market but business travel responded quickly to capacity availability. Australian did not expect overall demand to reach 85 per cent of pre-dispute levels before April. Diminished crew availability meant that some aircraft continued to lie idle. Rebuilding for Australian involved both the reintroduction of its own aircraft and the use of charter aircraft from Europe. At the end of November the airline was flying eleven of its own aircraft and eleven charter aircraft. That represented 110,000 seats a week (from 15 November) or 90 per cent of the number of passengers who had travelled on Australian in the same period in the previous year. Diminished demand meant that seats for all passengers wishing to fly would be available from December (but with very high load factors and lower flight frequencies). Australian's consolidated result to 31 August showed a loss of $11.1 million against a budgeted profit of $16.8 million. The main impact of the dispute had been felt from 24 August when the pilots stopped flying and the airline came to a halt. The estimated trading result for September was a loss of $28.8 million (bringing the year-to-date loss to $39.8 million). Trading projections for the full 1989–90 financial year indicated an operating loss, before tax, of $87.6 million.

For the airlines the costs of the dispute were without parallel. For the individual pilots concerned the results were disastrous. Australian, which now estimated it needed 385 pilots, continued recruiting within Australia and from overseas. More than one thousand applications had been received in Australia. Applications had come from overseas experienced A300, B727 and B737 captains and first officers, including pilots from major international airlines. The Australian

Federation of Air Pilots had self-destructed. Both major airlines now had their own award for pilots, the terms and conditions derived from individual contracts.

CHAPTER 22

1989–90

The deregulation of the domestic airline industry

On 27 August 1989, only days after the start of the pilots' strike and the grounding of the airlines, the federal government confirmed that it was now considering the merger of Australian Airlines and Qantas 'as an option'.[1] Ansett's general manager, Graeme McMahon, wrote briefly to Willis: 'We have noted several statements by you and the Prime Minister that merger of Qantas and Australian Airlines is an option available to the Government to ensure adequate funding of those airlines. We trust you would be aware, and understand, that if such a merger was to take place, Ansett would expect to be granted full international passenger and cargo rights. We would be happy to outline our reasons for this position, to the extent you and your advisors are not aware of them, should the option of merger of Qantas and Australian become the chosen course for the Government. In any event we do believe the merger would not be in the interests of this country.'[2] A Qantas board memo in March 1990 commented on the Ansett reaction to the Qantas–Air New Zealand merger option: 'It was clear that Ansett had a paranoia about the competitive impact of Qantas and Air New Zealand's wide-bodied jets on the very profitable operations of the domestic duopoly. [Qantas], therefore, was left with little option except to seek a shareholding in Air New Zealand in order to protect its commercial interests and to keep its strategic options open.'[3]

The disruption of the domestic aviation industry by the pilots' dispute had put these matters of policy on hold. As the dispute effectively came to an end at the end of November a link of a different kind was established between Qantas and Australian. The board of Australian, on 29 November, resolved to recommend to Willis the appointment of John W. Schaap, forty-three, as chief executive officer and managing director of the airline.[4] John Schaap's professional background was in marked contrast to James Strong's. He had spent his entire career in aviation, starting in 1963 as a reservations trainee with Qantas and rising by May 1988 to the position of director of airline operations. In July 1989 he was appointed general manager, passenger services. He was also a member of Qantas's Management Policy Committee.

John Schaap had one other significant qualification. In 1985, under a management agreement between Qantas and Air Pacific to help the financially troubled airline, he had been seconded to Air Pacific in Fiji as its chief executive. (It was his second secondment to the airline. In 1971 — when it was Fiji Airways — he was its reservations superintendent.) During his term with the airline as chief executive he had returned it to profitability, before rejoining Qantas in May 1988. He was appointed to Australian for a minimum period of three years from 16 January 1990 at a commencing salary of $175,000.

Schaap joined Australian with deregulation of the domestic aviation industry only ten months away. The airline was committed to a capital expenditure programme of $1.75 billion over the period 1988–89 to 1992–93. Total shareholders' equity was now $268.2 million of which still only $130 million was paid-up capital. It had received no capital injections since 1983. Australian also faced further capital expenditure of some $1 billion to fund strategic investments and the replacement of its A300 aircraft, scheduled for the mid 1990s. (On 1 December Harris had advised Willis that to bring the airline's projected gearing ratio at 30 June 1990 of 79 per cent interest-bearing debt to 21 per cent equity to the target of 60:40, a capital injection of $290 million was required before 30 June.) Schaap joined as Australian's forecasts to 30 June indicated an operating loss of $26.6 million. He also faced a period of rising interest rate expenses for the airline together with expected falls in passenger numbers and falls in yield that promised a profit squeeze in the years ahead. Though Australian had produced a record return to the Commonwealth in 1988–89 of $19.8 million in dividends, it did not expect to pay any future dividend until the 1992–93 financial year.

The disruption caused by the pilots' dispute had delayed action to attack what Harris and his board saw as the problem of the soft cost base of the airline. That necessary restructuring now had to be achieved much closer to deregulation than Harris wanted and was a high priority for Schaap. First, however, he had to rebuild the shattered airline.

Qantas, too, had suffered substantially from the effect on inbound tourism of the pilots' strike. The airline's chairman was now Bill Dix — appointed in December 1989. (Dix retired in 1990 as chairman of the Ford Motor Company of Australia Limited). Dix told Willis that estimates for the first six months of the 1989–90 year indicated a loss of $60 million. 'Action is in hand', he said, 'to reduce our flying programme, cut costs, freeze manpower, dispose of four older Boeing 747s and to at least maintain our share of the declining market'.[5] The airline was also facing a struggle for survival on its European routes where it was threatened by vigorous competition from Asian carriers.[6] Qantas now had a new chief executive. On 18 December 1989 the board unanimously appointed J. F. (John) Ward. Ward had joined the airline in 1969 and since April 1985 had served as deputy chief executive, deputy chief executive and chief operating officer, and (from July 1989) acting chief executive.

On 8 January 1990 the government announced that its compensation arrangements for the airlines that allowed them to retain staff who would otherwise have been subject to mass stand-downs would end. The acting minister for transport, Ros Kelly, said: 'The airlines now have increased seat capacity in their networks so that they are generally meeting demand. Comprehensive schedules for domestic air services are now in place.' The assistance arrangements, she said, 'do not compensate the airlines for other losses or for revenue or profits lost as a result of the domestic airline pilots' actions'.[7] Following the successful court action against the AFAP in November, and despite Hawke's wish that the airlines should not proceed, another hearing to assess the level of damages to be awarded to Australian, Ansett, East-West and IPEC began in January. Australian and Ansett each claimed some $3.5 million, East-West $570,000 and IPEC $127,000.[8] (On 12 February the court entered judgment for the airlines of $6.5 million plus costs. Australian's apportionment was $2,658,500.)[9]

On 31 January 1990 the board of Australian was advised that the airline had recruited 217 pilots, including sufficient A300, B727 and B737 captains to meet requirements. (Among the pilots recruited were 101 former members of the AFAP.)[10] Charter aircraft were to leave at the end of April. A series of 'welcome evenings' was held for all the new pilots. New industrial arrangements for pilots were planned. Management personnel down to check captains were to form a separate management group and seek umbrella coverage under another union. Talks were proceeding to establish a separate line pilots' union. Geoff Dixon told the board that load factors were extremely high and the airline was carrying some 98 per cent of the previous year's market.[11] On 23 January Ansett and Australian increased air fares by an average of 5 per cent to help recover the heavy losses incurred during the strike.

With the pilots' dispute behind them the airlines now faced political uncertainties. The prime minister, Bob Hawke, announced on 22 February that a federal election would be held on 24 March.

Of the 1,647 pilots belonging to the AFAP 1,300 remained unemployed. Ansett and Australian now had sixteen-page contracts with their pilots, replacing what had been a 178-page award. They could fly the old flying hours with little more than half the previous number of pilots. (On 20 March 1990 Schaap advised the board that very few vacancies were left in pilot ranks and all were expected to be filled within days.)[12] Ansett estimated its losses due to the strike at more than $120 million, Australian at more than $100 million. The loss to the domestic tourism industry was estimated by the Bureau of Tourism Research at between $230 million and $350 million.[13] Schaap told the *Independent Monthly* that Australian would have to pull back some capital spending programs as a result of the dispute and that the need to improve its debt–equity ratio was greater than ever. The equity injection needed, he said, had climbed from $240 million to about $300 million. That, said the newspaper, was 'an uncomfortable fact for whichever party wins the election'.

The Labor government was re-elected on 2 March. For the new minister for transport and communications, Kim Beazley, Australian's losses and forecast poor financial outlook meant a reappraisal of the timing of the desired privatisation of the airline and a decision on whether a capital injection would be necessary to maximise sale price. Forecasts indicated that interest expenses could be expected to grow by more than 60 per cent compared to 1989–90 — a direct result of cash forgone during 1989–90 and of fleet and infrastructure expenditure. Deregulation was expected to place severe pressures on passenger numbers and on fares. Market share erosion and falls in yield were expected, resulting in low operating profits and poor returns on assets and shareholders' funds until the industry stabilised.[14] A persuasive government document, 'Privatisation — The Australian Way', had been prepared and leaflets sent to airline unions that stated that Australian ownership of the airline would be protected through retention by the government of an 'Aussie Share'; overseas investment would be limited to between 10 and 15 per cent; no domestic shareholder would be able to buy more than 20 per cent of the share issue in the first five years after privatisation; and up to 10 per cent of the company's share capital would be set aside for exclusive purchase by employees of the airline. (It was, nevertheless, still in doubt whether any or all of these restrictions would be applied to Ansett.)

On 17 March 1990 the first of Australian Airlines' nine Boeing 737-400s, VH-TJE, arrived. It went into service during the month. The airline had options to buy an additional five. The 737-400 was a stretched version of the earlier 737-300, was three metres longer and had a capacity of 135 seats — 21 more than the 300. Australian's 737-400s had been ordered with additional features in order to operate at higher take-off weights than Boeing's standard 737-400. The aircraft were further modified to include two auxiliary fuel tanks, enhancing their suitability on Australian's longer routes.

At Qantas John Ward presented to his board a paper considering the implications for the airline of the newly re-elected government's commitment to structural changes in the Australian economy and to closer economic relations with New Zealand. (The original Closer Economic Relations treaty was signed in March 1983.) Ward's paper had important implications for the future of Australian Airlines. It recommended a fundamental change in Qantas's attitudes towards the impact of government policies on civil aviation. That change in Qantas attitude, said the paper, 'must be accompanied by a re-examination of the Company's commercial relationships, particularly with Ansett and Australian Airlines'.[15]

Ward saw the driving force for change at the political level coming from the government's concern that deregulation of Australia's domestic air services would fail to have any substantial effect; its conviction that the rising tide of consumerism demanded effective action to enhance competition; the worldwide trend to a more open trading environment; continued loosening up of the worldwide regulatory system for international air transport; and a conviction in the governments of both Australia and New Zealand that the future of their countries lay in following the European Economic Community's example and creating a single market throughout Australasia. Those strands, he said, 'have now all come together'. The government had become convinced 'that Australia can prosper only if there are substantial changes which enable it to compete in a world which is becoming increasingly open to the winds of competition'.[16]

There were good grounds for doubting that deregulation of the domestic aviation market would provide recognisable benefits for air travellers. While it was true that from October 1990 — when termination of the two-airline policy became effective — existing airlines and new entrants would be free to decide what routes they would fly and what fares they would offer, it was a less understood fact that practical barriers to entry into the relatively small market against two strongly entrenched carriers (with little spare capacity at passenger terminals) were formidable. Qantas thought that 'no substantial new operator is likely to obtain the necessary financial backing'. Ward noted: 'There have even been suggestions that in order to introduce keen competition into the domestic market, not only Air New Zealand but also other foreign airlines should be allowed to come in. The entry of any foreign carrier would have an adverse effect on Ansett and Australian Airlines ... and [be] even more damaging to Qantas.'[17]

These were all issues with which John Schaap, as a former senior Qantas executive, was familiar. He had still been with Qantas when, in 1989, the New Zealand government had agitated for an extension of CER to air transport, with Air New Zealand to be given rights to enter the Australian domestic market. A political will had emerged on both sides of the Tasman to create a single market for air transport in Australasia. 'If CER is to have any meaning', wrote John Ward, 'it must sooner or later involve opening up the trans-Tasman routes to the domestic airlines of both countries'. (Those routes were one of the mainstays of the Qantas network.) 'It will then be questionable', he wrote, 'whether it is worth Qantas' continuing to sacrifice the opportunities in the Australian domestic market in order to preserve the rest of its international network from the possible incursion of additional Australian carriers'.

For Australian these conclusions by Qantas had major implications. They brought up the question of Qantas's relationship with Ansett. 'One of the major objectives of the Company's [Qantas's] commercial arrangements with Ansett', wrote Ward, 'has been to hold in check their international aspirations'. (Qantas had entered into its close commercial agreement with Ansett in 1986. One other consideration had been the expectation of better financial results. Both these hopes had been disappointed. Ansett had pressed the New Zealand government for entry to international routes by designating Ansett New Zealand and had reiterated its desire to become Australia's second designated international carrier for passengers as well as freight.)[18] 'If Ansett', said Ward, 'are allowed to enter the trans-Tasman market — and still more so if they are designated as Australia's second freight carrier worldwide — the question of Qantas' access to the Australian domestic market will have to be re-opened. The whole basis for commercial collaboration between Qantas and Ansett will then be destroyed.' Moreover, he argued, if Ansett were given access to trans-Tasman routes Australian would have to be given similar opportunities. 'The Australian Government will then need to resolve the problem of its two wholly-owned carriers competing against each other both across the Tasman and in the Australian domestic market.' An obvious solution, he concluded, 'would be the amalgamation of Qantas with Australian Airlines'.[19]

In the international field Ward saw the 'shibboleth of competition' requiring Qantas and Air New Zealand to invade each other's routes with Ansett as a probable third Australasian carrier. Economic theorists went further, arguing that to maximise benefits to consumers foreign airlines should be given unrestricted access to Australasian ports and even to the domestic markets. 'In the real world', he wrote, 'this would lead to a considerable shrinkage of Australasia's locally-owned air transport industry and even perhaps its collapse'.

The best compromise, he concluded, 'might be for Qantas to enter into a merger — or at least an alliance — with Australian Airlines and Air New Zealand, while Ansett provided competition through services within Australia and New

Zealand and across the Tasman Sea'. He did not believe, however, that such an arrangement would be acceptable to Ansett. Ansett would also have to be given at least some international routes. 'History will show whether it is possible for two such groupings, with a relatively small population base, to survive.'[20] If the Australian government 'on mature consideration' decided to give Ansett full access to both freight and passenger traffic on international routes, wrote Ward, the restraints on Qantas would first need to be removed. That would entail 'at least' a full merger between Qantas and Australian Airlines, the transfer of the merged Qantas–Australian Airlines to private ownership, and a commitment that no impediment be placed in the way of a merger or similar arrangement between Qantas–Australian Airlines and Air New Zealand.[21]

On 20 April 1990 John Schaap wrote to the new minister for telecommunications and aviation support, Ros Kelly: 'The rebuilding of Australian Airlines in the aftermath of the mass resignation of our pilots last August is now almost complete and I am pleased to be able to inform you that from 26 April we will be flying a full schedule with our own aircraft and crews. All charter aircraft will have departed ... Our new pilot workforce consists mainly of former Australian Airlines pilots. These have been joined by expatriate Australians who have taken the opportunity to return home, recruits from the general aviation sector and around sixty very experienced pilots from overseas airlines ... We now have one of the youngest fleet of aircraft in the world. All our DC9 aircraft were phased out last year and we have commenced the introduction of the new Boeing 737-400.'[22] (For both Ansett and Australian a significant outcome of the dispute was a a virtual halving in pilot numbers. Graeme McMahon, at Ansett, commented: 'We have basically doubled productivity'. John Schaap said that there had been productivity increases in the cockpit of between 25 and 35 per cent.)[23]

Schaap told Australian's board on 26 April that development of a single Australasian market held greater opportunities, challenges and threats for Australian Airlines than did the forthcoming deregulation of the domestic market.[24] By June, however, it had become evident that government ministers were less enthusiastic than their advisers about the goal of extending closer economic relations with New Zealand in aviation. John Ward told the Qantas board: 'Political considerations, and considerations of Australia's national interests, have been given greater weight'.[25]

One consideration of the Minister for Transport and Communications had been the emergence of a new Australian airline, Compass, formed in anticipation of the impending deregulation of Australia's domestic aviation market. Compass, said Ward, 'to the surprise of many, has succeeded in raising more than the minimum of $50 million that it needed to get started'. (Compass Holdings Limited opened subscriptions for its share issue on 12 June 1990. The entire initial issue was fully subscribed within forty-eight hours. It was a huge success.) The minister was keen, he wrote, to give Compass 'a clear run in competition with Ansett and Australian Airlines before Air New Zealand is allowed to enter the Australian domestic market'. (James Strong, a year earlier, had reaffirmed in a letter to the Department of Transport and Communications Australian's attitude to any new airlines. 'I have made, on a number of occasions in diverse forums,' he wrote, 'many clear statements to the effect that our business strategy in relation to any new entrants will be to make life extremely difficult for them in terms of aggressive reaction on a commercial basis. This refers to pricing, scheduling and any other aspect of competitive performance.')[26]

Ward thought it 'not surprising' that the government was not presently contemplating a merger between its two publicly owned airlines. 'Australian is, if anything,' he wrote, 'even more hard pressed to reduce its gearing than Qantas itself. Putting two capital-hungry airlines together would do nothing to satisfy their capital needs.' He also told the Qantas board that if Qantas were to decide to revert to Australian Airlines in a commercial alliance the time was opportune. 'It is evident that Australian Airlines is agonising over its future ... If Qantas wishes to forge a new alliance it should therefore do so while the iron is hot.' If a close link were established between Qantas and Australian, he said, 'and especially if that link developed into a full merger, Qantas would almost certainly be the dominant partner'. Ward also recommended that Qantas sound out British Airways and other key international airlines on their interest in taking an equity or quasi-equity in Qantas.[27]

On 5 June 1990 Harris told his minister, Kim Beazley, that in the six-month period to 31 December 1989 Australian's consolidated operating result (before tax and abnormals) was a loss of $60.06 million compared to a profit of $83.956 million for the same period in the previous year. That deterioration in trading performance of $144.016 million was, he said, 'attributable entirely to the pilots' dispute'. He also told Beazley that he had had discussions with Sir Colin Marshall, chief executive of British Airways, on a possible future equity investment in Australian by British Airways as a strategic investor and would commence similar discussions in July with Singapore Airlines.[28]

Within Australian Airlines John Schaap, in mid year, announced a restructure of the airline's senior management, following a general spill of executive positions earlier in the year. In early June Gary Toomey, formerly chief financial executive, was appointed general manager finance and flight operations manager; Captain Dave Wiltshire, general manager flight operations.[29] In July Geoff Dixon was appointed general manager marketing and public affairs; John Anderson, general manager sales and customer service; Emmet Hobbs, general manager cargo; and Doug Gillies general manager corporate planning. (The emphasis of marketing and public affairs, said Schaap, was now specifically on pricing, product design, promotion and marketing planning and control.)[30] In August Schaap announced the appointment of Wally Mariani as general manager business enterprises and Rita Compton as manager human resources.[31] The restructuring process, however, was to affect every level of the airline. Australian planned to retrench up to 1,000 staff in the immediate future, ranging from lower middle executive level down through clerical staff ranks. Beazley wrote to Harris: 'I am aware, in general terms, that the Company is currently embarking on a restructuring and cost cutting program in an attempt to minimise current losses and better position itself for the future as a privatised company in a deregulated environment'.[32]

The new Australian management team took over as Qantas judged there was the prospect of a major world recession, triggered by the protracted and destabilising dispute in the Middle East. (The Gulf crisis had severely affected fuel prices. For Australian a variation of $1 in the crude oil barrel price represented $3 million in annual fuel costs.)[33] In the aviation industry Qantas saw the coming months as critical to the size and shape of the airline, with the government appearing set on a course of its partial privatisation. John Ward told his board that recent developments in Australian aviation policy, 'under the guise of micro-economic reform policies', were generally unfavourable to the company. Proponents of an 'open skies' regime (in essence allowing foreign airlines to service Australia without restriction or regard to traditionally negotiated traffic rights) were the main threat. 'Traffic rights', wrote Ward, 'are perhaps the most valuable assets the Company has to use. Without them we simply could not operate.' Continuation of the traditional regime in which access to sovereign air space was carefully negotiated had, he said, 'never been under greater threat [with] implications for what may well be irreparable harm to the ongoing viability of the Company'. There were, though, hopeful signs. Recent discussions with the minister, he wrote, 'indicate that the adverse impact of large scale liberalisation on the value of Qantas is at last becoming understood ... should partial privatisation proceed a more pragmatic policy approach may be adopted'.[34]

That Qantas assessment came as Australian Airlines, on 24 August 1990, made a presentation to Qantas 'to outline Australian's plans and strategies and to explain what we believe we can bring to Qantas as an alliance partner'. The thrust by the presentation team (led by John Schaap) was to demonstrate the superiority of Australian over Ansett. Since June 1988, it said, Australian had been the leading airline in the domestic market. For the June quarter of 1990 Australian out-carried Ansett by 1.34 million passengers to 1.29 million; for the year to 30 June Australian carried a total of 4.4 million passengers to Ansett's 4 million (figures, it said, that would have been much higher but for the pilots' dispute). Since the end of the dispute Australian had secured 47 per cent of the domestic air transport market compared with Ansett's 42.8 per cent. 'We not only expect to maintain our market dominance', said Australian, 'we expect to increase it'.

Far from being committed to Qantas as an alliance partner, Ansett and its associated companies, said Australian, 'have a declared interest in competing with the national carrier, both in passenger and freight operations'. Ansett was 'planning actively to create an international airline based in New Zealand. It is keen to operate Boeing 767 or Airbus A300 aircraft on regional routes to destinations such as Bangkok, Bali, Singapore and Japan.' Australian, however, had 'no plans to fly scheduled international services in its own right'.[35]

Ansett, in their separate presentation to Qantas, had, Qantas recorded, 'doubted the value of equity participation for cementing an alliance'. They had also been silent 'on the question of how the potential conflict of interest arising from the inevitable opening up of the trans-Tasman routes under the CER process was to be resolved'. No such problem, wrote Ward, arose with Australian Airlines, 'who disclaimed any desire to operate beyond the boundaries of Australia'.[36]

Qantas had advised both Ansett and Australian that 'in view of the link with the question of privatisation and of the Minister's express wish to be consulted beforehand, Qantas would be unable to come to a decision [on their alliance partner] until after the Special Federal Conference of the Australian Labor Party on 24 September at the earliest.'[37] That Special Federal Conference was required so that a vote could be taken on the radical change to the Labor Party platform required for the implementation of the Hawke Government's decision to privatise the Government-owned airlines. Conference approved the change with a considerable majority, endorsing the Government decision to privatise Australian and sell equity in Qantas. The choice of a domestic partner, Ward now told his board, could not be considered 'in isolation from the Government's historic decision to sell up to a 49 per cent stake in Qantas and up to 100 per cent of Australian Airlines'.

On 27 September 1990, three days after the Special Federal Conference, Ward told the Qantas board that the privatisation of Australian Airlines posed both an opportunity and a threat for Qantas. There was an opportunity to take a stake in the airline sufficient to ensure a binding and permanent relationship, and a threat that an airline or airlines hostile to Qantas might secure effective control of Australian. The minister, he said, was 'known to have a strong preference for selling the whole of Australian Airlines as it stands', leaving it to the purchaser or purchasers to satisfy the airline's capital requirements. 'Should Qantas decide to opt for a partnership with Australian Airlines', wrote Ward, 'it would therefore be advisable to move fast and make the running with the Government, rather than risk finding that the sale has been organised in a way which acts to Qantas' disadvantage'.

'On the other hand', he wrote, 'if Qantas opts for a partnership with Ansett (or finds itself in a position where this is the only realistic course open to it) Qantas will need to tie up an equity stake and shareholders' agreement urgently, in order to secure its position there'.

Either course required Qantas to put up a substantial amount of capital. A sum of $350 million had, however, been included in the company's business plan for such a purpose. It was enough to buy a substantial stake in Australian or Ansett. In either case Qantas needed to persuade the government to allow it to retain at least the bulk, if not all, of the funds, raised by reducing the government's shareholding in Qantas to 49 per cent, to enable it to cover its own capital needs plus the amount required to purchase its substantial stake in its domestic partner. 'This', wrote Ward, 'will not be easy'. Nevertheless, from the government's point of view, it would still receive the whole of the proceeds from the sale of Australian Airlines.[38]

The Qantas choice of a domestic partner had international implications. If it chose Australian, Ansett was likely to forge commercial links with Qantas's foreign competitors and obtain designation as Australia's second international carrier. The former was not of great concern. In Qantas's view Ansett was unlikely to be more effective in deflecting international traffic away from Qantas than Australian had been. Indeed it saw Australian as a more dangerous domestic opponent than Ansett if it were to be dominated by a foreign Qantas competitor.

The government was expected to press forward as rapidly as possible with the privatisation process. Nevertheless practical problems in managing this process meant that any public offer of shares in Qantas or Australian was not expected for at least a year. By that time, it was reasonable to assume, the Gulf crisis would be over, depressed stock markets returned to their former health and fuel prices back to a more acceptable level. Qantas judged that in likely 1991 market conditions realistic market values for each airline would be $1,200 million for Qantas and $550 million for Australian. (On the same valuation basis Ansett's market value was put at between $650 and $800 million.) Ward recognised that the Qantas calculations were highly sensitive to assumptions about the market value of the two government-owned airlines, the timing of the sales and the market conditions prevailing at the time.

From the government's point of view the threshold issue had been whether either or both airlines should be sold in their entirety. Domestically, in a completely deregulated aviation market (with no airline providing community services) there was no argument for the retention by government of any equity in Australian as such equity would not serve either competition policy or social justice aims. Australian could be sold in its entirety. Internationally different factors applied. International airline competition took place under treaty arrangements that set out the terms of bilateral air service agreements. There were strong arguments for keeping a majority government shareholding and selling only 49 per cent of the airline. (The government believed that the sale of Australian in favourable market circumstances would realise some $680 million.) Driving the whole process was the unavoidable fact that over the period to 1994–95 Qantas needed to invest some $6 billion and Australian some $1.6 billion in fleet replacement and expansion, and that to do so required equity injections of about $600 million for Qantas and $300 million for Australian. Government budgetary imperatives ruled out such capital injections. Additional debt to finance the airlines' needs, quite apart from its unacceptable cost and its effect on debt–equity ratios, was not an option given the global borrowing limits set for the airlines by the government. (The Qantas gearing in September 1990 stood at 78 per cent debt and 22 per cent equity, a ratio, Dix told Beazley, that was 'totally unacceptable'. Qantas's competitors, he said, who were re-equipping their fleets with the same or similar new aircraft as Qantas, operated at debt–equity ratios averaging 55:45.)[39]

Both Qantas and Australian Airlines were strong advocates of privatisation. Australian, in particular (when it became clear that the Government would make no further equity injection), pushed hard for such an outcome.[40] The airline, however, had its own views on the manner of its achievement. In examining potential equity partners Schaap looked for synergies to provide future expansion. That brought a focus on international airlines. Australian had recognised the future growth potential of the inbound market through its recent strategic alliances with United Airlines and British Airways. (Global links with British Airways were strengthened in August 1990 with the signing of a memorandum of understanding.)[41] A number of potential international airline investors had been identified. In the Asia-Pacific region Schaap listed Air New Zealand, Cathay Pacific, Japan Airlines, Singapore Airlines and Qantas; in Europe–UK, British Airways; in North America, American Airlines, Delta and United Airlines. While Schaap recognised that a Qantas link would provide considerable synergies it was his view that it 'would also only serve to combine the equity shortcomings of both Qantas and Australian into a common problem'.[42] (Australian's board had long held the view that government shareholders' funds might be utilised best by merging Qantas and Australian and then selling all or some of the merged equity. That concept had always been rejected by the government.)[43]

Australian's chairman, Ted Harris, advocated a two-stage sell-off of the airline, the first stage to be completed within six months. Harris proposed that 49 per cent of Australian be sold to foreign carriers and staff to allow an expansion of the equity base before the remaining 51 per cent was sold to the public.[44] (Harris thought $1 billion was a not unreasonable valuation of the airline.) His minister, Kim Beazley, however, favoured selling the entire airline immediately.[45]

These substantial issues were debated as Australian Airlines recorded a group operating loss of $13.737 million after tax for the financial year to 30 June. That loss followed the airline's record profit in the previous year of $70.84 million after tax. Consolidated operating profit before tax fell from the 1988–89 record level of $114.325 million to a loss of $62.016 million.[46] The pilots' dispute had cost the Australian Airlines group more than $200 million in pre-tax profit. 'The dispute is now behind us', said Harris. 'I am confident that the airline can return to profit this financial year.'[47]

In October Australian announced an order for three additional Boeing 737-400s, taking the total 737-400 order to fourteen. The order took to thirty the total number of 737 aircraft Australian either operated or had on order.[48] At the same time it announced the acquisition of 100 per cent of Victorian regional carrier, Sunstate Airlines, Mildura, and 100 per cent of Sunstate Airlines Queensland.

John Ward told the Qantas board on 2 October 1990: 'Events are likely to unfold very rapidly. If Qantas is to control its own destiny it needs to stay ahead of the game.' The airline, he said, would not be able to compete on its own in the environment that lay ahead. It had to form part of a larger grouping. 'Vital questions' were the choice of domestic ally, choice of international partners and 'how best to use the privatisation process to further Qantas' domestic and international relationships'. He proposed to keep both Ansett and Australian Airlines 'in play' by putting a consortium together under Qantas leadership that would offer to buy the whole of Australian Airlines and accept responsibility for meeting its capital requirements. At the same time Qantas would negotiate with Ansett and East-West for a substantial holding in their airlines (and a resolution of the problem of Ansett New Zealand). Ward thought it desirable for foreign airlines to acquire strategic stakes in Qantas.[49]

The government had one option that might have been more palatable to those in the Labor Party who still opposed privatisation. That option was the issue of 'quasi-equity', a device that would have enabled non-voting equity to be brought into the airlines. On the surface it would have satisfied the need for equity capital while at the same time leaving 100 per cent of voting shares in government hands. Various proposals of this kind were put to the government but were all seen, in the words of Ralph Willis (now minister for finance), as 'half-baked and likely to be discounted in financial markets'. More specifically, he said, 'they depended for real attraction on future options for conversion to full voting shares'. They thus 'seemed to be doing no more than postponing a decision to either go down the privatisation path or to make a capital injection from the budget. Better, it was thought, to bite the bullet now.'[50]

In October 1990 the government decided on the initial steps for the privatisation process, involving the establishment of a selling team to control the sale of equity in both Australian and Qantas. (The team was drawn mainly from the Asset Sales Task Force in the finance minister's department, a body that had been responsible for the sale of more than $2 billion of government assets in the previous three and a half years.) It was also decided that the first substantial step in the sales process should be a 'scoping study' of the issues that needed to be decided by the government before embarking on the sales process proper. That study began in

November 1990 and involved an initial valuation of the airlines, assessment of the possible methods of sale, and an evaluation of when to sell and whether the sales should be sequenced. The scoping study did not, however, keep the airlines at arm's length as mere providers of information. Each airline had pronounced views on the way it wanted matters to proceed.

As these first steps towards the privatisation of Australian were taken its commercial and regulatory environments changed fundamentally. Gone was the two-airline policy, which had sustained both TAA and its competitor in their decades of growth after World War II and given Australia a stable and technically advanced domestic airline industry. On 31 October 1990 the deregulation of the domestic airline industry came into effect.

CHAPTER 23

1990–92

'A little bit of history'

It was not the best of times to sell airlines. Dix wrote to Beazley that a shake-out in the world airline industry could be expected in the 1990s. 'This process', he wrote, 'is accelerating with the world's airlines now forced to make drastic reductions in services, staff and operating costs in response to the sharp fall in demand for air travel following the Gulf war'. (The profit collapse was evident well before the Iraqi invasion of Kuwait in August 1990.) Recession, coupled with rapid jet fuel price increases in the last half of 1990, brought fourth-quarter losses of $US1.7 billion for US carriers, almost all of it on domestic services. Eastern Airlines, in the United States, had collapsed. Both Pan American and Continental had been pushed to the brink, with both seeking survival through the US device of Chapter 11 bankruptcy protection. In 1990 airline members of IATA had reported combined losses of $US2 billion. British Airways, on 11 February 1991, announced staff cuts of 4,600. Scandinavian Airlines System planned staff reductions of 3,500, Belgium's Sabena 2,200, US Air 3,500 and the Dutch airline, KLM, 2,000. An IATA survey of its members estimated that the total airline industry had lost more than $US1.2 billion in January 1991 alone. The airline industry was, wrote Dix, 'in a state of crisis'. (Qantas had not been as severely affected as European and United

States airlines, but its load factors had fallen some 10 per cent to around 60 per cent.)[1]

Schaap told Australian's staff that 'things have deteriorated quite dramatically'. The economy, he said, had slumped, with many businesses large and small cutting back on staff and other expenditure. Australian had had to pay much more than budgeted for its fuel. 'With the introduction of deregulation, as expected there has been widespread discounting of air fares ... Our revenue yield has suffered a fall of more than 10 per cent since deregulation ... Each percentage point reduction translates to a $12 million per annum loss to the airline. Our forward bookings are slow ... businesses are being squeezed hard. Inbound tourist travel to Australia from overseas countries has been affected by the Gulf War.'[2] (A major factor in yield reduction had been, following deregulation, the entry of the new Compass Airlines on to a number of prime routes and the subsequent discount fare battle.) Schaap announced a major restructure of Australian Airlines in February 1991, following an efficiency review of the airline. That review had shown the need to focus on profitability and performance in individual business units in the group. Each business, said Schaap, was to have its own senior business manager responsible for its total operation and profitability. The units were identified as Australian Airlines, Australian Resorts, Regional Airlines, Catering, Westpac Travel (recently acquired by Australian) and Australian Cargo.

Both Willis and Beazley recognised that the Gulf War had destabilised the aviation industry but they still pressed for the rapid privatisation of both Qantas and Australian. The prime minister, Bob Hawke, had announced in Parliament on 8 November 1990 that the limit on individual foreign holdings in Australian by a foreign international airline would be increased from 15 to 25 per cent and an absolute aggregate limit was set for foreign holdings at 40 per cent. Government policy was that Australian Airlines remained majority Australian-owned.[3] The foreign investment limit in Qantas was set at 35 per cent. 'The foreign investment changes', said Hawke, 'offer clear opportunities for the New Zealand carrier to enter the Australian market'. The government, he said, would discuss with New Zealand 'the question of closer aviation relations'.[4]

Beazley indicated his opposition to any Qantas move to buy Australian Airlines. He told Parliament: 'The Government has not removed itself from ownership in the deregulated domestic aviation environment via a total sell-down of our holding in Australian to find ourselves coming in via the back door and still in a position of ownership in that [domestic] market'. The international aviation market, said Beazley, was different. It was not a deregulated market. The Australian side in bilateral arrangements with other countries was 'exercised of necessity by one airline'. In those circumstances, he said, 'the Government chose to maintain majority Government ownership ... and we see that as a totally different issue from those issues which are involved in domestic aviation'.[5]

There was a dilemma here for the government, which Beazley acknowledged in a letter to Dix. He noted the Qantas view of the desirability of a link between Qantas and one of the domestic airlines. 'A strong case could be made', Beazley said, 'that it would not be equitable to allow foreign airlines greater access to the domestic sector than Qantas'.[6] Qantas had another strength to further its strategy for the domestic market. It was well aware that the government's preferred outcome was the sale of Australian in its entirety. By the end of 1990 there had been no indications of any consortium (other than the one proposed by Qantas) being put together to acquire the whole of Australian, still less of any individual investor coming forward with an offer.

Ward reported: 'It is understood that, apart from their chairman, Australian Airlines are keen to establish a commercial link with Qantas. On the other hand, Sir Peter Abeles has told our chairman ... that Mr Murdoch is not prepared to sell his stake in Ansett, and that the same applies to TNT. Ansett/TNT have also failed to come forward with any proposals for resolving the existing conflicts of interests — notably over Ansett New Zealand.' Ward referred to the prime minister's 'allusion to the possibility of designating a second international freight carrier ... a matter which Qantas has contested with the utmost vigour'. Qantas believed that such a carrier (Ansett) would press for designation for the carriage of passengers also. 'Ansett's actions ... make it more and more difficult for Qantas to choose them in preference to Australian Airlines. Even if TNT and News Corporation were prepared to sell a substantial stake in Ansett to Qantas, the Minister's objections to re-entering the Australian domestic air transport market "via the back door" would apply no less to Qantas' acquisition of a stake in Ansett than to its acquisition of a stake in Australian Airlines.' A 25 per stake in Australian as a key member of a consortium, said Ward, 'would be sufficient to safeguard Qantas' position'. Qantas could also contend, he argued, that the eventual solution was to look to 'the complete privatisation of Qantas — which is bound to happen sooner or later'. For the government both the prospect of raising $1 billion by the 49 per cent sell-down (of Qantas) and the value of the government's residual 51 per cent stake, he said, 'will be considerably enhanced if Qantas is seen to have access to a reliable domestic feeder and distribution system'.

His conclusion was that Qantas could not continue for much longer its 'twin-track' policy towards Ansett and Australian 'without giving an appearance of vacillation and indecision which will damage Qantas in the eyes of the Government as well as the domestic airlines themselves'. Unless TNT and News Corporation were bluffing, he wrote, an association with Ansett would be largely on Ansett's terms. Qantas would have no equity stake in Ansett as a domestic partner, though TNT/News Corporation could take a stake in Qantas 'which would give them considerable leverage, if not control'. Qantas, he said, 'would then become Ansett's international arm instead of Ansett becoming Qantas' domestic partner'. Ward wanted the choice between Ansett and Australian to be made quickly.[7]

Beazley also had a strong motive for urgency in the privatisation process. The government wanted the sales agenda to be firmly under way before the next ALP Federal Conference in July 1991. But haste had its dangers. Dix pointed out to him and to the minister for finance, Ralph Willis, that Qantas might get a high price but from bidders who merely wanted to run it out of business and take over its routes.[8]

What was clear from various discussions by Australian with the government was that the Commonwealth had agreed on a general framework for selling government business enterprises (GBEs), and that it was fundamental to that framework that the government was in charge of the sales process (though the boards of Qantas and Australian would also be involved). Beazley said unequivocally that it would be politically unacceptable to have matters still unresolved by the time of the next Party Conference. It was also made clear that foreign airline shareholdings were an important part of the value of the shares to Australian investors and that foreign investors should be brought in by July. (Harris had been embarrassed in his discussions with Singapore Airlines on buying equity in Australian as Qantas had independently approached them about joining its proposed consortium to buy 100 per cent of Australian. 'We look like a bunch of hillbillies', said Harris.) Beazley emphasised his personal view that Qantas would have to accept that it could not buy Australian.

While these discussions progressed Qantas made a return presentation to Australian on the benefits of an alliance between the two-airlines (three months after Australian had made its August presentation to Qantas). Qantas, as the world's second oldest airline (KLM was the oldest) had proved its many strengths over seven decades. It had, though, two intrinsic weaknesses. It was the only international carrier denied the right to operate domestically in its own country and, as a long-haul airline, its base at Sydney was not a natural hub for high-density routes. The Qantas strategy reflected this position. The airline told Australian that it wanted to negotiate strong alliances with an Australian domestic airline, an Asian airline, a European airline and an American airline. The alliances, it said, would be initially commercially based but with future equity opportunities. The Australian board was told on 7 November 1990: 'Qantas now offers Australian Airlines an opportunity to join into a commercial alliance worldwide'. Schaap commented: 'No other airline can offer Australian home base support or has the same total commitment worldwide to Australian as Qantas. A long term commercial alliance with Qantas would hold very strong benefits for Australian, particularly if it also includes flow on benefits with other joint global alliance partners, and provides the opportunity for shared cost structures.' It was recognised that Qantas would not be in a position to enter into full alliance until the question of its shareholding was resolved.[9]

Qantas faced a very real danger from the volatile environment of the privatisation process. Although it had international interline rights that entitled it to carry international passengers on domestic routes in Australia it did not have the ability to service some 30 per cent of the international visitor market that wanted to travel beyond the key Australian gateway cities. Also, some 25 per cent of Australian residents travelling overseas needed to fly on internal routes not served by Qantas to link with their international flights. The danger to Qantas came from the possibility that both Ansett and Australian might make exclusive arrangements with other international carriers. That outcome would deny to Qantas the ability to access almost 30 per cent of the market into and from Australia. With Ansett seen as less and less desirable as a partner, an alliance with Australian was now a key goal.

Qantas continued to argue for a shareholding in Australian. Ward wrote on 14 February 1991: 'From the government's point of view the opportunity exists to achieve a significant increase in the value of *both* its airline assets by promoting a commercial alliance and shareholding relationship between them'. Qantas saw the optimum strategy for Qantas and Air New Zealand as continuance of their close collaboration, with Australian Airlines providing both with their Australian domestic link. A combined Qantas–Air New Zealand purchase of a significant shareholding in Australian was judged as the way to most effectively position all three airlines, as well as providing the Australian government with an excellent platform for the sale of the balance of Australian Airlines equity to other strategic investors (or though a public offering).[10]

Qantas, with the firm Baring Brothers, had carried out an evaluation of the merits of both domestic airlines as alliance partners. It had concluded that Qantas should seek a strong commercial alliance and a shareholding in Australian Airlines. Within government, however, there were conflicting views on the issue of a Qantas shareholding. They ranged from a prohibition on any shareholding at all to the acquisition of a non-controlling interest.[11] The Asset Sales Task Force and its advisers had not been prepared to canvass the option of a Qantas equity in Australian 'unless the Company indicated a preference for concluding a domestic alliance with Australian Airlines'. It was that attitude that had forced Qantas to declare its hand.[12]

Qantas, of course, had much to offer Australian in its proposed alliance. Most valuable was the provision of on-carriage from, and feeder traffic to, its international routes. Qantas carried 42 per cent of the international traffic to and from Australia. Its two international partners, Air New Zealand and Japan Airlines, carried 11 per cent and 2 per cent respectively, making a total for the coalition of some 55 per cent. A full alliance between Australian and Qantas also offered cost savings, particularly from the bulk purchasing of fuel, insurance and catering as well as other clearly achievable synergies for improving the bottom line of both airlines. Beyond these considerable contributions, and outweighing them by a factor of ten to one, lay the enormous benefits to be obtained from the flexibility of the merged fleet through the sharing of equipment. The Qantas Boeing 767-200s were the ideal aircraft to provide Australian Airlines with much greater capacity during peak traffic periods in Sydney (and later proved their worth in the battle for market share). The Qantas 747s, with their great capacity, were also available for handling the temporary and sometimes huge demand arising from special events. Indeed the fleet flexibility from a merged

Australian and Qantas provided the real commercial power underlying the proposed alliance.

Though there was opposition to a Qantas shareholding in Australian, other omens for a future link between them were good. John Schaap's move to Australian from Qantas had been one. Now there was a second. On 7 February 1991 Dix congratulated James Strong on his appointment as a director of Qantas Airways Limited and welcomed him to the board.[13]

Beazley had serious concerns about the Qantas financial position and had written to Dix 'requesting that vigorous action be taken to restore the airline to profitability'. He wanted advice on the scale and timing of staff reductions, including their bottom line implications, information on productivity improvements in selected staff categories and a briefing on Qantas strategies to enhance performance on the routes that offered the best prospect for profitability. He pressed also for improvements in the returns from non-core businesses, including Air New Zealand, and advice on whether these investments should be retained.[14]

Throughout all these considerations of high policy both Australian and Qantas had hanging over them the threat of terrorist activity resulting from the Iraqi move against Kuwait. The Iraqi leader, Saddam Hussein, had declared that Alliance attempts to retain possession of Kuwait meant a holy war. He called on all Muslims to strike at all participants in the multi-national force opposed to him. Australian's board was told on 27 February 1990 that past events had shown that the range of terrorist possibilities included bombing, grenade attacks, shooting and assassinations with 'a particular interest in aircraft, airports, airline offices and identifiable national institutions'. Intelligence reports all indicated 'that Australia is not being ignored as a potential target'.[15] The government advised Australian on 14 February that it had 'decided to rationalise responsibilities for airport security by making airport operators responsible [from 1 July 1991] for the counter terrorist presence, overall access control and the security of the air side areas of airports'.[16]

Australian had been taking steps to strengthen its weakening share of total industry airliner capacity within Australia. That capacity share had decreased significantly and was expected to continue decrease. By April 1991 Australian's share was 37.5 per cent, down from almost 43 per cent in November, 1990. ATI's share in the same period had also fallen — from 48.5 per cent to 42 per cent — and East-West's had dropped from 8.4 per cent to 7.2 per cent. The catalyst causing these declines had been the new Compass Airlines. Its capacity share (zero in November 1990) had grown to 18.3 per cent in April 1991. In November 1990 Australian's board had approved in principle the establishment of a wholly owned regional airline, Australian Regional. On 30 January 1991 it decided that Australian Regional enter into an operating lease for three BAe146 aircraft for a period of three years. 'Reductions in capacity share', the board was told, 'lead to declining market share'.[17] In February Australian acquired a shelf company belonging to Sunstate Airlines (Pinefield Pty Ltd) to trade under the name of Australian Airlink and be used exclusively for jet operations using BAe146s. (Australian Airlink was established as a separate company to distinguish its jet operations from Australian Regional Airlines [Queensland], which was a turboprop cost centre.) In March the board approved the purchase by Australian of the remaining 58.21 per cent equity in Eastern Australia Airlines.[18] (It had acquired its original 37.5 per cent shareholding in 1988 and later increased this to 41.79 per cent.)

Two markets where Australian was not present or competing effectively were the Western Australian intrastate market and the Queensland coast. The airline's 737-300s were not suitable for either market. (In Western Australia runways were inadequate and in Queensland they were too big for the average loads available.) 'In view of the general economic situation, the uncertainties flowing from the Gulf war and privatisation', the board was told, 'it is prudent to defer an entry into the Western Australian market for at least six months'.[19]

On 22 April 1991 the sale process for Australian Airlines and Qantas began. The minister for finance, Ralph Willis, issued a media release stating that Qantas and Australian Airlines were 'on the market'. The sale process for the airlines, he said, would comprise an initial trade sale followed by a public float to sell any remaining equity. 'The sale process for both airlines', said Willis, 'will begin immediately with the initial trade sale process for each airline commencing concurrently ... Offering to sell equity in both airlines concurrently will provide investors with the opportunity to consider buying a significant interest in both airlines.'[20] Qantas was barred from the trade sale.

That announcement was made with Willis and Beazley holding differing views on the issue of a Qantas investment in Australian. Beazley still opposed such investment.[21] On 18 April Dix had written to him reaffirming that it was the Qantas view 'that the best outcome in terms of maximising the values of both Australian Airlines and Qantas in the national interest is that there be a shareholding relationship between Qantas and Australian, thereby assuring that Qantas is not placed at a continuing disadvantage against other potential overseas airlines which may invest in Australian ... The Board believes that the logic of Qantas securing shareholding in Australian is convincing. However, if you and your Cabinet colleagues are not fully convinced of this at this time we would urge in the strongest terms that no decision be taken which would preclude this.'[22]

On the evening of that same day the chairman of the Labor Caucus Transport and Communications Committee, Neil O'Keefe, led a delegation to Beazley pointing out that the vast majority of Caucus strongly supported Qantas being permitted to invest in Australian Airlines. They hoped Beazley would reconsider his position. Cabinet, however, on the morning of 22 April, supported Beazley. (Considerable media speculation followed on the influence that both Sir Peter Abeles and Ted Harris had had on this Cabinet decision, given their close personal relationships with the prime minister.) Qantas issued a blunt media release on 23 April. 'It is difficult to understand', said the brief statement, 'why Qantas has been specifically excluded from participating in any form in domestic aviation in Australia while foreign competitors are being encouraged to do just that through equity investment in Australian Airlines'.[23]

The Qantas position was not as bad as it seemed. It did not expect serious bids for Australian at a high price from either North American or European carriers. It believed that even the strongest American carriers had better uses for their money. Within Europe the only serious contender was British Airways, but that airline was under pressure from powerful US competitors who were forcing their way on to the North Atlantic routes. It seemed logical to conclude that British Airways also had better uses for any spare capital than paying a large sum for a feeder-distribution network in Australia's small market.

The only natural ally for Qantas in a consortium was Air New Zealand but that airline did not have the necessary money, and there seemed little likelihood that Qantas would be allowed to finance or underwrite an investment by Air New Zealand in Australian. Japan was a natural participant for any consortium and Qantas had plans for further discussions with them. Singapore Airlines was a perceived danger to any friendly consortium. Its geographical position and superb airport made a hub at Singapore, with Australian providing an Australian feeder and distribution network, an excellent fit. Wild cards were Cathay Pacific and All Nippon.

It was an interesting chess game. Qantas had, to date, envisaged a consortium buying a controlling interest in Australian. Ward now thought this unrealistic. Assuming Australian was worth $400 million and Qantas twice as much, he wrote: 'Why should an intelligent airline which can acquire 20 per cent of the capital of Australian Airlines for $80 million pay the same amount for a 10 per cent interest in a "lame duck" Qantas which will continue to be in the grip of a politically motivated Government which is portrayed in the media as being unduly influenced by the owners of Ansett?'[24] (Beazley had reaffirmed in a letter to Dix on 6 June the government's decision that Qantas would not be permitted to invest directly in Australian during the sales process. 'In taking this decision', said Beazley, 'Cabinet was aware of Qantas' point of view'.)[25]

Australian's board had different worries. On 24 April, as Ward wrote his assessment of the Qantas position, Australian's board agreed that Harris should convey to Willis its 'strongly held view that the carriage of the sale process should be under the control of the Board and not with the Department of Finance'.[26] It did not contest the government's right to make the final decision but the board had grave concerns about the proposed sales process itself.[27] It recorded its concern 'that the Asset Sales Task Force appeared to have little or no concept of directors' legal and fiduciary responsibilities'.[28] Schaap told the airline's staff that Cabinet's approval of the 100 per cent sale of Australian was a positive one. 'The future owners of Australian', he wrote, 'are still unknown ... Qantas will not be permitted to buy shares since the Government has decided to withdraw completely from the domestic aviation industry.'[29] Harris continued his opposition to any shareholding by a partially privatised Qantas.

One other reason advanced by the government for banning Qantas from buying shares in Australian was its decision to continue the existing separation between international and domestic aviation. There was, paradoxically, no formal ban on Qantas buying into Ansett. Ansett, however, was now to be banned from acquiring an interest in Qantas. The ban on Qantas directly acquiring shares in Australian applied only during the actual airlines sales process. A direct investment by Qantas in a privately owned Australian Airlines after the privatisation of the airline was seen as a possibility. The government had also left open the possibility of Qantas making an indirect investment in Australian by the commitment of further funds to Air New Zealand to enable it to make such an investment on behalf of Qantas. (The Government had endorsed a resolution of the Special Labor Party Conference to include employee share schemes in the sale arrangements for both airlines.)

Aircraft's editor, Gerry Carman, commented in June:

The bell may well have tolled for our [sic] embattled international

> carrier, Qantas, courtesy its only shareholder, the Hawke goverment. Labor's veto on Qantas buying a slice of its domestic carrier, Australian Airlines, is tantamount to a final, brutal full-nelson on its financial jugular. It effectively stops the national carrier from establishing a guaranteed domestic passenger-freight feed while leaving the way open (indeed inviting) international competitors to grab up to 25 per cent of Australian ... The strenuous opposition of Australian Airlines' chairman, Ted Harris, to Qantas taking an equity stake in his airline may be right within the sphere of operations viewed from Franklin Street [Australian's headquarters] but is it in the best national [sic] interest? ... Shackling Qantas is not the way to success. It would not be alarmist to suggest that Qantas' long-term survival has been jeopardised.[30]

What was the government offering, in putting Australian up for sale? Australian's total shareholders' equity had increased 26 per cent from $254.481 million in 1989–90 to $320.466 million in 1990–91. Return on those funds from group operations (net profit) was 20.6 per cent (compared with a negative return of 5.39 per cent in 1989–90). The airline, in its corporate plan, had forecast a significant increase in operating profit for 1991–92 but this projection was based on a capital injection of $350 million in December 1991. (The government, however, had made it clear that a capital injection was not currently possible and that Australian's capital needs would be addressed during the sales process.) Australian's fleet of thirty-eight aircraft comprised sixteen Boeing 737-376s, ten Boeing 737-476s (one on lease to Malaysian), four Airbus A300s and eight Boeing 727-276s. At 30 June 1991 it employed 9,240 staff (down from 9,561 the year before). By May 1991 the Asset Sales Task Force had begun exploratory discussions with Qantas, Singapore Airlines, Air New Zealand, British Airways and some others. It was anticipated then that the trade sale component of the airline sales would be largely completed by the end of 1992.

Australian planned further staff reductions. At Qantas the board had also agreed to reduce total staff numbers. (Qantas staff had grown from some 15,000 in 1988 to over 20,000.) On 4 June 1991 Qantas announced its plans for large-scale retrenchments. Staff were to be reduced by 3,651 (13 per cent) to bring staff numbers down to 17,138 and provide annual savings of $161 million.[31]

In its annual report to 30 June 1991 Australian recorded a profit after tax of $65.985 million compared with a loss of $13.737 million in the previous year. Harris stated: 'The past year has been one of immense change for the domestic airline industry and for the Australian Airlines Group. We moved from recovery from the pilots' dispute at the commencement of the financial year into deregulation, the Gulf War and recession.' Australian had moved cautiously on discounting in the early stages of deregulation and had, as a consequence, lost market share. The annual report, however, affirmed a tougher approach. 'Australian Airlines will continue an aggressive pricing policy to ensure its markets are protected in whatever way is deemed necessary.' That was a direct challenge to Compass, whose executives began what Australian Airlines described as a long and malicious public campaign against Australian centring on alleged unsatisfactory access to airport terminals and predatory pricing.[32]

On 10 July 1991 the fledgling Australian domestic airline boldly announced that it intended to bid for Australian Airlines through a wholly owned subsidiary, Compass Aviation Developments Limited. Its chief executive, Bryan Grey, told the Stock Exchange that Compass planned to form a consortium of institutional investors with a view to acquiring not less than 51 per cent of Australian. Compass was now operating on eight routes and had six Airbus aircraft. Its overheads were estimated to be about one-third of Ansett's and Australian's. The *Financial Review* commented: 'John Schaap and Ted Harris may be gnashing their teeth at Grey's impertinence but, having started a new airline from scratch and forcing a drastic response from both Australian and Ansett, Grey has some runs on the board'.[33]

By the end of August 1991 other parties that had expressed interest in Australian Airlines included Brierley Investments Limited, Air New Zealand, Garuda Indonesian Airways, British Airways, Eva Airways and Northwest Airlines. (Eva was the airline subsidiary of the Taiwanese shipping company Evergreen.)[34]

Dix wrote to Willis on 12 July 1991 requesting access to the same Information Memorandum for Australian Airlines that was being provided to prospective purchasers. He did not get a response until 25 October when Willis, while refusing the request, hinted at other Qantas options. 'The Government's decision to ban *direct* [sic] investment in Australian Airlines by Qantas as part of the current sales process', he wrote, 'does not, of course, stop Air New Zealand from being a contender to purchase Australian Airlines. This gives an indication of what the Government is prepared to accept by way of an indirect investment by Qantas in Australian Airlines at this juncture.'[35]

The turmoil in Australian aviation was matched politically in Canberra. Hawke dumped his treasurer, John Kerin, on 6 December, replacing him with Ralph Willis. At the same time there were strengthening rumours that the prime minister himself would be challenged as leader by Paul Keating. The government of the nation was close to paralysis.

Bidders for the two-airlines, wrote the *Financial Review*, were nervous about the identity of their future business partner, 'given the pitfalls and contradictions inherent in the Government's quirky stance on airlines industry policy'. It was critical to assessing the value of Qantas to an outside shareholder, it wrote, 'whether the Government will back down on its policy of insisting that there be no mergers between Qantas and either of the two major domestic partners'.[36]

On 19 December the political drama reached its climax in the nation's capital. Paul Keating defeated the incumbent prime minister, Bob Hawke, in a Caucus ballot for the leadership of the Labor Party. On 23 December Bill Dix wrote to Keating: 'On behalf of the Qantas Board and Management please accept our congratulations on your appointment as Prime Minister'.[37] In the rearrangement of portfolios that followed, Senator Graham Richardson (for a brief period) became minister for transport and communications and Bob

Collins minister for shipping and aviation. Collins had full carriage of the aviation portfolio (except insofar as it impinged on privatisation, where Richardson had the leading role). For the confused world of Australian aviation, now launched on privatisation and at the end of the first year of deregulation, there was an immediate and dramatic change to the politically imposed parameters of the sales process. Keating, with great speed, took the Hawke–Abeles agenda out of the equation. The strategy to sell a much more valuable Qantas (with its own domestic base provided by an absorbed Australian) became realisable. The able and informed Bob Collins, supported by Willis, could now move forward towards the goal of a Qantas takeover of Australian and the full privatisation of the merged entity. The pragmatic Richardson accepted that such an outcome was politically saleable within Labor ranks.

Aircraft summarised that first year of deregulation. 'Deep fare discounts, unprecedented choice of services, unparalleled public interest in aviation, record numbers of passengers but generally low yields ... Simply, that was deregulation — the first twelve months.' Discounting, it said, had in some cases reached 60 per cent. 'By early September, Compass indicated it was ready to call a truce in the fares war but the majors would not bite. Angered by Compass' constant haranguing over a range of issues, from terminal leases to other perceived 'unfair' tactics, the majors escalated the fares war ... The blood on the carpet leading to airline board rooms thickened.'[38]

On 20 December 1991 Compass Airlines, which had begun flying operations on 1 December 1990, collapsed. Harris issued an angry statement: 'The collapse of Compass and the events immediately following the announcement of its inability to continue operations must rank amongst the most bizarre in Australian business history'. Compass, he said, had blamed everybody other than itself for its demise. Australian had at all times acted properly and fairly with respect to facilities for Compass and other parties. 'The reason for the collapse was that Compass sold its airline tickets at prices so heavily discounted that the company ceased to be able to meet its financial obligations.' Australian's response to the problem that had overwhelmed Compass, he said, had been to call upon all its resources over the Christmas holidays to transport those unfortunate people whom Compass had left stranded, namely customers who paid Compass for tickets that Compass was unable to honour. Compass, said Harris, by its unsustainable discounted fares, had created a short-term fragile market increase that had, inevitably, also proved unsustainable. (Throughout the discount fare war Australian had remained firm on its strategy that it would not be beaten on price.)[39]

The collapse of Compass on the eve of a change of prime minister, said a Qantas board memo, 'and associated changes in ministerial responsibilities provided an opportunity for the Company to press for a re-appraisal of Government aviation policy.'[40]

The Compass demise had taught the industry and the Australian public a lesson on both the limits of competition and the effects of deregulation. The great virtue of the two-airline policy had been stability; the great threat from deregulation was instability. Nowhere had this threat been more dramatically exemplified than in the United States. In the same month that Compass collapsed the venerable and once all-dominating international airline Pan American had also gone under. The Compass collapse was a footnote in the history of civil aviation; Pan American's collapse marked the end of an era.

There had been spectacular changes in the global environment in the preceding eighteen months. The Gulf War had ended in January with the rapid and dramatic defeat of the Iraqi army; the cold war with the Soviet Union had ended; the world had experienced continued economic decline and a prolonged global recession. In the aviation industry Pan American had been only one of a number of major international carriers that had disappeared. Mergers and acquisitions had reshaped the industry with the survivors forming new linkages to provide global networks. More carriers were expected to operate in the markets served by Qantas, many of them combinations of United States, European and Asian mega-carriers. An IATA report showed that the industry, in the previous twelve months, had lost some $US3.8 billion, or more than the aggregate of profits by all airlines over the preceding forty years. Ward told the Qantas board in January 1992: 'The Australian government's continued policies with respect to the development of new air service agreements and charter approvals continues to add to these pressures'.[41]

On 30 January 1992 Dix and Ward met Senator Richardson and the new aviation minister, Bob Collins, 'advancing the proposition that the time had come for the "winds of change" to sweep away the unsatisfactory compromises which are blocking Qantas' contribution to the national economy'.[42] They proposed that the whole of Qantas's ordinary shares should be offered for sale, instead of the 49 per cent previously envisaged, and that the Government should retain a 'golden share' with special powers. Qantas, said the proposal, should be released from the prohibition on operating domestic services and on purchasing a direct stake in a domestic carrier. Further, said Qantas, the Closer Economic Relations Agreement with New Zealand 'should be extended to create a single deregulated aviation market throughout Australasia, including all routes across the Tasman Sea'.

'It would be our intention', said the Qantas proposal, 'either individually or as part of a consortium, to bid for a strategic stake in Australian Airlines. We believe that this will enhance the price the Government will receive from its planned 100 per cent sale of Australian Airlines, as well as from the sale of Qantas itself.'[43] Dix told Collins on 5 February: 'My own view is that, providing the market can absorb the full amount, the most straightforward arrangement, and the one that would give rise to the fewest complications, would be for the Government to sell the whole of its ordinary shares to trade buyers, to the employees, and to the Australian public; and to rely entirely on the Government's regulatory powers, and on a newly-created "golden share" for the continuing control that it requires'.[44]

On 20 February a quite different initiative was discussed

at a meeting in Melbourne between Hawke, Abeles, Harris and Kelty. Abeles and Harris proposed that Australian Airlines and Ansett should combine to compete against Qantas. Press reports of the meeting alerted John Ward. The initiative was not developed further.

The devastation in the world's air transport industry over the past three years had severely affected Qantas but it had emerged in better condition than most airlines. The huge staff reductions had, with other cost-cutting measures, made it more competitive. Future aircraft orders had been adjusted to the reduced expectations of traffic growth. Still desperately undercapitalised, however, the injection of fresh equity capital was more urgent than ever. That need had driven the Qantas board and management to press for the full privatisation of the airline and the complete removal of government from its equivocal role as part owner of the airline, a position that precluded Qantas investment in the domestic airline industry.

The Qantas position was greatly strengthened by the change in Labor leadership, particularly as a result of the personal intervention by Paul Keating to distance the government from the previous Hawke–Abeles relationship. Freed from this albatross, Collins was able to advance more rational solutions to achieve the desired government outcomes. A government economic statement ('One Nation') issued in February by Keating announced radical changes to policies for air transport that had major implications for the privatisation process. It recognised 'that Qantas will not be able to compete effectively in international markets unless it is given the same opportunity as its foreign competitors to develop or acquire a domestic feeder and distribution system'. The new policy stated: 'The restrictions on Qantas' operations in the domestic market, and on its freedom to exercise its commercial judgment in forming and cementing an alliance with an Australian domestic carrier, will therefore be removed. This will be done with immediate effect, so that Qantas is free to bid for a stake in Australian Airlines if it wishes to do so'. The government also announced that subject to the agreement of the New Zealand government, 'air transport will be brought squarely within the ambit of the Closer Economic Relations Treaty'. That meant 'that all airlines of both countries will be able to operate as they wish in a single market within Australia and New Zealand and for the Tasman crossings'. (It was envisaged that this change would not come into effect until January 1994). Of equal moment was the decision that as part of its policy changes Australia's domestic airlines would no longer be excluded from international services. The Government, it said, 'will move cautiously in its approach to opening up international routes to domestic carriers'.[45] (The New Zealand government, however, made it plain that it would insist on full 'beyond rights' from Australia for Air New Zealand — a position that was unacceptable to Qantas.)

On 31 March 1992 Ward told the board: 'It has been learned that the Board of Australian Airlines has, by majority, requested that airline's management develop a paper highlighting the benefits of a shareholding by Qantas. It is understood that the Chairman of Australian and one other Board director [ex-ACTU official Gary Weaven] opposed this development'.[46] (It was Harris's firm view that Australian should be sold first as 'the easiest to get off the starting blocks', a view he put personally to Keating. Qantas, he urged, should then at some time be given domestic rights to ensure proper competition while Ansett — and Australian too — should be given the right to fly internationally if they wished. Market forces would then determine what happened. But, said Harris, the board of Australian was ignored.)[47]

Under the sales process firm expressions of interest for Australian Airlines and Qantas, including indicative bids, closed on 30 April 1992. Ward announced officially that Qantas was a bidder for a significant stake in Australian. (He also stressed that Qantas intended to pursue talks with Ansett.) In fact, the Qantas bid was for Australian in its entirety. On 30 April Ward wrote to the chairman of the Asset Sales Task Force, H.G. Heinrich: 'I am pleased to convey the interest of Qantas Airways Limited in acquiring the whole of the share capital (and therefore all the assets held and businesses carried on by) Australian Airlines Limited and its subsidiaries'. The two companies, he said, 'would continue to operate as separate entities — one specialising in domestic operations and the other in international carriage'. The acquisition by Qantas of the whole of the shares in Australian, he wrote, and its incorporation as a Qantas subsidiary 'would have significant macro-economic benefits for Australia. It would create a combined group under majority Australian ownership, capable of standing up to international competition. And it would do so at a lower overall capital cost.'

Qantas, said Ward, had formed preliminary views on the appropriate valuation range for 100 per cent of Australian but was not, given the need for further analysis, prepared to disclose this range. 'Consequently', he wrote, 'Qantas is only prepared, at this stage, to indicate a preliminary price of not less than $150 million'. The government, he said, 'would obtain maximum value from its shareholdings in both companies through Qantas' acquiring and retaining 100 per cent of Australian, with the Government benefiting through subsequent sale of 49 per cent of Qantas at an enhanced price and through an increase in the value of the 51 per cent of Qantas it currently intends to retain'.[48]

That Qantas offer was, of course, far less than the figure expected by the Asset Sales Task Force and a world away from the $1 billion valuation put on the airline by Harris. The position taken by Harris was that of a highly experienced, astute and commercial businessman. He was not, in the interests of the shareholder, prepared to talk down the value of a company about to be floated. When he came to Australian Airlines in 1987 the profit rose from $24.7 million (in the year to 30 June 1987) to $66.5 million in the following year and went up again in the next year to $108.5 million. The pilots' dispute had turned profits to losses but in the financial year that followed Australian announced a pre-tax profit of $113 million. (That, however, included a credit from over-provision in the pilots' superannuation fund of some $92 million.)[49] Overall these figures showed a five-times increase in profit since 1987. Harris's basis for valuing the airline was a price–

earnings ratio of 10 on earnings before tax which he described as 'a not unreasonable figure'. His valuation was supported in an independent assessment by Bankers Trust, who thought the airline could be sold for something in the order of $900 million to $1 billion.[50]

At the same time as Qantas announced its bid for Australian, Australian announced its intention to buy 49 per cent of Qantas. Neither the government nor Qantas saw the Australian bid as a credible one. The government was advised that such a reverse acquisition had the superficial attraction of enabling the subsequent sale of 100 per cent of Australian to the private sector (instead of the sale of only 49 per cent of a combined Qantas–Australian if Qantas absorbed Australian). Advice to the government by CS First Boston, however, was that Australian's proposal had major structural drawbacks and, from a financial standpoint, was unlikely to be a saleable proposition at all.

The board of Australian was proving an irritant for Senator Graham Richardson. Harris had written to him on 9 April (with all directors signing the letter) raising important issues about the final phase of the trade sale process. Richardson's reply on 30 April was blunt. He wrote: 'Your letter causes me considerable concern. For the Government's part it would expect, where the Commonwealth is the sole shareholder, compliance by the Board with Government policy and guidelines. Equally you can be assured that the Government is well aware of the Directors' obligations under the Companies Act and will respect them. For my part I cannot accept any approach that would involve providing the Board with a veto power over the sales process. I will not allow that process to be pre-empted or frustrated.'[51]

On that same day, 30 April, the chairman of British Airways, Sir Colin Marshall, wrote to Paul Keating about his airline's interest in the sales of both airlines. 'One of the important matters raised in our submission', he said, 'is our strong preference for a full merger of Qantas and Australian as part of the process'. British Airways, said Marshall, 'is the world's largest international passenger airline. Its operations are predominantly in the northern hemisphere with particular strengths in the European, North Atlantic and Asian markets. I believe that we are therefore the global carrier best placed further to develop Qantas, integrated with Australian Airlines, as a major Australian based international carrier.'[52]

By mid year it had become clear that there were only three main potential overseas bidders in the sales process — British Airways (in a combined Qantas–Australian), Singapore Airlines (with a prime interest in Qantas) and Air New Zealand–Brierleys (with a prime interest in Australian). The Singapore interest, however, was judged a defensive one.

The government made its decision on Australian's future with unexpected promptness. In early May Dix and Ward were still discussing with directors of Ansett the possibility of a future shareholding relationship between the two companies. Ansett representatives had indicated that the most sensible position would seem to be for Ansett to become a 100 per cent subsidiary of Qantas. That seemingly extraordinary proposition envisaged, however, that this would be achieved by a transfer to Ansett of shares in Qantas. Such a strategic shareholding in Qantas would have given Ansett effective control of the airline. Dix and Ward, of course, recognised at once what was being offered. 'We were very polite', said Ward. When Abeles later learned of the proposal he rejected it himself. He wanted no association with Qantas. In reality the proposal was little more than an opening gambit for further negotiations. Qantas was formally advised in writing that Ansett was withdrawing from negotiations. That, said Ward, left Qantas 'with clean hands' for what followed.[53]

On 22 May Dix and Ward met in Melbourne with the chairman of the Asset Sales Task Force, H.G. Heinrich. At that meeting the deal was agreed for the Qantas purchase of Australian Airlines. On 26 May all Qantas directors received a brief but dramatic message. 'There has been', they were told, 'an important and urgent development concerning privatisation. In short, Qantas has an immediate opportunity to purchase all the shares of Australian Airlines. The Government is seeking a signed agreement from Qantas this evening.' An essential element of the acquisition, said the message, was a price of $400 million. Directors were asked to confirm their agreement to a resolution that Qantas proceed with the acquisition and that their chairman be authorised to settle the final terms.[54]

Qantas had reassessed the price it was prepared to pay for Australian. It recognised that the opportunity provided by the change in Labor leadership had to be grasped quickly. There was no question but that a premium had to be paid. Australian Airlines, though currently operating unprofitably, was worth more to Qantas long term than the straight value of its assets. (The Australian Airlines Group incurred an operating loss of $38.454 million before abnormal and extraordinary items and tax for the year to 30 June 1992. The loss after tax and abnormal and extraordinary items was $49.335 million. Losses from abnormal items totalled $30.155 million, mainly as a result of provisions for employee redundancy costs. There was, though, a tax credit of $20.252 million for the year.)[55] While the figure of $400 million required by the government was almost three times the $150 million minimum first suggested by Qantas, Ward saw it as justifiable. Qantas had identified some $100 million a year achievable before tax from synergies. In rough terms that translated to $60 million after tax. A price–earnings multiple of about seven (which Ward saw as appropriate for airlines) gave an acceptable $400 million figure.[56] (In its 1992–1993 annual report Qantas stated that a decision had been taken 'to write off $282.3 million representing the intangible assets associated with the Australian purchase. That write-off confirmed the difference between the price Qantas had been prepared to pay to acquire Australian and the value it placed on the airline.)

In Canberra on 2 June the prime minister, Paul Keating, announced at a press conference what he described as 'a little bit of history'. The government, he said, had approved the sale of Australian Airlines to Qantas. 'A sale agreement will be signed tomorrow between Qantas and the Government', said the prime minister, 'under which Qantas will pay $400 million to the Government for 100 per cent of Australian Airlines then, subject to the processes of the Australian Labor Party, the Government will then propose to sell 100 per cent of Qantas by a trade sale and a public float, retaining a golden share for the national safeguards ... With the decision to sell 100 per cent of Qantas this will involve a major equity raising, recapitalising the airline on a competitive commercial basis and returning well over $1 billion to the Commonwealth Budget.' Settlement of the sale, said the prime minister, would be finalised by the end of September 'after which Australian Airlines will become a wholly-owned subsidiary of Qantas'.[57] Qantas had outbid all other offers for Australian Airlines by a substantial margin.[58] (The acquisition of Australian Airlines automatically cancelled Ansett's commercial agreement with Qantas.)

The government decision had broken the historic distinction between purely international and purely domestic Australian airlines, enabling its international airline, Qantas, to operate domestically. That decision also allowed Ansett to operate internationally. Having resolved its policy uncertainties the Government, which had previously resisted the New Zealand desire to expedite the inclusion of air transport within the CER treaty, now wished to establish a single market for air transport throughout Australasia. From November 1992 Air New Zealand was to be permitted to increase the number of destinations in markets beyond Australia (with reciprocal rights for Australian carriers beyond New Zealand). Additional Australian carriers were entitled from the same date to operate across the Tasman on a limited number of routes. That market was now open to new entrants on both sides of the Tasman.[59] (Qantas was protected from competition from other Australian carriers internationally by having its sole-designation status for existing routes preserved for five years.)

For airline passengers the government decision had immediate practical benefits. It meant that Qantas could use Australian Airlines' aircraft for those international routes for which they were appropriate, while Australian could use Qantas capacity on Australian domestic routes. The combined jet fleet of both airlines was eighty-four aircraft, with more than thirty-five on order or option. Qantas summarised the effects of the upheaval. 'The aviation industries of Australia and New Zealand', said a management appraisal, 'stand at a crossroads. The forces for change which have been unleashed by the Governments of both countries will have a momentous effect upon the airlines. Decisions taken within the next few months by the owners and managers of the companies involved will affect the shape of the aviation industry in Australasia for many years to come.'[60]

Aircraft commented: 'The Federal government's breathtaking move to merge and sell as a single entity its international and domestic carriers, Qantas and Australian Airlines, has ensured Australia will have at least one airline strong enough to compete in an increasingly concentrated international market dominated by a few mega-carriers'. *Australian Aviation* believed that the government's course of 'dramatic reform will change the nature of airline operations on both sides of the Tasman forever'. The decision to merge Qantas and Australian, it wrote, and sell 100 per cent of the merged entity 'has met with applause from almost every sector of the industry'.[61]

On 2 June Bob Collins (who had replaced Richardson as minister for transport and communications) advised the chairman of Qantas, Bill Dix, and the chief executive officer, John Ward, of their appointments to the board of Australian Airlines.[62] They attended their first Australian Airlines board meeting on 24 June and, the Qantas board learned, 'their reception was cordial'.[63]

For the management and staff of Australian the merger of the two-airlines had clear consequences. Ward wrote to the ACTU on 23 June: 'While both the chairman and I have publicly indicated that there would not be significant job losses emanating from the sale of Australian to Qantas, inescapably the realisation of synergies achieved during the integration of certain functions will produce surplus staff ... However, it is more likely to occur in relation to the senior management group, corporate functions or areas where integrated handling of both domestic and international aircraft is possible.' He undertook that there 'would be equity in the identification and separation of surplus staff in both Qantas and Australian'.[64] A guiding principle in the merger, said a board paper, was that 'the parties agree to work towards achieving a merged airline, operating at optimum desirable levels of efficiency and productivity'. Nevertheless it was set down formally that 'although Australian Airlines will continue to operate as a separate airline, synergies with Qantas operations will be sought wherever they do not severely impact on this status'.

Qantas moved swiftly to identify scenarios for the operation of the Qantas–Australian Airlines group. It was preferable, said a management paper on 29 June, 'where possible to co-locate the functions of the two-airlines. This is especially true for management functions ... With the amalgamation of many corporate functions it might well be possible to vacate Australian Airlines' existing head office facility.' It was planned to coordinate all scheduling functions and to amalgamate management and support functions in these areas. In the flight operations area all line functions were to remain separate but support functions amalgamated. Aircrew and cabin services resources were each to be amalgamated in central locations (though pilots and cabin crews were to remain employed by their existing airline). All engineering support and resource planning functions were to be amalgamated in a central location except for those needed for co-location with line facilities. Fuel purchasing was to be centralised.[65] Significant revenue and cost synergies were identified from the amalgamation of the two carriers' overseas offices.

Not only the management and staff of Australian were affected by the repercussions of the Qantas acquisition. On 27 July 1992 Dix asked Collins to arrange for the resignation of its chairman, Ted Harris, and all directors except John Schaap, John Ward and himself. 'This will in effect result', he wrote, 'in the Australian board comprising only three directors, namely J. W. Schaap, who will remain as managing director and chief executive officer, Mr J. F. Ward and myself'.[66]

Those resignations took effect on Monday, 14 September 1992, the day that the Commonwealth ceased to own shares in Australian Airlines Limited. That morning the sale of Australian to Qantas was settled in Canberra. Qantas gave to the Commonwealth its $400 million cheque for the purchase, the Commonwealth gave Qantas a share transfer for all the issued shares in Australian and a share certificate for 130 million shares. At a subsequent meeting of the directors of Australian Airlines Limited in the offices of the Department of Finance, in Langton Crescent, the share transfer was approved for registration. Those formalities brought to an end the long history of TAA/Australian Airlines as an independent entity.

A combined, commemorative edition of the staff newspapers of Qantas and Australian (*Qantas News* and *Network*) was published on settlement day. Bill Dix, Qantas Group chairman, wrote: 'Airline historians will look back on this day — on which Qantas formalises its purchase of Australian — as the most important date in the history of the nation's commercial aviation'.

Epilogue

For the Commonwealth government the merger of Qantas and Australian Airlines was only the first step in its broader strategy to achieve recapitalisation of the two airlines through privatisation. More change lay ahead. One of those changes was to see the former chief executive of Australian Airlines become the managing director of the enlarged Qantas.

The enlarged Qantas Group, now providing an integrated domestic and international service, had a combined fleet of 122 aircraft, one of the largest in the fast-growing Asia–Pacific market. Its jet fleet was one of the youngest in the world, with an average age of 5.1 years at 30 June 1993. Qantas flew overseas to 39 cities in 23 countries and to 47 destinations across Australia. It carried more than twelve million passengers a year.

In February 1993, in a trade sale, British Airways acquired a 25 per cent share of Qantas for $665 million. A formidable global partnership was formed. At completion of that sale the government provided Qantas with a capital injection of $1.35 billion.

In March 1993 Bill Dix was succeeded as chairman of Qantas by Gary Pemberton. It was decided that the merged Qantas–Australian would now trade under the single name of 'Qantas The Australian Airline'.

On 12 August 1993 John Ward stepped down as chief executive. On 26 October 1993 James Strong, former chief executive officer of Australian Airlines, was appointed managing director of Qantas Airways Limited.

It was not until mid-1995 that the government's strategic goals were finally achieved. In June there was a public float of the remaining 75 per cent of Qantas. The float closed in late July and was an outstanding success. Shares in Qantas traded (at a premium) on the Australian Stock Exchange from 31 July 1995.

Endnotes

Preface

1. Appendix B, report of Interdepartmental Committee, December 1943.
2. Abeles address to Perth luncheon, 29 November 1985. TAA archives.

Prologue

1. Recollection of Doug Laurie, Traffic Manager, 1946, who attended the meeting. Author interview with Laurie, 1994.
2. Hocking D. M. and Haddon-Cave C. P., *Air Transport in Australia*. Sydney: Angus and Robertson, 1951, p. 36.
3. *Air Communications Within and Beyond Australia*. Inter-Departmental Committee Report, Melbourne, October 1932. EJP.
4. Review of Civil Aviation in Australia, Department of Civil Aviation, Melbourne, 16 July 1945.
5. Hydson Fysh report to Qantas board, 24 October 1933. HFP.
6. Ibid.
7. Ibid.
8. Hocking and Haddon-Cave, *Air Transport*, p. 91.
9. Hudson Fysh, *Qantas at War*, Angus and Robertson, Sydney, 1968, p. 137.
10. Appendix B, report of Interdepartmental Committee, December 1943.
11. War Cabinet Agendum, No. 381/1943. EJP.
12. A. B. Corbett, *Post War Re-organisation*, Department of Civil Aviation, January 1943. Source: NL Mss 2413, Box K21818.
13. Ibid.
14. No author. *Wings Across Australia*, an early history of Trans-Australia Airlines. Produced by the public relations company, Eric White Associates. Undated.
15. Fysh to McMaster, 3 August 1944. Hudson Fysh papers, State Library (Mitchell) NSW.
16. Minister's second reading speech, Australian National Airlines Bill, 18 July 1945.
17. Quoted in *Wings Across Australia*.
18. Johnston to McVey, 3 August 1945. CAA archives, Canberra.

19. Johnston to McVey, 19 July 1945. CAA archives, Canberra.
20. Johnston to McVey, 27 July 1945. CAA archives, Canberra.
21. Fysh to Knollys, 24 August 1945. HFP.
22. McVey to Drakeford, 21 May 1945. CAA archives, Canberra.
23. *Sydney Morning Herald*, 15 December 1945.
24. *Trans-Australia Airlines — the first 21 years.* TAA publication, undated.
25. McVey's resignation from the Commission was noted at its meeting on 4 June 1946.
26. ANAC meeting minutes, 21 October 1946.
27. ANAC meeting minutes, 13 February 1946.
28. ANAC meeting minutes, 14 February 1946.
29. *Sydney Morning Herald*, 9 February 1946.
30. ANAC meeting minutes, 14 March 1946.
31. *Wings Across Australia.*
32. ANAC meeting minutes, 30 July 1946.
33. R. M. Ansett to ANAC, 13 March 1946. ANAC meeting papers.
34. McVey to Drakeford, 24 December 1945. EJP.
35. ANAC meeting minutes, 8 May 1946.
36. Holyman to Coles, appendix to ANAC meeting minutes, 8 May 1946.
37. Ibid.
38. Coles to Holyman, 1 May 1946. Appendix to ANAC meeting minutes, 8 May 1946.
39. Fysh to McMaster, 3 April 1946. HFP.
40. Fysh to McMaster, 12 April 1946. HFP.
41. *Wings Across Australia.*
42. Drakeford to Coles, 6 August 1946. TAA archives.
43. Brain report to ANAC, 3–14 June 1946.
44. ANAC meeting minutes, 14 June 1946.
45. ANAC meeting minutes, 16 July 1946.
46. Ibid.
47. McVey to Curtin, 15 May 1944. EJP.
48. McVey to Australian High Commission, London. 30 September 1944. EJP.
49. *Wings Across Australia.*
50. Watkins interview with the author, 1944.
51. Ian Sabey, *Challenge in the Skies: The Founding of TAA*, Hyland House, Melbourne, 1979 (quoted by Sabey).
52. J. L. Watkins, *Personal Memoirs of a Life in Aviation*, Sixth Pioneers Memorial Lecture, Royal Aeronautical Society, Australian Division, Canberra Branch, 19 November 1986.
53. ANAC meeting minutes, 27 August 1946.
54. Ibid.
55. Brain to Laurie, 12 June 1946. In Laurie's possession.
56. Brain to Laurie, 10 July 1946. In Laurie's possession.
57. Brain to Laurie, 6 August 1946. In Laurie's possession.
58. Laurie interview with author, 1994.

59. Ibid.
60. Ibid. Some reports give the flight time as two hours fifty minutes. Laurie's logbook entry (he was a passenger on the flight) shows three hours and five minutes.

1. Not the planned inauguration

1. General manager's report, 17 September 1946.
2. B. G. Woodgate, *Nothing Spectacular*, Sir Lawrence Wackett Memorial Lecture, 8 November 1988, RAeS Australian Division, Melbourne Branch.
3. General manager's report for the period 17 September to 2 October 1946.
4. Ibid.
5. Ibid.
6. *Aircraft*, October 1946.
7. Ibid.
8. Ibid.
9. Treasury memo, 11 September 1946. TAA archives.
10. ANAC meeting minutes, 2 October 1946.
11. Appendix to ANAC meeting minutes, 2 October 1946.
12. Author's interview with Watkins; and Sabey, *Challenge in the Skies.*
13. J. L. Watkins, Arthur William Coles, *With Zeal and Integrity*. Privately published, 1982.
14. J. L. Watkins, *Personal Memoirs of a Life in Aviation*. RAeS paper, Canberra, 19 November 1986.
15. Learman memo, 29 November 1946. TAA archives.
16. *Challenge in the Skies*.
17. Appendix to ANAC meeting minutes, 11 November 1946.
18. Ibid.

2. This socialised means of transport.

1. Ibid.
2. Appendix to ANAC meeting minutes, 9 December 1946.
3. *Aircraft*, April 1947.
4. Ibid.
5. Report by Brain to the ANAC, 24 December 1946.
6. David Corbett, *Politics and the Airlines*, George Allen & Unwin Ltd, London, 1965.
7. Eric Allen, *Australian Aviation*, September 1986.
8. ANAC meeting minutes, 24 March 1947.
9. Brain memo to Coles, 21 March 1947.
10. Ibid.
11. Appendix to ANAC meeting minutes, 24 March 1947.
12. Appendix to ANAC meeting minutes, 12 May 1947.
13. *Sydney Morning Herald*, 2 June 1947.
14. Ibid.

15. Appendix to ANAC meeting minutes, 2 June 1947.
16. *This Air Age*, Vol. I, No. 9, June 1947.
17. *Aircraft*, July 1947.
18. Appendix to minutes of ANAC meeting, 21 July 1947.
19. *This Air Age*, Vol. I, No. 10, July 1947.
20. *Sydney Morning Herald*, 28 July 1947.
21. *Sydney Morning Herald*, 29 July 1947.
22. ANAC meeting minutes, 4 August 1947.
23. Appendix to ANAC meeting minutes, 1 September 1947.
24. *Sydney Morning Herald*, 21 August 1947.
25. Appendix to ANAC meeting minutes, 24 November 1947.
26. *Aircraft*, December 1947.
27. *Aircraft*, August 1947.
28. ANAC meeting minutes, 27 October 1947.
29. Appendix to ANAC meeting minutes, 29 September 1947.
30. ANAC meeting minutes, 24 November 1947.
31. *Aircraft*, August 1947.
32. ANAC meeting minutes, 24 November 1947.
33. Ibid.
34. *Sydney Morning Herald*, 4 December 1947.
35. TAA publication *Trans-Air*, December 1947.
36. DCA Annual Report, 1946–47.
37. Appendix to ANAC meeting minutes, 22 December 1947.
38. *Aircraft*, January 1948.
39. ANAC meeting minutes, 27 January 1948.
40. Appendix to ANAC meeting minutes, 16 February 1948.
41. Ibid.
42. ANAC meeting minutes, 15 March 1948.
43. Appendix to ANAC meeting minutes, 16 April 1948.
44. *This Air Age*, Vol. 2, No. 4, March–April 1948.
45. ANAC meeting minutes, 15 March 1948.
46. ANAC meeting minutes, 16 April 1948.
47. *Wings Across Australia* and author's interview with John Watkins.
48. Ibid.
49. *Challenge in the Skies.*
50. J. L. Watkins, *Personal Memoirs of a Life in Aviation*, RAeS lecture, Canberra, 19 November 1986.
51. Author's interview with Watkins.
52. ANAC meeting minutes, 26–27 May 1948.
53. *This Air Age*, Vol. 2, No. 5, May–June 1948.
54. Quoted by Watkins in *Personal Memoirs of a Life in Aviation.*

3. The brink of remarkable developments

1. *Aircraft*, July 1948.
2. *Aircraft*, August 1948.
3. *Aircraft*, August 1948.

4. Appendix to ANAC meeting minutes, 3 September and 1 October 1948.
5. *Wings Across Australia.*
6. *Aircraft*, October 1948.
7. Appendix to ANAC meeting minutes, 3 September 1948.
8. *Aircraft*, November 1948.
9. DCA annual report 1947–48.
10. *Aircraft*, March 1949.
11. *This Air Age*, June–July 1949.
12. Appendix to ANAC meeting minutes, 10 December 1948.
13. *Politics and the Airlines*, p. 120.
14. Appendix to ANAC meeting minutes, 24 January 1949.
15. Appendix to ANAC meeting minutes, 21 March 1949.
16. Ibid.
17. Ibid.
18. Appendix to ANAC meeting minutes, 22 March 1949.
19. Appendix to ANAC meeting minutes, 23 May 1949.
20. ANAC meeting minutes, 25 July 1949.
21. Ibid.
22. *This Air Age*, June–July 1949.
23. *Aircraft*, September 1949.
24. *Aircraft*, August 1949.
25. Ibid.
26. *Aircraft*, October 1949.
27. Watkins report to Brain, 29 September 1949.
28. Ibid.
29. *Wings Across Australia.*
30. Ibid.
31. Ibid.
32. *Aircraft*, June 1950.
33. *This Air Age*, August 1950.
34. *Challenge in the Skies.*
35. *This Air Age*, April 1950.
36. ANAC meeting minutes, 8 May 1950.
37. *TAA, Its Place and Future in Australian Air Transport*. Paper prepared by TAA for the Cabinet Standing Committee on Civil Aviation Policy. 11 September 1950.
38. Ibid.
39. Ibid.
40. Ibid.
41. Appendix to ANAC meeting minutes, 2 October 1950.
42. Appendix to ANAC meeting minutes, 6 November 1950.
43. *Aircraft*, May 1950.
44. *Challenge in the Skies.*
45. *Politics and the Airlines*, p. 122.
46. *Wings Across Australia.*
47. *Politics and the Airlines*, p. 121.

48. ANAC meeting minutes, 17 January 1951.
49. Cabinet agendum undated, early 1951.
50. ANAC meeting minutes, 17 January 1951.
51. Brain to Walsh, 26 February 1951. TAA archives.
52. Walsh to Brain, 7 March 1951. TAA archives.
53. Brain to Walsh, 22 March 1951. TAA archives.
54. Appendix to ANAC meeting minutes, 6 April 1951.
55. *This Air Age*, May 1951.
56. Appendix to ANAC meeting minutes, 6 April 1951.
57. Appendix to ANAC meeting minutes. Review of decisions adversely affecting TAA. 12 May 1951.
58. Appendix to ANAC meeting minutes, 24 August 1951.
59. *Aircraft*, August 1951.
60. *Aircraft*, September 1951.
61. ANAC meeting minutes, 8 October 1951.
62. Brain to Johnston, 16 October 1951. TAA archives.
63. Ibid.
64. Ibid.
65. *Commonwealth Parliamentary Debates*, Vol. 215, November 1951.
66. ANAC meeting minutes, 23 November 1951.
67. Ibid.
68. Report and letter from Watt to Anthony, 15 January 1953.
69. Watt to Menzies, 11 February 1952. TAA archives.
70. *Civil Aviation Policy as Affecting TAA*. Paper submitted to Cabinet Sub-Committee by Watt, 22 March 1952. TAA archives.
71. Menzies to Holyman, 28 March 1952. TAA archives.
72. Ibid.
73. Ibid.
74. Watt to Anthony, 4 July 1952. TAA archives.
75. Ibid.
76. Watt to Anthony, 9 July 1952. TAA archives.
77. *Australian Financial Review*, 10 January 1952.
78. ANAC meeting minutes, 7 August 1952.
79. Appendix to ANAC meeting minutes, 29 September 1952.
80. S. Brogden, *Australia's Two-Airline Policy*, Melbourne University Press, Carlton, Vic., p. 99.
81. *Politics and the Airlines*, pp. 122–3.
82. Ibid.
83. Menzies to Holyman, 28 March 1952. TAA archives.
84. Appendix to ANAC meeting minutes, 12 May 1954, reviewing government policy decisions on matters affecting domestic airline operations in Australia. TAA archives.
85. Ibid., p. 123.
86. Minister's second reading speech, Civil Aviation Agreement Bill, 24 October 1952.

4. Opposing political philosophies

1. *Aviation Report*, 16 January 1953.
2. *Aircraft*, February 1953.
3. Ibid.
4. Watt to Anthony, 3 February 1953. TAA archives.
5. Director-General of Civil Aviation to Minister, January 1955. EJP.
6. Watt to Holyman, 17 February 1953. TAA archives.
7. Brain to Watt, 20 February 1953. TAA archives.
8. Appendix to ANAC meeting minutes, 3 March 1953.
9. Appendix to ANAC meeting minutes, 3 March 1953.
10. Watt to Holyman, 6 March 1953. TAA archives.
11. *Aircraft*, January 1953.
12. Notes on conference held at ANA with TAA on 28 March 1953. TAA archives.
13. Appendix to ANAC meeting minutes, 30 March 1953.
14. Edgar Johnston memo to Anthony, 12 November 1952 and undated, 1953. EJP.
15. Appendix to ANAC meeting minutes, 1 May 1953.
16. Anthony to Watt, 5 March 1953. TAA archives.
17. Appendix to ANAC meeting minutes, 23 January 1953.
18. *This Air Age*, February 1953.
19. ANAC meeting minutes, 5 June 1953.
20. *This Air Age*, August 1953.
21. Appendix to ANAC meeting minutes, 4 August 1953.
22. *This Air Age*, September 1953.
23. Cabinet agendum, 26 October 1953. TAA archives.
24. ANAC meeting minutes, 29 September 1953.
25. Cabinet agendum, 26 October 1953.
26. Appendix to ANAC meeting minutes, 27 October 1953.
27. Appendix to ANAC meeting minutes, 15 January 1954.
28. Watt to Brain, 27 January 1954. TAA archives.
29. Appendix to ANAC meeting minutes, 15 January 1954.
30. Management paper for the Commission, *Estimates for 1953–54*. TAA archives.
31. Ryland to Director-General, 17 March 1954. TAA archives.
32. Appendix to ANAC meeting minutes, 12 May 1954.
33. Ibid.
34. Appendix to ANAC meeting minutes, 14 April 1954.
35. Brain to G. Packer, Acting Chairman ANAC, 18 June 1954. TAA archives.
36. Chippindall to Anthony, 22 June 1954. TAA archives.
37. Watt to Townley, 21 September 1954. TAA archives.
38. Townley to Watt, 29 September 1954. TAA archives.
39. Appendix to ANAC meeting minutes, 16 August 1954.
40. Ibid.
41. Ibid.

42. Ibid.
43. Appendix to ANAC meeting minutes, 16 August 1954.
44. Appendix to ANAC meeting minutes, 26 October 1954.
45. Appendix to ANAC meeting minutes, 19 October 1954.
46. Ibid.
47. Author's interview with John Watkins, 1994.
48. Appendix to ANAC meeting minutes, 19 October 1954.
49. *This Air Age*, Special Supplement, November 1954.
50. Appendix to ANAC meeting minutes, 10 May 1955.
51. Appendix to ANAC meeting minutes, 16 December 1954.
52. Ibid.
53. Ibid.
54. Ibid.
55. Brain to Watt, handwritten, 3 February 1955. TAA archives.

5. Imminent collapse

1. Brain to Watt, 3 February 1955. TAA archives.
2. Extract from opinion of R. M. Eggleston QC, 2 March 1955. TAA archives.
3. Brain to Watt, 3 March 1955. TAA archives.
4. Holt to Watt, 18 February 1955. TAA archives.
5. Townley to Watt, 29 April 1955. TAA archives.
6. Watt to Brain, 18 November 1955. TAA archives.
7. *Aircraft*, March 1955.
8. Minutes of ANAC meeting, 8 March 1955.
9. Ibid.
10. Appendix to ANAC meeting minutes, 8 March 1955.
11. Ibid.
12. Fleet Planning Report by Ryland, 1 April 1955. TAA archives.
13. Ibid.
14. Appendix to ANAC meeting minutes, 27 July 1955.
15. *Aircraft*, August 1955.
16. Appendix to ANAC meeting minutes, 1 September 1955.
17. *This Air Age*, November 1955.
18. Appendix to ANAC meeting minutes, 1 September 1955.
19. *Financial Review*, 20 October 1955.
20. ANAC meeting minutes, 17 November 1955.
21. Appendix to ANAC meeting minutes, 25 January 1956.
22. Ibid.
23. Appendix to ANAC meeting minutes, 26 January 1956.
24. Ibid.
25. Ibid.
26. *This Air Age*, November 1956.
27. General Manager's report to the Commission, 13 November 1956.
28. *This Air Age*, October 1956.
29. Appendix to ANAC meeting minutes, 13 November 1956.

30. *Australian Financial Review*, 3 January 1957.
31. S. Brogden, *Australia's Two-Airline Policy*, Melbourne University Press, Carlton, Vic., 1968.

6. Inherent industry instability

1. S. Brogden, *Australia's Two-Airline Policy*, Melbourne University Press, Carlton, Vic., 1968.
2. Ibid. Quoted by Brogden.
3. Ibid.
4. *This Air Age*, January–February 1957.
5. *Financial Review*, 21 February 1957.
6. TAA study paper, 4 January 1957. TAA archives.
7. Ibid.
8. ANAC meeting minutes, 25 January 1957.
9. S. Brogden, *Australia's Two-Airline Policy*.
10. ANAC meeting minutes, 25 January 1957.
11. ANAC meeting minutes, 30 April 1957.
12. Ibid.
13. *Financial Review*, 13 June 1957.
14. Chippindall to Paltridge, 10 June 1957. Australian Archives, Vic. Regional Office.
15. Memorandum accompanying above letter.
16. Ibid.
17. Appendix to ANAC meeting minutes, 16 December 1957.
18. McDonald report to ANAC meeting, 3 September 1957.
19. *Financial Review*, 8 August 1957.
20. *This Air Age*, August 1957.
21. D. N. Gillison, *Civil Aviation Newsletter*, Special Issue, August 1957. CAA archives, Canberra.
22. ANAC meeting minutes, 30 August 1957.
23. *Financial Review*, 29 August 1957.
24. D. N. Gillison, *Civil Aviation Newsletter*, August 1957.
25. Ibid.
26. ANAC meeting minutes, 6 September 1957.
27. Statement to the Senate on Civil Aviation Policy, 6 September 1957. TAA archives.
28. Ibid.
29. ANAC meeting minutes, 26 September 1957.
30. *Financial Review*, 19 September 1957.
31. Appendix to ANAC meeting minutes, 4 November 1957. Australian Archives, Vic.
32. Ibid.
33. Appendix to ANAC meeting minutes, 16 December 1957.
34. Appendix to ANAC meeting minutes, 4 November 1957.
35. *This Air Age*, November 1957.
36. Appendix to ANAC meeting minutes, 4 November 1957.

37. *Financial Review*, 28 November 1957.
38. *Aircraft*, December 1957.
39. Ibid.

7. TAA's new competitor

1. S. Brogden, *Australia's Two-Airline Policy*.
2. Ibid.
3. *Financial Review*, 2 January 1958.
4. Appendix to ANAC meeting minutes, 13 February 1958 (a PMG Minute Paper).
5. Appendix to ANAC meeting minutes, 3 March 1958.
6. *Mt Isa Mail*, 6 February 1958.
7. *Northern Territory News*, 6 February 1958.
8. Appendix to ANAC meeting minutes, 3 March 1958.
9. Notes of meeting with Qantas by W. D. McDonald, 5 March 1958. TAA archives.
10. Letter from Ryland to Anderson, 21 March 1958. TAA archives.
11. Ryland to Anderson, 2 April 1958. TAA archives.
12. Turner to Anderson, 18 April 1958. Australian Archives, Vic. Regional Office.
13. Appendix to ANAC meeting minutes, 27 February 1958.
14. Watkins report, 21 February 1958. TAA archives.
15. Appendix to ANAC meeting minutes, 28 March 1958.
16. *Australia's Two-Airline Policy* (quoted by S. Brogden).
17. *Aircraft*, April 1958.
18. Appendix to ANAC meeting minutes, 28 March 1958.
19. McDonald to Paltridge, 29 April 1958. Australian Archives, Vic. Regional Office.
20. Ibid.
21. *Financial Review*, 3 April 1958.
22. Ibid.
23. J. Gunn, *Challenging Horizons, Qantas 1954–1970*, University of Queensland Press, 1988.
24. ANAC meeting minutes, 12 May 1958.
25. TAA archives, 21 May 1958.
26. *This Air Age*, June 1958.
27. Chairman's report to ANAC, 22 August 1958.
28. Ibid.
29. Appendix to ANAC meeting minutes, 22 August 1958.
30. Ryland report to ANAC, 21 August 1958.
31. Ibid.
32. Ibid.
33. *Financial Review*, 2 October 1958.
34. Australian Air Pilots' Association News Release, November 1958.
35. Appendix to ANAC meeting minutes, 12 June 1959.
36. Ibid.

37. ATA's managing director's report, *Financial Review* advertisement, 18 December 1958.

8. A political football

1. *Sydney Morning Herald*, 13 February 1959.
2. *Aircraft*, April 1959.
3. Ibid.
4. *This Air Age*, April 1959.
5. Appendix to ANAC meeting minutes, 19 February 1959.
6. McDonald to Paltridge, 20 November 1957. Australian Archives, Vic. Regional Office.
7. *Financial Review*, 9 July 1959.
8. Appendix to ANAC meeting minutes, 6 April 1959.
9. Appendix to ANAC meeting minutes, 15 May 1959.
10. *This Air Age*, May 1959.
11. Appendix to ANAC meeting minutes, 15 May 1959.
12. *Aircraft*, June 1959.
13. *Aircraft*, September 1959.
14. *This Air Age*, August 1959.
15. *Aircraft*, September 1959.
16. Ryland to Anderson, 8 April 1960. TAA archives.
17. Pascoe to Ryland, 4 March 1960. TAA archives.
18. Appendix to ANAC meeting minutes, 16 September 1959.
19. Appendix to ANAC meeting minutes, 23 November 1959.
20. Appendix to ANAC meeting minutes, 9 November 1959.
21. ANAC meeting minutes, 7 December 1959.
22. Report to Ryland, 20 April 1960. TAA archives.
23. Appendix to ANAC meeting minutes, 21 March 1960.
24. Report to Ryland, 20 April 1960. TAA archives.
25. Appendix to ANAC meeting minutes, 18 February 1960.
26. Chippindall press statement, undated. TAA archives.
27. *This Air Age*, January/February 1960.
28. Address by Chippindall, Brisbane, 7 March 1960. TAA archives.
29. *Financial Review*, 31 March 1960.
30. *Financial Review*, 19 May 1960.
31. Appendix to ANAC meeting minutes, 18 May 1960.
32. Paltridge to Taylor, 11 April 1960. TAA archives.
33. Fysh to Paltridge, 24 March 1960. TAA archives.
34. Chippindall to Fysh, 20 April 1960. TAA archives.
35. Fysh to Chippindall, 26 April 1960. TAA archives.
36. *Financial Review*, 14 April 1960.
37. Appendix to ANAC meeting minutes, 27 July 1960.
38. *Financial Review*, 12 May 1960.
39. Appendix to ANAC meeting minutes, 20 May 1960.
40. Appendix to ANAC meeting minutes, 23 June 1960.
41. Appendix to ANAC meeting minutes, 27 July 1960.

42. Appendix to ANAC meeting minutes, 27 July 1960.
43. *Aircraft*, November 1960.

9. Boundaries of competition

1. H. W. Poulton, *Law, History and Politics of the Australian Two-Airline System*, published by H. W. Poulton, Melbourne, 1981.
2. *Australia's Two-Airline Policy*.
3. Packer report to Chippindall, 2 May 1961. TAA archives.
4. Civil Aviation Report, Department of Civil Aviation, 1960–61.
5. *Financial Review*, 20 July 1961.
6. Ibid.
7. *Politics and the Airlines*.
8. Ibid.
9. ANAC meeting minutes, 15 September 1961.
10. *Financial Review*, 20 July 1961.
11. *Financial Review*, 28 September 1961.
12. *Age*, 31 October 1961.
13. Report to Commission by J. Chapman, Assistant General Manager, 26 September 1962. TAA archives.
14. Appendix to ANAC meeting minutes, 26 September 1962.
15. Ibid.
16. Ibid.
17. Ibid.
18. Appendix to ANAC meeting minutes, 26 September 1962.
19. *Financial Review*, 27 November 1962.
20. *Aircraft*, December 1962.
21. *This Air Age*, November 1962.
22. Appendix to ANAC meeting minutes, 6 February 1963.
23. TAA press statement, 19 March 1963. TAA archives.
24. *Financial Review*, 2 May 1963.
25. Appendix to ANAC meeting minutes, 23 May 1963.
26. Ibid.
27. *Financial Review*, 27 June 1963.
28. Appendix to ANAC meeting minutes, 24 July 1963.
29. *Financial Review*, 29 August 1963.
30. Appendix to ANAC meeting minutes, 18 November 1963.
31. Appendix to ANAC meeting minutes, 18 December 1963.
32. *Aircraft*, April 1964.
33. *This Air Age*, April 1964.
34. *Aircraft*, June 1964.
35. Ibid.
36. *Financial Review*, 8 May 1964.
37. Appendix to ANAC meeting minutes, 17 June 1964.
38. *Australian*, 16 July 1964.
39. Civil Aviation Report to Parliament, 1964–65.
40. *Financial Review*, 28 July 1964.

41. *Financial Review*, 31 August 1964.
42. *Financial Review*, 23 September 1964.
43. *Financial Review*, 29 September 1964.

10. Ansett's golden franchise

1. *Australian*, 1 March 1965.
2. *Financial Review*, 23 February 1965.
3. *Financial Review*, 1 March 1965.
4. Ibid.
5. *Financial Review*, 9 March 1965.
6. *This Air Age*, January–February 1965.
7. Appendix to ANAC meeting minutes, 24 March 1965.
8. Ibid.
9. Watkins to Manager, Canberra, 14 May 1965. J. L. Watkins papers.
10. Ibid.
11. *Australia's Two-Airline Policy*, p. 188.
12. Ibid., p. 190.
13. Watkins to Ryland, 13 September 1965. J. L. Watkins papers.
14. *This Air Age*, August 1965.
15. *This Air Age*, September 1965.
16. Chairman's memorandum to Minister, 21 October 1965. TAA archives.
17. *Financial Review*, 19 January 1966.
18. Chippindall to Minister, May 1966. Undated draft. TAA archives.
19. Appendix to ANAC meeting minutes, 2 February 1966.
20. DCA Annual Report, 1965–66.
21. *This Air Age*, February 1966.
22. Appendix to ANAC meeting minutes, 15 April 1966.
23. *Australian*, 14 July 1966.
24. Ibid.
25. *Age*, 5 August 1966.
26. *Australian*, 15 July 1966.
27. *Aircraft*, August 1969.
28. *Financial Review*, 3 August 1966.
29. Scherger to Swartz, 29 July 1966. TAA archives.
30. *Financial Review*, 24 August 1966.
31. *Financial Review*, 19 October 1966.
32. Appendix to ANAC meeting minutes, 16 November 1966.

11. A monopoly with two shareholders

1. *Financial Review*, 5 January 1967.
2. *Financial Review*, 17 January 1967.
3. *Sydney Morning Herald*, 3 January 1967.
4. John Gunn in the *Financial Review*, 13 February 1967.
5. *Aircraft*, February 1967.
6. *Nation*, February 1967.
7. *This Air Age*, April 1967.

8. Appendix to ANAC meeting minutes, 21 June 1967.
9. *This Air Age*, May 1967.
10. Article by John Watkins, *Aircraft*, June 1967.
11. *Aircraft*, June 1967.
12. Appendix to ANAC meeting minutes, 15 November 1967.
13. ANAC meeting minutes, 20 December 1967.
14. ANAC meeting minutes, 24 May 1968.
15. Scherger to Swartz, 26 January 1968. TAA archives.
16. Ibid.
17. Ibid.
18. ANAC meeting minutes, 21 February 1968.
19. *Australian*, 6 March 1968.
20. N. Blain, *Industrial Relations in the Air*, University of Queensland Press, 1984.
21. AFAP Newsletter, 19 March 1968. TAA archives.
22. Swartz to Ansett, 26 March 1968. TAA archives.
23. Minutes of marketing conference, Essendon, 18 April 1968. TAA archives.
24. Report prepared for R. R. Law-Smith, 30 June 1969. TAA archives.
25. *Financial Review*, 8 October 1968.
26. *Financial Review*, 5 November 1968.
27. *Financial Review*, 10 December 1968.
28. Appendix to ANAC meeting minutes, 5 February 1969.
29. *This Air Age*, special edition, January 1969.
30. *This Air Age*, March 1969.
31. Ibid.
32. Appendix to ANAC meeting minutes, 18 June 1969.

12. The affectionate antagonism of identical twins

1. *This Air Age*, January–February 1970.
2. Minutes of ANAC meeting, 9 February 1970.
3. Scherger to Cotton, 15 January 1970. TAA archives.
4. Ryland report to ANAC, 28 April 1970. TAA archives.
5. *Financial Review*, 28 April 1970.
6. Submission by Watkins to House of Representatives Select Committee on Aircraft Noise, 1970.
7. Ibid.
8. Scherger to Cotton, 8 April 1970. Appendix to ANAC meeting minutes, 8 April 1970.
9. Ibid.
10. Appendix to ANAC meeting minutes, 15 April 1970.
11. DCA Report, 1970–71.
12. Appendix to ANAC meeting minutes, 17 June 1970.
13. Ibid.
14. DCA Report, 1970–71.
15. Department of Civil Aviation Report, 1969–70.

16. Scherger to Cotton, 27 October 1970. TAA archives.
17. Scherger to Cotton, 25 November 1970.
18. Scherger to Cotton, 20 November 1970.
19. *Aircraft*, November 1970.
20. *Aircraft*, December 1970.
21. Scherger to Cotton, 11 February 1971. TAA archives.
22. *This Air Age*, April 1971.
23. Appendix to ANAC meeting minutes, 24 May 1971.
24. ANAC meeting minutes, 20 July 1971.
25. ANAC meeting minutes, 21 July 1971.
26. Scherger to Cotton, 17 August 1971. TAA archives.
27. Scherger to Cotton, 25 August 1971.
28. *Financial Review*, 7 December 1971.
29. Scherger to Cotton, 3 September 1971. TAA archives.
30. Cotton to Scherger, 8 February 1972.
31. Memo to Cotton from Scherger, 20 March 1972.
32. *Australian*, 23 March 1972.
33. *Age*, 8 April 1972.
34. ANAC meeting minutes, 10 May 1972.
35. *Finance Week*, 14 April 1972.
36. *Incentive*, May 1972.
37. Appendix to ANAC meeting minutes, 17 May 1972.
38. ANAC meeting minutes, 19 April 1972.
39. *Financial Review*, 21 March 1972.
40. Scherger to Cotton, 14 July 1972. Appendix to ANAC meeting minutes, 19 July 1972.
41. Cotton to Scherger, 29 August 1972. Appendix to ANAC meeting minutes, 20 September 1972.
42. Ibid.
43. Cotton to Scherger, 15 August 1972.
44. Statement issued by Cotton, 5 September 1972. TAA archives.
45. Appendix to ANAC meeting minutes, 20 September 1972.

13. At risk

1. *Sydney Morning Herald*, 5 December 1972.
2. Scherger to Jones, 21 December 1972. TAA archives.
3. *This Air Age*, January–February 1973.
4. Scherger to Jones, 22 February 1973. TAA archives.
5. Appendix to ANAC meeting minutes, 21 February 1973.
6. DCA press release, 20 February 1973. TAA archives.
7. Jones to Scherger, 28 March 1973. Appendix to ANAC meeting minutes.
8. Appendix to ANAC meeting minutes, 21 March 1973.
9. DCA annual report 1972–73 and *This Air Age*, June 1973.
10. Appendix to ANAC meeting minutes, 20 June 1973.
11. Scherger to Jones, 25 September 1973. TAA archives.
12. Ansett to Ryland, 7 June 1973. Appendix to ANAC meeting minutes.

13. Scherger to Jones, 14 June 1973. Appendix to ANAC meeting minutes.
14. ANAC annual report, 1972–73.
15. Scherger to Jones, 22 August 1973. Appendix to ANAC meeting minutes.
16. TAA press release, 30 August 1973.
17. Scherger to Jones, 5 September 1973. TAA archives.
18. Appendix to ANAC meeting minutes, 17 October 1973.
19. *This Air Age*, September–October 1973.
20. ANAC agenda item, 21 October 1973.
21. Scherger to Jones, 26 September 1973. Appendix to ANAC meeting minutes.
22. Appendix to ANAC meeting minutes, 20 February 1974.
23. *Aircraft*, February 1974.
24. Scherger to Jones, 21 December 1973. TAA archives.
25. *This Air Age*, December 1973.
26. C. J. Smith to L. L. McKenzie, 15 February 1974. TAA archives.
27. TAA press release, 21 June 1974. TAA archives.
28. ANAC annual report, 1973–74.
29. Scherger to Jones, 19 July 1974. TAA archives.
30. ANAC annual report, 1973–74.
31. Scherger to Jones, 5 March 1974. TAA archives.
32. Scherger to Jones, 15 March 1974.
33. *Wall Street Journal*, 19 June 1974.
34. Scherger to Jones, 15 November 1974. TAA archives.
35. Scherger to Jones, 15 November 1974. TAA archives.
36. Scherger to Jones, 9 December 1974. TAA archives.
37. Gough Whitlam, *The Whitlam Government 1972–75*, p. 435.
38. Scherger to Jones, 9 December 1974. TAA archives.
39. *This Air Age*, December 1974.

14. The harsh winds of worldwide economic downturn

1. Scherger to Jones, 31 January 1975. TAA archives.
2. Scherger to the Royal Commission on Australian Government Administration, 23 December 1974. TAA archives.
3. Minutes of special ANAC meeting, 23 January 1975. TAA archives.
4. Ibid.
5. Jones to Scherger, 20 February 1975. Appendix to ANAC meeting minutes, 19 March 1975.
6. Scherger to Jones, 12 May 1975. TAA archives.
7. Appendix to ANAC meeting minutes, 21 May 1975.
8. *Aircraft*, February 1976.
9. Ibid.
10. Court to Scherger, 26 June 1975. TAA archives.
11. Annual report of the Department of Transport 1974–75.
12. TAA annual report, 1974–75.
13. *Aircraft*, August 1975.
14. Report of the state of the economy by the ANAC to the Department of Transport.

15. Vial to Jones, 23 October 1975.
16. Vial to Jones, 3 September 1975. TAA archives.
17. Vial report to Jones, 6 October 1975. TAA archives.
18. Jones to Vial, 10 October 1975.
19. Vial to Jones, 20 October 1975. TAA archives.
20. C. J. Smith, Department of Transport, to Vial, 23 September 1975. TAA archives.
21. McKenzie to Smith, 25 September 1975. TAA archives.
22. *Aircraft*, February 1976.
23. *Aircraft*, February 1976.
24. Vial to Nixon, 27 January 1976. TAA archives.
25. Ibid.
26. Vial to Nixon, 30 January 1976.
27. Vial to Nixon, 18 February 1976.
28. Nixon to Law-Smith, 1 March 1976. TAA archives.
29. Appendix to ANAC meeting minutes, 17 March 1976.
30. Vial to Nixon, 5 March 1976. TAA archives.
31. Appendix to ANAC meeting minutes, 21 April 1976.
32. Nixon to Vial, 17 March 1976. TAA archives.
33. Vial to Nixon, 2 April 1976.
34. Vial to Nixon, 30 April 1976.
35. Vial to Nixon, 26 May 1976.
36. Halton to McKenzie, 7 April 1976. TAA archives.
37. McKenzie to Halton, 9 June 1976. TAA archives.
38. Halton to McKenzie, 16 September 1976. TAA archives.
39. Copy of Ansett letter included in appendices to ANAC meeting minutes, 21 July 1976.
40. Nixon to Vial, 11 June 1976. TAA archives.
41. Vial to McNiell, 12 October 1976. TAA archives.
42. Vial to Nixon, 19 October 1976. TAA archives.
43. Vial to McNeill, 12 October 1976. TAA archives.
44. Jephcott to Vial, December 1976 undated. TAA archives.
45. Report of the Committee of Inquiry into the Commonwealth's Transport Business Undertakings, 2 December 1976.

15. Arguments for change

1. Nixon to Vial, 1 May 1977. TAA archives.
2. ANAC meeting minutes, 15 June 1977.
3. Submission by the ANAC to the Review of Australian Air Transport Policy, September 1977.
4. Ibid.
5. Ibid.
6. Vial to Nixon, 16 December 1977. TAA archives.
7. Lyn McKenzie to F. Pascoe, Ansett general manager, 14 December 1977. TAA archives.
8. TAA press release, 24 October 1977. TAA archives.

9. Vial to Nixon, 27 October 1977. TAA archives.
10. Ibid.
11. Vial to Nixon, 24 November 1977. TAA archives.
12. Vial to Nixon, 19 December 1977. TAA archives.
13. ANAC annual report, 1976–77.
14. Vial to Nixon, 24 November 1977. TAA archives.
15. *Aircraft*, January 1978.
16. Nixon to Vial, 8 March 1978.
17. Ansett to Nixon, 4 May 1978. TAA archives.
18. *Financial Review*, 11 January 1978.
19. J. L. Watkins address, reported in *Aviation News* and the *Financial Review*, November 1977.
20. Department of Transport annual report, 1977–78.
21. *Travel Trade*, 20 June 1978. Comment by John Stackhouse.
22. Domestic Air Transport Review, released by Nixon 21 July 1987. TAA archives.
23. *Financial Review*, 24 July 1974.
24. Nixon to Law-Smith, 14 August 1978. TAA archives.
25. Ansett to Nixon, 18 August 1978. TAA archives.
26. ANAC annual report, 1978–79.
27. Vial to Nixon, 20 August 1978. TAA archives.
28. ANAC meeting minutes, 14 August 1978. TAA archives.
29. Appendix to ANAC meeting minutes, 14 August 1978. TAA archives.
30. *Australian*, 5 August 1978.
31. TAA archives.
32. ANAC annual report, 1977–78.
33. *Sydney Morning Herald*, 24 May 1979.
34. Appendix to ANAC meeting minutes, 30 August 1978.
35. TAA press release, 12 September 1978. TAA archives.
36. Appendix to ANAC meeting minutes, 18 October 1978.
37. Nixon to Vial, 6 December 1978.
38. Vial to Nixon, 12 December 1978. TAA archives.
39. J. L. Watkin's papers. This letter was not published by the *Age*.
40. *This Air Age*, December 1978.
41. Vial to Nixon, 11 December 1978. TAA archives.
42. McKenzie to DOT, 1 November 1978. TAA archives.
43. Nixon press statement, 2 February 1979. TAA archives.
44. *Financial Review*, 11 January 1979.
45. McKenzie report to the Commission, 26 February 1979. TAA archives.
46. Vial to Nixon, 20 February 1979. TAA archives.
47. Appendix to ANAC meeting minutes, 26 February 1979.
48. Ibid.
49. *Bulletin*, March 1979.
50. Vial to Bjelke-Petersen, 2 March 1979. TAA archives.
51. Nixon to Law-Smith, 16 April 1979. TAA archives.
52. Vial to Nixon, 9 April 1979. TAA archives.

53. *Laurie Oakes Report*, 23 May 1979.
54. *Sydney Morning Herald*, 16 May 1979.
55. Vial to Nixon, 3 August 1979. TAA archives.
56. Nixon to Vial, 9 August 1979. TAA archives.
57. *Financial Review*, 12 October 1979.
58. *Australian*, 31 October 1979.
59. *Age*, 10 October 1979.
60. *Age*, 12 October 1979.
61. Pascoe to McKenzie, 31 October 1979. TAA archives.
62. Law-Smith to Nixon, 23 October 1979.
63. *Age*, 24 November 1979.
64. *Financial Review*, 21 November 1979.
65. Nixon to Prime Minister, 22 November 1979. DOT archives.
66. Report on ANAC financial structure, 1979. TAA archives.
67. DOT press release, 5 December 1979. DOT archives.

16. The possible sale of TAA

1. *Bulletin*, 22 January 1980.
2. TAA press release, 20 January 1980. TAA archives.
3. *Australian*, 18 January 1980.
4. Law-Smith letter to ANAC Commissioners, 7 March 1980. TAA archives.
5. *Penthouse*, undated 1980.
6. Draft TAA press release, 8 January 1980. TAA archives.
7. *This Air Age*, February–March 1980.
8. *Australian*, 26 March 1980.
9. *Age*, 25 March 1980.
10. *Sunday Mail*, Adelaide, 13 April 1980.
11. Ibid.
12. Law-Smith memo to TAA staff, 14 April 1980. TAA archives.
13. *Australian*, 18 April 1980.
14. Law-Smith to Hunt, 24 April 1980. TAA archives.
15. Ibid.
16. Appendix to ANAC meeting minutes, 28 April 1980.
17. Law-Smith to Bjelke-Petersen, 1 May 1980. TAA archives.
18. Law-Smith to Hunt, 8 May 1980. TAA archives.
19. News Release by Hunt, 21 May 1980. TAA archives.
20. Law-Smith to Hunt, 5 June 1980. TAA archives.
21. Law-Smith to Hunt, 2 June 1980. TAA archives.
22. *Age*, 13 June 1980.
23. *Sydney Morning Herald*, 28 April 1980.
24. *Australian*, 4 July 1980.
25. DOT annual report, 1979–80.
26. Law-Smith to Everingham, 19 August 1980. TAA archives.
27. Appendix to ANAC meeting minutes, 25 August 1980.
28. *Australian* and *Sydney Morning Herald*, 12 August 1980.

29. Advice by First Assistant Secretary, Air Transport Policy Division to Minister, 17 July 1980. DOT archives.
30. Hunt press release, 19 September 1980. TAA archives.
31. Minutes of ANAC meeting, 22 September 1980.
32. *This Air Age*, October 1980.
33. TAA PR briefing memo, 13 January 1981. TAA archives.
34. DOT news release, 8 January 1981. DOT archives.
35. Michael G. Kirby. *Domestic Airline Regulation: the Australian Debate*, CIS Research Studies in Government Regulation. Australian National University, 1981.
36. *Bulletin* (article by Greg Sheridan), 24 March 1981.
37. Ball to NT Transport Minister, 16 January 1981. TAA archives.
38. *Financial Review*, 9 March 1981.
39. *Financial Review*, 5 March 1981.
40. *Financial Review*, 13 March 1981.
41. *Australian*, 12 March 1981.
42. Hunt telex to Law-Smith, 13 March 1981. TAA archives.
43. TAA press release, 21 April 1981. TAA archives.
44. *Financial Review*, 22 April 1981.
45. *Age*, 6 April 1981.
46. Law-Smith to Hunt, 1 May 1981. TAA archives.
47. TAA internal memo, 10 March 1981. TAA archives.
48. Appendix to ANAC meeting minutes, 25 May 1981.
49. *Aircraft*, July 1981.
50. TAA annual report, 1980–81.
51. *Courier Mail*, 9 September 1981.
52. Law-Smith to Hunt, 25 November 1981. TAA archives.
53. *This Air Age*, November 1981.

17. The fruits of government fiat: technical insolvency

1. DOT news release, 4 January 1982.
2. *Bulletin*, 26 January 1982.
3. *Age*, 6 January 1982.
4. *Financial Review*, 8 January 1982.
5. TAA news release, 12 January 1982. TAA archives.
6. Hunt to Law-Smith, 2 March 1982. TAA archives.
7. *This Air Age*, January 1982.
8. *Age*, 13 February 1982.
9. Law-Smith to Hunt, 26 February 1982. TAA archives.
10. TAA press release, 10 February 1982. TAA archives.
11. Law-Smith to Hunt, 16 February 1982. TAA archives.
12. DOT Halton minutes, 10 February 1982. DOT archives.
13. *Business Review Weekly*, 20 February 1982.
14. *Financial Review*, 11 February 1982.
15. Abeles letter to all Ansett staff, 19 February 1982. TAA archives.
16. Abeles to Law-Smith, 19 February 1982. TAA archives.

17. TAA press release, 19 February 1982.
18. Leslie to Hunt, 27 January 1982. DOT archives.
19. *Bulletin*, 30 March 1982.
20. *Executive News*, undated, 1982.
21. J. C. Dawson, address to the 7th Australian Transport Research Forum, Hobart, 1982. TAA archives.
22. *Financial Review*, 5 March 1982.
23. Dawson letter to the author, 4 December 1995.
24. Appendix to ANAC meeting minutes, 22 March 1982.
25. *Bulletin*, 13 April 1982.
26. *Business Review Weekly*, 15 May 1982.
27. Ball memo, 12 May 1982.
28. *Australian Business*, 24 June 1982.
29. Law-Smith to Fife, 11 June 1982. TAA archives.
30. Statement by Fife, 8 June 1982. TAA archives.
31. *Sydney Morning Herald*, 4 August 1982.
32. Hunt to Law-Smith, 18 June 1982. TAA archives.
33. *Australian*, 12 June 1982.
34. *Financial Review*, 26 July 1982.
35. Fife to Law-Smith, 23 July 1982. TAA archives.
36. Fife to Law-Smith, 13 July 1982. TAA archives.
37. ANAC annual report, 1981–82.
38. Law-Smith to Fife, 23 August 1982. TAA archives.
39. *This Air Age*, August 1982.
40. *This Air Age*, August 1982.
41. Law-Smith to Fife, 25 October 1982. TAA archives.
42. Ibid.
43. TAA internal report attached to above letter. TAA archives.
44. Law-Smith to Fife, 17 December 1982. TAA archives.
45. *Australian*, 9 December 1982.
46. Appendix to ANAC meeting minutes, 13 December 1982.
47. Confidential Departmental submission, 19 January 1983. DOT archives.
48. Ibid.
49. Ibid.
50. Appendix to ANAC meeting minutes, 28 January 1983.
51. *Network*, February 1983.
52. Information paper, Transport Commission, Western Australia, February 1983.
53. Law-Smith to Fife, 9 March 1983. TAA archives.
54. Law-Smith to Beazley, 11 March 1983. TAA archives.
55. Appendix to ANAC meeting minutes, 28 February 1983.
56. Appendix to ANAC meeting minutes, 28 February 1983.
57. Law-Smith to Beazley, 31 March 1983. TAA archives.
58. Appendix to ANAC meeting minutes, 23 May 1983.
59. Law-Smith to Beazley, 14 March 1983.
60. Beazley to Law-Smith, 3 May 1983. TAA archives.

61. Law-Smith to Beazley, 25 August 1983.
62. Ball staff memo, 7 June 1983. TAA archives.
63. Law-Smith to Beazley, 18 October 1983. TAA archives.
64. Beazley to Law-Smith, 9 December 1983.
65. Appendix to ANAC meeting minutes, 24 October 1983.
66. Ball memo to all TAA pilots, 6 October 1983.
67. *Financial Review*, 13 October 1983.
68. Press release by W. A. Department of the Premier and Cabinet, 12 October 1983.
69. *Australian Business*, 2 November 1983.
70. Appendix to ANAC meeting minutes, 28 November 1983.
71. *Network*, December 1983.

18. The grip of uncertainty

1. *Bulletin*, 31 January 1984.
2. Appendix to ANAC meeting minutes, 23 January 1984.
3. *Financial Review*, 5 March 1984.
4. Ball memo to staff, May 1984.
5. Beazley to Smith, 4 June 1984. TAA archives.
6. Beazley to Smith, 4 September 1984. TAA archives.
7. ANAC report to the Minister, September 1984. TAA archives.
8. ATI to Flight Engineers' Association, 23 November 1984. TAA archives.
9. Ball to Flight Engineers' Association, 28 November 1984. TAA archives.
10. TAA press release, 10 December 1984.
11. Minister's press release, 12 December 1984. TAA archives.
12. Statement by Department of Aviation, 13 December 1984. TAA archives.
13. Appendix to ANAC meeting minutes, 21 January 1985.
14. *Business Review Weekly*, 15 March 1985.
15. *Aircraft*, April 1985.
16. Department of Aviation press statement, 30 April 1985. TAA archives.
17. Minister's news release, 12 March 1985. TAA archives.
18. Appendix to ANAC meeting minutes, 27 May 1985.
19. TAA press release, 27 May 1985.
20. Smith to Morris, 31 May 1985. TAA archives.
21. *Financial Review*, 24 July 1985.
22. *Financial Review*, 27 July 1985.
23. Bureau of Economics Occasional paper 72. *Competition and Regulation in Domestic Aviation: Submission to Independent Review*, Australian Government Publishing Service, Canberra, 1985.
24. ANAC Submission to Independent Review of Economic Regulation of Domestic Aviation. TAA publication, August 1985.
25. Smith to Morris, 8 August 1985.
26. *Australian*, 5 September 1985.
27. *Canberra Times*, 5 September 1985.
28. General Manager memo, 9 September 1985. TAA archives.
29. TAA press release, 9 September 1985.

30. TAA annual report, 1984–85.
31. Smith to Morris, 2 September 1985. TAA archives.
32. TAA press release, 3 October 1985.
33. *Canberra Times*, 23 November 1985.
34. *Aircraft*, December 1985.
35. Ibid.

19. A new name, a new management

1. *Australian*, 6 November 1985.
2. *Bulletin*, 21 January 1986.
3. Abeles address to The Decision Makers' Luncheon, Perth, 29 November 1985. TAA archives.
4. TAA press release, 20 December 1985.
5. Minutes of ANAC meeting, 20 January 1986.
6. *Concept of Stability of the Domestic Air Transport Industry: a Historical Review, 1945–1986*. DOT review. TAA archives.
7. Ibid.
8. Ibid.
9. Ibid.
10. *Financial Review*, 27 February 1986.
11. Smith to Morris, 21 March 1986. TAA archives.
12. TAA press release, 17 April 1986.
13. M. Rush to Arthur Robinson & Hedderwicks, solicitors, 28 May 1986. TAA archives.
14. *Financial Review*, 6 May 1986.
15. Appendix to ANAC meeting minutes, 30 June 1986.
16. Strong memo to all pilots, 12 June 1986. TAA archives.
17. Strong to TAA marketing conference, 19 July 1986. TAA archives.
18. Appendix to ANAC meeting minutes, 28 July 1986.
19. *Age*, 9 August 1986.
20. TAA press release, 9 June 1986.
21. TAA 1985–86 annual report.
22. TAA press release, 9 June 1986.
23. Appendix to ANAC meeting minutes, 25 August 1986.
24. Media release by Bruce Lloyd, shadow minister for aviation. 12 August 1986. TAA archives.
25. *Aircraft*, September 1986.
26. *Financial Review*, 4 August 1986.
27. Appendix to ANAC meeting minutes, 22 September 1986.
28. Australian press release, 12 October 1986.
29. Appendix to ANAC meeting minutes, 27 November 1986.
30. Appendix to ANAC meeting minutes, 22 December 1986.
31. Tilton memo, 8 January 1987.
32. Strong memo, 27 January 1987.
33. Smith to Morris, 22 December 1986. TAA archives.
34. Lini to Morris, 19 January 1987. DOT archives.

35. Department of Aviation minutes of meeting with Strong, 5 February 1987. DOT archives.
36. Appendix to ANAC meeting minutes, 19 January 1987.
37. Appendix to ANAC meeting minutes, 27 July 1987.
38. Report to ANAC, 23 February 1987. TAA archives.
39. Appendix to ANAC meeting minutes, 19 January 1987.
40. *The Australian Way*, staff journal, July 1987.
41. Appendix to ANAC meeting minutes, 19 January 1987.
42. *Australian*, 7 March 1987.
43. *Financial Review*, 3 April 1987.
44. *Financial Review*, 25 May 1987.
45. *Interavia*, July 1987.
46. Press release, 17 July 1987.
47. ANAC annual report, 1986–87.
48. Media Release by Minister, 5 June 1987. TAA archives.
49. *Aircraft*, July 1987.
50. *Business Review Weekly*, 7 August 1987.
51. *Financial Review*, 4 August 1987.
52. *Financial Review*, 18 August 1987.
53. Smith to Morris, 4 May 1987. TAA archives.
54. Appendix to ANAC meeting minutes, 31 August 1987.
55. Ibid.
56. *Financial Review*, 19 August 1987.
57. *Age*, 21 August 1987.
58. *Age*, 24 August 1987.
59. Evans to Smith, 30 September 1987. TAA archives.
60. *Sydney Morning Herald*, 8 October 1987.
61. *Australian*, 8 October 1987.
62. Second Reading Speech by Senator Evans, Australian Airlines (Conversion to Public Company) Bill 1987.

20. No soft option

1. Appendix to ANAC meeting minutes, 30 November 1987.
2. Scott Hawker, Bain & Company Limited company report, *TNT, A Global Transportation Company*, November 1987. TAA archives.
3. Appendix to ANAC meeting minutes, 11 December 1987.
4. Strong to G. Keneally, Minister for Transport, S. A., 15 January 1988. TAA archives.
5. Harris to Evans, 12 February 1988. TAA archives.
6. ANAC meeting agenda item, 8 February 1988.
7. *Financial Review*, 5 April 1988.
8. *Financial Review*, 7 April 1988.
9. *Financial Review*, 6 April 1988.
10. Ibid.
11. *Financial Review*, 11 April 1988.
12. Qantas board memo from Ward, 28 March 1990. Qantas archives.

13. Media statement by Minister Evans, 27 April 1988. TAA archives.
14. Appendix to ANAC meeting minutes, 26 April 1988.
15. Annual report, 1987–88, Australian Airlines Limited.
16. *Aircraft*, September 1988.
17. Appendix to Australian Airlines board meeting, 23 August 1988.
18. Australian Airlines board minutes, 7 March 1989.
19. Agenda item, Australian Airlines board meeting, 14 April 1989.
20. Appendix to Australian Airlines board meeting, 14 February 1989.
21. Australian Airlines press release.
22. *Financial Review*, 19 February 1989.
23. *Australian*, 14 March 1989.
24. Michael Johnson, *Meeting the Capital Needs of Qantas and Australian Airlines*. Public Sector Research Centre, University of New South Wales, April 1989.
25. *Network*, Australian Airlines staff magazine, April 1989.
26. *Sydney Morning Herald*, 4 April 1989.
27. Ibid.
28. Author's interview, March 1966.
29. Ibid.
30. Ibid.
31. Harris to Willis, 17 May 1989.
32. Ibid.
33. Minutes of Australian Airlines board meeting, 3 April 1989.
34. Caucus Discussion paper by Gareth Evans, February 1988.
35. Harris to Willis, 19 July 1989.
36. Australian Airlines Limited annual report, 1988–89.
37. Board report, 27 July 1989.

21. High drama

1. *Age*, 25 August 1989.
2. *Financial Review*, 25 August 1989.
3. Ibid.
4. *Weekend Australian*, 26–27 August 1989.
5. *Weekend Australian*, 26–27 August 1989.
6. *Financial Review*, 15 September 1989.
7. *Financial Review*, 18 September 1989.
8. *Australian*, 21 September 1989.
9. *Age*, 22 September 1989.
10. *Age*, 11 December 1989. 'History of the Dispute'.
11. Australian Airlines board agenda item, 31 January 1990.
12. Australian Airlines board minutes, 25 October 1989.
13. Ibid.
14. *Age*, 11 December 1989.

22. The deregulation of the domestic airline industry

1. *Canberra Times*, 28 August 1989.

2. McMahon to Willis, 6 September 1989. DOT archives.
3. Qantas board memo, 28 March 1989. Qantas archives.
4. Harris to Willis, 30 November 1989. Australian Airlines archives.
5. Dix to Willis, 3 January 1990. Qantas archives.
6. Dix to Beazley, 11 April 1990. Qantas archives.
7. Ministerial statement, 8 January 1990.
8. Australian Airlines board agenda item, 31 January 1990.
9. Board agenda item, 28 February 1990.
10. *Network*, February 1990.
11. Board minutes, 31 January 1990.
12. Board paper, 20 March 1990.
13. *Independent Monthly*, March 1990.
14. Briefing notes prepared for Schaap, 19 March 1990. Australian Airlines archives.
15. Qantas board memo, 26 April 1990. Qantas archives.
16. Ibid.
17. Ibid.
18. Qantas board paper, 26 June 1990.
19. Qantas board memo, 26 April 1990.
20. Ibid.
21. Ibid.
22. Schaap to Kelly, 20 April 1990. Australian Airlines archives.
23. *Independent Monthly*, March 1990.
24. Board minutes, 26 April 1990.
25. Qantas board memo, 26 June 1990. Qantas archives.
26. Strong to DOT, 10 March 1989. Australian Airlines archives.
27. Ibid.
28. Harris to Beazley, 20 June 1990. Australian Airlines archives.
29. *Network*, June 1990.
30. *Network*, July 1990.
31. *Network*, August 1990.
32. Beazley to Harris, August 1990. TAA archives.
33. Appendix to Australian Airlines board minutes, 26 September 1990.
34. Ward memo to Qantas board, 24 August 1990. Qantas archives.
35. Australian Airlines presentation to Qantas, 24 August 1990. Australian Airlines archives.
36. Qantas board memo, 27 September 1990. Qantas archives.
37. Ibid.
38. Ibid.
39. Dix to Beazley, 13 September 1990. Qantas archives.
40. Paper by minister for finance, received by Asset Sales Task Force, 19 February 1991. DOT archives.
41. *Network*, September 1990.
42. Australian Airlines board paper, 26 September 1990.
43. Australian Airlines board minutes, 16 October 1990.
44. Australian Airlines board minutes, 26 September 1990.

45. *Financial Review*, 25 September 1990.
46. Australian Airlines annual report, 1989–90.
47. *Network*, September 1990.
48. Australian Airlines media release, 11 October 1990.
49. Qantas board memo prepared by Roger Robertson, general manager corporate planning and Ward, 2 October 1990. Qantas archives.
50. Paper by minister for finance, received by Asset Sales Task Force, 19 February 1999. DOT archives.

23. A little bit of history

1. Dix to Beazley, 21 February 1991.
2. *Network*, February 1991.
3. Ibid.
4. Hawke statement to Parliament, 8 November 1990. TAA archives.
5. Hansard, 14 November 1990.
6. Beazley to Dix, 1 November 1990. Qantas archives.
7. Qantas board memo, 28 November 1990. Qantas archives.
8. The source of these comments cannot be quoted.
9. Australian Airlines board agenda item, 7 November 1990.
10. Qantas board paper, 2 February 1991. Qantas archives.
11. Qantas board memo, 28 February 1991. Qantas archives.
12. Ibid.
13. Qantas board minutes, 7 February 1991.
14. Beazley to Dix, 6 February 1991. Qantas archives.
15. Australian Airlines board agenda paper, 27 February 1991.
16. Beazley to Harris, 14 February 1991. Australian Airlines archives.
17. Australian Airlines board agenda item, 30 January 1991.
18. Australian Airlines board agenda item, 27 March 1991.
19. Ibid.
20. Media release, minister for transport, 22 April 1991.
21. Qantas board memo, 24 April 1991.
22. Dix to Beazley, 18 April 1991. Qantas archives.
23. Qantas News Release, 23 April 1991. Qantas archives.
24. Qantas board memo, 24 April 1991. Qantas archives.
25. Beazley to Dix, 6 June 1991. Qantas archives.
26. Minutes of Australian Airlines board meeting, 24 April 1991.
27. Minutes of Australian Airlines board meeting, 29 May 1991.
28. Australian Airlines board minutes, 23 May 1991.
29. *Network*, April–May 1991.
30. *Aircraft*, May 1991.
31. *Australian*, 6 June 1991.
32. Australian Airlines board agenda item, 29 January 1992.
33. *Financial Review*, 12 July 1991.
34. Qantas board memo, 28 August 1991. Qantas archives.
35. Willis to Dix, 25 October 1991. Qantas archives.
36. *Financial Review*, October 1991.

37. Dix to Keating, 23 December 1991.
38. *Aircraft*, November 1991.
39. Australian Airlines board agenda item, 30 October 1991.
40. Qantas board memo, 6 February 1992.
41. Qantas board memo, 30 January 1992.
42. Qantas board memo, 6 February 1992.
43. Dix to Collins, 5 February 1992.
44. Ibid.
45. Statement of revised Government policy. Attachment to Qantas board memo, 4 March 1992.
46. Qantas board memo, 31 March 1992.
47. Author's interview with Harris, March 1996.
48. Ward to Henrich, 30 April 1992. Qantas archives.
49. Australian Airlines annual report, 1990–91.
50. Author's interview with Harris, March 1996.
51. Richardson to Harris, 30 April 1992. Australian Airlines archives.
52. Marshall to Keating, 30 April 1992. Qantas archives.
53. Author's interview with Ward, March 1996.
54. Memo to all Qantas directors, 26 May 1992. Qantas archives.
55. Australian Airlines news release, 10 September 1992.
56. Author's interview with Ward, March 1996.
57. Joint statement by the prime minister, Paul Keating, the minister for finance, Ralph Willis and the minister for transport and communications, Bob Collins, 2 June 1992. Qantas archives.
58. Attachment to Qantas board memo, 2 July 1992.
59. Ibid.
60. Ibid.
61. *Australian Aviation*, August 1992.
62. Collins to Dix and Ward, 2 June 1992. Qantas archives.
63. Qantas board memo, 2 July 1992.
64. Ward to L. Ayres, senior industrial officer, ACTU, 23 June 1992.
65. Qantas board paper, 29 June 1992.
66. Dix to Collins, 27 July 1992. Qantas archives.

Bibliography

Baitsell, J. M. *Airline Industrial Relations: Pilots and Flight Engineers*. Boston: Harvard University, 1966.

Behr, J. *Royal Flying Doctor Service in Australia 1928–1979*. Manuscript in the possession of the Federal Council of the Royal Flying Doctor Service of Australia.

Blain, N. *Industrial Relations in the Air*. St Lucia, Qld: University of Queensland Press, 1984.

Brogden, S. *Australia's Two-Airline Policy*. Carlton, Vic.: Melbourne University Press, 1968.

Butler, C. A. *Flying Start: The History of the First Five Decades of Civil Aviation in Australia*. Sydney: Edwards & Shaw, 1971.

Corbett, C. *Politics and the Airlines*. London: George Allen & Unwin Ltd, 1965.

Davis, R. E. G. *A History of the World's Airlines*. London: Oxford University Press, 1964.

Eric White Associates, *Wings Across Australia*. Unpublished manuscript, Trans-Australia Airlines Archives. Melbourne, 1965.

Gibson, R. J. *Australia and Australians in Civil Aviation: An Index to Events from 1832 to 1920*. Vol. 1. Sydney: Qantas Airways Ltd, 1971.

Gunn, J. *The Defeat of Distance, Qantas 1919–1939*. St Lucia, Qld: University of Queensland Press, 1985.

———. *Challenging Horizons, Qantas 1939–1954*. St Lucia, Qld: University of Queensland Press, 1987.

———. *High Corridors, Qantas 1954–1970*. St Lucia, Qld: University of Queensland Press, 1988.

Hocking, D. M., and Haddon-Cave, C. P. *Air Transport in Australia*. Sydney: Angus & Robertson, 1951.

Poulton, H. W. *Law, History and Politics of the Australian Two Airline System*. Parkville, Vic.: H. W. Poulton, Parkville, 1982.

Sabey, I. *Challenge in the Skies*. Melbourne: Highland House, 1979.

Stroud, J. *Annals of British and Commonwealth Air Transport 1919–1960*. London: Putnam, 1962.

Index